MW00986878

A Geometry of Music

OXFORD STUDIES IN MUSIC THEORY
Series Editor Richard Cohn

Studies in Music with Text, David Lewin

Music as Discourse: Semiotic Adventures in Romantic Music, Kofi Agawu

Playing with Meter: Metric Manipulations in Haydn and Mozart's Chamber Music for Strings, Danuta Mirka

Songs in Motion: Rhythm and Meter in the German Lied, Yonatan Malin

Tonality and Transformation, Steven Rings

A Geometry of Music: Harmony and Counterpoint in the Extended Common Practice, Dmitri Tymoczko

For Chuck + his girls 10/18/17

A Geometry of Music

Harmony and Counterpoint in the Extended Common Practice

DMITRI TYMOCZKO

OXFORD
UNIVERSITY PRESS
2011

Oxford University Press, Inc., publishes works that further
Oxford University's objective of excellence
in research, scholarship, and education.

Oxford New York
Auckland Cape Town Dar es Salaam Hong Kong Karachi
Kuala Lumpur Madrid Melbourne Mexico City Nairobi
New Delhi Shanghai Taipei Toronto

With offices in
Argentina Austria Brazil Chile Czech Republic France Greece
Guatemala Hungary Italy Japan Poland Portugal Singapore
South Korea Switzerland Thailand Turkey Ukraine Vietnam

Published by Oxford University Press, Inc.
198 Madison Avenue, New York, New York 10016

www.oup.com

Library of Congress Cataloging-in-Publication Data
Tymoczko, Dmitri, 1969–
A geometry of music : harmony and counterpoint
in the extended common practice / Dmitri Tymoczko.
p. cm. — (Oxford studies in music theory)
Includes bibliographical references and index.
ISBN 978-0-19-533667-2
1. Harmony. 2. Counterpoint. 3. Musical analysis. I. Title.
MT50.T98 2010
781.2—dc22 2009046428

Oxford Web Music

Visit the companion website at:
www.oup.com/us/ageometryofmusic

For more information on Oxford Web Music, visit www.oxfordwebmusic.com

19 18 17 16 15 14 13 12 11

Printed in the United States of America
on acid-free paper

To the memory of my father, who predicted I'd someday get tired of rock and want to understand other musical styles as well.

ACKNOWLEDGMENTS

In college, I met four people who had a profound impact on my life. Milton Babbitt gave me permission to be a composer, showing me that a serious artist could also be a rigorous thinker. Stanley Cavell opened my ears to philosophy, demonstrating that rigorous thinking could begin with scrupulous honesty. Hilary Putnam, who seemed to know everything, reawakened my interest in science and math. And Noam Elkies taught me what true intellectual and musical excellence looked like, setting standards that I am happy to try to uphold, even though I might never actually meet them.

As a graduate student, I learned how to be a professional musician from Edmund Campion, Steve Coleman, Bevan Manson, David Milnes, and David Wessel. Later, my colleagues at Princeton University provided me with a supportive home, encouraging my nonconformist and cross-disciplinary tendencies. (Paul Lansky and Steve Mackey in particular taught me not to worry about the slings and arrows of outraged forefathers.) Rick Cohn, Dan Harrison, Fred Lerdahl, and Joe Straus all nurtured my fledgling theoretical career. Rick's theoretical work was also quite influential, as it pioneered the use of geometry to model chromatic voice leading. Conversations with Clifton Callender, Ian Quinn, and Rachel Hall were crucial to developing a number of the ideas in this book, as can be seen from our various co-authored papers. I still cherish the memory of fall 2004, when Cliff, Ian, and I—and occasionally Noam Elkies—exchanged excited emails about the links between music and geometry.

Rick Cohn, John Halle, Dan Harrison, Christopher Segall, Bill Sethares, and Jason Yust all read very large portions of the manuscript, providing countless substantive and organizational suggestions. Jason's highly professional copyediting, performed on short notice, caught a number of embarrassing errors. Students in Princeton's Music 309, a mixed undergraduate/graduate theory course, read a first draft of the entire manuscript and offered many useful comments. One of these students, Andrew Jones, produced the audio examples on the book's companion website. Another, Jeff Levenberg, proofread the book and produced the index. Still more comments were provided by Kofi Agawu, Fernando Benadon, Poundie Bernstein, Elisabeth Camp, Mark Dancigers, Robert Gjerdingen, Philip Johnson-Laird, Jon Kochavi, Yuhwon Lee, Steve Rings, Dean Rosenthal, Lauren Spencer, and Dan Trueman. Students in Music 306 (a later iteration of 309) caught an infinite number of typos while the book was in page proofs.

Suzanne Ryan at Oxford University Press was a firm and relentless advocate; her calm presence helped guide this unusual book past some formidable obstacles. As series editor, Rick Cohn was a benevolent overseer from first to last. Important financial support was provided by Princeton University, the Radcliffe Institute for Advanced Study, and the Guggenheim Foundation.

Finally, conversations with my wife, Elisabeth Camp, have provided more than a decade of intellectual stimulation, emotional support, and just plain fun. Since 2008, conversations with our son Lukas have been equally rewarding, though somewhat less relevant to the concerns of this book.

CONTENTS

ABOUT THE COMPANION WEBSITE

www.oup.com/us/ageometryofmusic

The website contains audio files corresponding to each of the musical examples, as well as a few additional soundfiles and movies that further illustrate points in the text. It is primarily intended to assist readers who have trouble playing or imagining the notated examples.

INTRODUCTION

When I was about 15 years old, I decided I wanted to be a composer, rather than a physicist or mathematician. I had recently switched from classical piano to electric guitar, and although I exhibited no obvious signs of compositional talent, I was fascinated by the amazing variety of twentieth-century music: the suavely ferocious *Rite of Spring,* which made tubas sound cool; the encyclopedic *Sgt. Pepper,* which contained multitudes; the hypnotic repetitions of Philip Glass, whose spirit seemed also to infuse the music of Brian Eno and Robert Fripp; and the geeky sophistication of art rock and new wave. I was aware of but intimidated by jazz, which seemed to be perpetually beyond reach, like the gold at the end of a rainbow. (Told by my guitar teacher that certain chords or scales were jazzy, I would inevitably find that they sounded flat and lifeless in my hands.) To a kid growing up in a college town in the 1980s, the musical world seemed wide open: you could play *The Rite of Spring* with your rock band, write symphonies for electric guitars, or do anything else you might imagine.

I was somewhat surprised, therefore, to find that my college teachers—famous academics and composers—inhabited an entirely different musical universe. They knew nothing about, and cared little for, the music I had grown up with. Instead, their world revolved around the dissonant, cerebral music of Arnold Schoenberg and his followers. As I quickly learned, in this environment not everything was possible: tonality was considered passé and "unserious"; electric guitars and saxophones were not to be mixed with violins and pianos; and success was judged by criteria I could not immediately fathom. Music, it seemed, was not so much to be composed as constructed—assembled painstakingly, note by note, according to complicated artificial systems. Questions like "does this chord sound good?" or "does this compositional system produce likeable music?" were frowned upon as naive or even incoherent.

I studied many things in college: seventeenth-century masses, eighteenth-century Lutheran chorales, and twentieth-century avant-garde music. I learned about Heinrich Schenker, who purported to reduce all good tonal pieces to a small number of basic templates. I absorbed mathematical tools for constructing and deconstructing atonal compositions. But I did not learn anything whatsoever about jazz, Debussy, Ravel, Shostakovich, Messiaen, or minimalism. In fact, even the music of Wagner and Chopin was treated with a certain embarrassment—acknowledged to be important, but deemed suspiciously illogical in its construction. Looking back, I can see that the music I encountered was the music my teachers knew how to talk about. Unfortunately, this was not the music I had come to college wanting to understand.

Twenty years later, things are different, and a number of the barriers between musical styles have fallen. Many composers have returned to the tonal ideas that my own teachers deemed irrelevant. Electric guitars now mix freely with violins, and everything is indeed permitted. But despite this new freedom, tonality remains poorly understood. We lack even the most rudimentary sense of the musical ingredients that contribute to the sense of "tonalness." The chromatic music of the late nineteenth century continues to be shrouded in mystery. We have no systematic vocabulary for discussing Debussy's early 20th-century music or its relation to subsequent styles. Graduate students in music often know nothing about bebop, or about how this language relates backward to classical music and forward to contemporary concert music. As a result, many young musicians are essentially flying by the seat of their pants, rediscovering for themselves the basic techniques of modern tonal composition.

The goal of this book is to understand tonality afresh—to provide some new theoretical tools for thinking about tonal coherence, and to illuminate some of the hidden roads connecting modern tonality to that of the past. My aim is to retell the history of Western music so that twentieth-century tonality appears not as an aberration, the atavistic remnant of an exhausted tradition, but as a vital continuation of what came before. I hope that this effort will be useful to composers who want new ways to write tonal pieces, as well as to theorists, performers, and analysts who are looking for new ways to think about existing music.

While my primary audience consists of composers and music theorists, I have tried to write in a way that is accessible to students and dedicated amateurs: technical terms are explained along the way, and only a basic familiarity with elementary music theory (including Roman numeral analysis) is presumed. (Specialists will therefore need to endure the occasional review of music-theoretical basics, particularly in the early chapters.) More than anything else, I have attempted to write the sort of book I wish had existed back when I first began to study music. It would make me happy to think that these ideas will be helpful to some young musician, brimming with excitement over the world of musical possibilities, eager to understand how classical music, jazz, and rock all fit together—and raring to make some new contribution to musical culture.

PART I

Theory

CHAPTER 1

Five Components of Tonality

The word "tonal" is contested territory. Some writers use it restrictively, to describe only the Western art music of the eighteenth and nineteenth centuries. For them, more recent music is "post-tonal"—a catch-all term including everything from Arvo Pärt's consonances to the organized sonic assaults of Varèse and Xenakis. This way of categorizing music makes it seem as if Pärt, Varèse, and Xenakis are clearly and obviously of a kind, resembling one another more than any of them resembles earlier composers.

"Tonal" can also be used expansively. Here, the term describes not just eighteenth- and nineteenth-century Western art music, but rock, folk, jazz, impressionism, minimalism, medieval and Renaissance music, and a good deal of non-Western music besides. "Tonality" in this sense is almost synonymous with "non-atonality"—a double negative, most naturally understood in contrast to music that was deliberately written to contrast with it. The expansive usage accords with the intuition that Schubert, the Beatles, and Pärt share musical preoccupations that are not shared by composers such as Varèse, Xenakis, and Cage. But it also raises awkward questions. What musical feature or features lead us to consider works to be tonal? Is "tonality" a single property, or does it have several components? And how does tonality manifest itself across the broad spectrum of Western and non-Western styles? Faced with these questions, contemporary music theory stares at its feet in awkward silence.[1]

The purpose of this book is to provide general categories for discussing music that is neither classically tonal nor completely atonal. This, in my view, includes some of the most fascinating music of the twentieth century, from impressionism to postminimalism. It also includes some of the most mysterious and alluring music of Chopin, Liszt, and Wagner—music that is as beloved by audiences as it is recalcitrant to analytical scrutiny. My goal is to try to develop a set of theoretical tools that will help us think about these sophisticated tonal styles, which are in some ways freer and less rule-bound than either eighteenth-century classical music or twentieth-century modernism.

---

1 Fétis (1840/1994), who popularized the term "tonality" in the early nineteenth century, was one of the first scholars to try to provide a general account of the phenomenon. (For more on the early history of the term "tonality" see Simms 1975 and Dahlhaus 1990.) More recently, Joseph Yasser (1975), Richard Norton (1984), William Thomson (1999), Brian Hyer (2002), Carol Krumhansl (2004), and Matthew Brown (2005) have offered different perspectives on the subject.

More specifically, I will argue that five features are present in a wide range of genres, Western and non-Western, past and present, and that they jointly contribute to a sense of tonality:

1. *Conjunct melodic motion.* Melodies tend to move by short distances from note to note.
2. *Acoustic consonance.* Consonant harmonies are preferred to dissonant harmonies, and tend to be used at points of musical stability.
3. *Harmonic consistency.* The harmonies in a passage of music, whatever they may be, tend to be structurally similar to one another.
4. *Limited macroharmony.* I use the term "macroharmony" to refer to the total collection of notes heard over moderate spans of musical time. Tonal music tends to use relatively small macroharmonies, often involving five to eight notes.
5. *Centricity.* Over moderate spans of musical time, one note is heard as being more prominent than the others, appearing more frequently and serving as a goal of musical motion.

The aim of this book is to investigate the ways composers can use these five features to produce interesting musical effects. This project has empirical, theoretical, and historical components. Empirically, we might ask how each of the five features contributes to listeners' perceptions of tonality: which is the most influential, and are there any interesting interactions between them? For instance, is harmonic consistency more important in the context of some scales than others? Theoretically, we might ask how the various features can *in principle* be combined. Is it the case, for example, that diatonic music necessarily involves a tonic? Conversely, is chromatic music necessarily non-centric? Finally, we can ask historical questions about how different Western styles have combined these five tonal ingredients—treating the features as determining a space of possibilities, and investigating the ways composers have explored that space.

This book is primarily concerned with the theoretical and historical questions. I am a musician, not a scientist, and although I will sometimes touch on perceptual issues, I will largely leave empirical psychology to the professionals. Instead, I will ask how composers *have combined* and *might combine* the five features. Part I of the book develops theoretical tools for thinking about the five features. Part II uses these tools to argue for a broader, more continuous conception of the Western musical tradition. Rather than focusing narrowly on the eighteenth and nineteenth centuries (the so-called "common practice period"), I attempt to identify an "extended common practice" stretching from the beginning of Western counterpoint to the music of recent decades. The point is to retell the history of Western music in such a way that the tonal styles of the last century—including jazz, rock, and minimalism—emerge as vibrant and interesting successors to the tonal music of earlier periods.

My central conclusion is that the five features impose much stronger constraints than we would intuitively expect. For example, if we want to combine conjunct melodic motion and harmonic consistency, then we have only a few options, the most important of which involve acoustically consonant sonorities. And if we want to combine harmonic consistency with limited macroharmony, then we are led to a collection of very familiar scales and modes. Thus the materials of tonal music are, in Richard Cohn's apt description, "overdetermined," in the sense that they are special or distinctive for multiple different reasons.[2] This suggests that when we look closely, we should find important similarities between different tonal styles: since there are only a few ways to combine the five features, different composers—from before Palestrina to after Bill Evans—will necessarily use the same basic techniques. In the second part of this book I make good on this claim, tracing common practices that connect the earliest examples of Western counterpoint to music of the very recent past.

1.1 THE FIVE FEATURES

Let's consider the five features in more detail, with an eye toward understanding why they might be so widespread throughout Western and non-Western music. A preference for *conjunct melodic motion* likely derives from the features of the auditory system that create a three-dimensional "auditory scene."[3] An eardrum, in effect, is a one-dimensional system that can only move back and forth. From this meager input our brains create a vivid three-dimensional sonic space consisting of individually localized sounds: the phone ringing in front of you, the honk of a car horn outside your window, and the sound of a droning music theorist off to your right. To accomplish this dazzling transfiguration, the brain relies on a number of computational tricks, one of which is to group sonic events that are nearby in pitch.[4] Thus, a sequence like Figure 1.1.1a tends to be heard as belonging to a single sound source, whereas Figure 1.1.1b creates the impression of multiple sources. In this sense, small melodic steps are intrinsic to the very notion of "melody."

Acoustic consonance, or intrinsic sonic restfulness, is another very widespread musical feature.[5] Many styles make heavy use of consonant intervals such as the octave and perfect fifth, assigning them privileged melodic and harmonic roles. Scales containing a large number of consonant intervals are found in seemingly independent musical cultures, and there is evidence from infant psychology that the preference for consonance is innate.[6] At present, however, we do not know

Figure 1.1.1 Small movements sound melodic (*a*), while large registral leaps create the impression of multiple melodies (*b*).

2 See Cohn 1997.

3 See Bregman 1990, Narmour 1990, and Vos and Troost 1989. Huron 2007 contains data about statistical properties of Western melodies, including conjunct melodic motion.

4 Wessel (1979) suggests that the relevant variable might be the "spectral centroid," which in normal listening circumstances is highly correlated with pitch.

5 Izumi (2000) and Hulse et al. (1995) indicate that nonhuman animals such as monkeys and birds can distinguish consonance from dissonance.

6 Crowder, Reznick, and Rosenkrantz 1991, Zentner and Kagan 1996 and 1998, Trainor and Heinmiller 1998, Trainor, Tsang and Cheung 2002, and McDermott and Hauser 2005.

for certain how universal or innate this preference is. Fortunately, this issue is largely irrelevant in the present context: what matters is just that many listeners, both Western and non-Western, do have a fairly deep-seated preference for consonant sonorities.

Slightly more general than acoustic consonance is *harmonic consistency*, or the use of sonorities that resemble one another. For example, Figure 1.1.2a features a series of major and minor chords, all audibly similar. Their resemblance gives the passage a kind of smoothness, and we experience the chords as belonging together. Likewise, Figure 1.1.2b uses a series of very dissonant chromatic clusters that also seem to belong together. By contrast, Figure 1.1.2c uses very different-sounding harmonies, switching aimlessly between different sonic worlds. This sort of harmonic incongruity is quite unusual in Western music, and often provokes spontaneous laughter—suggesting that the expectation of harmonic consistency is very strong, even though it is rarely discussed.

Figure 1.1.2 Harmonic consistency using consonant sonorities (*a*) and dissonant sonorities (*b*). Sequence (*c*) does not exhibit harmonic consistency.

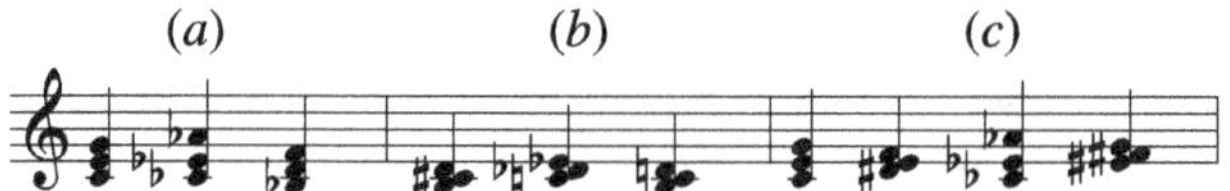

In most Western and non-Western music, pitches are drawn from a relatively small reservoir of available notes—typically, between five and eight.[7] As a result, Western music has a two-tiered harmonic consistency: at the local (or instantaneous) level, a passage like Figure 1.1.3 presents a series of major and minor chords, which are audibly related, while over larger time spans it articulates a scale by using only seven different notes. The scale can thus be considered a kind of "large" or *macro* harmony that subsumes the individual chords.[8] Even though there is no one instant at which this larger harmony is presented, it nevertheless has a significant effect on our listening experience: scale-based melodies are easier to remember than nonscalar melodies, and notes outside the scale sound more pungent than notes in the scale. As we will see, macroharmonies can be relatively consonant, like the diatonic or pentatonic scale, or relatively dissonant, like the chromatic scale. They can also participate in larger-level voice leadings analogous to those connecting individual chords.

Finally, we often hear some pitches or notes as being more important (or "central") than others. These pitches tend to serve as points of musical arrival, to which others are heard as "leading" or "tending." Thus, one and the same sequence of notes—such as that in Figure 1.1.4—can be heard in a variety of ways. If we hear it in a musical

---

7 Burns 1999 and Dowling and Harwood 1986. The range "five to eight" recalls familiar facts about the limitations on human short-term memory (see Miller 1956 on "seven plus or minus two").

8 Thanks to Ciro Scotto for suggesting this term.

Figure 1.1.3 Major and minor triads belonging to the same diatonic scale.

Figure 1.1.4 A single melody will sound different in different harmonic contexts.

context where C is the most stable pitch, then it sounds like a beginning that is in need of some sort of continuation, ending with a comma rather than a period. But in a context where F is stable, it sounds more complete, as if it ends with a period or exclamation point. Centricity is again a very widespread feature of human music, appearing in a large number of seemingly unrelated musical cultures. However, different styles can emphasize the tonic note to different extents: as Harold Powers once noted, there is a much stronger feeling of centricity in Indian music than in Renaissance polyphony.[9]

Of these five features, harmonic consistency is clearly the most culturally specific. The idea that music should consist of rapidly changing chords is a deeply Western idea, in a double sense: it is deep, insofar as it characterizes much Western music since before the Renaissance; and it is Western, since there are many cultures in which the notion of a "chord progression" simply plays no role. (Many traditional non-Western styles are purely monophonic, or feature an unchanging "drone" harmony; however, there are now a large number of syncretistic styles that combine Western harmonies with non-Western melodic and rhythmic ideas.) Acoustic consonance is also somewhat culture-specific: although many cultures make some use of consonant intervals, and although some have recognizably Western conceptions of consonance, other non-Western styles sound quite dissonant to Western ears. By contrast, the three other features—conjunct melodic motion, limited macroharmony, and centricity—are common to virtually all human music. This near universality may be attributable, at least in part, to features of our biological inheritance.[10]

Now for an important disclaimer. While I think that typical Western listeners *prefer* music that exemplifies the five features, I do not mean to suggest that such music is intrinsically *better* than any other kind of music. "Tonal," for me, is not synonymous with "good." (Nor is "popular," for that matter: there is plenty of unpopular, nontonal music that I happen to like, from Nancarrow to Xenakis to Ligeti.) In particular, I have no interest in arguing that atonal composers are misguided, fighting against biology, or anything of the sort. Instead, the purpose of this book is an affirmative one: to develop new theoretical tools for thinking about tonality, and to provide new insights into the relations between various musical styles. My hope is that this investigation will be useful to composers and theorists of all varieties, as even the advocates of atonality will stand to gain from a deeper understanding of that which they are trying to avoid.

9 Powers 1958.

10 Dowling and Harwood 1986, Narmour 1990.

1.2 PERCEPTION AND THE FIVE FEATURES

This book is primarily concerned with what composers do, rather than what listeners hear: the goal is to describe various ways in which the five features have been or might be combined. But it is not possible to avoid perceptual issues altogether. After all, readers have a right to wonder whether my five features do indeed contribute to the experience of tonality, and if so, whether they are the only factors that contribute.

The first question can be easily answered: all one needs to do is constrain randomly generated notes according to each of the five features. Insofar as the constraints cause random music to sound increasingly tonal, or at least ordered, then I am right about their psychological importance. Furthermore, the same experiment can be used not just to show *that* these features have important psychological effects, but also *what particular psychological effects they have.* This is useful because familiar styles tend either to combine many of the features, and hence be fully tonal in a traditional sense, or else to abandon most of them à la radical atonality. Consequently, existing musical works do not always help us to understand the specific contributions made by each of our five components individually.

I strongly urge you to try this experiment for yourself: the results are not subtle, and they demonstrate the powerful psychological effects that can be obtained with simple musical means. (In particular, I encourage you to use the book's companion website, which contains a number of illustrative examples.[11]) Unfortunately, this is a case where a musical experience is worth a thousand words: no amount of merely verbal description on my part will substitute for your own investigation. Nevertheless, it is worth trying to describe these effects, if only to persuade you to actually perform the experiment. Figure 1.2.1a presents a series of completely random three-note chords, with pitches chosen arbitrarily from the range C2 to C7. It provides a baseline against which subsequent examples can be judged. (Some people, myself included, find this sort of random texture to be oddly appealing.) Figure 1.2.1b constrains the randomness by requiring that the notes move just a few semitones from chord to chord. What results is very rudimentary sort of counterpoint, consisting of three independent melodic strands. Although it is considerably less random-sounding than the pointillistic texture of (*a*), the harmonic structure of the sequence still sounds somewhat indistinct, providing the ear with relatively little to grab onto. Figure 1.2.1c combines conjunct melodic motion with harmonic consistency, requiring that each chord be a "stack of fourths." The melodic lines, rather than wandering aimlessly, now seem to create chords with a distinctive harmonic identity, which in turn gives the passage a feeling of increased consistency.[12] (This example might seem reminiscent of some Stravinsky or Hindemith.) Finally,

---

11 www.oup.com/us/ageometryofmusic

12 With a little practice it is easy to distinguish harmonically consistent sequences from those involving random, unrelated chords. However, it should be said that some chords (such as the major triad or stack of fourths) have a very distinctive sound, while others (such as C-C♯-D♯) are more generic. It takes more compositional work to create a palpable sense of harmonic consistency using these generic chords.

Figure 1.2.1d restricts the chords to the same diatonic scale. To complete the transition from utter randomness to something recognizably tonal, I have replaced the "fourth chords" of (*c*) with more consonant diatonic triads. Although the result will not win any composition prizes, it does demonstrate that a kind of rudimentary tonalness is in fact generated by my five features. Indeed, the differences between Figures 1.2.1a–d are striking and unmistakable, even for a layperson with no specialized musical training.

Informal experiments like these suggest that, for typical listeners, the five features play an important role in determining the tonalness (or perhaps "orderedness") of musical stimuli. Furthermore, I strongly suspect that for many listeners, "tonalness," "orderedness," and "pleasantness" are correlated: all else being equal, music displaying many of the five features will be preferred to music that does not.[13] This constitutes the testable psychological theory lurking at the core of this book. Personally, I think it would be interesting to try to determine not just *that* the five features have important psychological effects, but also their relative importance. What makes a larger difference to listeners' perceptions, harmonic consistency, acoustic consonance, or conjunct melodic motion? We lack even the most rudimentary data that would allow

Figure 1.2.1 Four randomly generated sequences. Sequence (*a*) is completely random; (*b*) exhibits efficient voice leading; (*c*) exhibits harmonic consistency and efficient voice leading; (*d*) exhibits harmonic consistency, efficient voice leading, and limited macroharmony.

13 Some preliminary studies, conducted by John Muniz, Cynthia Weaver, and Asher Yamplosky (graduate students at Yale University), suggest that conjunct melodic motion may contribute more to "orderedness" than "pleasantness." Disentangling these issues is a subject for future research.

us to answer this question. One of my hopes is that some psychologist readers will be motivated to undertake the obvious experiments suggested by the ideas I will be discussing.

Figure 1.2.1 shows that the five features *can* contribute fairly dramatically to the sense of tonality. But are they *necessary* for creating tonal effects? And if so, are they the only such features or are there others?

In some ways, I think the question is misguided. The point here is not to police the use of the word "tonality" by setting strict limits on what may or may not be described with the term, but rather to replace the crude opposition "tonal/atonal" with a more nuanced set of distinctions. You can decide for yourself whether to use "tonal" to describe (say) diatonic music without a tonal center, or chromatic music with a strong sense of harmonic consistency; my job is just to show that the term "tonality" typically applies to music that exhibits my five basic features. I should also point out that I am neglecting important issues such as rhythm, motivic variation, timbre, form, performance, and rubato, all of which can contribute to the sense of tonality. (My goal is not to provide a complete theory of all music, but rather to discuss a few general features whose musical importance is for the most part unquestioned.) That said, however, I confess that it is difficult for me to imagine that I would ever want to use the term "tonal" to describe music in which acoustic consonance plays no role, in which there is no conjunct melodic motion or harmonic consistency, in which no tone is heard as central, and which does not limit itself to a relatively small number of pitch classes over short stretches of time. In this sense, it seems that at least some of the five features are necessary for tonality, at least as I personally understand it.

Throughout the twentieth century, composers devised new musical languages—some idiosyncratic, some very widely used—intended to replace traditional tonality. It is instructive to subject these alternative systems to the experimental test described above: that is, to constrain random musical notes according to their basic principles, and to listen for the perceptual differences that result.[14] To that end, Figure 1.2.2 uses "constrained randomness" to investigate one of the most prominent alternatives to tonality, the twelve-tone system.[15] On a first (or even tenth) listening, I do not find the sequences in Figure 1.2.2 to be dramatically different from randomly generated sequences such as Figure 1.2.1b. Indeed, if someone were to present the three passages in a psychology experiment, I doubt I would notice that one was random while the other two were not. This is not to say that twelve-tone structure makes *no* audible difference, or that one cannot learn to hear the coherence in Figure 1.2.2, but rather

14 It is exceedingly difficult to judge the effects of a musical syntax if we only encounter it in the context of complete compositions, since compositional skill may mask the contributions of the syntax itself.

15 Figure 1.2.2a uses three successive rows to generate a sequence of 12 three-note chords. Figure 1.2.2b sets the row in counterpoint against its inversional and retrograde-inversional forms, producing a series of 12 three-note chords. I have borrowed the 12-tone row from Schoenberg's first consistently twelve-tone piece, his Op. 25 Suite for piano.

Figure 1.2.2 Randomly generated twelve-tone music.

that the psychological effects here are relatively subtle—considerably less dramatic than those produced by our five features.

Does this show that twelve-tone music is aesthetically problematic? Or that the twentieth-century quest for alternatives to traditional tonality is fruitless? Not at all.[16] But it does suggest that twelve-tone rows produce less powerful psychological consequences than harmonic consistency, conjunct melodic motion, acoustic consonance, macroharmony, and centricity.[17] And while twelve-tone music is just one twentieth-century musical system, similar comments might be made about other approaches. To my mind, this suggests that the five features are unusually powerful tools for creating musical coherence. To say this is not to deny that alternative tools may in principle exist, but simply to reiterate the basic point that tonality constitutes a fairly unique solution to some elementary compositional problems. If this is right, then the task of providing an alternative to tonality is much more difficult than one might intuitively have imagined.

1.3 FOUR CLAIMS

The argument of this book revolves around four basic claims, each of which concerns ways in which the five features can interact with or constrain one another. In this section I'll briefly outline these claims as a way of foreshadowing some of my central preoccupations.

16 First, it is possible that there are gifted listeners who respond strongly and immediately to the non-random features of the sequences in Figure 1.2.2. Second, it is possible that with extensive training ordinary listeners can sensitize themselves to the sequences' structure—as when one gradually starts to discern the details in an all-gray painting. Third, it is possible that there are specific compositional techniques that can make twelve-tone structure psychologically transparent. Fourth, it is possible that some listeners simply enjoy random pitch structures. And fifth, it is possible that twelve-tone music can be attractive in ways that make up for any potential absence of interesting pitch structure.

17 Schoenberg (1975, p. 215) observed that "composing [using twelve-tone techniques] does not become easier, but rather ten times more difficult" (see also Dubiel 1997).

1.3.1 Harmony and Counterpoint Constrain One Another

Imagine a composer, Lyrico, who would like to combine conjunct melodic motion with harmonic consistency; that is, he would like to write melodies that move by short distances while using harmonies that are structurally similar to one another. Intuitively, it might seem that there are innumerable ways to satisfy these two constraints—that there is an entire universe of syntaxes consistent with these fundamental principles. But in fact, there are just a few ways in which they can be combined.

Consider the simplest possible situation. Suppose Lyrico decides to combine an unchanging "drone" harmony with a moving melodic voice. Harmonic consistency is thus obtained trivially: the chords in the passage will all be similar because *there is only one chord*. Let us further imagine that Lyrico chooses to use a C major chord as his drone. If he were to confine the melody to the notes of this chord, the result would be a series of unmelodic leaps (Figure 1.3.1a). This is because its notes are all reasonably far apart. To obtain conjunct melodic motion, Lyrico can therefore introduce "passing tones" that connect the chord tones by short melodic steps. The result, shown in Figure 1.3.1b, is a *scale* covering an entire octave, in which successive notes are connected by relatively small distances, and in which chord tones alternate with nonchordal "passing tones." Lyrico can now write melodies that move freely along this scale, alternating between stable and unstable notes.

But suppose Lyrico wakes up one day in a more ornery mood and decides to use the dissonant chromatic cluster {B, C, D♭} as his drone. Here the compositional situation is reversed: where the major chord is consonant, and has its notes spread relatively far apart, this chord is very dissonant and has all its notes close together. Consequently, by confining himself to the notes of the chord, Lyrico can obtain conjunct melodies, as in Figure 1.3.2. However, it takes a large number of passing tones to connect the D♭ in one octave to the B in the

Figure 1.3.1 (*a*) Confining a melody to the notes of the C major chord produces large leaps, so it is necessary to add "passing tones" (*b*).

Figure 1.3.2 (*a*) Confining a melody to the notes of the cluster {B, C, D♭} produces conjunct melodic motion, but changing octaves requires a large number of passing tones (*b*).

next. Since the resulting scale does not exhibit a regular alternation of stable "chord tones" and unstable "passing tones," it is difficult to hear the nonharmonic tones as connective devices that simply decorate an underlying harmony.

These two examples suggest a general moral: *harmony and melody constrain one another.* Different types of chords suggest different musical uses. In particular there is a fundamental difference between chords like {C, E, G}, whose notes are all far away from each other, and chords like {B, C, D♭}, whose notes are clustered close together. When a chord's notes are clustered close together, it is possible to create conjunct melodies that use only the chord's notes, but it is not possible to create scales that have a regular alternation between chord tones and passing tones. When a chord's notes are relatively spread out, it is not possible to create conjunct melodies by using only the notes of the chord, but it *is* possible to create scales with a nice arrangement of chord and non-chord tones.

Now consider a more sophisticated problem. Suppose Lyrico decides to write a C major chord followed by an F major chord, its transposition by ascending perfect fourth. As shown in Figure 1.3.3, *every* note in the C major chord is near some note in an F major chord: C is common to both, E is one semitone from F, and G is two semitones from both F and A. This means that Lyrico can write a sequence of C and F major chords that articulates *three separate melodies*, each moving by small distances. This is *counterpoint*—a group of simultaneous melodies, or *voices*, articulating mappings, or *voice leadings*, between successive chords. For example, the first voice leading in Figure 1.3.3b maps G to A, E to F, and C to C. This voice leading is *efficient* because all the voices move by short distances. Clearly, efficient voice leading is simply conjunct melodic motion in all parts of a contrapuntal texture.

Figure 1.3.3 (*a*) Every note of the C major triad is near some note of the F major triad. (*b*) It is possible to use a series of C and F major triads to construct three simultaneous melodies.

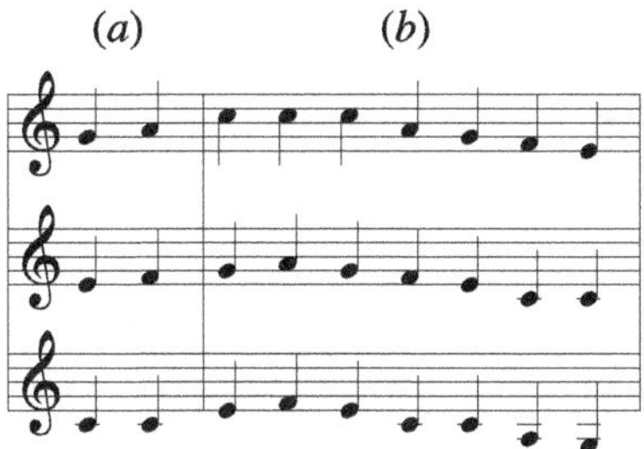

As it happens, the major chord is particularly well suited for contrapuntal music. Figure 1.3.4 shows that any two major chords can be connected by stepwise voice leading in which no voice moves by more than two semitones. This means that Lyrico can write a harmonic progression *without worrying about melody*; that is, for any sequence

Figure 1.3.4 Any two major triads can be linked by stepwise voice leading; in the case of the tritone, this requires four voices.

of major triads, there is always some way to connect the notes so as to form stepwise melodies. Conversely, Lyrico can write any melody whatsoever without worrying about harmony, as there will always be some way to harmonize it with a sequence of efficient voice leadings between major chords.

But what if Lyrico writes the chromatic cluster {B, C, D♭} followed by {E, F, G♭}, its transposition by ascending fourth? Here, none of the notes of the first chord are within two semitones of any note in the second, and hence there is no way to combine a sequence of these chords so as to produce conjunct melodies (Figure 1.3.5). At the same time, however, the chromatic cluster can do things that the C major chord can't: Figure 1.3.6 shows that it is possible to write contrapuntal music in which individual melodic lines move by short distances *within* a single, unchanging harmony. Clearly, this is possible only because the chord's notes are all clustered together, ensuring that there is always a short path between any two of them. The resulting music produces a feeling of burbling within stasis, a kind of melodic activity within overall harmonic restfulness.[18]

Once again, we see that different kinds of chords are useful for different purposes. Chords that divide the octave very unevenly, such as {B, C, D♭}, are ideally suited for static music in which harmonies do not change. By contrast, chords that divide the octave relatively evenly, like C major, can be connected to their transpositions by efficient voice leading, and are therefore suited for contrapuntal music in which harmonies change quickly. Remarkably, the most nearly even chords in twelve-tone equal temperament are the familiar chords of Western music: perfect fifths, triads, seventh chords, ninth chords, and familiar scales. Besides being well suited for contrapuntal music, these chords are all *acoustically consonant,* or restful and stable-sounding. This, then, is an example of Cohn's "overdetermination," a situation in which a familiar musical object is remarkable for multiple reasons: nearly even chords are interesting not just because they permit the combination of harmonic consistency and conjunct melodic motion, but also because they can be acoustically consonant.[19]

Figure 1.3.5 Chromatic clusters cannot always be linked by efficient voice leading.

Figure 1.3.6 Chromatic clusters allow conjunct melodic motion to be combined with harmonic stasis.

More generally, it would seem that composers who wish to combine harmonic consistency and conjunct melodic motion have relatively few options: they can either use familiar sonorities in more or less familiar ways, or they can use chromatic chords whose notes are clustered

18 This sort of texture was popularized during the 1960s by composers such as Ligeti and Lutosławski; precursors to the technique include Bartók's *Out of Doors* ("Night Music") and Ruth Crawford Seeger's String Quartet.

19 This observation has been made by Agmon (1991) and Cohn (1996), in the special case of the triad. Both writers explained the specialness of the triad in terms of the way it is embedded in a larger collection. In the following chapters, I provide an account that applies to consonant chords more generally and that does not presuppose embedding into a larger scale.

together. The next few chapters will elaborate on this point, using the notion of *near symmetry* to explain exactly how chord structure constrains contrapuntal function. Later chapters will trace the practical consequences of this interdependence, considering a range of superficially different styles, from Renaissance polyphony to contemporary jazz, and showing that they all utilize fundamentally similar procedures. Our theoretical work will demonstrate that these similarities are not simply the byproduct of historical influence, but also of the more fundamental ways in which the five features constrain one another. In other words, they testify to the fact that there are only a few ways to combine harmonic consistency and stepwise melodies.

1.3.2 Scale, Macroharmony, and Centricity are Independent

My second claim is that we need to distinguish the closely related phenomena of scale, macroharmony, and centricity. A *scale*, as I use the term, is a means of measuring musical distance—a kind of musical ruler whose unit is the "scale step." Relative to the C diatonic scale, the notes E and G are two scale steps apart, since there is precisely one white note between them (Figure 1.3.7).[20] These same notes are one step apart relative to the pentatonic scale C-D-E-G-A and three steps apart relative to the chromatic scale. Similarly, C and E are two steps apart relative to the diatonic and pentatonic scales, and four apart relative to the chromatic scale. The three scales therefore give us three different ways of measuring musical distance, and three different estimates of the relative sizes of the intervals C-E and E-G. In principle, we should not ask whether the intervals C-E and E-G are "the same size" unless we also specify a particular musical "ruler." As we will see, the richness of tonal music lies partly in the way it exploits these various conceptions of musical distance.

If a scale is a musical ruler, then a *macroharmony* is the total collection of notes used over small stretches of musical time. Typically, macroharmonies are also scales: a composer might (for example) use only the white notes on the piano keyboard, while also exploiting the unit of distance defined by adjacent notes (the "scale step"). But in

Figure 1.3.7 Scale steps provide a means of measuring musical distance. The intervals C-E and E-G are two steps large relative to the diatonic scale (*a*), two and one steps large relative to the pentatonic scale (*b*), and four and three steps large relative to the chromatic scale (*c*).

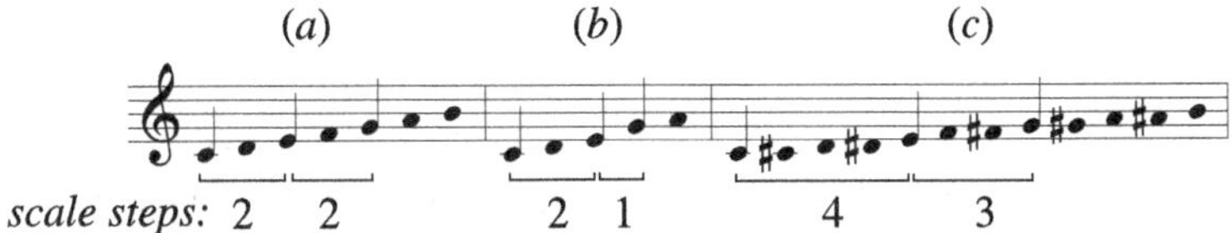

20 Here and elsewhere, I use the term "C diatonic scale" to refer to the notes of the C major scale (i.e. the white notes) without suggesting that the note C is special in any way. I use the term "C major" (or "C ionian") in contexts where C is a tonal center.

Figure 1.3.8 The music makes use of two scales to create a chromatic macroharmony.

principle it is possible to separate the two phenomena. Figure 1.3.8 shows a passage of "polytonal" music in which the upper staff moves systematically along the C diatonic scale, while the lower staff moves along G♭ pentatonic. To explain how this music works, we need to postulate two different scales, one for each staff. (Of course it would be possible to combine the notes in both staves into a single chromatic scale, but the resulting collection would be useless for explaining why the individual voices move as they do.) Here, then, is a passage of music that uses pentatonic and diatonic scales to create a chromatic macroharmony. The concept of "scale" allows us to describe the structure within each voice, while the concept "macroharmony" allows us to describe the global harmony they produce.

A second fundamental distinction is between *macroharmony* and *centricity*. "Centricity" refers to the phenomenon whereby a particular pitch is felt as being more stable or important than the others. (In traditional tonality this is the tonic note; in modal theory, it is the "final.") Chapters 4 and 5 will suggest that macroharmony and centricity are completely independent: it is entirely possible, for example, to write diatonic music in which no note is heard as a tonal center, just as one can write chromatic music with a very clear center. There is, however, a strong historical association between the two, with diatonic music often being centric and chromatic music centerless. The explanation for this connection lies in the fact that some prominent musicians believed that the diatonic scale had a unique "natural" tonic, and hence that a centerless chromaticism was the main alternative to traditional tonality. Other musicians, believing that centricity and macroharmony were independent, felt free to explore a much wider range of scales and modes. Chapter 5 will thus propose that the cleavage between the "scalar" and "chromatic" traditions, exemplified by composers such as Debussy and Schoenberg, was exacerbated by a fundamental disagreement about the relationship between macroharmony and centricity.

Together, scale, macroharmony, and centricity are the three principal components of what I think of as the "general theory of keys"—a set of tools for describing music that is tonal in the broad sense, even though it may not conform to the specific conventions of eighteenth-century tonality. One of this book's goals is to consider various sorts of "generalized keys" in Western music. Particularly interesting here is the gradual emergence of a musical language that combines a wide variety of macroharmonies and tonal centers. The earliest Western music explored the tonal centers contained within a relatively static and largely diatonic macroharmony (Figure 1.3.9).[21] Classical music, which reduced the available modes to just major and minor, created large-scale harmonic contrasts by juxtaposing different scalar collections (e.g. G major and C major). It was only in the last decades of the nineteenth century that these two procedures were combined, as composers began to feel free to use *any*

21 The presence of unnotated accidentals (*musica ficta*) complicates matters somewhat.

Figure 1.3.9 (*a*) In earlier music, composers emphasized different centers within a single fixed diatonic collection. (*b*) In classical music, composers restricted the available modes to two, creating long-term harmonic change by emphasizing *different* major or minor scales. (*c*) Only in the twentieth-century were these two techniques systematically combined, creating a much wider range of tonal areas to choose from.

of the seven modes of *any* of the twelve diatonic collections. This scalar vocabulary was further extended with the use of additional nondiatonic scales—including the pentatonic, whole tone, melodic minor, harmonic minor, and octatonic—creating hundreds of possible combinations of macroharmony and tonal center. What results is a dazzling proliferation of "generalized keys" providing a wealth of alternatives to traditional major and minor modes.

1.3.3 Modulation Involves Voice Leading

My third claim is that tonal music makes use of the same voice-leading techniques on two different temporal levels: *chord progressions* use efficient voice leading to link structurally similar chords, and *modulations* use efficient voice leading to link structurally similar scales.[22] As a result, tonal music is both self-similar and hierarchical, exploiting the same procedures at two different time scales.

Figure 1.3.10 shows the opening of the last movement of Clementi's D major Piano Sonata, Op. 25 No. 6. The two parallel phrases present a series of three-voice chord progressions: I–V^6–I followed by I–IV–I and then V^7/V–V. The bottom staff shows that we can find a higher-level harmonic motion relating two diatonic collections: the first six measures limit themselves to the seven notes of D major, while the rest of the phrase abandons the G♮ in favor of the G♯. As we will see in Chapter 4, this modulation, or motion between macroharmonies, can be represented as a voice leading in which the G♮ *moves by semitone* to G♯. This means that the music exhibits two sorts of efficient voice leading: on the level of the half measure, there is a sequence of eight efficient voice leadings between triads; while on a larger temporal level there is a

22 This is not all that modulation does, of course, but it is typically part of it.

Figure 1.3.10 Two levels of voice leading in Clementi's Op. 25 No. 6.

single efficient voice leading between D major and A major scales, occurring somewhere near the seventh measure of the example.

Figure 1.3.11 shows that similar processes occur in twentieth-century music. The top system depicts the main theme of Debussy's prelude "Le vent dans la plaine," which uses the pitches of E♭ natural minor. When the theme returns, B♭ moves by semitone to B♭♭, producing a collection that is enharmonically equivalent to F♯ melodic minor ascending. Debussy's "modulation" is thus analogous to Clementi's, although it involves modes that Clementi himself would never have used. Here, then, we have a familiar tonal technique appearing in the context of a significantly expanded modal vocabulary. As we will see in Chapter 9, this same technique has been used by a number of twentieth-century composers, including Stravinsky, Shostakovich, and the minimalists. There are also a few non-Western styles that use voice leading to link closely related scales.[23]

The idea that tonal music is hierarchically self-similar is central to the work of Heinrich Schenker, who claimed that tonal pieces consisted of recursively embedded patterns. The theory I have described is similar to Schenker's insofar as I consider

23 Morton 1976 and Hall 2009.

Figure 1.3.11 Voice leading between macroharmonies in Debussy's "Le vent dans la plaine."

tonal music to utilize efficient voice leading at two temporal levels. Unlike Schenker, however, I view macroharmonies and scales (rather than chords or melodic lines) as the primary vehicles of long-range harmonic progression: for me, the long-term voice leading in Figure 1.3.10 connects the D and A major *scales* rather than D and A major tonic triads. By contrast, a Schenkerian would likely interpret the passage—and indeed the entire piece—as involving chord progressions at all hierarchical levels. In Chapter 7 I will return to these issues, suggesting that my approach, though perhaps less unified than Schenker's, more closely reflects the cognitive processes involved in composition.

1.3.4 Music Can Be Understood Geometrically

My fourth claim is that geometry provides a powerful tool for modeling musical structure. This is because there exists a family of geometrical spaces that depict the voice-leading relationships among virtually any chords we might care to imagine. Some of these (such as the familiar "circle of fifths") are relatively simple, but others (such as the Möbius strip containing two-note chords) are considerably more complex. One goal of the book is to provide a user-friendly introduction to these musico-geometrical spaces, explaining how they work, and showing how they allow us to visualize a wealth of musical possibilities at a glance.

Suppose, by way of illustration, that our friend Lyrico decides to write music using only the seven triads in the C diatonic collection. After a little exploration, he finds that some of these are closer together than others: for example, he can turn a C major triad into an A minor triad by moving only one note by one diatonic step, whereas he must move each voice to turn C major into D minor (Figure 1.3.12). Pondering this a little further, Lyrico eventually realizes that the diatonic triads can be linked in a "circle of thirds" (Figure 1.3.13), where each chord can be connected to its neighbors by a single-step motion. This circle allows him to define a kind of "distance" according to which C major and A minor are one step apart (since they are adjacent on the circle) while C major and D minor are three steps apart (since there are two chords between them).

Now suppose that Lyrico's rival Avanta becomes frustrated with all this conservatism. "Why limit yourself to just the triads in that one seven-note scale?" she asks, stamping her foot. "There's a whole world out there beyond the white notes, you know!" Avanta then proceeds to demonstrate some of the musical possibilities not represented in Lyrico's simple circular model: she shows that in the familiar chromatic scale, the C major chord can be linked to *four* separate triads by single-semitone voice leading, and to *seven* triads by a pair of semitone steps (Figure 1.3.14). What is the analogue, in Avanta's expanded musical world, to Lyrico's circular map? How can she depict the voice-leading possibilities between *all* the triads in the chromatic scale?

Figure 1.3.12 Voice leading between diatonic triads.

The answer turns out to be surprisingly complicated: instead of a simple seven-chord circular model, Avanta needs the three-dimensional, 40-chord lattice shown in Figure 1.3.15. This figure provides a map of all the contrapuntal possibilities available to a composer who wants to use traditional triads, but is willing to step outside the confines of a single diatonic scale. This complex-looking construction provides the first hint that ordinary musical questions might sometimes lead to nontrivial geometrical answers. In fact, Chapter 3 shows that Avanta's lattice lives in what mathematicians would call "the interior of a twisted triangular two-torus," otherwise known as a triangular doughnut. This space contains all possible three-note chords in any conceivable scale and any conceivable tuning system. Analogous spaces depict

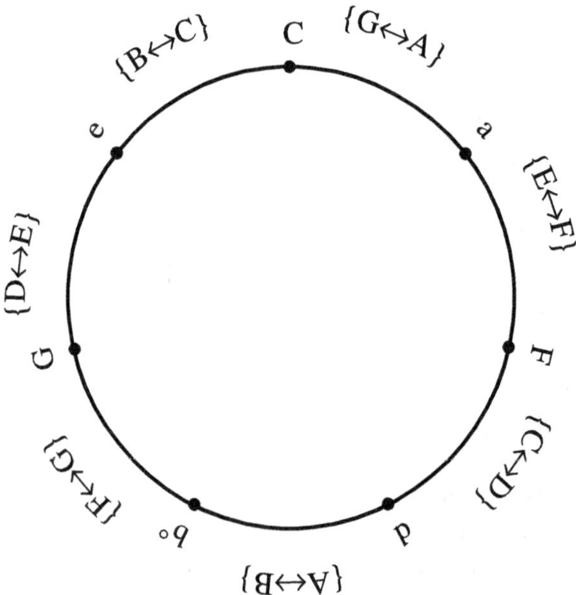

Figure 1.3.13 Single-step voice-leading between diatonic triads can be modeled with a circle.

Figure 1.3.14 (*a*) One-semitone voice leading and (*b*) two-semitone voice leading among triads.

Figure 1.3.15 This three-dimensional graph represents single-semitone voice leading between major, minor, augmented, and diminished triads—represented by dark spheres, light spheres, dark cubes, and light cubes respectively. Chords on the same horizontal cross-section are related by major-third transposition; vertical motion corresponds to semitonal transposition, and the top face is glued to the bottom with a 120° twist. We will explore this figure more thoroughly in Chapter 3.

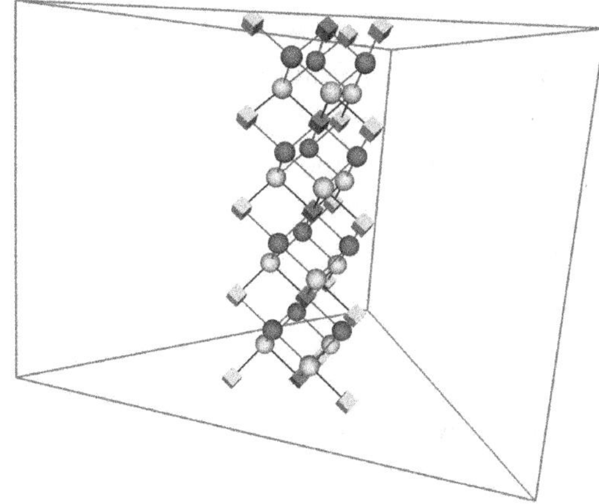

voice-leading relations among four-note chords, five-note chords, and so on. We will use them throughout this book, both for modeling chords and scales and for analyzing specific pieces.

For now, it is enough to note that the world of chromatic voice leading, as represented by Figure 1.3.15, is significantly more complicated than the simple circle representing diatonic triads. Because of this complexity, the fundamental logic animating nineteenth-century music has not always been clearly understood: theorists have sometimes depicted chromaticism as involving whimsical aberrations, departures from compositional good sense, rather than as the systematic exploration of a complex but coherent terrain. This has in turn led historians and composers to depict nineteenth-century chromaticism as pushing tonal logic to its breaking point, such that the step to complete atonality became all but inevitable. I will argue against this point of view, using new geometrical tools to demonstrate that the music of Chopin and Wagner can be just as rigorous as the music that preceded it.

1.4 MUSIC, MAGIC, AND LANGUAGE

Having sketched some major themes, let me now step back to make a few remarks about my approach to music theory. In this book I am primarily interested in the idealized composer's point of view: my goal is to describe conceptual structures that can be used to *create* musical works, rather than those involved in perceiving music. I stress the adjective "idealized," as my goal is not to undertake a historical investigation of the way past composers *actually* conceived of their music, but rather to describe concepts contemporary composers might find useful—in other words, to answer the question "what concepts would be helpful if I wanted to compose music like this?" Music theory, understood in this way, helps composers steal from one another in a sophisticated fashion, allowing us to appropriate general procedures and techniques rather than particular chords or melodies. Of course it can also help performers and analysts understand music "from the inside," by showing how composers make use of the options available to them.

Of course, composer-based music theory cannot ignore listeners entirely: the point is to write music that other people want to listen to, and this can only occur if composers are dealing with musical features that listeners care about. But though composers and listeners need to be synchronized in general, there is room for considerable divergence when it comes to the details. For example, classical composers evidently considered it important to conclude a piece in the tonic key, even though listeners are relatively insensitive to this feature of musical organization.[24] This means that theorists should not assume that the cognitive structures involved in *making* music are the same as those involved in *perceiving* it: ideas that are central to the composer's craft, such as the principle that a classical sonata should recapitulate the second theme in the tonic key, may have only a glancing relevance to ordinary listeners.

I find it useful here to consider the analogy with magic. A stage magician uses various tricks to *cause* the audience to have extraordinary experiences—bunnies seem to disappear, beautiful assistants seem to be sawed in half, and so on. Enjoying a magician's performance does not require you to understand how the tricks are done; in fact, understanding may actually diminish your astonishment. Nor is the magician's "ideal audience" composed of professional magicians: the point is to perform the trick for people who will genuinely be *fooled*. In much the same way, I understand composition to be a process of using technical musical tools to ensure that audiences have certain kinds of extraordinary experiences. When composing, I make various choices about chords, scales, rhythm, and instrumentation to create feelings of tension, relaxation, terror, and ecstasy, to recall earlier moments in the piece or anticipate later events. But I do *not* in general expect listeners to be consciously tracking these choices. Listeners who do ("ooh, a dissonant ♯9 chord in the trombones, in polyrhythm against the flutes and inverting the opening notes of the piece!") are like professional magicians watching each others' routines—at best, engaged in a different

24 Cook 1987, Marvin and Brinkman 1999.

sort of appreciation, and, at worst too intellectually engaged to enjoy the music as deeply as they might.

One might contrast this approach with an alternative, on which the composer's and listener's perspectives are thought to be more closely aligned. Here the relevant analogy is not to magic, but to language: the idea is that composers write music that contains various sorts of patterns, including familiar sequences of chords and keys, thematic recurrences, and so on, while the listener's job is to recover these patterns. Expert listeners recover more patterns than inexpert listeners, and are consequently more qualified to pass aesthetic judgment on particular pieces of music. Insofar as some composers place patterns in their music that cannot be decoded aurally by expert listeners, their compositions are thereby aesthetically flawed.[25] On this view, music essentially involves a language-like transmission of syntactic patterns from producer to receiver.

The linguistic model is attractive, and there is no doubt some truth to it. But I think it understates the extraordinary distinctiveness of human language. Linguistic abilities are remarkable both for their accuracy and for their homogeneity: if you say "there is a tiger nearby," I have no trouble repeating the sentence word for word, writing it down, or explaining what it means. Furthermore, almost any English speaker can effortlessly distinguish grammatical utterances such as "there is a tiger nearby" from nongrammatical ones like "nearby tiger is." By contrast, musical abilities are both *heterogeneous* and fairly *in*accurate. First, there is an enormous spectrum ranging from congenital amusics to gifted listeners with extraordinarily accurate absolute pitch. These individuals have radically different musical capabilities as both producers and consumers of music. Second, while competent language-listeners are typically also competent language-speakers, this is not the case for music: most people enjoy listening to music, while only a few enjoy creating it. Third, even expert listeners lose a large amount of the "signal" in even moderately complicated music. I have had more than three decades of musical training, and yet I—like most other "expert" listeners—would have trouble notating, or recreating at the piano, the notes and rhythms in a ten-second excerpt from an unfamiliar four-voice Baroque fugue. Musically, in other words, I am analogous to a person who cannot reliably understand all the words in the sentence "there is a tiger nearby."[26]

These differences no doubt reflect the fact that music largely lacks semantic content. A listener who does not understand "be quiet, there's a tiger nearby" is a serious danger to himself and others; consequently, there is tremendous pressure for speakers and listeners to converge on the same interpretation of sentences. By contrast, a listener who does not follow the detailed syntax of a Beethoven symphony, but who nevertheless enjoys it, creates no problems whatsoever. In some important sense *it*

25 See Babbitt 1958, Lerdahl 1988, Raffman 2003, and Temperley 2007.

26 Of course, musical signals are in some respects more complex than spoken sentences: listening to a Bach fugue is like listening to four people speak at the same time. But this should make us wonder why we tolerate higher information content in music.

simply does not matter whether you follow all the details of a piece's syntax; what matters is that you follow the piece well enough to enjoy what you hear. For in the end, the composer's well-being depends on your willingness to listen, not on whether you interpret music in the same way that he or she does. Or to revert to our earlier analogy: what is important is not that you understand the magic trick, but simply that you feel the force of the illusion.

I should pause here to mention that I have a personal perspective on these issues, since I sometimes create music with the aid of algorithms and computers. In these cases I can be fairly removed from the underlying syntactical structure of the music I create, whether that be some complex melodic process, a gradually shifting probability distribution over the twelve chromatic notes, or a harmonic structure derived from a mathematical analysis of Mozart's music. Here my compositional role is that of a gatekeeper or judge, selecting the computer-generated passages that strike me as intuitively compelling, and arranging them, in a collage-like fashion, so as to produce the best musical effect. (Typically, I augment these algorithmic passages with music composed intuitively, producing a final product that blends the human and the inhuman.) The fact that some people seem to *like* this music only serves to highlight the oddness of the linguistic approach. For here the composer is only vaguely aware of the structures that, on the linguistic model, the listener is supposed to be recovering. Given that I am not at all sure that *I* am hearing these structures accurately, it seems presumptuous for me to demand much more from my listeners. Instead, I am hoping that listeners will be *directly affected* by the music in the same way I am—that is, tickled, amused, impressed, or awed.

Faced with this situation, I draw several morals.

First, there is a potential for real divergence between what we might call "composer's grammar" and "listener's grammar." Listeners may potentially grasp only a fraction of the underlying syntax of a Bach fugue, a Beethoven symphony, or a John Coltrane solo. (Some authors have claimed that this is particularly true when we consider the artificial syntaxes of twentieth-century atonality, and this may be true; but the more important point is that there will be significant gaps whenever we consider music of any complexity.[27]) In this sense, listening is like trying to catch up to a train that is forever just beyond your reach; indeed, the very fact that we miss so much structure is no doubt part of what leads us to study scores, or listen repeatedly to the same pieces. This means that there are at least two separate projects that music theorists can engage in: modeling what composers actually do, and modeling what listeners actually experience. We should be careful not to conflate these by acting as if listening is "composing in reverse."

27 See Lerdahl (1988, 2001) and Raffman (2003). Lerdahl asserts that it is desirable for "composer's grammar" and "listener's grammar" to be close together, and suggests this is true for classical music. Furthermore, he postulates lossless musical perception, in which listeners have subconscious but completely accurate access to most of the details in a musical score. He therefore believes the gap between composer and listener is significantly less severe than I do.

Second, we should be careful not to assume that there is any one thing that "listening" is. It is possible that some listeners are adept at recovering a large amount of the structure in muscial pieces, but many listeners are not. The heterogeneity of musical abilities makes it difficult to abstract away from individual variation in favor of some idealized "competent" listener. Can we describe as "competent" the listener who loves Beethoven, but who performs poorly on standard ear-training tests? What about the listener who hates music but perceives it very accurately? Does the "ideal" musical listener have absolute pitch? A perfect memory for every musical detail? Is the point of listening to music to experience aesthetic enjoyment, or is it to recover a kind of musical "syntax" that the composer placed in his or her music? Personally, I suspect there is no uncontroversial answer to these questions: there simply is no "competent" or "ideal" listener that is analogous to the "idealized speaker" of contemporary linguistics.

Third, listeners' perceptions may in some respects be more crude and statistical than we would initially think. We do not determine the meaning of sentences by estimating the proportion of nouns to verbs, but we do respond very strongly to relatively crude global features of the musical stimulus. Does the piece use consonant or dissonant harmonies? Does it restrict itself, over moderate spans of musical time, to a small set of notes, and do these notes themselves change over larger time spans? Do melodies in general move by short distances? The answers to these questions tell us an enormous amount about how untrained listeners will respond to a piece. Hence my five features might be compared to a set of basic tools which composers can use to perform their musical magic.

Fourth, musical heterogeneity poses special problems for composers, who confront an audience of widely varying interests and abilities. Traditional tonal composers dealt with this by writing music that was immediately attractive, largely by virtue of exploiting the five features. Many composers also built into their music layers of additional, more complicated structure—complex thematic and formal interrelationships, intricate rhythmic devices, sophisticated contrapuntal tricks, and so on. The result was a kind of music that listeners could engage with in multiple ways: laypersons could simply enjoy a piece for the gross statistical features it shared with many other compositions in the same style, while cognoscenti could become more involved in the subtleties particular to that work.

I find it fascinating that so many twentieth-century musicians chose to abandon this strategy. Composers such as Schoenberg, Webern, Berg, and Varèse—and later Babbitt, Boulez, Cage, Xenakis, and Stockhausen—wrote music that listeners often found quite unpleasant. In many cases, this was because these composers rejected not just acoustic consonance, but also harmonic consistency, conjunct melodic motion, limited macroharmony, and centricity. Some early modernist composers may have hoped that ordinary listeners would adapt to this new musical style, adjusting their ears to the absence of familiar musical structures and coming to enjoy atonality as deeply and directly as traditional music. But after several decades of avant-garde exploration, composers began to realize that this might never occur. The *locus classicus* of this new perspective is Milton Babbitt's 1958 manifesto "Who Cares if You Listen?"—in which he cheerfully acknowledged that his music was not enjoyed by laypersons, but only by a specialist musical community analogous to the specialist community of professional mathematicians.[28]

Rather than criticizing this point of view, let me just say that I am interested in music that does not make this choice: I like music that brings people together, rather than dividing them, and I think the traditional strategy—writing immediately attractive music that also contains deeper levels of structure—is as potent as it ever was. (Indeed, it may be all the more necessary in an economic and cultural environment in which notated music is somewhat marginal.) In this book, therefore, I will be primarily concerned with effects that can be achieved *within* a broadly attractive sound-world. From a technical standpoint, this restriction is relatively unconstraining, as a large number of avant-garde techniques are easily applied within a consonant harmonic context: it is perfectly possible, for example, to write music that is diatonic, or more generally macroharmonically consonant, while also being serial, aleatoric, indeterminate, wildly polyrhythmic, and so on.[29] Thus, the choice between superficial accessibility and off-putting dissonance is not forced on us by our interest in particular musical techniques. Instead, it is a relatively independent reflection of our own aesthetic preferences.

1.5 OUTLINE OF THE BOOK, AND A SUGGESTION FOR IMPATIENT READERS

The book is divided into two halves, with the theoretical material front-loaded into the first five chapters. Chapter 2 reviews basic theoretical concepts and introduces simple geometrical models of musical structure, representing pitches as points on a line and pitch classes as points on a circle. These models are then used to investigate the relations between conjunct melodic motion, harmonic consistency, and acoustic consonance. Chapter 3 introduces higher-dimensional "maps" of musical space, providing powerful tools for visualizing the interactions between harmony and counterpoint. Chapter 4 introduces scales, describing them as musical "rulers" that allow musicians to measure the distance between notes; it then identifies a set of familiar scales that are interesting for a number of distinct reasons. Finally, Chapter 5 describes the components of the generalized theory of keys. It proposes various tools for representing macroharmony and centricity, and contrasts two traditions in twentieth-century music: the *chromatic tradition,* which largely abandons scales in favor of highly chromatic textures, and the *scalar tradition,* which makes use of an expanded range of scales and modes. Since Chapters 2–4 are the most technically demanding portion of the book, Appendix F provides a series of study questions to help reinforce the material. These questions make good homework assignments when the book is used in a classroom.

28 Babbitt 1958.

29 Avant-garde techniques have been used in consonant contexts by composers like Conlon Nancarrow, Paul Lansky, Steve Reich (Cohn 1992), and "totalists" such as Mikel Rouse (Gann 2006).

The second part uses these ideas to reinterpret the history of Western music. Chapter 6 proposes that there is an "extended common practice" stretching from the beginning of Western counterpoint to the tonal music of the twentieth century. What links these different styles is the combination of harmonic consistency and conjunct melodic motion: the idea that music should have a two-dimensional coherence, both harmonic (or vertical) and melodic (or horizontal). Chapter 7 uses geometrical models to investigate the functional harmony of the classical period, briefly considering the relation between traditional harmonic theory and the views of Heinrich Schenker. Chapter 8 explores the ways in which nineteenth-century composers exploited efficient voice leading in chromatic space, suggesting that there is more structure to chromatic music than we might expect. Chapter 9 argues that twentieth-century tonal composers used scales to counteract the trend toward a saturated chromaticism, fusing chromatic voice-leading techniques with the limited macroharmony of earlier periods. Finally, Chapter 10 treats what I call the "modern jazz synthesis," a contemporary common practice that unites impressionist chords and scales, chromatic voice leading, and the functional harmony of the classical era.

The design of the book means that readers will need to absorb a considerable amount of theoretical material before reaching the analytical payoff in the second half. Readers who are less interested in theory for its own sake may therefore want to read the book out of order. Chapter 8 can largely be read directly after Chapters 2 and 3, although the discussion of *Tristan* will be enhanced by familiarity with the material in §§4.8–10. Chapter 9 can be read directly after Chapter 4. This abbreviated path hits the main theoretical highlights (new tools for understanding voice leading and scales), as well as the most important analytical applications: to the chromatic tonality of Schubert, Chopin and Wagner, and to the twentieth-century scale-based tonality of Debussy, Stravinsky and Reich. When using the book in an advanced undergraduate theory class, I have assigned pieces from Chapters 8–9 as homework assignments early in the semester, while students are still reading the introductory chapters. (For instance, I assign Chopin's E minor prelude and F minor mazurka in the week when students are reading Chapter 3.) That way, students have an opportunity to work with the music on their own before being introduced to my own particular perspective on these remarkable works.

Finally, a word of encouragement: it is possible to understand the gist of later chapters even while remaining somewhat fuzzy about the technical material in Chapters 2–4. So don't be afraid to forge ahead, returning to earlier sections as the need arises.

CHAPTER 2

Harmony and Voice Leading

The enterprise of "musical set theory" aspires to catalogue all the chords available to contemporary composers. Unfortunately, this project turns out to be more complicated than one might imagine. This is, first, because chords have an intrinsic and sophisticated geometry, with distance being determined by voice-leading size. Second, basic musical concepts such as "transposition," "inversion," "triad," and "chord type" can all be *relativized* to scales; thus two chords may belong to the same category relative to one scale but not another. (To make matters worse, we can also do set theory in an unquantized space that admits a continuous infinity of notes between B and C. This perspective can even teach us useful lessons about the discrete world of ordinary musical experience.) Third, chord tones themselves can be differentiated in terms of their importance, leading to phenomena such as rootedness and centricity. Finally, in the most sophisticated versions of set theory, the objects of comparison may themselves be chord progressions, with musical categorization proceeding flexibly and according to an ever-changing variety of symmetry operations (to be discussed shortly).

The next four chapters will try to address these issues, describing a new approach to chords and rebuilding "musical set theory" from the ground up. This chapter introduces the basic concepts and definitions. We begin with elementary geometrical models of musical structure, representing notes as points on a line (*pitch space*) and on a circle (*pitch-class space*). We then turn to higher-order objects—chord progressions and voice leadings—that describe motion through time. (Because this formalism sets the stage for much of the rest of the book, I encourage you to work through the study questions in Appendix F.) Next we consider the importance of symmetry in music theory, asking under what conditions harmonic consistency and conjunct melodic motion can be combined. This leads to our first significant theoretical result: a general understanding of the interdependence between acoustic consonance, efficient voice leading, and harmonic consistency.

2.1 LINEAR PITCH SPACE

Sound consists of small fluctuations in air pressure, akin to changes in barometric pressure. These fluctuations are heard as having a definite pitch when they repeat themselves (at least approximately) after some period of time t (Figure 2.1.1). The

Figure 2.1.1 Pitched sounds are periodic. The fundamental frequency is equal to $1/t$, where t is the duration of the cycle.

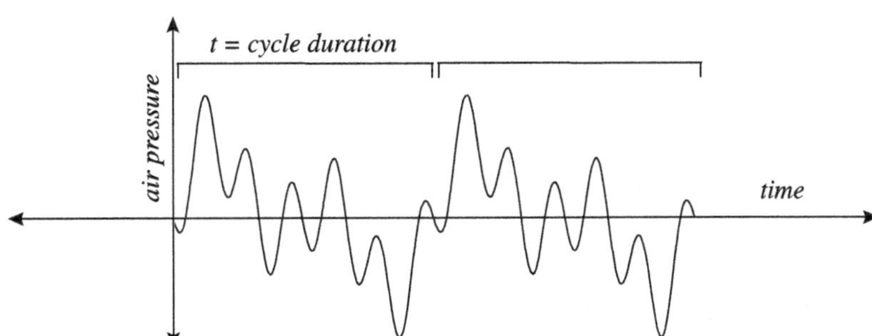

reciprocal of the period, $1/t$, is the *fundamental frequency* of the sound—a number that measures how many repetitions occur per unit of time. Musicians without absolute pitch are sensitive not to fundamental frequencies as such, but rather to the *ratios* between them. Suppose, on Tuesday, a typical person whistles a tune whose pitches have frequencies $f, g, h, \ldots$. On Wednesday, if asked to reproduce the tune, she is likely to whistle the frequencies $cf, cg, ch, \ldots$, where c is some number close to one. Musicians say that the whistler has *transposed* the notes, changing their fundamental frequencies so as to preserve the ratios between them. This suggests that frequency ratios represent a kind of musical distance, and that listeners are more attuned to the distances between notes than to their absolute positions in frequency space.[1]

Musicians do not like to work with fundamental frequencies, since ratios are awkward and division is hard; furthermore, we typically measure numerical distances using subtraction rather than division. It is useful, therefore, to relabel pitches by mapping every fundamental frequency f onto a number p according to an equation of the form

$$p = c_1 + c_2 \log_2 (f/440)$$

Don't be put off by the logarithm: the important point is that in the new system, the whistler whistles the pitches $p, q, r, \ldots$ on Tuesday, and $p + x, q + x, r + x, \ldots$ on Wednesday. The distance between two pitches p and q is now calculated by subtraction ($|p - q|$) rather than division (f/g).

The equation in the preceding paragraph has two constants, c_1 and c_2, the first of which determines the number corresponding to the frequency A440, and the second of which determines the size of the octave. In this book, I will always choose $c_1 = 69$ and $c_2 = 12$. This creates a linear *pitch space* in which the unit of distance is the *semitone* and middle C is (arbitrarily) assigned the number 60. (Note that the term "semitone" is defined in continuous space, without presupposing any particular temperament or chromatic scale.) As shown in Figure 2.1.2, labels for familiar equal-tempered pitches

1 Transposition preserves these distances, since $f/g = cf/cg$. McDermott and Hauser (2005) suggest that this measure of musical distance is innate and that it is common to at least some nonhuman animals. Dowling and Harwood (1986) suggest it is a musical universal.

Figure 2.1.2 Linear pitch space is a continuous line, containing a point for every conceivable pitch.

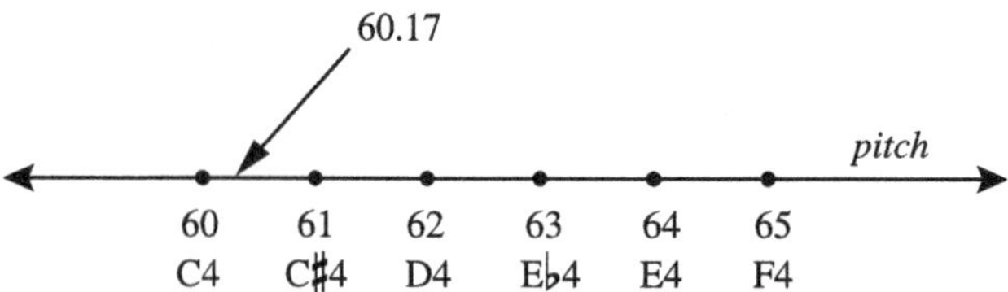

can be determined by counting keys on an ordinary piano, so that the C♯ above middle C is 61, the D above that is 62, and so on. Since the space is continuous, we can use fractional numbers, labeling the pitch 17 hundredths of a semitone (or *cents*) above middle C as 60.17. In principle, we could eschew letter-names for the remainder of this book, conducting the discussion entirely in numerical terms. For clarity, however, I will use familiar letter names whenever possible. These should be taken as shorthand for numerical pitch labels: "C♯4" and "61," like "Bob Dylan" and "Robert Zimmerman," are different ways of referring to the same thing.

2.2 CIRCULAR PITCH-CLASS SPACE

In linear pitch space octaves are not special, and the distance 12 is no different from any other. However, human beings hear octave-related pitches as having the same quality, color, or—as psychologists call it—*chroma*.[2] (As Maria puts it in *The Sound of Music,* the note "Ti" brings us *back* to "Do.") Music theorists express this by saying that two pitches an octave apart belong to the same *pitch class*. Geometrically, pitch classes can be represented using a circle (Figure 2.2.1). A single point in this space

Figure 2.2.1 Circular pitch class space. The number 0.17 refers to the pitch class seventeen cents above the pitch class C, while the number 2.5 refers to the pitch class D‡, or D quarter-tone sharp, halfway between D and E♭.

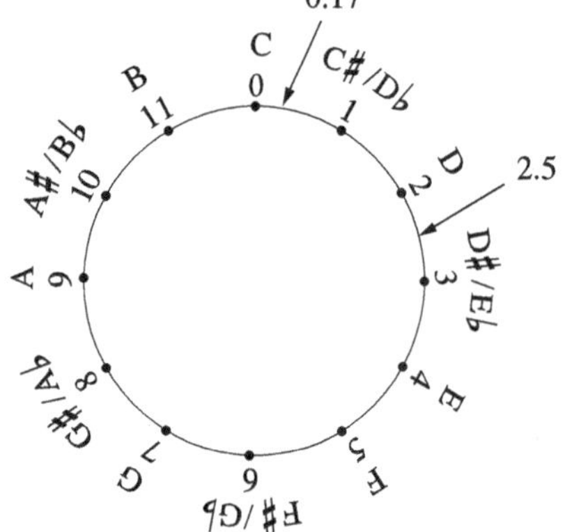

2 Octave equivalence seems to be nearly universal in human cultures (Dowling and Harwood 1986), and there is some evidence for it in nonhuman animals (Wright et al. 2000).

corresponds to the quality that is common to all the pitches sharing the same chroma: thus, the point "2" represents the quality ("D-ishness") that is shared by the pitches D0, D1, D2, D3, and so on.[3] Alternatively, we can take points on the circle to represent *categories* of notes all sharing the same chroma.

It is important to understand that pitch and pitch-class space are not separate and independent: pitch-class space is formed out of pitch space when we choose to ignore, or abstract away from, octave information.[4] As a result, many properties of linear pitch space are transferred to circular pitch-class space. For example, it is not necessary to devise a new system of naming pitch classes, as we can simply use pitch names in the range $0 \leq x < 12$ to refer to the chromas they possess (Figure 2.2.1). The terms "above" and "below" also inherit their meaning from pitch space: the phrase "the pitch class a quarter tone above pitch class D" simply refers to the chroma possessed by any pitch a quarter tone above any pitch with chroma D. (Of course, since pitch-class space is circular, it is not meaningful to say that one pitch class is absolutely above or below another; the pitch class E is both two semitones above D and ten semitones below it.) Finally, the *distance* between two pitch classes can be defined as the shortest distance between any two pitches belonging to those pitch classes. Thus, when a musician says "pitch class E is four semitones away from C," this means that for every pitch with chroma C, the nearest pitch with chroma E is precisely four semitones away.

Ultimately, pitch classes are important because they provide a language for making generalizations about pitches. The statement "pitch class E is four semitones above C" implies the statements "E4 is four semitones above C4," "E5 is four semitones above C5," and so on. Since it would take too long to list these statements individually, musicians instead use the convenient shorthand that pitch classes provide. Readers may find it useful here to consider the analogy between pitch class and time of day. The question "what's the distance from C to C♯?" is exactly analogous to "how long is it from 8 AM to 9 AM?" The answer "there is one hour between 8 AM and 9 AM," means that on any given day, 9 AM occurs precisely one hour after 8 AM. (Similarly, we can say "9 AM is one hour after 8 AM" or even "9 AM is 23 hours before 8 AM," much as we might observe that pitch class A is both one semitone above and eleven semitones below G♯.) Here we use time of day to summarize infinitely many facts about times: the statement "there is one hour between 8 AM and 9 AM" implies that there is one

3 Here I am using scientific pitch notation, in which numbers refer to octaves, with octave 4 ranging from middle C to the B above and with octave 5 starting at the next C. (Thus B4 is a semitone below C5.) Note that there is a subtle difference between the languages of psychology and music theory: psychologists say that the pitches D3 and D4 *possess* the same chroma ("D-ishness"), while music theorists say that the pitches *belong to* the same category ("the pitch class D"). The difference is analogous to the contrast between whiteness (a property) and the collection of all white things (a group). Points in pitch-class space can be taken to represent either of these.

4 Consequently, pitch-class space is circular only in an abstract sense. One shouldn't think of it as being embedded in a larger two-dimensional space, the way an ordinary circle exists on a two-dimensional piece of paper. Instead, one should think of it as a one-dimensional space unto itself. Here it can be useful to imagine a pointlike inhabitant of the space: from its perspective, "circularity" consists in the fact that a "straight line"—for example, a counterclockwise path—eventually returns to its starting point.

hour between 8 AM and 9 AM on Monday, August 8, 2006, one hour between 8 AM and 9 AM on Tuesday, August 9, 2006, and so on *ad infinitum*.

One unusual feature of this book is that I use *paths in pitch-class space* to represent intervals, or particular ways of moving from one pitch class to another.[5] The motivation here is that progressions like the first three in Figure 2.2.2 are closely related: in each case a C moves up by four semitones to an E, with the only difference being the octave in which the motion occurs. In the final three cases, C also moves to E, but differently—by eight descending semitones or 16 ascending semitones. We can capture what is similar about the first three cases, and their difference from the others, by modeling intervals using phrases such as "start at C and move up by four semitones." These combine an initial pitch class (C), a direction (up), and a distance (4), and can be notated $C \xrightarrow{+4} E$. Geometrically, these phrases correspond to ways of moving around the pitch-class circle: $C \xrightarrow{+4} E$ is represented by a four-semitone clockwise (ascending) path, whereas $C \xrightarrow{-8} E$ is represented by an eight-semitone *counterclockwise* (descending) path. (Motions can even wrap around the circle one or more times, as shown on the figure.) By contrast, music theorists have traditionally represented motion in pitch-class space using phrases like "start at C and move to E however you

Figure 2.2.2 The passages in (*a*)–(*c*) are similar in that they move C to E by four ascending semitones. The passages in (*d*)–(*f*) also move C to E, but differently—by eight descending semitones or by sixteen ascending semitones. We can capture what is similar about (*a*)–(*c*) by modeling these progressions as paths in pitch-class space. The progressions in (*a*)–(*c*) move C to E clockwise by four semitones along the pitch-class circle; (*d*) and (*f*) move eight semitones counterclockwise, and (*e*) moves sixteen clockwise semitones.

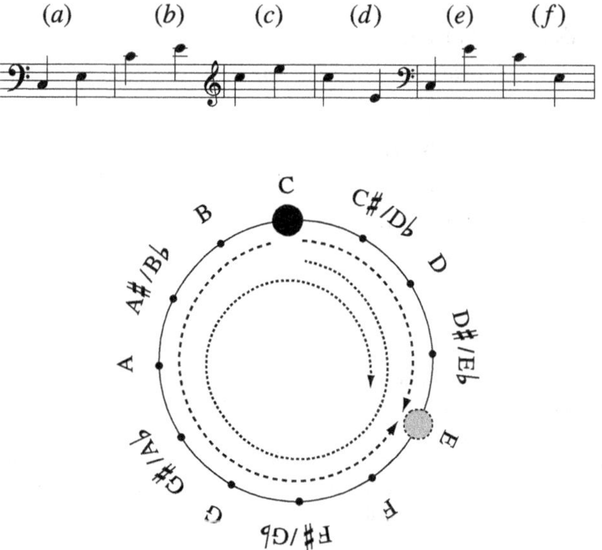

5 For more on paths in pitch-class space see Tymoczko 2005 and 2008b. Mazzola 2002 contains related ideas.

want." This gives us no way to formalize the elementary musical observation that the first three progressions in Figure 2.2.2 are particularly closely related.[6]

2.3 TRANSPOSITION AND INVERSION AS DISTANCE-PRESERVING FUNCTIONS

Since musicians are primarily sensitive to the distances between notes, we have reason to be interested in the distance-preserving transformations of musical space. It turns out that there are only two of these—*transposition* and *inversion,* corresponding to the geometrical operations of *translation* and *reflection*. These transformations play an important role in many different musical styles, and are central to contemporary music theory.

Transposition, discussed in §2.1, moves every pitch in the same direction by the same amount: the transposition of pitch p by x semitones, written $\mathbf{T}_x(p)$, is equal to $p + x$ (Figure 2.3.1). The distance moved represents the *size* of the transposition: virtually any listener can immediately distinguish a passage of music from its transposition by five octaves, while even the most subtle absolute-pitch listeners, extensively trained at the best conservatories, cannot discern the effects of transposition by 0.00001 of a semitone.

The second type of distance-preserving transformation, inversion, turns musical space upside-down. (Warning: music theorists use the term "inversion" in two unrelated senses, which go by the names of "registral inversion" and "pitch-space inversion"; I am talking about the second of these.[7]) Figure 2.3.2 depicts inversion as it operates on the theme of Bach's A minor prelude from Book II of the *Well-Tempered Clavier*. Where the left hand of (*a*) begins with an ascending octave leap, followed by a series of descending semitones, the left hand of (*b*) begins with a *descending* octave leap followed by a series of ascending semitones. In other words, the direction of motion has changed while the distances remain the same. (The passages in the upper

Figure 2.3.1 Transposition moves every point in the same direction by the same amount. Here, the arrows indicate ascending transposition by two semitones.

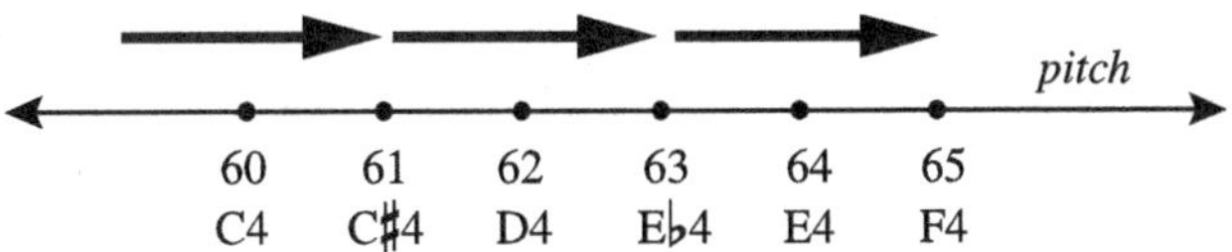

6 Traditional pitch-class intervals can sometimes be useful, however—for instance when we would like to categorize root progressions in functionally tonal music (§7.1).

7 *Registral inversion* changes the octave in which notes appear (for instance, transforming a root position chord C4-E4-G4 into a first-inversion E4-G4-C5). In §2.4 I call this "the O symmetry." *Pitch-space inversion* turns all of pitch space upside-down (for instance, transforming a major chord C4-E4-G4 into a minor chord G4-E♭4-C4). In §2.4 I call this "the I symmetry."

Figure 2.3.2 (*a–b*) Inversionally related passages in Bach's A minor prelude, WTC II. (*c*) Inversion as reflection in pitch space. Here, the note A3 is unaltered by the inversion, so the inversion can be written I^{A3}_{A3}. All other notes move by twice their distance from A3.

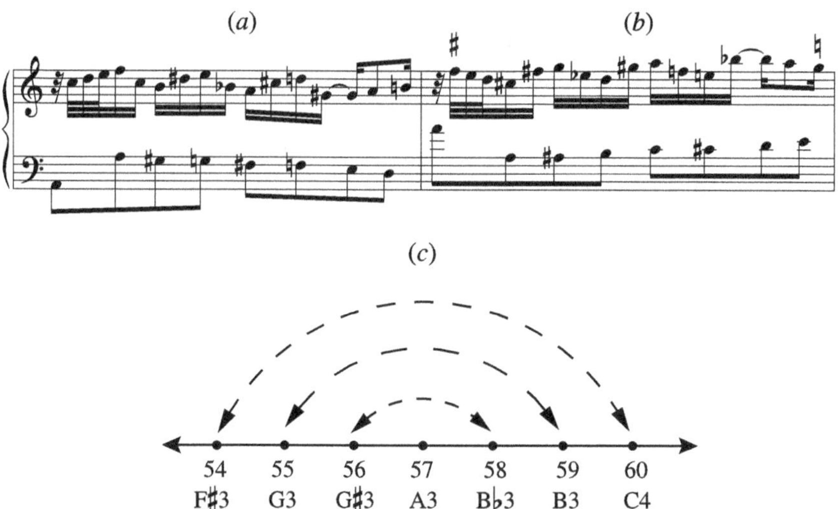

staff are also related by inversion, although the first and last notes are altered slightly.) Because they are *direction reversing*, inversions change the character of musical passages more dramatically than transpositions: nobody would ever mistake the inverted form of Bach's theme for the original. Nevertheless, inversionally related chords often sound reasonably similar, at least in the grand scheme of things: the chords in Figure 2.3.3a contain a minor third, a minor seventh, and a perfect fifth, and sound reasonably restful, while those in (*b*) contain a perfect fifth, a tritone, and a minor second, and have a distinctive, dissonant "bite."[8] For this reason, many twentieth-century composers consider inversionally related chords to be similar.

Figure 2.3.3 The chords in each measure are inversionally related, and sound more similar to each other than to either of the chords in the other measure.

Inversion can be represented mathematically by subtraction from a constant value: the inversion that maps pitch x to pitch y, written $\mathbf{I}^x_y(p)$, is $(x + y) - p$.[9] Geometrically, inversion corresponds to *reflection:* if we were to place a two-sided mirror at point A3 on Figure 2.3.2c, then every pitch would be sent to the place where its reflection

8 Major and minor triads are of course importantly different, even though they are related by inversion; nevertheless, they are more similar to one another than to three-note chromatic clusters. With other chords, inversional relationships are even more striking: in informal tests with undergraduate music majors, students could easily distinguish the two categories of chords in Figure 2.3.3, but had much more trouble distinguishing the inversionally related chords within each category.

9 The notation is a tad confusing, since the variables x and y serve to *label* the function $\mathbf{I}^x_y(p)$. For a particular choice of x and y, we get a general function that takes any pitch p as input, and outputs another pitch. Thus $\mathbf{I}^{A3}_{B3}(p)$ is a function acting on any pitch p; when p = A3, the function outputs B3.

Figure 2.3.4 In circular pitch class space, transposition corresponds to rotation, while inversion corresponds to reflection.

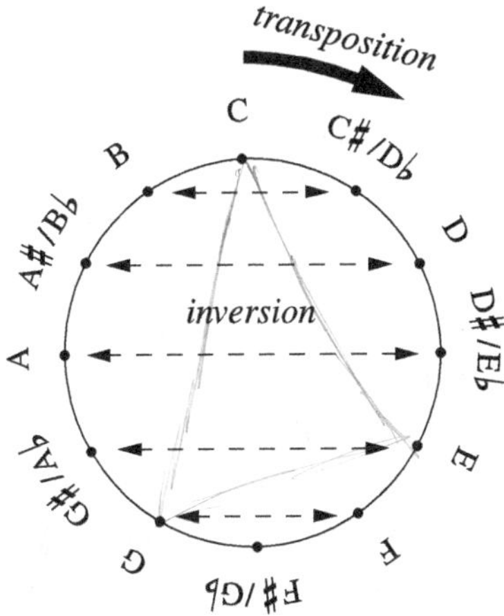

would be. The point A3 is a *fixed point* of the inversion, since it is unaltered by the reflection. Every inversion has a fixed point, although it may lie between piano keys: for instance, the inversion that maps E4 to F4 has a fixed point at E‡4—the E quarter-tone sharp halfway between E4 and F4.[10] (Note that inversions move each pitch by twice its distance to this fixed point.) Inversions, unlike transpositions, cannot be distinguished by their size, since for any distance x, an inversion will move some pair of pitches by that amount.

Transposition and inversion can also be defined in pitch-class space. Figure 2.3.4 shows that transposition is represented by *rotation* while inversion is represented by reflection: the inversion around C sends every pitch class to the point where its image would appear, if there were a pointlike mirror at C. Note that every pitch-class inversion fixes *two* antipodal points on the circle, whereas pitch inversion fixes only a single point.[11] Our earlier mathematical formulas continue to apply: if p is a pitch class, then its transposition by x semitones is $p + x$, while the inversion that sends x to y is $(x + y) - p$. However, when operating with pitch classes we should always add or subtract 12 until the result lies in the range $0 \leq x < 12$. This can lead to odd-looking equations like $6 + 3 + 1.5 + 1.5 = 0$, since 12 and 0 are equivalent in pitch-class arithmetic.[12]

2.4 MUSICAL OBJECTS

Understanding music is a matter of ignoring, or abstracting away from, information: we interpret the violinist's C4 and the cellist's C4 to be two instances of the same pitch, ignoring subtle differences in timbre and instrument. Similarly, we conceptualize the violinist's note, a little sharp and ever-so-slightly before the beat, as an in-tune note played on the beat. We can model this process using the mathematical concept of symmetry: to abstract away from musical information is to define a collection of *symmetry operations* that leave the object's "essential identity" unchanged. Mathematicians say that objects related by a symmetry operation belong to the same *equivalence class*—the group of objects that are mutually "equivalent" under

10 The fixed point of $\mathbf{I}_y^x$ is $(x + y)/2$.

11 Pitch inversion around middle C sends F♯4 to F♯3, preserving the chroma of the note, but changing its register. If we ignore octaves, F♯ becomes a second fixed point of the inversion.

12 Pitch-class arithmetic is simply a continuous version of what mathematicians call "modular" (or "clock") arithmetic. Transposing pitch class 2.5, or D‡, by −5 semitones produces $2.5 - 5 = -2.5$. To move this pitch into the range $0 \leq x < 12$, we add 12, shifting the octave. The result is the pitch class 9.5, or A‡.

the effects of the symmetry operation. These equivalence classes can in turn be taken to represent the *properties* or *attributes* the objects share, much as the group of all white things can be taken to represent the property of whiteness. As we will see, many different music-theoretical concepts can be understood in this way.

We can begin by defining a *basic musical object* as an ordered series of pitches, uncategorized and uninterpreted.[13] Basic musical objects can be ordered in time or by instrumental voice: thus the object (C4, E4, G4) could represent an ascending C major arpeggio or a simultaneous chord in which the first instrument plays C4, the second E4, and the third G4 (Figure 2.4.1). (Instruments can be labeled arbitrarily; what matters is simply that we distinguish them somehow.) Basic musical objects are so particular as to be uninteresting. Until we have defined some symmetry operations, some way of grouping objects into larger categories, the object (C4, E4, G4) is absolutely different from and absolutely unrelated to (E4, C4, G4). Of course, the fact that we instinctively consider them to be similar shows that we categorize musical objects unthinkingly; indeed, it is difficult to conceive of music without grouping objects together in *some* way.

Figure 2.4.1 The basic musical object (C4, E4, G4) can appear either harmonically or melodically.

During the early eighteenth century, Jean-Philippe Rameau articulated the modern notion of a chord, classifying basic musical objects based on their pitch-class content rather than their order or registral arrangement.[14] Rameau implicitly suggested that three basic operations preserve the "chordal" or "harmonic" identity of a musical object: octave shifts, permutation (or reordering), and cardinality change (or note duplication). For instance, one can transform (C4, E4, G4) by reordering its notes to produce (E4, G4, C4), transposing the second note up an octave to produce (C4, E5, G4), or duplicating the third note to produce (C4, E4, G4, G4)—all without changing its right to be called a "C major chord." Furthermore, as shown in Figure 2.4.2, these transformations can be combined to produce an endless collection of objects, all representing the same chord: (E4, G4, C5), (G3, G4, C5, E4), (E2, G3, C4, E4, E5), and so on. To be a C major chord is simply to belong to this equivalence class—or in other words, to contain all and only the three pitch classes C, E, and G. We can therefore represent the C major chord as the unordered set of pitch classes {C, E, G}. (Note that I use curly braces to represent unordered collections, reserving parentheses for ordered collections.) Geometrically, chords correspond to particular collections of points on a circle, as in Figure 2.4.2.

Traditional theory uses terms like "major chord" and "minor chord" to represent *chord types*, or collections of transpositionally related chords. We can interpret these terms as referring to equivalence classes formed by *four* symmetry operations: octave shifts, permutations, cardinality changes, and transpositions (Figure 2.4.3).[15] (Note

---

13 For more on this general approach to chord classification, see Callender, Quinn, and Tymoczko 2008.

14 See Lester 1974 and Rameau 1722/1971.

15 Octave shifts allow us to change the octave of just *one* note in an object. Transposition, by contrast, moves *all* the notes in an object in exactly the same way. (If we were to let transposition act on just

Figure 2.4.2 (*a*) All of these musical objects represent the C major chord, and are related by some sequence of octave shifts, permutations (or rearrangement of voices), and note duplication. (*b*) The C major chord can be represented by an unordered set of points in pitch-class space.

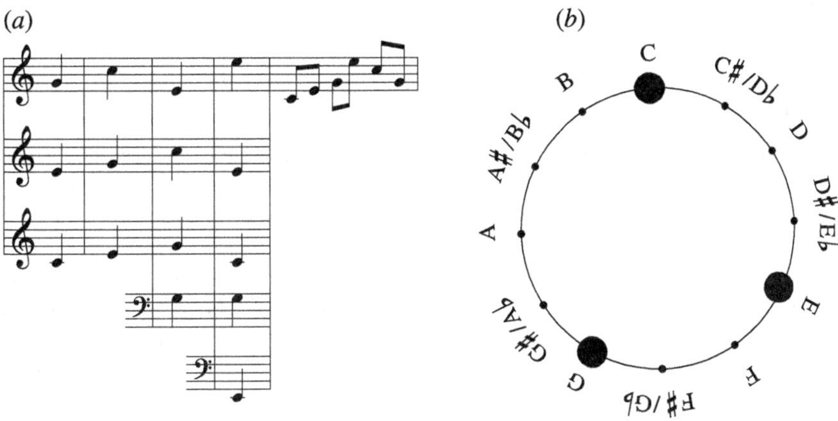

Figure 2.4.3 (*a*) All of these musical objects represent major chords, and are related by some combination of octave shifts, reordering of voices, note duplication, and transposition. (*b*) Any two major chords relate by rotation on the pitch-class circle and divide the pitch class circle into arcs that are 4, 3, and 5 semitones large, moving clockwise from the root. The figure shows the C and D major triads.

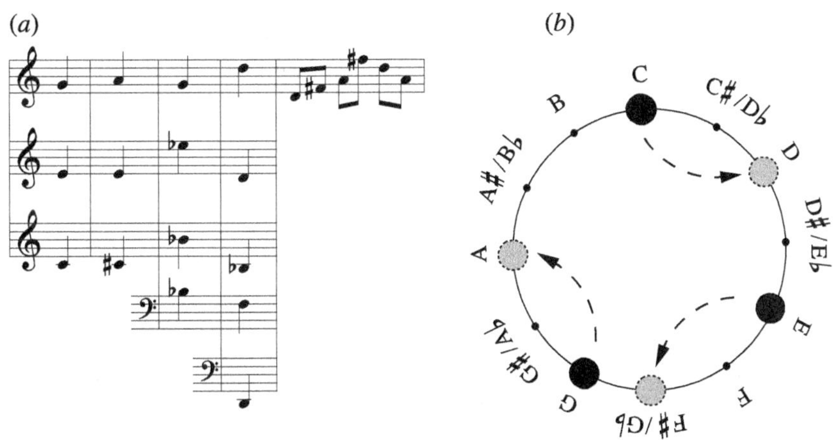

that contemporary music theorists sometimes prefer the term *transpositional set class* to the more colloquial "chord type.") Geometrically, two chords belong to the same type if one can be rotated into the other in circular pitch-class space (Figure 2.4.3b). Such chords will share the same sequence of distances between their adjacent notes:

---

one of the notes in an object, then we could transform any *n*-note object into any other, and we would no longer be able to make any distinctions among them.) It is also worth noting that the "cardinality change" operation is rather delicate mathematically; for details, see Callender, Quinn, and Tymoczko 2008.

for example, major chords divide the pitch-class circle into arcs of four, three, and five semitones, reading clockwise from the root.

Since inversionally related chords share many properties (and sound reasonably similar), contemporary theorists often group them together as well. Music theorists say that two objects belong to the same *set class* if they are related by any combination of *five* symmetry operations (the "OPTIC" symmetries): octave shifts (O), permutations (P), transpositions (T), inversions (I), and cardinality changes (C) (Figure 2.4.4).[16] Figure 2.4.5 shows that the C major chord divides pitch-class space into arcs that are four, three, and five semitones large, reading clockwise from C, while its inversion, the C minor chord, divides the pitch-class circle into arcs that are four, three,

Figure 2.4.4 (*a*) Each of the five OPTIC operations allows you to transform a musical object in some way. Musical objects belong to the same *set class* if they can be transformed into each other (or into some third chord) by some sequence of OPTIC transformations. (*b*) These objects all belong to the same set class, and relate to the initial (C4, E4, G4) by octave shift, reordering of voices, transposition, inversion, or cardinality change.

(*a*)

Operation	**Allowable Action**
Octave	Move *any* note into a new octave.
Permutation	Reorder the object, changing which voice is assigned to which note.
Transposition	Transpose the object, moving *all* of its notes in the same direction by the same amount.
Inversion	Invert the object by turning it "upside down."
Cardinality change	Add a new voice duplicating one of the notes in the object.

(*b*)

16 Huron (2007, p. 121) expresses some doubt about the musical significance of both chord types and set classes; however, in my experience students readily confuse inversionally related three-note chords such as those in Figure 2.3.3. Furthermore, when listening to sequences such as Figure 1.2.1c I can easily determine what set class is being used, though I sometimes have trouble identifying which inversion is present.

and five semitones large reading *counterclockwise from G.* Chords belonging to the same set class will always share the same sequence of arc lengths, although this sequence may progress either clockwise or counterclockwise around the pitch-class circle.

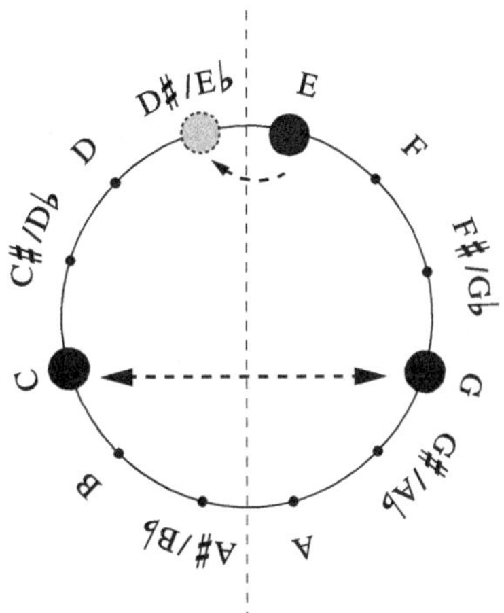

Figure 2.4.5 Major and minor chords relate by inversion, and divide the pitch-class circle into arcs that are 4, 3, and 5 semitones large, proceeding either clockwise (major) or counterclockwise (minor).

A specific example will help reinforce this approach to chord classification. Figure 2.4.6 begins with the basic musical object (E4, G4, B♭4, D5)—a half-diminished chord starting on the E above middle C. We then exploit the octave symmetry to produce (E3, G4, B♭3, D4). The permutation symmetry then rearranges the voices in which the notes appear, transforming (E3, G4, B♭3, D4) into (E3, B♭3, D4, G4); now the order of the voices corresponds to their registral order. We then use the transposition symmetry to shift the entire object up by semitone, giving (F3, B3, D♯4, G♯4)—recognizable as the first chord in Wagner's *Tristan*. Next, we apply the I symmetry to invert the chord around the point halfway between A3 and B♭3, transforming (F3, B3, D♯4,

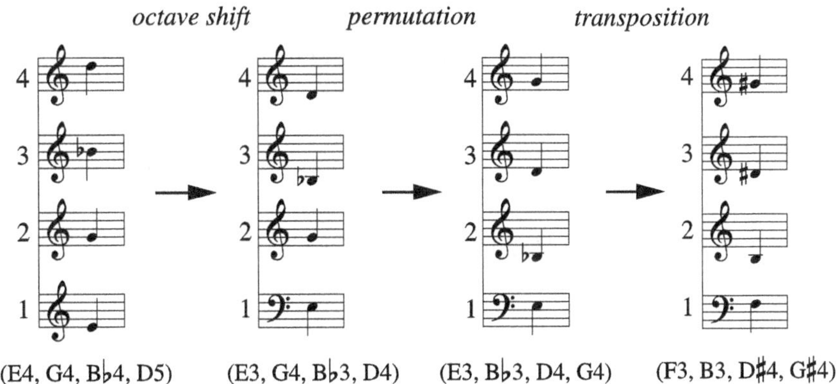

Figure 2.4.6 Using OPTIC operations to transform musical objects.

G♯4) into (D4, G♯3, E3, B2). The octave and permutation symmetries can then be used to give us (E3, G♯3, D4, B4), which is the second chord in *Tristan*. Finally, we can use cardinality changes to create additional voices that double notes already in the chord.

Musical classification thus proceeds by the progressive discarding of information. When we understand music as a sequence of pitches, we disregard many specific features of the acoustic signal, such as timbre, vibrato, duration, and rhythm. When we think in terms of pitch classes, we disregard the particular octave in which notes appear. To form chords, we ignore even more information, considering only the pitch-class content of a group of notes, rather than their order or multiplicity. Finally, we form chord types (or set classes) by focusing on the distances between a chord's notes rather than its pitch classes. Thus when we say that an object is a major chord, we are neglecting an enormous number of musical details, leaving behind something that is very abstract—an ordered sequence of clockwise distances around the pitch-class circle.

Although chords, chord types, and set classes are central to contemporary theory, they are not the only possibilities to consider. In certain situations it may be useful to talk about unordered sets of *pitches* rather than pitch classes ("chords" of pitches), or to distinguish the *multiset* {C, C, E, G}, which contains two copies of the pitch class C, from {C, E, G}, which contains only one C. We may at other times want to consider "tone rows" or *ordered* sequences of pitch classes, such as (C, E, G). (Order is particularly important when modeling melody, of course.) As shown in Figure 2.4.7, each of these terms corresponds to a unique combination of the five OPTIC symmetries. These alternatives all represent potentially useful ways of classifying musical objects, and there is no one optimal degree of abstraction: since different musical purposes require different kinds of information, we need to remain somewhat flexible about how we conceptualize music. To this end, it can be quite instructive to work out the musical significance of all 32 combinations of the OPTIC symmetries.

Figure 2.4.7 Music-theoretical terms and the symmetry operations to which they correspond. A "chord" is a group of musical objects related by octave shifts, permutations, and note-duplications, while a "multiset" is a group of objects related by octave shifts and permutation. (Thus, when we are talking about multisets, the number of times a note appears is important; when we are talking about chords it is not.) In a "tone row," as defined by Schoenberg, order is important: we are permitted only to shift octaves and introduce note duplications.

Term	Symmetry
chord	OPC
"chord type" or transpositional set class	OPTC
set class	OPTIC
multiset of pitch classes	OP
chord (of pitches)	PC
"tone row" (ordered set of pitch classes)	OC

2.5 VOICE LEADINGS AND CHORD PROGRESSIONS

Having reviewed some basic objects of music theory, our next task is to consider *progressions*, or sequences of musical objects, as musical entities in their own right. In other words, we will shift from an object-based approach (whose subject is single chords such as {C, E, G}) to a transformational approach (whose subject is progressions such as "C4, E4, G4 followed by C4, F4, A4").[17] This increased level of abstraction can be a little confusing, and readers may want to brace themselves for a slight uptick in the level of theoretical difficulty.

We can classify progressions using the very same OPTIC symmetries described in the preceding section. The main complication is that progressions are "higher-order" constructions containing multiple individual objects, which means that each symmetry can be applied in two different ways: we can either apply the *exact same* operation to each object in a progression or we can use different versions of the same symmetry on the progression's two objects. Take the progression (C4, E4, G4)–(C4, F4, A4), whose first object is (C4, E4, G4) and whose second is (C4, F4, A4). To apply the permutation symmetry *uniformly* is to reorder each of the two objects in precisely the same way, for instance producing (E4, G4, C4)–(F4, A4, C4) (Figure 2.5.1). (Here we have moved the first note in each object to the end.) *Individual* permutations apply different reorderings to the two objects in the progression, and can produce results such as (C4, E4, G4)–(F4, C4, A4). (Here we leave the first object unchanged, while switching the first two notes in the second object.) The distinction between "individual" and "uniform" can be applied to the other symmetries as well: the progression (C4, E4, G4)–(C4, F4, A4) can be transposed uniformly to produce (D4, F♯4, A4)–(D4, G4, B4) and individually to produce (D4, F♯4, A4)–(E♭4, A♭4, C5). Since each of the five OPTIC symmetry operations can be applied uniformly, individually, or not at all, there are many more categories of progressions than there are of individual objects.

Figure 2.5.1 (*b*) relates to (*a*) by uniform permutation. To get from (*a*) to (*b*) move all notes downward by one staff, shifting the bottom staff to the top. (*c*) relates to (*a*) by individual permutation, since it applies different permutations to each chord. Similarly, (*d*) and (*e*) relate to (*a*) by uniform and individual transposition, respectively.

Of these, two are particularly important for our purposes: *voice leadings*, which describe how individual musical "voices" move from chord to chord, and *chord progressions*, which describe successions of harmonies with no regard for musical

17 The shift from objects to transformations is central to Lewin 1987, though he favors group-theoretical models of harmonic relationships, whereas I am oriented toward geometrical models that represent counterpoint as well. For more, see Tymoczko 2007, 2008a and 2009b.

voices. Intuitively, voice leadings can be represented by phrases such as "move the C major triad to a C♯ diminished triad by shifting the note C up by semitone," while chord progressions correspond to phrases such as "move the C major triad to the C♯ diminished triad however you want." Mathematically, it turns out that voice leadings arise from *uniform* applications of the permutation symmetry, while chord progressions arise from *individual* applications of the permutation and cardinality-change symmetries. (These individual transformations destroy the identity of musical "voices," since they change the two chords in different ways.) One way or another, voice leadings and chord progressions will occupy us for the rest of the book.

We'll begin with *voice leadings in pitch space,* which represent mappings from one collection of pitches to another.[18] For example, Figure 2.5.2a presents the voice leading (G2, G3, B3, D4, F4)→(C3, G3, C4, C4, E4), in which the voice sounding G2 in the first chord moves to C3 in the second chord, the voice sounding G3 in the first chord continues to sound G3 in the second, the voice sounding B3 moves up to C4, and so on. (Note that I use an arrow to represent voice leadings.) Since the overall order in which the voices are listed is not significant, one could also represent this voice leading as (F4, D4, G2, B3, G3)→(E4, C4, C3, C4, G3); what matters is simply that we describe how the notes in one chord move to those in the next.[19] Voice leadings are like the atomic constituents of musical scores, the basic building blocks of polyphonic music.

Figure 2.5.2 Three voice leadings between G^7 and C.

Clearly, the voice leading in Figure 2.5.2b is closely related to that in Figure 2.5.2a; all that has changed is the octave in which some voices appear. We can represent what is common to them by writing (G, G, B, D, F)$\xrightarrow{5,\,0,\,1,\,-2,\,-1}$(C, G, C, C, E). This indicates that one of the voices containing G, whatever octave it may be in, moves up five semitones to C; the other voice containing G is held over into the next chord; the B moves up by semitone to C; and so on. I will refer to such octave-free voice leadings as *voice leadings between pitch-class sets* or *pitch-class voice leadings.*[20] The numbers above the arrow, here (5, 0, 1, −2, −1), are paths in pitch-class space that describe how the voices move (§2.2). The two pitch-space voice leadings in Figure 2.5.2a–b are both *instances* of the pitch-class voice leading (G, G, B, D, F)$\xrightarrow{5,\,0,\,1,\,-2,\,-1}$(C, G, C, C, E). Figure 2.5.2c is

18 More formally, voice leadings in pitch space are equivalence classes of pairs of basic musical objects (ordered pitch sets) generated by uniform applications of the permutation symmetry.

19 In other words, we do not change the voice leading when we apply permutation uniformly.

20 Mathematically, voice leadings in pitch-class space are equivalence classes of progressions generated by uniform applications of the octave and permutation symmetries. Previous theorists (Roeder 1984, 1987, 1994, Lewin 1998, Morris 1998, Straus 2003) define voice leadings using traditional pitch-class intervals rather than "paths in pitch-class space" (§2.2). Hence they do not, for instance, distinguish one-semitone ascending motion from eleven-semitone descending motion. For more, see Tymoczko 2005, 2006, 2008b, and Callender, Quinn, and Tymoczko 2008.

not an instance of this voice leading, since G moves to C by seven descending semitones rather than five ascending semitones. (The specific path matters!) For simplicity, I will omit the numbers over the arrow when the number of semitones moved by each voice lies in the range $-6 < x \leq 6$. Thus I will write (G, G, B, D, F)→(C, G, C, C, E) for the pitch-class voice leading in Figures 2.5.2a–b. This indicates that each voice moves by the *shortest possible path* to its destination, with the arbitrary convention being that tritones ascend.

Pitch-class voice leadings are abstract schemas that are central to the enterprise of Western composition. Without them, a composer would need to conceptualize the voice leadings in Figure 2.5.3 as being entirely unrelated, and this would pose overwhelming burdens on his or her memory. It is far simpler, and more practical, to understand the two voice leadings as examples of a single principle: *you can transform a C major triad into an F major triad by moving the E up by semitone and the G up by two semitones*. The concept "pitch-class voice leading" is simply a tool for formalizing such principles, and thus for modeling one important aspect of the composer's craft. Of course, in actual compositions voice leadings are always represented by specific pitches, and composers always think very carefully about register. Nevertheless, it is also true that composition requires a general sense of the various "routes" from chord to chord, and these routes are precisely what pitch-class voice leadings describe.

Figure 2.5.3 Two instances of the same voice-leading schema.

Geometrically, a pitch-space voice leading corresponds to a collection of paths in linear pitch space. Figure 2.5.4a represents the pitch-space voice leading in Figure 2.5.2a, with the dotted lines showing how each pitch moves to its destination. Similarly, a pitch-class voice leading can be represented as a

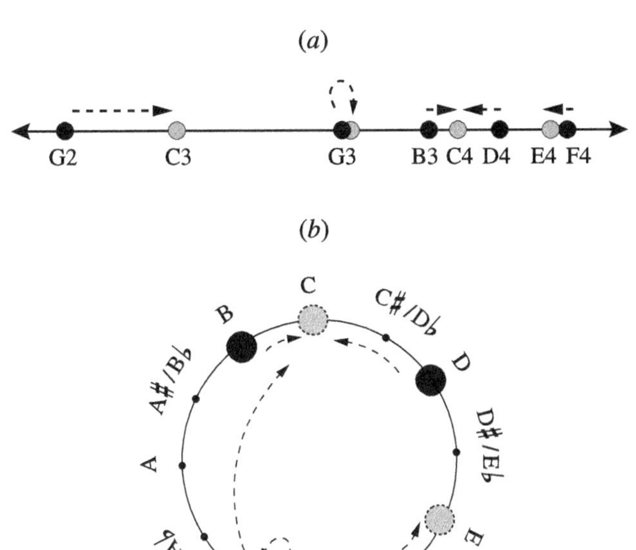

Figure 2.5.4 (*a*) Voice leadings in pitch space can be represented as paths on a line. (*b*) Pitch-class voice leadings can be represented as paths on a circle. These paths can move in either direction by any distance, and may complete one or more circumferences of the circle.

collection of paths in circular pitch-class space. In principle these paths can be arbitrarily long, with notes taking one or more complete turns around the pitch-class circle. Indeed, any collection of paths on the pitch-class circle, between any points whatsoever, defines a voice leading in pitch-class space. In some cases, it can be useful to represent voice leadings by a continuous process (which could be shown as a movie) in which each note glides along the appropriate path to its destination, beginning and ending at the same time.[21]

By contrast, *chord progressions* (as I define them) are simply successions of chords, with no implied mappings between their notes. Typically, the term "chord progression" is understood to refer to a sequence of unordered *pitch-class sets*. Thus {C, E, G, B♭}⇒{E, G♯, B}, or C[7]⇒E, is a chord progression whose first chord is {C, E, G, B♭} and whose second chord is {E, G♯, B}, but which does *not* associate the note C with any particular note in the second chord.[22] (Note that I use the double arrow for chord progressions, reserving the single arrow for voice leadings.) However, we could also define a *pitch-space chord progression* as a pair of unordered pitch sets, as in {C4, E4, G4}⇒{C4, F4, A4}. Again, there is no implication that the note E4 moves to F4 or to any other pitch in the chord. (When we are talking about chord progressions in pitch or pitch-class space, we are focusing on the harmonies and ignoring how individual voices might happen to move.) Figure 2.5.5 shows that chord progressions can be modeled as successions of unordered points in either linear pitch space or circular pitch-class space. Geometrically, we can imagine each chord occupying its own individual frame of a movie, with the motion between them being instantaneous and giving us no reason to associate any pair of notes.

Figure 2.5.6 summarizes this discussion, showing that each of these different theoretical concepts applies the five OPTIC symmetries in different ways.

Figure 2.5.5 The chord progression {C, E, G, B♭}⇒{E, G♯, B}.

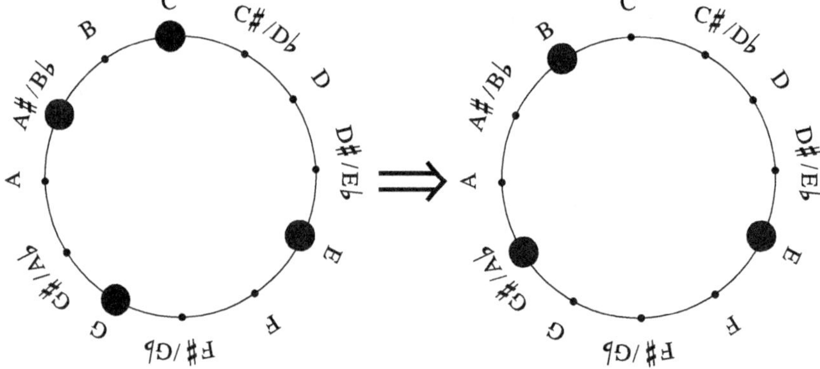

21 On the companion website I have provided a series of movies of this sort.

22 Mathematically, chord progressions result from the individual application of the octave, permutation, and cardinality-change symmetries.

Term	Symmetry
voice leading in pitch space	uniform P
voice leading in pitch-class space	uniform OP
pitch-space chord progression	individual PC
chord progression	individual OPC
path in pitch-class space	uniform O (one-note progressions only)

Figure 2.5.6 Music-theoretical terms for progressions, along with the symmetries that generate them.

2.6 COMPARING VOICE LEADINGS

We'll now start to think about how voice leadings relate to one another. The interesting wrinkle is that we'll consider not just *uniform* relationships, in which the same operation applies to both objects in a voice leading, but also their *individual* counterparts.

2.6.1 Individual and Uniform Transposition

The voice leadings (C, E, G)→(C, F, A) and (G, B, D)→(G, C, E) are very similar, exhibiting the same musical pattern at different transpositional levels: each holds the root of a major triad fixed, moves the third up by semitone, and the fifth up by two semitones (Figure 2.6.1). Since we transpose both chords in the same way, the two voice leadings are *uniformly transpositionally related,* or *uniformly T-related.* The voice leadings (C, E, G)→(C, F, A) and (G, B, D)→(F♯, B, D♯) are also similar, albeit slightly less so; each maps the root of the first chord to the fifth of the second, the third of the first chord to the root of the second, and the fifth of the first chord to the third of the second. Figure 2.6.1b shows that one voice leading can be transformed into the other by applying a *different* transposition to each chord: (C, E, G) is seven semitones away from (G, B, D), but (C, F, A) is *six* semitones away from (F♯, B, D♯). These voice leadings can thus be said to be *individually transpositionally related,* or *individually T-related.*

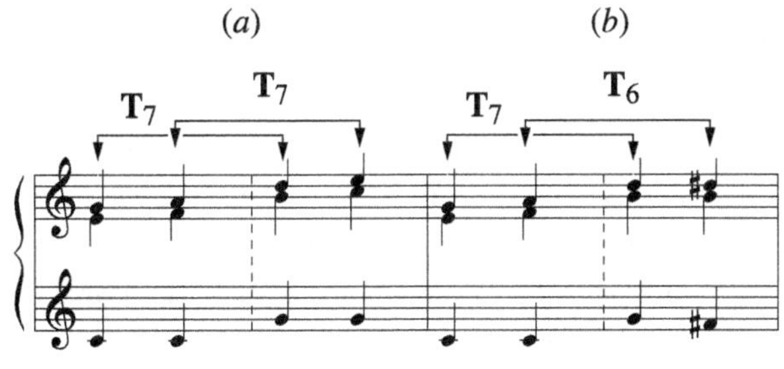

Figure 2.6.1 Uniformly and individually T-related voice leadings.

2.6.2 Individual and Uniform Inversion

The distinction between individual and uniform relatedness extends naturally to inversion. Figure 2.6.2a shows that (C, E, G)→(C, F, A) can be inverted to produce (G, E♭, C)→(G, D, B♭). These are *uniformly inversionally related* (or *uniformly I-related*) voice

Figure 2.6.2 Uniformly and individually I-related voice leadings. Here, pitch-space inversion around E𝄳4 (E quarter-tone flat, halfway between E♭4 and E) sends C4 to G4, E4 to E♭4, F4 to D4, G4 to C4 and A4 to B♭3.

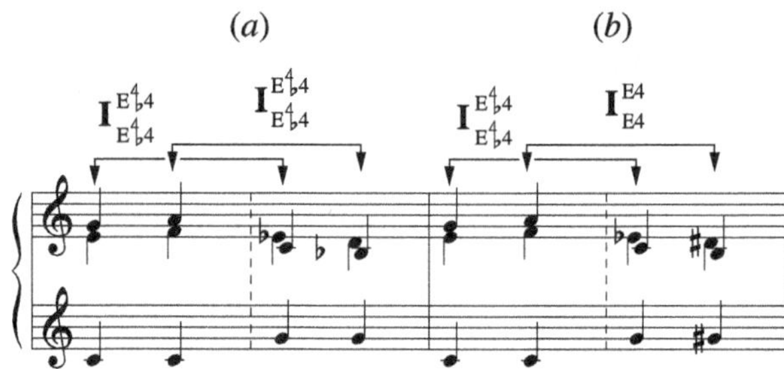

leadings. By contrast, (C, E, G)→(C, F, A) and (G, E♭, C)→(G♯, D♯, B) are *individually inversionally related,* or *individually I-related,* since it takes *two different* inversions to transform the first into the second. (Figure 2.6.2b inverts the first chord around E𝄳4, or E quarter-tone flat, while inverting the second around E4.) Note that as I am using the term, "individual I-relatedness" requires that each chord in the first voice leading be related by some inversion to the corresponding chord in the second voice leading; it is not permissible to invert only one of the two chords.

The significance of uniform transposition is clear, as it moves the same musical pattern to a different transpositional level. Uniform I-relatedness is somewhat more abstract: (C, E, G)→(C, F, A) sounds rather different from (C, E♭, G)→(B♭, D, G), which is uniformly I-related to it. Note however that the two voice leadings are mirror images of each other: the first moves one voice by zero semitones, one voice up by one semitone, and one voice up by two semitones; the second moves one voice by zero semitones, one voice *down* by one semitone, and one voice *down* by two semitones. The distances are the same but the directions have been reversed. Some theorists have asserted that individually I-related voice leadings are perceptually or metaphysically similar.[23] From our perspective, what is more important is that the answers to theoretical questions often come in I-related pairs. For example, suppose we want to catalogue voice leadings between major and minor triads in which no voice moves by more than a semitone; since the inversion of any such "semitonal" voice leading is also semitonal, each of these voice leadings has an inversionally related partner (Figure 2.6.3). This makes it much easier to conceptualize and remember them.

The musical significance of *individual* T and I relationships is perhaps even less clear, since the voice leading $(\text{C, E, G})\xrightarrow{0,\,1,\,2}(\text{C, F, A})$ sounds like a standard I–IV chord progression, while $(\text{C, E, G})\xrightarrow{-1,\,0,\,1}(\text{B, E, G}\sharp)$, individually T-related to it, evokes Schubertian chromaticism. Nevertheless, there is a sense in which the two are similar: each relates structurally analogous notes (moving the root of the first chord

23 These include Hauptmann, Riemann, and contemporary "neo-Riemannians." For more discussion, see Tymoczko 2008b and forthcoming.

Figure 2.6.3 The semitonal voice leadings between major and minor triads. Since inversion preserves the distance moved by each voice, these voice leadings can be grouped into uniformly I-related pairs.

to the fifth of the second, the third of the first chord to the root of the second, and the fifth of the first to the third of the second); and the voices in the second voice leading end up exactly one semitone lower than in the first (moving by −1, 0, and 1 semitones rather than 0, 1, and 2). Very similar points can be made about individually I-related voice leadings.[24] We will see that it is often advantageous to focus on these sorts of relationships, as they allow us to make interesting analytical observations that would otherwise be very hard to express.

For example, Figure 2.6.4 compares the opening progressions in Wagner's *Tristan*, Brahms' Op. 76 No. 4, and Debussy's *Prelude to "The Afternoon of a Faun."*[25] I think it is likely that both Brahms and Debussy, despite their ambiguous feelings about Wagner, had *Tristan* somewhere in the backs of their minds: the opening gesture, by which a half-diminished seventh chord slides chromatically to a dominant seventh, is unmistakably Tristanesque. (Note that Brahms' opening chord even uses the same pitch classes as Wagner's.) But rather than blatantly copying *Tristan*, both Brahms and Debussy do something *similar to* yet *different from* the earlier piece. The concept of individual T-relatedness provides a precise way to describe this sense of "similarity-with-difference": what Brahms and Debussy did, essentially, was transpose the second chord in *Tristan* up by semitone. (In Debussy's case, he also transposes the entire voice leading by tritone, rearranging the voices somewhat.) In all three cases, the result is a two-semitone voice leading between half-diminished and dominant seventh chords, an unfamiliar chromatic motion linking familiar chords. Furthermore,

24 Individual transposition adds a constant to the numbers representing the paths in a voice leading; individual inversion subtracts these numbers from a constant (see Tymoczko 2008b).

25 I have removed Wagner's "voice crossings," as will be discussed in Chapter 8.

all three voice leadings move root to root, third to third, fifth to fifth, and seventh to seventh. Yet at the same time, the connection to *Tristan* has been disguised: what has been borrowed is not the progression itself, but rather something more abstract—a general voice-leading schema rather than a particular way of resolving the half-diminished chord. (Thus we see how theoretically savvy composers can steal without getting caught!) Whether this is a matter of defusing, one-upping, or "correcting" Wagner is an interesting critical question.

Figure 2.6.4 The opening progressions in Wagner's *Tristan* (*a*), Brahms' Intermezzo Op. 76 No. 4 (*b*), and Debussy's *Prelude to "The Afternoon of a Faun."*

In classical music, individually T-related voice leadings often appear in sequential contexts. Figure 2.6.5a presents a nice example from the opening of Mozart's C minor Fantasy, K. 475. The music invokes a relatively standard chromatic sequence in which iv⁶–V⁷ chord progressions move downward by major second: beginning with A^7, we have f^6–G^7 followed by what we expect to be e♭⁶–F^7. But Mozart transposes the last chord up by semitone so that the final pair is individually T-related to the pair preceding it, with the sequence ending on F♯⁷ rather than the expected F^7. This maneuver, which transforms a minor-key iv^6–V^7 progression into a major-key iii^6–V^7 progression, is reasonably common in tonal music. Figure 2.6.5b cites an analogous progression from the recapitulation of the first movement of Beethoven's E♭ major Piano Sonata, Op. 31 No. 3.[26] Here the sequence moves downward by diatonic thirds, with each chord preceded by its applied dominant. If the passage were strictly sequential, it would cycle through all seven diatonic triads before returning to the tonic E♭; however, Beethoven arranges an earlier return by inserting a descending diatonic *second* into the sequence of thirds. Once again, the structural similarity of the voice leadings

Figure 2.6.5 Individually T-related voice leadings in sequential passages from Mozart (*a*) and Beethoven (*b*).

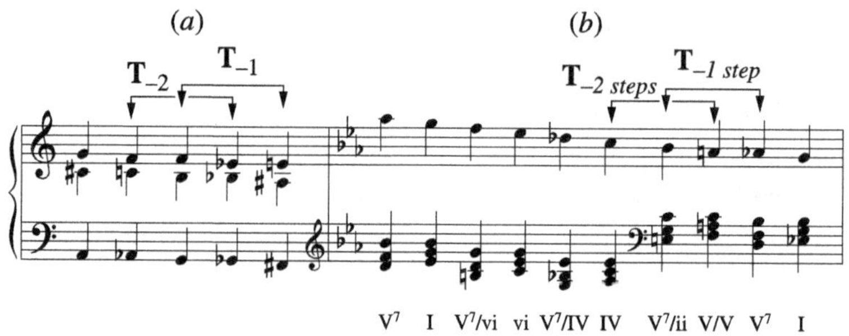

26 A very similar sequence appears at m. 45 of the first movement of Beethoven's F major piano sonata, Op. 54.

masks the deviation from strict sequential procedure: we hear successive voice leadings as being similar, even though they are not related by exact transposition. Again, the concept of "individual T-relatedness" provides a precise tool for describing this sort of similarity.

2.7 VOICE-LEADING SIZE

Polyphonic music uses independent melodies to articulate efficient voice leadings between meaningful harmonies (Figure 2.7.1). To be sure, it also involves following many other rules that are particular to specific styles and time periods: in some genres, for example, parallel perfect fifths are forbidden, while in others they are allowed. (Similarly, in some genres the bass is more likely to move by leap, while in others the bass is essentially similar to the other voices.) Later chapters will deal with these style-specific nuances. For now, I want to focus on the basic conditions under which polyphony itself is possible.

Clearly, to write this sort of music, composers need to be able to compare the overall efficiency, or "size," of different voice leadings. But how is this done? In some situations, comparisons seem unproblematic: for instance, a voice leading that moves just one note by just one semitone seems obviously smaller than a voice leading that moves three notes by six semitones each. But other cases are considerably more difficult. Is (C, E, G)→(D♭, F, A♭) larger or smaller than (C, E, G)→(C, E, A)? The first voice leading moves its voices by a greater total distance (three semitones vs. two semitones), while in the second, the largest distance moved is greater (two semitones vs. one semitone). Which is more important? Is the smaller voice leading the one that minimizes the total amount of motion or the largest distance moved by any voice?

Although pedagogues have long enjoined their students to use small voice leadings, they have never bothered to provide specific answers to these sorts of questions. (Students, it seems, are supposed to intuit which of the available voice leadings is the smallest.) More recently, theorists have proposed a variety of very precise methods of measuring voice-leading size. Unfortunately, musical practice does not allow us to adjudicate between these different proposals, leaving us with many plausible but incompatible solutions to the same problem. Rather than adopting one of these, my strategy here is to try to remain as neutral as possible about the issue. (Precision is a virtue only when it is not arbitrarily imposed!) Happily, it turns out that "reasonable" measures of voice-leading size agree about a number of important cases.

Figure 2.7.1 The opening phrase of the Bach chorale "O Herzensangst." This music can be represented as the sequence of voice leadings (E♭, G, E♭, B♭)→(E♭, B♭, E♭, G) $\xrightarrow{-7,-2,0,5}$ (A♭, A♭, E♭, C)→(A♭, F, D, B♭). I have ignored the starred ("nonharmonic") note at the end of the first measure.

Figure 2.7.2 The principle of avoiding crossings tells us that (*a*) should be no larger than (*b*) and (*c*) should be no larger than (*d*).

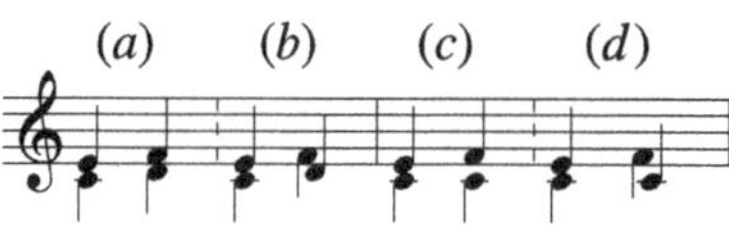

I consider a measure of voice-leading size to be "reasonable" if it satisfies two basic requirements: first, it should depend only on *how far* the individual voices move, with larger motion leading to larger voice leadings; and second, it should judge voice leadings with *voice crossings* to be larger (or at the very least, no smaller) than their natural uncrossed alternatives. This is illustrated by Figure 2.7.2. The first requirement is basic to the very notion of voice-leading size; the second mandates a kind of musical "division of labor," according to which it is preferable to have more voices moving by small amounts, rather than fewer voices moving by larger amounts. (The connection between avoiding voice crossings and the division of musical labor is not obvious, although it can be proved mathematically.[27]) Thus Figure 2.7.3a, in which two voices move by three and four semitones, should be at least as small as Figure 2.7.3b, in which one voice moves by seven semitones. Both principles are consistent with Western musical practice, and to my knowledge no composer, theorist, or pedagogue has ever proposed a method of measuring voice leading that violates either principle.[28]

Figure 2.7.3 Generally speaking, Western composers prefer smaller amounts of motion in more voices (*a*) to larger amounts of motion in fewer voices (*b*). The pattern in (*a*) is common in the inner voices in classical music; (*c*) provides an example from the Bach chorale "Nun lob' mein' Seel' den Herren."

Appendix A summarizes the technical issues involved in measuring voice leading. For our purposes, the important point is that the two constraints are powerful enough to imply a number of theoretical results: for instance, they imply that the more evenly a chord divides the octave, the smaller the voice leadings to its various transpositions; they also imply that E and A♭ major triads can be linked to the C major triad by smaller voice leadings than any other major triads. Indeed, the constraints are so powerful that, in many contexts, it is unnecessary to specify a particular method of measuring voice leading, because all reasonable metrics will agree. For most of this book, we will therefore be able to speak of "large" and "small" voice leadings without getting into the details of how to measure voice leading. Readers should feel comfortable trusting their musical intuitions, interpreting the term "efficient voice leading" as a synonym for "voice leadings in which all voices move by short distances."

---

27 See Tymoczko 2006.

28 It bears repeating that this notion of voice-leading size is meant to model composers' behavior rather than listeners' experience. See Callender and Rogers 2006 for some work on listeners' judgments of voice-leading distance.

2.8 NEAR IDENTITY

So far we have grouped chords into categories based on transpositional and inversional equivalence. But this insistence on *exact* equivalence is actually quite restrictive: in many contexts, it is useful to describe two chords as being similar even though they are not exactly the same.[29] This is particularly important when investigating matters of intonation and tuning: for instance, music theorists might speak about the "acoustically pure perfect fifth {C, G}," the "equal-tempered fifth {C, G}," the "quarter-comma meantone perfect fifth {C, G}" and so on. The language suggests that these different tunings are variations on the same object, which may come in a variety of closely related forms. Yet from our perspective the different tunings of {C, G} belong to different chord types, since no transposition or inversion relates them. Thus there is a mismatch between ordinary musical thinking and the extremely precise terminology we have been developing.

The problem is not limited to matters of tuning and intonation. The dominant seventh chord {C, E, G, B♭} is in the grand scheme of things rather similar to the minor seventh {C, E♭, G, B♭}, which differs only in that it has an E♭ rather than E♮. Although they do not belong to the same set class, the two chords are clearly more similar to each other than either is to the dissonant cluster {F♯, G, A♭, A}. Consequently, {C, E, G, B♭}⇒{C, E♭, G, B♭} feels like a progression between two more-or-less similar chords, while {C, E, G, B♭}⇒{F♯, G, A♭, A} is quite jarring, connecting very different harmonies. Our discussion, rather than trying to model to this fact, has instead treated harmonic identity as an all-or-nothing affair.

It therefore seems that exact identity stands at one end of a *continuum* of musical relatedness. The equal-tempered chord {C, E, G, B♭} is exactly identical to itself, and is very closely related to the just-intonation chord {C, E, G, B♭}. Both of these chords are somewhat related to the minor-seventh chord {C, E♭, G, B♭}, and are not very similar at all to the chromatic cluster {F♯, G, A♭, A}. Notice that these "degrees of relatedness" seem to mirror facts about voice leading: there is a very small voice leading from the equal-tempered {C, E, G, B♭} to its just-intonation counterpart, and a reasonably small voice leading from {C, E, G, B♭} to {C, E♭, G, B♭}, but it takes a relatively large voice leading to get from {C, E, G, B♭} to {F♯, G, A♭, A}. This suggests that we may be able to use voice leading to model at least some of our intuitions of musical similarity.[30]

Metaphors of distance are useful here. We can think of the acoustically pure perfect fifth {0, 7.01} as being *close* to the equal-tempered fifth {0, 7}, as if the two chords were nearby in some abstract "space of all chords." Conversely, the chord {3, 4} is

29 The notion of similarity is central to the work of Ian Quinn (1996, 2001, 2006).

30 In principle, voice leading provides just *one* of many possible notions of musical distance. We might sometimes want to conceive of musical distance harmonically (based on common tones or shared interval content), or in a way that privileges membership in the same diatonic scale—so that the F major triad is closer to C major than E major is. (See, for example, Quinn 2001, 2006, and 2007, and Tymoczko, forthcoming.) However, we will see that conceptions based on voice leading are extremely versatile and can be useful in a wide range of contexts.

much farther from {0, 7} than {0, 7.01} is, since it takes a larger voice leading to connect {3, 4} to {0, 7}. Chapter 3 will show that this talk of distance is not just a metaphor: it is possible to describe geometrical spaces containing all chords with a particular number of notes, and in which the distance between any two chords corresponds to the size of the minimal voice leading between them. Musical "similarity" can therefore be represented by distance in these spaces. In anticipation of this discussion, I will say that chords are "near" or "close to" each other when they can be linked by efficient voice leading.

We can extend these ideas to chord types as well. Two chord types can be said to be similar if there is a relatively small voice leading between their transpositions. Thus the diminished triad is closer to the minor triad than to the chromatic cluster, since there is a very small voice leading taking C diminished to C minor, but no similarly small voice leading connecting any diminished triad to any chromatic cluster.[31] Another way to make the point is to say that any particular diminished triad is *nearly transpositionally related* to any minor triad: for example, C diminished is nearly transpositionally related to F minor, since {C, E♭, G♭} is *near* {C, E♭, G} which is in turn transpositionally related to {F, A♭, C}. In the same spirit, we could say that {C, D♭, G} is *nearly inversionally related* to {E♭, G, A}, meaning that {C, D♭, G} is near {C, D, F♯}, which is inversionally related to {E♭, G, A}. What results is a more flexible conception of harmonic similarity: rather than considering two chords to be similar only when they are *exactly* related by transposition or inversion, we can consider them similar when they are nearly (or *approximately*) related by these same transformations. This is useful insofar as actual composers are often more concerned with approximate than with exact musical relationships.

2.9 HARMONY AND COUNTERPOINT REVISITED

In Chapter 1, we observed that Western music has a kind of two-dimensional coherence: vertical or harmonic principles dictate that chords should be audibly similar, while horizontal or contrapuntal principles dictate that chords should be connected by efficient voice leading. Figure 2.9.1 shows these constraints operating in a wide range of different Western styles, including classical music, contemporary jazz, late-nineteenth-century chromaticism, and even modern atonality. To be sure, composers often deviate from these norms for expressive reasons—just as, when driving, one sometimes takes a scenic detour rather than following the most direct route. And to be sure, different styles always involve additional constraints over and above these very basic norms. But the norms themselves are relatively robust, shared by a wide range of styles spanning several centuries.

31 The single-semitone voice leading (C, E♭, G♭)→(C, E♭, G) links diminished to minor, but it takes at least four semitones to link a diminished triad to a chromatic cluster.

Figure 2.9.1 Harmonic consistency and efficient voice leading in a range of styles. (*a*) A common upper-voice pattern for the classical I–IV–I–V–I chord progression. (*b*) A common jazz-piano "left-hand voicing" for the descending-fifths progression D^7–G^7–C^7–F^7. The voicings add ninths and thirteenths and omit roots, fifths, and elevenths, as is common in jazz. (*c*) Two celebrated examples of Wagnerian chromaticism; the first is a simplification of the opening of *Tristan* and the second is the opening of *The Ring's* "Tarnhelm" motif. (*d*) Chromatic clusters of the sort often found in late twentieth-century music, particularly in the music of Ligeti and Lutosławski.

So under what circumstances is it possible to find an efficient voice leading between nearly transpositionally or inversionally related chords? In other words, how is it possible to write music that is both harmonically and melodically coherent?

Chapter 1 noted that this is possible when a chord divides the octave very evenly or very unevenly. Here I want to replace the contrast "even/uneven" with the more powerful concept of *near symmetry*. It turns out that one can combine harmonic consistency and efficient voice leading only by using *nearly symmetrical* chords, which are typically near chords that are *completely symmetrical* under transposition, inversion, or reordering. Nearly even chords (such as the major triad) are near the symmetrical chords that divide the octave perfectly evenly (such as the augmented triad). Clustered chords (such as {B, C, C♯}) are near the symmetrical chords that contain many copies of one specific pitch class (such as the "triple unison" {C, C, C}). But there are other symmetrical chords as well: transpositionally symmetrical chords such as {C, C♯, F♯, G}, which do not divide the octave particularly evenly, and inversionally symmetrical chords such as {C, D, E}, which are neither particularly even nor particularly uneven. Thus an approach based on symmetry leads to a much deeper understanding of the fundamental connection between harmony and counterpoint—opening our eyes to new compositional possibilities and revealing regularities latent in the music of the past.

We will begin by considering efficient voice leading between chords *exactly* related by transposition or inversion; then, at the end of the section, we will broaden the discussion to include near transposition or near inversion.

2.9.1 Transposition

A chord is transpositionally symmetrical if it is unchanged by some transposition. Thus, when we transpose an augmented triad by a major third, we produce the same pitch classes we started with. Figure 2.9.2 shows that there are two kinds of transpositionally symmetrical chords, those that divide the pitch-class circle evenly and those

Figure 2.9.2 Transpositionally symmetrical chords either divide the octave evenly (*a*), or can be decomposed into equal-size subsets that themselves do so (*b*). Here, the transpositionally symmetrical chord {C, F, F♯, B} can be decomposed into tritones {C, F♯} and {B, F}.

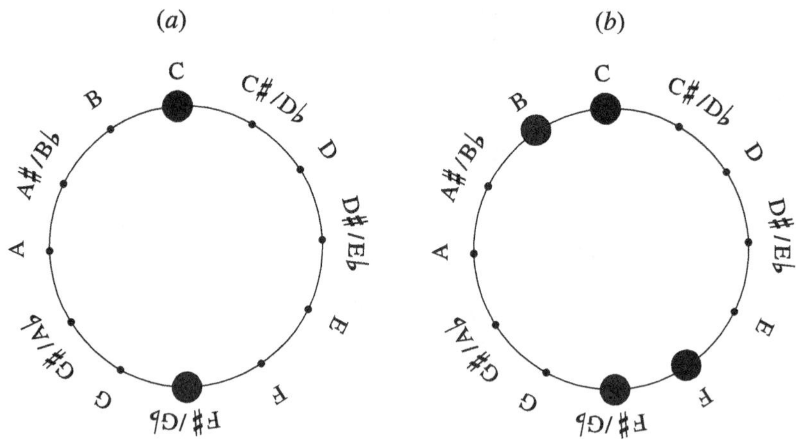

that can be decomposed into equal-size subsets that do so.[32] For example, {B, C, F, F♯} does not divide the circle into four even parts, but it can be decomposed into a pair of tritones that each divide the circle in half.

If a chord is near one of these symmetrical chords, then it can be linked by efficient voice leading to some of its transpositions. Consider {C, E, G}, which is near {C, E, G♯} since the voice leading (C, E, G)→(C, E, G♯) is small. It follows that the E major chord must also be near the C augmented triad. This is because we can transpose the small voice leading (C, E, G)→(C, E, G♯) uniformly by ascending major third, obtaining (E, G♯, B)→(E, G♯, C). This is an efficient voice leading from E major to C augmented. Figure 2.9.3 shows that we can retrograde this second voice leading and attach it to the earlier one, producing (C, E, G)→(C, E, G♯)→(B, E, G♯). Here we have the conjunction of two small voice leadings. Removing the middle chord will give a small voice leading from C major to E major: (C, E, G)→(B, E, G♯). In other words, if C major is close to an augmented triad, then its major third transposition must also be close to that same augmented triad, and since C and E major are both close to the same chord, they must also be close to each other.

Of course, there is nothing particularly special about major or augmented chords. Take any chord A close to a symmetrical chord S that is unchanged by transposition $\mathbf{T}_x$. Then $\mathbf{T}_x(A)$ will also be close to $\mathbf{T}_x(S)$, which is the same as S; and since A and $\mathbf{T}_x(A)$ are both near S, they are also near each other. Speaking somewhat metaphorically, the symmetrical chord passes on its symmetry to nearby chords in the form of efficient voice leading. These nearby chords are not themselves symmetrical, but they are *nearly* so, which is to say that they can be linked to their x-semitone transpositions by efficient voice leading. It follows that transpositional symmetry is

32 See Starr and Morris (1977).

Figure 2.9.3 Any chord that is near an augmented triad can be connected to its major-third transposition by efficient voice leading.

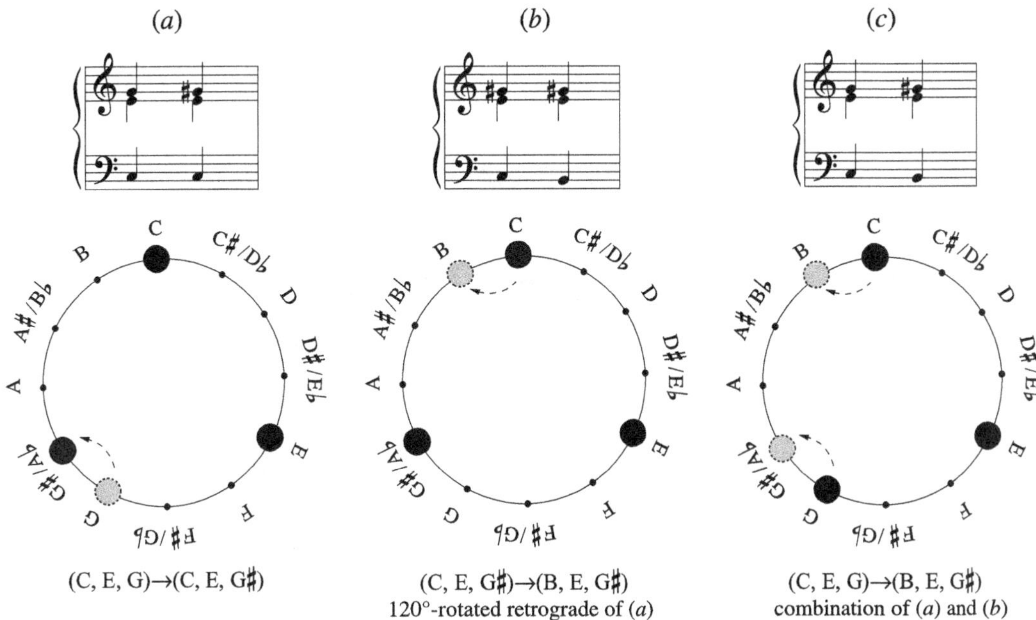

a limiting case of efficient voice leading: as chord *A* moves closer and closer toward a transpositionally symmetrical chord, the size of the minimal voice leading between *A* and $\mathbf{T}_x(A)$ decreases, reaching zero when the chord is exactly symmetrical.

Let's consider a second example. The chord {B, C, E, F♯} appears commonly in jazz, but does not divide the octave particularly evenly. However, it is near the transpositionally symmetric {B, C, F, F♯}, which contains two separate tritones. Beginning with the small voice leading (B, C, E, F♯)→(B, C, F, F♯), we transpose by tritone to produce (F, G♭, B♭, C)→(F, G♭, B, C) (Figure 2.9.4). Retrograding this and gluing it to the original voice leading, we obtain (B, C, E, F♯)→(B, C, F, F♯)→(B♭, C, F, G♭). Removing the middle chord gives (B, C, E, F♯)→(B♭, C, F, G♭), which efficiently links tritone-related chords. Chapter 10 will show that this sort of voice leading plays a role in jazz "tritone substitutions." For now, however, the focus should be on the general form of the argument: since chord *A* is close to the tritone-symmetrical chord *S*, then so is the tritone transposition of *A;* and since *A* and its tritone transposition are close to the same chord, they must also be close to each other.

Figure 2.9.4 Since both {C, E, F♯, B} and its tritone transposition are close to {B, C, F, F♯} (*a*–*b*), they are close to each other. In (*c*), we retrograde the voice leading in (*b*) and attach it to (*a*). Removing the middle chord gives us the voice leading in (*d*).

There is one complication that should be mentioned here. Suppose a three-note chord, such as {C, F, F♯}, is near a transpositionally

Figure 2.9.5 A larger chord can take advantage of the symmetries of a smaller chord, but it requires additional voices.

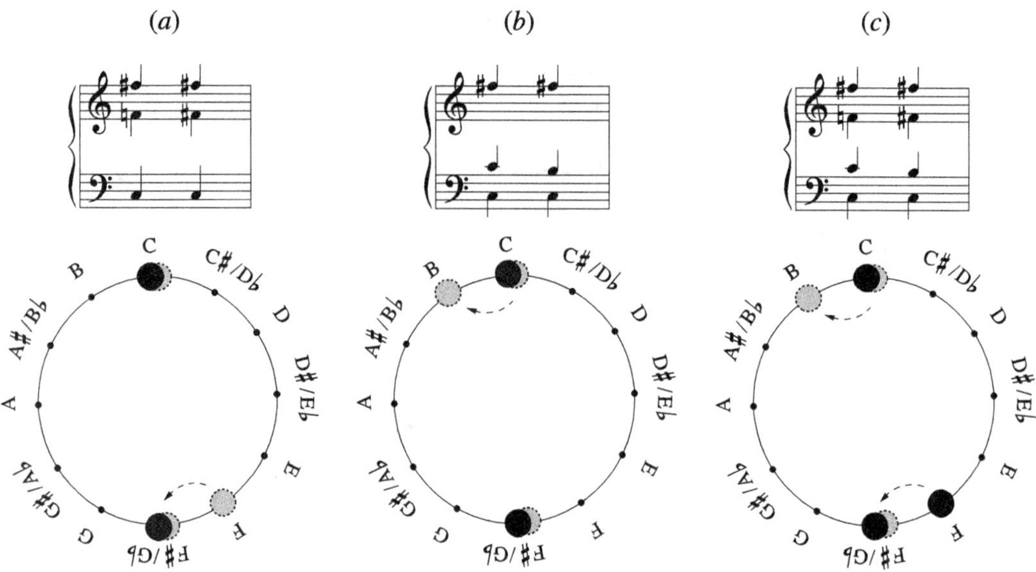

symmetrical two-note chord, such as {C, F♯} (Figure 2.9.5). Proceeding as we did earlier, we begin with the three-voice voice leading (C, F, F♯)→(C, F♯, F♯); retrograding and transposing by tritone we obtain (F♯, C, C)→(F♯, B, C). Note that we cannot simply glue these two voice leadings together, since (C, F♯, F♯) is not the same as (F♯, C, C). However, if we double a voice in each voice leading, we can attach them. What results is a *four-voice* voice leading between {C, F, F♯} and its tritone transposition, (C, C, F, F♯)→(C, C, F♯, F♯)→(B, C, F♯, F♯) or (C, C, F, F♯)→(B, C♯, F♯, F♯) upon removing the middle chord. The fourth voice is the price the three-note chord has to pay for exploiting the symmetry of a two-note chord. In general, extra voices will *always* be necessary whenever a larger chord exploits the symmetries of a smaller chord. In Chapter 7 we will see that there are common tonal routines, such as the voice leading (C, C, E, G)→(A, C, F, F), which exploit this very procedure (§7.2). It follows that the familiar major triad is special not just because it divides the octave into three nearly even parts, but also because it is reasonably close to the tritone.

2.9.2 Inversion

A chord will be unchanged by inversion if its notes are arranged symmetrically around an "axis of symmetry" crossing the pitch-class circle at two antipodal points, with tones placed freely on either of these points. For example, Figure 2.9.6 shows that the axis of the inversionally symmetrical {C, D, E} contains the notes D and A♭; since C and E are arranged symmetrically around this axis, inversion around D leaves the chord unchanged.

The nonsymmetrical chord {C, D♯, E} is near {C, D, E}, since the voice leading (C, D♯, E)→(C, D, E) is small. Inverting this entire voice leading around the fixed

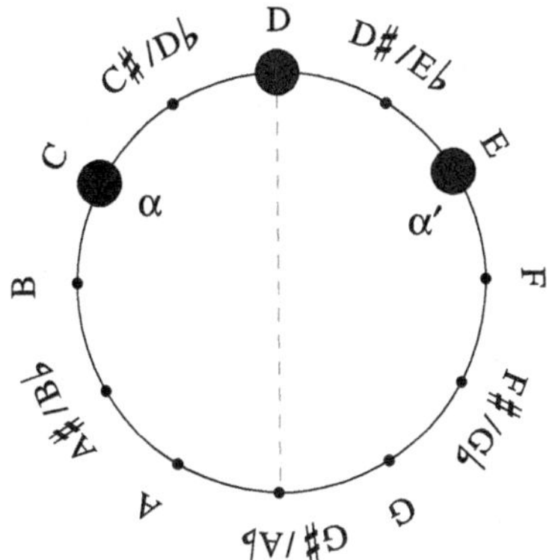

Figure 2.9.6 To form an inversionally symmetrical chord, choose two antipodal points to act as an axis of symmetry—here, {D, A♭}. One can place notes on either axis point (or both), as they will be unaffected by the inversion. For any points not lying on the axis, such as α, one must also add its inversional partner, symmetrically placed on the other side of the axis. Here, α is 60° counterclockwise from the upper axis point, while α' is 60° clockwise from that point. The antipodal points can also lie *between* equal-tempered pitch classes.

Figure 2.9.7 Any chord that is near an inversionally symmetrical chord can be connected to its inversion by efficient voice leading.

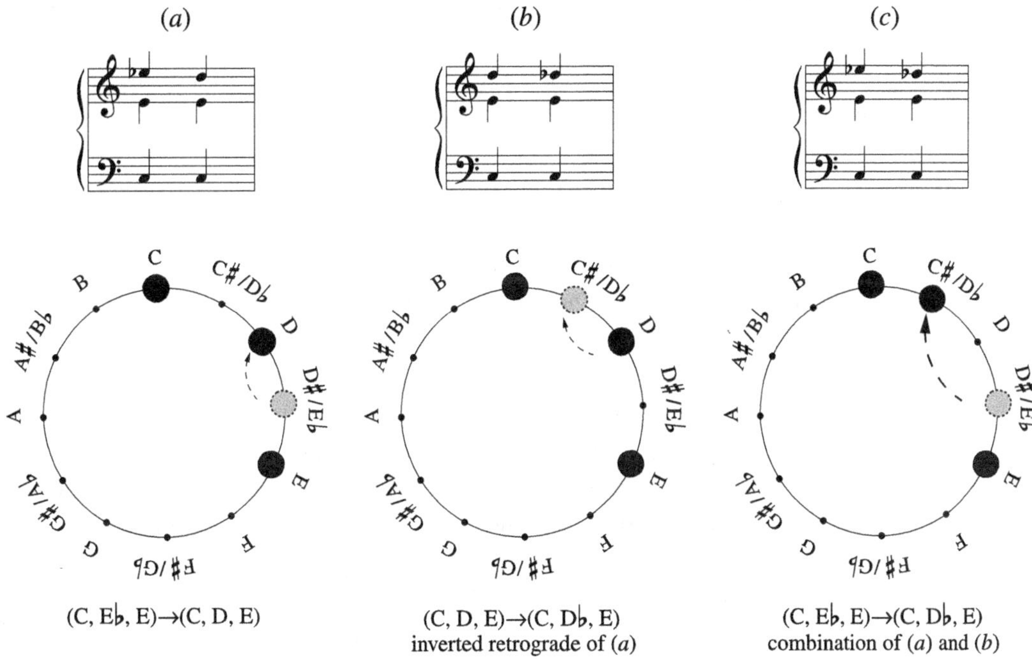

point D produces (C, D♭, E)→(C, D, E). Reversing this voice leading and gluing it to the earlier one produces (C, D♯, E)→(C, D, E)→(C, D♭, E). Removing the middle chord gives us a small voice leading between inversionally related chords: (C, D♯, E)→(C, D♭, E) (Figure 2.9.7). As in the transpositional case, the inversionally symmetrical chord passes its symmetry on to nearby chords: if chord *A* is near a chord *S* that is invariant under some inversion $\mathbf{I}_y^x$, then $\mathbf{I}_y^x(A)$ will also be near *S*, and hence *A* and $\mathbf{I}_y^x(A)$ can be linked by efficient voice leading.

Figure 2.9.8 provides a real-world example. We begin with the efficient voice leading (F, A♭, C♭, E♭)→(F, A♭, C♭, D), which uses a single-semitone motion to transform the F half-diminished chord into a fully diminished seventh. The next voice leading inverts the first uniformly around A4/B♭4, producing an efficient voice

Figure 2.9.8 The F half-diminished chord is close to a diminished seventh chord (*a*). Inverting this voice leading uniformly around A4/B♭4, we get an efficient voice leading from E^7 to the same diminished chord. In (*c*), we retrograde the voice leading in (*b*) and attach it to (*a*). Removing the middle chord (*d*) gives us an efficient voice leading from the F half-diminished chord to E^7, a voice leading that plays a central role in Wagner's *Tristan*.

leading from the E dominant seventh to the same diminished seventh chord. In Figure 2.9.8c we reverse this and glue it to the first voice leading. Removing the symmetrical chord gives us an efficient voice leading from F half-diminished to E^7, strongly reminiscent of the opening of *Tristan*. We conclude that this celebrated nineteenth-century progression exploits the near I-symmetry of the half-diminished and dominant seventh chords.

2.9.3 Permutation

The third symmetry is a little bit different from the others. Suppose we model chords as *multisets* that may contain multiple copies of a single note. From this point of view, the chord {C, C, C} is different from {C, C}, since they have a different number of copies of the note C. Let's also imagine that (contrary to fact) we could somehow keep track of these different copies, which we can represent with subscripts like $\{C_a, C_b, C_c\}$. Now consider $(C_a, C_b, C_c) \rightarrow (C_c, C_a, C_b)$, a voice leading that permutes the notes in the chord {C, C, C}. Since none of the voices in this voice leading actually moves, we can say that {C, C, C} is *permutationally symmetrical*. "Permutation symmetry" is just a fancy synonym for "has multiple copies of one or more of its notes."

Permutationally symmetrical chords are themselves rather boring, but the *nearby* chords are quite interesting. The chromatic cluster {B, C, D♭} is near {C, C, C} since (B, C, D♭)→(C, C, C) is small. Retrograding and reordering voices, we obtain (C, C, C)→(C, D♭, B). Gluing the two voice leadings together gives us (B, C, D♭)→(C, C, C)→(C, D♭, B); upon removing the middle chord, we obtain (B, C, D♭)→(C, D♭, B), a small voice leading from {B, C, D♭} to itself. (Figure 2.9.9 attempts, somewhat lamely, to illustrate.) Once again, the symmetrical chord passes its symmetry on to nearby chords: given a small voice leading $A \rightarrow S$, from chord A to the permutationally symmetrical chord S, we can permute both chords uniformly to obtain the small voice leading $\boldsymbol{P}(A) \rightarrow \boldsymbol{P}(S)$, or $\boldsymbol{P}(A) \rightarrow S$, since S is permutationally symmetrical. Retrograding and gluing together gives us $A \rightarrow S \rightarrow \boldsymbol{P}(A)$; upon removing the middle chord, we have $A \rightarrow \boldsymbol{P}(A)$, an efficient voice leading between A and itself. The general procedure here is precisely the same as in the cases of transposition and inversion; the only difference is the nature of the symmetry.

Figure 2.9.9 Any chord that is near a chord with pitch-class duplications can be connected to its untransposed form by efficient voice leading.

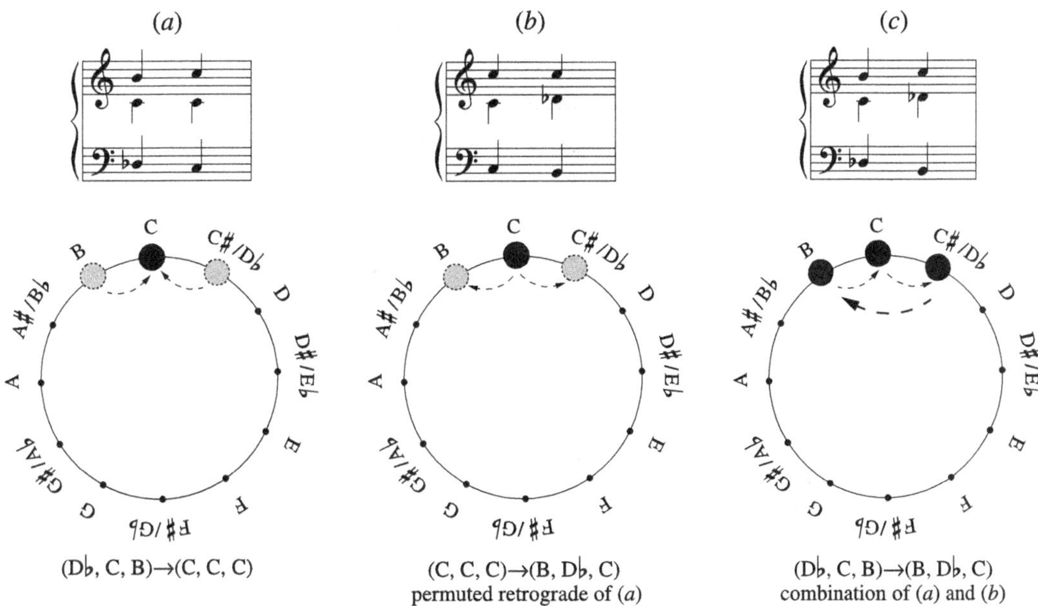

It may seem surprising to place permutation alongside transposition and inversion, since we are accustomed to thinking of chords as inherently unordered objects. But the discussion in §2.4 should ameliorate any feelings of unease: we form chords by abstracting away from the order of the notes in a musical object, just as we form set classes by abstracting away from the distinction between transpositionally and inversionally related objects. And just as transpositionally symmetrical chords are special (because there are fewer transpositions to abstract away from) so too are permutationally symmetrical chords (because there are fewer orderings to abstract away from). Voice leading reveals this "specialness" by providing a musical mechanism for rearranging the notes in an unordered chord. As a result, it should not be too surprising that there is a close analogy between permutational symmetry and the more familiar symmetries considered previously. Transpositional near-symmetry guarantees efficient voice leading between transpositionally related chords; inversional near-symmetry guarantees efficient voice leading between inversionally related chords; and permutational near-symmetry guarantees efficient voice leading between a chord and itself. Here we see the advantages of a more flexible approach to chord classification, in which we embrace a wide variety of musical transformations. From our point of view, permutation is just another kind of symmetry, with its own distinctive collection of musical consequences.

The arguments in this section show that *if* a chord is near a symmetrical chord then it will inherit this symmetry in the form of efficient voice leadings. One might also wonder whether the converse is true: is it the case that *if* there is an efficient voice leading from a chord *A* to one of its transpositions or inversions, then chord *A* is nearly symmetrical under transposition, inversion, or permutation? That is, is it the case that our three symmetries are *the only symmetries there are*—the only symmetries we need to understand if we want to know how to combine efficient voice leading with harmonic consistency? Basically, the answer is "yes," at least insofar as we understand the term "harmonically consistent" to mean "using chords that are approximately related by transposition or inversion."[33] It follows that every instance of efficient voice leading between structurally similar chords—in any scale or tuning system—can be understood in terms of the three basic symmetries we have just discussed. This is precisely what will allow us, in Part II, to interpret a large number of Western musical practices as variations on the same basic techniques.

It is very important to realize that the symmetrical chords relevant to voice leading will *not* necessarily lie on the ordinary piano keyboard. The familiar pentatonic scale, {C, D, F, G, B♭} or {0, 2, 5, 7, 10}, is quite close to the chord that divides the octave into five equal pieces: {0, 2.4, 4.8, 7.2, 9.6}. Consequently, the pentatonic scale can be efficiently linked to its transpositions, as in (C, D, F, G, B♭)→(C, D, F, G, A). While both of these chords belong to the equal-tempered universe, and can be played on an ordinary piano, the perfectly even five-note chord does not. Yet this missing chord nevertheless exerts its influence on twelve-tone equal-tempered music; indeed, twelve-tone equal-tempered five-note chords can be linked to their transpositions by efficient voice leading only if they are close to this phantasmic and elusive chord. This is just one of many cases where a deep understanding of the discrete musical universe requires us to think in continuous terms. Even though we are ultimately concerned with equal-tempered music, we find that we can understand this music best when we consider the continuous space in which equal temperaments are embedded.[34]

33 It is relatively easy to demonstrate the connection between efficient voice leading and near symmetry; the harder point is to explain the circumstances under which nearly symmetrical chords are near chords that are perfectly symmetrical. (This becomes clear only when we examine the geometrical spaces described in Chapter 3.) With respect to the first issue, here is a simple argument connecting efficient voice leading and near symmetry. Suppose there is some function $\mathcal{F}$ over the pitch classes, which could be a transposition or an inversion or something else altogether. Now let us suppose that there is some efficient voice leading between chords A and $\mathcal{F}(A)$. We can therefore represent $A \rightarrow \mathcal{F}(A)$ as the product of two separate voice leadings $(a_i, a_j, a_k, \ldots) \rightarrow (a_x, a_y, a_z, \ldots) \rightarrow (\mathcal{F}(a_x), \mathcal{F}(a_y), \mathcal{F}(a_z), \ldots)$. The first of these rearranges the notes of A while the second simply applies $\mathcal{F}$ to each note. (The first voice leading need not be a permutation, and it may involve doublings.) Now consider $(a_x, a_y, a_z, \ldots) \rightarrow (a_i, a_j, a_k, \ldots)$ and $(a_x, a_y, a_z, \ldots) \rightarrow (\mathcal{F}(a_x), \mathcal{F}(a_y), \mathcal{F}(a_z), \ldots)$. These voice leadings must be approximately equal. (This follows from the fact that the original voice leading is efficient, and hence moves none of its voices very far.) The first rearranges the notes of A, the second applies $\mathcal{F}$ to each note; hence there is some rearrangement that is approximately equal to applying $\mathcal{F}$. This is just what it means to be nearly symmetrical under $\mathcal{F}$.

34 John Clough (in unpublished work) and Rick Cohn (1996, 1997) articulated a special case of the central claim of this section, observing that major and minor triads are a semitone away from augmented chords, and that this allows them to be connected by efficient chromatic voice leading. (Cohn further generalizes to chromatic scales whose size is divisible by three, and speculates that analogous claims can be made about tetrachords and hexachords in the standard chromatic scale.) This section generalizes this important observation by articulating a somewhat broader principle: if a chord A is near a chord that is $\mathcal{F}$-symmetrical, then A and $\mathcal{F}(A)$ can be connected by efficient voice leading. I also observe that the converse of this statement is true: if A and $\mathcal{F}(A)$ can be connected by efficient voice leading, then A is nearly symmetrical under $\mathcal{F}$ (see the preceding note). Furthermore, my notion of "nearness" is somewhat more general, since I consider chords like {C, E, G} to be "near" {C, F♯}. I also show that the symmetrical chord need not appear in the relevant scale—for instance, the diatonic collection is near the equiheptatonic collection, which does not appear in the twelve-tone chromatic scale.

Finally, note that nothing really changes when we adopt the more flexible notion of harmonic relatedness discussed in §2.8. For suppose we would like to find an efficient voice leading between two chords *A* and *B* that are *nearly*—rather than precisely—transpositionally or inversionally related. Since *A* is nearly transpositionally or inversionally related to *B*, there is a small voice leading $\mathcal{F}(A) \rightarrow B$, where $\mathcal{F}$ is some transposition or inversion. And if the voice leading $A \rightarrow B$ is small, then the voice leading $A \rightarrow \mathcal{F}(A)$ must also be small, as both *A* and $\mathcal{F}(A)$ will be close to *B*. In the cases of musical interest, $\mathcal{F}$ will be some nonzero transposition or inversion, which means that *A* is itself nearly symmetrical.[35] (The same argument shows that *B* must also be nearly symmetrical.) Thus, expanding our notion of "harmonic consistency" does not expand the realm of musical possibilities: a chord *A* can be linked by efficient voice leading to one of its *near*-transpositions or *near*-inversions only if *A* is itself nearly symmetrical under transposition, inversion, or permutation.

2.10 ACOUSTIC CONSONANCE AND NEAR EVENNESS

We now return to acoustic consonance, the second of our five basic components of tonality. Recall that Western listeners tend to agree that certain chords sound stable and restful, or consonant, while others sound unstable and harsh, or dissonant. Many, though not all, Western styles exploit this difference: consonant sonorities tend to appear as musical destinations or at points of rest, while dissonant sonorities tend to be more active and unstable. To be sure, the distinction between consonance and dissonance is extremely complex, and it maps only indirectly onto the concept of musical stability. (There are situations when an acoustically consonant sonority behaves as if it were musically unstable.) But to a first approximation, it is reasonable to say that in many musical styles, dissonant sonorities tend to resolve to consonant sonorities.

Acoustic consonance is somewhat imperfectly understood, and there are a number of theories about what produces it.[36] Nevertheless, there is broad agreement on some basic principles. The eighteenth-century mathematician Jean-Baptiste Fourier showed that any periodic mathematical function can be represented as the sum of sine and cosine waves whose frequencies are integer multiples of a single frequency *f* (Figure 2.10.1). In the case of a musical sound, these sine waves are called *partials*.

---

35 There are some subtleties here that I am glossing over. More precisely, the cases of musical interest are those where $\mathcal{F}$ is either an inversion or nontrivial transposition, or where $\mathcal{F}$ is the identity operation and the voice leading $\mathcal{F}(A) \rightarrow B$ involves some nontrivial permutation. When these conditions are not met, then our argument simply records the boring fact that any chord can be transformed into some other chords by moving its notes by small distances: for example, that a major triad can be transformed into a minor triad by lowering its third. The musically interesting cases are those in which small voice leadings lead to an interesting reshuffling of the resulting notes. For instance, if we think of a minor triad as a major triad with lowered third, then the voice leading (C, E, G)→(B, E, G) is interesting because it does *not* simply lower the third; instead, it is an efficient voice leading in which the root of the major triad becomes the *fifth* of the minor triad. Here, we are exploiting the near symmetries of the underlying chords.

36 Helmholtz (1863/1954), Terhardt 1974, Burns 1999, Sethares 1999, Cariani 2001, Tramo et al. 2005.

Figure 2.10.1 The periodic sound on the left has frequency *f*. (Two repetitions of the waveform are shown.) This sound can be analyzed as the sum of the sine waves on the right, with periods *f*, 2*f*, and 6*f*.

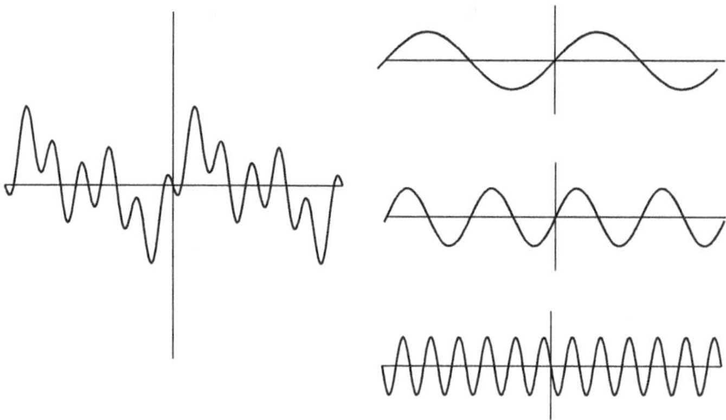

The nineteenth-century German psychologist Hermann von Helmholtz proposed that two pitches are consonant if their partials are aligned, or else are sufficiently far apart so as not to interfere. Dissonance is caused when partials are close together, but not perfectly aligned; this creates a sense of "roughness" or harshness. (Twentieth-century auditory physiologists have shown that the ear's basilar membrane decomposes incoming sound waves into sine waves, more or less as Fourier described.) Although there is much disagreement about just how complete this story is, most contemporary psychologists believe that it is at least partly right.[37]

Western instruments typically produce periodic sounds that, when analyzed as Fourier described, have relatively strong lower partials (*f*, 2*f*, 3*f*, 4*f*, etc.). The partials of several such "harmonic" sounds will match when their fundamental frequencies are related by simple whole-number ratios.[38] Consequently, as Pythagoras discovered roughly 2700 years ago, the most consonant intervals have fundamental frequencies in simple ratios: 2:1 (octave), 3:2 (perfect fifth), 4:3 (perfect fourth), 5:4 (major third), and 6:5 (minor third). A larger chord will be consonant when it contains a preponderance of consonant intervals, and this in turn requires that its notes be relatively evenly distributed in pitch-class space.

For small chords there is a particularly elegant connection between near evenness and acoustic consonance. The most consonant three-note chord, the major triad, contains the first three distinct pitch classes in the harmonic series, with fundamental frequencies in a 3:4:5 ratio. Figure 2.10.2 shows that the triad divides the frequency-space octave into three exactly equal pieces. When we take the logarithm of these frequencies, passing from frequency space into pitch space (§2.1), we move from an equal division of the (frequency-space) octave into a nearly even division of the

37 In particular, writers such as Tramo et al. (2005) have suggested that the relevant neural circuitry may involve timing information rather than spatial information.

38 The consonance of an interval therefore depends on the timbre (or overtones) of the sound. Sethares (1999) provides compelling examples of this phenomenon.

Figure 2.10.2 The frequencies {330, 440, 550} divide a frequency-space octave (between 330 and 660) perfectly evenly. In pitch space, the chord divides the octave *nearly* evenly, into pieces that are approximately 5, 4, and 3 semitones large. Note that the acoustically pure C♯ (72.9) is not quite the same as the equal-tempered C♯ (73).

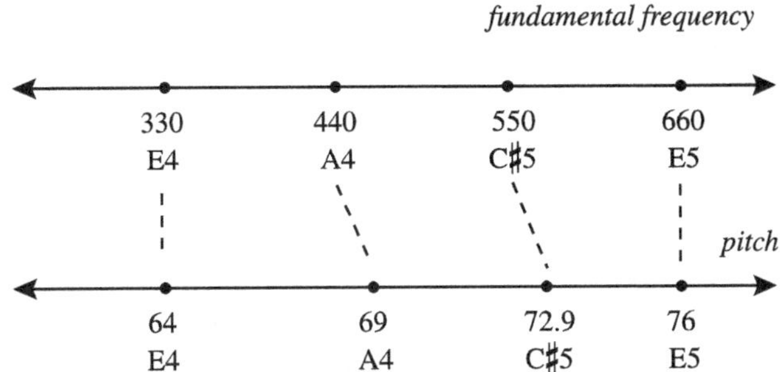

Figure 2.10.3 Highly consonant chords divide the octave nearly evenly.

Notes	Name
{C, G}	Perfect fifth
{C, E, G}	Major triad
{C, E♭, G}	Minor triad
{C, E, G, A}	Major triad "add six"
{C, E, G, B♭}	Dominant seventh chord
{C, E, G, B}	Major seventh chord
{C, D, E, G, A}	Pentatonic scale
{C, E, G, B♭, D}	Dominant ninth chord
{C, D, E, F, G, A}	Diatonic hexachord
{C, E, G, B♭, D, F♯}	Dominant "sharp eleven"
{C, D, E, F, G, A, B}	Diatonic scale
{C, D, E, F♯, G, A, B♭}	Melodic minor ascending

(log-frequency, pitch-space) octave. (A similar point holds for the perfect fifth, which contains the first two distinct pitch classes in the harmonic series and evenly divides the frequency-space octave.) Thus, for small chords, maximal consonance directly implies near evenness. And though the situation is somewhat more complicated in the case of larger chords, it remains true that highly consonant chords always divide the octave relatively evenly (Figure 2.10.3).[39]

In other words—and this being one of the most important ideas in the entire book, it is worth a little interjective buildup—the basic sonorities of Western tonal music are optimal for two distinct reasons: considered as individual sonic objects,

39 With four notes, the dominant seventh chord divides the frequency-space octave precisely evenly, but is not maximally consonant. However, it is fairly consonant, and the more consonant chords (such as the major triad with added sixth) are also quite even. Huron (1994) estimates the most common twelve-tone equal-tempered chords of various sizes; his maximally consonant chords are always nearly even.

they are acoustically consonant and hence sound pleasing in their own right; but since they divide the pitch-class circle nearly evenly, they can also be connected to their transpositions by efficient voice leading. Any composer who cares about harmonic consistency would therefore have reason to choose these chords, even if he or she did not care a whit about acoustic consonance. Or to put the point in the form of a parable: suppose God asked you, at the dawn of time, to choose the chords that humanity would use in its music. There are two different choices you might make. You might say, "Well, God, I'm a somewhat cerebral type and I'd like to combine efficient voice leading and harmonic consistency, since this will allow me to praise You with glorious polyphony." And God would hand you a suitcase containing nearly even chords, including the perfect fifth, the major triad, and dominant seventh chord.[40] On the other hand, you might say, "You know, God, I'm kind of a hedonist, and at the end of a hard day of hunting and gathering I'd really like to hear chords that *sound good*—chords whose intrinsic consonance will put a smile on my face." And in this case, God would hand you a suitcase containing... the perfect fifth, the major triad, the dominant seventh chord. In other words, he would hand you *the very same chords,* no matter which choice you made.

It follows that the development of Western counterpoint is something of an amazing accident. No doubt musicians originally chose consonant chords because they "sounded good" in some primary sense—they were acoustically consonant and hence felt restful and harmonious. But during the early history of Western music it gradually became apparent that these chords were special in another way as well: they could be used to write *contrapuntal* music that was also *harmonically consistent.* This realization led to the marvelous efflorescence of Western contrapuntal technique, as composers over the centuries explored an ever-increasing range of voice-leading possibilities between an ever-increasing range of consonant chords. (This efflorescence, and its numerous variations and ramifications, is the subject of Part II.) Ultimately, this was possible because of the nonobvious connection between efficient voice leading, harmonic consistency, and acoustic consonance—a connection that we now understand as a simple consequence of the hidden symmetries of circular pitch-class space.[41]

---

40 This suitcase might contain some other chords as well: consonance implies near evenness, but not the reverse. However, in the twelve-tone equal-tempered system, the most nearly even chords are reasonably consonant.

41 It bears repeating that I am generalizing claims made by Eytan Agmon and Richard Cohn. Agmon (1991) notes that the diatonic triad is special because it can be connected to each of its diatonic transpositions by particularly efficient voice leadings; Cohn (1996, 1997) notes that the chromatic major triad is capable of participating in "parsimonious" voice leadings to three separate minor triads. ("Parsimonious" voice leadings, in Cohn's parlance, are voice leadings in which just one voice moves and it moves by just one or two semitones.) Here I extend these points in several ways. First, rather than limiting myself to Cohn's parsimonious voice leadings, I consider efficient voice leading more generally. Second, while Agmon and Cohn focus on the triad as an object in some particular scale, my point is true of chords in any scale whatsoever—diatonic, chromatic, or even in continuous unquantized space. Third, I point out that analogous facts hold for acoustically consonant sonorities more generally: while Agmon and Cohn seem to privilege the triad even in comparison to the perfect fifth, dominant seventh chord, and diatonic scale, I suggest that the consonant sonorities are all essentially in the same boat. Finally, I show that acoustic consonance *implies* near evenness, which in turn implies the ability to move by efficient voice leading to all of a chord's transpositions or inversions; for Agmon and Cohn, these are separate properties that sometimes happen to coincide.

CHAPTER 3

A Geometry of Chords

We now turn to geometrical models in which chords are represented as points in higher dimensional spaces. As we will see, these "chord spaces" are a good deal more interesting than the plain-vanilla space of ordinary Euclidean experience, containing twists, mirrors, Möbius strips, and their higher dimensional analogues. Besides being extraordinarily beautiful, these geometrical models clearly illustrate musical principles that can otherwise be quite difficult to grasp.[1] In particular, we can use them to construct "voice-leading graphs" that depict the basic contrapuntal relations between the familiar chords and scales of Western music, graphs that will serve as the principal analytical tools of the second half of this book.

3.1 ORDERED PITCH SPACE

Chapter 2 introduced the *basic musical object,* or ordered sequence of pitches. Figure 3.1.1 shows that there are two ways to represent these objects geometrically. In Figure 3.1.1a we represent ordered pairs of notes using a gray circle for the first note and a black circle for the second. (We need different colors because the pairs are ordered, and we need to differentiate the first note from the second.) In Figure 3.1.1b, the horizontal axis represents the first pitch while the vertical axis indicates the second. Each model therefore has two *degrees of freedom:* in the first, we can move either circle independently of the other; in the second, we can move along one axis while holding fixed our position on the other. It is more or less a matter of convenience whether we wish to represent two-note objects using two points in a one-dimensional space, as we did in Chapter 2, or one point in a two-dimensional space. However, the models are different in at least one important respect. It is easy to see how to ignore octave and order in the first, linear model: we simply represent all notes using same color (thereby ignoring order) and wrap the line into a circle (thereby ignoring octaves and reproducing pitch-class space). But it is not at all clear how we should modify the two-dimensional representation in those situations where we wish to ignore these musical parameters.

1 The ideas in this chapter are based on Tymoczko 2006 and 2008b, which are in turn inspired by earlier geometrical work on "chord-type spaces," including Roeder 1984, 1987, 1994, Cohn 2003, and Callender 2004. For a comprehensive account of a wide range of geometrical spaces, see Callender, Quinn, and Tymoczko 2008.

Figure 3.1.1 Two ways to represent the ordered pair (C4, E4). The first uses two points in a one-dimensional space—here, the gray circle represents the first note, and the black ball the second. The second uses a single point in a two-dimensional space.

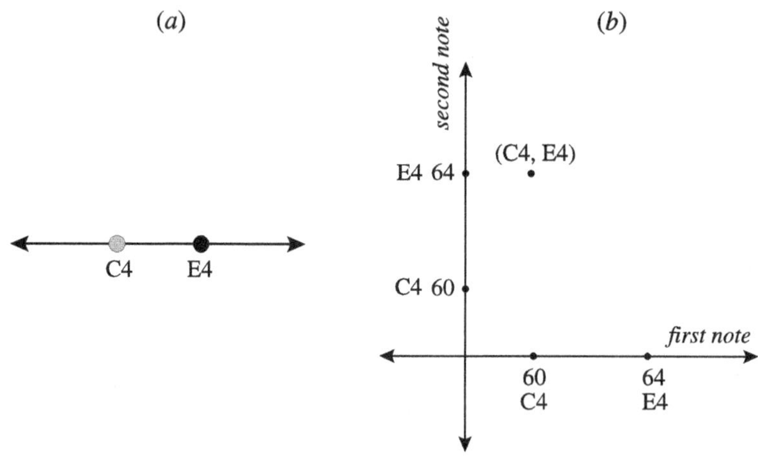

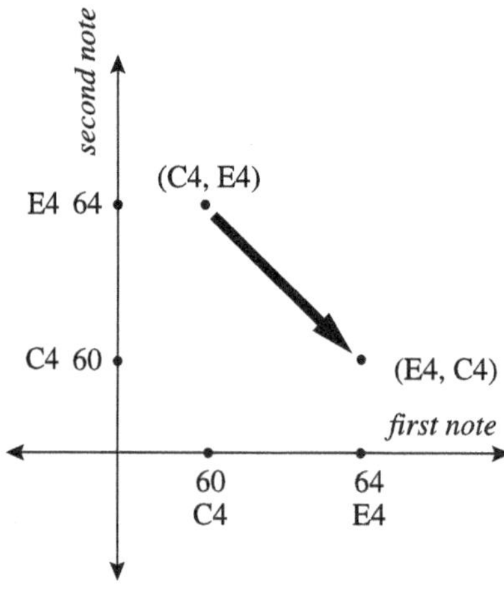

Figure 3.1.2 A voice leading can be represented as a line segment in the plane. Here, the voice leading (C4, E4)→(E4, C4), in which the first and second voices trade notes.

In the one-dimensional space, progressions between objects are represented by collections of paths (cf. Figure 2.5.4). In the two-dimensional space, progressions can be represented by line segments such as that in Figure 3.1.2, which depicts a situation in which the voices trade notes. Figure 3.1.3 uses line segments to model a two-voice passage from Josquin's *Missa l'homme armé*. With a little practice, it becomes easy to translate two-voice music into a series of line segments in the space. Any two-voice passage of music, in any style whatsoever, can be depicted in this way.

Horizontal and vertical line segments represent motion in a single voice (Figure 3.1.4). Parallel motion, in which the two voices move in the same direction by the same amount, is represented by lines parallel to the 45° NE/SW diagonal, while perfect *contrary* motion—in which the voices move the same distance in opposite directions—is represented by lines parallel to the 45° NW/SE diagonal. It turns out to be somewhat more convenient to rotate the space clockwise by 45°, so that parallel motion is horizontal and perfect contrary motion is vertical. Chords on the same horizontal line now relate by transposition; chords on the same vertical line sum to the same value when pitches are represented numerically. (This follows from the fact that perfect contrary motion subtracts from one voice what it adds to the other.) Oblique motion now moves along the 45° diagonals: motion in the first voice occurs along the NW/SE diagonal, while motion in the second occurs along the NE/SW diagonal. This rotation does not change the space in any way; we are simply changing our perspective on it.

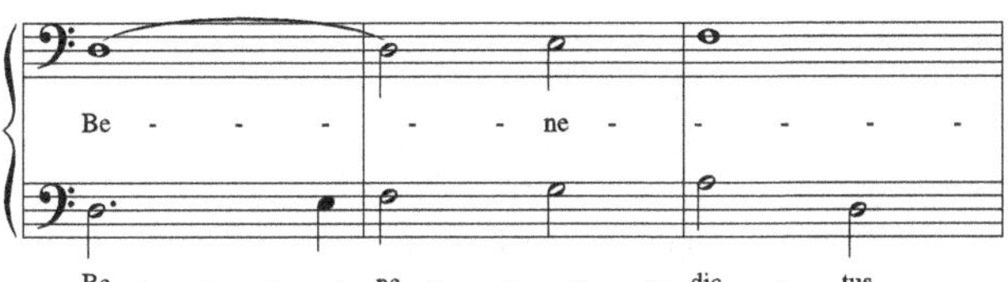

Figure 3.1.3
A passage from Josquin represented in two-dimensional space.

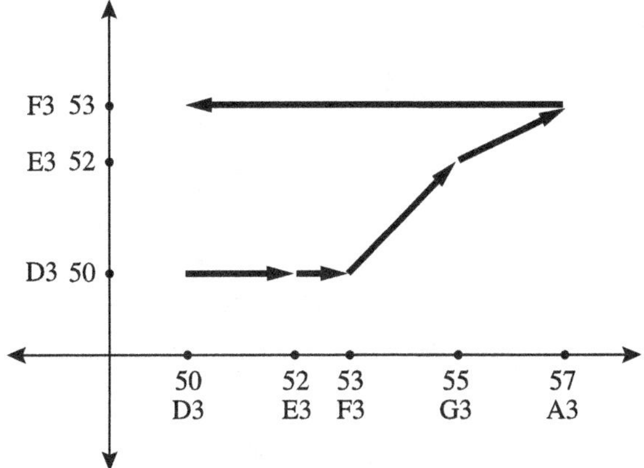

Figure 3.1.4 Rotating two-note ordered pitch space.

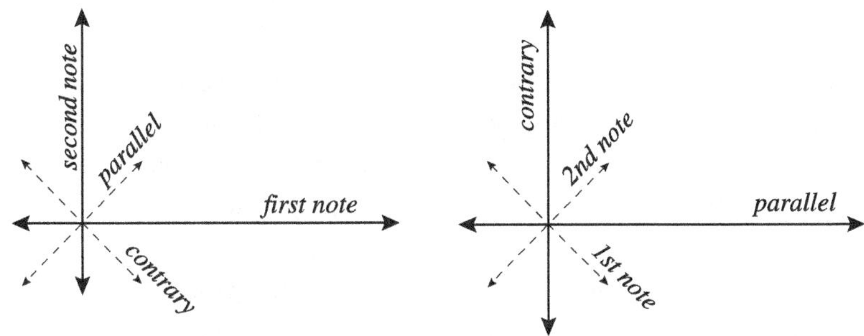

Figure 3.1.5 depicts an extended portion of two-dimensional ordered pitch space, with the axes rotated as just described. The most striking feature of this graph is its *periodicity:* like a piece of wallpaper, it consists of a single pattern (or "tile") that is repeated to cover the larger plane. The figure contains four complete tiles. The points in the lower left quadrant are related by octave transposition to the corresponding points in the upper right: the first element in each pair is the same, while the second element in the lower left pair is one octave below the second element in the upper right pair. Moving from the lower left quadrant to the corresponding point in the upper right will therefore transpose the second note up by an octave. Similarly, moving from the upper left to the corresponding point in the lower right shifts the *first* element up by an octave. Since any quadrant can be connected by a series of diagonal motions to one of the quadrants in Figure 3.1.5, and since diagonal motion between quadrants always corresponds to octave transposition in one voice, the rest of the infinite space can be generated from this figure.

Figure 3.1.5 A portion of infinite, two-dimensional ordered pitch space.

(F♯3, F♯4) (G3, G4) (G♯3 G♯4) (A3, A4) (B♭3, B♭4) (B3, B4) (C4, C5) (C♯4, C♯5) (D4, D5) (E♭4, E♭5) (E4, E5) (F4, F5) (F♯4, F♯5)

| (G3, F♯4) (A♭3, G4) (A3, G♯4) (B♭3, A4) (B3, A♯4) (C4, B4) | (C♯4, C5) (D4, C♯5) (E♭4, D5) (E4, E♭5) (F4, E5) (F♯4, F5) |

(G3, F4) (A♭3, G♭4) (A3, G4) (B♭3, A♭4) (B3, A4) (C4, B♭4) (C♯4, B4) (D4, C5) (E♭4, C♯5) (E4, D5) (F4, E♭5) (F♯4, E5) (G4, F5)

| (A♭3, F4) (A3, F♯4) (B♭3, G4) (B3, G♯4) (C4, A4) (C♯4, A♯4) | (D4, B4) (E♭4, C5) (E4, C♯5) (F4, D5) (G♭4, E♭5) (G4, E5) |

(G♯3, E4) (A3, F4) (B♭3, G♭4) (B3, G4) (C4, A♭4) (C♯4, A4) (D4, B♭4) (D♯4, B4) (E4, C5) (F4, D♭5) (F♯4, D5) (G4, E♭5) (G♯4, E5)

| (A3, E4) (B♭3, F4) (B3, F♯4) (C4, G4) (D♭4, A♭4) (D4, A4) | (E♭4, B♭4) (E4, B4) (F4, C5) (G♭4, D♭5) (G4, D5) (A♭4, E♭5) |

(A3, D♯4) (B♭3, E4) (B3, F4) (C4, F♯4) (D♭4, G4) (D4, G♯4) (E♭4, A4) (E4, B♭4) (F4, B4) (F♯4, C5) (G4, C♯5) (G♯4, D5) (A4, D♯5)

| (B♭3, E♭4) (B3, E4) (C4, F4) (D♭4, G♭4) (D4, G4) (E♭4, A♭4) | (E4, A4) (F4, B♭4) (F♯4, B4) (G4, C5) (G♯4, C♯5) (A4, D5) |

(B♭3, D4) (B3, D♯4) (C4, E4) (D♭4, F4) (D4, F♯4) (E♭4, G4) (E4, G♯4) (F4, A4) (F♯4, A♯4) (G4, B4) (A♭4, C5) (A4, C♯5) (B♭4, D5)

| (B3, D4) (C4, E♭4) (C♯4, E4) (D4, F4) (E♭4, G♭4) (E4, G4) | (F4, A♭4) (F♯4, A4) (G4, B♭4) (G♯4, B4) (A4, C5) (A♯4, C♯5) |

(B3, C♯4) (C4, D4) (C♯4, E♭4) (D4, E4) (E♭4, F4) (E4, F♯4) (F4, G4) (F♯4, G♯4) (G4, A4) (G♯4, A♯4) (A4, B4) (B♭4, C5) (B4, C♯5)

| (C4, C♯4) (C♯4, D4) (D4, E♭4) (E♭4, E4) (E4, F4) (F4, F♯4) | (F♯4, G4) (G4, A♭4) (A♭4, A4) (A4, B♭4) (B♭4, B4) (B4, C5) |

(C4, C4) (C♯4, C♯4) (D4, D4) (E♭4, E♭4) (E4, E4) (F4, F4) (F♯4, F♯4) (G4, G4) (G♯4, G♯4) (A4, A4) (B♭4, B♭4) (B4, B4) (C5, C5)

| (C♯4, C4) (D4, C♯4) (E♭4, D4) (E4, E♭4) (F4, E4) (F♯4, F4) | (G4, F♯4) (A♭4, G4) (A4, G♯4) (B♭4, A4) (B4, A♯4) (C5, B4) |

(C♯4, B3) (D4, C4) (E♭4, C♯4) (E4, D4) (F4, E♭4) (F♯4, E4) (G4, F4) (A♭4, G♭4) (A4, G4) (B♭4, A♭4) (B4, A4) (C5, B♭4) (C♯5, B4)

| (D4, B3) (E♭4, C4) (E4, C♯4) (F4, D4) (G♭4, E♭4) (G4, E4) | (A♭4, F4) (A4, F♯4) (B♭4, G4) (B4, G♯4) (C5, A4) (C♯5, A♯4) |

(D4, B♭3) (D♯4, B3) (E4, C4) (F4, D♭4) (F♯4, D4) (G4, E♭4) (G♯4, E4) (A4, F4) (B♭4, G♭4) (B4, G4) (C5, A♭4) (C♯5, A4) (D5, B♭4)

| (E♭4, B♭3) (E4, B3) (F4, C4) (G♭4, D♭4) (G4, D4) (A♭4, E♭4) | (A4, E4) (B♭4, F4) (B4, F♯4) (C5, G4) (D♭5, A♭4) (D5, A4) |

(E♭4, A3) (E4, B♭3) (F4, B3) (F♯4, C4) (G4, C♯4) (G♯4, D4) (A4, D♯4) (B♭4, E4) (B4, F4) (C5, F♯4) (D♭5, G4) (D5, G♯4) (E♭5 A4)

| (E4, A3) (F4, B♭3) (F♯4, B3) (G4, C4) (G♯4, C♯4) (A4, D4) | (B♭4, E♭4) (B4, E4) (C5, F4) (D♭5, G♭4) (D5, G4) (E♭5, A♭4) |

(E4, G♯3) (F4, A3) (F♯4, A♯3) (G4, B3) (A♭4, C4) (A4, C♯4) (B♭4, D4) (B4, D♯4) (C5, E4) (D♭5, F4) (D5, F♯4) (E♭5, G4) (E5, G♯4)

| (F4, A♭3) (F♯4, A3) (G4, B♭3) (G♯4, B3) (A4, C4) (A♯4, C♯4) | (B4, D4) (C5, E♭4) (C♯5, E4) (D5, F4) (E♭5, G♭4) (E5, G4) |

(F4, G3) (F♯4, G♯3) (G4, A3) (G♯4, A♯3) (A4, B3) (B♭4, C4) (B4, C♯4) (B4, C♯4) (C5, D4) (C♯5, E♭4) (D5, E4) (E♭5, F4) (E5, F♯4)

| (F♯4, G3) (G4, A♭3) (A♭4, A3) (A4, B♭3) (B♭4, B3) (B4, C4) | (C5, C♯4) (C♯5, D4) (D5, E♭4) (E♭5, E4) (E5, F4) (F5, F♯4) |

(F♯4, F♯3) (G4, G3) (G♯4, G♯3) (A4, A3) (B♭4, B♭3) (B4, B3) (C5, C4) (C♯5, C♯4) (D5, D4) (E♭5, E♭4) (E5, E4) (F5, F4) (F♯5, F♯4)

What about the lower left and upper left quadrants? Here, the relationship is somewhat harder to grasp. Imagine that there were a hinge connecting them, so that the bottom-left quadrant could be lifted out of the paper and flipped onto the upper left. This transformation maps each pair in the lower quadrant onto a pair with the same pitch content, but in the reverse order. Geometrically, the transformation is a *reflection:* a pair in the lower left quadrant gets sent to the spot where its reflection would appear if the common border were a mirror. When we move a dyad from the lower left quadrant to its reflected image in the upper left, we therefore switch the order of its notes. The two rightmost quadrants are related in exactly the same way.

Figure 3.1.6 Ordered pitch space is like a piece of wallpaper.

Figure 3.1.6 depicts symbolically the relationship between the four tiles, using a right-side-up human face to represent the lower left tile. The upper left quadrant is upside down relative to the lower left: if they were connected by a hinge along their common border, then either could be flipped over so as to coincide with the other. Similarly, the lower right tile is upside-down relative to the upper right. The lower right tile is also upside-down relative to the lower *left* tile, but in this case they cannot be related by reflection along their common border—that process would exchange left and right, but not up and down.

3.2 THE PARABLE OF THE ANT

Imagine now that an ant is walking along the wallpaper in Figure 3.1.6. Suppose that you and I are gambling types and decide to bet on whether the ant will touch a pipe in the next 30 seconds. For the purpose of settling the bet, it does not matter which tile the ant is on; what matters is whether it touches *any* pipe in *any* tile. We could therefore represent the ant's trajectory on a single tile, as in Figure 3.2.1. (Perhaps we use a single tile because we want to record our game for posterity while being environmentally conscious and using the minimum amount of paper.) That is, we arbitrarily select one tile from Figure 3.1.6 and take the ant's position to be the point on this tile corresponding to its position on the tile it actually occupies.

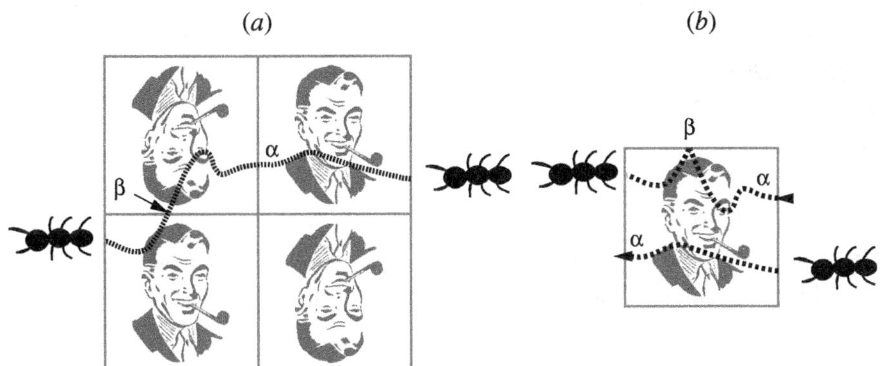

Figure 3.2.1 An ant's path can be represented on a single tile.

Although the underlying idea is simple, the structure of the resulting single-tile space is complex. For example, at the point marked α, the ant disappears off the lower left edge, only to reappear on the upper right. This is reminiscent of early video games such as *Asteroids* or *Pac-Man,* in which objects could move off one side of the screen to reappear on the other. Unlike those games, however, the ant leaves the *lower* half of the figure only to reappear on the *upper* half and vice versa, as if the left edge were attached to the right in a twisted fashion. The mathematical name for such a space is a *Möbius strip*.

Now consider point β in the ant's trajectory. In the single-tile representation the ant appears to "bounce off" the figure's upper edge, as if it were a mirror, or the bumper of a pool table. But we can see from Figure 3.2.1a that the ant's actual trajectory is straight. Nothing intrinsic to the ant's motion produces the change in direction—rather, it is the structure of the wallpaper on which it walks. The ant, being unaware of the wallpaper pattern, would have no knowledge that anything unusual was occurring.

Note that the placement of the left and right boundaries is essentially arbitrary. For the purpose of settling the bet, one could equally depict the ant's trajectory on

Figure 3.2.2 (*a*) The choice of left and right boundaries is arbitrary. (*b*) We could even represent the wallpaper without any left and right boundaries at all, if we stretched it horizontally and used the third dimension to attach the two edges. (*c*) The choice of upper and lower boundaries is not arbitrary, since this figure has no pipe.

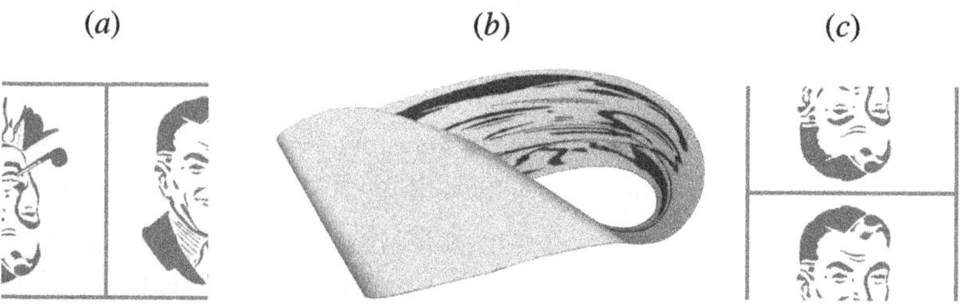

Figure 3.2.2a, which contains two half faces, one upside down and the other right side up. Though bizarre from an artistic point of view, it is perfectly adequate for gambling, since all parts of the figure are represented. If we were to stretch the figure horizontally, forming a rectangle rather than a square, we could even represent the tile in three dimensions *without any left or right boundaries whatsoever*—as in Figure 3.2.2b.[2] By contrast, the location of the upper and lower boundaries is *not* arbitrary. Figure 3.2.2c shows that we cannot settle our bet using the space consisting of two halves of two vertically adjacent tiles, since that space contains two copies of the top half of the figure but none of the lower half.

All this talk about ants, wallpaper, and gambling may seem like a distraction from the serious goal of understanding music. But in fact, the Parable of the Ant has introduced the fundamental concepts needed in the rest of this chapter. The key idea is that we can form a similar structure by "folding up" the two-dimensional *musical* space in Figure 3.1.5. In this case, ignoring what tile we are on corresponds to ignoring the *order* and *octave* of a pair of notes. In other words, the resulting space represents two-note chords as musicians are accustomed to thinking of them. Thus the Parable of the Ant, rather than being a frivolous digression, has actually marked the beginning of our investigation into a remarkable convergence between music theory and contemporary geometry.

3.3 TWO-NOTE CHORD SPACE

Our goal is to "fold" the infinite space of Figure 3.1.5 so as to glue together all the different points representing the same chord: (C4, E4), (E4, C4), (E5, C2), and so on. The result will be a new geometrical space, analogous to our single tile of wallpaper,

2 By using the third dimension, we can attach the figure's boundaries in the appropriate, twisted way. However, the figure remains *intrinsically two-dimensional,* since the ant can move in just two perpendicular directions at any point. The fact that we represent it using three dimensions simply reflects the difficulty of embedding the two-dimensional space in a Euclidean world. For a good nontechnical introduction to these issues, see Weeks 2002.

Figure 3.3.1 Two-note chord space. The left edge is "glued" to the right, with a twist.

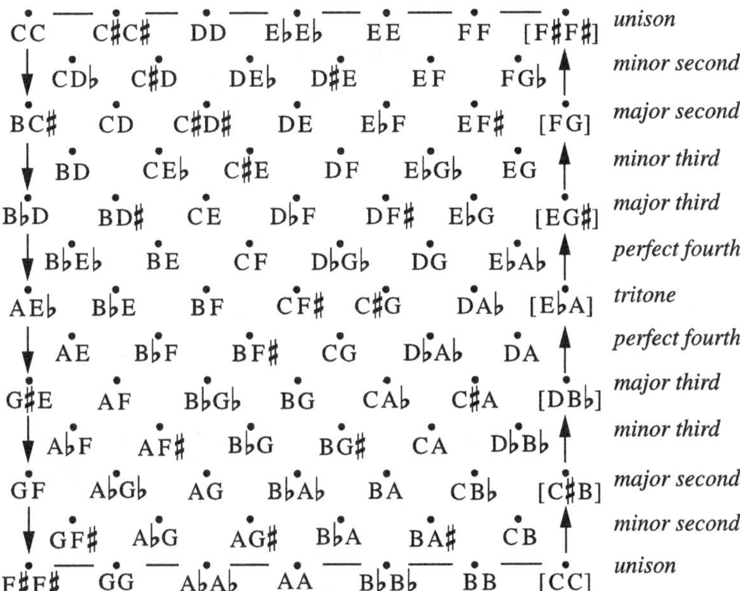

in which points represent two-note *chords*—or unordered pairs of pitch classes—rather than ordered pairs of pitches.

Happily, the detailed work has already been done. The "wallpaper space" described in the preceding section was modeled on Figure 3.1.5, and we can immediately adapt our earlier results.[3] Since each of the quadrants in Figure 3.1.5 contains precisely one point for every unordered set of pitch classes, any of them can be used to represent two-voice music. The *two-note chord space* shown in Figure 3.3.1 consists in a single quadrant of Figure 3.1.5, with octave designations removed to reflect the fact that we have discarded octave information. Although the points are labeled using ordered pairs, this ordering is not significant: the point CD♭ represents the ordering (D♭, C) just as much as it represents the ordering (C, D♭). Accordingly, I will sometimes refer to this point as {C, D♭} or {D♭, C}.

In §3.1, we rotated the coordinate axes so that parallel musical motion is represented by horizontal geometrical motion. This is again true in our new, "folded" space: horizontal motion represents parallel motion in both voices, while vertical motion represents contrary motion in which the two voices move in opposite directions by the same distance. (Oblique motion, in which one voice stays fixed, is again represented by the 45° diagonals.) It follows that chords on the same horizontal line of Figure 3.3.1 are related by transposition: the top edge of the figure, for example, contains unisons—two-note chords in which both voices sound the same pitch

3 People sometimes wonder why two-note chord space is a Möbius strip rather than the surface of a doughnut (or "torus"). The answer is that a torus models the space you get when you ignore octave *but not order*. On a torus, the point (C, E) is different from the point (E, C). While there are some musical purposes in which it is useful to distinguish these two orderings, there are many more in which it is not.

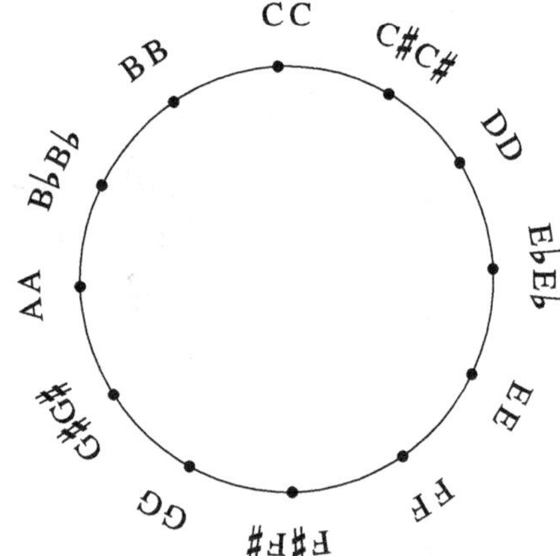

Figure 3.3.2 The boundary of two-note chord space is an (abstract) circle, since you can move in one direction to return to your starting point. The circle is very similar to pitch-class space.

class.[4] Unisons can also be found on the bottom edge of the figure, with two of them—{C, C} and {F♯, F♯}—appearing on both edges. (Chords on the right side of the figure are enclosed in brackets, indicating that they also appear on the left side.) These duplications are different representations of the same chord, artifacts of the doomed attempt to depict a Möbius strip in two Euclidean dimensions. *Intrinsically*, the Möbius strip has only one edge: what appear as distinct line segments containing unisons are actually two halves of an abstract "circle," since horizontal motion along the edge eventually returns to its starting point (§2.2). Figure 3.3.2 shows that this abstract circle is very similar to pitch-class space, with the only difference being that its points represent not single pitch classes but musical states in which two voices articulate the same pitch class.

The other intervals are also found on horizontal line segments, one in the top half of the figure and one in the bottom. The horizontal line segment just below the top edge, and just above the bottom edge, contains minor seconds. (Again, these apparently different line segments are attached at their endpoints, forming two halves of an abstract circle.) Major seconds are just below the minor seconds on the top half and just above the minor seconds on the bottom. As the interval between the two notes gets larger, dividing the octave more evenly, the lines representing them move toward the center. Consequently, the horizontal line at the midpoint of the figure contains tritones, which divide the pitch-class circle into two halves.[5]

Chords on the same vertical line can be linked by exact contrary motion: for instance, the voice leading (C, F♯)→(D♭, F) moves C up by semitone and F♯ down by semitone, and joins two chords on the same vertical line. It follows that every dyad lies on the same vertical line as its tritone transposition.[6] Since exact contrary

4 In these geometrical spaces, it is convenient to represent chords as *multisets* that can have multiple copies of particular pitch classes (§2.4). From this standpoint {C, E, E} is different from both {C, C, E} and {C, E}. We will return to this point shortly.

5 The (abstract) circle containing tritones is therefore half as long as the (abstract) circles containing the other intervals. This is the analogue, in continuous musical space, of the statement that there are half as many (twelve-tone equal-tempered) tritones as there are instances of the other (twelve-tone equal-tempered) intervals.

6 One can always connect tritone-related dyads by contrary motion: given the dyad {C, E}, one can move C up by tritone to F♯, and E down by tritone to A♯.

motion preserves the sum of a chord's pitch classes, chords on the same vertical line always sum to the same value. Thus {C, F♯}, {G, B}, and {A♭, B♭}, which lie on the vertical line at the center of Figure 3.3.1, all sum to six using pitch-class arithmetic.[7] (*Note:* this fact will be important later on, so make sure you understand it.) The pitch classes on the left edge of Figure 3.3.1 sum to zero. The sum of the chords in the vertical cross section increases as one moves rightward until we reach the right edge, whose chords again sum to zero (equivalent to twelve in pitch-class arithmetic). Finally, motion along the 45° diagonals alters just one note, so that (C♯, E) lies 45° northeast of (C, E). (Note, however, that diagonal motion can no longer be thought of as moving the "first note" rather than the "second note" because we are now neglecting order.[8]) It is worth emphasizing that two-note chord space is *continuous*, containing every conceivable chord in every conceivable tuning system. A chord like (C𝄲, E) (C quarter-tone sharp, E), though not labeled on the example, lies 45° northeast of (C, E), halfway to (C♯, E).

3.4 CHORD PROGRESSIONS AND VOICE LEADINGS IN TWO-NOTE CHORD SPACE

Our Möbius strip can be used to represent any chord progression and any voice leading between two-note chords. To represent a progression like {C, E}⇒{F, A} simply identify the initial point, {C, E}, and the final point, {F, A}. It is not necessary to choose any particular path between them, because a chord progression does not specify exactly *how* the individual notes move (§2.5). It is as if the music magically teleports, disappearing at {C, E} and instantaneously reappearing at {F, A}, without occupying any of the places in between.

A voice leading, by contrast, is represented by a particular *path* between chords, with the *size* of the voice leading corresponding to the *length* of the path. The simplest way to find this path is to imagine each voice making a continuous glissando, beginning and ending at the same time. For example, (C, E)→(E♭, G) moves each voice up by three semitones. If each voice made a continuous glissando, the music would pass through a series of major thirds: (D♭, F), (D, F♯), and countless others not accessible with an ordinary piano. These all lie on the horizontal line segment shown on Figure 3.4.1. Similarly, the voice leading (B, D)→(A♭, F) moves each voice by three semitones in contrary motion. This voice leading passes through the chords {B♭, E♭}, {A, E}, and a variety of other non-equal-tempered chords. It is therefore represented by the vertical line segment on the figure.

A little experimentation will show that the boundaries of the figure behave exactly like the boundaries of our earlier wallpaper space. To see this, imagine making a smooth glissando from (E♭4, G4) to (F4, A4). Figure 3.4.2 indicates that the

---

7 The sum of the pitch classes {B, G}, or {11, 7}, is 6, because we add or subtract 12 from our result until we obtain a number in the range $0 \leq x < 12$; $11 + 7 = 18$, and $18 - 12 = 6$ (§2.3).

8 Instead, we should think of it as moving particular notes: when we move northeast from {C, E}, we raise C to C♯. In actual musical contexts the C might belong to either voice, and might appear above or below the E.

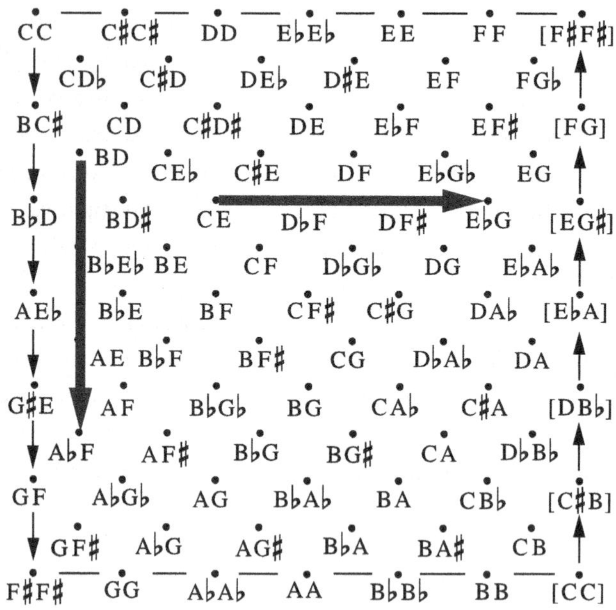

Figure 3.4.1 Voice leadings are represented by line segments. Parallel motion is horizontal, while perfect contrary motion is vertical. The voice leadings (C, E)→(E♭, G) and (B, D) → (A♭, F) are shown.

glissando is initially represented by rightward motion on the top half of the strip, from {E♭, G} to {E, G♯}. However, the point {E, G♯} is represented *both* on the top half of the right edge and on the bottom half of the left edge. As we move from (E4, G♯4) to (F4, A4), the glissando now appears on the bottom half of the figure, moving from the lower-left {E, G♯} to {F, A}. Thus, as in the Parable of the Ant, the music disappears off the upper right edge only to reappear on the lower left. Alternatively, consider the smooth glissando from (C4, D4) to (E4, D4)—in which the

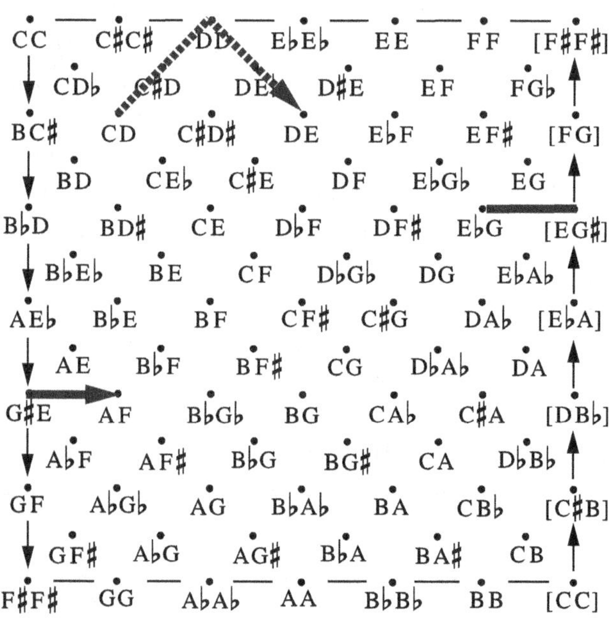

Figure 3.4.2 The horizontal boundaries act like mirrors, whereas the vertical boundaries are glued together with a "twist." Voice leadings thus disappear off the left edge to reappear on the right, and vice versa. Here, the voice leadings (E♭, G) → (F, A) and (C, D) → (E, D) are shown.

first voice moves from C4 to E4 while the second voice remains fixed. The resulting path, illustrated in Figure 3.4.2, is represented by a line segment that begins at {C, D} and moves diagonally northeast to {D, D}. (Recall that motion in just a single voice always lies along a 45° diagonal.) However, the second half of the path is represented by a line segment moving diagonally *southeast* from {D, D} to {E, D}. As in the Parable of the Ant, what causes the apparent "change in direction" is the structure of the underlying space: musically, the first voice moves smoothly upward from C4 to E4, and does not do anything strange at D4.

Voice leadings are therefore represented by what might be called "generalized line segments" that can bounce off a mirror boundary, or disappear off one side of the figure only to reappear on the other. There is, in fact, a one-to-one correspondence between these "generalized line segments" and voice leadings: for every generalized line segment there is a voice leading in pitch-class space, and for every voice leading in pitch-class space there is a generalized line segment. In principle, there can be infinitely many generalized line segments linking any two chords, each represented by a different pattern of reflections off the horizontal boundaries and "disappearances" off the left and right edges.

The total amount of horizontal motion in a voice leading can be calculated algebraically by adding the pitch-class paths in the two voices. A voice leading like $(C, E)\xrightarrow{2,\,1}(D, F)$ moves its two voices by a total of $2 + 1 = 3$ semitones, and is therefore represented by a generalized line segment whose horizontal component moves 3 units to the right.[9] $(C, E)\xrightarrow{-7,\,-2}(F, D)$ moves its voices by $-7 + -2 = -9$ semitones, and therefore moves 9 units to the left (Figure 3.4.3). Similarly, if one writes the voice leading so that the first two notes are in the same order as they are on Figure 3.3.1, then the total amount of *vertical* motion can be determined by subtracting the second path from the first. For example, $(C, E)\xrightarrow{2,\,1}(D, F)$ moves by a total of $2 - 1 = 1$ unit upward, while $(B, D)\xrightarrow{-3,\,3}(A\flat, F)$ moves its voices by $-3 - 3 = -6$ units upward, or 6 units downward.[10] (The first of these voice leadings is shown in Figure 3.4.3, the second in Figure 3.4.1.) However, contact with *any* of the four "edges" of the strip exchanges "downward" and "upward": $(C, E)\xrightarrow{5,\,-2}(F, D)$ moves its voices by $5 - (-2) = 7$ upward units, but it reaches the upper mirror boundary after just four of these; the remaining three steps are therefore taken in a descending direction (Figure 3.4.3). Similarly, the voice leading $(C, E)\xrightarrow{-7,\,-2}(F, D)$ moves its voices by $-7 - (-2) = -5$ units, but when the path disappears off the left edge to reappear on the right, the direction turns upward. These algebraic principles provide a more systematic alternative to the method of imagining each voice making a continuous glissando. For an even simpler method readers can download a free computer program that plots voice leadings on the Möbius strip automatically.[11]

9 A "unit" is the distance between adjacent vertical cross sections containing equal-tempered chords. Since there are twelve of these, the Möbius strip has a width of 12 units.

10 A "unit" is the distance between adjacent horizontal lines containing equal-tempered chords; again, the Möbius strip is twelve units high.

11 See the companion website for links to the "ChordGeometries" program.

Figure 3.4.3 Four voice leadings between {C, E} and {D, F}, as represented on the Möbius strip. The amount of rightward motion can be calculated by adding the paths in the two voices; the amount of upward motion can be calculated by subtracting the second path from the first.

(*a*)

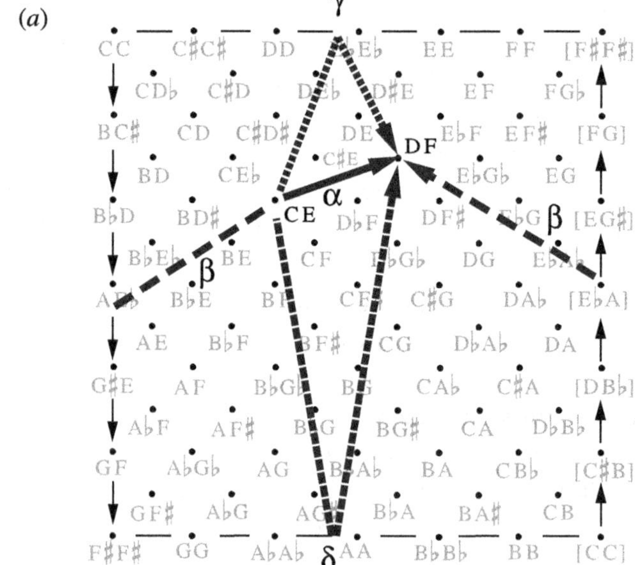

(*b*)

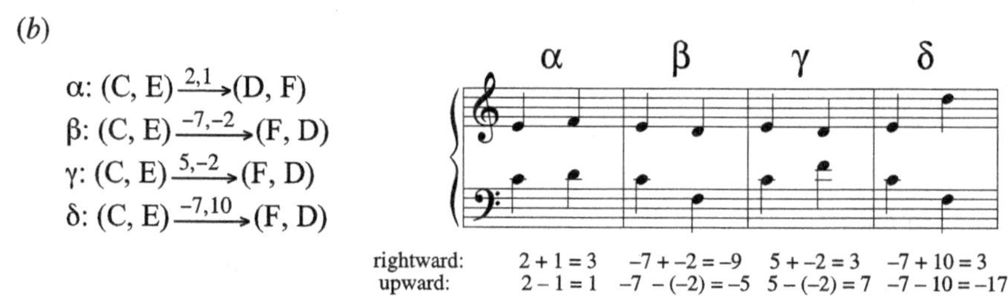

α: (C, E) 2,1 → (D, F)
β: (C, E) −7,−2 → (F, D)
γ: (C, E) 5,−2 → (F, D)
δ: (C, E) −7,10 → (F, D)
α β γ δ
rightward: 2 + 1 = 3 −7 + −2 = −9 5 + −2 = 3 −7 + 10 = 3
upward: 2 − 1 = 1 −7 − (−2) = −5 5 − (−2) = 7 −7 − 10 = −17

3.5 GEOMETRY IN ANALYSIS

Figure 3.5.1 uses the Möbius strip to graph the eighth phrase of the *Allelujia Justus et Palma,* one of the earliest examples of Western counterpoint. The music begins by tracing out a pair of triangles, each of which represents a four-chord unit that returns to its starting point. (The triangles share a side because the last two chords of the first unit are also the first two chords of the second.) Having completed the second triangle, the music moves back to the initial {G, D} dyad, disappearing off the left edge and reappearing on the right. The final voice leading retraces the (G, D)→(E, E) motion that begins the phrase.

All of this, I believe, is considerably easier to see in Figure 3.5.1b than in traditional musical notation. The geometrical patterns virtually jump off the page, without any effort or concentration on the analyst's part, whereas the corresponding musical patterns are much harder to identify. This is largely because our visual system is optimized for perceiving geometrical shapes such as triangles, but not for perceiving musical structures as expressed in standard musical notation. Translating the music into geometry thus allows us to bring our formidable visual pattern-matching skills to bear on musical analysis.

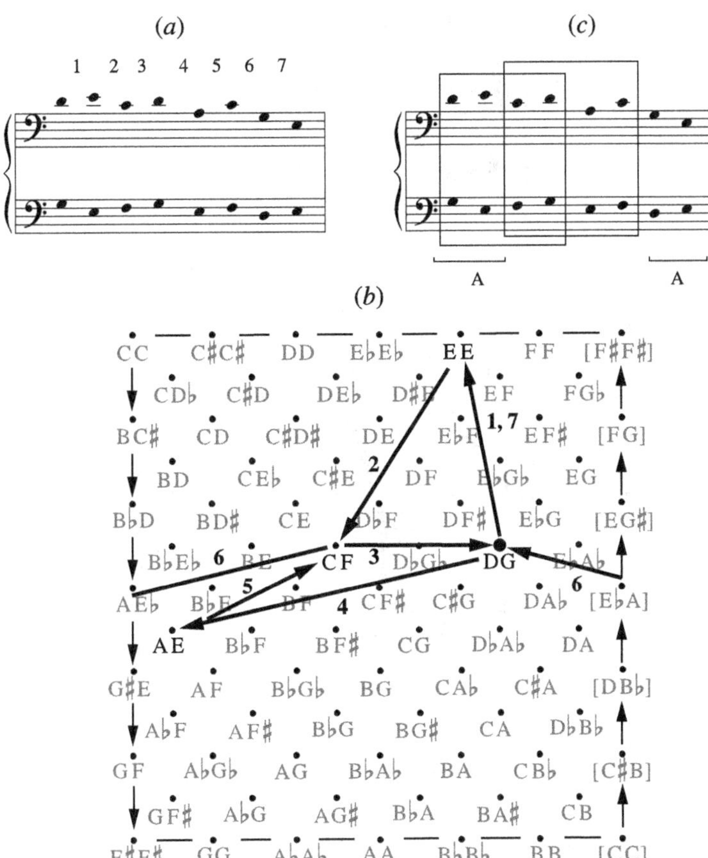

Figure 3.5.1 Plotting a phrase from the *Allelujia Justus et Palma* (*a*) on the Möbius strip (*b*) reveals interesting musical structure (*c*).

Figure 3.5.2 provides a more sophisticated example.[12] We begin with four voice leadings from the opening of Brahms' Intermezzo, Op. 116 No. 5. Figure 3.5.2b graphs the voice leadings in two-note chord space, representing each measure as a pair of line segments forming an open angle. We can imagine sliding the pair {X1, X2} so that X1 nearly coincides with Y1, and X2 nearly coincides with Y2. This represents the most obvious analysis of the passage, according to which voice leading Y1 is a slight variation of X1, and Y2 is a slight variation of X2. (That is, X1 moves its two voices by semitonal contrary motion, whereas Y1 moves by slightly skewed contrary motion; X2 moves in a skewed fashion, while Y2 moves in pure contrary motion.) Geometrically, however, it is clear that (Y1, Y2) is also the *mirror image* of (X1, X2). Hence we can move the pair (X1, X2) off the left edge so that it exactly coincides with (Y1, Y2), as in Figure 3.5.2c. (Remember that an upward-pointing arrow becomes a downward-pointing arrow when it moves off one side of the figure to reappear along the other.) On this interpretation, Y2 is exactly equivalent to X1, and Y1 is exactly equivalent to X2. Figure 3.5.2d represents this musically, heightening the comparison by switching hands and reordering dyads. Now both pairs begin with perfect contrary motion and move to less perfectly balanced motion, with melodies in each staff being transpositionally related.

12 This example first appeared in Callender, Quinn, and Tymoczko 2008.

(*a*)

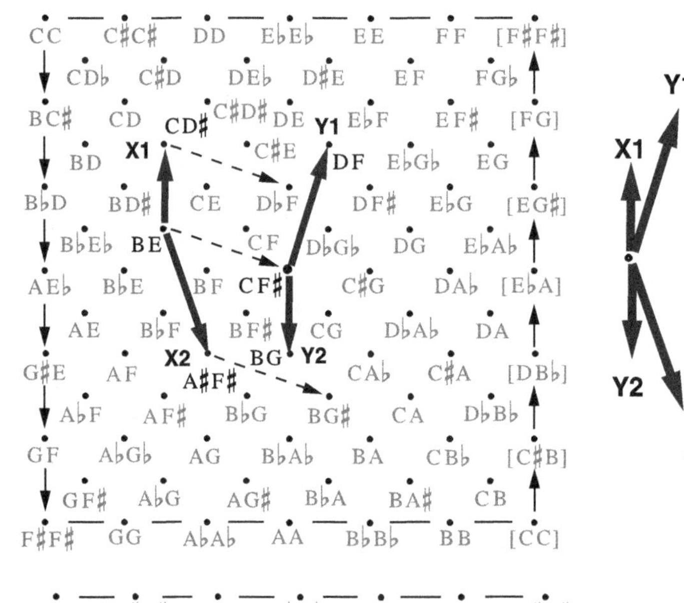

(*b*)

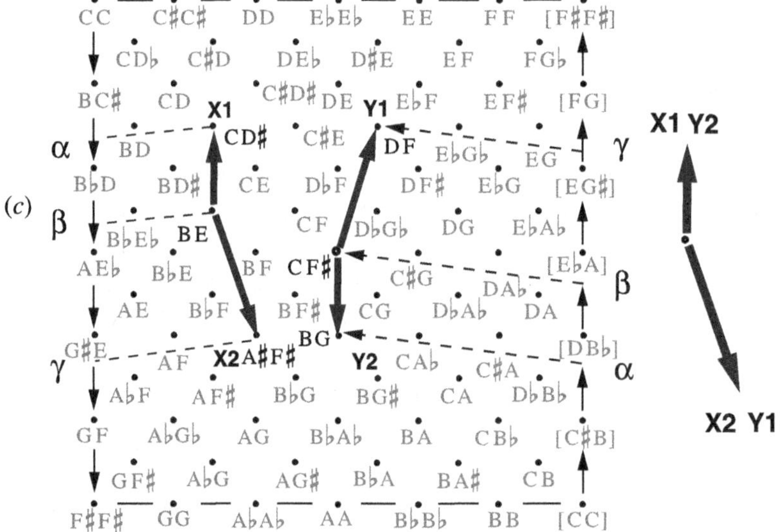

(*c*)

(*d*)

Figure 3.5.2 (*a*) Two passages from Brahms' Op. 116 No. 5, as plotted on the Möbius strip (*b*). It is natural to view Y1 and Y2 as variants of X1 and X2, respectively. However, it is clear from the graph that Y2 and Y1 are also mirror images of X1 and X2. This means we can move the pair {X1, X2} off the left edge of the figure so that it coincides with {Y1, Y2} (*c*). On this reading, Y2 is related to X1, and Y1 is related to X2 (*d*). Here, "P" and "N" stand for "perfect" and "near perfect" contrary motion.

Figure 3.5.3 There are many ways to notate a C major chord.

Playing through Brahms' piece, I have always been dimly aware of these relationships—you feel in your fingers the difference between the precisely contrary motion and the less balanced motion, and you feel the purely semitonal motion in the right hand of measures 1–2 moving to the left hand of mm. 3–4. However, it is quite difficult to see the relationship in the musical notation, and rather hard to describe it using traditional terminology. By contrast, Figure 3.5.2b makes it obvious that the passages are mirror images—a fact that Brahms, with all his love for invertible counterpoint and other forms of compositional trickery, would no doubt have enjoyed.

In these sorts of cases, geometry can help to sensitize us to relationships that might not be immediately apparent in the musical score. Ultimately, this is because conventional musical notation evolved to satisfy the needs of the performer rather than the musical thinker: it is designed to facilitate the translation of musical symbols into physical action, rather than to foment conceptual clarity. This is precisely why one and the same chord can be notated in such a bewildering variety of different ways (Figure 3.5.3). Learning the art of musical analysis is largely a matter of learning to overlook the redundancies and inefficiencies of ordinary musical notation. Our geometrical space simplifies this process, stripping away musical details and allowing us to gaze directly upon the harmonic and contrapuntal relationships that underlie much of Western contrapuntal practice.

3.6 HARMONIC CONSISTENCY AND EFFICIENT VOICE LEADING

Let's pursue this further by returning to a more abstract question. Suppose you are a composer who wants to write two-part note-against-note counterpoint, in which transpositionally related dyads are linked by "stepwise" voice leading (or voice leading in which no voice moves by more than two semitones). Under what circumstances is this possible? In other words, how can we combine harmonic consistency and efficient voice leading with just two voices?

The question can be answered simply by inspecting two-note chord space. Transpositionally related dyads can be found on two horizontal line segments, one in the lower half of the strip and one in the upper half, equidistant from the central line of tritones; we are therefore looking for short line segments connecting points on these line segments. One solution is immediately clear, since we can move any chord horizontally to its transpositions. Unfortunately, these voice leadings involve parallel motion in the two voices, and are therefore somewhat unsatisfactory. If the goal is to write contrapuntal music that suggests *independent* melodies, then it will not do to move the voices in the same direction all the time; this would sound like a single melody being doubled at two pitch levels, rather than two distinct melodic voices.

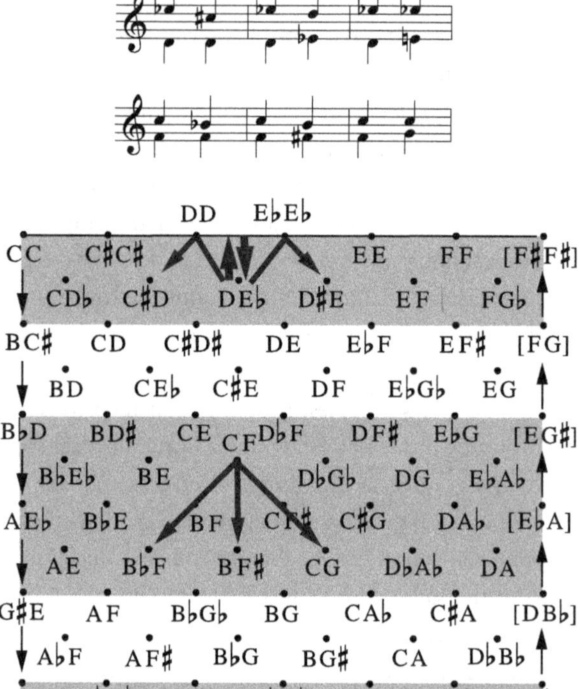

Figure 3.6.1 Even dyads and uneven dyads can both be connected to their transpositions by stepwise voice leading.

A second solution involves nearly even chords, which occupy horizontal line segments near the center of the space. Thus tritone-related perfect fifths can be linked by semitonal voice leading, represented geometrically by a vertical arrow (Figure 3.6.1, second line of music). In addition, they can be linked to their fifth transpositions by oblique voice leading in which one voice moves by two semitones. Major thirds, since they lie farther away from the center of the figure, can be linked only to their tritone transpositions by stepwise voice leading. Analogous voice leadings are available for the non-twelve-tone-equal-tempered intervals larger than a major third: in each case, the voice leading between tritone-related chords is the shortest, and is represented by a vertical line, with the other acceptable transpositions represented by slightly diagonal lines.

There is also a third and even less obvious possibility: chords that divide the octave very *unevenly*—such as minor and major seconds—can be linked to themselves by short line segments reflecting off the nearby mirror boundary. For instance, the voice leading (D, E♭)→(E♭, D) connects a minor second to itself by stepwise contrary motion, and is represented by a vertical arrow. (Analogous voice leadings again exist for any of the non-twelve-tone-equal-tempered intervals smaller than the major second.) Given any such voice leading, we can always transpose the second chord by a small amount without much increasing the voice leading's size. Consequently, small dyads can also be connected by stepwise voice leading to their one-semitone (or smaller) transpositions. For these chords the short vertical arrows connect a chord to itself, while for nearly even dyads the vertical arrows connect a chord to its tritone transposition (Figure 3.6.1). Geometrically, the clustered chords reach their nearby transpositions by bouncing off the mirror, while nearly even chords cross the center of the Möbius strip, thereby taking advantage of its "twist."[13] Thus we see that our earlier conclusions about symmetry are manifest in the structure of the two-dimesional space.

3.7 PURE PARALLEL AND PURE CONTRARY MOTION

Are we completely certain that these three possibilities are the *only* ones? Some readers might think this is obvious, while others may (justifiably) wonder whether there might be additional features of Möbius-strip geometry that we have overlooked. How do we know we have accounted for all the relevant musical alternatives?

Let me address this worry by noting that any two-voice voice leading can be decomposed into two components, one involving pure contrary motion and the other involving pure parallel motion (Figure 3.7.1). The "pure contrary" component moves the notes by the same amount in opposite directions, while the "pure parallel" component moves the notes by the same amount in the same direction. Geometrically, the "contrary" component will be confined to a vertical slice of the Möbius strip, such as that in Figure 3.7.1b, while the transpositional component will move horizontally. This decomposition into parallel and contrary is nothing other than high school vector analysis, which dissects arbitrary vectors into their x and y components.[14] Musically, the goal of the decomposition is to focus on the *relative* motion among the voices, ignoring the parallel motion they all share.

Now consider any efficient voice leading between transpositionally related dyads. The purely contrary component of this voice leading will connect transpositionally related dyads lying in the same vertical slice of the Möbius strip. It is visually obvious that the contrary component must either bounce off the mirror or cross the midpoint of the line. In the former case, it will be smaller when the chord is uneven; in the latter case, it will be smaller when the chord is even. Simple examination of the cross section shows that there are no other possibilities: if a dyad is neither particularly even nor particularly uneven, then it simply cannot participate in purely contrary voice leadings of the sort we are interested in.

We will periodically find it useful to abstract away from a voice leading's parallel component in this way. Geometrically, this involves restricting our attention to a cross section of chord space—the vertical line in Figure 3.7.1b rather than the entire

---

13 Note that Western composers typically conceive of two-note chords as subsets of larger triadic collections, and hence are not concerned with (two-voice) "harmonic consistency" as described in this section. My goal is simply to illustrate general principles in the simplest geometrical setting; as we will shortly see, the same basic principles hold in higher dimensions as well.

14 Given the voice leading $(x_1, x_2) \xrightarrow{d_1, d_2} (y_1, y_2)$ we can transpose the first chord by $(d_1 + d_2)/2$ semitones so that the two voices move by the same amount in opposite directions. This is the "pure contrary" component of the voice leading. The purely transpositional voice leading moves both voices by $(d_1 + d_2)/2$ semitones.

Figure 3.7.1 Any voice leading can be decomposed into parallel and contrary components. Here, the voice leading (E, B)→(F♯, B) (α) combines the parallel (E, B)→(F, C) (β), which moves both voices up by semitone, with the contrary (F, C)→(F♯, B) (γ), which moves the voices semitonally in opposite directions. Pure parallel motion is represented geometrically by horizontal lines, while pure contrary motion is vertical. This means that the pure contrary component of any voice leading will remain within a cross section of the space (*b*), containing dyads whose pitch classes sum to the same value.

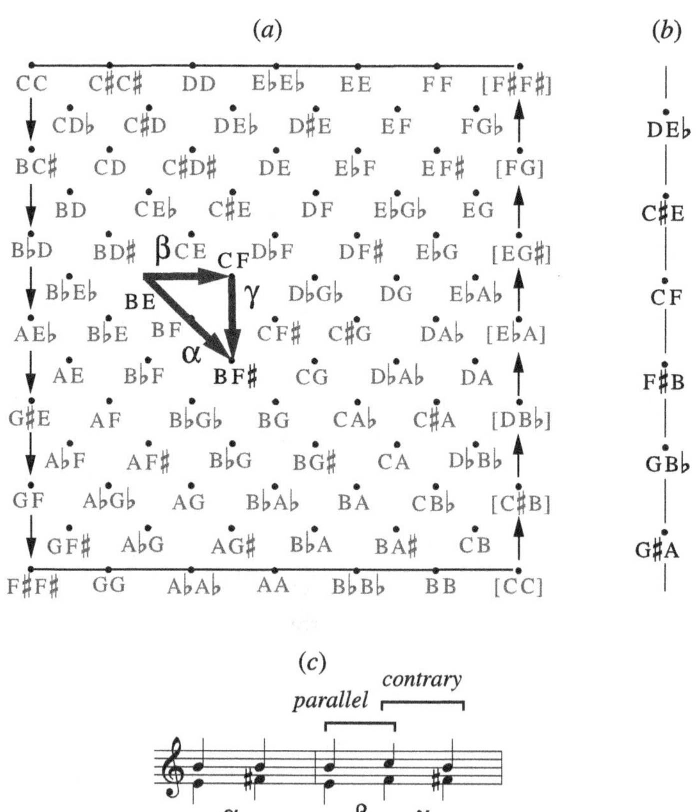

Möbius strip. However, although every cross section of the space contains precisely the same chord types, not all of these appear in twelve-tone equal-tempered forms. Consider the chord {C𝄲, E𝄳} (C quarter-tone sharp, E quarter-tone sharp), which lies halfway between {C♯, E} and {C, F}.[15] Although this chord cannot be played on an ordinary piano, it is a major third, transpositionally related to familiar chords like (C, E). (Geometrically, {C𝄲, E𝄳} lies on the same horizontal line as {C, E} and {D♭, F}, halfway between them.) Clearly, no vertical cross section of the Möbius strip will contain twelve-tone equal-tempered major and minor thirds, even though *every* such cross section contains some representative of every chord type.

15 This is because C𝄲 is a quarter tone above C, halfway between C and C♯, while E𝄳 is a quarter tone below F, halfway between F and E. The voice leading (C, F)→(C𝄲, E𝄳) therefore involves pure contrary motion.

When restricting our attention to a single cross section, it is therefore convenient to relabel its points so that all twelve-tone equal-tempered intervals are on equal footing. Figure 3.7.2a identifies points according to the interval they represent: 01 for minor second, 02 for major second, and so on, with the symbols "T" and "E" referring to ten and eleven, respectively. These new labels can be understood as referring to chord *types*, rather than particular chords: the label 04, for instance, refers to any major third, rather than the particular pitches C and E.[16] Note that the cross section is redundant: major thirds can be represented both by 04 or 08, just as perfect fifths are represented both by 05 and 07. (Remember that our chords are unordered.) This means that the contrary component of any voice leading can be represented in this abstract space in two different ways (Figure 3.7.3). Removing this redundancy produces a true "set class" space in which each point corresponds to a chord type; however, this involves some unpleasant mathematical complexities, so we will need to learn to live with the redundancy.

It turns out that line segments in the cross section represent collections of voice leadings, all "individually T-related" to one another (§2.6). This is because the operation of "individual transposition" alters the horizontal component of a voice leading while leaving the vertical component unchanged. Figure 3.7.4 shows that the voice leading (E, B)→(F, B♭) is represented by a purely vertical line segment, with no horizontal component whatsoever. The voice leading (G, D)→(F♯, B) is related to it by individual transposition: we transpose the first chord up by minor third, which corresponds to sliding it rightward by three places, while we transpose the second chord up by one semitone, which amounts to sliding it rightward by one place. This introduces a purely horizontal component into the voice leading while simply shifting the

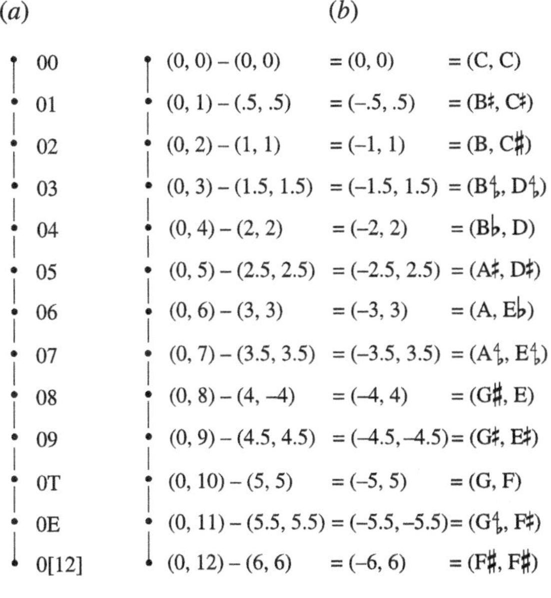

(a)
00
01
02
03
04
05
06
07
08
09
0T
0E
0[12]
(b)
(0, 0) – (0, 0) = (0, 0) = (C, C)
(0, 1) – (.5, .5) = (–.5, .5) = (B𝄲, C𝄲)
(0, 2) – (1, 1) = (–1, 1) = (B, C♯)
(0, 3) – (1.5, 1.5) = (–1.5, 1.5) = (B𝄳, D𝄳)
(0, 4) – (2, 2) = (–2, 2) = (B♭, D)
(0, 5) – (2.5, 2.5) = (–2.5, 2.5) = (A𝄲, D𝄲)
(0, 6) – (3, 3) = (–3, 3) = (A, E♭)
(0, 7) – (3.5, 3.5) = (–3.5, 3.5) = (A𝄳, E𝄳)
(0, 8) – (4, –4) = (–4, 4) = (G♯, E)
(0, 9) – (4.5, 4.5) = (–4.5,–4.5)= (G𝄲, E𝄲)
(0, 10) – (5, 5) = (–5, 5) = (G, F)
(0, 11) – (5.5, 5.5) = (–5.5,–5.5)= (G𝄳, F𝄲)
(0, 12) – (6, 6) = (–6, 6) = (F♯, F♯)

Figure 3.7.2 (*a*) It is useful to label the cross sections such that every equal-tempered interval is represented. (*b*) To translate these abstract labels into labels for particular chords in a cross section, subtract a constant from each number in the label so that its elements sum to the same value. Here, for example we recover the sum-0 cross section from the more abstract labels.

16 Geometrically, we are investigating the *projection* of chords onto the cross section, rather than some particular slice of the space. This is because we are using the cross section to *represent* the larger space.

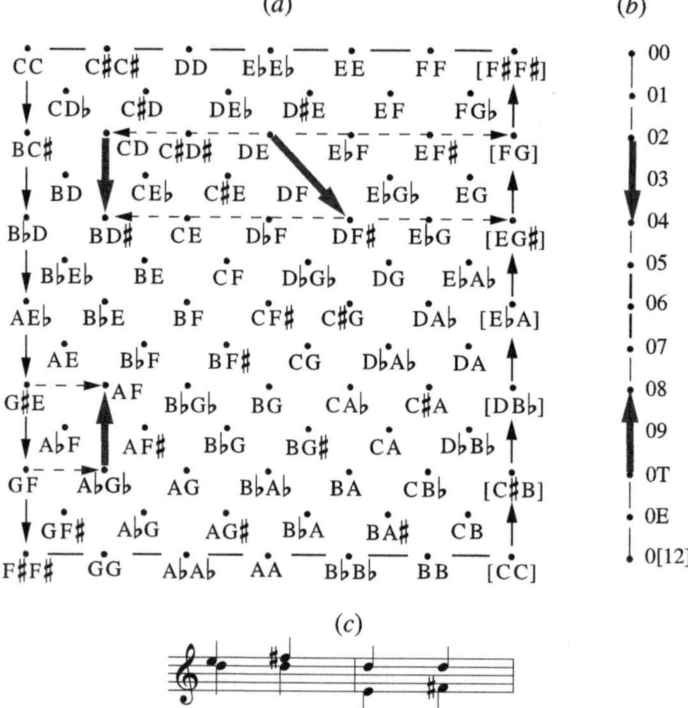

Figure 3.7.3 There are always two equally good ways to move the contrary component of a voice leading into a particular cross section. Either of the arrows in (*b*) can represent the voice leadings in (*c*).

(*a*)

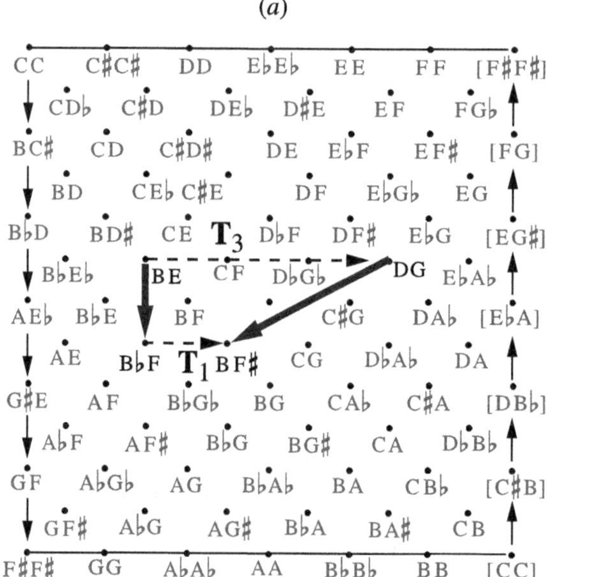

(*b*)

00
01
02
03
04
05
06
07
08
09
0T
0E
0[12]

(*c*)

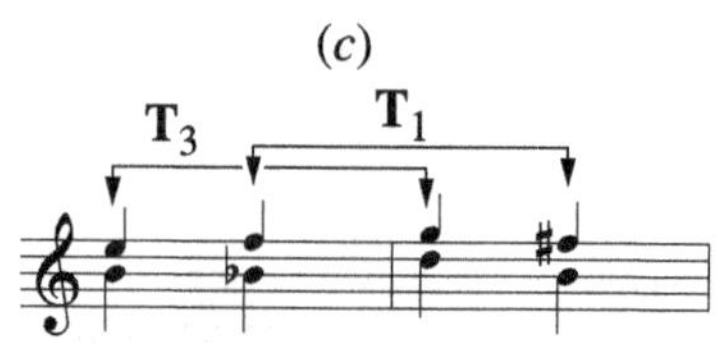

Figure 3.7.4 Individually T-related voice leadings can be moved into the same cross section so that their purely contrary components coincide. Here, the voice leadings in (*c*) share the same pure contrary component (*b*).

contrary component rightward. Consequently both (G, D)→(F♯, B) and (E, B)→(F, B♭) are represented in the cross section by the line segment (0, 7)→(0, 5). Thus we see that limiting our attention to the cross section of the Möbius strip is equivalent to focusing on the qualities shared by individually T-related voice leadings. This is just one of many cases where we find unexpected connections between purely musical ideas and relatively straightforward geometrical operations.

3.8 THREE-DIMENSIONAL CHORD SPACE

Having considered two-note chords, the next task is to describe the analogous spaces containing three-note chords, four-note chords, and so on. These higher-dimensional spaces are fundamentally similar to our two-dimensional Möbius strip, and it is usually possible to reason about them by extrapolating from the simpler space we have just explored. Readers might therefore want to make sure they are comfortable with the Möbius strip before proceeding onward.

Suppose you wanted to model music consisting of *three* distinct voices—say trumpet, saxophone, and trombone. Figure 3.8.1 shows that it takes three dimensions to record the possible musical states of the trio, with the x-axis representing the trumpet, the y-axis the saxophone, and the z-axis the trombone. If you were to examine a large volume of this three-note ordered pitch space, you would find that it again has a repeating, periodic structure—being divisible into three-dimensional "tiles" containing one representative of every three-note chord, exactly like Figure 3.1.5. Once again, focusing on a tile of the space is the geometrical analogue to ignoring octave and order information. But since the "tile" has three dimensions, our musical space is now a three-dimensional piece of wallpaper—perfect for covering the walls of your four-dimensional bedroom.[17]

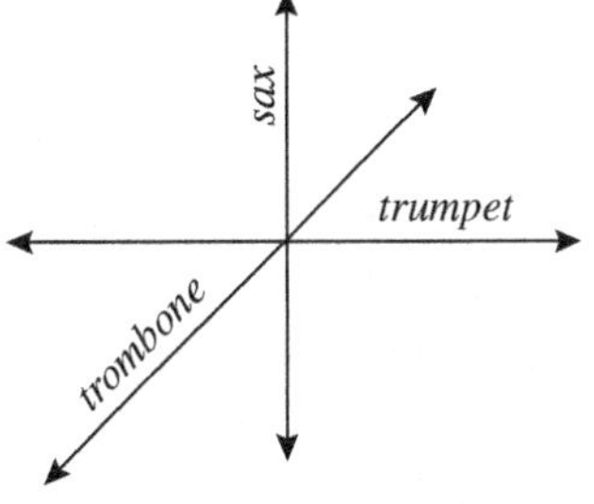

Figure 3.8.1
It takes three dimensions to model three instruments.

Figure 3.8.2 depicts one of these tiles. The space is a triangular prism. Augmented triads, dividing the octave into three equal parts, lie on the vertical line at its center, and are represented as dark cubes. (For clarity, only twelve-tone equal-tempered triads are shown.) Chords that divide the octave nearly evenly are found near the center, with the equal-tempered major and minor triads depicted as dark and light spheres, respectively.[18] More and more uneven chords are found farther and farther from the center. At the boundary are chords with multiple copies of some note: chords with

17 In general, the boundary of a space has one less dimension than the space itself: thus two-dimensional walls enclose three-dimensional rooms, and three-dimensional walls enclose four-dimensional rooms.

18 The cubic lattice at the center of the strip was first discovered, in a somewhat more abstract representation, by Douthett and Steinbach (1998). (See Appendix C.) The nineteenth-century theorist Carl Friedrich Weitzmann (1853) came very close to describing the figure, as Cohn (2000) discusses.

Figure 3.8.2 A single "tile" of three-note chord space is a triangular prism. Minor triads are light spheres, major triads are dark spheres, and augmented triads are cubes. The dark spheres on the edges of the prism are triple unisons. The lines in the center of the space connect chords that can be linked by voice leading in which only a single voice moves, and it moves by only a single semitone.

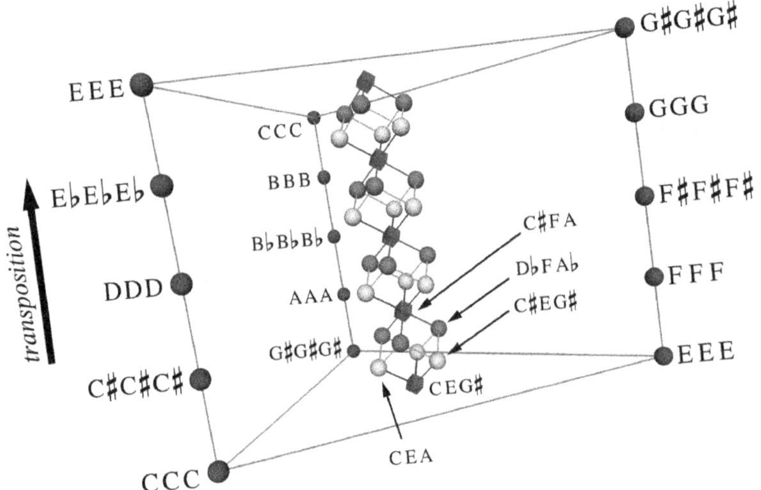

two copies of some pitch class are found on the sides of the prism, while triple unisons are found on its edges. (Triple unisons are maximally uneven, containing three copies of a single pitch class.) And although the illustration depicts only a few familiar equal-tempered chords, the space itself is again continuous: *any* possible unordered set of pitch classes corresponds to some point in the prism, including microtonal chords such as {0.17, 2.5, 8.999}.

As before, voice leadings are "generalized line segments" that stretch from one point to another. Ascending parallel motion in all three voices corresponds to ascending vertical motion on the prism.[19] Here, however, line segments disappear off the top face and reappear on the bottom, rotated by one third of a turn. Thus as the three voices ascend in parallel from {C, C, C} to {E, E, E}, the associated line segment in Figure 3.8.2 ascends along the left edge of the figure. When the line segment reaches {E, E, E}, it reappears on the bottom face of the figure, on the right corner. It then climbs up the front right edge to {G♯, G♯, G♯}. When it reaches the top of this edge, it moves up the rear edge of the figure and begins to climb again until reaching {C, C, C}. This means that we should imagine the triangular faces to be "glued together" with a 120° twist. Since the line containing triple unisons returns eventually to its starting point, it can be considered an (abstract) circle. The same is true for the three line segments containing all the transpositions of any other chord.

19 On the Möbius strip, parallel motion is represented by horizontal rather than vertical motion, but this difference is merely orthographical.

Once again, three-dimensional chord space can help clarify musical relationships that would otherwise be very hard to describe. Figure 3.8.3a presents four chromatic sequences from the first movement of Brahms' C minor Piano Quartet, each of which uses descending semitonal voice leading to connect major and minor triads. In the first two sequences, Brahms lowers the major triad's root to form a minor triad (as indicated by "r^{-1}") while in the last two sequences, he lowers the major triad's third ("t^{-1}"). Note that the sequences repeat at three different transpositional levels, as can be seen by comparing successive major or minor triads: the first and last sequences descend by semitone, the second ascends by minor third, and the third ascends by perfect fifth. At first glance, there does not seem to be any clear structure here; the impression is of a kind of intuitive play, as if Brahms had arbitrarily chosen four unrelated sequences from among countless essentially similar possibilities.

When we consider the music geometrically, however, we see that Brahms is actually moving quite systematically along the lattice at the center of three-note chord space (Figure 3.8.3b). Starting from any major triad, there are only two semitonal descents that will produce a minor triad (labeled "*a*" and "*b*" on the lattice); the two available paths correspond to the possibility of lowering the major triad's root or third. From here, one must move the root downward by semitone to form an augmented triad. (Brahms typically skips this triad, though it does appear in the second sequence.) There are then three geometrical paths to choose from (labeled "1," "2," and "3" on the lattice), corresponding to the three major triads that can be reached by lowering a note of the augmented triad, and producing three different root relationships to the starting chord. (The possible relationships are descending semitone, ascending minor third, and ascending perfect fifth, precisely as in Brahms' piece.) Clearly, there are six sequences that can be formed in this way, since there are two possibilities for the initial move and three possibilities for the second (Figure 3.8.3c). What is interesting is that Brahms uses four of these six options, composing a group of sequences that are *contrapuntally* similar (by virtue of using descending stepwise voice leading) while *harmonically* distinct (by virtue of using a variety of different root progressions). The result is a sort of developing or continuous variation, in which the same basic procedure (descending semitonal voice leading among major and minor triads) produces subtly different results. And even though this process of developing variation might at some level be intuitive or improvisational, it nevertheless exhibits very clear structure. By showing us the field in which Brahms' intuition necessarily operates, geometry helps us understand this structure, while also leading us to expect that we will find these same sequences in other pieces as well. Chapter 8 will return to this thought, using the very same lattice to interpret chromatic procedures in music as diverse as that of Schubert and Jimi Hendrix.

Once again, it is sometimes useful to consider just the horizontal cross section of our three-note chord space—which, being two-dimensional, is much easier to draw. As before, these horizontal cross sections contain chords whose pitch classes

Figure 3.8.3 (*a*) Descending sequences from the first movement of Brahms' C minor Piano Quartet, Op. 60. (*b*) These result from moving downward along the equal-tempered lattice at the center of chord space. (Major chords are dark spheres, minor chords light spheres.) (*c*) There are six basic sequences that can be formed in this way, depending on whether one lowers the root or the third of the initial major triad, and whether the sequence descends by semitone (D1), ascends by seven semitones (A7), or ascends by three semitones (A3).

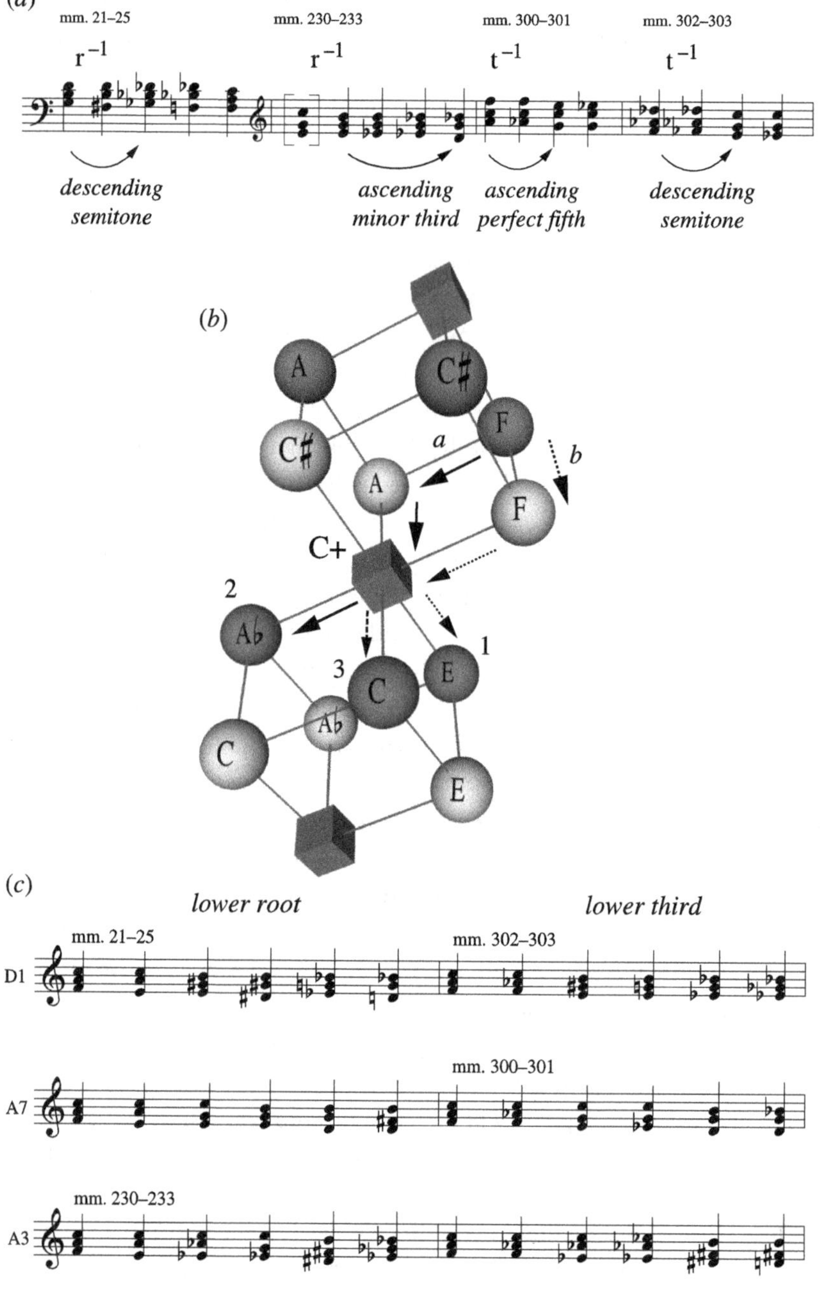

sum to the same value (Figure 3.8.4).[20] If a chord appears on the triangular cross section, then so do its transpositions by ascending and descending major third. This is because transposing a three-note chord by four semitones does not change the sum of its pitch classes: 4 + 4 + 4 = 0 in pitch-class arithmetic. The three transpositions of each chord are arranged symmetrically around the triangle, so that 120° rotation transposes each by major third. Chords in the same triangular cross section can be linked by "pure contrary" voice leadings in which the amount of ascending motion exactly balances the amount of descending motion. For example, Figure 3.8.5 shows that {E, A, B} and {F, G♭, D♭} can be linked by the voice leading (E, A, B)→(F, G♭, D♭), which is represented by a line segment lying entirely within the triangle. Here, one voice ascends by semitone, one voice ascends by two semitones, and one voice descends by three semitones, so that the total amount of ascending motion is 1 + 2 − 3 = 0.

Figure 3.8.4 (*a*) A horizontal slice of three-note chord space is a triangle containing chords summing to the same value; here the chords sum to 0. (Only equal-tempered chords are shown.) (*b*) These triangular cross sections are analogous to the vertical "slices" of two-note chord space, which also contain chords summing to the same value.

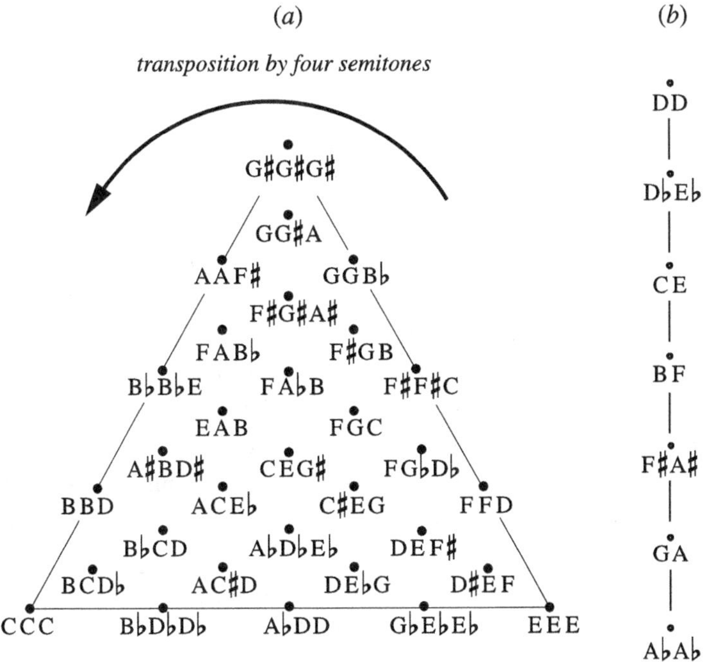

20 Roeder 1984 and Callender 2004 explore these cross sections, using them to represent set classes. Cohn 1998b also notes that major-third-related triads sum to the same value and can be connected by pure contrary motion.

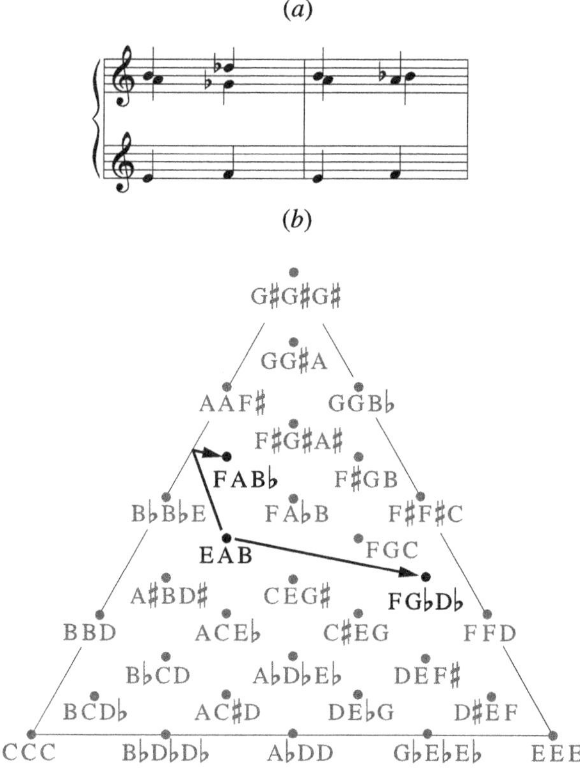

Figure 3.8.5
(*a*) Two voice leadings in which the total amount of ascending motion perfectly balances the total amount of descending motion. (*b*) These voice leadings are contained in a cross section of three-note chord space. The second voice leading, which has voice crossings, bounces off the triangle's mirror boundary; the first does not.

Since Figure 3.8.4 shows only equal-tempered chords summing to zero, certain chord types do not appear. (In particular, there are no major triads.) Again, though, every *chord type* appears in every cross section: if we were to transpose {C, E, G} up by one third of a semitone, we would obtain a major triad whose pitch classes sum to zero.[21] (This chord would appear on Figure 3.8.4a precisely in the same place that the C major triad appears on its cross section.) As in §3.7, we can therefore construct an abstract representation of the cross section in which all equal-tempered chord types appear (Figure 3.8.6). The arrows to the left of the triangle show how to interpret motion in the space: horizontal motion raises or lowers the last note in the chord; motion along the up-and-left diagonal raises or lowers the middle note in the chord; and motion along the other diagonal raises and lowers the last *two* notes in the chord. (Of course, raising two notes is equivalent to lowering the other when we factor out pure parallel motion, which is what we are doing when we consider only the cross section.[22]) Figure 3.8.7 explains how to plot the pure contrary component of a voice leading in this space.

---

21 The pitch classes in an equal-tempered major triad must sum to either eleven, two, five, or eight; by transposing up by a third of a semitone, we add one to these sums. This is analogous to the fact that perfect fourths do not appear in Figure 3.8.4b, since equal-tempered fourths sum to an odd number, and Figure 3.8.4b contains pitch classes that sum to four.

22 Mathematically, $(0, 1, 1) + (-1, -1, -1) = (-1, 0, 0)$, which says that $(0, 1, 1)$ and $(-1, 0, 0)$ are related by pure parallel motion $(-1, -1, -1)$.

Figure 3.8.6 An abstract representation of the cross sections of three-dimensional chord space. In this abstract representation, the labels do not sum to the same value. (Compare Figure 3.7.2.)

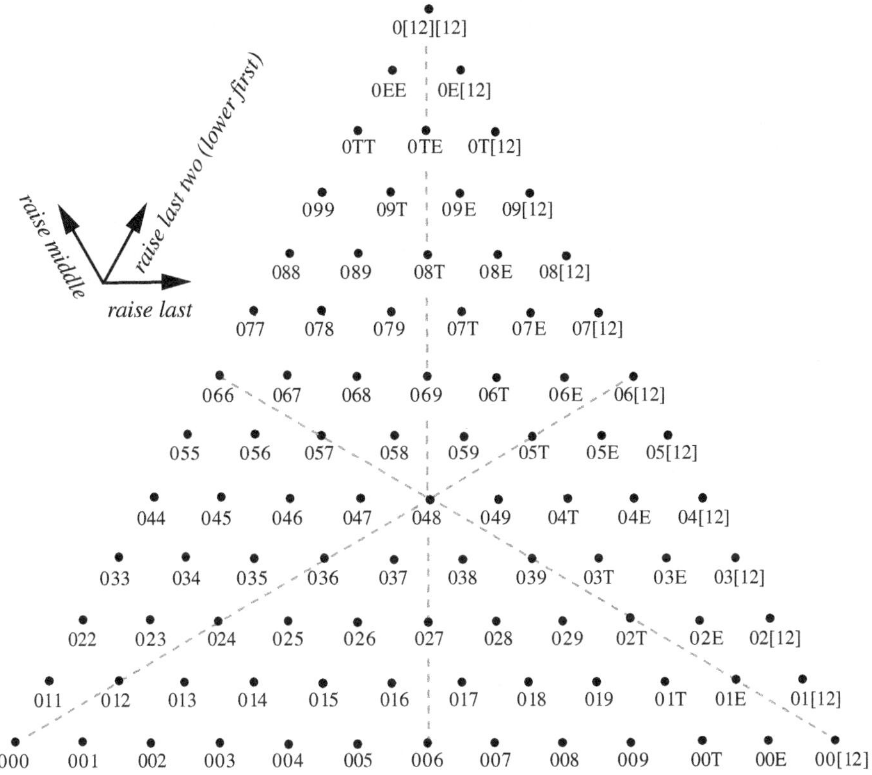

Finally, observe that the structure of the space again demonstrates the relation between evenness and efficient voice leading. Suppose you want to find an efficient (three-voice) voice leading between transpositionally related three-note chords. As in §3.7, we decompose our voice leading into pure parallel and pure contrary components. Since the original voice leading is small, then both the pure parallel and pure contrary components will also be small. It is clear from Figure 3.8.8 that there are just two basic possibilities: either the chord is near the center and the pure contrary component links it to its four- or eight-semitone transposition, or it is near the edge and the line segment links it to itself.[23] The situation is precisely analogous to the two-dimensional case, except that here the contrary component connects *major-third*-related (rather than tritone-related) chords. This fact has important musical consequences, as we will shortly see.

23 Of course, it is trivially possible that the voice leading has no contrary component, and moves all voices in parallel by the same amount.

Figure 3.8.7 To plot the purely contrary component of a voice leading in the triangular cross section, reorder it (uniformly) so that the first chord is in ascending order spanning less than an octave, then transpose the chords (individually) so that they both start on C, with the first voice moving by zero semitones. One can then use the arrows to the left of the figure to determine the path representing the voice leading. For example, to represent (C, E, G)→(C, F, A) we need to raise the middle voice by one semitone, represented by one-step diagonal NW motion; we then raise the third voice by two semitones, which requires moving two units to the right. Combining these vectors gives us the path representing the voice leading's pure contrary component (*center of figure*). Contact with a boundary exchanges the position of two voices: for example, (C, F, F♯)→(C, G, F♯) can be represented by two diagonal steps to the NW from 056 (*left side of figure*). However, the first of these steps brings us to the boundary, which exchanges the position of the second and third voices. Thus, instead of moving the middle voice up by semitone, we now have to move the *third* voice up by semitone; this is represented by a one-step rightward motion. Geometrically, it looks as if our arrow has reflected off the mirror boundary. Note that we cannot represent this voice leading with a direct line from 056 to 067, since the voice crossing requires that the line reflect off the mirror boundary: thus where the two arrows 047→057 and 057→059 can be combined into a single arrow, the two arrows 056→066 and 066→067 cannot.

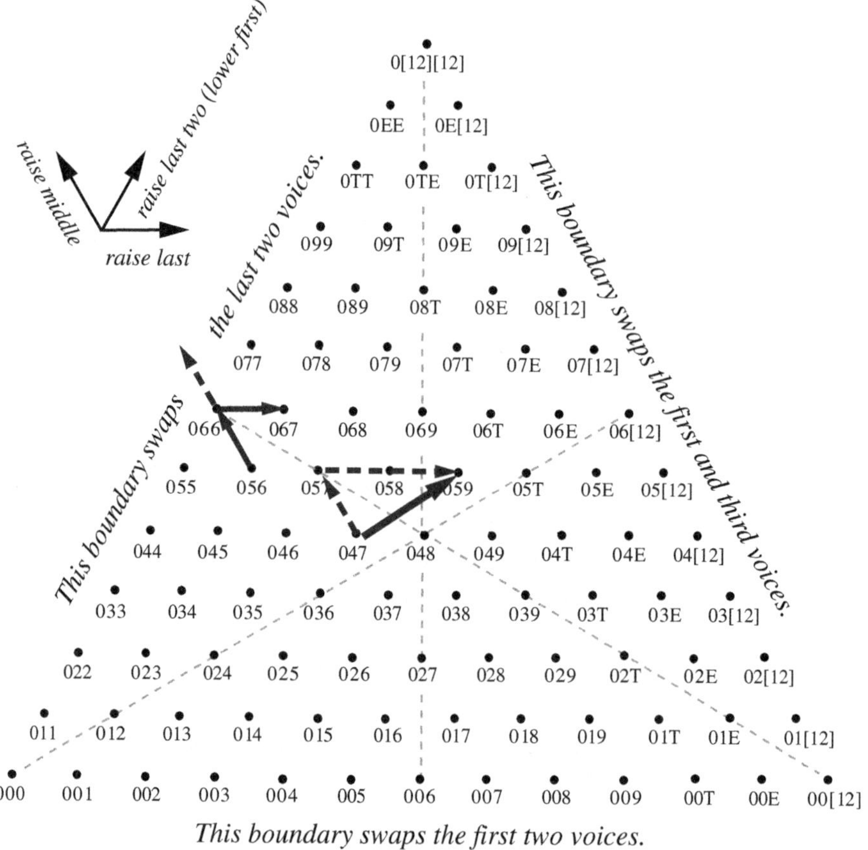

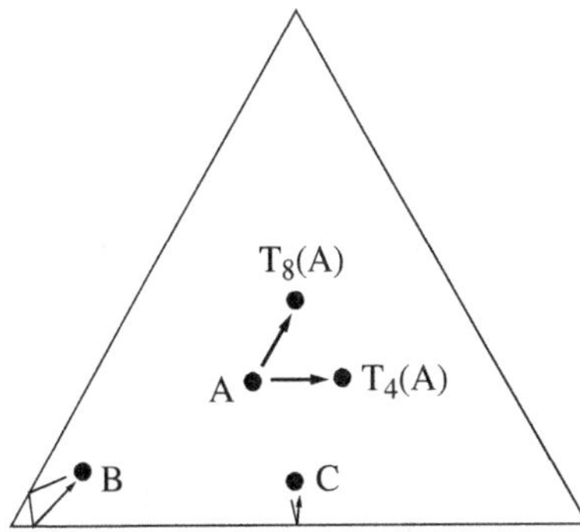

Figure 3.8.8 Efficient pure contrary voice leading between transpositionally related three-note chords. Chord A divides the octave nearly evenly; it and its transpositions are near the center of the space. Chords B and C have notes that are clustered together, and are near the boundary.

3.9 HIGHER DIMENSIONAL CHORD SPACES

Attempting to visualize higher dimensional spaces is an exercise in diminishing returns: while one might barely manage four dimensions, it becomes increasingly difficult to picture five, six, or more. Nevertheless, it will be useful in what follows to have a rough understanding of the geometry of the higher dimensional chord spaces. Accordingly, I will ask the reader's indulgence as I try to describe the spaces representing four-note, five-note, and even larger chords.

We have seen that it takes a separate dimension to model each individual musical voice. Thus, it takes four dimensions to represent the state of a four-instrument ensemble, five dimensions to represent the state of a five-instrument ensemble, and so on. When we abstract away from order and octave, we find that each of these spaces is periodic, a higher dimensional piece of wallpaper consisting of many equivalent copies of the same pattern or tile.

Figure 3.9.1 displays the tiles in the two-, three-, and four-dimensional cases. The two-dimensional tile is our familiar Möbius strip, a rectangle whose left edge is glued to its right with a half twist. For the sake of generality, however, it is useful to forget the term "rectangle," and to imagine the space as a *two-dimensional prism*—the shape that results when we drag the (one-dimensional) left edge horizontally rightward to form a two-dimensional figure. The resulting structure has two "faces" (here, the left and right edges), which are one-dimensional line segments. Chords on the same vertical line sum to the same value; hence every chord is on the same vertical line segment as its tritone transposition. As we drag the left face horizontally rightward, we transpose each chord upward. We can obtain new chords in this way until we have transposed by six semitones, at which point the left and right faces contain the same chords. These two faces need to be glued together with a "twist" that gives the space a circular structure: because of this twist, we can eventually return to our starting point by moving perpendicular to the face (§3.3).

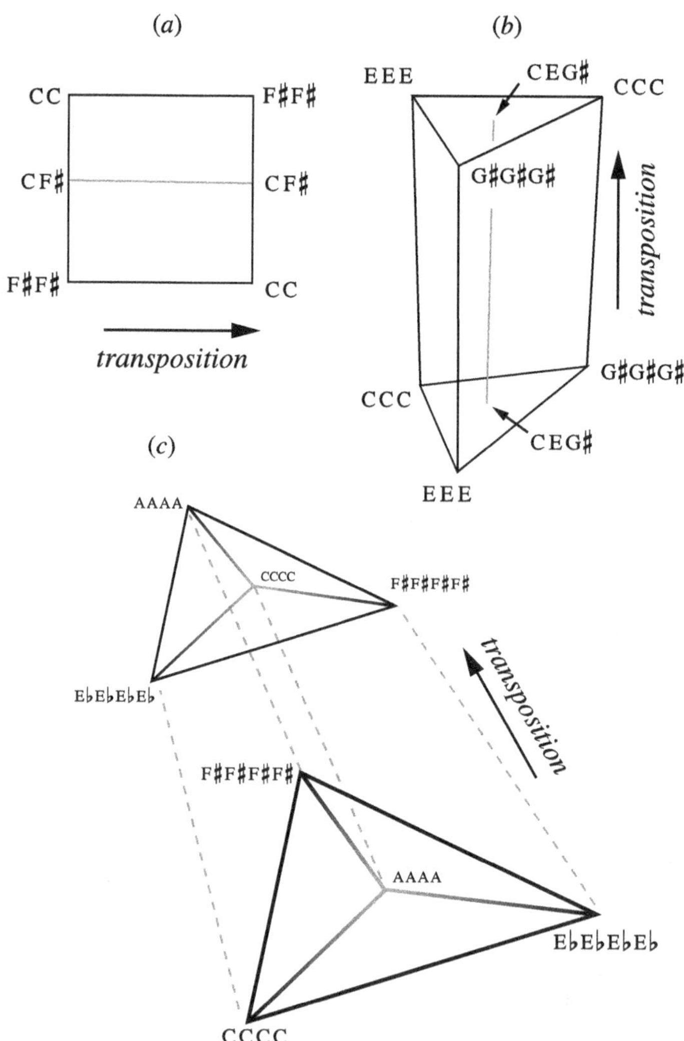

Figure 3.9.1 Chord space in two, three, and four dimensions.

The three-dimensional tile is also a prism, the shape that results from dragging the bottom face, a triangle, vertically upward. The resulting structure again has two faces, which are now two-dimensional triangles rather than one-dimensional line segments. Each triangular face contains three-note chords summing to the same value, so that every chord is on the same face as its major-third transposition. Dragging the bottom triangle upward transposes each chord upward; we drag it until the chords have been transposed by four semitones, at which point the top face contains the same chords as the bottom. These two faces must then be glued together with a "twist" that matches the appropriate chords—here, a 120° rotation. This "gluing" produces a triangular doughnut and introduces a circular structure in to the space: once again, if we move perpendicular to the triangle, we eventually return to where we started.

Figure 3.9.1c illustrates the four-dimensional shape that tiles the space of four-note chords. Readers will not be surprised to find that it, too, is a prism. Here the faces are *tetrahedra*, the three-dimensional analogues of triangles. Each tetrahedral cross section contains pitch classes that sum to the same value. Consequently, if a chord is on the cross section, then so is its minor third transposition.[24] The four vertices of the tetrahedron contain quadruple unisons related by *minor* third—here, {C, C, C, C}, {E♭, E♭, E♭, E♭}, {F♯, F♯, F♯, F♯} and {A, A, A, A}—while the chord at the center divides the octave perfectly evenly and contains the pitch classes {C, E♭, F♯, A}. To form the prism, drag the tetrahedron into the *fourth* dimension, represented by dotted lines on Figure 3.9.1c, thereby transposing every chord upward. We can drag it until its chords have been transposed by minor third, at which point the transposed tetrahedron contains the same chords as the initial one. These again need to be attached by a "twist" that connects the appropriate chords and transforms the prism into a kind of four-dimensional doughnut.

The general pattern should now be clear. In each dimension, chord space is an n-dimensional prism, formed by dragging a "generalized triangle" through an additional dimension (Figure 3.9.2).[25] The generalized triangle is the *face* of the prism, containing chords summing to the same value. Consequently, each n-element chord is on the same face as its transposition by $12/n$ semitones. (This is because transposing n notes by $12/n$ adds $12n/n = 12$ to their sum, and in pitch-class arithmetic we discard multiples of 12.) Dragging the face into the additional dimension transposes each chord upward; it can be dragged until the chords have been transposed by $12/n$ semitones, at which point it contains the same chords as those on the initial face. The two duplicate faces are glued together with a "twist" that matches the appropriate chords, introducing a circular structure and creating the higher dimensional analogue of a twisted doughnut.

Nonmathematical readers should not wrack their brains trying to picture these spaces in too much detail. Instead, focus on the important structural features they all share:

Figure 3.9.2 A simplex (or "generalized triangle") is bounded by n points, all connected by line segments. One-, two-, and three-dimensional simplexes are line segments, triangles, and tetrahedra, respectively.

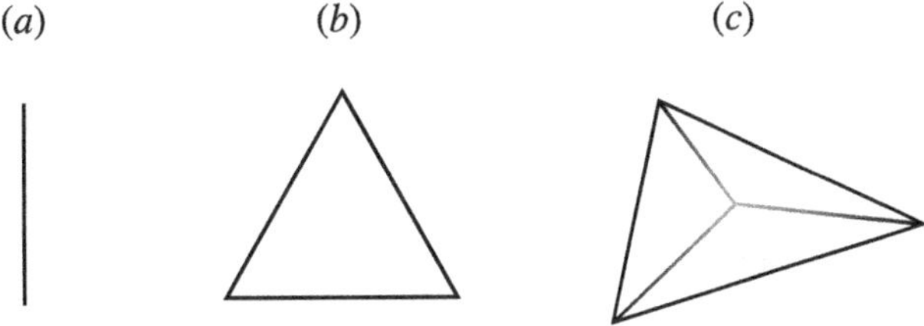

24 Transposing a four-note chord by three semitones adds $3 + 3 + 3 + 3 = 0$ to their sum, in pitch-class arithmetic.

25 A generalized triangle, or "simplex," is an n-dimensional figure enclosed by $n + 1$ points, all connected by lines. Thus, in one dimension, it is a line segment (two points connected by a line segment); in two dimensions, it is a triangle (three points connected by line segments); in three dimensions, it is a tetrahedron (four points connected by line segments); and so on. One can form an $(n + 1)$-dimensional simplex by adding a single point to an n-dimensional simplex.

1. In each space, points correspond to chords and line segments correspond to voice leadings, with the length of the line segment representing the size of the voice leading. Consequently, nearby chords can be linked by efficient voice leading, while distant chords cannot.
2. A chord's "evenness" determines its distance from the center. Chords that divide the octave precisely evenly are found at the very center of the space, while nearly even chords are nearby. Chords whose notes are clustered together are found near the boundary of the space, as far from the center as possible.
3. Chord space is made up of "layers," or cross sections, each containing chords summing to the same value. There are n instances of every n-note chord type in each layer. These can be obtained by repeatedly transposing by $12/n$ semitones. The transpositions are arranged symmetrically around the center of the cross section, with their distance from the center determined by the chord's evenness. The geometrical *symmetries* of the cross section relate the different forms of each chord type.
4. Each cross section of the space is a generalized triangle. The boundaries of the generalized triangle contain chords like {C, C, E, G}, which have multiple copies of some pitch class.[26]
5. Nearly even chords can be linked to their transpositions by very efficient voice leading. An n-note chord is particularly close to its transposition by $12/n$ semitones, since they are near the center of the same horizontal cross section.
6. Voice leading that remains within the layers represents pure contrary motion in which the amount of ascending motion perfectly balances the amount of descending motion. Moving perpendicular to these layers corresponds to pure parallel motion, in which every note moves in the same direction by the same amount. Any voice leading can be decomposed into parallel and contrary components, as in high school vector analysis (§3.7).
7. The top and bottom "layers" of the prism are glued together in a twisted fashion, endowing the space with a circular, doughnut-like structure. For this reason, a voice leading in which every voice ascends by octave will be represented by a line segment that passes through each cross section n different times, moving through each of its transpositions before returning to its starting point. The trajectory it follows will be a circle in the abstract sense.
8. The remaining boundaries of the figure—the ones that are not glued together—act like mirrors. Voice leadings bounce off these mirrors, like balls off of the bumpers of a pool table. "Clustered" chords near the edges of the space can be linked to their untransposed forms by efficient voice leading, bouncing off nearby mirrors to return to their starting point.

26 The number of pitch classes in the chord determines which part of the boundary it inhabits: vertices contain chords like {C, C, C}, with only one pitch class; edges contain chords like {C, C, G}, with two pitch classes; faces contain chords like {C, C, E, G}, with three pitch classes; and so on (see Figure 3.8.5 for the three-dimensional case).

Appendix B provides a more detailed mathematical description of the spaces, for readers who are so inclined.

3.10 TRIADS ARE FROM MARS; SEVENTH CHORDS ARE FROM VENUS

Musically, the most important consequence of all this geometry is the following: since a nearly even n-note chord occupies the same cross section of the space as its transposition by $12/n$ semitones, such chords can be linked by particularly efficient voice leading.[27] Thus, nearly even two-note chords are very close to their six-semitone transpositions, nearly even three-note chords are very close their four- and eight- semitone transpositions, nearly even four-note chords are very close to their three-, six-, and nine-semitone transpositions, and so on. This is illustrated in Figures 3.10.1 and 3.10.2.

Figure 3.10.1 Two-note chords are particularly close to their tritone transpositions; three-note chords are particularly close to their major-third transpositions; and four-note chords are particularly close to their minor-third and tritone transpositions.

Suppose, then, that a composer is interested in exploiting efficient voice leadings between two major triads or two dominant seventh chords. Theoretically, we should expect an abundance of major-third relations between the triads and minor-third relations between the dominant sevenths. And when we look at actual music, we see that this is indeed the case. Direct juxtapositions of minor-third-related dominant seventh chords already occur in baroque and classical music, while direct juxtapositions of major-third-related seventh chords are very rare; similarly, major-third-related triads sometimes occur across phrase boundaries, as when V/vi moves directly to I, while there is no analogous convention associating minor-third-related triads.[28] Figure 3.10.3 indicates that this asymmetry also characterizes the more chromatic music of the nineteenth century. In Schubert, major-third-related triads occur about 1.5 times more often than minor-third-related triads, while minor-third-related dominant seventh chords occur about 14 times more often than major-third-related dominant seventh chords.[29] (In Chopin, major-third-related

27 Mathematically inclined readers will note that I am presupposing the Euclidean metric for simplicity. However, at least some of the statements made in this section are metric independent; furthermore, reasonable voice-leading measures are all approximately consistent with each other. For more information, see Hall and Tymoczko 2007.

28 Bach's chorales contain a number of cross-phrase triadic juxtapositions, with major-third root-relationships outnumbering minor-third relationships by almost 2:1. In Mozart's piano sonatas, there are several juxtapositions of minor-third-related dominant sevenths, but no major-third-related dominant sevenths. Major-third-related major triads also occur several times, whereas minor-third-related major triads are more rare and typically occur only in sequences with stepwise descending voice leading (§8.4).

29 The methodology here was crude but, hopefully, unbiased: I programmed a computer to look through MIDI files for simultaneously sounding chords that were either triads or seventh chords. I then tallied up the root progressions of each type. Note that since minor-third-related triads can be connected by reasonably efficient voice leading, we would still expect these progressions to appear periodically.

Figure 3.10.2 A geometrical representation of the closeness between (*a*) tritone-related perfect fifths and (*b*) major-third-related triads. These figures show just a portion of the relevant geometrical spaces, and connect chords by lines if they can be linked by single-semitone voice leading.

(*a*)

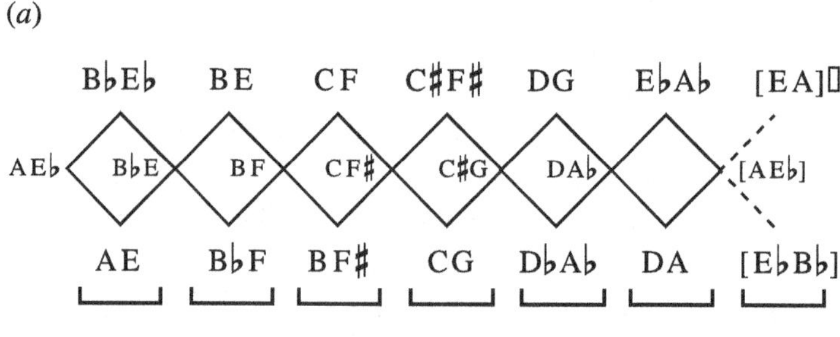

(*b*)

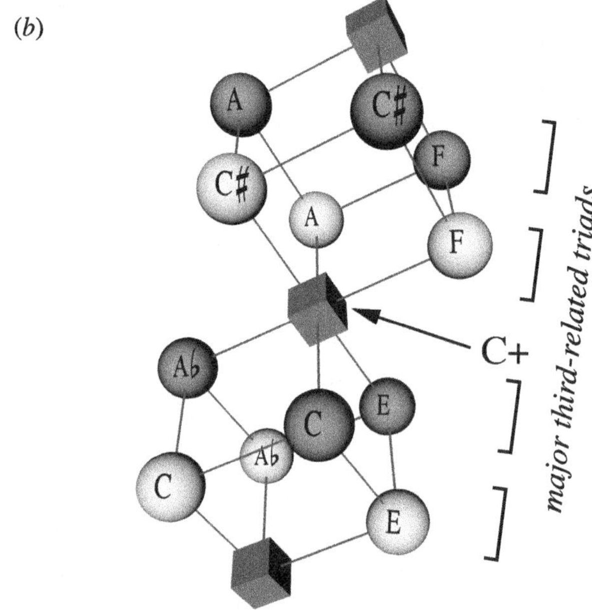

major triads occur about 1.6 times more often than minor-third-related triads, and minor-third-related dominant-seventh chords occur about 2.2 times more often than major-third-related dominant sevenths.) This suggests that composers' harmonic choices are indeed guided by the voice-leading relationships we have been exploring. To be sure, composers are not guided *exclusively* by voice-leading considerations, and individual artistic preference no doubt plays a significant role. Nevertheless, there is clear evidence that Western musicians are sensitive to the relationships that are modeled by our geometrical spaces.

Figure 3.10.4 turns to a very different sort of music, analyzing the basic three-chord progression of Nirvana's "Heart-Shaped Box." The first two chords, A and F,

Figure 3.10.3 Nondiatonic chord progressions in a large number of pieces by Schubert and Chopin. The leftmost column indicates root motion: thus "+1" indicates a progression where the root moves upward by semitone, while "–3" refers to one where the root moves downward by three semitones. The next two pairs of columns distinguish progressions between two major triads and two dominant seventh chords. The boldface numbers show that major triads are more likely to be connected by major third than by minor third, while the reverse is true for dominant sevenths.

Root	**Schubert**		**Chopin**	
Motion	Maj. triads	Dom. 7th	Maj. triads	Dom. 7th
+1	22%	5%	32%	1%
–1	10%	1%	22%	4%
+2	-	9%	-	4%
–2	-	10%	-	6%
+3	10%	**17%**	8%	**5%**
–3	16%	**25%**	7%	**15%**
+4	**18%**	0%	**13%**	1%
–4	**21%**	3%	**12%**	8%
+5	-	26%	-	52%
–5	-	2%	-	5%
6	3%	1%	6%	1%
#	**560**	**163**	**630**	**239**

are pure triads related by major third.[30] The final D^7 chord has four notes, retaining the fifth of the F major triad as the seventh of D. (Note that every chord contains the note A, which appears as root, third, and fifth in turn.) We can understand this last voice leading as an incomplete manifestation of the efficient voice leading between F^7 and D^7 chords. This is not to say that Kurt Cobain necessarily conceived it as such; rather, it is to say that the voice leading between the last two chords is contained within a very familiar seventh-chord schema and exploits the same musical facts that make the more familiar schema possible. From our point of view, the interesting fact is that Cobain's switch from triads to seventh chords goes hand in hand with the switch from major-third motion to minor-third motion. There are countless other examples of this phenomenon: for instance, the Beatles' "Glass Onion" juxtaposes major-third-related triads in the verse and minor-third-related dominant sevenths in the chorus. Figure 3.10.5 presents a similar progression from Schumann, which alternates between the "major-third system" of closely related triads (represented geometrically by the cubic lattice of Figure 3.10.2b) and the "minor-third system" of closely related seventh chords (to be discussed shortly).[31] As we will see, a large amount of chromatic music can be understood in this way (Figure 3.10.6).

---

30 Though not articulated by independent instruments, the voice leading is relatively clear.

31 Note that this progression is slightly more complicated insofar as it connects an F *minor* chord to the following A^7; nevertheless, this major-third root motion still permits efficient voice leading.

Figure 3.10.4 Nirvana's "Heart-Shaped Box" switches from major-third root motion to minor-third root motion when it switches from triads to a seventh chord. The upper three voices in the last voice leading of (*a*) are contained within the common four-voice voice leading in (*b*).

Of course, it is always possible to add a small purely parallel component without drastically increasing the size of a voice leading. So, for example, starting with the pure contrary voice leading (C, G)→(C♯, F♯), one can transpose the second chord up by semitone to produce (C, G)→(D, G), a relatively efficient voice leading between fifth-related perfect fifths. Applying the same procedure to (E, G♯, B)→(E♭, A♭, C) yields (E, G♯, B)→(E, A, C♯) (Figure 3.10.7). Figure 3.10.8 identifies, for chords with two to five notes, the transpositions that can be obtained by combining pure contrary motion with a small parallel component. The perfect fourth (or equivalently, the fifth) is the only interval appearing in every row of the table, which means that nearly even chords of any size can be linked to their perfect-fourth transpositions by relatively efficient voice leading. (Here again we have an example of a familiar musical object being optimal for multiple reasons: the perfect fourth is both extremely consonant while also being a uniquely useful interval of transposition, allowing for efficient voice leading in a broad range of circumstances.[32]) This fact is of obvious relevance to tonal music,

Figure 3.10.5 (*a*) A voice leading from the "Chopin" movement in Schumann's *Carnaval*. Here, an F minor triad moves by major third to an A dominant seventh. (The bass, tenor, and soprano give us a pair of major-third-related triads, with the alto moving semitonally from the doubled third to the seventh.) The next progression moves the A^7 chord to an $E♭^7$. Once again the shift from triads to seventh chords accompanies a shift in root motion. (*b*) A comparison of Schumann's "Chopin" and Nirvana's "Heart-Shaped Box." In Schumann's progression, the switch to seventh chords occurs at the second chord in the passage: doubling the third of the F minor triad, he uses the semitonal motion A♭→G to create an A^7 chord. In the Nirvana progression, the switch does not occur until the final chord, where the C of F major is held over to become the seventh of D^7.

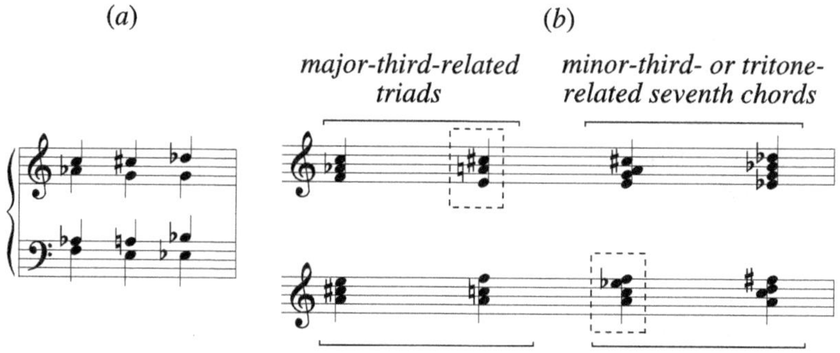

32 More precisely, the perfect fourth is very close to some interval contained within the interval cycle that results when we divide the octave precisely evenly, no matter how many parts we divide it into.

Figure 3.10.6 Triads and seventh chords in mm. 18–20 of the first movement of Schubert's B♭ major Piano Sonata (*a*), mm. 14–15 of the third-movement trio (*b*), the "Tarnhelm" motive from mm. 37–39 of Scene III of Wagner's *Das Rheingold* (*c*), mm. 11–12 of Mozart's C minor Fantasy, K. 475 (*d*), the eighteenth-century "omnibus" progression (*e*), and mm. 44–45 of Chopin's *Nocturne*, Op. 27 No. 2 (*f*).

Figure 3.10.7 Adding a small parallel component (*p*) to a small purely contrary voice leading (*c*) still produces an efficient voice leading.

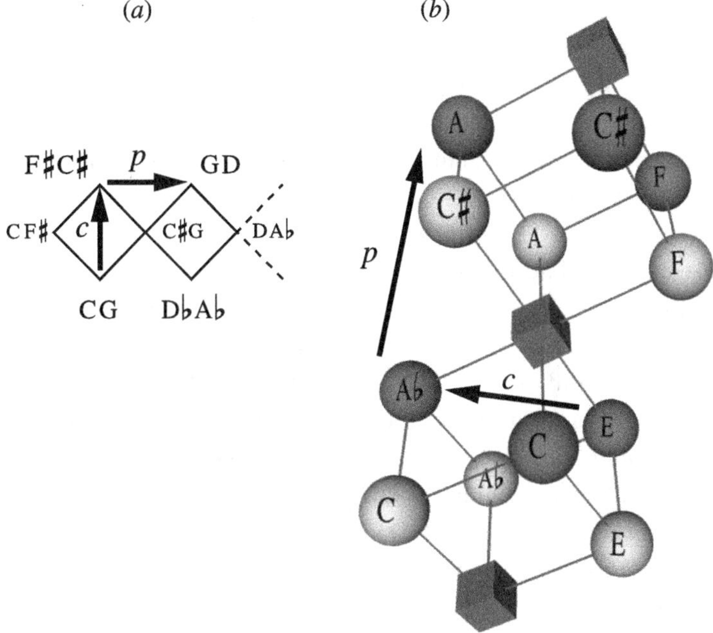

which exploits fourth-progressions between triads, seventh chords, ninth chords, and diatonic scales.

One feature of Figure 3.10.8 deserves further comment. A five-note chord can be linked by pure contrary motion to its 2.4, 4.8, 7.2, and 9.6 semitone transpositions. Since none of these transpositions lie in twelve-tone equal temperament, any voice leading between familiar transpositionally related five-note chords must have at least some parallel component. If the purely contrary voice leading involves transposition

Figure 3.10.8 The transpositions that permit pure contrary motion for chords of various cardinalities. Nearby equal-tempered transpositions are also shown.

Cardinality	Pure Contrary Motion	Nearby Equal-Tempered Transpositions
2-note chords	6 semitones	perfect fourth
3-note chords	±4 semitones	minor third, perfect fourth
4-note chords	±3, 6 semitones	major second, major third, perfect fourth
5-note chords	±2.4, ±4.8 semitones	perfect fourth

by 2.4 semitones, then the purely parallel component must be at least 0.4 semitones large. However, if the purely contrary voice leading involves transposition by 4.8 semitones, then it is necessary to add only 0.2 semitones of pure parallel motion. It follows that from a twelve-tone equal-tempered perspective, very even five-note chords will seem to be closest to their five-semitone transpositions. (And indeed, the pentatonic scale can be linked to its five-semitone transposition by single-semitone voice leading.) In continuous pitch-class space, we would see that the pentatonic scale is *also* quite close to its 2.4-semitone transposition, but this symmetry disappears when we view music through a twelve-tone equal-tempered grid. Here again we see that it is sometimes useful to adopt the continuous perspective, even when we are primarily interested in equal-tempered music.

In later chapters, we will find that these sorts of voice-leading relationships underwrite three major compositional practices. First, as discussed above, composers often use maximally efficient voice leading to move from one chord to another, creating an abundance of major-third relations among triads and an abundance of minor-third relationships among seventh chords. Second, composers often use maximally efficient voice leading to *replace* one chord with another, as when a jazz musician replaces a dominant seventh chord with its tritone transposition (e.g. B^7 replacing F^7). Here, rather than connecting two actually existing chords, efficient voice leading is used to substitute a surprising chord for one that we would otherwise expect; the jazz "tritone substitution" is the most familiar example of this practice, though Chapter 7 will uncover a similar procedure ("third substitution") in classical harmony. Finally, composers often combine efficient voice leading with small amounts of *descending* parallel motion, producing harmonic sequences where all voices slowly sink downward. In the triadic case, this leads to sequences such as those in Figure 3.8.3, with roots moving by descending minor second, ascending minor third, or ascending fifth.[33] In Chapter 8 we will study their seventh-chord analogues in the music of Chopin and Wagner, and in Chapter 9 we will observe Shostakovich and Reich applying the same procedure to seven-note scales. The value of geometry lies in the way it provides a unified perspective on all of these

33 It is notable that the descending versions of these patterns are so much more common than their ascending analogues; the asymmetry likely reflects a more general tendency for small intervals to descend (Vos and Troost 1989).

seemingly disparate musical activities, helping us to see that they involve different ways of exploiting the fundamental geometry of musical space.

3.11 VOICE-LEADING LATTICES

Obviously, the problem with higher dimensional chord spaces is that we can't visualize them; since each individual musical voice requires its own dimension, we quickly lose the ability to present musical information in a clear and intuitive manner. One solution is to depict only the portion of the space directly relevant to our musical needs. In this book we will typically be interested in voice-leading relationships among nearly even chords belonging to familiar scales. Happily—and somewhat surprisingly—it turns out that there are simple three-dimensional lattices representing all of the relevant musical relationships.[34]

There are two types of graph most directly relevant to our needs. The first depicts chords whose size (number of notes) exactly divides the size of the scale containing them. These can be used to represent nearly even two-, three-, four-, or six-note chords in twelve-note chromatic space. (This is because two, three, four, and six all divide twelve.) These lattices are circular "necklaces" of cubes of various dimensions, each linked to its neighbors by shared vertices. The second kind of structure arises when the number of notes in the chord is *relatively prime* to the number of notes in the scale—which is to say that no positive integer other than one divides both numbers. Here the relevant voice-leading facts are represented by a necklace of cubes sharing a common *face* with their neighbors. This type of lattice can be used to represent five- or seven-note chords in twelve-tone chromatic space, and chords of any size in any seven-note scale.[35]

Figure 3.11.1 presents a pair of examples. The first represents single-semitone voice leadings among perfect fifths and tritones. (Consult Figure 3.3.1 to see how this figure sits in continuous space.) Each square contains two perfect fifths and two tritones, with tritones being common to adjacent squares. (The square on the right edge shares a vertex with that on the left, forming a "circle of squares.") As shown in the figure, there are two possible paths from one shared vertex to the next, representing the two ways of sequentially raising or lowering the tritone's notes.[36] Contrast this with Figure 3.11.1b, which depicts single-step voice leadings among thirds and

34 For our purposes a "lattice" is a graph whose vertices lie on a regular cubic grid, with vertices connected by edges only when they are adjacent on the grid. Strictly speaking, our graphs are only *locally* lattice-like, since they contain topological twists, but the term "lattice" is evocative and I will use it. Douthett and Steinbach (1998) describe the first class of lattices considered in this section, while Tymoczko (2004) describes the second.

35 In principle, there is also a third category of lattices that results when the number of notes in the chord shares a common divisor with the number of notes in the scale. Though these lattices are typically not needed, you may enjoy exploring their structure.

36 For example, the two single-semitone displacements A→B♭ and E♭→E will transform the tritone {A, E♭} into {B♭, E}. If we first raise A→B♭ and then E♭→E, we move along the upper half of the leftmost square on Figure 3.11.1a; while if we first raise E♭→E and then A→B♭, we move along the lower half.

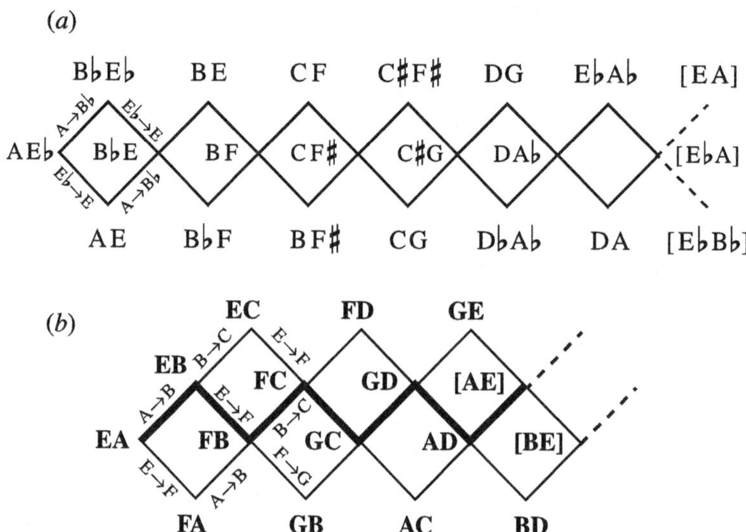

Figure 3.11.1 The two fundamental kinds of discrete lattices. The first is a circle of squares linked by shared vertices, representing single-semitone voice leading among equal-tempered tritones and perfect fifths. The second is a circle of squares linked by common edges, representing single-step voice leading among *diatonic* fourths and thirds.

fourths in the C diatonic scale. (In making this graph, I have represented diatonic scale steps, such as C-D or E-F, as having equal size; Chapter 4 explores this idea in detail.) Where the squares in the earlier figure are linked by a common vertex, those in Figure 3.11.1b share a common *edge*. Here, each square contains three diatonic fourths and one diatonic third: fourths zigzag through the center of the figure like the stripe on Charlie Brown's sweater, while thirds lie on the external vertices. Once again, the voice leadings within each square represent different ways of ordering the same pair of single-step motions: for example, to move from {E, A} to {F, B}, we could either raise E to F and then A to B; or we could raise A to B and then E to F. The first path goes by way of {F, A} while the second moves through {E, B}.

One finds closely analogous structures in higher dimensions. For example, suppose we want to graph voice-leading relationships among nearly even three-note chords in the chromatic scale. Since three evenly divides twelve, the lattice contains three-dimensional cubes linked by a common vertex (Figure 3.11.2a). As we have learned, the shared vertex is an augmented triad, with the edges of the cubes representing different ways that the augmented triad's notes can be raised or lowered by semitone: for instance, we can move from C♯ augmented to C augmented by first lowering F, then C♯, then A; alternatively, we could first lower A, then C♯, then F. Each of these sequences traces out a different series of edges on the top cube of Figure 3.11.2a. (Note that the chords on a single cube draw their notes from two semitonally adjacent augmented triads and hence belong to the same hexatonic scale.[37]) By contrast,

37 For example, the chords on the cube containing F, A, and C♯ major all belong to the hexatonic scale C-C♯-E-F-G♯-A, to be discussed in the next chapter.

Figure 3.11.2 (*a*) The cubic lattice at the center of three-note chromatic space. The shared vertex is the augmented triad; the edges represent different ways of raising or lowering the augmented triad's notes by semitone. (*b*) The cubic lattice at the center of three-note diatonic space. Here, the cubes share a face with their neighbors.

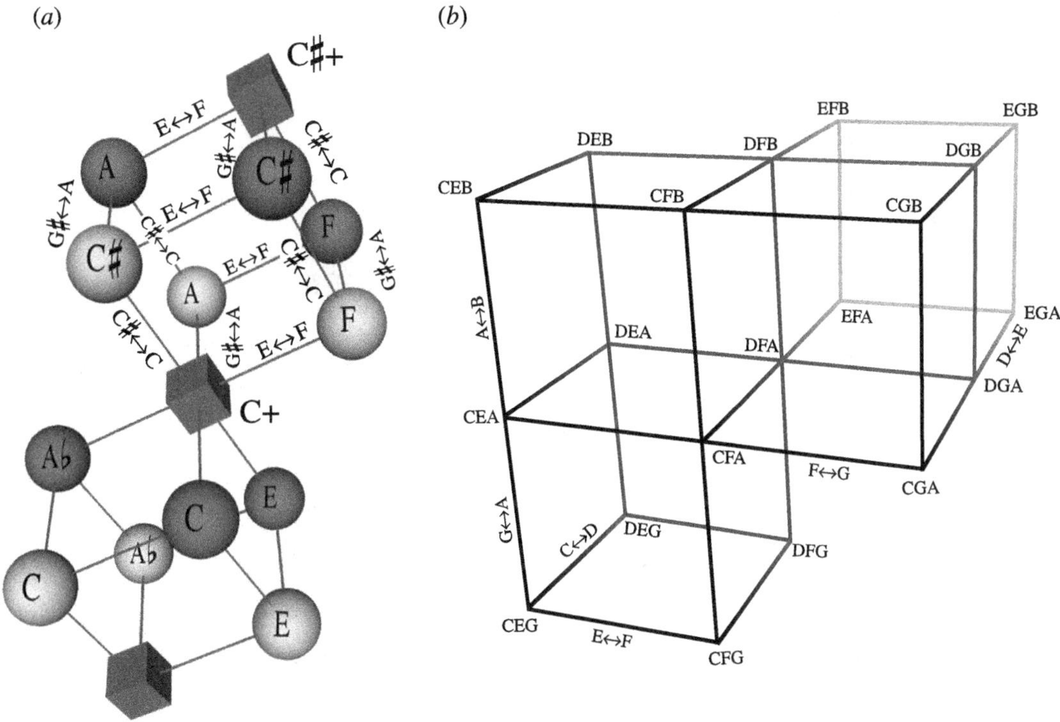

nearly even three-note *diatonic* triads are represented by a lattice of the second kind, since three and seven have no common divisor. The resulting graph, shown in Figure 3.11.2b, consists of a series of stacked cubes, each sharing a *face* with its neighbors. This graph is analogous to the linked squares of Figure 3.11.1b, though its structure is somewhat more complex. We will return to it momentarily.

The first type of lattice is relatively easy to understand. If the number of notes in the chord exactly divides the number of notes in the scale, then the scale contains chords that are *perfectly* even.[38] These sit at the very center of (continuous) chord space and form the vertices shared by the lattice's adjacent cubes. The remaining edges on the lattice identify the various ways in which one can successively raise or lower each note of this perfectly even chord.[39] Thus the edges in Figure 3.11.1a show how one can succes-

38 Strictly speaking, this is true only when we measure distance using "scale steps" (discussed in Chapter 4). However, in the familiar chromatic scale, scale-step distances are equivalent to log-frequency distances. At the moment, the chromatic scale is our primary concern.

39 Since the chord has n notes, there are at first n possible notes to lower; having lowered one note, there are $(n - 1)$ remaining possibilities, and so on. Geometrically, the various sequences of "lowerings" outline an n-dimensional cube. To see this, note that one can construct an n-dimensional cube whose vertices consist of all the points with individual coordinates that are either 0 or 1: in two dimensions, the

Figure 3.11.3 (*a*) The lattice at the center of four-note chromatic space is a circle of four-dimensional cubes linked by a shared vertex. The shared vertex is the diminished seventh chord. The labels "bFr" and "dFr" designate "French sixth" chords on D and B; these points appear to lie close to each other on the interior of the cube, but this is an artifact of the three-dimensional representation. (*b*) The edges of the four-dimensional cube represent the different ways of raising or lowering the notes of the diminished seventh chord.

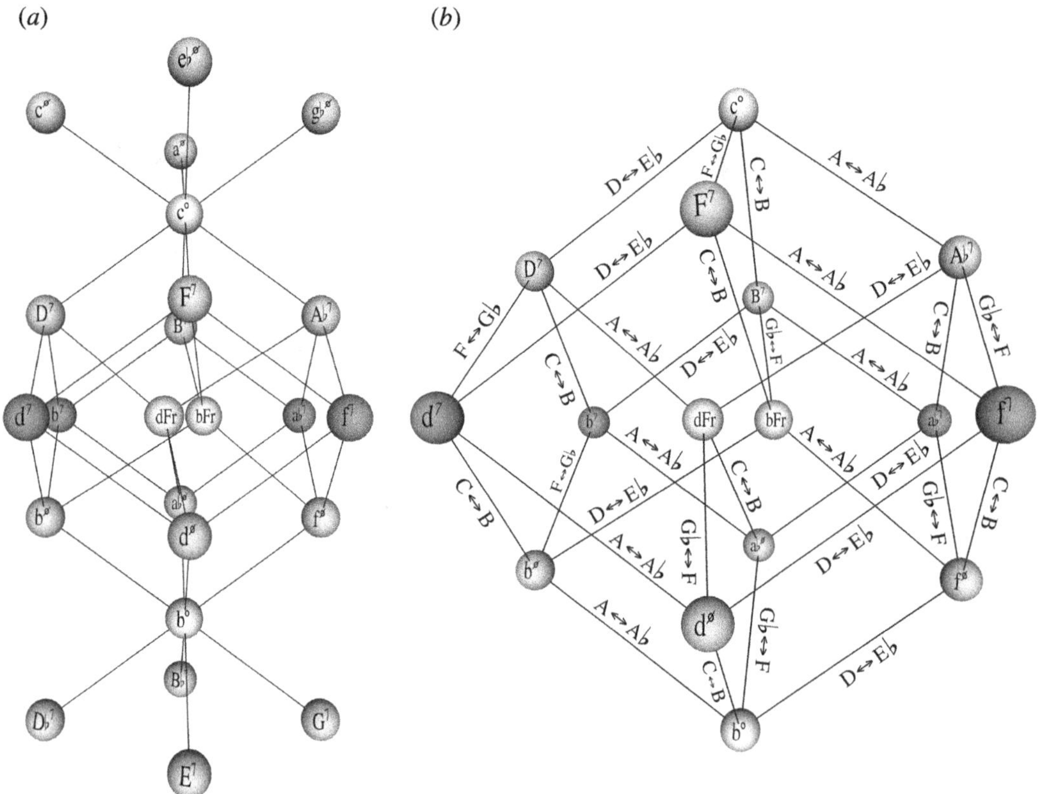

sively raise or lower the notes of the tritone by semitone, while those in Figure 3.11.2a show how one can raise or lower the three notes of the augmented triad. Figure 3.11.3 illustrates the four-dimensional case. Here we have a series of four-dimensional cubes—also known as "tesseracts"—linked to their neighbors by shared vertices. (Figure 3.11.3 projects this four-dimensional structure into what looks like three Euclidean dimensions, much as we can draw the outlines of a three-dimensional cube using a two-dimensional piece of paper.[40]) As expected, the shared vertices are diminished seventh chords, with the edges recording the various ways of sequentially raising or lowering

points (0, 0), (0, 1), (1, 0), and (1, 1); in three dimensions, the points (0, 0, 0), (0, 0, 1), (0, 1, 0), (1, 0, 0), (1, 1, 0), (1, 0, 1), (0, 1, 1) and (1, 1, 1); and so on. The edges of the cube can be traced out by starting at the point (1, 1,..., 1), and considering all the ways of successively "lowering" coordinates (changing them from 1 to 0), until (0, 0,..., 0) is reached.

40 Actually, the illustration is two-dimensional, but our brains automatically construct a three-dimensional scene. In a true four-dimensional representation any two intersecting lines in the tesseract would form 90° angles, but in the three-dimensional projection this is not possible. Similarly, in four dimensions the two "French Sixth" chords are far apart, whereas in three dimensions they seem close.

their notes. Chords on a single "tesseract" draw their notes from two semitonally adjacent diminished seventh chords, and hence belong to the same octatonic scale. Thus chords on the hypercube containing F^7, D^7, B^7, and $A\flat^7$ all belong to the octatonic scale D-E♭-F-G♭-A♭-A-B-C. Readers may be relieved to learn that this is the most complicated lattice we will need to use in this book. Although an analogous (six-dimensional!) structure represents nearly even six-note chromatic chords, its chords can typically be interpreted as incomplete forms of familiar seven-note scales.

The second type of lattice appears when the size of the chord and the size of the scale have no common divisor. In this case, the scale will not contain any *perfectly* even chords; instead, it will contain *nearly* even chords that form a *near interval cycle*—that is, a circular sequence of notes all but one of which are linked by the same interval, with the unusual interval being either one scale step larger or smaller than the rest.[41] Three examples are shown in Figure 3.11.4: two- and three-note chords in diatonic space, and seven-note chords chromatic space. In each case, it is possible to

Figure 3.11.4 When the size of the chord and the size of the scale are relatively prime, the maximally even chord is a "near interval cycle"—a circle of notes all but one of which are linked by the same interval, with the unusual interval being just one step different from the others. Because of this, the chords can be linked by a chain of single-step voice leadings. (*a*) Diatonic fifths linked by single-step voice leading. (*b*) Third-related diatonic triads linked by single step voice leading. (*c*) Diatonic scales linked by single-semitone voice leading.

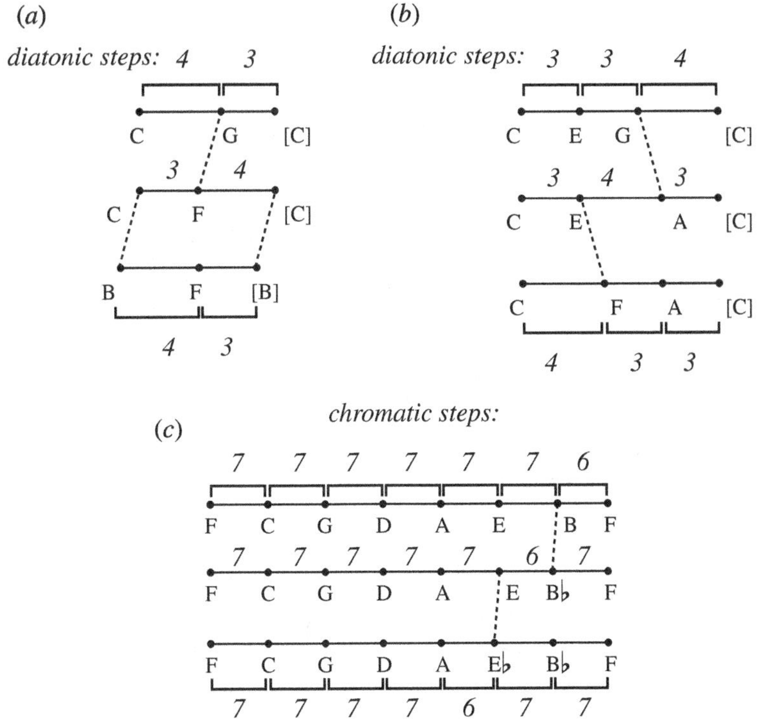

41 These scales were studied by Clough and Myerson (1985), Clough and Douthett (1991), and Erv Wilson (in unpublished work).

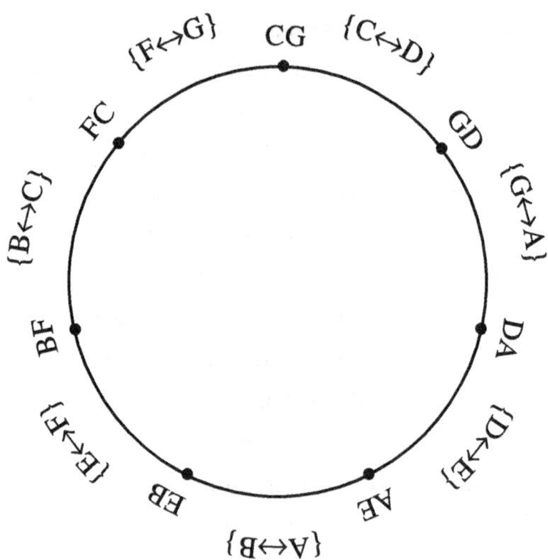

Figure 3.11.5 Single-step voice leading links near interval cycles into a circle, structurally analogous to the familiar circle of fifths. Here, the circle of two-note diatonic fifths, each linked to its neighbors by single-step motion.

Figure 3.11.6 A "generalized circle of fifths" is near, but not exactly at, the center of chord space. In (*a*), the circle of diatonic fifths zigzags through the center of the Möbius strip. In (*b*), the circle of diatonic triads zigzags three-dimensionally through the center of three-note chord space.

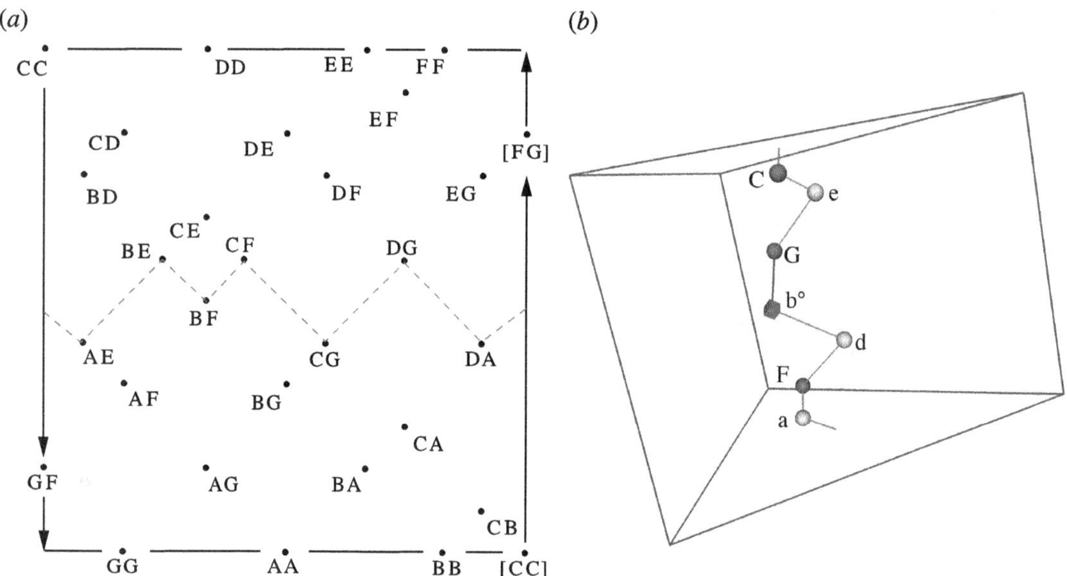

shift the position of the unusual interval by moving a single note by just one scale step. Consequently, these chords can be linked by a sequence of single-step voice leadings somewhat analogous to the familiar circle of fifths (Figure 3.11.5).[42] This

42 Here I am considering the circle of fifths to represent single-semitone voice leadings among diatonic scales: (C, D, E, F, G, A, B)→(C, D, E, F♯, G, A, B)→(C♯, D, E, F♯, G, A, B)→.... Theorists sometimes consider the circle of fifths to be a sequence of fifth-related pitches, such as C→G→D→..., but this perspective is not germane to the current discussion.

"generalized circle of fifths" will lie *as close as possible* to the center of chord space (at least for chords belonging to that particular scale), but it will not be exactly *at* the center (Figure 3.11.6).

Figure 3.11.7 arranges our circle of diatonic fifths in a regular zigzag pattern.[43] These diatonic fifths are the most nearly even two-note chords in diatonic space. To add the second-most even chords, we can *rearrange the order of the voice leadings on the central zigzag*. For example, we move from {A, E} to {B, F} along the zigzag by way of the sequence (A, E)→(B, E)→(B, F), first raising A to B, and then E to F. But suppose we were to reorder these two single-step shifts: raising the E in {A, E} produces the diatonic third {A, F}, while raising the A in {A, F} brings us to {B, F}. Geometrically, these reordered voice leadings complete the square on the left side of Figure 3.11.7b. By continuing this process we can generate all the single-step voice leadings among diatonic thirds and fourths, thus reconstructing the lattice in Figure 3.11.1b.

Remarkably, this same process of "rearranging" is sufficient to construct all the voice-leading lattices of the second type. By way of illustration, let's generate a voice-leading graph representing nearly even seven-note chords in chromatic space. The diatonic circle of fifths is shown in Figure 3.11.8a: here we move from C diatonic to G diatonic by the semitonal shift F→F♯, from G diatonic to D diatonic by the shift C→C♯, and so on. This circle lies as close as we can get to the center of seven-note

Figure 3.11.7 (*a*) The two-note diatonic "circle of fifths," represented as a regular zigzag. (*b*) To include diatonic thirds, simply reverse the order of every pair of voice leadings, for instance by letting E→F operate on the fifth {A, E}. This converts the zigzag into a series of squares each sharing a common edge.

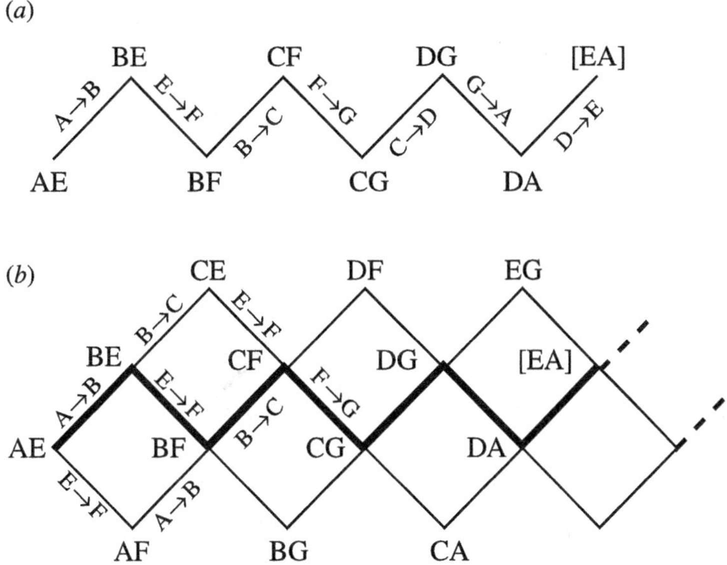

43 By regularizing the zigzag, we are again making the decision to treat all "scale steps" as having the same size.

chord space, given twelve-tone equal temperament. Figure 3.11.8b adds the second-most even seven-note chord by rearranging adjacent voice leadings as described in the previous paragraph: C→C♯ takes C diatonic to the G "acoustic scale" (or D melodic minor ascending) while F→F♯ takes G acoustic to D diatonic. (Note that the resulting graph is two-dimensional, even though seven-note chords live in seven dimensions!) We can even create a three-dimensional version of the graph by scrambling the order of *three* successive voice leadings on the diatonic circle of fifths. Here we begin with a three-dimensional zigzag that moves alternately up, right, and into the paper. We then apply all six reorderings of three adjacent voice leadings to a generate a cube: for instance, the scales on the lower left cube in Figure 3.11.9 result from applying to C diatonic the six different orderings of F→F♯, C→C♯, and G→G♯. (Note that F→F♯ is always represented by a vertical line, while C→C♯ is always horizontal, and G→G♯ always moves into the paper.) The resulting three-dimensional lattice, which describes voice-leading relationships among the four most even twelve-tone equal-tempered chords in seven-dimensional space, is structurally analogous to the graph of three-note diatonic triads shown in Figure 3.11.2b. Here the circle of fifths zigzags three-dimensionally through the center of the space, much as the circle of thirds zigzagged through the two-dimensional Figure 3.11.8.[44]

Figure 3.11.8 (*a*) The familiar circle of fifths connects fifth-related diatonic scales by single-semitone voice leading. (*b*) To include the second-most even five-note chords scramble the order of adjacent voice leadings, for instance by letting C→C♯ operate on C diatonic before F→F♯ does.

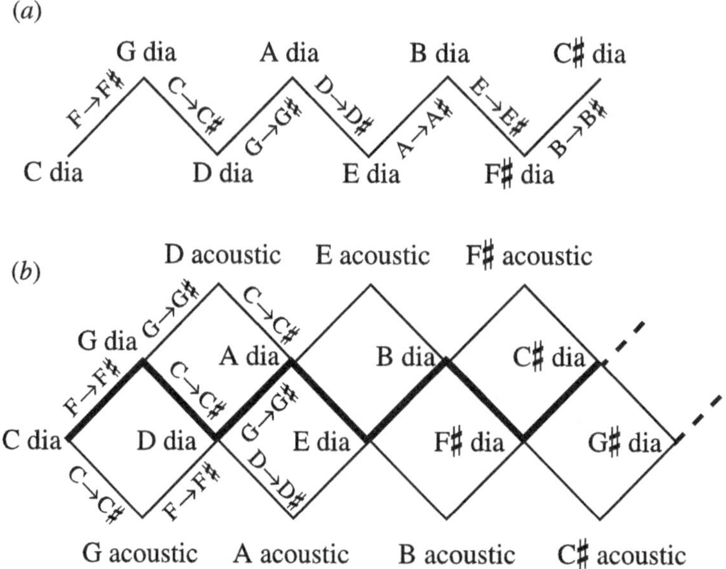

44 In principle, we could continue this process by adding a fourth or even fifth dimension to the graph, thus extending the lattice so that it covers more and more of seven-dimensional chord space.

Figure 3.11.9 We can extend the scale lattice to three dimensions. The result depicts single-semitone voice leading among the four most even seven-note chromatic chords. We will discuss these scales in the next chapter.

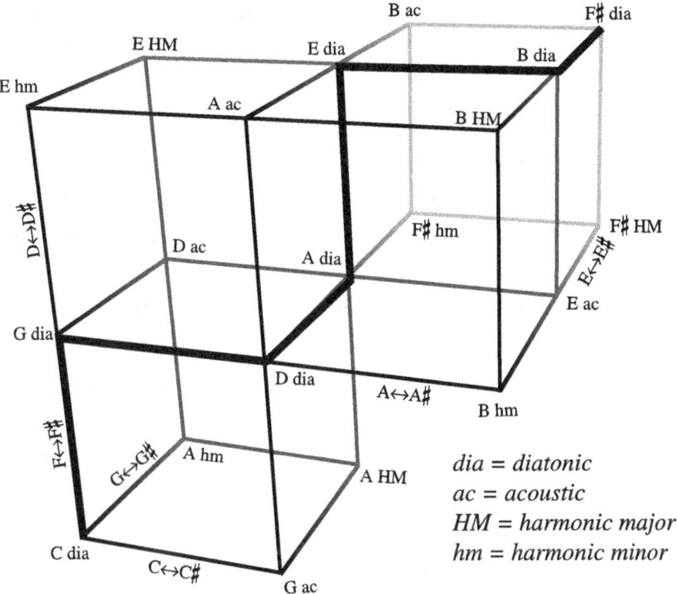

Again, the key point is that the lattices in our second category—representing objects as diverse as diatonic seventh chords, octatonic triads, and familiar seven-note scales—are all structurally similar. At their center is a generalized circle of fifths that zigzags through two, three, or more dimensions. These chords are *near interval cycles* linked by a chain of single-semitone voice leadings. The rest of the lattice is generated by rearranging its voice leadings: for a two-dimensional graph, begin with a two-dimensional zigzag and switch the order of each pair of adjacent voice leadings, producing a sequence of squares sharing a common edge (as in Figures 3.11.7 and 3.11.8b); for a three-dimensional graph, begin with a three-dimensional zigzag (up, right, in) and scramble the order of every three consecutive voice leadings, producing a series of stacked cubes sharing a common face (as in Figure 3.11.9). This process of "scrambling" adds successively less even chords to the lattice, extending it farther and farther from the center of chord space. (Thus, where the dimension of the first kind of graph is controlled by the size of the chords we want to represent, the dimension of this second kind of graph is controlled by the number of distinct chord types we are interested in.) We will return to these structures throughout the book, using the "scale lattice" to represent voice leadings among familiar seven-note scales and using the three-note diatonic lattice to represent familiar classical voice-leading patterns.

Music theorists tend to take it for granted that we can use discrete lattices to represent voice-leading relationships, in large part because these discrete structures preceded the more comprehensive geometrical spaces we have discussed in this chapter. But on reflection, it is actually quite remarkable that (say) the one-dimensional circle of fifths can faithfully represent voice-leading relationships among seven-note diatonic scales. After all, diatonic scales are seven-note objects inhabiting a *seven-dimensional space,* and we have no reason to expect that six of these dimensions would turn out to be irrelevant. And yet it turns out that for most practical purposes we can make do by representing diatonic voice leadings on the familiar circle of fifths. This suggests that the circle of fifths is quite a special structure which lies within seven-note chord space in a very particular way. Other lattices are *not* special in this way and do *not* accurately model voice-leading distances, even though they might appear to do so. In general, it is extremely difficult to distinguish "faithful" lattices (such as the circle of fifths) from unfaithful lattices (such as the familiar *Tonnetz*). To understand these structures in a deep and principled way, we must reflect on how they are embedded within the continuous spaces described here. Those of you who want to explore this issue further should consult Appendix C. Those who are more interested in music analysis can instead focus on internalizing the two types of lattice described in this section. The important point is that it is typically sufficient to understand the discrete lattices, and to be able to construct the graph germane to a particular musical situation.

3.12 TWO MUSICAL GEOMETRIES

We have now developed two geometrical representations of the same musical facts—the circular pitch-class space of Chapter 2 and the higher dimensional spaces discussed in this chapter. These two representations are complementary, in the sense that relationships that are difficult to understand in one are often easier to understand in the other. Let's conclude by considering some of the strengths and weaknesses of the two models.

In some ways, the circular space of Chapter 2 is simpler and more convenient than its higher dimensional counterparts. In this chapter we've created individual spaces for chords of various sizes: the space of two-note chords is two-dimensional, the space of three-note chords is three-dimensional, and so on. But there is no analogous description of the space of *all* chords.[45] Furthermore, it can be very difficult to visualize relationships among larger chords, since a new dimension is required for each additional voice. By contrast, the circular representation uses a single circle to depict chords of any size, and there is no sense that two-note chords and three-note chords occupy fundamentally different worlds. Nor are there any special problems associated with large chords, as we can always add more points to the circle.

Moreover, the spaces discussed in this chapter do not provide a natural way to represent the similarity between chords with the same pitch-class content but different "doublings." For example, the collections {C, E, E, G} and {C, E, G, G} are repre-

45 We can actually construct these spaces, but they are infinite-dimensional and almost impossible to visualize. Furthermore, distance in the resulting spaces does not accurately represent voice-leading size (see Callender, Quinn, and Tymoczko 2008).

Figure 3.12.1 Two collections of paths linking the points {C, E, G} and {D, F, A}. On the left, the three-voice voice leading (C, E, G)→(D, F, A); on the right, the four-voice (C, C, E, G)→(F, A, D, F).

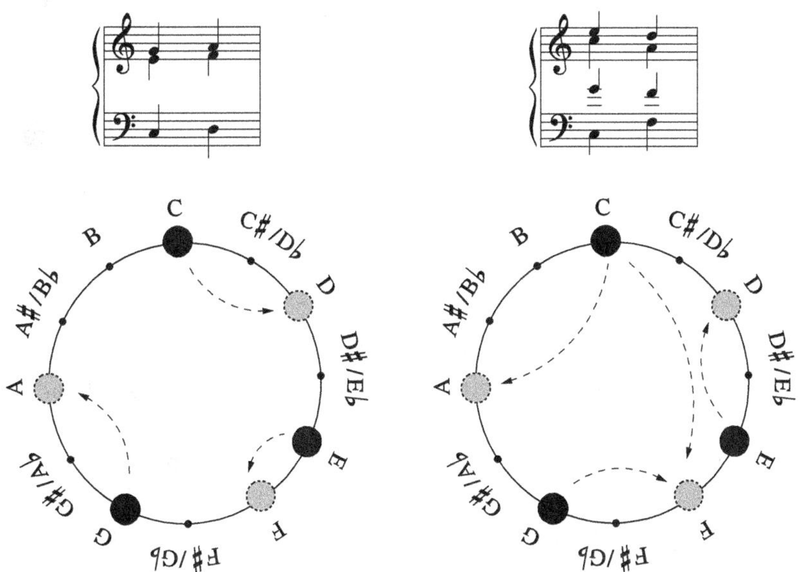

sented by widely separated points in four-note chord space, yet they are musically quite similar; ordinarily, both would be considered C major chords. This problem is again ameliorated in the circular representation, which does not require us to distinguish the number of times each note appears: the chords {C, G}, {C, C, G} can both be modeled using the same two points on the circle, C and G. Voice leadings with "doublings" can be represented as different collections of paths between the same sets of points. Thus Figure 3.12.1 models the voice leadings (C, E, G)→(D, F, A) and (C, C, E, G)→(F, A, D, F) as two different ways to link the same configurations of black and gray points on the circle. Once again, the circular model seems more flexible than the higher dimensional alternative.

The problem with the circle, however, is that it is easy to use but hard to understand. One could stare at circular pitch-class space for a long time without ever realizing that voice leadings can be decomposed into purely parallel and purely contrary components. And important voice-leading relationships can sometimes be hard to see. (Quick: which of its transpositions is the chord in Figure 3.12.2 closest to? Now look at Figure 3.11.8 and ask yourself the same question.) Nor does circular space make manifest structural relations such as those we uncovered in the *Allelujia Justus et Palma* or the Brahms C minor Piano Quartet. So at least in some cases, the circular model will obscure important features of musical structure.

By contrast, higher dimensional chord spaces provide a powerful set of visual tools for thinking about music. We can describe the process of musical abstraction—the ignoring of octave and order information—as a matter of concentrating on a single "tile" of musical wallpaper. Abstract concepts like "individual T-relatedness" (or even "scalar transposition") can be translated into concrete visuospatial terms.

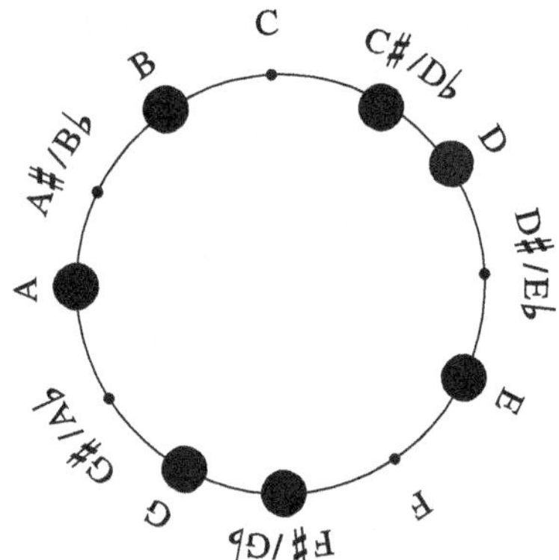

Figure 3.12.2 In circular pitch-class space, it is not immediately obvious which of this chord's transpositions it is closest to.

Plotting music in the spaces can yield insight into its structure (§3.5). And though the higher dimensional spaces are unwieldy, lattices such as those in §3.11 can be used to convey a large amount of musical information very quickly, mapping a wealth of compositional possibilities in a clear and extremely efficient manner. To use such lattices is to exploit the higher dimensional chord spaces described in this chapter, even if we do not explicitly represent the whole space from which they are drawn.

In all of these ways, then, the higher dimensional spaces provide useful complements to the simpler, circular model of Chapter 2. Ultimately, a deep understanding of music likely requires fluency with *both* models. (As the physicist Richard Feynman once put it, "every theoretical physicist who is any good knows six or seven different theoretical representations for exactly the same physics."[46]) By learning multiple ways to represent the same music, we can develop flexibility of mind and deepen our grasp of the underlying structures—even if, in the end, we prefer one representation to another. Readers who do not share my aesthetic appreciation for the higher dimensional chord spaces may therefore still be able to appreciate them as part of a program of music-theoretical calisthenics. In stretching our minds to understand these exotic structures, we will surely strengthen our appreciation for the richness latent in ordinary musical notation.

3.13 STUDY GUIDE

Readers who want to improve their understanding of musical geometry should practice three basic skills. First, representing voice leadings on the two-note Möbius strip of Figure 3.3.1. Second, representing single chords, as well as the pure contrary component of three-note voice leadings, on Figure 3.8.6. (It may also be useful to try representing pure contrary two-note voice leadings on Figure 3.7.2a.) And third, constructing the lattices describing voice-leading relationships among musically interesting objects—for instance, the most even two-note chords in the pentatonic and

46 Feynman 1994, p. 162.

whole-tone scales, the most even three-note chords in the diatonic and whole-tone scales, the most even four-note chords in the diatonic and octatonic scales, and the most even five-note chords in the chromatic scale. (In constructing these lattices, use the various graphs in this chapter as guides, and consider the scale step to be a unit of distance.) After practicing these particular tasks, the more general geometrical principles should start to become clear. It may also be helpful to read the chapter once, spend some time with the questions in Appendix F (perhaps augmented by the more detailed discussion in Appendix B), and then return to the chapter a second time, repeating as necessary. In the end, passive reading is no substitute for a little bit of active, hands-on exploration. Just as nobody will ever learn to play the piano simply by reading about it, nobody will learn geometry unless they pick up a pencil and start working through some exercises.

Readers who are hungry to explore analytical applications can turn directly to Chapter 8, which is concerned with chromatic voice leading. Chapter 9 also uses the geometry of seven-dimensional scale space to investigate twentieth-century music, though it should be read after Chapter 4. The geometrical spaces described in this chapter also appear in Chapter 6, where they provide a framework for retelling the history of Western music. However, this chapter is probably best read after the remaining theoretical material in Part I.

CHAPTER 4

Scales

Now we're ready to incorporate scales into our developing theoretical apparatus. We'll begin by modeling scales as "musical rulers" that allow us to measure distances in pitch and pitch-class space. We'll then investigate a number of familiar scales, including the pentatonic, diatonic, chromatic, and melodic minor. This leads to a discussion of the relation between modulation and voice leading. Finally, we investigate *scalar* and *interscalar* transpositions—concepts that are useful not just for understanding scalar music, but also for understanding voice leading more generally. The upshot is that there is an interesting duality, or complementarity, between chord and scale. Not only can chordal concepts (e.g. voice leading) help us understand scalar processes (e.g. modulation), but the reverse is also true; concepts like *scalar transposition* provide useful tools for understanding relationships between chords.[1]

4.1 A SCALE IS A RULER

Intuitively, the opening of *The Sound of Music's* "Do, Re, Mi" (Figure 4.1.1) involves three repetitions of the same musical pattern: when composing each phrase, Richard Rogers simply "did the same thing" at different pitch levels. (This, of course, is part of the song's cheery didacticism—it's supposed to teach kids music.) But we are hard pressed to describe this sense of sameness using the ideas developed so far. From the standpoint of Chapter 2, (C, D, E) and (D, E, F) are fundamentally different objects, since they are not related by transposition, inversion, or any other combination of OPTIC symmetries.

The difficulty, of course, is that we are thinking chromatically rather than diatonically. Instead of describing F as being one semitone above E, we should describe it as being one *scale step* above E. Once we start to think diatonically we realize that each phrase begins with two ascending scale steps, with the entire pattern moving up by step at each repetition. The moral is that a scale provides us with an alternative measure of musical distance, and that we must be careful to choose the right distance metric for the job. In principle, any collection of pitches can be a scale: a scale's notes do not have to be very close to one another, nor are they required to repeat after every

1 The ideas in this chapter are based on Tymoczko 2004 and 2008b.

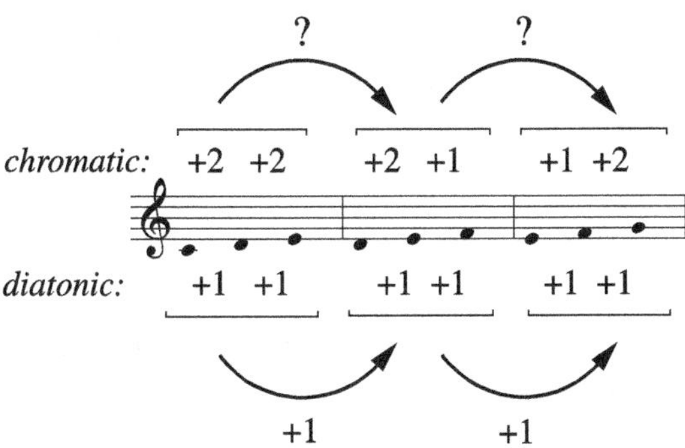

Figure 4.1.1 The opening notes of the first phrases of "Do, Re, Mi," interpreted chromatically and diatonically. The numbers represent intervals as measured relative to the two scales.

octave, nor is it necessary that scales have "first" or "tonic" notes (Figure 4.1.2). All the scale needs to do is to tell us how to move up and down by 1 unit, or *scale step*.[2]

Octave-repeating scales, which contain each of their pitches in every possible octave, can be represented as points in circular pitch-class space.[3] When depicting them geometrically we can choose whether the visual layout should reflect chromatic or scalar distance. (*Note:* throughout this chapter, the term "chromatic" refers to the continuous, log-frequency measure of §2.1, rather than to distances along some chromatic scale.[4]) For example, Figure 4.1.3a uses chromatic distance, representing C and D as farther apart than E and F, while Figure 4.1.3b uses scalar distances, placing the seven notes around the circle so that steps all appear to be the same size. We can do something similar even when working with the higher dimensional chord spaces of the previous chapter. For example, Figure 4.1.4a draws the two-note Möbius strip, labeling only the dyads in the C diatonic scale. Points are connected by lines when they can be linked by voice leading in which both voices move by diatonic step:

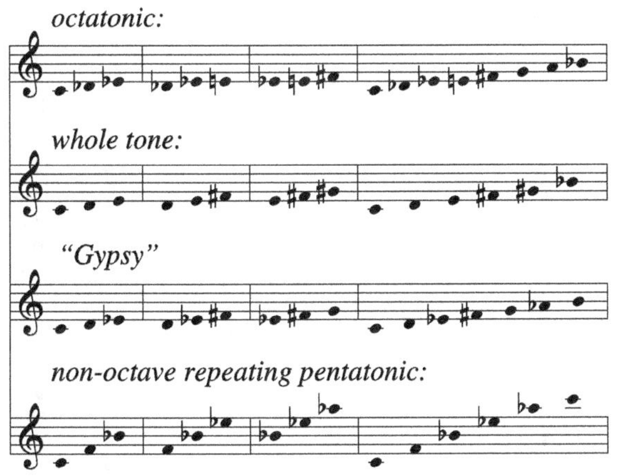

Figure 4.1.2 The "Do, Re, Mi" pattern in other scales.

2 Clough and Meyerson (1985) use the term "diatonic length" to refer to the scale-specific measure of musical distance.

3 Non-octave-repeating scales, though musically quite interesting, occur only sporadically in Western music; we will not discuss them here.

4 Only in equal temperaments do scale distances correspond to log-frequency distances.

the roughly horizontal lines represent parallel motion within the scale; the roughly vertical lines represent contrary motion within the scale. The irregularity of the resulting grid reflects the fact that the scale's steps are not all the same chromatic size. Figure 4.1.4b redraws the graph using scalar distance, so that the grid is perfectly regular and all scale steps appear to be equally large.[5]

Figure 4.1.3 An octave-repeating scale is a circular arrangement of pitch classes. It can be drawn either using chromatic distance (*a*) or scalar distance (*b*).

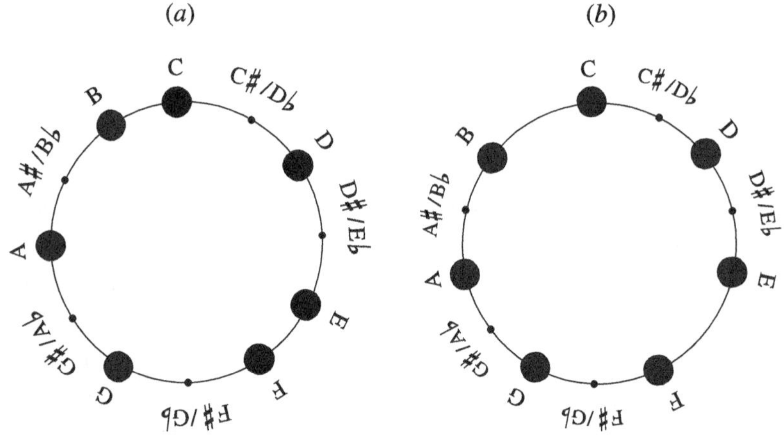

Figure 4.1.4 Two-dimensional chord space, drawn using chromatic distance (*a*) and scalar distance (*b*). Only the white notes are labeled.

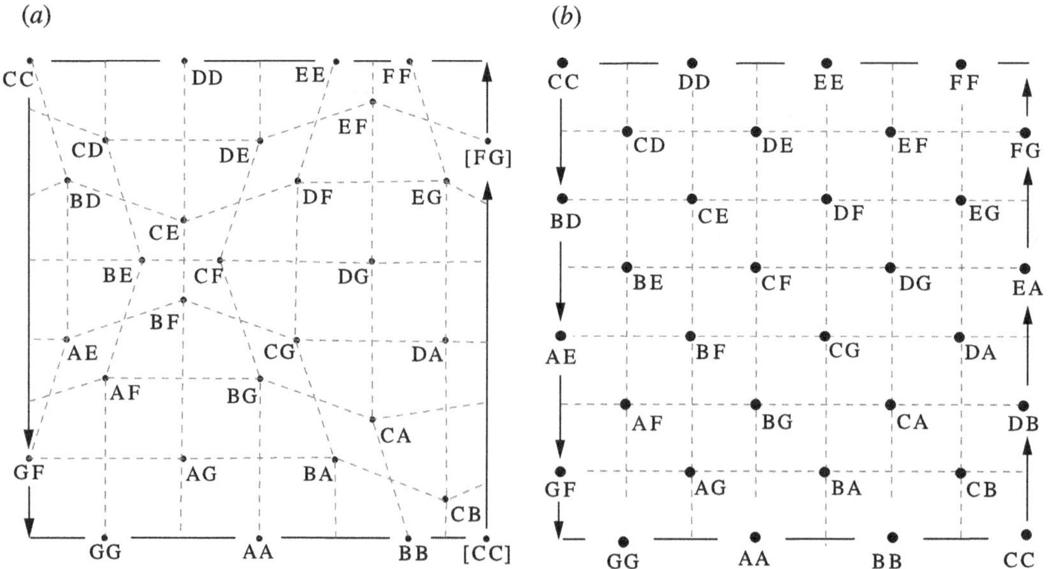

5 You may find it interesting to draw lines representing single-step voice leading among perfect fifths and major thirds; this produces the discrete lattice in Figure 3.11.1b.

To my eye, Figure 4.1.4a has a three-dimensional quality, resembling a crumpled piece of paper or an aerial view of a hilly city, such as San Francisco. This impression of three-dimensionality testifies to the way our visual system has evolved to manipulate multiple kinds of distance. When we look down at San Francisco, we need to infer the *intrinsic* length of the city blocks from their *apparent* length on our retinas. Intrinsically the blocks are all (roughly) equal, since San Francisco is a grid city, but the blocks appear different, since some travel uphill. (When seen from above, these uphill blocks look shorter, as we lose the vertical dimension.) These two visual distances are closely analogous to the two musical distances we have been discussing. Just as the hot air balloonist needs to juggle multiple visual distances when looking down at San Francisco, so too does the musician need to realize that the line segments in Figure 4.1.4a have the same diatonic length, but different chromatic sizes. Remarkably, all of this is encapsulated in the crumpled appearance of Figure 4.1.4a—demonstrating once again that geometry can help us understand abstract music-theoretical relationships.

4.2 SCALE DEGREES, SCALAR TRANSPOSITION, AND SCALAR INVERSION

Since a scale provides a measure of musical distance, it also defines scale-specific notions of transposition, inversion, chord type, and set class. These allow us to adapt the ideas of the previous chapters to our new scalar perspective.

We begin by assigning numbers to the notes in the scale—arbitrarily selecting some note as scale degree 1, labeling the note immediately above it scale degree 2, the note two steps above it scale degree 3, and so on (Figure 4.2.1). (The choice of a first scale degree is a mere notational convenience and does not imply that this note is more significant than the others.) Scale degree numbers are analogous to numerical pitch-class labels, with one trivial difference: while music theorists label pitch classes starting from zero, they label scale degrees starting from one.[6] Note that while scale degree *numbers* are dependent on the arbitrary choice of a first scale degree, scalar distances are not—in C diatonic, for instance, the scalar distance between C and D is always one scale step, no matter what the first scale degree happens to be. Musicians refer to these distances in a somewhat confusing way, using the terms "a second," "a third," and "a fourth" to refer to scalar distances of one, two, and three steps, respectively.

Transposition and inversion are the two distance-preserving operations in chromatic space. We can define new operations of *scalar transposition* and *scalar inversion* that preserve scalar distances. To transpose relative to a scale, simply add a constant to each scale degree (Figure 4.2.2). (Here we use "scale degree arithmetic"—for an

---

6 It would be possible to bring the two conventions in line, for instance, by labeling scale degrees starting from zero. This would make scale degree labels formally identical to pitch-class labels.

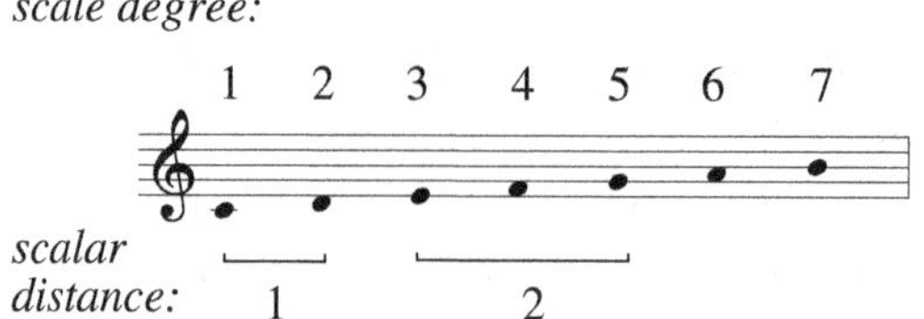

Figure 4.2.1 Scale degrees and scalar distances. A scalar distance of one step is called a "second," a distance of two steps is "a third," and so on.

n-note scale, we add or subtract n until the result lies between 1 and n, inclusive.[7]) To invert relative to a scale, choose a fixed point that will remain unaffected by the inversion. Any note x scale steps above the fixed point gets sent to the note x scale steps *below* the fixed point, and vice versa. Scalar inversion can be represented algebraically by subtraction from a constant value: in C major, we invert (C, D, F) around the fixed point E by subtracting each scale degree from 6, transforming 1, 2, 4 into 5, 4, 2, or (G, F, D).[8] The mathematics is identical to that in §2.2, only using scale degree numbers rather than chromatic pitch-class labels.

Relative to a scale, two chords belong to the same chord type (transpositional set class) if they are related by scalar transposition. Thus, relative to C harmonic minor, the chords {B, D, F} and {C, E♭, G} are both "triads," and hence transpositionally related, even though one is diminished and the other is minor (Figure 4.2.3). Relative to C harmonic minor, {A♭, B, E♭} is *not* a triad, because A♭ and B are only *one* scale step apart. (Chromatically, of course, it is an A♭-minor triad and is transpositionally related to C minor.) This shows that the same chords can be transpositionally related relative to one scale, but not another.[9] Scalar "set classes" can be defined in the obvious way, as groups of chords related either by scalar transposition or scalar inversion. Thus {C, D, F} and {D, F, G} belong to the same set class relative to C harmonic minor, because they are related by scalar inversion around E♭.

Figure 4.2.2 (*a*) To transpose up by three scale steps, add 3 to each scale degree number. (*b*) To invert around E (scale degree 3), subtract each scale degree number from 6 (= 3 × 2). In both cases, use "scale degree arithmetic," adding or subtracting 7 until the result lies between 1 and 7.

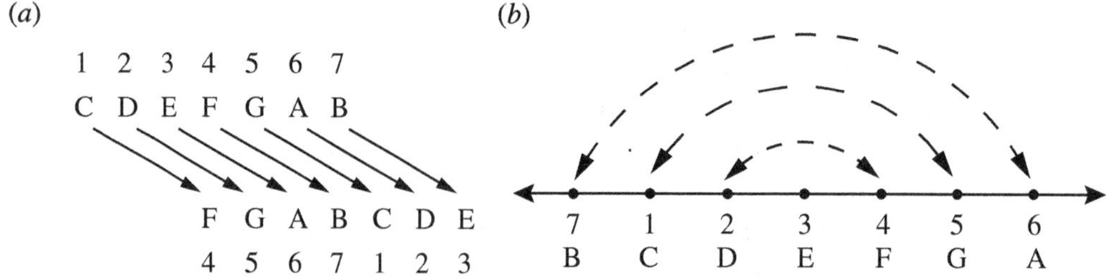

7 To transpose (F, G, A) up by three steps in the C diatonic scale, add 3 to (4, 5, 6) obtaining (7, 8, 9). Then subtract 7 from any numbers larger than 7, producing (7, 1, 2).

8 To invert around fixed point x, one subtracts each scale degree from $2x$.

9 In a scalar context, letter names often indicate distance. Thus, {A♭, B, E♭} has a step while {C, E♭, G} does not.

Figure 4.2.3 Relative to the C harmonic minor scale, these chords all belong to the same transpositional set class, and are therefore triads. {A♭, B, E♭} is not a member of this set class, and is not a triad, even though it is related to {C, E♭, G} by chromatic transposition.

It is even possible to assign scale degree numbers to notes that are not in the scale. Relative to C diatonic, the note C♯ can be considered scale degree 1.5, since it lies halfway between scale degrees 1 and 2 (Figure 4.1.3). Similarly, E𝄲 (E quarter-tone sharp) can be considered scale degree 3.5, since it is halfway between scale degrees 3 and 4. It follows that scalar transposition and inversion can act on notes *outside the scale!* For example, we can shift (C, D, E) up by half a scale step to produce (C♯, D♯, E𝄲), or we can invert (C, D, D♯) around D♯ to produce (F, E, D♯).[10] Proceeding in this way, we can apply scalar transposition and inversion completely promiscuously—shifting *any* collection of notes by any fraction of a scale step.

This suggests the perverse musical strategy of writing music that uses the C diatonic scale to measure musical distance, while not privileging its notes in any way. For example, Figure 4.2.4 repeatedly transposes the C major triad by one and a half scale steps, producing {E♭, G♭, B♭}, {F, A, C} and {G♯, B𝄲, D♯}.[11] The resulting music is *guided* by the diatonic scale without emphasizing the white notes themselves. A brilliant music theorist, gifted with extremely sharp ears and a somewhat demented musical imagination, might even be able to discern the presence of the scale from the deformations it introduces as chords move through musical space. I stress that I am not recommending this as a practical possibility; my point is simply that a musical scale is very similar to what mathematicians call a *metric,* or a method of measuring distance. In principle, a scale can function in this way even in highly chromatic contexts such as Figure 4.2.4. This is just to repeat the point that a *scale* need not also be a *macroharmony.*

Figure 4.2.4 This music uses the C major scale to measure distance, while also containing notes foreign to the scale (compare Figure 4.1.1).

10 Inversion around a point halfway between two scale degrees sends scale tones to scale tones. Here, for example, C and D get sent to F and E.

11 G♭ is 1.5 scale steps above E, since it is halfway between F and G. Similarly, B𝄲 is 1.5 scale steps above A, since it is halfway between B and C. Note that we are using the log-frequency metric to measure fractions of a scale step (§2.1).

4.3 EVENNESS AND SCALAR TRANSPOSITION

Listeners are typically aware of both scalar and log-frequency distance at the same time. We know that (D, E, F) is in some sense "the same" as (C, D, E), but we also know that (E, F) is different from (D, E). Ordinary musical terminology adopts this twofold perspective, asserting that (E, F) and (D, E) are both "seconds" (one-step intervals), while adding the qualification that the first is "minor" and the second is "major."[12] Scalar music is interesting precisely because of this doubleness. When moving musical patterns along a scale, composers inevitably transform their material in subtle ways, creating a pleasing mixture of identity and difference.

For scalar music to be successful, these induced variations must be small—otherwise, listeners would not be able to treat (D, E, F) as being essentially similar to (C, D, E). Figure 4.3.1a presents an example of a scale that fails spectacularly in this regard. Scalar transposition transforms (C, C♯, D) (analogous to "Do, a deer") into (C♯, D, B♭) ("Re, a... *drop?!!?!?*"), creating an eight-semitone step that sounds nothing whatsoever like the one-semitone step between C and C♯. By contrast, Figure 4.3.1b presents a relatively even three-note scale, in which scalar transposition is completely successful and gestures retain their shape as they are transposed. Such passages are common in Western music, demonstrating that scalar terminology can be useful even when we are investigating objects that are not traditionally considered to be scales.

Clearly, scalar transposition will be precisely equal to chromatic transposition when the scale's notes are distributed perfectly evenly in pitch-class space—as in the case of the familiar whole-tone scale. When the scale is *nearly* even, then the two forms of transposition will be nearly but not exactly the same. In some ways this latter situation is preferable: scalar transposition along a perfectly even scale does not introduce any variations into the music and can become boring rather quickly. A bit of unevenness therefore adds musical interest by introducing a degree of variation. Interestingly, we can also make an analogous point about chords. When a chord divides the octave *perfectly* evenly, efficient voice leading typically involves parallel motion in all voices and does not create the effect of independent melodic

Figure 4.3.1 (*a*) An uneven scale, in which the step between D and B♭ is much larger than the others. (*b*) A small but nearly even scale, containing only the notes {C, E, G}.

12 "Major" and "minor" here mean "big" and "little," as in *Ursa major* and *Ursa minor;* they do not refer to the major and minor tonalities.

Figure 4.3.2 (*a*) Chords that divide the octave completely evenly can be connected to their transpositions by efficient but parallel voice leading. (*b*) Slightly uneven chords can be connected to their transpositions by voice leading in which the voices move by different distances, creating the sense of counterpoint. (*c*) Along a completely even scale, scalar transposition introduces no variation into music. (*d*) A small amount of unevenness creates slight amounts of variation, which can often be desirable.

lines (Figure 4.3.2). A little bit of unevenness is preferable here as well, allowing us to escape parallelism by causing the voices to move unequally. We might therefore say that both scales and chords are subject to the *Goldilocks Principle*—not too much evenness, because that would be boring, and not too little, because that would lead to musical disorder.

Near evenness therefore plays at least three fundamentally different roles in musical life: the nearly even collections can be linked to their transpositions by efficient voice leading, they include the acoustically consonant chords, and they also allow for scalar transpositions that introduce moderate but not overwhelming amounts of variation into musical textures. It is somewhat remarkable that these three separate considerations all point in the same musical direction. Intuitively, one would think that the requirements for constructing contrapuntal music had nothing in common with the requirements for constructing effective scales, and this in turn might lead to the expectation that composers had an enormous amount of freedom in creating alternative musical languages. The *overdetermination* of Western chords and scales leads to the very opposite conclusion. For insofar as composers are interested in harmonic consistency, acoustic consonance, *or* scalar transposition, they will necessarily find themselves gravitating toward the same familiar musical objects.

4.4 CONSTRUCTING COMMON SCALES

Since scales typically function as macroharmonies, tonal composers have reason to be interested in scales containing many consonant intervals. And since the octave is the most consonant of the intervals, composers have reason to use scales that are maximally saturated with octaves—that is, scales in which each note has an octave both above it and below it. But this, of course, is just to say that the scale is *octave repeating*. Octave-repeating scales are therefore overdetermined in their own modest way: besides being easy to use and remember, they also contain as many octaves as they possibly can.

The second-most consonant interval, the acoustically pure perfect fifth, is just a hair's breadth larger than its familiar equal-tempered cousin. Suppose you would like to construct an octave-repeating scale that is maximally saturated with acoustically pure fifths—that is, you would like as many notes as possible to have fifths both above them and below them. It has been known for thousands of years that a finite scale can never have pure fifths above and below *each* of its notes; the best one can do is construct scales in which all but two notes have this property—in other words, "stacks of fifths" such as those in Figure 4.4.1. If the scale divides the octave nearly evenly, then the final note of the stack is *nearly* a perfect fifth away from the initial note.[13] Figure 4.4.1 identifies three salient possibilities: a stack of five perfect fifths falls approximately 0.9 semitones short of three octaves, a stack of seven perfect fifths exceeds four octaves by about 1.137 semitones, and a stack of twelve perfect fifths overshoots seven octaves by nearly 0.25 semitones.[14] We can therefore build nearly even scales containing four, six, and eleven perfect fifths, otherwise known as the pentatonic, diatonic, and chromatic scales. The pentatonic has a "near fifth" approximately equal to a minor sixth; the diatonic has a "near fifth" approximately equal to a tritone; and the chromatic scale has a "near fifth" a bit smaller than the perfect fifth. Different tuning systems will assign slightly different sizes to these intervals, depending on how exactly they compromise between the demands of evenness and acoustic purity. We will return to this issue momentarily.

Let us now play the same game with thirds. Suppose you would like to create a scale maximally saturated with acoustically pure major or minor thirds. Figure 4.4.2 shows that three acoustically pure major thirds, or four acoustically pure minor thirds, are about half a semitone away from an octave. To extend these stacks further would create very small melodic intervals that would be awkward to sing and play, and this is rarely done in Western music. Instead, musicians consider the cycle C-E-G♯-C to be closed, containing two pure thirds (C-E and E-G♯) and one "near major

Figure 4.4.1 (*a*) A stack of five perfect fifths falls 0.9 semitones short of three octaves. (*b*) A stack of seven perfect fifths overshoots four octaves by 1.14 semitones. (*c*) A stack of twelve fifths overshoots seven octaves by 0.25 semitones. (Note that the B♯ is not quite the same as C♮.) By eliminating the top note of each stack we can form a relatively even scale with one "imperfect fifth."

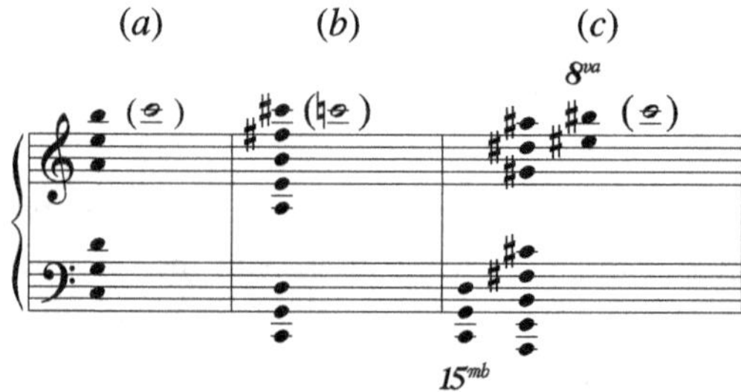

13 Carey and Clampitt (1989) unpack the term "almost" using the mathematics of continued fractions.

14 Beyond twelve notes, a stack of fifths has microtonal intervals about a quarter of a semitone large, which are very difficult to sing. We will not consider these scales here.

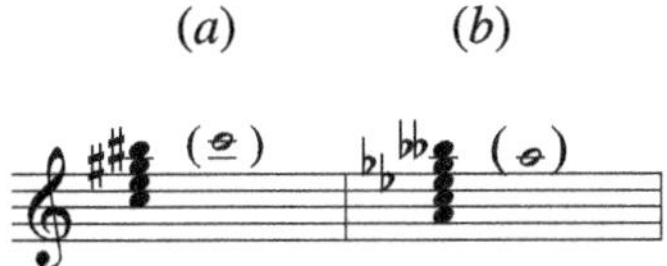

Figure 4.4.2 (*a*) A stack of four major thirds falls 0.41 semitones short of an octave. (*b*) A stack of five minor thirds overshoots an octave by 0.62 semitones.

third" (G♯-C). (Modern equal temperament of course regularizes the thirds so that they are exactly the same size, with the resulting augmented triad dividing the octave into three precisely even parts.) Similarly, four minor thirds are considered to form a closed cycle A-C-E♭-G♭-A, consisting of three pure minor thirds and one "near minor third"—or in equal temperament, four completely equal intervals.

Unlike our stacks of perfect fifths, these thirds-cycles are too small to serve as satisfying macroharmonies. However, we can *combine* cycles to make larger collections. The hexatonic scale (Figure 4.4.3a) combines two augmented triads at a distance of a perfect fifth. This scale is maximally saturated with major thirds while also containing a large number of perfect fifths. However, it does not divide the octave particularly evenly, since its steps are (approximately) one and three semitones large. The octatonic scale (Figure 4.4.3b) is analogous to the hexatonic, but is built with minor-third cycles; it contains a large number of *minor* thirds and perfect fifths. Because its steps are one and two semitones large, it is considerably more even than the hexatonic scale. Hexatonic and octatonic are close cousins, being structurally similar and playing important roles in nineteenth- and twentieth-century music. A third possibility, the *whole-tone scale* (Figure 4.4.3c), combines two augmented triads at a distance of a major second; although it is not particularly saturated with consonances, it is perfectly even. In principle, we could use diminished seventh chords to construct a perfectly even eight-note scale, although it is not available in twelve-tone equal temperament.

We can also form two-octave stacks of major and minor thirds, as in Figure 4.4.4. The thirds can be arranged to produce four familiar scales: diatonic, "acoustic" (or melodic minor ascending), harmonic minor, and "harmonic major."[15] The acoustic scale is so-called because it is approximately equal to the first seven pitch classes of the harmonic series; it is usually labeled relative to the ordering (C, D, E, F♯, G, A, B♭),

Figure 4.4.3 (*a*) The hexatonic scale combines two augmented triads at a distance of a perfect fifth. (*b*) The octatonic scale combines two diminished sevenths at a distance of a perfect fifth. (*c*) The whole-tone scale combines augmented triads at a distance of a major second; it is perfectly even, but contains no perfect fifths.

15 In principle, there is a fifth possibility, C-E-G♯-C-E♭-G♭-A, which has two instances of a single note. In some tuning systems these two Cs are slightly different.

Figure 4.4.4 Four scales can be represented as nearly even stacks of three major thirds and four minor thirds: diatonic (*a*), acoustic (*b*), harmonic minor (*c*), and harmonic major (*d*).

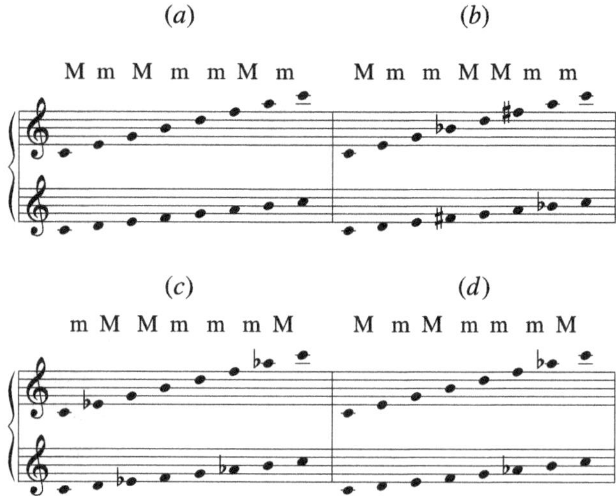

known as the "C acoustic collection."[16] (This is equivalent to either the mixolydian mode with raised fourth degree or the lydian with lowered seventh.) The harmonic scales are the only ones we have considered that are not inversionally symmetrical: the harmonic minor is ubiquitous in classical music, while its inversion, the so-called harmonic major scale, was investigated by nineteenth-century musicians such as Weitzmann and Rimsky-Korsakov.[17] It can be described as a major scale with lowered sixth degree or as a harmonic minor scale with raised third.

Figure 4.4.5 categorizes our eight scales based on their step sizes. The scales on the left—diatonic, acoustic, whole tone, and octatonic—have steps that are at most two semitones large, and thirds (two-step scalar intervals) that are either three or four semitones large.[18] These scales are important because they permit composers to import traditional compositional techniques to new scalar environments: by selecting adjacent scale tones, a composer can create melodies that are recognizably stepwise (i.e. whose notes are linked by one- or two-semitone intervals); and by selecting scalar "thirds" a composer can create chords that are recognizably "tertian" (i.e. whose

---

16 The first thirteen harmonic partials of C are roughly equal to the pitch classes C-C-G-C-E-G-B♭-C-D-E-F♯-G-A, with the eleventh and thirteenth partials (F♯ and A) being rather flat relative to their equal-tempered counterparts. The acoustic scale is the best equal-tempered approximation to these notes.

17 See Riley 2004.

18 In their twelve-tone equal-tempered versions; other versions of the scales have steps that are *approximately* one or two semitones large, and thirds that are *approximately* three or four semitones large. Not surprisingly, these scales have been thoroughly investigated, by writers such as Berger (1963), Lendvai (1971), Gervais (1971), Whittall (1975), Pressing (1978, 1982), van den Toorn (1983), Howat (1983), Antokoletz (1984, 1993), Perle (1984), Russom (1985), Forte (1987, 1990, 1991), Taruskin (1985, 1987, 1996), Parks (1989), Cohn (1991), Rahn (1991), Larson (1992), Callender (1998), Clough, Engebretsen, and Kochavi (1999), Quinn (2002), Zimmerman (2002), Caballero (2004), and Rappaport (2006). See Tymoczko 1997, 2002, and 2004 for more.

Figure 4.4.5 The scales in (*a*) have steps that are either one or two semitones large, and thirds that are three or four semitones large. Those in (*b*) have at least one step that is three semitones large. The top three scales in (*b*) have thirds that are three or four semitones large. The pentatonic scale is enclosed in a box because it is a subset of the diatonic.

adjacent notes are linked by three- or four-semitone intervals). The scales in the second group—harmonic minor, harmonic major, hexatonic, and pentatonic—have at least one step that is three semitones large, and hence lead to more exotic melodies. However, the first three scales have thirds that are three or four semitones large, and can again be used to construct "tertian" chords. By contrast, pentatonic thirds are four or five semitones large, which means that stacks of pentatonic thirds tend to sound like "fourth chords" (that is, chords whose notes are five *chromatic* steps apart). Figure 4.4.6 shows that twentieth-century tonal composers often used the pentatonic scale to create the impression of "fourthiness."

In twelve-tone equal temperament, our scales have another useful property as well: they contain *every* chord that does not itself contain a "chromatic cluster" such as {C, C♯, D}.[19] The scales thus provide a technique for managing a greatly extended harmonic vocabulary that nevertheless stops short of atonality's extremes—that is, composers can construct harmonies by freely choosing notes from one of these scales, secure in the knowledge that they will never generate a dissonant chromatic cluster. Conversely, the scales provide a ready "reservoir" of melodic notes with which to accompany any cluster-free chord. Note in particular that "polychords," formed by superimposing two triads, can always be embedded within one of these scales. In this sense, they fit naturally with the extended tertian sonorities characteristic of twentieth-century tonal music.

A final word about tuning and temperament. Temperament enters the picture because of the need to balance the demands of regularity and acoustic purity. A Pythagorean twelve-tone chromatic scale contains acoustically pure fifths, but does not divide the octave precisely evenly. Conversely, the twelve-tone equal-tempered chromatic scale sacrifices purity in the name of evenness—with all its steps

19 Note that from this point of view the pentatonic scale is redundant, since it is a subset of the diatonic.

Figure 4.4.6 Diatonic fourths and pentatonic thirds. In (*a*), from mm. 34–35 of Debussy's "La fille aux cheveux de lin," diatonic fourths give way to pentatonic thirds. In (*b*), from Ligeti's *Piano Concerto* (second movement, mm. 60–61) diatonic fifths are superimposed on pentatonic fourths (the inversions of pentatonic thirds). In (*c*), Herbie Hancock uses pentatonic thirds in the fifth chorus of "Eye of the Hurricane," from the album *Maiden Voyage*. (*d*) Pentatonic thirds at the end of the chorus of the Decemberists' "Here I Dreamt I Was an Architect."

being precisely the same size, but its fifths being very slightly impure.[20] Beyond these two alternatives are a variety of other options, such as just intonation and meantone tuning, each enforcing a slightly different compromise between evenness and euphony. The important point is that the scales we have been considering will be interesting no matter which intonational compromise we favor, simply because they divide the octave fairly evenly, while also containing a large number of consonances.[21]

20 Similarly, in the just major scale, six of the seven thirds are acoustically pure, but one of the six perfect fifths is not; alternative tuning schemes redistribute the unevenness differently among the various intervals.

21 In some alternative tuning systems there may be possibilities not considered here. For example, Paul Erlich (personal communication) has pointed out that in 22-tone equal temperament, it is possible to construct scales with five minor thirds and two major thirds.

That so many of them can be played on the ordinary piano keyboard is testimony to the power and flexibility of the twelve-tone equal-tempered system.

4.5 MODULATION AND VOICE LEADING

Figure 4.5.1 presents the transition section from the first movement of Mozart's G major Piano Sonata, K. 283. The first three bars are sequential, transposing the same music up one step at each repetition, while the last three bars contain a second sequence, now transposed up two steps at a time. As the music repeats, the accidentals change: F♮ moves to F♯ in measure 4 and C♮ moves to C♯ in m. 6.

Suppose we ask a naive question: why say that Mozart's music changes scale? Why not say instead that Mozart uses a *nine*-note scale containing all the white notes plus F♯ and C♯? The answer lies in the music's sequential structure: we would like to say that the leaps (D, F), (E, G), and (F♯, A), are two-step scalar intervals, but there can be no scale in which (D, F), (E, G), and (F♯, A) are all two steps apart.[22] Thus, if we wish to claim that the passage is a sequence—the same pattern repeated at different musical levels—we are required to postulate changes in the underlying scale.

In fact, we are forced to postulate *specific voice leadings* between scales. This is because the sequence of scalar intervals will be preserved only if we assert that the F moves *up by semitone* to the F♯, and the C♮ moves *up by semitone* to C♯. To see why, look at the last six notes in the fourth bar of the example, D-F-E-G-F♯-A. Presumably, we would like to say that the music here consists in a repeating "up two, down one" pattern. But if this is right, then the F♮ and F♯ must occupy the same

Figure 4.5.1 (*a*) The transition from the first movement of Mozart's G major Piano Sonata, K. 283. (*b*) The passage involves two voice leadings between scales.

22 Such a scale would have to contain E, F, F♯, and G, in which case the interval E-G would be at least three scale steps large.

abstract position: the note F♮ is one step above E, the note F♯ is one step below G, and the distance E-G is two scale steps. The only way these facts are consistent is if the scale degree that used to be located at F has somehow moved to F♯—or in other words, if there has been a voice leading between scales.

We conclude that a piece's *scalar* structure can determine specific voice leadings between its *macroharmonies*. It is our desire to analyze the music using scale steps, and in particular to do justice to its sequential structure, that requires us to postulate specific scalar voice leadings. I find it useful here to imagine a frog hopping in a regular way around a gently drifting circle of lily pads—say, forward by two lily pads, back by one lily pad, forward by two, back by one, and so on (Figure 4.5.2). As the frog hops, the fourth lily pad moves into a new position, with the others remaining fixed. Clearly, to describe the frog's motion perspicuously, we need to measure in units of lily pads. (It would be somewhat odd to describe it as hopping forward by 10 centimeters, backward by 3 centimeters, and so on, oblivious to the fact that the size of its jumps is determined by the position of the pads!) But we also need to take into account the fact that the lily pads are themselves shifting: the phrase "lily pad #3" acts as a kind of variable that can refer to various locations in physical space.[23] In much the same way, we often want to analyze music using scale steps even while the scales themselves are changing. In these contexts a scale degree is a kind of abstract address ("the musical location one step above E and one step below G") that can point to a variety of different chromatic locations (such as F♮ or F♯).[24]

We can now see that traditional modulation is typically a two-stage business. Modulation is often initiated by voice leading between scales—the fourth degree gets raised by semitone, the leading tone gets lowered, and so on (Figure 4.5.3). This change of scale permits the introduction of the new key's V^7 chord, setting the stage

Figure 4.5.2 A frog, hopping along a circle of gently shifting lily pads.

23 The idea of a scale degree as pointer is captured by Agmon's two-dimensional model of the diatonic system (Agmon 1989), which plays a role in forthcoming work by Steven Rings.

24 Some music uses variable scale degrees that can come in multiple forms. For example, the seventh scale degree in classical minor-key music can occur either as a raised leading tone or as a lowered subtonic. Here, it is as if the lily pads were moving much more rapidly, with the abstract address "seventh scale degree" shifting from leading tone to flatted seventh on a measure-by-measure (or even beat-by-beat) basis. Unfortunately, it would take us too far afield to consider flexible scale degrees in more detail.

Figure 4.5.3 (*a*) Classical modulation as a two-stage process. Here a modulation from A major to E major, in which the scale shifts before the tonal center (represented by the boxed note). Thus we first change D to D♯ and then shift the tonic (boxed) note from A to E. (*b*) In twentieth-century tonality, one frequently finds a change of scale without a change of tonal center. For example, The Who's "I Can't Explain" moves from E mixolydian in the verse to E major in the chorus; here the tonal center stays fixed while D moves to D♯.

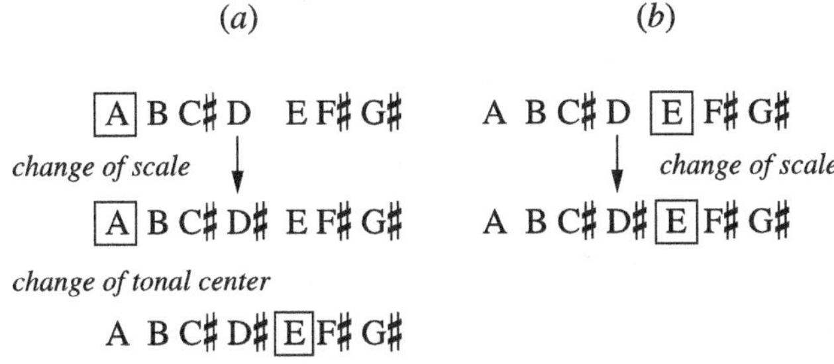

for a shift in the tonal center. Thus, in the typical modulation from tonic to dominant, the raising of the fourth scale degree occurs *prior* to the conclusion of the V^7–I cadence in the new key. (In fact, it sometimes takes a while for our ears to be convinced that the scale shift represents a genuine change in tonic, rather than a passing melodic inflection.) In classical music, shifts between parallel keys (such as C major and C minor) are unique insofar as they do not involve any change of tonic. But in twentieth-century tonality, we encounter a much wider range of tonic-preserving modulations, including all the shifts between parallel diatonic modes.

It is important to understand that the points I have been making do not depend in any way on notation. The question is about conceptualizing music in terms of scalar distances, and this does not require that the music be notated at all—in the case of our Mozart example, it merely requires that it be useful to conceptualize the distances F-A and F♯-A as *thirds,* and hence to infer that the note F has *moved to* F♯. Nevertheless, notation can often help us determine voice-leading relationships among scales. Suppose we imagine that the seven letter names A–G represent distinct musical voices, so that there is an "A" voice, a "B" voice, and so on. Accidentals can then be taken to indicate how the letter-voices move: thus when Mozart replaces F♮ with F♯, he signals that the "F voice" has moved up by semitone to F♯. In other words, standard musical notation faithfully reflects the fact that the first modulation in Figure 4.5.1 occurs by way of the voice leading (C, D, E, F, G, A, B)→(C, D, E, F♯, G, A, B), while the second occurs by way of (C, D, E, F♯, G, A, B)→(C♯, D, E, F♯, G, A, B).

Of course, scalar voice leading can occur in nonmodulatory contexts as well. Consider, for example, the passages in Figure 4.5.4. In the first, the notation suggests that the G in a B♭ major scale moves down to G♭, creating B♭ harmonic major, while in the second it suggests that F moves up to F♯, producing G harmonic minor. We can experience this difference without musical notation: for instance, an improvising musician might play the diminished chord in Figure 4.5.4a, anticipating a continuation whereby the G♭ moves downward to F, while on another occasion the same

Figure 4.5.4 Spelling often indicates a difference in musical function. Here, the chord {A, C, E♭, G♭} would typically lead back to a B♭ major triad, while {A, C, E♭, F♯} would lead to G minor. Spelling can be interpreted as indicating specific voice leadings between scales.

improviser might play the same chord anticipating a continuation where the F♯ rises to G. Our musical expectations are powerful enough that the same chord can even sound different in these two contexts. (Certainly, when imagining the passages in my head I experience them quite differently.) Here again, notation can clarify matters, even though the actual phenomena do not depend on notation itself.

4.6 VOICE LEADING BETWEEN COMMON SCALES

In twelve-tone equal temperament, the four most even seven-note scales are the diatonic, acoustic, harmonic minor, and harmonic major. Consequently, their voice-leading relations are modeled by one of the lattices described in §3.11 and repeated here as Figure 4.6.1.[25] As mentioned earlier, the diatonic circle of fifths zigzags three-dimensionally through the center of the figure, moving successively up, right, and into the paper. It turns out that the remaining scales are also linked by a chain of single-semitone voice leadings. For instance, beginning with A harmonic major, we find

A harmonic major→A harmonic minor→D acoustic→E harmonic major→E harmonic minor → A acoustic →....

This is a second "circle of fifths" whose unit of sequential repetition is three scales long. These scales wind their way around the diatonic circle, somewhat in the manner of a double helix. However, the two strands are not quite the same shape: where the diatonic circle takes a right-angled turn after every step, the nondiatonic strand moves in a straight line through each acoustic collection.

25 In twelve-tone non-equal-tempered contexts, we would find similar lattices whose vertices are minutely displaced.

Figure 4.6.1 Voice leadings among seven-note scales. The diatonic circle of fifths (dark solid line) starts at C diatonic (lower left front), while the nondiatonic circle (dashed line) starts at G acoustic (lower right front).

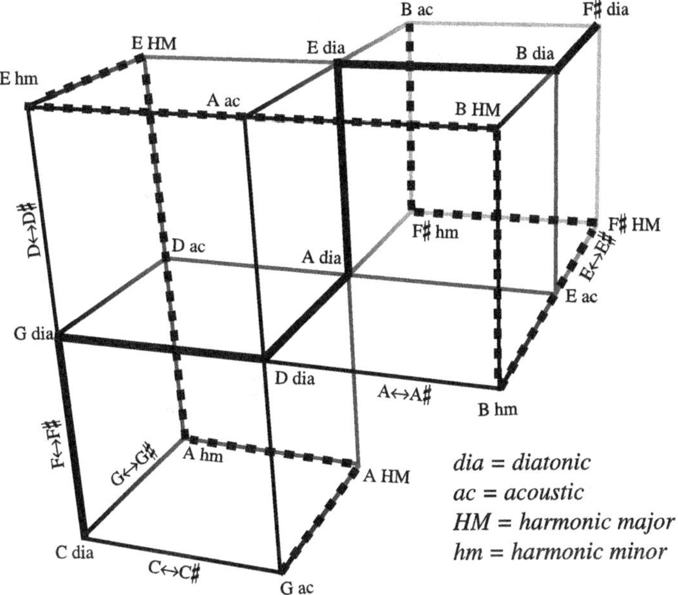

The harmonic and acoustic scales are closely related to the transpositionally symmetrical whole-tone, hexatonic, and octatonic scales. Figure 4.6.2 shows that we can change whole tone into acoustic by a voice leading in which a single pitch class "splits" into its chromatic neighbors; because of the whole-tone scale's sixfold transpositional symmetry, there are six possible acoustic scales that can be reached in this way.[26] Similarly, octatonic can be transformed into acoustic by the reverse process—a transformation in which a major second "merges" into its central note. (Again, since the octatonic scale is transpositionally symmetrical, there are four ways to "merge" into an acoustic collection.) Octatonic can move to harmonic major or minor by a more complicated process of "merging": here, we fuse three notes spanning a minor third, producing the minor second in the center of the span—for instance, {C♯, D♯, E} becomes {D, E♭}, transforming C octatonic into G harmonic minor. (There are eight such possibilities for every octatonic scale, four leading to harmonic major and four leading to harmonic minor.) Finally, the hexatonic can be transformed into harmonic major or minor by the reverse process: here, a minor second such as {G♯, A} splits to become a three-note scale fragment whose outer notes span it, such as {G, A♭, B♭}. There are six such possibilities for every hexatonic scale, three leading to harmonic major and three leading to harmonic minor.

26 Callender (1998) uses the words "split" and "fuse" to refer to these "non-bijective" voice leadings (§4.9). Related discussions of scale-to-scale voice leading (though not always using those terms) can be found in Perle 1984, Taruskin 1996, Howat 1983, Antokoletz 1993, and Tymoczko 2004.

Figure 4.6.2 (*a*) To transform a whole-tone scale into an acoustic, "split" one note into its two chromatic neighbors. (*b*) To transform an octatonic scale into an acoustic, "merge" a major second into the note at its center. (*c*) To transform an octatonic scale into a harmonic major or minor, "merge" three notes spanning a minor third into the semitone they enclose. (*d*) To transform a hexatonic collection into a harmonic major or minor, "split" a semitone into a three-note scale-fragment enclosing it.

Figure 4.6.3 describes these relationships using an inverted pyramid, with the three transpositionally symmetrical scales on the top line. The middle line contains the nondiatonic seven-note scales, while the diatonic scale is at the bottom. Scales are connected by line segments if they can be linked by particularly efficient voice leading: either a "split" or "merge" described in the preceding paragraph, or one of the single-semitone voice leadings represented on Figure 4.6.1. The numbers above each line indicate the presence of multiple possibilities for that particular kind of voice leading. Thus the notation "←6" on the line connecting whole tone to acoustic indicates that there are six different ways to "split" a note of the whole-tone scale, creating six different acoustic collections. By contrast, "1→" points in the opposite direction, because for any particular acoustic scale there is only one way to "merge" its notes to create a whole-tone collection.

The table in Figure 4.6.4 shows how the nondiatonic seven-note collections can be used to connect transpositionally symmetrical scales. Every scale shares six of its seven notes with the octatonic scale to its left, and five of six notes with the whole-tone or hexatonic scale above it. (For example, G acoustic and D♭ acoustic share six notes with C♯-D octatonic and five notes with D♭ whole tone.) In addition, each seven-note scale shares six of its notes with some diatonic collection. Figure 4.6.5 tries to convey the same information graphically: the central core features the full cycle of 36 seven-note nondiatonic scales, each linked to its neighbors by single-semitone voice leading. On the outside of this central circle runs the diatonic circle of fifths; another can be found within the central circle. (Here, the double-headed arrows connect scales sharing six of their seven notes: the A harmonic major collection, for example, shares six notes with A diatonic; while the next collection along the non-diatonic

Figure 4.6.3 Voice leadings among familiar scales. The transpositionally symmetrical scales are at the top. The harmonic and acoustic scales mediate between these and the diatonic. The numbers indicate how many scales of each type can be connected by the voice leadings described in Figures 4.6.1 and 4.6.2. Thus the whole-tone scale can be connected to six different acoustic scales by a "split," while every acoustic scale can be connected to only one whole-tone scale by a "merge."

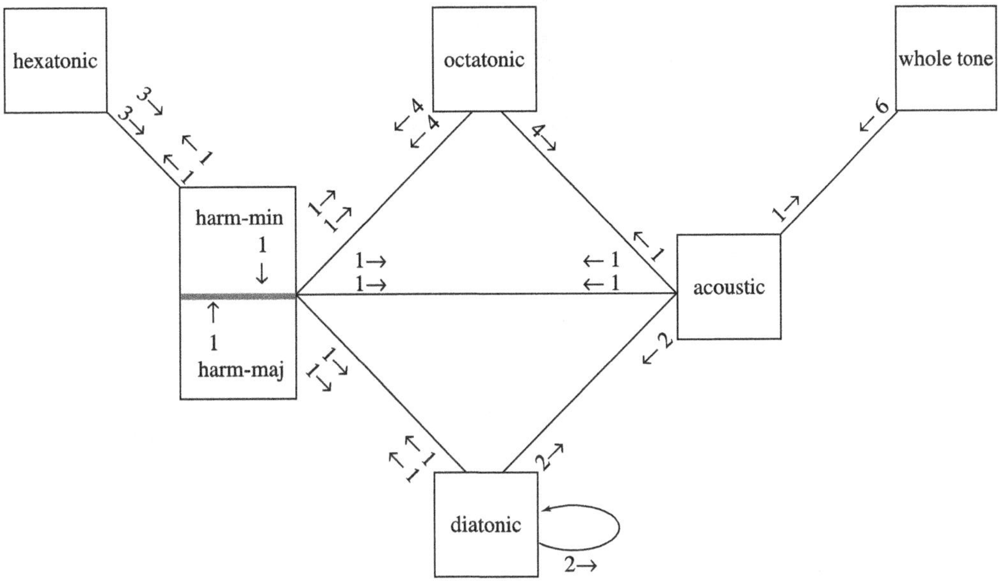

circle, A harmonic minor, shares six notes with C diatonic.) The labels along the central circle indicate the nearest octatonic, whole-tone, and hexatonic scales. This exotic and almost alchemistical graph provides a way to visualize all the voice leadings we have been discussing. I encourage you to verify that Figures 4.6.1, 4.6.3, and 4.6.5 provide different perspectives on the same basic relationships.

Figure 4.6.4 Each scale in the table shares six of its seven notes with the octatonic scale to its left, and contains five of the six notes in the whole-tone or hexatonic scale above it.

	C wt	**D♭ wt**	**C-D♭ hex**	**C♯-D hex**	**D-E♭ hex**	**D♯-E hex**
C-D♭ oct	C ac	E♭ ac	D♭ hm	B♭ hm	G hm	E hm
	F♯ ac	A ac	F HM	D HM	B HM	A♭ HM
C♯-D oct	E ac	D♭ ac	F hm	D hm	B hm	A♭ hm
	B♭ ac	G ac	A HM	F♯ HM	E♭ HM	C HM
D-E♭ oct	D ac	F ac	A hm	F♯ hm	E♭ hm	C hm
	A♭ ac	B ac	C♯ HM	B♭ HM	G HM	E HM

Figure 4.6.5 A geometrical representation of the voice leading between diatonic, acoustic, harmonic major/minor, whole-tone, hexatonic, and octatonic scales. Here "wt 1" and "wt 2" refer to the C♯ and D whole tone scales, respectively; "oct 1," "oct 2," and "oct 3" refer to the C♯-D, D-E♭, and D♯-E octatonic scales; and "hex 1," "hex 2," "hex 3," and "hex 4" refer to the C♯-D, D-E♭, D♯-E, and E-F hexatonic scales.

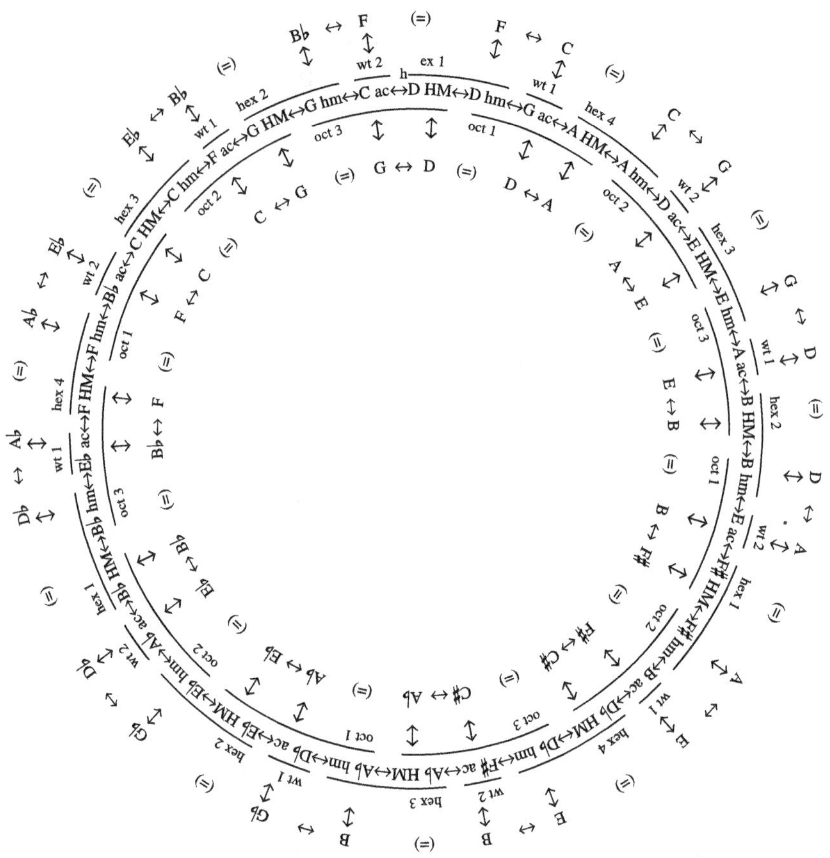

4.7 TWO EXAMPLES

The previous section placed the acoustic and harmonic scales *between* the diatonic and the transpositionally symmetrical scales, since each shares six notes with some diatonic collection, while also being very close to some octatonic, whole-tone, and hexatonic collections. (This is represented by the fact that the harmonic and acoustic scales occupy the central line of the inverted pyramid in Figure 4.6.3.) And in fact, twentieth-century composers often use acoustic and harmonic collections to mediate between these different harmonic worlds. For example, at the end of the central section of "Mouvement," Debussy moves from F♯ mixolydian to C whole tone by way of the E acoustic scale (Figure 4.7.1). This acoustic collection is as close as possible to the other two, sharing five of the whole-tone scale's six notes, and six of the diatonic scale's seven notes. In this way, Debussy creates a smooth transition from familiar diatonic modality to the much more exotic world of the whole-tone scale. This was one of

Figure 4.7.1 At the end of the B section of *Mouvement,* Debussy moves from F♯ mixolydian to the C whole tone by way of the F♯ mode of E acoustic.

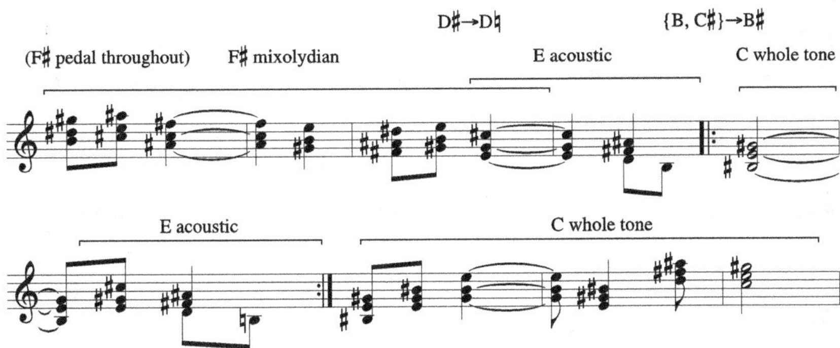

his favorite compositional techniques, with similar progressions appearing repeatedly throughout his works.[27]

For a more complicated example, consider "Sunlight Streaming in the Chamber," the first of Prokofiev's 1916 *Five Poems of Anna Akhmatova* (Figure 4.7.2). The music begins with a repeating figure that echoes the opening of Stravinsky's *Petrouchka,* composed just a few years earlier. I interpret the underlying harmony here as an E major triad, which can be connected to the following C major by semitonal voice leading. C major then initiates a stepwise descent through B minor, A major, G major, and F♯ major, each generating familiar scales. The music then shifts suddenly to C diatonic, moving toward a half cadence on an F♯ half-diminished seventh. The second half of the song begins by alternating between E minor (with added C) and A^9 chord (with G in the bass), vaguely suggesting ii–V in D major. The piece then shifts to D acoustic (A melodic minor) for six measures, ending with a turn to C-D♭ octatonic. This is the first appearance of the octatonic scale in the piece and it has a somewhat surprising effect, giving the impression of a question mark or raised eyebrow rather than an exclamation point.

Figure 4.7.3 graphs Prokofiev's scales using the two-dimensional scale lattice of Figure 3.11.8. The diatonic and acoustic collections form a compact region of the graph: the four diatonic collections (C, G, D, and A) are all adjacent on the zigzag of fifths, with the two acoustic collections (D and E) connected to these scales by single-semitone voice leading.[28] Although the music does not always exploit these connections, there are a number of transitions that do so. (For instance, the move from B melodic minor to A diatonic, or the progression from C diatonic to G diatonic to D diatonic.) Overall, there are six shifts involving single-semitone voice leading, five or six two-semitone shifts, one or two three-semitone shifts, and one four-semitone shift (Figure 4.7.4). It is interesting that the more dramatic shifts occur at the beginning and end of the song, with the smoother motions concentrated in the middle.

27 See Chapter 9 and Tymoczko 2004.

28 Note that I am considering the opening to be in E mixolydian rather than E major; if one wishes to assert the presence of E major, then there are five diatonic collections in the piece.

Figure 4.7.2 An outline of Prokofiev's Op. 27 No. 1.

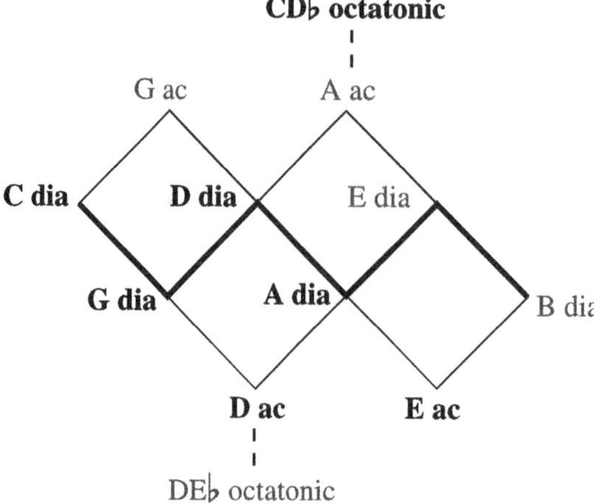

Figure 4.7.3 The scales in Prokofiev's piece form a connected region.

E/A dia	2/3
G dia	3
E ac	1
A dia	1
D dia	2
E ac	2
D dia	2
E ac	2
C dia	1
G dia	1
D dia	1
G dia	1
D dia	2
D ac	4
CD♭ oct	

Figure 4.7.4 Prokofiev typically modulates by relatively efficient voice leading, with the most dramatic changes occurring at the beginning and end of the piece. Here, the numbers refer to the total number of semitonal shifts required to connect each scale to its successor: thus, the number "3" in the second line indicates that it takes 3 semitonal shifts (G→G♯, A→A♯, C→C♯) to change G diatonic into E acoustic.

The final modulation deserves some comment. Had Prokofiev wanted to create a smooth transition from the antepenultimate D diatonic scale to the concluding CD♭ octatonic, he could have done so, since both scales share almost all their notes with A acoustic. (See Figure 4.7.3, where this is obvious.) However, the penultimate acoustic collection does *not* share a large number of notes with the final octatonic scale. (It does however share five notes with the preceding D diatonic.) Nevertheless, this D acoustic scale still has audible links to both the diatonic and octatonic scales, since it is "nearly transpositionally related" to both (§2.8). In other words, the mediation here is one of internal intervallic structure rather than particular common tones: Figure 4.7.5 shows that the acoustic scale shares the step-interval sequence 2-1-2-2-2 with the diatonic and the sequence 2-1-2-1-2 with the octatonic. Consequently, the piece articulates a gradual transition at the level of interval content, with the acoustic scale containing more tritones than the diatonic, but fewer than the octatonic, fewer fifths than the diatonic, but as many as the octatonic, and so on.[29]

Overall, Prokofiev's music suggests a somewhat loose and playful structure—the sense is of a relatively intuitive use of closely related scales, rather than a more logical or systematic exploration. Nevertheless, it is significant that he uses closely related scales that *can be* linked by efficient voice leading, and that he often modulates so as to highlight these connections. It is also relevant that his scalar vocabulary consists entirely of scales we have discussed, suggesting that our abstract, scale-theoretic considerations do indeed capture his actual concerns. Chapter 9 continues this line of argument, demonstrating that the techniques we have identified

29 This sort of transition occurs frequently in twentieth-century music, for instance at the opening of Debussy's "Fêtes" (the second of the *Nocturnes*) and the third of Prokofiev's *Ten Pieces*, Op. 12.

Figure 4.7.5 In Prokofiev's piece the acoustic scale mediates between diatonic and octatonic in a somewhat abstract way. On the left side of (*a*) we see that the A acoustic scale can mediate between D diatonic and the C-D♭ octatonic, sharing almost all of its notes with both collections. However, the right side of (*a*) shows that Prokofiev presents the D acoustic scale instead. (*b*) When we consider intervallic structure, we see that the acoustic is similar to both diatonic and octatonic, sharing step patterns 2-1-2-1-2 with the octatonic and 2-1-2-2-2 with the diatonic.

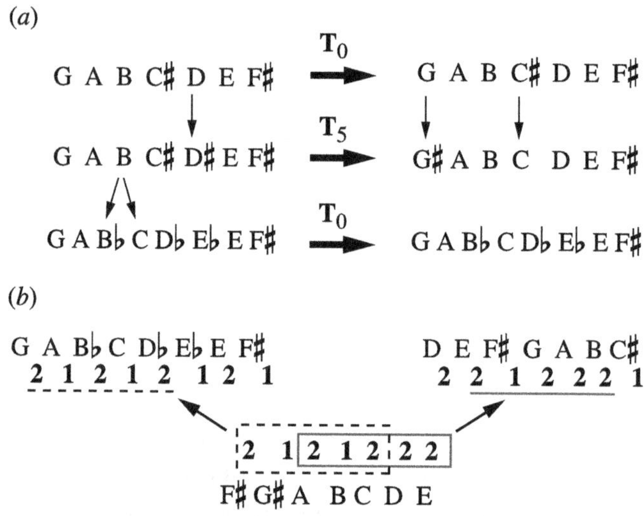

here are symptomatic of a much more general practice stretching from late nineteenth-century tonality to contemporary jazz and postminimalism.

4.8 SCALAR AND INTERSCALAR TRANSPOSITION

Figure 4.8.1 shows two appearances of the subject of Shostakovich's Fugue in E minor, one in E aeolian, and the other in G mixolydian.[30] The two forms of the subject are related by a double process of transposition: a *scalar* transposition downward by diatonic step, from aeolian to mixolydian, combined with *chromatic* transposition upward by five semitones, from G diatonic to C diatonic (Figure 4.8.2). Though this combination of scalar and chromatic transposition can occasionally be found in earlier centuries, it plays a central role in twentieth-century tonal composition, particularly in the works of composers such as Debussy, Ravel, Stravinsky, Shostakovich, Steve Reich, and John Adams. By way of illustration, Figure 4.8.3 cites rehearsal 13 of Debussy's "Fêtes," where scalar transposition upward by two steps combines with

30 The theme itself does not contain the aeolian mode's F♯. However, it is present both in the key signature and the countersubject.

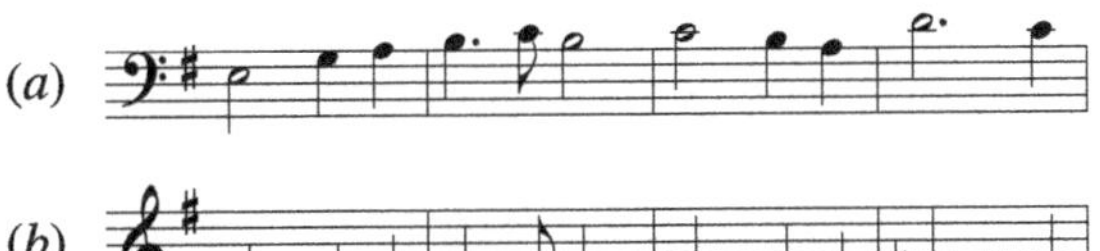

Figure 4.8.1 The subject in Shostakovich's Fugue in E minor, Op. 87 No. 4, as it appears at the opening of the piece and in m. 22.

Figure 4.8.2 The two forms of the subject relate by scalar and chromatic transposition.

Figure 4.8.3 Rehearsal 13 of Debussy's "Fêtes" (*Nocturnes* II).

chromatic transposition downward by three steps. The resulting voice leading shifts A♭ dorian into A♭ lydian, raising G♭, C♭, and D♭.

Note that these two kinds of transposition can sometimes combine to produce a simple change of accidentals, as in the opening of the Rondo from Clementi's Piano Sonata, Op. 25 No. 2 (Figure 4.8.4). The theme, which originally begins on scale degree 5 in G major, returns on scale degree 1 of D major, with C♯ replacing C♮. Though one could say that Clementi simply moved the note C♮ up by semitone, it is also possible to describe the relationship as combining two separate transpositions: scalar transposition *down* by four scale degrees followed by chromatic transposition *up* seven semitones. These two transpositions nearly cancel each other out, leaving behind the single-semitone shift C→C♯ as a residue. As we will see, there

Figure 4.8.4 The D-major theme in the Rondo from Clementi's Piano Sonata, Op. 25 No. 2, originally begins on scale degree 5 in G major, but returns in the transition with C♮ replaced by C♯. The two forms of the theme can be related by a combination of scalar and chromatic transposition.

are a number of musical circumstances in which it is profitable to think in precisely this way.

If scalar transposition moves a musical pattern along a single scale, then a slightly more general process of "interscalar transposition" moves a pattern *from one scale to another.*[31] Figure 4.8.5 tracks the main motive of Bach's D minor invention as it moves from D harmonic minor scale to F major and D melodic minor ascending (G acoustic). Although the scale changes, each form of the motive uses precisely the same set of scalar intervals. In fact, if we label the notes of D harmonic minor and F major in the standard way, we can use the very same scale degree numbers to describe the first two passages in the figure. In this sense, we can say that they are related by *zero-step interscalar transposition*. Similarly, if we label the degrees of D melodic minor starting from D, then Figure 4.8.5a relates to (*c*) by *two-step* interscalar transposition—meaning that each note of Figure 4.8.5c is two scale degrees higher than the corresponding note of Figure 4.8.5a. Of course, the number of steps involved in an interscalar transposition depends on our arbitrary choice of the first scale degree. What is important is the fact that two passages are related by interscalar transposition, not the particular label we apply to the relationship.

Figure 4.8.5 Three forms of the motive in Bach's D minor two-part invention. Scale degrees are shown above each example.

31 See Santa 1999 and Hook 2007a. Hook (2007b and 2008) and Tymoczko (2005) explore the relation between key signatures and interscalar transpositions.

Figure 4.8.6 identifies interscalar transpositions in Debussy, Stravinsky, and Shostakovich. The first two examples involve interscalar transposition from the diatonic scale to the acoustic. The third is interesting insofar as its "scales" are simple triads. (This is the gimmick of Shostakovich's A major fugue; it is a "bugle fugue" that treats triads as if they were scales.) Thus in Figure 4.8.6c, the main theme originally appears in the A major triad (top line); when it returns in minor, at m. 21, it has moved to a new three-note scale, F♯ minor. This is interscalar transposition by zero steps (middle line). Eventually, in the stretto, the theme is transposed diatonically along the A major scale (bottom line). Thus the bottom two lines of Figure 4.8.6c are connected by descending-step interscalar transposition.[32]

Figure 4.8.6 Interscalar transposition in the opening of Debussy's "Fêtes" (*a*), Stravinsky's *Rite of Spring* (*b*), and Shostakovich's A major fugue (*c*).

32 Transposing (C♯, A, F♯) down by step produces (A, F♯, C♯). A zero step interscalar transposition takes (A, F♯, C♯)—or "third, root, fifth" in the minor triad—to (C♯, A, E), or "third, root, fifth" in the major triad.

One terminological point: the previous examples describe what might be called "interscalar transpositions in pitch-class space," since they link octave-repeating scales with the same number of notes. There is an even more general musical transformation that relates scales of different sizes, which we can call "interscalar transposition in *pitch space*." Figure 4.8.7 presents examples from Debussy and Steve Reich. These transformations introduce octave-dependent changes into the music: for example, the D5 in the top line of Figure 4.8.7a gets mapped to C, whereas the D4 gets mapped to B♭. Consequently, we cannot speak of "what happens to the pitch class D"; instead, we need to speak about what happens to specific pitches in specific registers. By contrast, when the scales have the same number of notes, then all pitches in a pitch class are transformed in exactly the same way. (For example, the interscalar transposition in Figure 4.8.6a moves every D up by three semitones.) This in turn means that these interscalar transpositions can be modeled as voice leadings between pitch-class sets. This is precisely why they will be important in what follows.

Figure 4.8.7 (*a*) "Fêtes" presents the same pattern of scalar intervals in the seven-note dorian mode and the six-note whole-tone scale. (*b*) Steve Reich's *Variations for Winds, Strings, and Keyboards* presents the same pattern of scalar intervals in the six-note diatonic hexachord and the five-note pentatonic scale.

4.9 INTERSCALAR TRANSPOSITION AND VOICE LEADING

In the final sections of this chapter I want to switch gears somewhat, exploring the connections between scale theory and voice leading. To prepare for this discussion we need to make a subtle conceptual shift: instead of thinking of chords as being embedded within larger scales, we will start to think of them as *scales unto themselves*. In other words, we will think of the C major chord as being a "scale" whose three scale degrees are C, E, and G, respectively. (This is just what we did in discussing Figure 4.8.6c,

Shostakovich's A major fugue.) This will allow us to represent the voice leading (C, E, G)→(B, E, G) as an interscalar transposition that sends the first scale degree of the C major triad to the third scale degree of the E minor triad (C→B), the second scale degree to the first (E→E), and the third scale degree to the second (G→G). Once we start thinking in this way, we will see that there is a deep connection between the notion of an "interscalar transposition" and the general problem of identifying efficient voice leadings between chords.

To understand why, notice that scalar and interscalar transpositions represent a very special kind of voice leading: not only are they free of voice crossings, but they remain so *no matter how their voices are distributed in pitch space.* (For this reason, I will say that they are "strongly crossing free.") For example, the first voice leading in Figure 4.9.1 has no crossings no matter how we change the register of its individual voices. By contrast, the second voice leading is only *weakly* crossing free, since transposing its lowest voice up by an octave creates a crossing between the bottom two voices. Given a strongly crossing-free voice leading, we can always arrange its voices so that each chord spans less than an octave, with ascending steps in one chord being sent to ascending steps in the other (Figure 4.9.2).[33] But this in turn implies that the voice leading is a scalar or interscalar transposition, since it sends any scalar interval in the first chord to the same scalar interval in the second.

Figure 4.9.1 The voice leading in (*a*) is strongly crossing free: no matter what octave its voices are in, there will never be crossing. The voice leading in (*b*) is crossing free but not strongly so, since a crossing is created when the lowest voice moves up by octave (*c*).

Figure 4.9.2 In a strongly crossing-free voice leading, the voices can be transposed by octave so that each chord is in "close registral position," spanning less than an octave. Ascending steps in one collection are sent to ascending steps in the other.

The connection to voice leading lies precisely here: in §2.7, we saw that, for any "reasonable" measure of voice-leading size, removing voice crossings never makes the voice leading larger. (See also Appendix A.) This means that we can take any voice leading and, by repeatedly removing voice crossings and changing the octave in which voices appear, eventually produce a scalar or interscalar transposition. Since octave shifts don't affect the voice leading, and since removing crossings never makes it larger, the final voice leading is guaranteed to be at least as small as the original (Figure 4.9.3). Consequently, there is always a maximally efficient voice leading between

33 Conversely, any voice leading that can be arranged in this way is an interscalar transposition.

Figure 4.9.3 Repeatedly octave-transposing and removing crossings will eventually produce a strongly crossing-free voice leading. (*a*) Transposing the bass voice up by octave produces a crossing (*b*). Switching the bass and tenor in the first chord removes the crossing (*c*). Transposing the tenor up by octave produces another crossing (*d*). Switching soprano and alto in the first chord removes this crossing (*e*), yielding a strongly crossing-free voice leading. Since removing crossings never makes a voice leading larger, the voice leading in (*e*) is at least as small as that in (*a*).

any two chords that is a scalar or interscalar transposition.[34] It follows that the concept of interscalar transposition will be relevant wherever efficient voice leading is important.

Let me illustrate with a few concrete examples. Figure 4.9.4 identifies the minimal voice leading between C major and A minor triads. If we consider each triad to be a scale, with root, third, and fifth being its first, second, and third scale degrees, then the voice leading is an interscalar transposition by one ascending step.[35] Similarly, the most efficient voice leading between the C major and C minor triads is an interscalar transposition by zero steps (root to root). The figure also shows that the most efficient voice leading between C^{ø7} and E♭^{7} chords is an interscalar transposition by three steps (root to seventh), and the most efficient voice leading between F diatonic and G acoustic scales is an interscalar transposition by one descending step (scale degree one to scale degree seven).[36] Geometrically, interscalar transpositions can be represented as collections of crossing-free paths between two concentric circles, as in Figure 4.9.5. Appendix A shows that these voice leadings correspond to paths that do not "bounce off" the mirror boundaries of higher-dimensional chord space.

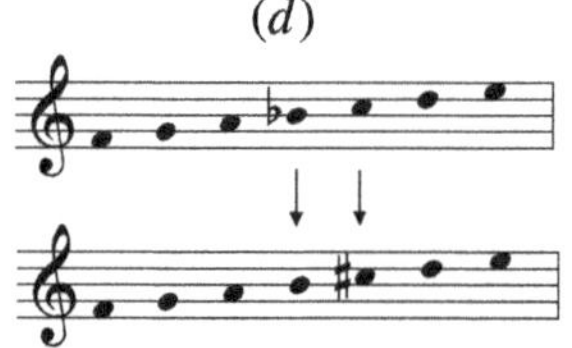

Figure 4.9.4 The minimal voice leading between C major and A minor triads (*a*), between C major and C minor triads (*b*), between C^{ø7} and E♭^{7} chords (*c*), and between F diatonic and G acoustic scales (*d*). All are interscalar transpositions.

34 Here and for the remainder of this section, I use "voice leading" to mean "voice leading without doublings, in which every note in one chord is mapped to exactly one note in the other." Mathematically, these are called *bijective* voice leadings. We will return to the issue of doublings at the end of the section.

35 Here and in what follows, I always consider the root of a traditional chord to be its first scale degree.

36 Considering G to be the first scale degree of the G acoustic collection. If we consider the scale to be D melodic minor and number its scale degrees from D, then the relevant interscalar transposition is two ascending steps.

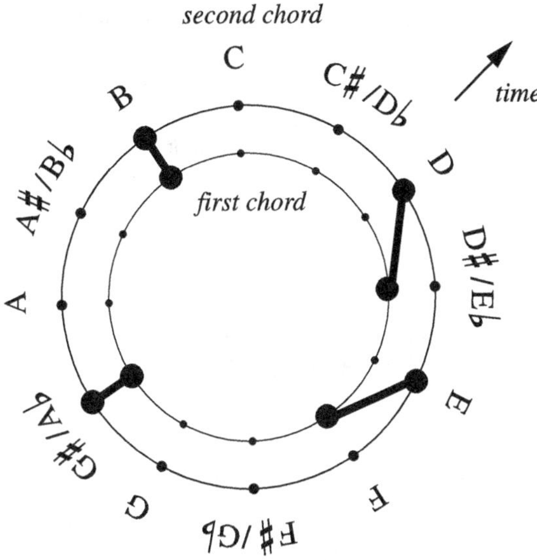

Figure 4.9.5 Strongly crossing-free voice leadings can be represented geometrically by non-intersecting paths connecting two concentric circles. Here the music progresses radially outward, from the inner circle to the outer. The voice leading (F, G♯, B, D♯)→(E, G♯, B, D) holds G♯ and B constant, moving F and D♯ down by semitone.

Throughout this book I have emphasized that Western music involves the simultaneous satisfaction of two independent constraints—a vertical constraint that requires chords to be structurally similar, and a horizontal constraint that dictates that they be connected by efficient voice leadings. Clearly, to satisfy these constraints, a composer must be able to *find* the efficient voice leadings between arbitrary chords. This need is all the more pressing when we reflect that composers regularly ask questions that require sorting through a large number of possibilities. Suppose, for example, you write the chord in Figure 4.9.6, and decide to move it to some nearby dominant seventh; to solve this problem, it is (in principle) necessary to search 288 different voice leadings to all twelve dominant sevenths. It is rather remarkable, therefore, that composers, theorists, and even beginning music students manage to find efficient voice leadings so quickly, and with so little apparent effort.

Our discussion helps explain how this can be possible. Rather than searching *all* the different voice leadings between chords, musicians need consider only the small number of interscalar transpositions. For example, if you want to find a minimal voice leading between the C half-diminished and F dominant seventh chords, it is sufficient to consider the four interscalar transpositions shown in Figure 4.9.7—mapping the root of the half-diminished to the root, third, fifth, and seventh of the dominant seventh chord, respectively. This reduces the number of potential voice leadings by a factor of six, from twenty-four down to four. (For larger chords the reduction of effort is even more

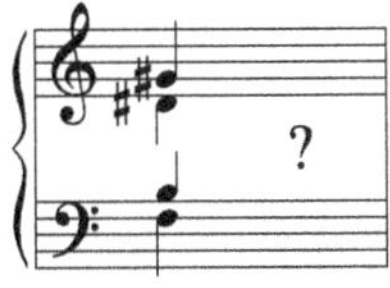

Figure 4.9.6 Suppose a composer decides to connect this F half-diminished seventh chord to some dominant seventh chord by maximally efficient voice leading. There are almost three hundred possible voice leadings to consider. Yet musicians manage to solve problems like this very quickly.

Figure 4.9.7 In order to find the minimal voice leading between two chords, it is necessary to check only the interscalar transpositions between them. Here, the first interscalar transposition maps the root of $C^{ø7}$ to the root of F^7, the second maps root to third, the third maps root to fifth, and the fourth maps root to seventh. Having chosen a destination for the root, the rest of the voice leading is completely determined by the fact that it is an interscalar transposition.

dramatic.) Thus when harmony teachers enjoin their students to avoid voice crossings, they are actually achieving two distinct aims: they are encouraging a kind of composition in which the voices remain registrally separate, and hence easy to distinguish aurally, while also drastically reducing the "search space" that students must consider when looking for efficient voice leadings. This last point, though rarely discussed, is arguably central to the whole enterprise of Western composition: for if "crossed" voice leadings could be smaller than their uncrossed counterparts, it would be enormously more difficult to combine harmonic consistency with efficient voice leading—simply because it would be very hard to sort through all the voice-leading possibilities.

It follows that there are both *perceptual* and *conceptual* reasons to expect that voice crossings should be infrequent, since crossings make life difficult for both listener and composer. And when we look at actual music we find that voice crossings are indeed rare, occurring only 5% of the time even in the most polyphonic of styles.[37] Furthermore, when they *do* occur it is often profitable to interpret them as embellishments of more basic, crossing-free paradigms. For example, the opening of Palestrina's motet "Adoramus Te," shown in Figure 4.9.8, can plausibly be said to be based on crossing-free voice leadings in the bottom staff—with the crossing not only serving to add melodic interest, but also allowing Palestrina to evade the parallel fifths and octaves that would otherwise occur.[38] (Notice that in this passage the top three voices typically articulate voice leadings between complete triads, with the bass adding doublings—a technique that we will explore later.) Chapters 6 and 7 will generalize this observation by showing that a large majority of voice leadings, in a large range of music, can be understood as embellishments of a few basic templates, all of which are strongly crossing free. This in turn suggests that composers really do privilege the crossing-free voice leadings, perhaps thinking of voice crossings as surface-level embellishments to be used only on special occasions.

37 The figure "5%," which refers to the percentage of voice leadings containing crossings, is based on a statistical survey of a large number of MIDI files of vocal compositions by fifteenth and sixteenth-century composers. There is some evidence that the rate of voice crossings gradually decreases over this period. Note that some of these voice leadings are only weakly crossing-free.

38 These sorts of voice crossings are quite common in Renaissance music, for example in the opening phrase of Lassus' *Prophetiae Sibyllarum*.

Figure 4.9.8 The opening phrase of Palestrina's "Adoramus Te" can be interpreted as embellishing a fundamentally crossing-free template.

One word of caution: for simplicity, I have been considering voice leadings without doublings, in which the number of voices is equal to the number of notes in each of the two chords. However, it sometimes happens that a minimal voice leading maps multiple notes in the one chord to a single note in the other. For example, the first voice leading in Figure 4.9.9 is smaller than any of the four-voice voice leadings between the C and E major seventh chords. This, clearly, is not an interscalar transposition.[39] Fortunately, in many practical applications, we can ignore this complication, restricting our attention to voice leadings without doublings. (Figure 4.9.10 demonstrates that, for nearly even three- and four-note chords, maximally efficient voice leadings are almost always doubling free.) In the grand scheme of things, this is quite fortunate, for otherwise the composer's task of finding efficient voice leadings would be considerably more difficult than it already is.

Figure 4.9.9 The five-voice voice leading on the left is smaller than any of the four-voice alternatives. Here, three voices move by one semitone, whereas the smallest four-voice alternative moves one voice by three semitones and one voice by one semitone. Voice leadings containing doublings cannot be identified using the techniques discussed in this chapter.

	All Chords	Nearly Even
2 notes	0%	**0%**
3 notes	10%	**1%**
4 notes	29%	**2%**
5 notes	48%	8%
6 notes	61%	19%
7 notes	69%	14%
8 notes	73%	11%

Figure 4.9.10 The probability that the minimal voice leading between two randomly chosen *n*-note chords will involve "doublings," as in Figure 4.9.9. The first column represents the likelihood of doublings when the chords are selected randomly from all pairs of *n*-note chords, while the second represents the likelihood when chords are restricted to the four most even *n*-note chords. Nearly even chords with four or fewer notes thus require doublings only rarely.

39 More precisely, it is not an interscalar transposition between four-note chords; it *is* an interscalar transposition between the five note chords {C, E, E, G, B} and {E, G♯, B, B, D♯}, but it is not obvious how to figure out which notes to double. There exist efficient algorithms for solving this problem, but the details are too technical to discuss here (see Tymoczko 2006 and 2008b).

4.10 COMBINING INTERSCALAR AND CHROMATIC TRANSPOSITIONS

Let me end by showing how scale theory can be used to model the intuitive knowledge possessed by sophisticated tonal composers. To begin, note that the interscalar transpositions linking any transpositions of the same two chord types will always be related by individual transposition. For instance, the scalar transpositions linking the C major triad to itself are individually transpositionally related to the interscalar transpositions linking the C major to the E major triad, and indeed to those connecting any other major triads (Figure 4.10.1). This is because transposition can never introduce voice crossings into a voice leading, even when applied individually.

From this it follows that we can decompose any strongly crossing-free voice leading from C to E major into two parts: a scalar transposition that moves each note down by some number of scale steps (relative to the C major triad) and a chromatic transposition that moves each note up by some number of semitones. This voice leading will be efficient when these two components nearly cancel out—as, for instance, when a one-step descending scalar transposition nearly neutralizes the

Figure 4.10.1 (*a*) The scalar and/or interscalar transpositions between any transpositions of the same two chord types are always individually T-related. (*b*) The minimal voice leading between C and E major triads can therefore be analyzed as the combination of a one-step descending scalar transposition with a four-semitone ascending chromatic transposition. (*c*) More generally, the minimal (three-voice) voice leading between any major triads can be depicted as combining chromatic and scalar transposition. As the chromatic transposition increases, the descending scalar transposition increases as well, so that the two forms of transposition cancel out.

four-semitone ascending chromatic transposition (Figure 4.10.1). In fact, we can produce a similar decomposition of any strongly crossing-free voice leading between *any* two major triads. Again, the voice leadings will be efficient when the two transpositions combine to leave each voice roughly where it was: thus in Figure 4.10.1c the descending scalar transposition increases as the ascending chromatic transposition does.

Figure 4.10.2 uses this idea to organize the efficient voice-leading possibilities between half-diminished and dominant seventh chords. Here, we represent voice leadings between half-diminished and dominant sevenths as combining an *interscalar* transposition (from C half-diminished to C dominant seventh) with a chromatic transposition to some other dominant seventh. Again, there is an inverse relationship between the two transpositions, so that one counteracts the other. Thus we see that *efficient voice leadings occur when scalar or interscalar transpositions neutralize the effects of chromatic transpositions.*

The upshot is that we can provide a surprising and nontrivial answer to what might otherwise seem like a hopeless question: what is it that a composer knows, when she knows all the most efficient voice leadings from one type of chord to another? For example, what does a composer know when she can easily identify the most efficient path between *any* particular half-diminished and dominant seventh chords? Our answer is: *she knows how to combine interscalar and chromatic transpositions.* That is, in the particular case of half-diminished and dominant sevenths, she knows how to combine the four templates in Figure 4.10.2a with the various chromatic transpositions. Thus a seemingly complicated musical skill—knowing *all* the most efficient voice leadings between two chord types—reduces to a much simpler kind of knowledge, knowing how to combine two familiar kinds of transposition.

In the second half of the book, I show how this idea allows us to understand chromatic music "from the inside," revealing some of the remarkable ways in which nineteenth-century composers explored the contrapuntal possibilities available to them. For now, let me simply offer a few hints about what is to come. Figure 4.10.3 analyzes the first four resolutions of the half-diminished seventh chord in the prelude to Wagner's *Tristan,* showing that the first two involve interscalar transposition by zero steps, whereas the last two involve interscalar transposition by ascending step. Besides helping us understand these relationships, scale theory can prompt us to ask new questions: for example, we might find ourselves wondering whether Wagner uses the other two interscalar transpositions in his opera, or whether he ever substitutes one scalar transposition for another. Similarly, Figure 4.10.4 contains a series of progressions that resolve a seventh chord into a triad. Scale theory can show us that the first two voice leadings are closely related, since they map the root of the seventh chord to the root of the triad, whereas the third maps the root to the fifth.[40] Finally, consider the situation of a composer who wants to identify efficient (three-voice) voice leadings from major to minor triads. Having absorbed the ideas in this chapter,

---

40 Here we can conceive of the triad as a four-note scale with one doubled note.

Figure 4.10.2 (*a*) The four interscalar transpositions from the C half-diminished seventh chord to the C dominant seventh. (*b*) The minimal voice leading between the C half-diminished and F dominant seventh chords combines the third of these interscalar transpositions with chromatic transposition upward by five semitones. (*c*) The minimal (four-voice) voice leading between any half-diminished and dominant seventh chords combines one of these interscalar transpositions with a chromatic transposition. Again, as the chromatic transposition increases, the descending interscalar transposition increases as well, so that the two forms of transposition cancel out.

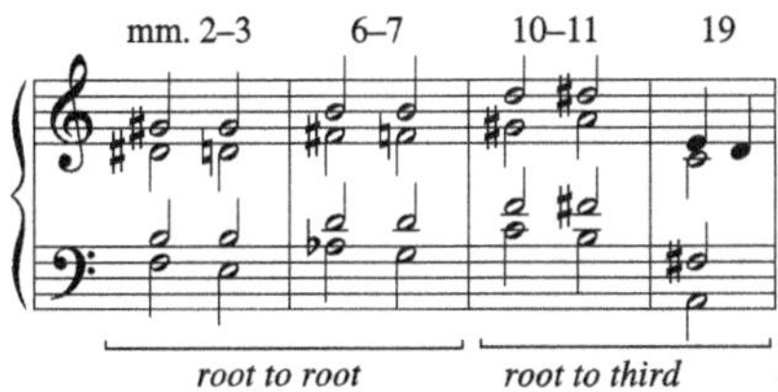

Figure 4.10.3 The first four resolutions of the half-diminished seventh chord in Wagner's *Tristan*. The first two map root to root, while the second two map root to third.

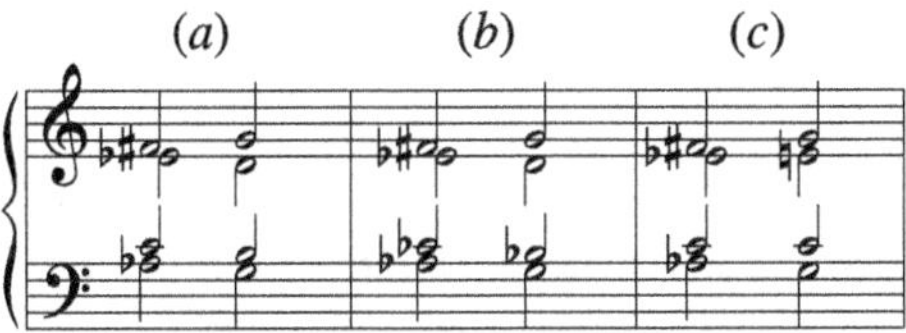

Figure 4.10.4 Three chromatic voice leadings. The first two map the root of the first chord to the root of the second, and can be considered interscalar transpositions from a seventh chord to a triad with doubled root. The last maps the root of the first chord to the fifth of the second.

the composer will see that there are really just three basic possibilities: once the destination of the root is chosen, the rest of the interscalar transposition is determined. Each possibility gives rise to a family of voice leadings, all related by individual transposition and hence sharing the same basic voice-leading structure.

The broader moral is that there is indeed a close connection between chord concepts and scale concepts. Fundamentally, a scale is a large chord, and a chord is just a small scale: both participate in efficient voice leadings, and both can be represented using the same basic geometries; composers develop musical motifs by transposing them along familiar chords, as if chords were just very small scales (Figs. 4.3.1b and 4.8.6c); and efficient voice leading frequently involves interscalar transposition or strongly crossing-free voice leadings. In fact, it even turns out that there is a close analogy between the idea of decomposing voice leadings into scalar and chromatic transpositions, and the idea of analyzing them into pure parallel and pure contrary components. Thus there are significant theoretical advantages to adopting a unified perspective that treats chords and scales similarly.

Those of you who are interested in pursuing this idea in greater technical detail should consult Appendix C, while those who are impatient for analysis can instead turn to Chapters 8 and 9. Everyone else is encouraged to proceed to Chapter 5 in an orderly fashion.

CHAPTER 5

Macroharmony and Centricity

Having discussed harmony, counterpoint, and acoustic consonance, we'll now turn to macroharmony and centricity, the last of the five features. First, we'll explore the ways in which composers might combine harmonic and macroharmonic consistency. Then we'll develop two analytical tools for quantifying macroharmony: *pitch-class circulation graphs,* which record how fast a piece cycles through the pitch classes, and *global macroharmonic profiles,* which represent the relative proportion of large collections in a piece. We'll then introduce *pitch-class profiles* to describe both "local" centricity (or rootedness) and "global" centricity (or tonicity). Together, these tools amount to a "generalized theory of keys" allowing us to conceptualize the possibilities between complete atonality and traditional scale-based tonality.

5.1 MACROHARMONY

When we think about harmony, we automatically think about chords. In fact, we are so fixated on chords that we sometimes forget they tell only part of the story. To counteract this tendency, Figure 5.1.1 uses the same chords to construct two very different sequences: the first, containing twelve triads from the C diatonic scale followed by twelve triads from the F♯ diatonic scale, is placid and restful; the second, alternating between C and F♯ diatonic scales, is considerably more angular and energetic. The difference suggests that musical experience is strongly colored by what we have heard recently: after a number of white notes, a C diatonic triad will sound relatively consonant, while after a sequence of black notes, it will sound more jarring and out of place. It is as if previously heard notes linger in our memory, mixing with what we are currently hearing to create a harmonic penumbra—a "macroharmony" extending beyond the boundaries of the temporal instant.

In thinking about macroharmony we need to ask at least four questions:

1. Does the music articulate identifiable macroharmonies other than the total chromatic?
2. How fast do these macroharmonies change?
3. Are the various macroharmonies in the piece structurally similar—that is, related by transposition or nearly so?
4. Are the macroharmonies consonant or dissonant?

Figure 5.1.1 Two sequences containing the same chords, but in different order. The first sounds considerably less chromatic than the second.

From this point of view, our two sequences are very different. The first is both *macroharmonically consistent* (which is to say that it articulates a pair of diatonic collections, related by transposition) and *macroharmonically consonant* (since those collections are themselves relatively consonant). The second is macroharmonically consistent only in a trivial sense, since it cycles through the complete chromatic collection every two measures or so. More important, it is *macroharmonically dissonant,* because the chromatic scale is itself fairly dissonant. As a result, the second sequence sounds considerably less "tonal" than the first, even though they use exactly the same triads.

Note that our questions echo those we might ask about ordinary harmonies: macroharmonies, like harmonies, can be consonant or dissonant, and sequences of macroharmonies can be harmonically consistent just as chord progressions can. Thus Figure 5.1.2 exhibits a *macroharmonic* transition from mild dissonance to greater consonance and back, somewhat akin to a classical V^7–I–V^7 progression. (To say this is just to repeat the basic point that traditional Western music uses similar techniques on different time scales.) In fact, in some twentieth-century music macroharmony becomes the primary bearer of harmonic significance. Mechanical, repetitive, or random chord changes can create a sonic "wash" in which changes in macroharmony become more salient than the individual chords. Listening to Debussy's "Voiles," Stravinsky's "Dance of the Adolescents," or Reich's *Different Trains,* it is motion *between* macroharmonies that really strikes the ear. Harmonic states are

Figure 5.1.2 Each section of Debussy's "Voiles" uses a different scale. The switch from whole tone to pentatonic to whole tone moves from greater dissonance to greater consonance and back again.

here intermediate between chord and key, lasting longer and containing more notes than classical chords, but also moving faster than classical keys.

5.2 SMALL-GAP MACROHARMONY

Suppose we would like to write music that is harmonically consistent while also confining itself to a macroharmony with five to eight pitch classes. How should we go about doing this?

One strategy is just to choose a collection of similar chords that together contain no more than five to eight notes. For instance, we could chose A minor, F major, and D♭ major, which together form a six-note hexatonic scale (Figure 5.2.1). This works well until we get bored of our chords, at which point we notice—somewhat ruefully—that the macroharmony is quite limited. First, the *only* major or minor triads it contains are those with roots on F, A, and D♭. Second, it contains only a small number of chord types: if, for example, we later decide to use stacks of fourths (such as F-B♭-E♭ or F-B-E), we must choose another macroharmony, since the hexatonic scale contains no fourth chords whatsoever. The problem, it turns out, is that the hexatonic scale has a number of three-semitone "gaps" between successive notes—or to coin a term, it is a "3-gap macroharmony." Because of this, there are no fourth chords in the collection, and no triads with roots other than F, A, or D♭.[1]

Figure 5.2.1 One way to combine harmonic and macroharmonic consistency is to choose a set of chords that together contain a relatively small number of notes. Here, the A minor, F major, and D♭ major triads contain the pitches of a hexatonic scale.

By contrast, a macroharmony whose steps are at most two semitones large (i.e. a "2-gap macroharmony") will always contain both a triad and a fourth chord above each of its notes. This is because harmonic terms like "triad" and "fourth chord" typically allow for some variation in interval size. For example, the term "triad" refers to a stack of three- or four-semitone intervals. Consequently, for each chord tone there are two semitonally adjacent options to choose from: given the root C, we can put the third at either E♭ or E♮, and given the third E♮, we can put the fifth at either G♮ or G♯. In a 2-gap macroharmony, one of these options will always be contained within the scale.

The principle here is related to what I call the "Fundamental Theorem of Jazz," which states that *you can never be more than a semitone wrong.*[2] The basic idea is that when trying to fit a particular chord into a 2-gap macroharmony, one only needs to shift its notes by semitone at most. This is illustrated in Figure 5.2.2. The connection

1 For instance, neither of the fourths above D♭ is in the collection, since both G♭ and G fall in the gap between F and A♭.

2 While the name "Fundamental Theorem of Jazz" is a joke, the principle does play an important role in jazz theory.

to jazz lies in the fact that improvisers often make use of 2-gap macroharmonies; consequently, any note they play will either belong to the macroharmony or can be a chromatic neighbor to one of its notes. Practically speaking, this means that if one finds oneself accidentally playing a note outside the macroharmony, it can always be reinterpreted as a chromatic neighbor to an adjacent macroharmonic tone. In fact, with a 2-gap macroharmony, the improviser is free to shift either upward *or* downward by semitone. (If a particular note is not in a 2-gap macroharmony, then both of its chromatic neighbors are.[3]) This is quite useful, since out-of-macroharmony notes can be instantly corrected, without the improviser having to think about exactly how he or she has gone wrong.

Figure 5.2.2 In a 2-gap macroharmony, out-of-scale notes can be moved into the scale by semitone, in either direction.

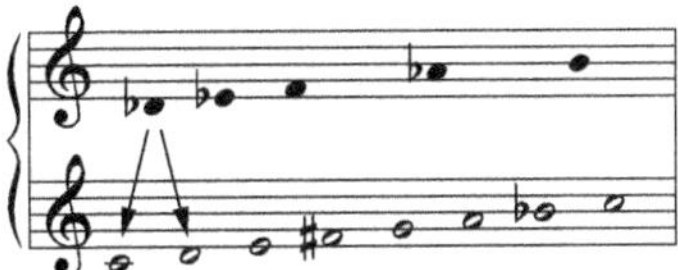

Observe that there is a difference between "having small gaps" and the "near evenness" of Chapter 4. In a nearly even scale, scalar transposition resembles chromatic transposition, which means that we can take a harmony that is *inside* the scale and transpose it *along* the scale without distorting it much. In a 2-gap macroharmony, any note is at most one semitone away from some note in the macroharmony, which means that we can take *any sonority whatsoever* and "squeeze" it into the macroharmony without distorting it much. This difference is illustrated by Figure 5.2.3. Note, in particular, that a collection can be nearly even while still having large gaps (e.g. the major triad). Conversely, a collection can have reasonably small gaps while still being somewhat uneven.[4]

Figure 5.2.3 Near evenness and gaplessness. Chords can be transposed along a nearly even scale with minimal distortion (*a*). In a gapless scale (*b*), chords outside the scale can be "squeezed" into the scale with minimal distortion. Here, the E minor triad is squeezed into the C acoustic scale by shifting B down by semitone.

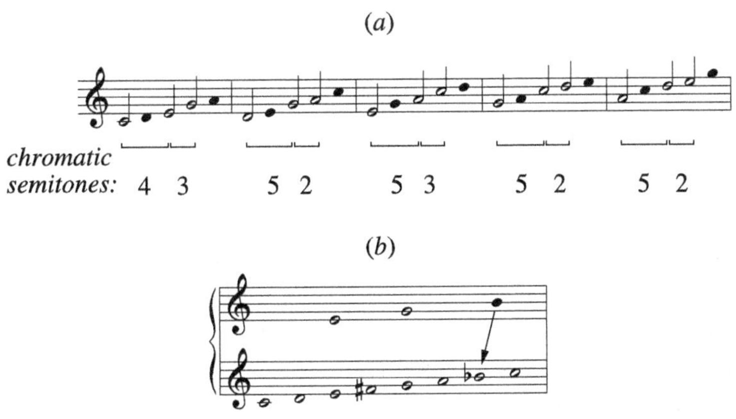

3 In a 3-gap macroharmony, one can never be more than a semitone wrong, but there may be no choice about whether to slide upward or downward by semitone.

4 For example, the eight-note collection {C, C♯, D, D♯, E, F♯, G♯, B♭} has its semitones distributed unevenly.

Figure 5.2.4 Set classes representing 2- and 3-gap macroharmonies.

Size	2-gap	3-gap
5 notes	—	pentatonic "dominant ninth" C-C♯-E♭-F♯-A C-C♯-E-F♯-A
6 notes	whole tone	*17 set classes*
7 notes	diatonic acoustic C-C♯-D-E-F♯-G♯-B♭	*19 set classes*
8 notes	*8 set classes*	*16 set classes*

Nevertheless, it is true that the most even collections generally have the smallest gaps, relative to other collections of that size. Figure 5.2.4 shows that the twelve-tone equal-tempered system has four five-note 3-gap macroharmonies, including the pentatonic scale, the "dominant ninth" chord, and the "diminished seventh plus one" chord. There is only one six-note 2-gap macroharmony (the whole-tone scale), while there are 17 six-note 3-gap macroharmonies. The three seven-note 2-gap macroharmonies are the diatonic, acoustic, and "whole tone plus one" scales. Finally, there are eight eight-note 2-gap collections, including the octatonic scale. Once again, we find familiar musical objects—such as the diatonic and acoustic scales—turning up in a variety of different theoretical contexts. And once again, we see that the goal of combining elementary tonal features (in this case harmonic and macroharmonic consistency) places nontrivial constraints on the composer. It is relatively easy to write music that exhibits harmonic or macroharmonic consistency, but more difficult to write music that exhibits both at once: we cannot simply choose harmonies and macroharmonies willy-nilly, mixing and matching them to our hearts' content.

5.3 PITCH-CLASS CIRCULATION

We'll now develop some tools for quantifying macroharmony, starting with graphs that represent how many pitch classes are used over various spans of musical time. The concept is easiest to explain by way of an example. Figure 5.3.1 shows that if we look at every three consecutive notes of the opening of Bach's F major two-part invention, we find on average 2.4 distinct pitch classes. Similarly, if we look at every four-note window of the music, we find on average 2.9 pitch classes. Figure 5.3.1c compiles this data into a *pitch-class circulation graph*, which shows how many pitch classes are found in windows of various sizes. Such graphs are very crude tools that do not tell us anything about the character of the macroharmonies; furthermore, they can be influenced by textural features independent of the music's underlying

Figure 5.3.1 (*a*) The theme of Bach's F major two-part invention, along with the number of pitch classes in the first several three- and four-note windows. (*b*) A table listing the average number of pitch classes per window in the excerpt, for window sizes between 1 and 10 notes. (*c*) The same information expressed as a graph.

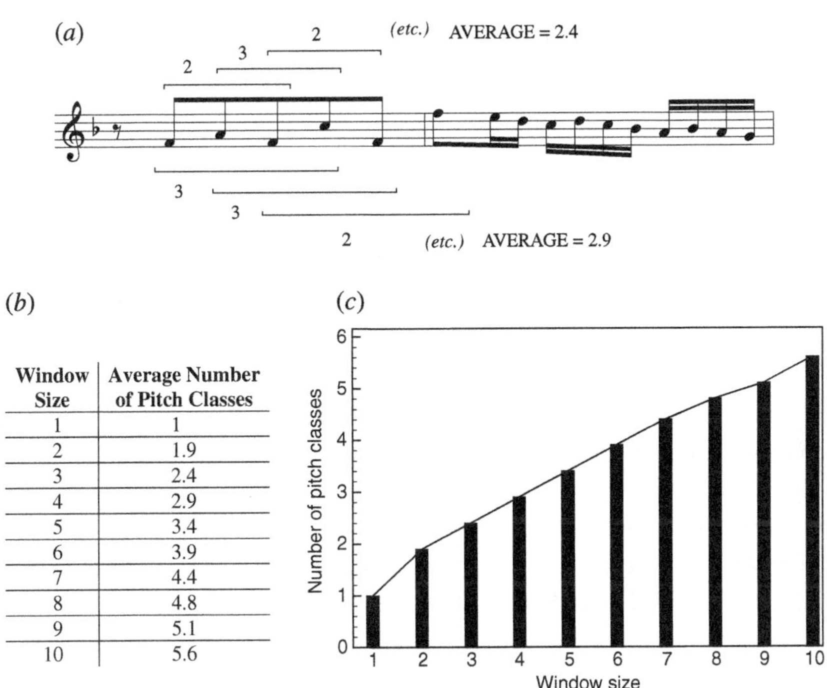

Window Size	Average Number of Pitch Classes
1	1
2	1.9
3	2.4
4	2.9
5	3.4
6	3.9
7	4.4
8	4.8
9	5.1
10	5.6

harmonic structure.[5] But by providing a rough picture of how fast a piece of music moves through the available notes, they can help us get a quantitative grip on how "chromatic" it is.

Figure 5.3.2 graphs the pitch-class circulation in a number of familiar pieces. Palestrina's *Pope Marcellus Mass* is at the bottom, while Webern's *Piano Variations,* Op. 27 is at the top. These two curves have a similar shape, rising quickly and flattening out rather sharply. The quick rise reflects the fact that, over short time scales, the two composers both tend to exhaust a particular collection of notes—the seven diatonic notes in Palestrina's case and the twelve chromatic notes in Webern's. The point at which the graphs level off tells us how large the macroharmony is, with Palestrina's leveling off below Webern's since the diatonic scale is smaller than the chromatic. The flattening itself indicates the relative absence of macroharmonic change: Webern's twelve-tone piece systematically cycles through the only twelve notes available to him,

5 Since pitch-class circulation graphs measure the number of pitch classes per note attack, they are susceptible to differences in tempo, with slower pieces often appearing to be more chromatic than faster pieces. The presence of tremolo or other repetitions also tends to artificially decrease the "chromaticism" of the music. Furthermore, in constructing these graphs it is necessary to "linearize" simultaneous attacks, so that one comes before the other. (This can be done in a random fashion, hoping that the size of the data set will wash away any inaccuracies introduced by the process.) For these reasons, these graphs should be taken with a grain of salt, as providing a very general picture that may not always be accurate in its precise details.

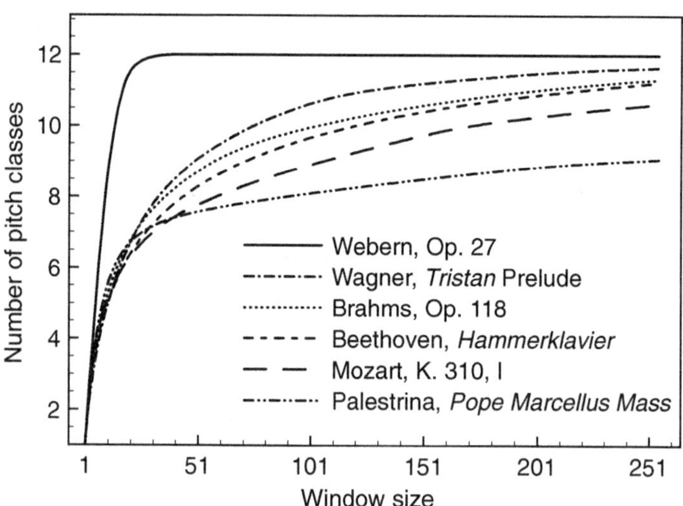

Figure 5.3.2 Pitch-class circulation in several well-known pieces.

and as a result his graph reaches a completely horizontal plateau; Palestrina's occasional use of nondiatonic notes creates a very gradual slope over larger spans of time. Each piece is *macroharmonically static,* since any two of its mid-length segments will contain roughly the same pitch classes.

Between these extremes lies most of the music of the classical tradition. Figure 5.3.2 shows that pieces by Mozart, Beethoven, Brahms, and Wagner exhibit a distinctive harmonic profile, with their graphs rising very quickly and then leveling off much more gradually. (In fact, a typical 10-note excerpt of classical music contains roughly half the pitch classes in a typical 100-note excerpt.[6]) The quick rise reflects the fact that the music again cycles through a collection of available notes, as in Palestrina and Webern. The more gradual flattening indicates that the macroharmonies are *themselves* changing, albeit at a much slower rate. Modulation here ensures a slow but steady supply of fresh pitch classes, causing the graph to level off much more gradually.

Figure 5.3.2 is consistent with a truism of music history: that chromaticism gradually increased over time, beginning with modest explorations during the baroque and classical eras, thriving during the nineteenth century, and culminating in complete atonality. Our graph shows that from Palestrina through Wagner, later composers do indeed tend to utilize faster rates of pitch-class circulation, reflecting increasingly rapid modulations to increasingly distant tonal areas, increasing use of altered chords, and so on. (Of course, some of this is selection bias: including composers such as Gesualdo and Satie would complicate the matter considerably.) Furthermore, as we will see below, there is relatively little difference between the rate of pitch-class circulation in the highly chromatic tonal music of Max Reger and the fully atonal music of Schoenberg. In this sense, atonality does represent a relatively natural response to the saturated chromaticism of late nineteenth-century tonality. We will return to this thought below.

6 Statisticians would say that these graphs are *log-linear* to within window sizes of about 256 notes.

5.4 MODULATING THE RATE OF PITCH-CLASS CIRCULATION

In most Western music, the rate of pitch-class circulation is itself a harmonic variable to be manipulated. For example, Figure 5.4.1 graphs the rate of pitch-class circulation found in selected Chopin Etudes, the first book of Debussy's Preludes, the individual numbers of Stravinsky's *The Rite of Spring,* and a selection of Shostakovich's Op. 87 Preludes and Fugues. All four works display enormous variation, ranging from Palestrina-like sections that use just a few pitch classes, to highly chromatic sections

Figure 5.4.1 Pitch-class circulation in Chopin's *Etudes* (*a*) and Debussy's *Preludes* (*b*). Both collections cover an enormous range, comparable to that of the entire classical tradition (compare Figure 5.3.2).

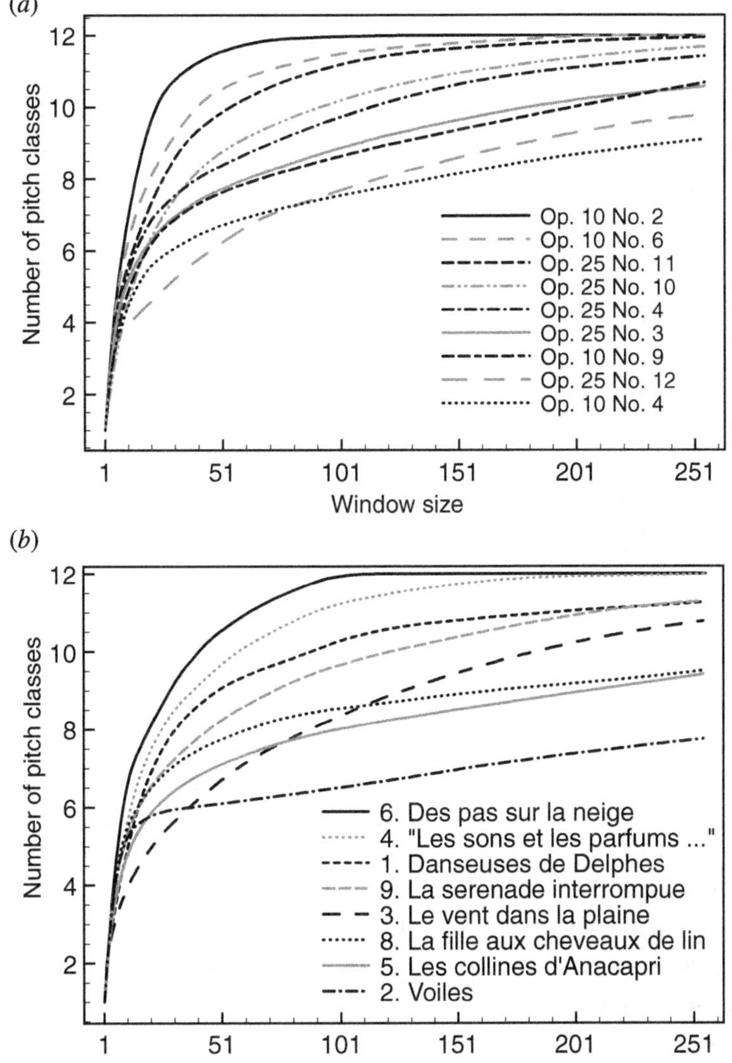

Figure 5.4.1 (Continued) Pitch-class circulation in Stravinsky's *Rite of Spring* (*c*) and Shostakovich's *Preludes and Fugues* (*d*). Again, the pieces cover a large range.

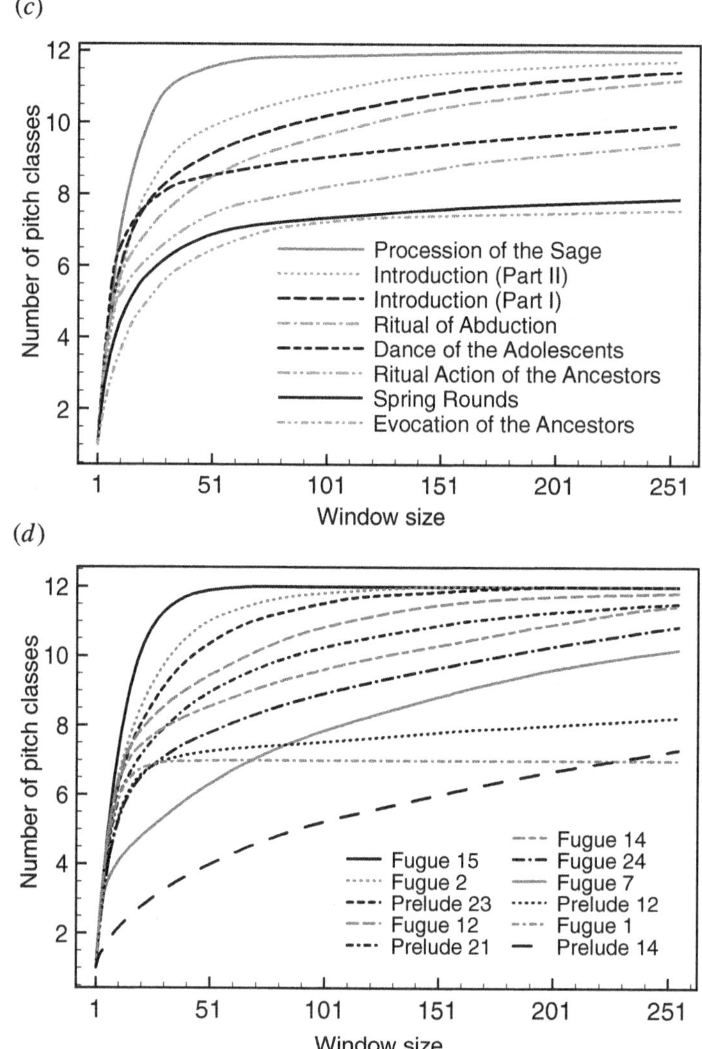

in which all twelve notes are in play. This of course reflects a common technique for creating large-scale form: composers can generate long-term harmonic change by juxtaposing moments of relative calm—in which the music remains fixed in a small macroharmony—with passages of more rapid and aggressive chromaticism.

This diversity in the rate of pitch-class circulation stands in stark contrast to the homogeneity of much atonal music. Figure 5.4.2 graphs the pitch-class circulation in Schoenberg's Op. 11 piano pieces and Webern's Op. 27 variations. The outer movements of both pieces are almost indistinguishable from one another, while their middle movements are ever so slightly less chromatic. The difference between Figures 5.4.1 and 5.4.2 is truly remarkable: where Chopin, Debussy, Stravinsky, and Shostakovich embraced a vast array of macroharmonic states, a diversity comparable to that of the *entire history of Western music,* Schoenberg and Webern restricted

Figure 5.4.2 Pitch-class circulation in Schoenberg's Op. 11 and Webern's Op. 27 piano pieces. The individual movements of each piece are much more similar than in Figure 5.4.1.

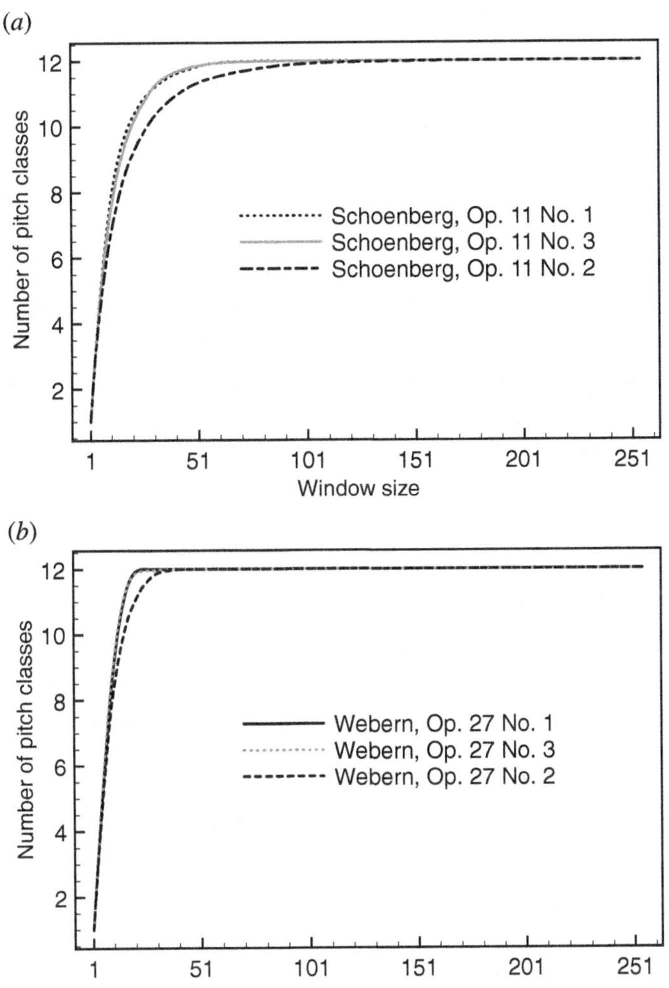

themselves to a much narrower region of musical space. This no doubt helps explain why some listeners find atonal music to be somewhat static. In writing music with a consistently fast rate of pitch-class circulation, atonal composers deprived themselves of one important tool for creating large-scale harmonic change.

It is notable that historians have sometimes used *stylistic* categories to describe the macroharmonic diversity in the music of Debussy, Stravinsky, and Shostakovich. The low-circulation passages are said to evoke particular genres—the diatonicism of ancient music, the pentatonicism or exoticism of non-Western music, and so on—while the high-circulation passages are associated with modernism. In this way, composers favoring macroharmonic diversity are sometimes made out to be polyglots, stylistic magpies who borrow from many different sources. In some cases, this characterization is accompanied by an evaluative narrative, as if diatonicism represents a regressive, backward-looking tendency, while thoroughgoing chromaticism represents a progressive or forward-looking attitude. Macroharmonic diversity is thus associated with stylistic mawkishness, testifying to an incomplete embrace of modernity.

Of course, it is true that many twentieth-century composers were interested in evoking a range of styles. Nevertheless, I think we should be careful to separate the issue of style from the purely harmonic effects that stylistic juxtaposition can create. Rather than seeing Debussy, Stravinsky, and Shostakovich as stopping short of a complete and consistent chromaticism, I would therefore prefer to describe them as embracing *modulation*—writing music that presents a wealth of different macroharmonic states and that changes the rate of pitch-class circulation to reinforce larger formal boundaries. (In fact, I suspect that critics have sometimes resorted to stylistic categories in part because we lack precise theoretical terms for talking about phenomena such as pitch-class circulation.) From this point of view, it is thoroughgoing chromaticism that is conservative, as it abandons macroharmonic change in favor of musical textures that are harmonically uniform in the large. In this respect it recalls the macroharmonic stasis of the earliest Western music.

5.5 MACROHARMONIC CONSISTENCY

Pitch-class circulation graphs show us *how fast* pitch classes are passing by, but do not provide any sense of what the macroharmonies actually are; as a result, they cannot distinguish between quickly modulating diatonic music and nondiatonic music in which all twelve pitch classes are constantly in play. This can be seen by comparing Schoenberg's Op. 11 No. 1 with John Coltrane's solo on "Giant Steps" (Figure 5.5.1). Both pieces have almost identical rates of pitch-class circulation, even though Schoenberg's music is intuitively "more chromatic" than Coltrane's.

What we need are *global macroharmonic profiles* that identify the five- to eight-note macroharmonies used in a particular piece. Given an excerpt of music, we can exhaustively tabulate all the three-note chord types, four-note chord types, five-note chord types, and so on.[7] Figure 5.5.2 presents the six- and seven-note collections in Schoenberg and Coltrane's pieces. As we would expect, the graph of Coltrane's solo is highly peaked, reflecting the fact that it is saturated with diatonic scales and scale fragments. By contrast, Schoenberg's piece features a much more even distribution of chord types, not strongly emphasizing any particular six- or seven-note collection. (On these graphs, the x-axis is labeled using Allen Forte's hard-to-decipher numerical labels for set classes; what is important here is just the overall difference in shape—Coltrane's graph is much more peaked than Schoenberg's.[8]) We can therefore say

7 As before, the analysis here is simplistic but hopefully unbiased: I simply "linearize" simultaneous attacks by arpeggiating them in an essentially random way, and then count up the successive macroharmonies in the piece. That is, for each note i and each size n, I identify the n-note chord type that begins with note i.

8 For Forte's labeling system, see Straus 2005 or Forte 1973. In general, the more chromatic set classes (such as 0123) have smaller numbers, while more even chord types have larger ones.

Figure 5.5.1 Schoenberg's Op. 11 and John Coltrane's *Giant Steps* solo have identical rates of pitch-class circulation (*a*), even though Coltrane's solo is tonal (*b*).

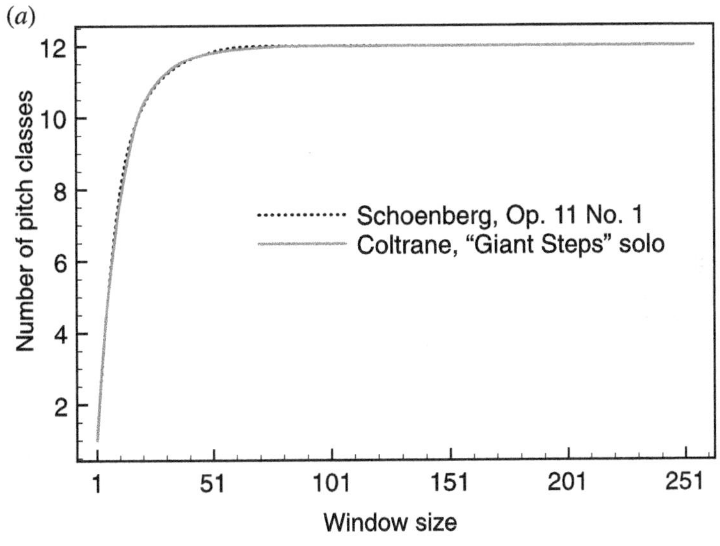

that Coltrane's solo is macroharmonically consistent in a way that Schoenberg's piece is not: Coltrane emphasizes one particular seven-note collection, while Schoenberg makes relatively indiscriminate use of almost all the available seven- and eight-note macroharmonies.[9] To be sure, Coltrane's music *modulates* very quickly, thus ensuring a high overall rate of pitch-class circulation; but unlike Schoenberg, the local structure of his music clearly articulates familiar scales.

One can make a similar distinction among musical styles in which pitch classes circulate more slowly. Figure 5.5.3 contrasts Debussy's "La fille aux cheveux de lin" with Satie's "Theme of the Order," from *Sonneries de la Rose + Croix*. The opening of Debussy's piece very clearly articulates E♭ natural minor and G♭ acoustic scales, separated by a brief cadence on E♭ major. Satie's piece, although it uses relatively few accidentals, does so sporadically and without a clear system; as a result it is difficult to separate the music into regions exemplifying recurring macroharmonies. Yet both pieces have relatively low rates of pitch-class circulation, and are in this sense "not very chromatic."

9 Of course, Schoenberg's music is macroharmonically consistent by virtue of using the chromatic scale, but this is trivial.

Figure 5.5.2 The relative preponderance of different chord types in pieces by Schoenberg and Coltrane. Coltrane's graph is highly peaked at points representing familiar tonal collections. Schoenberg's piece does not emphasize any larger collections to the same extent. The *x*-axis uses a variant of Forte's (1973) set-class labels, where a half-integer *i* + .5 represents the inversion of chord *i*. Thus, the harmonic major scale, 32.5, is the inversion of the harmonic minor, 32.

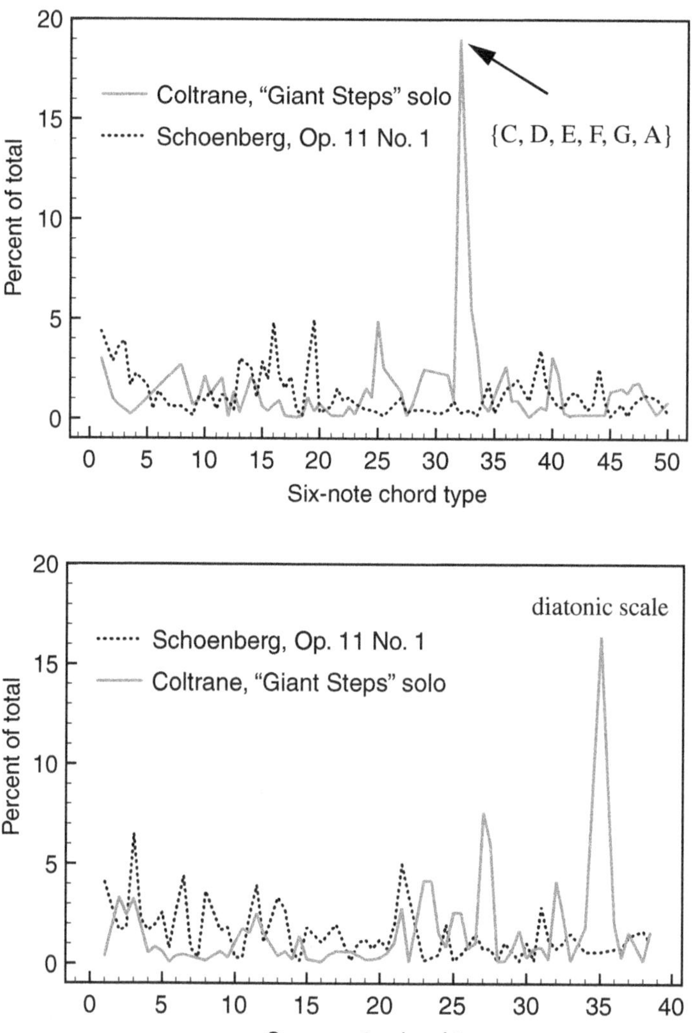

Taken together, these four pieces demonstrate that the informal music-theoretical term "chromatic" involves the interaction of at least two independent variables: rate of pitch-class circulation and the degree of emphasis on particular macroharmonies. Figure 5.5.4 tries to represent the situation visually. Music such as Schoenberg's, which combines a high rate of pitch-class circulation with a low degree of macroharmonic consistency, will be heard as very chromatic; conversely, music such as Debussy's, with a low rate of pitch-class circulation and a high degree of macroharmonic consistency, will be heard as non-chromatic. Pieces such as "Giant Steps" or Satie's "Theme"

Figure 5.5.3 Debussy's "La fille aux cheveux de lin" (*a*) and Satie's "Theme of the Order," from *Sonneries de la Rose + Croix* (*b*).

are somewhat more difficult to classify, because the simple opposition between "chromatic" and "non-chromatic" breaks down: Coltrane's piece has faster pitch-class circulation than Satie's, but more clearly articulates specific macroharmonies; while Satie's circulates through the pitch classes more slowly, but without articulating identifiable macroharmonies. Each is somewhat chromatic in its own distinctive way.

Figure 5.5.4 The rate of pitch-class circulation is independent of the degree of emphasis on particular macroharmonies. The four pieces we have been discussing stake out four different regions in the space of musical possibilities.

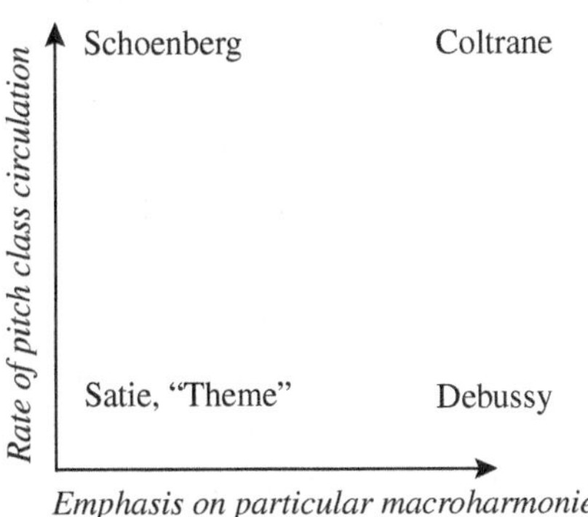

Global macroharmonic profiles can also be useful analytically. For example, Figure 5.5.5 identifies the most prominent seven- and eight-note collections in the opening four sections of *The Rite of Spring*. The introduction is relatively chromatic, superimposing multiple tonalities without emphasizing any familiar macroharmony. (The melodic minor scale is the most prominent seven-note collection, but it appears only 9% of the time.) The "Dance of the Adolescents" features a larger preponderance of harmonic and melodic minor scales—chiefly because its famous opening chord is a harmonic minor collection,

Figure 5.5.5 The most common large collections in the first four sections of the *Rite of Spring*. Each section has a distinct macroharmonic profile.

	Introduction	**Dance of the Adolescents**	**Ritual of Abduction**	**Spring Rounds**
Prevalent Seven-note Collections	melodic minor (9%)	harmonic minor (18%) melodic minor (16%) diatonic (8%)	*subsets of the octatonic*	diatonic (53%)
Prevalent Eight-note Collections	*Various chromatic collections:* (0, 1, 2, 3, 5, 6, 8, 9) (12%) (0, 1, 3, 4, 5, 6, 7, 8) (8%)	*supersets of the above*	octatonic (18%)	*supersets of the diatonic*

while the final section emphasizes the A mode of F acoustic.[10] While neither of the opening sections involves much explicitly octatonic material, the "Ritual of Abduction" is highly (18%) octatonic. Finally, "Spring Rounds" is extremely diatonic (55%). Overall, these figures indicate that Stravinsky's piece exhibits a large-scale transition from the highly chromatic opening to the very diatonic "Spring Rounds," a transition mediated by familiar nondiatonic scales. This transition might be compared to those we encountered in Debussy and Prokofiev (§4.7), though spread out over a much longer span of time.

The Rite of Spring can be usefully contrasted with Shostakovich's Op. 87 Preludes and Fugues. Both pieces belong to the twentieth-century extended-tonal tradition, drawing on tonal techniques while also featuring moments of extreme chromaticism, superimposition of multiple scales, and other modernistic devices. However, where Stravinsky makes relatively frequent use of nondiatonic scales, the Preludes and Fugues are profoundly and almost stubbornly diatonic. Figure 5.5.6 shows that the diatonic scale is the most prominent macroharmony in almost every one of Shostakovich's 48 preludes and fugues, sometimes by an enormous degree.[11] (Indeed, in the first fugue it is the *only* macroharmony.) In fact, Shostakovich's minor-mode pieces are even more diatonic than Bach's—largely because Shostakovich eschews V–i progressions in favor of diatonic cadences that hearken back to a pre-tonal modality. In this respect, Shostakovich's pieces are more neo-classical than post-impressionist; like Copland, Piston, and many other mid-twentieth-century composers, the Preludes and Fugues tend to move between diatonicism, chromaticism, and polytonality without exploring nondiatonic scales. This is part of what endows the music with its distinctive austerity.

10 See Tymoczko 2002 for related observations.

11 One of the few exceptions, the F♯ minor fugue, is built on the seventh mode of G harmonic major; we discuss it in Chapter 9.

Figure 5.5.6 (*a*) The height of each bar represents the proportion of seven-note macroharmonies that are diatonic. The diatonic scale is the most common seven-note collection in all but four of Shostakovich's *Preludes and Fugues*, and in some pieces it is the only macroharmony. The most common non-diatonic collection is represented by a thin gray line; in only four movements does it rise above the black line. (*b*) Shostakovich's minor-key pieces are considerably more diatonic than Bach's minor-key Preludes and Fugues. In particular, Shostakovich rarely uses the harmonic and melodic minor scales, preferring the natural minor.

(*a*)

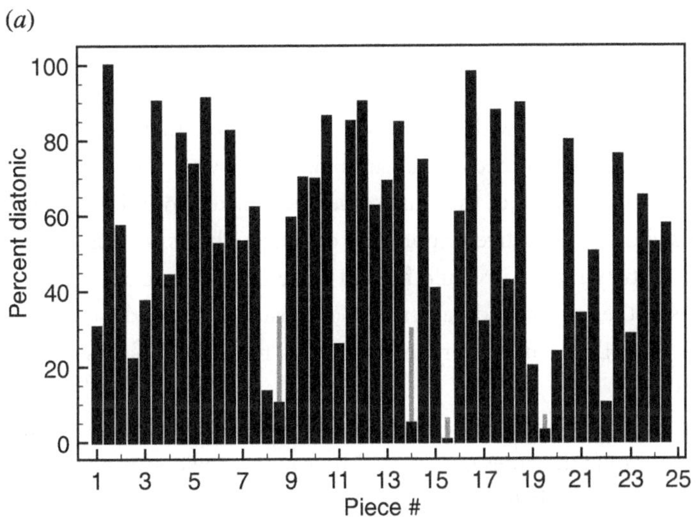

(*b*)

	Bach	Shostakovich
Harmonic minor	25%	5%
Diatonic	20%	56%
Melodic minor	12%	3%

5.6 CENTRICITY

In many musical passages, a particular note is felt to be more prominent, important, or stable than the others—in other words, to be a tonal "center." The concept of centricity is complicated, in part because it encompasses two closely related phenomena: *rootedness,* which applies to individual chords, and *tonicity,* which refers to prominence over longer stretches of musical time. Rootedness and tonicity are music-theoretical cousins, sharing a number of physiognomic characteristics while being of distinct parentage. And just as the line between chord and macroharmony is sometimes blurry, so too is the distinction between rootedness and tonicity: in impressionist or minimalist music, it can be difficult to say whether the most important tone is a root, a tonic, or something in between. For this reason, it is useful to try to develop a unified approach to the two phenomena, without presupposing that there will always be a sharp line dividing them.

Elementary music theory teaches that the "root" of a tertian chord is the lowest note when the chord is arranged as an ascending chain of thirds: thus, E is the root of

Figure 5.6.1 Two progressions that use the same pitch classes, but sound very different.

the collection {E, G, B}, regardless of musical context. (I tell students that to find the root, they must first write the chord in *snowman form.*[12]) But this is an oversimplification: though the two progressions in Figure 5.6.1 use the same pitch classes, the first sounds like i–iv in E minor, while the second sounds more like V–I in C major. A more flexible theorist might therefore describe the chords in Figure 5.6.1b as G and C chords with "added sixths." This shows that a sophisticated notion of "root" cannot rely on mechanical rules like "the lowest note in a chain of thirds is always the root"; instead, we must sometimes make more delicate psychological judgments about the relative importance of notes. This issue arises all the time in twentieth-century music: it would be odd to describe Figure 5.6.2 as a series of 16 repetitions of the same chord, rather than a transition from a dissonant sonority (in which the notes D, E♭, and F♯ predominate) to a more consonant sonority featuring C, E, and G.

Contemporary theorists often use *pitch-class profiles* to represent differences of importance among the notes in a chord. These useful devices are bar graphs in which the *x*-axis represents pitch class and the *y*-axis represents a subjective assessment of prominence, stability, or importance.[13] The simplest conception of a chord is binary; notes can be either inside the chord or outside of it, but no further differentiations are made. This approach can be modeled using two-tiered pitch-class profiles, with notes in the chord being assigned the value 1 and the rest being assigned 0 (Figure 5.6.3). The musical cases we have been considering require finer gradations of prominence. For example, Figure 5.6.4 shows how we might describe the progressions in Figure 5.6.1: the first profile assigns higher prominence to the pitch classes E and A,

Figure 5.6.2 The same notes are attacked on every sixteenth note, but there is a palpable transformation over the course of the measure.

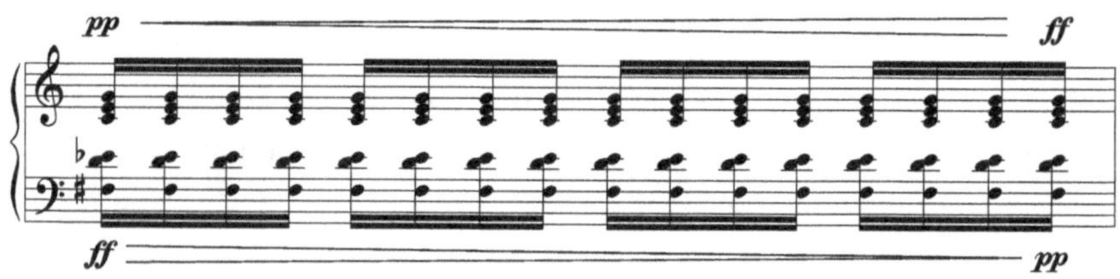

---

12 That is, as a stack of thirds, which looks like a self-supporting snowman. (Other inversions seem to have a snowball floating unsupported in the air.) For seventh chords, you need "extended snowman form."

13 These sorts of graphs originate with Krumhansl and Shepard 1979. Related graphs have been used by Deutsch and Feroe (1981) and are central to the work of Fred Lerdahl (2001). I discuss Lerdahl in Appendix E.

Figure 5.6.3 The simplest model of a chord is a binary one: notes are either in the chord or outside of it.

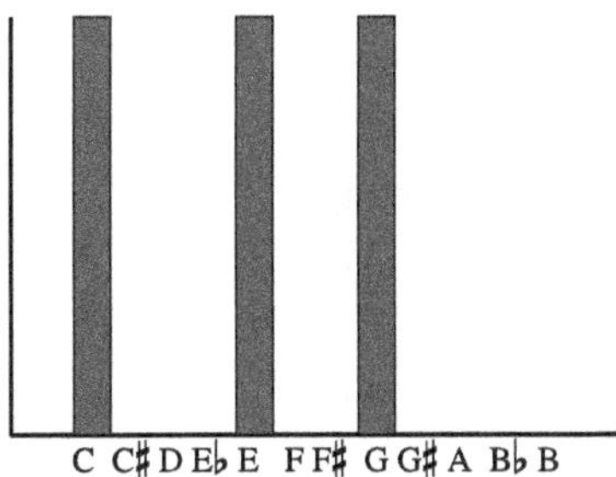

while the second assigns higher prominence to G and C. Figure 5.6.5 represents the music in Figure 5.6.2, where there is a gradual shift from D, E♭, and F♯ to C, E, and G. In these cases, the notion of chord membership becomes fuzzy, admitting a range of values between 0 and 1.

We can also use pitch-class profiles to represent global centricity, or tonicity.[14] Three-tiered profiles provide a simple but effective way to visualize musical modes: notes outside the macroharmony are assigned the value 0, non-centric notes inside the macroharmony are assigned the value 1, and centric notes are assigned the value 2.[15] Thus, Figure 5.6.6 represents C lydian, G ionian, C phrygian, and G locrian modes. In

Figure 5.6.4 Pitch-class profiles can be used to reflect the fact that chord tones differ in terms of their importance. Here, (*a*) and (*b*) represent the two progressions in Figure 5.6.1.

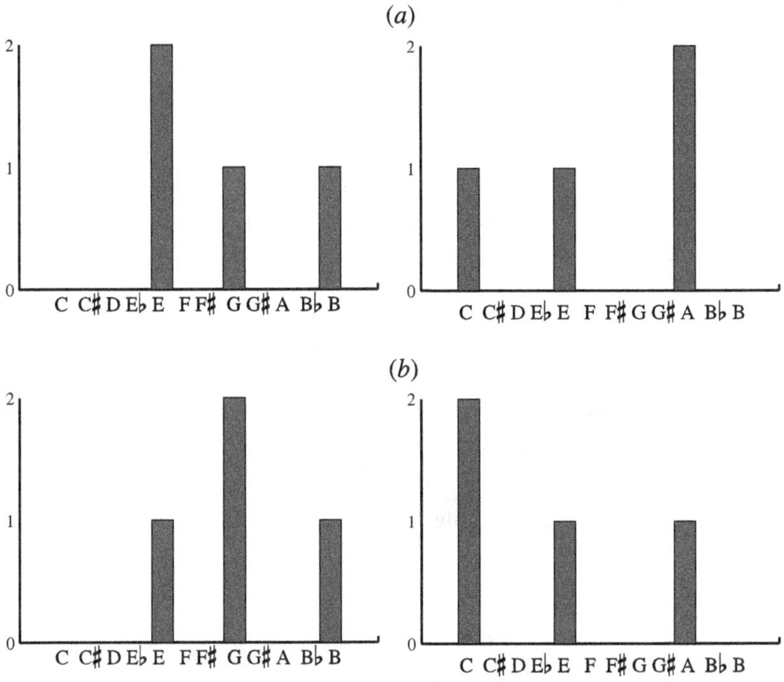

14 Note that local and global centricity can conflict in fascinating ways. For example, in C major, the tonic note can sometimes be unstable, such as when it acts as a neighboring tone to the third of a V^7 chord. Relative to the local harmony, C is less stable than B; relative to the global key, however, the leading tone is less stable than the tonic. Remarkably, our minds can encompass both perceptions at once, with global pitch-class profiles playing a role even in the presence of conflicting local harmonic states.

15 The numerical values here are arbitrary; what is more important is the relative prominence of the various notes. However, in some circumstances, we could use different numerical strengths to record different degrees of musical prominence. For example, Harold Powers (1958, p. 456) contrasts South Indian

Figure 5.6.5 The music of Figure 5.6.2 can be represented as a continuous interpolation between these two graphs, with the more prominent notes becoming less so, and the less prominent notes becoming more so.

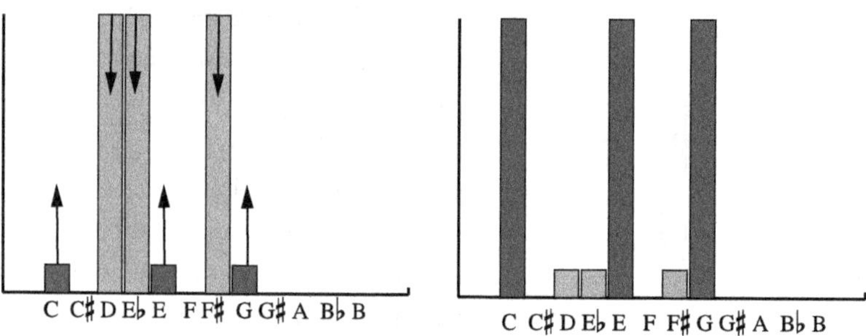

some theoretical contexts we may want to draw more fine-grained distinctions: for example, there is a palpable difference between an E phrygian mode in which the fifth scale degree is emphasized, and an E phrygian mode in which the fourth scale degree is important (Figure 5.6.7).[16] We could capture this with a four-tiered model that distinguishes tonal center, second-most important tone, within-macroharmony notes, and outside-macroharmony notes. Figure 5.6.8a goes even further by proposing a five-tiered pitch-class profile for the key of C major: here, C is most important, G the second-most important, E the third-most important, the remaining diatonic notes fourth-most important, and the black notes last. (This graph is strongly reminiscent of what Fred Lerdahl calls the "basic space" for C major, discussed in Appendix D.) In extreme cases, we may even want to use graphs such as that in Figure 5.6.8b, where we have continuous gradations of pitch-class stability. Here it is impossible to draw sharp distinctions between notes "inside" the macroharmony and those outside it.

An interesting piece, in this regard, is the "Petit airs au bord du ruisseau" from Stravinsky's *Histoire du soldat*. This playful bagatelle has an almost flirtatious relation to traditional scale-based tonality: the piece uses five fixed scale degrees (G-A-B-D-E) and two mobile degrees that appear in distinct flavors (F vs. F♯ and C vs. C♯). While some parts of the music clearly articulate distinct scales, others juxtapose different forms of the "mobile" scale degrees to create a mild form of polytonality

---

ragas with Gregorian modality, writing "the drone-tonic is much more prominent with respect to the other notes of any given raga than is any tone of a Gregorian piece, even the tenor of a psalm-tone." We could express this by adjusting the height of the tonic note in our graph.

16 Gregory Barnett (1998, pp. 266ff) uses secondary pitches (among other considerations) to argue that seventeenth-century ideas about "key" derive from "church keys" rather than traditional modal theory. Powers (1981, p. 453) offers some related observations about tonal differences between Renaissance motets sharing the same final. Historians such as Powers (1958, 1981, 1992) have rebelled against overly simple conceptions of modality, pointing out that earlier musicians understood the phenomenon to include characteristic melodic gestures, complex pitch hierarchies, and so on. The point is well taken, but I think contemporary theorists sometimes have reason to use a basic definition according to which, for instance, "D dorian" simply means "the white notes with D as tonal center." (Barnett 1998 uses the term "tonality" as a synonym for this minimalist definition of "mode.") There is nothing wrong with using modern concepts to analyze earlier music.

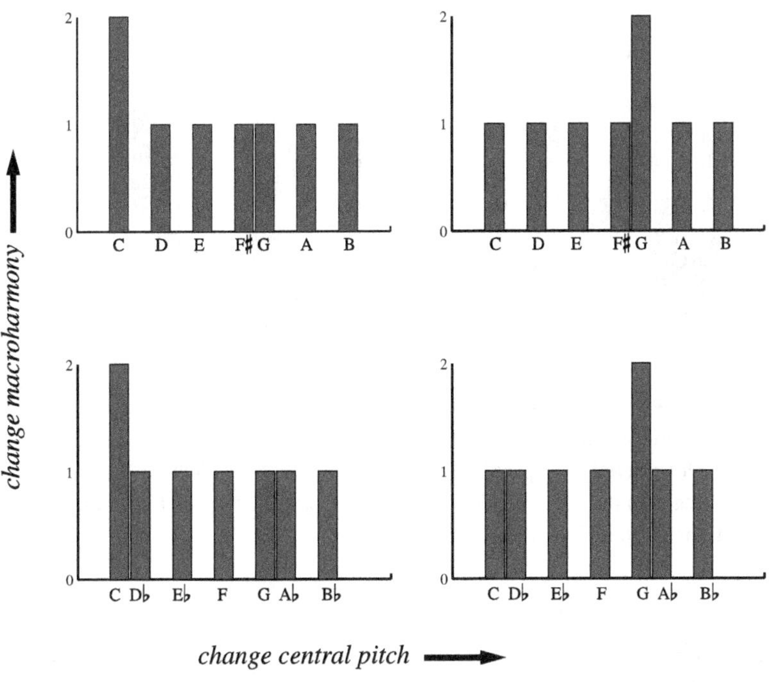

Figure 5.6.6 Pitch-class profiles for C lydian, G ionian, G locrian, and C phrygian (clockwise from upper left).

Figure 5.6.7 The melody in (*a*) emphasizes the notes E and A, while that in (*b*) emphasizes E and B. Though both might be said to be "in E phrygian," there is an important difference between them. We might represent this difference by using pitch-class profiles that identify the second-most important note in a mode.

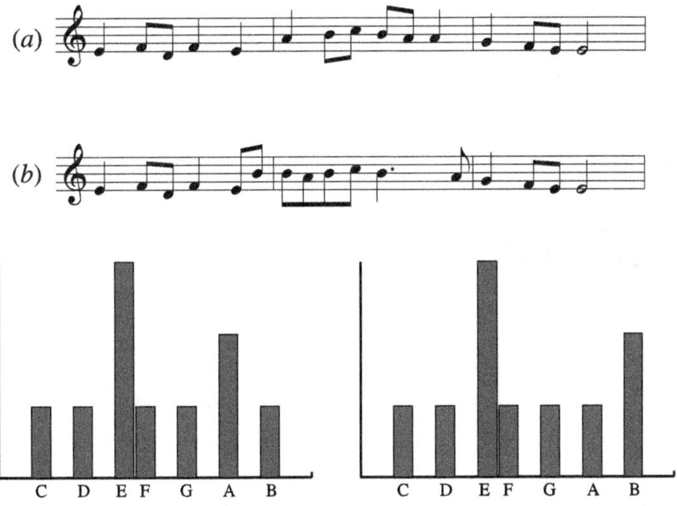

(Figure 5.6.9). Interestingly, there is only one point in the piece where a single line sounds distinct forms of the mobile notes in direct succession; for the most part, it is as if the music were "locally scale-based" within each instrument. (This is precisely what leads me to consider F and F♯ to be two different forms of the same scale degree, rather than analyzing the music using a nine-note scale.) Figure 5.6.9b

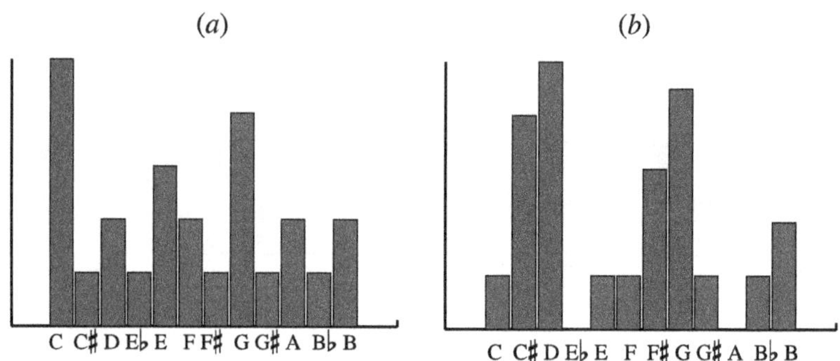

Figure 5.6.8 A five-tiered pitch-class profile representing the key of C major (*a*) and a profile that does not represent any common key (*b*).

Figure 5.6.9 Stravinsky's "Petit airs," from *Histoire du soldat* uses five "fixed" pitches (G, A, B, D, E) and two "mobile" pitch classes (C/C♯, and F/F♯) (*a*). We can represent the music using a four-tiered pitch profile (*b*), in which the "mobile" pitch classes are assigned a lower weighting than the fixed pitch classes. Here, A is assigned the highest value, indicating that it functions as a tonic.

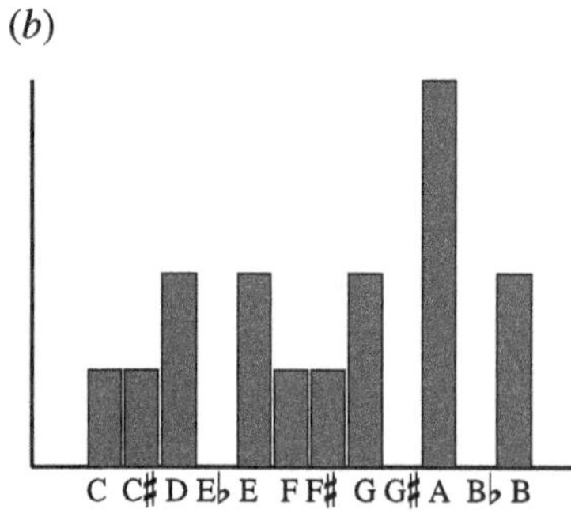

uses a pitch-class profile to represent the somewhat blurred tonality of this movement: here, the profile indicates that I consider A the central pitch; the "fixed" scale degrees are assigned the value 1, indicating their relative stability, while the mobile scale degrees are assigned lower values, indicating their status as fluctuating, "secondary" pitches. But as the graph shows, these notes are more significant than those that do not appear at all.

Global pitch-class profiles represent a psychological or conceptual phenomenon—the felt or imagined importance of the different pitch classes. However, the

Figure 5.6.10 (*a*) The distribution of pitch classes in the opening phrase of Mozart's Jupiter Symphony. (*b*) A three-tiered pitch-class that matches Mozart's distribution reasonably well.

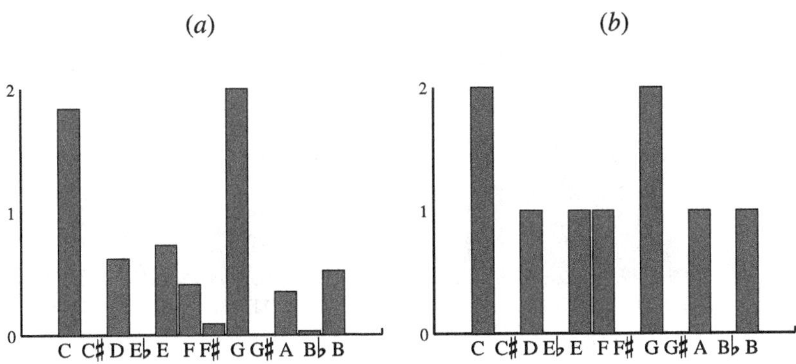

statistical distribution of notes in a piece often correlates reasonably well with the three-tiered pitch profiles we would intuitively describe them with.[17] (Terminological note: I distinguish *pitch-class distributions,* which measure the statistical frequencies of notes in a piece, from *pitch-class profiles,* which represent subjective assertions about psychological importance.) For example, Figure 5.6.10 shows the frequencies of the pitch classes in the first 23 measures of the first movement of Mozart's Jupiter Symphony. This statistical distribution resembles a three-tiered pitch-class profile in which both C and G are assigned the value 2, while the remaining diatonic notes are assigned the value 1—an arrangement that captures the intuitive sense that C and G are most stable in the key of C major, and that the diatonic tones are more stable than the nondiatonic tones. Note that we cannot recover *all* the information about pitch prominence simply by counting pitch classes, since G appears more frequently than C. But this should not be surprising, as there are many ways of generating centricity besides note repetition. What is interesting is that a very crude count of the pitch classes provides a reasonable guide to the relative importance of the notes.

Indeed, pitch-class distributions can sometimes reveal interesting facts about the tonality of specific passages. For example, Figure 5.6.11 records the note frequencies of the three solos in "Freedom Jazz Dance," from the Miles Davis Group's *Miles Smiles.* The piece is an example of "modal jazz," in which the rhythm section plays a relatively static riff emphasizing B♭. Though the music is ostensibly in a single key, the pitch-class distributions are all very different, suggesting that the three soloists have different interpretations of the piece's "B♭-ness." Davis's distribution suggests B♭ dorian, with B♭, C, D♭, F, and G occurring most frequently, while Shorter's is more suggestive of B♭ mixolydian, emphasizing A♭, B♭, C, D, and F. Hancock's is considerably more chromatic than either of these, and the relative lack of A, C, and G♭ may suggest B♭ octatonic. In Chapter 9, we will see that some of these differences result from the fact that the soloists do, in fact, play different

17 This observation derives from Krumhansl and Schmuckler 1986. See also Krumhansl 1990 and 2004. Chapter 9 of Huron 2007 contains a particularly informative discussion.

Figure 5.6.11 Pitch-class distributions of the three solos in "Freedom Jazz Dance," from the album *Miles Smiles*. Each soloist emphasizes different pitches, suggesting different ways of conceiving of the key.

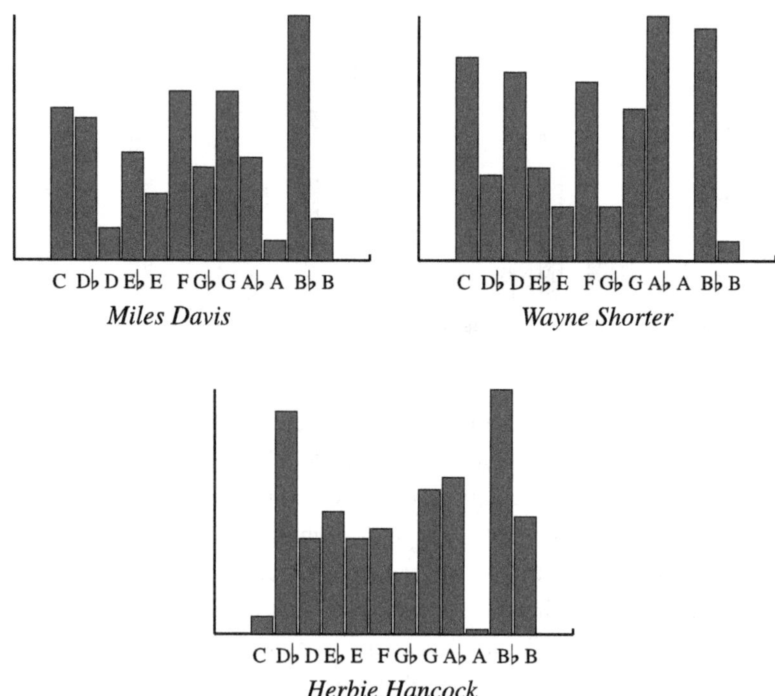

scales over the fixed B♭ ostinato. But scales are not the whole story. Even within a single scale, the musicians choose to emphasize different notes, creating very different shadings of the underlying B♭ tonality.

Compositionally, I find pitch-class profiles to be extremely useful devices. I like to ask: could I construct (or improvise) music that reflects Figure 5.6.8b? Could I write music that realizes Figure 5.6.12, in which both C and D♭ are perceived as equally important? The basic technique here is simply to make sure that the more prominent notes in the pitch-class profile are accented in various ways. Figure 5.6.13 provides an excerpt from a short computer-composed etude, in which pitch-class profiles were used as probability tables that determine the likelihood of each note's appearing. Another example, from a more conventional piece, is given in Figure 5.6.14. In composing this music, I began with the idea of "coloring" a single tonic note with a variety of secondary pitches. The pitch profiles in (*b*) provided an intuitive guide, allowing me to construct a sequence of improvisatory lines that gradually broadened the music's macroharmonic content. The result is a kind of blurred, burbling texture, in which the note A is a vey clear tonal center. (Note that the rhythmic language gradually congeals in concert with the harmonies, moving from indeterminate

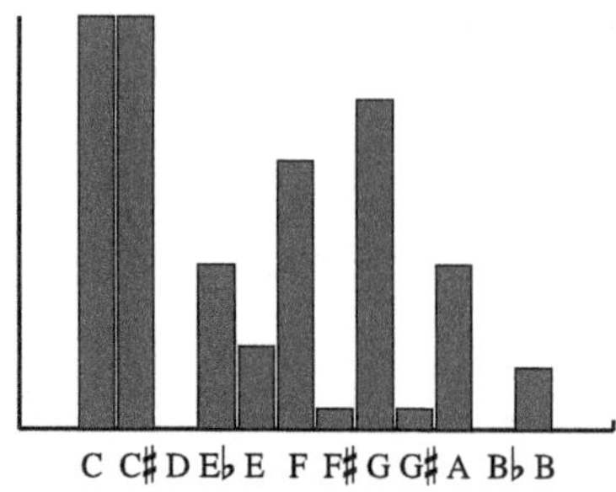

Figure 5.6.12 A hypothetical profile in which C and D♭ are equally important.

Figure 5.6.13 Three pitch-class profiles, along with a passage of computer-generated music embodying the third. Readers with access to the internet can hear a short computer-generated etude on the companion website that moves between the three profiles.

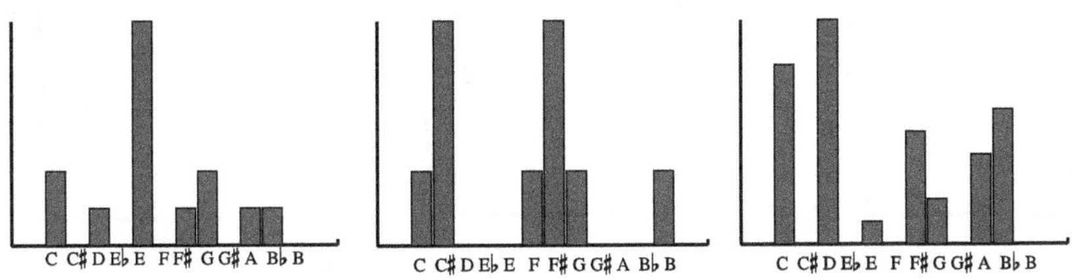

to determinate notation.) It seems to me that there is an enormous amount of unexplored musical territory here, representing the no-man's-land between traditional tonality and full-on atonality. Pitch-class profiles, by helping us visualize this territory, can help us imagine ways to explore it.

5.7 WHERE DOES CENTRICITY COME FROM?

Broadly speaking, theorists have explained centricity in two ways. *Internal* explanations assert that the structure of a group of notes is sufficient to pick one out as a tonal center, without any effort on the composer's part. *External* explanations focus on what composers do, asserting that composers make notes more prominent (or stable) by playing them more frequently, accenting them rhythmically or dynamically, placing them in registrally salient positions, and so on. Rather than being a property of collections considered abstractly, centricity is a property of collections as they are used in actual music.

Figure 5.6.14 The opening three phrases of my piece *Cathedral* (one phrase per line), along with the three pitch-class profiles that inspired them.

Internalists typically cite principles such as the following:

I1. A note is more prominent if it is the lower note of one or more consonant intervals (perfect fifth, major third, or minor third) in the macroharmony.
I2. A note is more prominent if it does not form sharp dissonances (tritone, or minor second) with any note in the macroharmony.

Principle I1 suggests, for example, that C is the most prominent tone in the collection {C, E, G} and that the note B is poorly suited to be the tonic of the C diatonic scale, since there is no scale tone a perfect fifth above it. There is actually some psychological evidence in favor of this view: in an interesting series of experiments, Erkki Huovinen has shown that listeners, when asked to identify the tonic of a series of notes, generally prefer a note that has a perfect fifth above it.[18] Other theorists, such as Schoenberg and Ramon Fuller, have used these ideas to argue that ionian and aeolian are the most natural or appropriate modes of the diatonic scale.[19]

By contrast, external explanations assert that pitch classes become stable or prominent by

E1. Appearing more frequently;
E2. Being held for longer durations;
E3. Being accented dynamically;
E4. Being accented rhythmically;
E5. Being accented registrally (in other words, occurring as melodic high points and low points);
E6. Being the target of stepwise melodic motion, particularly stepwise contrary motion converging on a particular pitch class; and
E7. Being doubled at the octave, or paired with the note a fifth above.

These external explanations all focus on notes as they are deployed compositionally.[20]

Note that the two approaches suggest two drastically different views about what is and is not musically possible. For suppose internal factors are relatively weak: in this case, composers can easily override "internal" centric tendencies, choosing to emphasize notes by a variety of external means. However, if internal factors are strong then composers are ill-advised to disregard them—for by attempting to emphasize something other than a collection's "natural" tonal center, they may create music that is unconvincing, inconsistent, or otherwise aesthetically deviant. It is interesting that

18 See Huovinen 2002.

19 Schoenberg 1911/1983, Fuller 1975.

20 Cultural factors sometimes play an essential role in determining centricity. For example, many nineteenth-century pieces are structured around tonic chords that rarely appear. To understand these pieces, one must hear them as yearning for a consummation that is continually deferred. In these and other cases, appropriate determination of the tonal center requires initiation into a cultural practice, rather than simple examination of the formal properties of the music. (See Huron 2007, for more.) Some writers, such as Reti (1958) and Huovinen (2002) go so far as to consider centricity to be something that the *listener* does, rather than a property of musical stimuli as such; on this account, centricity is a result of "tonal focusing" by which listeners organize pitch material around a primary tone.

Figure 5.7.1 (*a*) Diatonic music with no clear center. (*b*) Chromatic music with a clear center.

these two views played a crucial role in early twentieth-century music history, with a number of prominent Germanic musicians (including Schoenberg and Schenker) inclined toward internalism, and a number of non-Germanic musicians (including Debussy) taking the opposite view.[21] The divergence between nonscalar atonality and scalar "extended tonality" can thus be traced, at least in part, to this difference of music-theoretical opinion: for Schoenberg and others, centricity was a matter of a natural law, and hence it was necessary to choose between traditional tonality and the wholesale abandonment of centricity. For composers in the French and Russian traditions, centricity was a compositional choice, and thus it was possible to contemplate musical styles that made use of new modes and scales.

My own sympathies lie very much with the external view: in most practical cases, I believe the internal contributions to centricity are relatively weak and can easily be overridden. Consequently it is entirely possible to write diatonic music that is acentric, or chromatic music that emphasizes a particular note (Figure 5.7.1). I do not

21 Schoenberg's view was that the diatonic scale has an inherent tonal center, but that the chromatic scale does not; see, for example, Chapter 20 of his *Theory of Harmony* (1911/1983). Perle (1996) echoes Schoenberg's conclusions almost a century later. For the opposite view, see Helmholtz (1863/1954, pp. 365–366). Helmholtz's externalism was shared by composers such as Grieg, Debussy, and Stravinsky.

consider either kind of music to be "unnatural."[22] Nor do I have any problem with any of the diatonic modes (or any other mode of any other scale): I am entirely convinced by the music of the Renaissance, of Debussy, Ravel, and Shostakovich, and of contemporary jazz and rock; I enjoy those numerous passages of twentieth-century music that make use of symmetrical scales while still asserting a tonal center; and as a composer I believe I can make virtually any note of virtually any collection sound like a tonic. (This last conviction has been reinforced by my experience with computers: by emphasizing particular notes through repetition, duration, loudness, and stepwise melodic motion, it is easy to create the effect of centricity in otherwise random sequences.) Any theorist who wants to argue against these convictions would have to fight an uphill battle: indeed, the very claim that the phrygian mode is deficient, or that centric music cannot use symmetrical scales, strikes me as evidence of a limited musical imagination.

5.8 BEYOND "TONAL" AND "ATONAL"

I want to close this chapter—and by extension, the theoretical half of the book—by showing how we can use these ideas to orient ourselves relative to the broad spectrum of contemporary musical styles. I'll begin by contrasting two twentieth-century movements: the *chromatic tradition,* which rejects five- to eight-note macroharmonies in favor of the chromatic scale; and the *scalar tradition,* in which limited macroharmonies continue to play a significant role. I'll then suggest that our inquiry into the five basic components of tonality might help us envision new possibilities lying between these two extremes.

5.8.1 The Chromatic Tradition

A standard trope of music history asserts that the chromatic tradition originates in the extended tonality of post-Wagnerian chromaticism. According to this narrative, composers such as Strauss and Reger began to make heavy use of chromatic voice leading, to the point where familiar analytical concepts began to lose their purchase: pitch-class circulation increased, traditional scales became less important, and centricity became less obvious, with key-defining progressions (such as I–ii–V^7–I) gradually disappearing. Later composers, feeling that it was unreasonable to retain acoustic consonance while abandoning the other components of tonality, created atonality as we know it.

In my view, this narrative is essentially right: macroharmony was indeed the first casualty in the war on tonality, and highly chromatic "wandering tonality" does begin to approach atonality both in its rate of pitch-class circulation and in the absence

22 Interestingly, the internal view has been defended both by radical atonal composers and by conservative opponents of atonality, including Schoenberg (1911/1983, p. 394) and William Thomson (1991, pp. 87–88). Thus, although these two writers have diametrically opposed aesthetic orientations, they have a similarly limited conception of tonal possibilities.

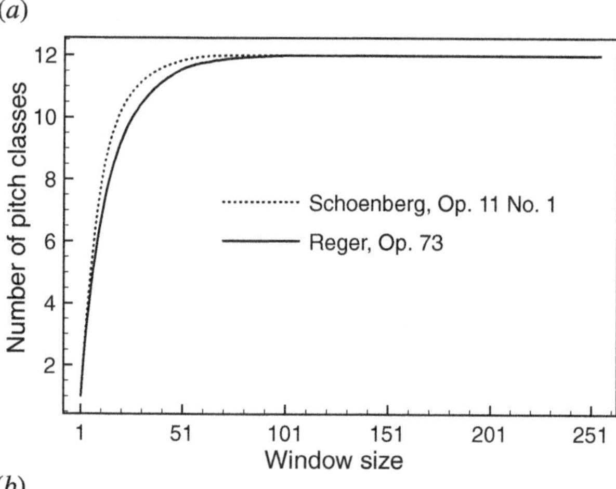

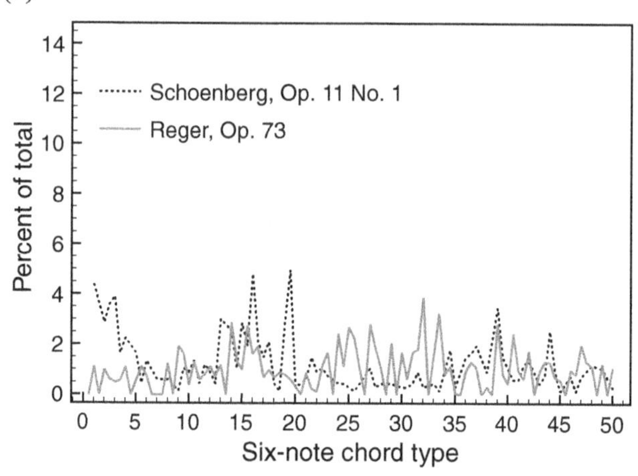

Figure 5.8.1 (*a*) Reger's tonal music sometimes circulates through the pitch classes almost as fast as Schoenberg's atonal music. (*b*) Some of Reger's pieces exhibit a very broad distribution of macroharmonies, comparable to that found in atonal music. Again, set-classes on the *x*-axis are labeled using Allen Forte's system, so that "15" corresponds to his set "7–15."

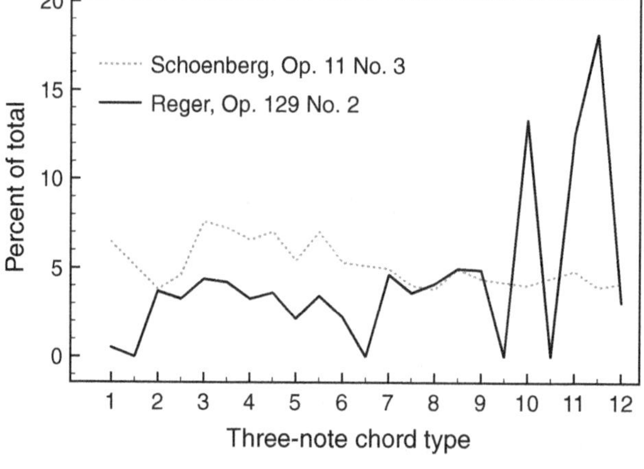

Figure 5.8.2 Reger's highly chromatic tonal music often exhibits more harmonic consistency than Schoenberg's atonal music. Here, the "spike" indicates that the music is saturated with major and minor triads.

of traditional macroharmonies.[23] Figure 5.8.1 shows that Reger's music sometimes circulates quickly through the twelve pitch classes while also abandoning clearly articulated macroharmonies. (The road to atonality, one might say, was paved with chromatic voice leading.) That said, there is still an important step from Reger to Schoenberg. For not only did Schoenberg "emancipate the dissonance," treating any possible combination of notes as a potential

23 See Proctor 1978.

harmony, but he also took the much more radical step of rejecting harmonic consistency—in other words, the very idea that harmonies should be structurally similar to one another. By way of illustration, Figure 5.8.2 contrasts the distribution of three-note chords in Schoenberg's Op. 11 No. 3 and Reger's Op. 58 No. 5: where Reger's graph is strongly peaked at the familiar major and minor triads—which together account for more than a third of the three-note chords in the piece—Schoenberg's graph is much flatter, suggesting a much more even distribution of chord types. In this respect, Schoenberg's music goes far beyond the simple rejection of tonality: by abandoning harmonic consistency, he took the radical step from "everything is permitted" to "everything is permitted *at all times*." Not only was he willing to use any collection of notes as a harmony, but he was also willing to use an enormous range of chord types within very short temporal spans.[24]

It is worth asking whether this feature of Schoenberg's music might have been an *unintended byproduct* of the decision to abandon consonant chords. We have seen that harmonic consistency and conjunct melodic motion can be combined only under very special circumstances, typically involving acoustically consonant chords. It follows that composers who abandon consonance may put themselves in a difficult situation, sacrificing their ability to achieve the traditional two-dimensional coherence of Western music. Certainly, it is suggestive that the music of the second Viennese school often occupies two opposite poles: pointillistic textures that are harmonically consistent (as in the opening of Webern's *Concerto for Nine Instruments*), and conjunct passages that use a very wide range of harmonies (as in the opening of *Pierrot Lunaire*'s "Die Kreuze").[25] It seems possible that atonal composers did not explicitly *choose* to abandon harmonic consistency or conjunct melodic motion; instead, this choice may have been forced upon them by their prior rejection of acoustically consonant chords.

It is also clear that there are some specific ways in which atonal music resembles random music. Figure 5.8.3a shows that the pitch-class circulation graph of the first movement of Schoenberg's Op. 11 is nearly indistinguishable from that of an equally long series of random pitches. Figures 5.8.3b–c compare the distributions of harmonies in Schoenberg's piece with those in random sequences. Again, both atonality and random music contain a broad and relatively even distribution of chord types. Finally, Figure 5.8.3d contrasts the frequency of pitch classes in a Schoenberg movement with those in random sequences: the graphs are both relatively flat, reflecting the absence of clear points of tonal emphasis. (It is worth recalling that Schoenberg's later twelve-tone method was *explicitly designed* to promote flat pitch-class profiles of this sort: as Schoenberg emphasized, doubling or repeating notes could potentially give rise to feelings of centricity, which would be reflected by unevenness in the pitch-class profile.[26]) Taken together, the figures suggest that there is some truth to a

24 Curiously, this has been relatively little discussed in the literature, even though the abandonment of harmonic consistency is (to my ear, at least) a fairly salient feature of Schoenberg's music.

25 Of course, there are many passages that exhibit neither efficient voice leading nor harmonic consistency.

26 Schoenberg 1975, p. 219; Huron 2007 makes a similar point.

Figure 5.8.3 (*a*) Pitch-class circulation in Schoenberg and in random notes. (*b*) Distribution of six-note macroharmonies in Schoenberg and in random notes. (*c*) Distribution of three-note harmonies in Schoenberg's Op. 11 No. 3 and in random notes.

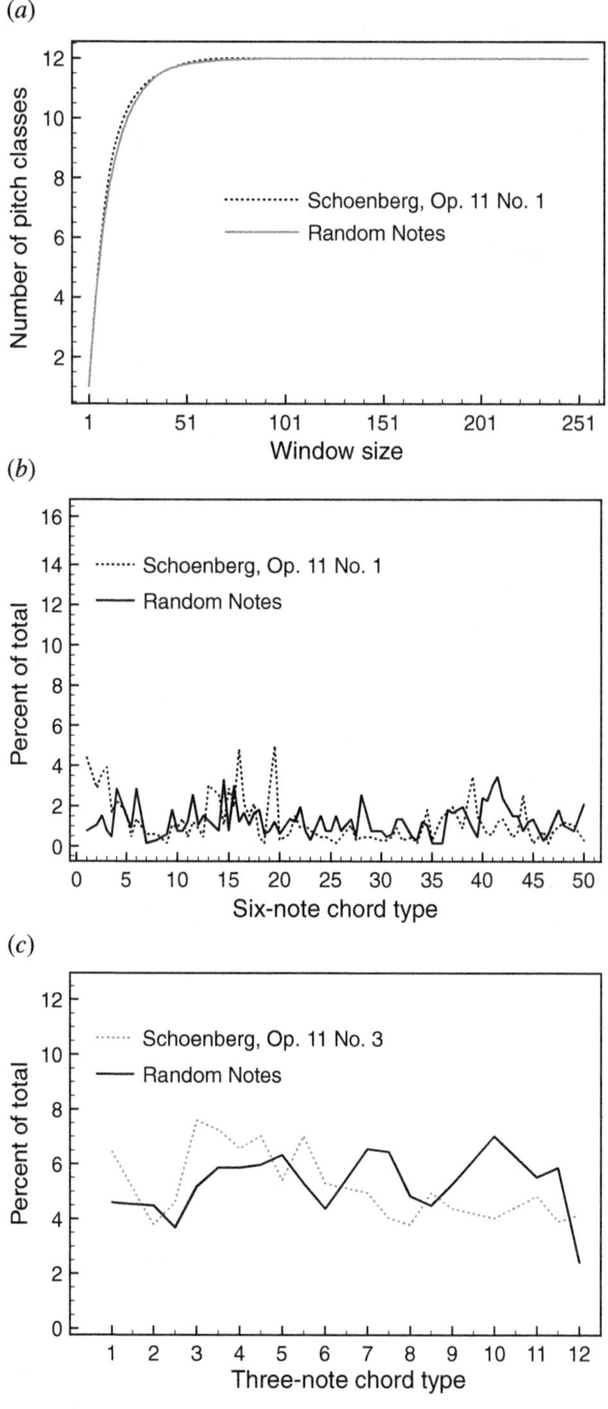

Figure 5.8.3 (*d*) Pitch-class distributions in Schoenberg's Op. 11 No. 1 (*left*) and in random notes (*right*).

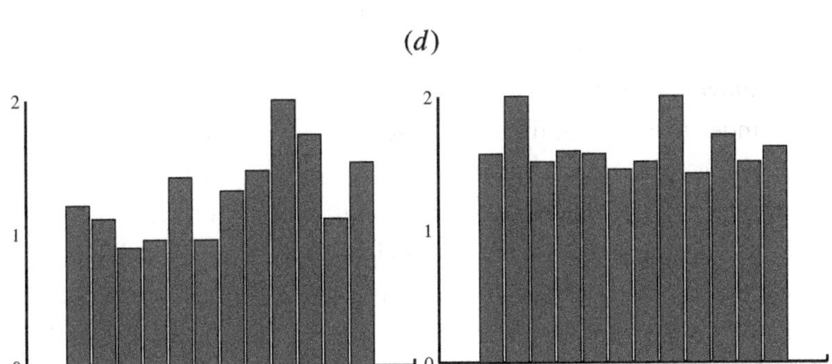

common ("naive") response to atonality—namely, "it sounds random." Statistically speaking, atonal music is often remarkably similar to random notes, and listeners perceive this fairly accurately.

Of course, in abandoning tonality, Schoenberg and other atonal composers attempted to substitute alternative methods of musical organization for those we have been considering—some of which, such as the twelve-tone method, involve the *order* of pitch sequences rather than their unordered pitch content. Discussions of atonal music often focus on the difficulties involved in perceiving this alternative organization: sympathetic observers sometimes explain atonality's unpopularity by comparing it to a language that is very difficult to learn, while more critical commentators, such as Fred Lerdahl and Diana Raffman, suggest that atonal music may be organized according to principles that are beyond *any* human perceptual understanding.[27] The preceding discussion suggests that we might want to reconsider this line of argument. For appreciating atonal music requires more than simply learning to appreciate alternative methods of musical organization; it also requires learning *not* to respond to those statistical features that the music shares with random sequences of notes. And insofar as a listener fundamentally dislikes the *sound* of random pitches, then it may not matter how atonal pieces are organized: after all, mere ordering does not typically convert unpleasant stimuli into pleasant ones. (Imagine someone causing you pain, or feeding you disgusting food, according to a perceptible and highly structured pattern!) If this is right, then atonal music is not so much analogous to a language that is hard to understand; instead, it is more like a taste that many people do not see the point of acquiring. To put it crudely: people dislike atonal music, not because they have a hard time understanding it, but *because they think it sounds bad*.[28]

---

27 See Babbitt 1958, Lerdahl 1988, and Raffmann 2003. Babbitt compares atonal music to advanced mathematics, rather than a complex language, but the point is similar.

28 I should clarify that I am not denying that many listeners have a cognitive, language-like relation to music; instead, I am suggesting that direct sensory pleasure also plays a significant role. My claim is that, in some cases, the unpleasantness of the musical stimuli may be more important than the perceptibility of underlying structure: pleasant-but-random is perhaps preferred to unpleasant-but-structured.

None of this implies that highly chromatic music actually *is* bad or otherwise aesthetically flawed: on the contrary, I think moments of extreme chromaticism (and even randomness) can often be artistically compelling. However, I do think that we might have reason to resist the claim that fans of atonality constitute a cognitive elite, or that the enjoyment of atonal music is a straightforward function of unusual powers of musical understanding. For these claims tend to rely on the rather dubious suggestion that *if* people understood atonal music *then* they would like it—a claim that is no more likely to be true of Schoenberg and Babbitt than it is of heavy metal or polka. Instead, I think it is better to describe the aficionados of atonality as having managed to acquire a taste for highly chromatic musical textures: like the taste for clam chowder ice cream, this is one that people often do not care to cultivate. But that neither makes it worthy of approval nor condemnation—instead, it is just one of the myriad different specialized pleasures whose pursuit makes contemporary society so colorful.

5.8.2 The Scalar Tradition

Diametrically opposed to atonality is the "scalar tradition" that makes extensive use of familiar scales and modes. This tradition encompasses at least six major twentieth-century movements—impressionism, neoclassicism, jazz, rock, minimalism/postminimalism, and neo-Romanticism—and a good deal of other music as well (including, to various extents, music of Scriabin, Stravinsky, Bartók, and Shostakovich). Of course, the scalar tradition is itself diverse: some styles (including mid-century neoclassicism and contemporary rock) are predominantly diatonic, while others (including impressionism and jazz) make much greater use of nondiatonic scales; some composers write largely scalar music, while others juxtapose familiar scales with chromatic or even atonal passages. Nevertheless, we will see in Chapter 9 that there are enough

Figure 5.8.4 Nondiatonic scales in nineteenth-century music. In (*a*), a fragment of the "Gypsy" scale (G-A-B♭-C♯-D-E♭-F♯) in Grieg's Lyric Piece "Gjetergutt" ("Shepherd's Boy"), Op. 54 No. 1. In (*b*), the acoustic scale in Liszt's "Angélus! Prière aux anges gardiens"), *Années de pèlerinage,* Year 3.

Figure 5.8.5 (*a*) The two-dimensional modulatory space of twentieth-century diatonic music. Horizontal motion corresponds to scalar transposition; vertical motion chromatic transposition. The figure's left and right edges are glued together, as are its top and bottom edges. (*b*) The three-dimensional space of twentieth-century scalar music. Each plane of the figure is analogous to (*a*); vertical motion changes the underlying scale.

(*a*)

C mixolydian	D aeolian	E locrian	F ionian	G dorian	A phrygian	B♭ lydian
B mixolydian	C♯ aeolian	D♯ locrian	E ionian	F♯ dorian	G♯ phrygian	A lydian
B♭ mixolydian	C aeolian	D locrian	E♭ ionian	F dorian	G phrygian	A♭ lydian
A mixolydian	B aeolian	C♯ locrian	D ionian	E dorian	F♯ phrygian	G lydian
A♭ mixolydian	B♭ aeolian	C locrian	D♭ ionian	E♭ dorian	F phrygian	G♭ lydian
G mixolydian	A aeolian	B locrian	C ionian	D dorian	E phrygian	F lydian
F♯ mixolydian	G♯ aeolian	A♯ locrian	B ionian	C♯ dorian	D♯ phrygian	E lydian
F mixolydian	G aeolian	A locrian	B♭ ionian	C dorian	D phrygian	E♭ lydian
E mixolydian	F♯ aeolian	G♯ locrian	A ionian	B dorian	C♯ phrygian	D lydian
E♭ mixolydian	F aeolian	G locrian	A♭ ionian	B♭ dorian	C phrygian	D♭ lydian
D mixolydian	E aeolian	F♯ locrian	G ionian	A dorian	B phrygian	C lydian
D♭ mixolydian	E♭ aeolian	F locrian	G♭ ionian	A♭ dorian	B♭ phrygian	C♭ lydian

(*b*)

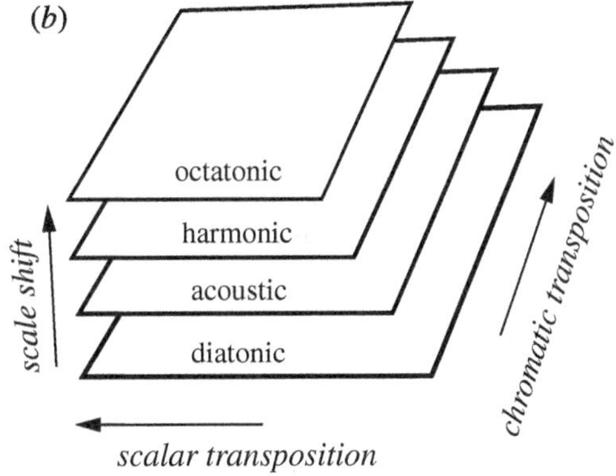

commonalities among twentieth-century composers to justify talk of a scalar "common practice."

Like the chromatic tradition, the scalar tradition has its origins in the late nineteenth century. Composers such as Chopin, Liszt, Mussorgsky, Rimsky-Korsakov, Grieg, and Fauré began experimenting with the various modes of the diatonic scale, as well as with whole-tone, octatonic, and melodic and harmonic minor scales (Figure 5.8.4).[29] Historians have often conceptualized this tradition *extrinsically*—as reflecting "folk" influences external to the functionally harmonic tradition. But we can also understand the scalar tradition intrinsically, as representing an expansion and generalization of traditional compositional practices. In particular, twentieth-century scalar composers were the first to systematically combine three fundamental musical operations: change of tonal center, change of scale, and chromatic transposition. These operations are represented geometrically in Figure 5.8.5. Here, each plane represents the combination of chromatic and scalar transposition, while motion between scales is represented by vertical motion between the planes.[30] The resulting modal system

29 Samson 1977 emphasizes the late nineteenth-century divergence between scalar and chromatic traditions.

30 This diagram should be understood as an abstract representation of musical possibilities; it is not a portion of the geometrical spaces described in Chapter 3.

Figure 5.8.6 Twentieth-century scalar composers potentially have a very wide range of scales and modes to work with.

Scale Type	Number of Scales	Number of Notes	Mode Types	Total Number of Modes
Pentatonic	12	5	5	60
Whole tone	2	6	1	12
Hexatonic	4	6	2	24
Diatonic	12	7	7	84
Acoustic	12	7	7	84
Harmonic Min.	12	7	7	84
Harmonic Maj.	12	7	7	84
Octatonic	3	8	2	24
Chromatic	1	12	1	12
TOTAL	70		39	468

provides a truly vast range of different key areas (Figure 5.8.6): instead of seven modes or 24 major and minor keys, composers now have more than 450 different tonal areas to chose from!

Within the scalar tradition, we can distinguish chordal from "pandiatonic" (or perhaps "panscalar") approaches: chordal music preserves the two-tiered "chord within scale" organization of earlier Western music; while pandiatonic music effaces the role of chords as scales themselves begin to assert a more central harmonic role.[31] (As mentioned earlier, Debussy's "Voiles" is an early example of this second practice.) The distinction between these two approaches thus mirrors the distinction between the chromaticism of composers like Reger and that of true atonality: Reger's music, like traditional tonality, preserves harmonic consistency, limiting itself to a small number of recognizable chord types, while pandiatonic music (like more radical atonality) abandons harmonic consistency altogether. This is illustrated graphically in Figure 5.8.7. Once again, we see that the binary opposition between "chromatic" and "nonchromatic" (or "tonal" and "atonal") blurs a number of more specific music-theoretical distinctions.

Returning now to a question broached earlier in this chapter: is it really true that Western music became more chromatic over the course of its history? Clearly, there is a sense in which it has: the progression from Palestrina to Mozart to Schubert to Wagner to Reger to Schoenberg exhibits a steady and quantifiable increase in chromaticism (Figure 5.3.2). What is left out of this story is that late nineteenth-century composers had already begun to rebel against this trend. This scalar tendency gathered steam throughout subsequent decades, culminating in an unprecedented explosion of diatonicism in the works of composers such as Shostakovich, Riley, Reich, Glass, Pärt, Górecki, Adams, Bryars, and ter Veldhuis, not to mention jazz, rock, and other popular forms of music. (The trend is also evident in the renewed appre-

31 The term "pandiatonic" was invented by Nicolas Slonimsky in the first edition of *Music Since 1900* (Slonimsky 1994). It has been applied both to diatonic music lacking harmonic consistency and to diatonic music lacking centricity. Here, I use it in the former sense.

Figure 5.8.7 In both the scalar and chromatic traditions, there are genres exhibiting harmonic consistency (top row) as well as genres in which harmonic consistency does not play as an important a role (bottom).

		Limited Macroharmony	
		YES	**NO**
Harmonic Consistency	**YES**	traditional scale-based tonality (Debussy, Jazz)	"triadic atonality" (Gesualdo, Reger)
	NO	pandiatonicism (*Voiles*)	complete atonality (Schoenberg, Babbitt)

ciation for early music.) Thus, where early twentieth-century historians might have seen a relentless, ever-increasing drive toward chromaticism, twenty-first century musicians confront a very different environment, in which early twentieth-century scalar music seems as much a harbinger of things to come as a relic of the past.

5.8.3 Tonality Space

Of course, the chromatic and scalar traditions represent just a portion of the huge tapestry that is twentieth-century music. Figure 5.5.4 depicted twentieth-century music as lying on a two-dimensional continuum, whose axes represented the rate of pitch-class circulation and the explicitness of macroharmony. While the scalar tradition lies on the far right of the graph, and while complete atonality is in the lower left corner, there is a considerable amount of music that does not fit into either category. Many of Prokofiev's pieces, for example, make free use of accidentals without attempting to stay within a single scale for very long. Similarly, composers such as Stravinsky, Milhaud, Bartók, and Shostakovich explored polytonal textures in which familiar musical materials are superimposed, creating the effect of clashing keys.[32] Still others—such as the Messiaen of the *Quartet for the End of Time* or *Vingt regards sur l'enfant-Jésus*—wrote music that embraces many different techniques, being at different points traditionally tonal, polytonal, completely atonal, or several of these at once (Figure 5.8.8).

Among these myriad approaches, György Ligeti's "non-atonality" stands out as being particularly relevant to the present discussion. Though dissonant, his music

32 Although several eminent composers and theorists have critiqued the notion of polytonality (Bartók 1976, pp. 365–366, Hindemith 1937/1984, Vol. 1, p. 156, Forte 1955, and Samson 1977, p. 256), the term seems unobjectionable to me. Some music can be segregated into relatively independent musical streams, each with its own sonic character—for instance, when two timbrally distinct instruments are widely separated spatially or in register. Here the auditory streams do not completely fuse, allowing us to distinguish independent scales, macroharmonies, and even tonal centers in each stream.

Figure 5.8.8 Messiaen's "Première communion de la Vierge" (*Vingt regards sur l'enfant-Jésus* No. 11) combines an octatonic-infused tonality with atonal upper-register gestures.

often exhibits a harmonic consistency that contrasts with the more classical atonality of Schoenberg, Stockhausen, or Babbitt. This is in large part due to Ligeti's innovative use of chromatic clusters—and more specifically, to his "micropolyphonic" technique of moving multiple voices within a fixed chromatic collection. As I mentioned in Chapter 1, this "micropolyphony" constitutes a uniquely modern solution to the problem of combining conjunct melodic motion with harmonic consistency, one that exploits the *near-permutation symmetry* of very uneven chords (§1.3.1, §2.9). (Alternatively, we can say that Ligeti's music exploits the mirror boundaries of the higher-dimensional chord spaces, rather than taking advantage of their twists [§3.6]). I find it remarkable that there are just two general techniques for combining conjunct melodies with consistent harmonies, the first involving nearly even chords and underwriting the tonal procedures of the last five hundred years, the second involving clustered chords and featuring in the atonality of the 1960s. It is particularly interesting that this second solution arose almost *fifty years* after the first experiments with atonality—as if it took that long for composers to abandon the doomed project of writing traditional music with nontraditional sonorities, and to instead embrace a more radical approach that exploits the distinctive virtues of nontraditional, clustered chords. In a real sense, this music is unclassifiable: atonal by virtue of its dissonance, but tonal in its aspiration to combine harmonic consistency with conjunct melodic motion.

One of my goals here has been to identify concepts that allow us to think about the full spectrum of musical possibilities, ranging from traditional tonality to outright atonality. From this point of view, the five basic components of tonality are useful insofar as they demarcate a collection of conceptual possibilities—as if each were a musical "vector" pointing into its own abstract dimension. Together, these (metaphorical) vectors span a region that could be called "tonality space." We can situate unfamiliar pieces or genres within this metaphorical space by asking questions such as those in Figure 5.8.9. The first set of questions concerns chords and melodies, and generalizes the traditional concerns of harmony and counterpoint; the second extends notions such as "mode," "key," and "tonic" to a broader range of macroharmonic possibilities. Collectively, they replace the opposition "tonal"/"atonal" with a much more fine-grained set of categories, more appropriate to the richness of contemporary musical practice.

Composers can use these questions to situate themselves within the world of musical possibilities. For some, this may be a matter of settling in a relatively small

LOCAL
1. Does the music use a small set of similar-sounding chords?
1a. How consonant are these chords?
1b. Do these chords progress freely or are certain progressions favored?
2. Does the music use efficient voice leading?
2a. Does this voice leading take place in chromatic space or in another scale?
2b. Does it exploit near symmetries, as discussed in Chapter 2?
2c. Can it be usefully modeled with the geometrical spaces of Chapter 3?

GLOBAL
3. How fast do pitch classes circulate?
4. Does the music articulate clear macroharmonies?
4a. Are these macroharmonies structurally similar to each other?
4b. How consonant are the macroharmonies?
4c. How fast do macroharmonies change?
4d. Does the music exploit efficient voice leading between these macroharmonies?
4e. Does the music exploit "polytonal" effects by juxtaposing multiple scales or macroharmonies, each retaining their own identity?
5. Is there a sense of tonal center?
5a. Are there important secondary pitches?

Figure 5.8.9 Questions that help us situate music in tonality space.

region of tonality space for the majority of their careers. (A strategy that is perfectly reasonable insofar as one has a strong preference for a very particular kind of music, or if one wants to appeal to audiences who do.) Others—following in the footsteps of Stravinsky, Bartók, Shostakovich, Messiaen, Ligeti, and John Adams—may prefer to compose music that traverses a broader range of tonality space, sometimes within the span of a single piece. Unimaginative critics may decry this as a matter of polystylistic or postmodern inconstancy, but it is perhaps better described as a desire to embrace the full range of musical opportunities, an attitude encapsulated in Mahler's famous remark that composers create musical worlds "with all the technical means available."[33] For composers of a maximalist bent, tonality space is the field in which contemporary music operates, just as the 24 major and minor keys set the boundaries of eighteenth-century musical exploration.

To my mind there is a lot of fertile ground here. Having completed the theoretical portion of the book, my hope is that some of you will feel inspired to think about how to combine the five features—whether by making creative use of nearly symmetrical chords, exploring the voice-leading spaces of Chapter 3, manipulating interesting scales in novel ways, exploiting unusual pitch-class profiles, devising new combinations of scale, macroharmony, and centricity, or by doing something else entirely. Those who are uncertain about how to proceed may benefit from the analyses in Part II, which consider the ways in which previous composers have solved this problem. Besides deepening our appreciation for the music of the past, these analyses may suggest new directions to composers of the present.

33 See De La Grange 1973, p. 330.

PART II

History and Analysis

CHAPTER 6

The Extended Common Practice

In the second half of the book, we'll employ our theoretical apparatus to ask specific analytical and historical questions. Chapter 6 uses the five components of tonality as a framework for reinterpreting the history of Western music, suggesting that a number of broadly tonal styles use very similar compositional techniques. The remaining chapters take up specific issues raised by this overarching narrative. Chapter 7 discusses the harmonic syntax of eighteenth-century tonality, using geometrical models to investigate general questions about chord progressions, sequences, and key distances. Chapters 8, 9, and 10 are mostly analytical, focusing on chromatic harmony, twentieth-century scalar music, and jazz. Here the point is to demonstrate that the theoretical apparatus is useful for explicating *specific pieces* as well as more general historical trends.

Ultimately, the goal of Part II is to argue that Western tonal music constitutes an *extended common practice* stretching from the eleventh century to the present day. By now, this thesis should not be too surprising: since the five components of tonality constrain each other in interesting and nonobvious ways, composers who wish to combine them have only a few alternatives at their disposal. The simple fact is that many composers from before Josquin to after John Coltrane *have* wanted to combine these features, and hence have struggled with a problem that has a relatively small number of solutions. We should therefore expect that when we dig deep enough, we will start to find interesting similarities among their approaches.

Chapter 6 illustrates this point by considering brief passages from five very different musical styles. The first is eleventh-century, two-voice note-against-note counterpoint—the earliest and most basic form of Western polyphony. The second illustrates the vocal counterpoint of the Renaissance. The third exemplifies the functional harmony of the baroque and classical eras, and embodies two related innovations: the establishment of purely harmonic conventions and the increasingly systematic use of modulation. The fourth style highlights nineteenth-century composers' growing awareness of chords as objects in *chromatic* space, while the fifth illustrates twentieth-century approaches to nondiatonic scales. Since my goal is to argue that there are similarities between these five very different kinds of music, my discussion will necessarily abstract away from numerous historical particulars. This is precisely why I consider brief passages, rather than entire pieces. I trust you will agree that my examples capture the spirit of the genres they represent.

6.1 DISCLAIMERS

There are several ways in which my approach might strike some readers as being anachronistic. First, I will generally model chords as unordered collections of pitch classes, and counterpoint as voice leadings in pitch-class space. These ideas, though originating in the theories of Lippius and Rameau, are more commonly associated with the twentieth century. It is therefore worth repeating that my goal is to describe music in a way that is useful to contemporary musicians, rather than to explain how earlier composers actually thought. I should also reiterate that the very notion of "pitch class" involves a significant degree of abstraction: every composer in every era thinks carefully about octave, instrument, and register, distinguishing perfect fourths from perfect fifths and root position from second-inversion triads. Were this a hands-on guide to composition, I would need to spend a great deal of time considering the various ways pitch-class voice leadings can be embodied in real music. However, my purpose here is to provide more general theoretical tools for understanding tonality—and in this context, an abstract approach is perfectly appropriate.

The other major point of anachronism is that I am not going to worry much about tuning and intonation. These are, of course, major preoccupations of music theory, and tuning systems have coevolved with harmony in fascinating ways: just intonation, which permits acoustically pure thirds, burgeoned alongside the development of triadic harmony; while more equal temperaments accompanied the increasing use of distant modulations.[1] That said, standard tuning systems are in the grand scheme of things reasonably similar, and can all be represented by very similar geometrical structures. To be sure, tuning colors music in important ways and can make a real difference to our listening experience. But it does not fundamentally affect the very general theoretical relationships that are our main subject.

Finally, since this chapter surveys musical pieces spanning a millennium, it will necessarily omit many details. Professional music historians, who devote their lives to understanding history in all its marvelous specificity, will look in vain for the nuanced discussions that are their stock-in-trade. They may even feel, at some points, that my descriptions are uncomfortably close to the potted histories of introductory music appreciation classes. I make no apologies for this. It seems to me that there *are* some fairly systematic connections between Western styles, and that these connections have often been ignored. Insofar as conventional scholarship de-emphasizes or disregards these general facts—perhaps in something like the way that a fish ignores the water in which it swims—then I think it is worthwhile to try to discuss them, even at the risk of seeming somewhat naive.[2]

---

1 For nontechnical (and wildly different) introductions to this subject, see Isacoff 2001 and Duffin 2006.

2 Here I am inspired by Jared Diamond (1997), who attempts to uncover broad geographical factors that constrain and influence the progress of human history. My geography is abstract and mathematical.

6.2 TWO-VOICE MEDIEVAL COUNTERPOINT

Figure 6.2.1 returns to the *Allelujia Justus et Palma,* first published in the eleventh-century treatise *Ad Organum Faciendum* (*How to Write Counterpoint*), and discussed previously in §3.5. Although it stands at the very beginning of the Western polyphonic tradition, the piece clearly exemplifies a number of our five features.

1. *Conjunct melodic motion.* In general the voices move by step, with contrary motion preferred to parallel motion. There are no prohibitions against parallel fifths or octaves.
2. *Acoustic consonance.* The Montpelier organum treatise, roughly contemporaneous with *Ad Organum Faciendum,* considers steps, sevenths, and tritones to be forbidden dissonances. Thirds and sixths are imperfect consonances which can be used only in the middle of phrases; unisons, fourths, and fifths are perfect consonances which can be used anywhere. This accurately describes the musical examples in *Ad Organum Faciendum,* though that text does not discuss imperfect consonances.[3]
3. *Harmonic consistency.* There is no robust notion of harmonic consistency, or "chord" in the modern sense. Instead, intervals are categorized by consonance and dissonance.
4. *Macroharmony.* The lines move within an enriched diatonic system containing seven and a half notes: C, D, E, F, G, A, and B♭/B♮. The last of these is a flexible note that exists in both a "soft" (B♭) and a "hard" (B♮) form. These two forms do not intermix; one does not progress directly to the other, and care is taken to avoid clashes between different note forms in

Figure 6.2.1 The *Allelujia Justus et Palma* from *Ad Organum Faciendum.* Open and closed noteheads represent the two different musical voices.

3 See Blum 1959. Note that I mean to be including compound intervals in this list: thus, an octave and a third (15 or 16 semitones) is an imperfect consonance, while an octave and a fifth (19 semitones) is a perfect consonance.

different voices. The two flavors of B allow composers to avoid the tritones E-B♭ and F-B.

5. *Centricity*. Cadences are articulated by contrary motion onto a unison or octave, with one voice moving by step and the other moving by step or third. By modern standards there is only a weak sense of centricity, and the music often seems to float freely in diatonic space.

No less than the music of the high Baroque, then, our simple medieval style requires the simultaneous satisfaction of harmonic and contrapuntal constraints: the principal harmonic constraint is that intervals must be consonant, with perfect consonances predominating and imperfect consonances appearing more rarely; contrapuntally, the main requirement is that the music should feature a pair of conjunct melodies, often moving in contrary motion. Early medieval music-theory treatises attempt to help composers satisfy both constraints, typically by listing useful progressions in mind-numbing detail—"when one part ascends a step, the other, beginning at the octave above may descend two steps and be at the fifth"; "when one part repeats a note, the other, beginning at the fourth above, may ascend by step to the fifth"; and so on.

Let us see if we can use two-note chord space to describe these principles more efficiently. Figure 6.2.2 labels the consonances in our simplified medieval system, using dark type for the perfect consonances and lighter type for imperfect consonances. Perfect consonances are linked by line segments when it is possible to connect them by stepwise voice leading, and by dotted line segments when they can be connected by "near-stepwise" voice leading—that is, voice leading in which one voice moves by step and the other by third. To a good first approximation, learning to compose in this style involves internalizing the structure of this graph: perfect

Figure 6.2.2 Perfect and imperfect consonances in our simplified medieval system, displayed on the Möbius strip. Solid lines in the interior of the figure correspond to stepwise voice leadings, while dashed lines show nearly stepwise voice leadings.

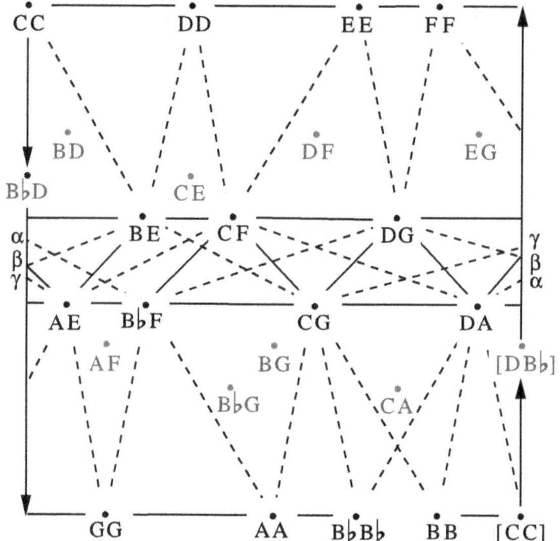

consonances account for about 90% of the intervals in the *Allelujia,* with the two voices moving stepwise or near stepwise 70% of the time.[4] These numbers suggest that our Möbius strip does indeed encapsulate the basic compositional knowledge possessed by early medieval composers, acting as a kind of musical "game board" on which they plied their trade.

Figure 6.2.3 traces out the seventh phrase of the *Allelujia* on the game board. For clarity, I have shifted the location of the left and right boundaries, and have omitted the imperfect consonances.[5] Five of the eight voice leadings use near-stepwise voice leading to connect perfect fourths and unisons (or fifths and octaves). This is much clearer on the Möbius strip than in the musical notation; we can see at a glance that the phrase largely consists of line segments connecting boundary points (octaves or unisons) to the nearest perfect fourth/fifth on the inside of the strip. The geometrical representation also shows that the latter part of the phrase contains a hidden repetition of the opening: the initial dyads (G, G)→(E, A)→(F, F) form a wedge on the lower left

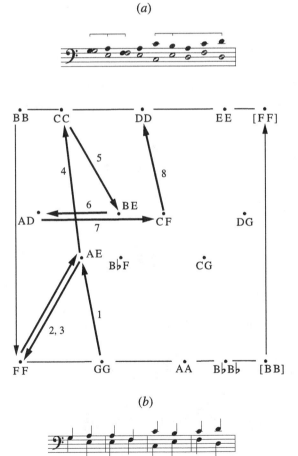

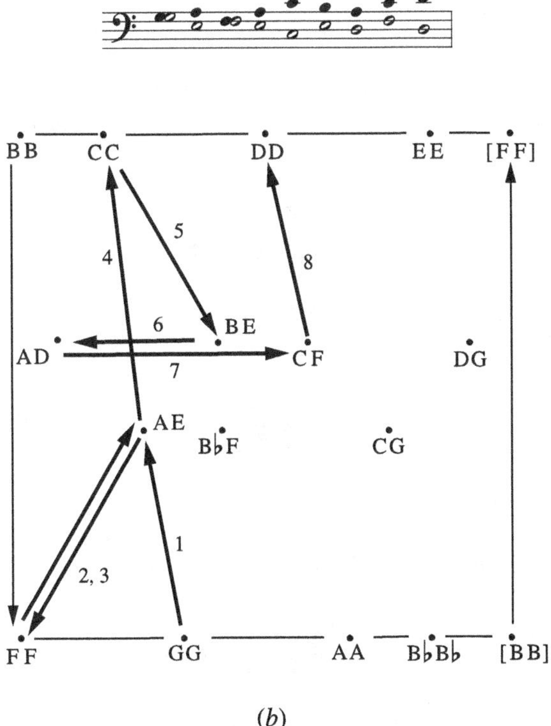

Figure 6.2.3 (*a*) The seventh phrase of the *Allelujia Justus et Palma,* traced out on the Möbius strip. (*b*) The phase contains four "nearly stepwise" voice leadings connecting a perfect fifth to an octave (or perfect fourth to a unison).

4 Stepwise motion in both voices counts for about 30% of the progressions, while near-stepwise motion adds another 40%; individually, each voice moves stepwise about 50% of the time.

5 As explained in §3.2 the placement of the left and right boundaries is arbitrary.

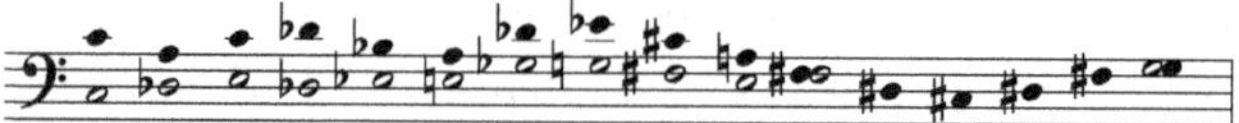

Figure 6.2.4
Octatonic organum.

of the Möbius strip, which is echoed by wedge (C, C)→(E, B)→...→(D, D) above it. (See also the brackets above the musical notation.) However, the repetition is interrupted by a pair of parallel fifths that bring the music to {D, A} and {F, C}.

One might think the consonant quality of this music derives primarily from the fact that it uses consonant intervals. But as we saw in Chapter 5, its placid sonic character is also a function of its macroharmony. Figure 6.2.4 illustrates this point with a piece of "octatonic organum" that parodies the *Allelujia*'s opening phrase: though the parody uses only consonant intervals, it is more suggestive of a black mass or satanic ritual than medieval Christian piety. This demonstrates quite clearly that the appeal of early music is as much a function of the macroharmony as of the vertical intervals themselves—a lesson that suggests contemporary composers need to pay as much attention to macroharmony as to harmony proper.

6.3 TRIADS AND THE RENAISSANCE

Figure 6.3.1 presents the opening of "Tu pauperum refugium," the second part of Josquin's motet "Magnus es tu, Domine."[6] As in the *Allelujia Justus et Palma,* the music is

Figure 6.3.1
The opening of Josquin's "Tu pauperum refugium." Beneath the staff, I have shown how the music contains a series of efficient three-voice voice leadings between three-note chords.

6 This piece was published anonymously in 1504, and has been attributed to both Finck and Josquin (see Judd 2006). It has been analyzed by writers such as Salzer and Schachter (1989), Berry (1976), Joseph (1978), and Judd (2006).

largely diatonic, using stepwise melodic motion to articulate consonant harmonies. But there are also some fundamental differences between the styles.

Consonance and counterpoint. Parallel fifths and octaves are no longer used. Fourths over the bass typically resolve to thirds, as if they had been reclassified as dissonances (Figure 6.3.2). However, fourths are tolerated between upper voices, giving them an ambiguous status between consonance and dissonance.[7] Diminished triads sometimes appear in first inversion, even though they contain a dissonant tritone. As a result, Josquin's music is significantly less austere than the earlier medieval style.

Harmonic consistency. The music creates a much stronger effect of harmonic consistency, with fully 85% of the four-voice sonorities being triadic. The occasional use of diminished chords reinforces the sense that triads are syntactical objects: it is as if the diminished chord's triadic status (i.e. its transpositional relatedness to major and minor triads in diatonic space) trumps the fact that it contains a dissonance. Although it might be anachronistic to treat every sonority in the piece as representing an underlying triad, there seems to have been a move toward this way of thinking. Certainly, one gets the impression that the transition toward conceiving of triads as harmonic things-in-themselves is well underway.

Macroharmony and centricity. The music makes use of a wider range of accidentals, occasionally producing mild macroharmonic change. Cadences are often articulated by specific melodic and harmonic formulas, some of which anticipate the V–I progressions of later music (Figure 6.3.2). To a modern ear, there is more sense of a "tonal center" than in the medieval style. However, the music continues to have a somewhat "floating" quality, and many passages are only weakly centered.

Figure 6.3.2 In Josquin's music, fourths typically resolve to thirds (*a*), diminished triads sometimes appear in first inversion (*b*), and cadences sometimes anticipate the functional harmony of later centuries (*c*).

7 The ambiguous status of the fourth is addressed by early fifteenth-century theorists such as Prosdocimus de Beldemandis (see Kaye 1989 and Gut 1976).

In the rest of this section I want to look more carefully at these differences, with the goal of understanding how they might relate to the music-theoretical constraints discussed earlier.

6.3.1 Harmonic Consistency and the Rise of Triads

The triadic quality of Josquin's music can be traced, in part, to simple combinatorial facts about the diatonic scale. To see this, notice that it is almost impossible to write three-voice counterpoint using only perfect consonances. This is illustrated in Figure 6.3.3, which locates the perfect consonances in three-note chord space; chords here are quite far apart, and only a few are connected by lines representing stepwise voice leading. (In fact, there are only three ways to connect three-note perfect consonances by stepwise voice leading, and two of these produce parallel octaves.[8]) Readers who try to compose under these conditions will quickly develop a renewed appreciation for imperfect consonances, which are virtually necessary for creating elegant three-voice counterpoint.[9]

Now suppose that you would like to use three-note chords containing only perfect and imperfect consonances—that is, thirds, fourths, fifths, sixths, and their

Figure 6.3.3 There are only a few three-note chords containing only perfect consonances, and they are spread throughout three-note chord space (*a*). (Note that we are viewing chord space from above, looking down through the triangular faces; compare the side view in Figure 3.8.2, where the triangular faces are on the top and bottom.) As a result, there are only a few ways to connect them with stepwise voice leadings (*b*), particularly if one wants to avoid parallel octaves.

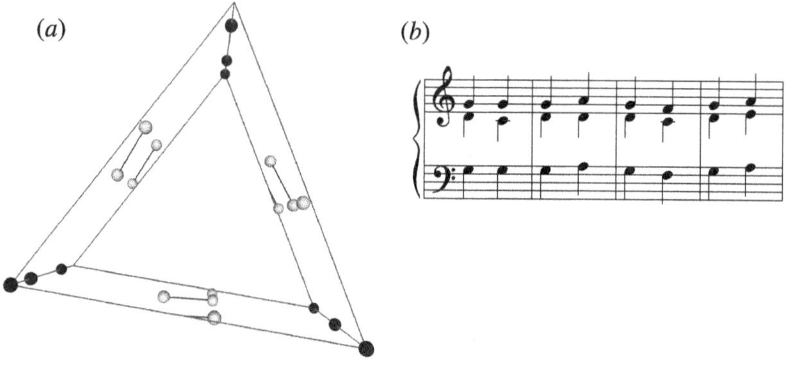

8 If we relax the requirement of stepwise motion, we obtain a few more options, but not enough for compositional comfort.

9 There is some medieval music in which only the perfect consonances are *stable*. However, this music typically utilizes a large number of unstable sonorities in metrically weak positions.

Figure 6.3.4 Doubled consonances (*a*) and triads (*b*).

compounds. It turns out there are only two possibilities: *doubled consonances,* containing multiple copies of some note, and *triads,* containing no doublings at all (Figure 6.3.4). The chords in the second category are sonically richer than those in the first, simply by virtue of containing three distinct pitch classes. But they are also related in another way as well: considered as unordered sets of pitch classes, they are all related by diatonic transposition. It follows that a relatively *weak* notion of harmonic consistency—the mere preference for triads over doubled consonances—automatically generates a much stronger kind of consistency. To my mind this is a profound fact, suggesting that harmonic consistency might arise as the *unbidden byproduct* of more basic musical preferences: composers who favor three-pitch-class consonances, purely on the basis of their richer note content, will inevitably use chords related by scalar transposition.

In fact, a fondness for triadic harmonies is already evident in the three-voice compositions of the late fourteenth century.[10] Figure 6.3.5 traces the development of this norm throughout the following decades.[11] In Dufay's music, complete triads account for about 46% of the three-voice chords and 78% of the four-voice chords—numbers

Figure 6.3.5 The percentage of consonant sonorities that are complete triads rather than "doubled" intervals, by composer date of birth. The percentage is reasonably high throughout the Renaissance, and increases over time.

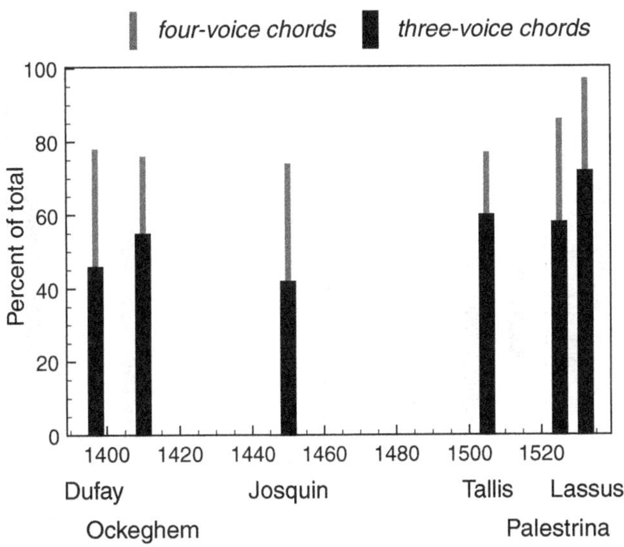

10 See Crocker 1962, Rivera 1979, Kaye 1989.

11 The data in this section come from more than 150 MIDI files of four-voice Renaissance vocal music.

that increase to 72% and 97% in the music of Lassus.[12] The ratio of four-voice to three-voice chords increases as well, with three-voice sonorities being more prevalent in Dufay and Ockeghem, and four-voice sonorities predominating later. Indeed, it is likely that the desire for triadic harmonies explains this gradual standardization of four-voice textures, since it is very difficult to write three-voice music that consistently articulates complete triads, particularly if one wants to avoid second-inversion chords. A fourth voice allows for significantly greater compositional freedom, permitting composers to use complete triads while still leaving enough flexibility to write interesting melodic lines.

6.3.2 "3 + 1" Voice Leading

Four-voice textures would seem to pose a challenge for our geometrical approach, since they require a four-dimensional space in which doublings are not perspicuously represented.[13] Happily, a sizable proportion of Josquin's voice leadings involve what I call *the 3 + 1 schema:* here, three voices articulate a strongly crossing-free voice leading between complete triads (§4.9), while a fourth voice adds doublings. This fourth voice is typically the bass, which often leaps from root to root; the other three voices are typically in close position and often move as efficiently as possible. (See Figure 6.3.1, bottom staff.) Figure 6.3.6 shows that these "3 + 1" voice leadings account for a significant portion of the four-voice triadic voice leadings in a broad sample of Renaissance music. These figures suggest that the eighteenth-century ten-

Figure 6.3.6 The percentage of four-voice triadic voice leadings that are factorizable in a "3 + 1" manner, with three voices articulating strongly crossing-free voice leadings between complete triads, arranged by composer birth year.

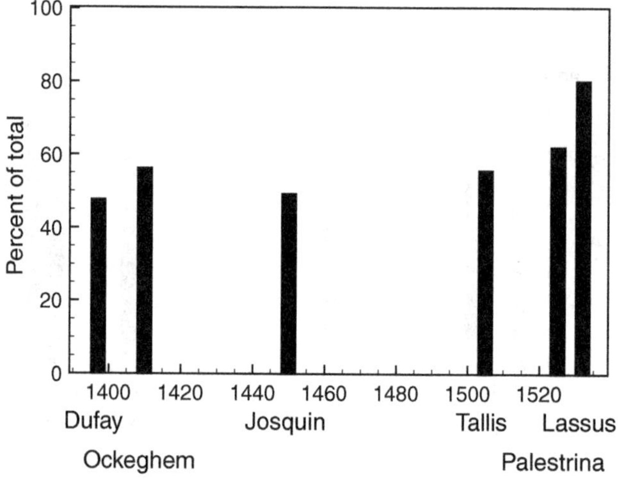

12 Because there are many more doubled consonances than complete triads, even the 50:50 ratio for three-note chords suggests a preference for complete sonorities.

13 For example, in four-note space the chord {C, C, E, G} is somewhat distant from {C, E, G, G} (§3.12).

dency to conceive of harmony as "a bass line plus some relatively homogenous upper voices"—exemplified most clearly by figured-bass notation—might actually originate in the Renaissance.

It follows that we can often use three-note chord space to analyze four-part Renaissance music: we simply focus on three of the voices, treating the fourth as an "odd man out" subject to its own rules. Figure 6.3.7 locates the diatonic triads in three-note chord space, with the lines indicating single-step voice leading. The seven diatonic triads form a crooked chain running through the center of the space, with the top chord connected to the bottom as explained in Chapter 3. In §3.11, we described this circle of triads as being analogous to the diatonic circle of fifths, since it links a series of structurally similar chords by single-step voice leadings. We now see that we can use it to model many of the voice leadings in Renaissance counterpoint.

Suppose, for example, you would like to move three voices from C major to F major. The most efficient way to do this is to take two clockwise steps along the circle, producing the voice leading (C, E, G)→(C, E, A)→(C, F, A) or (C, E, G)→(C, F, A). Each clockwise move raises a single voice by step: the first moves G to A, while the second moves E to F (Figure 6.3.8). Alternatively, however, we can move from C to F by taking five *counterclockwise* steps, producing (C, E, G)→(B, E, G)→(B, D, G)→(B, D, F)→(A, D, F)→(A, C, F), or (C, E, G)→(A, C, F). Each counterclockwise move lowers one voice by step, yielding a voice leading whose voices descend by a total of five steps. By taking one or more complete turns around the circle, we can generate other voice leadings between C major and F major, all of which are strongly crossing free. In

Figure 6.3.7 The diatonic triads form a chain that runs through the center of three-note chord space, with adjacent triads linked by single-step voice leading. (*b*) This "circle of thirds" is analogous to the familiar circle of fifth-related diatonic scales, and can be used to represent any three-voice, strongly crossing-free voice leading between triads.

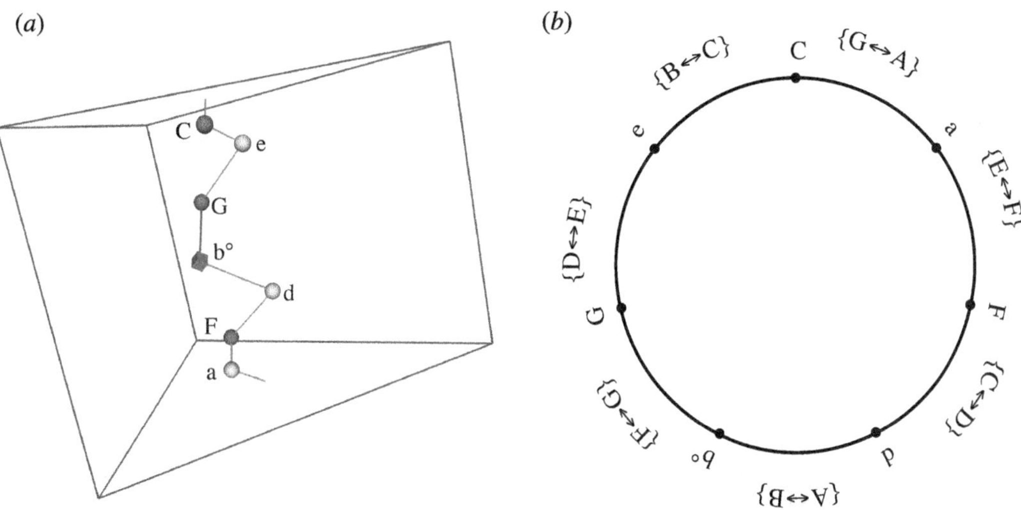

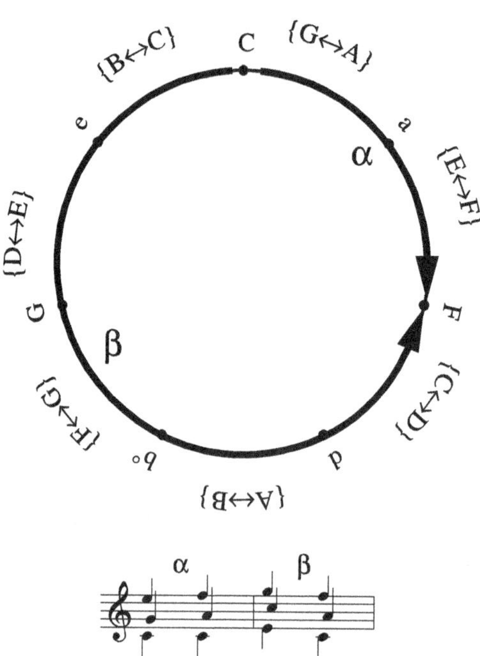

Figure 6.3.8 Two strongly crossing-free voice leadings between C and F, represented on the circle.

fact, the circle models *all* possible strongly crossing-free voice leadings between any two triads in the C diatonic scale.

Figure 6.3.9a plots the opening phrase of "Tu pauperum refugium" as a series of paths in three-note chord space. Figure 6.3.9b shows how these voice leadings would be represented on the circle; in both views, the music takes the most direct path between successive triads. This is characteristic of the excerpt: indeed, of the twelve numbered voice leadings on Figure 6.3.1, all but one takes the shortest path along the triadic circle.[14]

To give a sense of the utility of the circle—and of the ubiquity of the voice leadings it represents—Figure 6.3.10 turns to a style worlds apart from Josquin. Here we see that many common guitar fingerings also articulate strongly crossing-free voice leadings in their upper voices. (Of course, in pop music, efficient voice leading results more from guitarists' attempts to

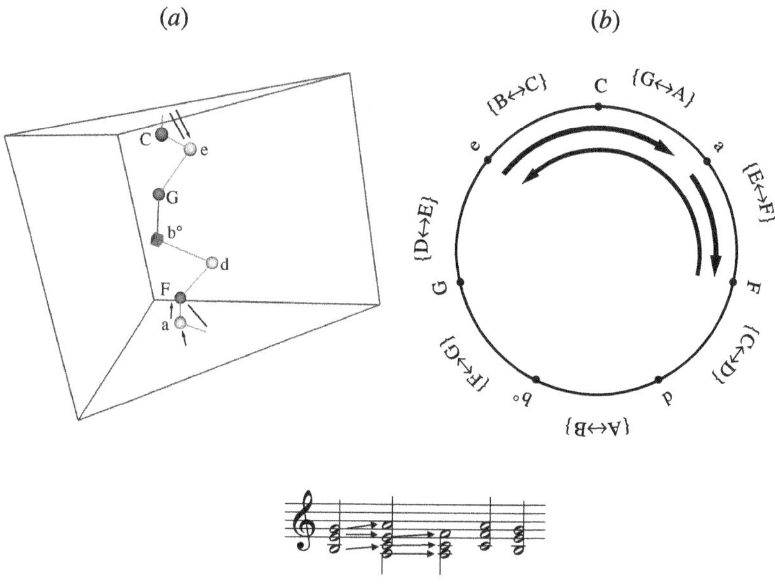

Figure 6.3.9 Four voice leadings from the opening of Josquin's "Tu pauperum refugium" plotted in three-note chord space (*a*) and on the diatonic circle of thirds (*b*).

14 The exception is (D, F, A)→(B, E, G♯), which is less efficient than (D, F, A)→(E, G♯, B). However, the latter voice leading is unusable because it creates both parallel fifths and a melodic augmented second. Furthermore, it is actually *less* efficient when considered as a voice leading in chromatic space—involving seven semitones of motion as opposed to five.

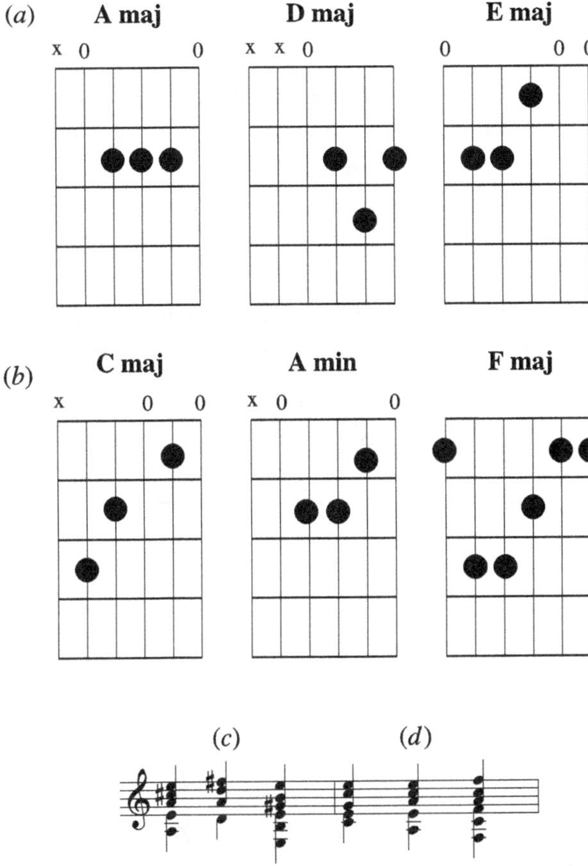

Figure 6.3.10 (*a–b*) Two common chord progressions, as they are often played on a guitar. (*c–d*) The notes produced by these fingering patterns. The top three voices articulate strongly crossing-free voice leadings that can be represented on the triadic circle.

minimize their physical motions than from an explicit concern for polyphony.) The distance between these two examples—one representing the high art of the Renaissance, the other representing the vernacular of our own time—suggests that our triadic voice leadings feature in a very broad range of music.

6.3.3 Fourth Progressions and Cadences

We now turn to a feature of Renaissance practice that is not altogether obvious in the brief Josquin excerpt. Figure 6.3.11 shows that root progressions by perfect fourth and fifth become increasingly prevalent from Josquin on: where the root progressions in Dufay and Ockeghem are about evenly divided between steps, thirds, and fourths, fourths account for more than 50% of the progressions in Josquin and almost 60% in Palestrina.[15] This trend continues into the eighteenth century, reaching more than 70% in the Bach chorales. One possible explanation lies in the fact

15 Note that I am using use "fourth" to mean "fourth or fifth or any of their compounds." In constructing the graph I also eliminated progressions such as (C4, C4, E4, G4)→(C4, C4, E4, A4), which could be interpreted as resulting from linear motion in the top voice; third progressions were counted only when at least two voices change.

that these progressions make it particularly easy to harmonize stepwise melodies. Figure 6.3.12 shows that if we start with a C major chord, with any of its notes in the soprano, we can harmonize any melodic step with either the progression C major→F major or C major→G major. By contrast, steps and thirds are not nearly so useful: third progressions from a fixed triad can harmonize only two stepwise motions; while step progressions can easily lead to parallel fifths and octaves.[16] (To avoid these parallels, composers typically use chord inversions, or move the upper voices inefficiently.)

Figure 6.3.11 Root progressions by composer, with S = second, T = third, and F = fourth. Over the course of the Renaissance, there is an increasing preference for fourth progressions, a trend that continues into the classical tradition.

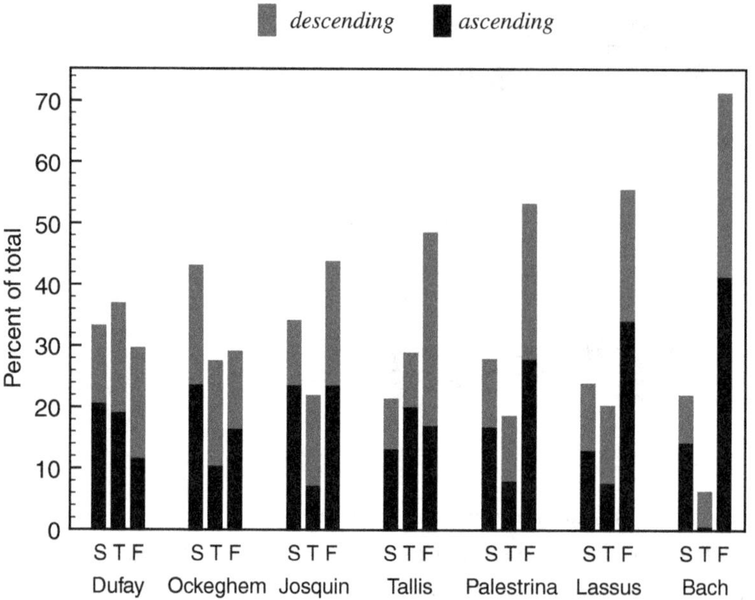

Figure 6.3.12 Fourth progressions allow a composer to harmonize a wide range of stepwise melodies in a "3 + 1" fashion, with the upper voices moving by strongly crossing-free voice leadings and the bass moving from root to root. Root motions by second and third are comparatively less flexible, either because they do not harmonize many stepwise melodies or because they can create forbidden parallels.

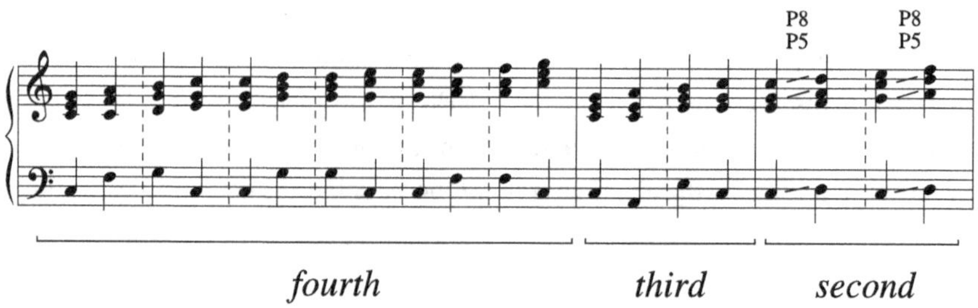

16 Common tones may also be a factor: step-related triads have no common tones, fourth-related triads have one, and third-related triads have two. The Goldilocks Principle perhaps favors the middle option.

From this point of view, fourth progressions are particularly handy tools, being easy to use while also providing a wealth of melodic options.

Of course, fourth progressions play a critical role at cadences, too. Recall from §6.2 that medieval cadences often feature two voices converging by stepwise contrary motion onto a unison or octave (Figure 6.3.13). Suppose we want to add a third voice to this cadence, ending on either a triple unison C, or the open fifth C-G-C. (In particular, suppose we want the bass to sound the pitch class on which the voices converge, so that the acoustic root of the chord reinforces the converging melodies.[17]) One possible harmonization is shown in Figure 6.3.13b: with the F♯, this is a standard medieval double leading-tone cadence; with the F♮, it suggests a tonal vii°6–I progression. (Another variant, with B♭ and D♭, produces a "phrygian cadence," common in both Renaissance and classical music.) A second option, shown in Figure 6.3.13d, very closely resembles the V–I progression. When we examine four-voice harmonizations, the situation is even more dramatic, as virtually all the available options evoke familiar cadences.[18] Rather than being arbitrary conventions, then, these cadential formulas may arise as relatively obvious solutions to the basic problem of harmonizing two converging stepwise voices.

We see, then, that Renaissance music involves two different kinds of fourth progressions. Within-phrase progressions have little or no cadential function and do not necessarily create the sense of tension and release. In particular, these progressions typically feature 3 + 1 voice leading rather than the converging stepwise voices of the cadential formulas (cf. the first voice leading in Figure 6.3.1). By contrast,

Figure 6.3.13 (*a*) A basic medieval two-voice cadential pattern, in which two voices converge onto an octave by stepwise motion. (*b–c*) Three-voice harmonizations producing a common medieval cadence (with the F♯), a vii°6–I cadence (with the F♮), or a phrygian cadence (with F♮ and D♭). (*d*) A three-voice harmonization resembling a V–I cadence. (*e*) A failed harmonization producing parallel fifths. (*f–h*) Four-voice extensions of the preceding schemas. The V–I form (*g*) cadences on a sonority containing only perfect consonances.

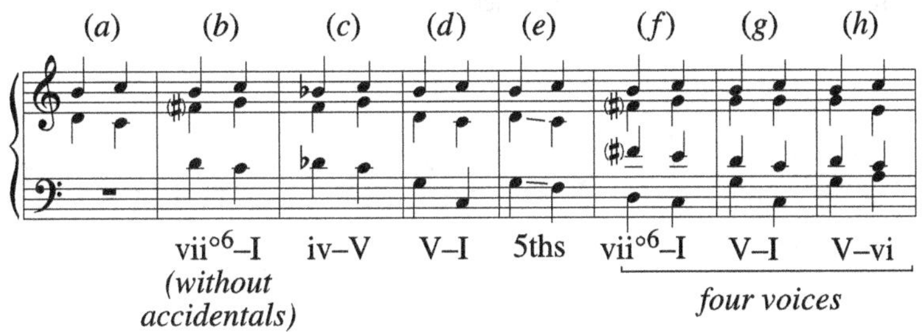

17 Not all medieval cadences are like this, of course: one sometimes finds progressions such as (G3, B3, D4)→(F3, C4, C4), but it is reasonable to suppose that musicians would incline toward cadences in which the pitch class in the bass is also the object of melodic convergence, as these would presumably create a stronger sense of emphasis on a single pitch class.

18 These ideas derive from Randel (1971), who suggests that the increasing popularity of the V–I cadential form is the result of two factors: first, a preference for concluding on open fifths rather than complete triads, and second, an increasing preference for four-voice textures. See also Lowinsky 1961.

cadential fourth progressions *do* exhibit a clear pattern of tension and release, and almost always employ converging melodic voices. One interesting possibility is that functional tonality arose out of the gradual fusion between these two types of progression—in other words, the within-phrase fourth progressions gradually acquired the tension-release quality of the cadential formulas, articulating the music into a sequence of short "harmonic cycles," each concluding with its own tension-resolving V–I progression. We will return to this idea in the next chapter.

6.3.4 Parallel Perfect Intervals

Finally, a word about the prohibition on parallel perfect fifths and octaves. Many theorists have proposed that the prohibition is connected to the phenomenon of auditory streaming: on this account, parallel motion by perfect fifth or octave tends to destroy the sense that the music is composed of *independent* musical voices, since it leads us to "fuse" the voices into a single melody.[19] While I am sympathetic to this explanation, it seems to me that the prohibition might also reflect structural features of diatonic scale itself. Figure 6.3.14 shows that parallel diatonic fifths almost always produce parallel chromatic fifths; by contrast, parallel diatonic thirds do not produce the same degree of chromatic parallelism, since the diatonic scale contains a more even distribution of major and minor thirds. To me, this difference is at least as striking as the difference in the acoustic quality of the intervals. Figure 6.3.14 illustrates this point by comparing two sorts of parallel motion in Messiaen's nine-note "mode 3." Here three-step scalar intervals are always four semitones large, while four-step scalar intervals alternate between six and seven semitones. I find that the passages exhibit a roughly similar degree of "voice independence,"

Figure 6.3.14 Parallel motion within the diatonic scale (*a–c*) and in Messiaen's "Mode 3" (*d–e*). Underneath each interval I have written its chromatic size in semitones. The brackets identify chromatic motion that is not parallel.

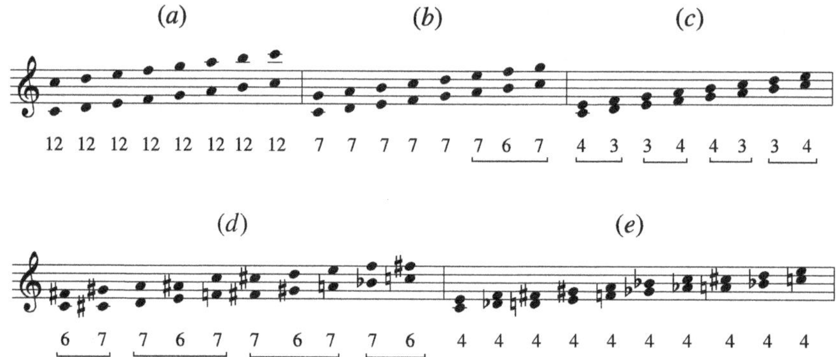

19 See Huron 2001 and the references therein.

even though one of them contains parallel perfect fifths and the other doesn't. This suggests scale structure plays at least some role in explaining the prohibition on forbidden parallels.[20]

* * *

Let me conclude this discussion by reinforcing two general points. First, there are a number of features of Renaissance practice that prefigure later styles, including triadic harmonies, the 3 + 1 arrangement of the voices, the avoidance of parallel perfect intervals, and the increasing use of root progressions by perfect fifth. These facts should perhaps make us hesitate before drawing too sharp a distinction between the musical languages of Palestrina and Bach.[21] Second, and perhaps more important, several features of Renaissance syntax can be seen as relatively obvious solutions to very basic compositional goals—ensuring voice independence, writing consonant music using three-note sonorities, and harmonizing stepwise convergence onto a unison. In hindsight, we can see these developments as exploiting relatively obvious possibilities lying dormant in the diatonic system.

In saying this, I do not mean to propose a deterministic or Hegelian view of music history according to which music was fated to develop as it actually did: one can certainly imagine alternate histories in which, say, Western composers never developed an aversion to parallel perfect fifths. But I do think that composers, like all artists, are opportunists, quick to take advantage of whatever possibilities present themselves. And the fundamental moral of Part I is that the five components of tonality impose nontrivial constraints on composers' choices, boxing them in on some sides while allowing them to move freely in other directions. One might make an analogy here to a mountaineer ascending a cliff: though the climber is in principle free to move in any direction, the structure of the rock will naturally suggest certain routes, offering handholds and footholds that will guide any sensible person's decisions. In much the same way, we can sometimes tell reasonably compelling stories about why music might have developed as it did. The trick for the historian is to make room for contingency while also capturing the way in which music history sometimes follows the path of least resistance, like a climber ascending a cliff by way of a particularly inviting chute.

---

20 One point in favor of the acoustic explanation is that parallel perfect fourths are permitted in classical three-voice counterpoint, whereas parallel perfect fifths are not. (This marks an interesting difference between fifths and octaves: parallel octaves remain objectionable no matter how the octaves are arranged in register, whereas fifths can always be converted to unobjectionable fourths by a suitable transposition of voices.) However, it is not clear whether we should try to find principled explanations for every feature of traditional practice. In fact, very occasional parallel perfect fifths, embedded in complex contrapuntal textures, may not significantly weaken voice independence.

21 Well-meaning scholars have sometimes been overzealous in their attempts to complicate this picture. For example, Harold Powers (1992, pp. 11–12) denies each of the following claims: "the modal system was displaced by the tonal system," "modality evolved into tonality," and "the ancestors of our major and minor scales were the Ionian and Aeolian modes." It seems to me that these three truisms are unobjectionable when properly understood; by rejecting them completely, Powers commits an error as egregious as the oversimplifications he warns against.

6.4 FUNCTIONAL HARMONY

Where our early medieval excerpt exhibited the basic two-dimensional coherence of Western music, combining recognizable melodies with consonant harmonies, the Renaissance passage added a much more robust notion of harmonic consistency. Our next example features two further innovations. First, chords are now constrained to move according to a small number of ("functional") harmonic conventions. These conventions go hand-in-hand with a much stronger emphasis on the tonic, so that centricity is often significantly clearer than in earlier music. Second, keys now participate in their own meaningful progressions, as modulation becomes more systematic and encompasses a wider range of macroharmonic states. The result, as I have said, is a musical style that is hierarchically self-similar, with the same fundamental procedures appearing on both the level of the scale and that of the chord.

Figure 6.4.1a presents the opening of one of J. S. Bach's harmonizations of the chorale melody "Herr Christ, der ein'ge Gott's sohn." Where the progressions in Josquin's "Tu pauperum refugium" are extremely free, those in Bach's chorale can be summarized by the simple map in Figure 6.4.1b. Such maps embody the new conventions central to eighteenth-century harmony—for instance, that ii chords often move to V chords, but not vice versa. The bottom staff of the figure shows that the music again uses the 3 + 1 schema, with the upper three voices in close position and moving in a strongly crossing-free manner, and with the bass obeying its own principles. The

Figure 6.4.1 (*a*) The first phrase of Bach's chorale "Herr Christ, der ein'ge Gott'ssohn" (No. 303 in the Riemenschneider edition) and a reduction of the upper voice counterpoint. (*b*) A simple model of the chord progressions it contains. Chords can move freely rightward, but can move leftward only by following the arrows.

similarity to Figure 6.3.1 suggests that functionally tonal music *augments* Renaissance voice-leading practices with new and distinctive harmonic rules.[22]

This last observation is surprisingly controversial. A number of theorists, influenced by Heinrich Schenker, seem to deny that functional tonality involves purely harmonic conventions.[23] Instead, they claim that what *appear* to be independent harmonic laws can actually be derived from new voice-leading principles indigenous to the classical era. We will consider this view more carefully in the next chapter. For now, though, let us note that we have good historical reasons for claiming that functionally tonal music obeys purely harmonic laws. To put it crudely: Renaissance music uses efficient voice leading, avoids parallel fifths and octaves, and allows triads to progress in a very free fashion; classical music observes many of the same voice-leading conventions, but also requires chords to move in particular ways. Moreover, twentieth-century tonal music often permits parallel fifths and octaves while still conforming to the harmonic schemas of the classical era. It seems exceedingly natural to represent this situation as shown in Figure 6.4.2. Here, the so-called "common practice period" is depicted as lying at the intersection of *two* separate common practices: a contrapuntal common practice that includes the music of the Renaissance, and a harmonic common practice that includes a good deal of twentieth-century music. Theorists who renounce harmonic laws risk effacing these two common practices, and hence obscuring the connections between Renaissance music, classical tonality, and more recent rock and jazz.

Functional harmony is also notable insofar as it charts coherent paths through the space of possible keys. This can be seen in the opening phrases of one of Bach's settings of the hymn "Ein' feste Burg," shown in Figure 6.4.3. The music begins in D major but modulates to A major at the end of the first phrase; it then turns to B minor to start the second phrase, returning to the tonic D major at the end. As discussed earlier, these modulations involve *particular voice leadings between scales:* the first raises G to G♯, the second raises A to A♯, and the last cancels these two changes by returning to the opening collection. Figure 6.4.4 shows how these modulations appear on the scale lattice of §4.6: the music begins by taking minimal steps between adjacent collections, and ends by moving diagonally back to its starting point. Such voice leadings represent a higher dimensional analogue to the contrapuntal processes linking individual chords.

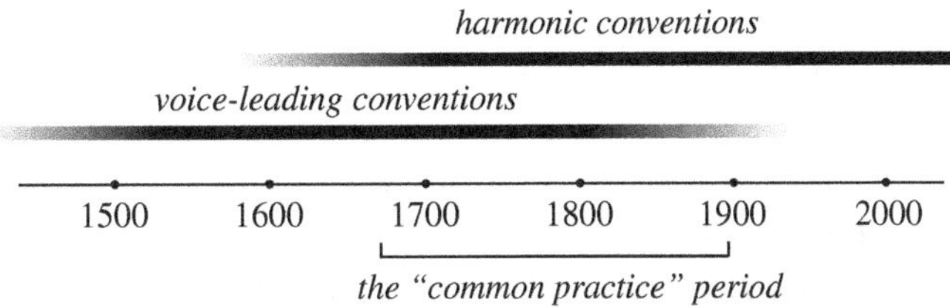

Figure 6.4.2 The "common practice period" as the intersection of two common practices.

22 To be fair, functionally tonal music may involve a few new rules, such as the requirement that the leading tone resolve upward. Nevertheless, the vast majority of its contrapuntal rules are inherited from earlier styles.

23 See, for example, Salzer 1982, Schenker 2001, and Beach 1974.

Figure 6.4.3 The first two phrases of one of Bach's harmonizations of "A Mighty Fortress is Our God" (Riemenschneider No. 20).

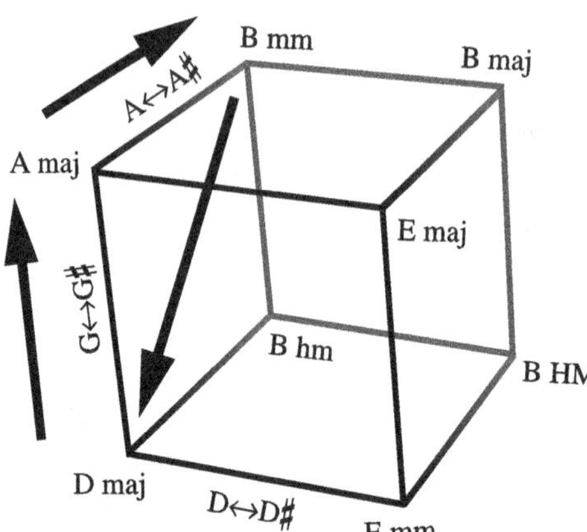

Figure 6.4.4 The modulations in Figure 6.4.3, graphed on a portion of the scale lattice.

When I first began to study tonal harmony, the chord-by-chord constraints seemed to be the most important and distinctive feature of the style. I thought the regular flow from tonic to subdominant to dominant provided music with a powerful and historically unprecedented level of structure—one that differentiated it from the less principled harmonic languages of other eras. Twenty-five years later, it now seems to me that systematic modulation is at least as important, providing a powerful tool for producing large-scale harmonic change while also creating a remarkable sort of self-similar musical texture. It is interesting, therefore, that modulation continues to feature prominently in twentieth-century music, even in styles that have abandoned the chord-to-chord constraints of the classical era. Indeed, one could even argue that systematic relations among macroharmonies are the most significant and enduring legacy of the functional tradition.

6.5 SCHUMANN'S CHOPIN

We'll approach our next style with a bit of musical analysis. Figure 6.5.1 summarizes the chords used in Schumann's "Chopin," a wonderful little piece of musical portraiture. The harmony here is not radical: it opens in A♭ major, turns briefly to B♭ minor, and immediately returns to A♭ major at the start of the example's third bar. Bar four moves to F minor, featuring a chromatic passage in which the tenor and bass exchange the notes E♮ and G. The major point of interest lies in the last bar: beginning at F minor we move to a shocking A^7 chord which then progresses to $E♭^7$, the dominant of A♭. It is precisely the sort of daring harmonic gesture that

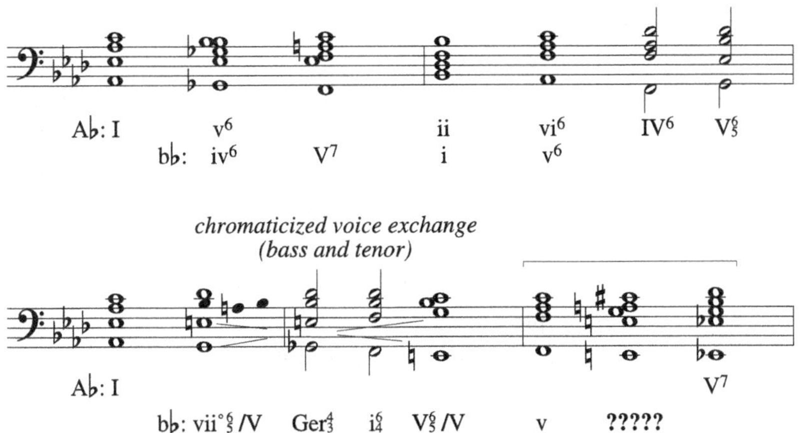

Figure 6.5.1 A harmonic summary of Schumann's "Chopin." Each whole note in the summary corresponds to a measure in the actual work.

characterizes Chopin's music—at once willful and completely convincing to the ear. One can well imagine the young Schumann playing the passage with a wink.

Now, what can we say about this A^7 chord? Where does it come from and what does it mean? It is, to begin with, a chord without a name. Without the G♮, one might call it a "Neapolitan," but according to harmony textbooks such chords typically behave rather differently. Were this a piece of contemporary jazz, we might call the A^7 a "tritone substitution" for the dominant $E\flat^7$, though the name seems more than a little anachronistic here. We could perhaps invent a new term for the chord, calling it a "Schumann seventh" or some such. Or we could name it with reference to other keys, asserting that it has been "borrowed" from either D major or D minor. But these descriptions merely serve as labels for our puzzle, rather than solutions. What we want to know is why Schumann might have written such a chord, and why it sounds so shocking and so beautiful at one and the same time.

Figure 6.5.2 The last measure of "Chopin" can be interpreted as a four-voice passage in which each voice moves by semitone.

The obvious answer is that the chord is connected by efficient chromatic voice leading to both the preceding F minor and the following $E\flat^7$. Figure 6.5.2 shows that we can model the music as having four distinct musical voices, each moving by semitone. Our exotic A^7 chord is a chromatic passing chord—a moment of musical liquidity that "fills the gaps" between the perfectly respectable diatonic sonorities surrounding it. But it would be wrong to dismiss it as a *mere* agglomeration of linear passing tones with no vertical significance, since the purported passing tones form a familiar dominant seventh chord that has *already occurred in the piece.* (In m. 3 of the figure, neighboring motion briefly converts an E diminished seventh into an A dominant seventh.) To downplay the vertical significance of the A^7 chord is to miss the fact that Schumann could have chosen any number of different passing or neighboring chords, and that this particular sonority appears twice in a very short span of time.

What makes the chord interesting, therefore, is its twofold status. Contrapuntally, we can think of it as a mere collection of passing tones. Harmonically, however, it has its own individuality and significance. Furthermore, the A^7 chord suggests keys—D major and D minor—that are intuitively quite "distant" from the tonic A♭. Thus the A^7 is simultaneously close and not close to the chords surrounding it: it is *melodically* close, since A^7 can be connected by efficient voice leading to both F minor and E♭^{7}; but it is *tonally* distant, since the keys of D major and D minor are in some sense "far" from the tonic A♭ major. It is precisely this conflict that produces the feeling that the A^7 chord is both out of place and yet profoundly right.

Geometrically, both of these distances can be modeled with the voice-leading spaces of Chapter 3. Key distances can be represented using the seven-dimensional space depicting voice-leading relationships among familiar scales, as we will see in the next chapter. Chord distances can be represented using the lower dimensional spaces containing triads and seventh chords. In four-note chromatic space, for example, A^7 is quite close both to E♭^{7} and the doubled triad F-A♭-A♭-C. In more traditional tonal contexts, the proximity of A^7 and E♭^{7} is not apparent, since chords are restricted to a particular major or minor scale; thus, to move from A^7 to E♭^{7} one must not only change chords, but also change scales via modulation. The essence of nineteenth-century harmony lies in the elimination of this modulatory step: in "Chopin," Schumann temporarily abandons the diatonic world in favor of a direct manipulation of chromatic relationships. This involves replacing a relatively simple diatonic geometry with the much more complex geometry of chromatic possibilities—a shift that is illustrated, in the three-note case, by Figure 6.5.3. The contrast between these figures shows at a glance why chromatic music can be so hard to understand.

Figure 6.5.3 Voice leading relations among diatonic triads (*a*) are much less complex than those among chromatic triads (*b*).

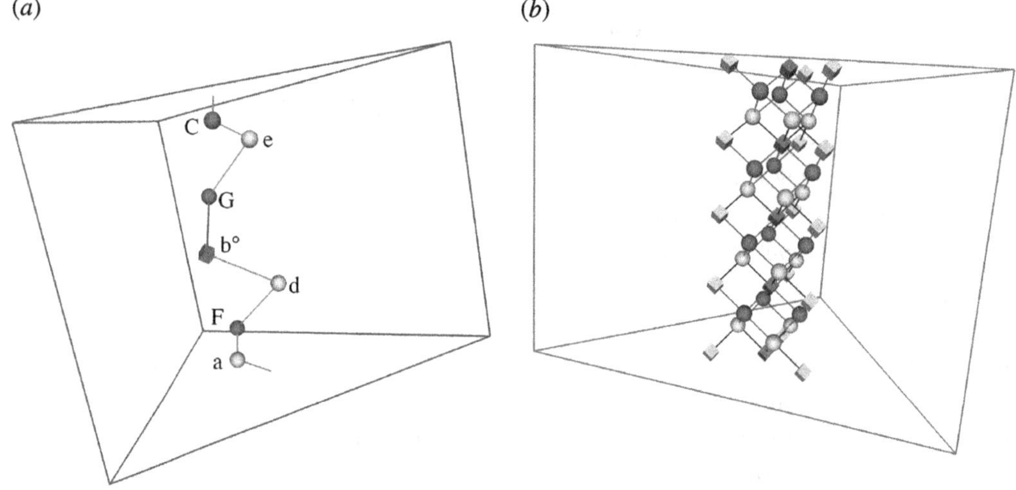

6.6 CHROMATICISM

Schumann's musical portrait could serve as the frontispiece to the entire tradition of nineteenth-century chromaticism, a genre that is characterized by the increasing tendency to conceive of chords as objects in chromatic space. This tendency manifests itself in two musical techniques, one pedestrian and the other more radical. The pedestrian technique uses chromatic chords to embellish or decorate familiar tonal progressions without fundamentally unseating the conventions of functional harmony. The more radical technique abandons functional norms in favor of direct chromatic voice leading between triads and seventh chords. These direct chromatic moves serve a variety of musical functions, acting as neighboring chords, passing chords, bridges to distantly related keys, and motivic progressions in their own right. It is this second technique that has led theorists to propose that nineteenth-century musical syntax is fundamentally dual, combining a diatonic "first practice" inherited from the classical era, with a newer "second practice" based on chromatic relationships.[24]

Figure 6.6.1 illustrates this fundamental change from diatonic to chromatic frames of reference. Relative to the diatonic scale, each voice in Figure 6.6.1a moves by a single step, so that there is no gap between successive notes. Relative to the chromatic scale, however, G moves to A by *two* chromatic steps. As nineteenth-century composers began to think more chromatically, it became increasingly tempting to try to fill this gap. In Figure 6.6.1b, for example, the added note between G and A produces two different sonorities, a C augmented triad on the way up and an F minor triad on the way down.[25] From this perspective, the two chords result from the same fundamental musical process of filling in gaps.

Figure 6.6.1 (*a*) Relative to the diatonic scale each voice moves by the smallest possible distance. (*b*) Relative to the chromatic scale, there are gaps that can be filled in. The resulting progression appears in the nineteenth-century song "You tell me your dream, I'll tell you mine."

Contemporary terminology sometimes seems designed to obscure this fact, describing the F minor chord as being *borrowed* from the key of C minor. I am somewhat suspicious of this metaphor of "borrowing." Musical keys are not lending libraries, and there are no borrower's cards that can be used to verify whether the F minor chord is indeed on loan

24 This view has been defended by Mitchell (1962), Proctor (1978), and Cohn (1996, 1997, 1998a). See also the essays in Kinderman and Krebs 1996. Antecedents can be found in Kurth 1920 and Weitzmann 1860.

25 In principle, of course, one could use the F minor chord on the way up, and the C augmented on the way down, but this would be less effective. In C–f–F, the single-semitone shift A♭→A occurs after the root motion has already happened, and sounds like a "correction" of the final chord. In C–C+ –F, the chromatic alteration intensifies the C chord, and makes the root change more dramatic when it happens.

from C minor. Moreover, the idea of "borrowing" potentially reinforces a compartmentalized approach to chromatic harmony, one that presents the style as a series of disconnected idioms with no common structure. (For example, in one popular textbook "borrowed" chords appear eight chapters before augmented triads, thus making it seem as if the chords in Figure 6.6.1 have no relationship.[26]) Rather than focusing on assigning labels to chords (such as "borrowed chord" or "augmented sixth"), I would prefer to focus on the underlying musical procedures relating them, which in many cases is chromatic voice leading. Otherwise, it can be very difficult to understand the fundamental logic animating chromatic music.[27]

In the previous example, chromaticism decorates a familiar progression. Figure 6.6.2 exhibits the more radical kind of chromaticism as it operates in the middle phrase of Chopin's E major prelude. Almost all the unusual moves in this passage can be interpreted in light of two different voice-leading "systems": one connecting triads whose roots relate by major third, and the other connecting seventh chords whose roots relate by minor third or tritone. We begin with the major-third system, moving from E major to C major by way of the voice leading (B, D♯, F♯)→(B, D, G); this connects V in E to V in C. The music then hints at dominants of F major, D minor, and A♭ major, each expressed in a slightly different way: the dominant of F is a dominant seventh chord, the dominant of D is both a triad and a diminished seventh, and the dominant of A♭ is both a diminished and dominant seventh. Finally, we return to E

Figure 6.6.2 The second phrase of Chopin's E major prelude. Beneath the excerpt I provide simplified voice leadings that illustrate the major- and minor-third systems.

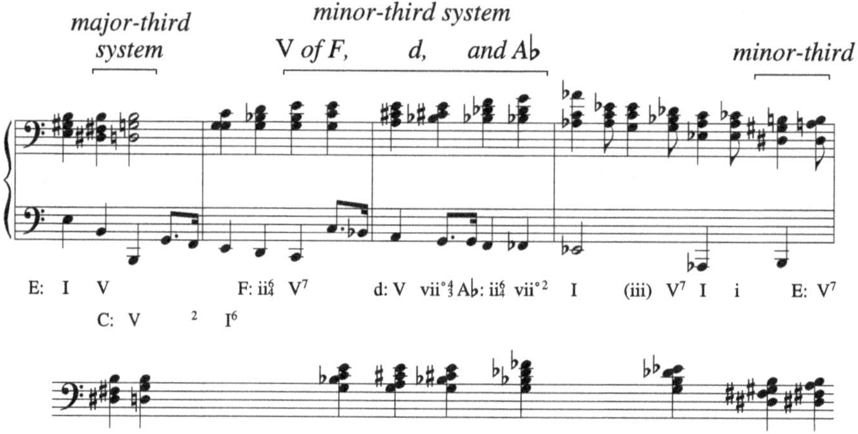

26 Aldwell and Schachter 2002. "Mode mixture" is not even included in the section on chromaticism, but is considered a completely different procedure. Kostka and Payne (2003) treat modal mixture and augmented triads in Chapters 21 and 26, respectively, but give little sense of the relation between them. Perhaps the best pedagogical treatment is in Gauldin (1997), who treats mode mixture and augmented triads in different chapters, but who includes an introductory discussion that clarifies the similarities between them.

27 I don't wish to suggest that there is never any role for the notion of "borrowing" or modal mixture, only that we should be careful not to invoke these ideas reflexively and without justification.

by way of a single-semitone voice leading connecting G♯ minor to an (incomplete) B^7 chord. Below the example I have provided a hypothetical "background" in which the contrapuntal logic is easier to see. We can think of these voice leadings as basic templates which Chopin has embellished in a relatively straightforward way.

A more involved example is given by the scherzo to Schubert's C major String Quintet (Figure 6.6.3).[28] The piece is exuberantly simple and folksy, presenting the same melodic material in a variety of distant keys. Five of Schubert's eleven modulations involve the major-third system: three directly juxtapose major-third-related tonic triads, while two more connect a tonic triad with what turns out to be the dominant of the following key. Three of the remaining modulations involve minor-third-related dominants: the initial feint to D minor connects V^7/IV to the minor-third-related V/ii (which here appears without its seventh), while the modulation from A♭ to G connects C^7 (itself obtained via a semitonally ascending sequence of seventh chords) directly to E♭^{7}, which is in turn reinterpreted as an augmented sixth of G. (This passage is cleverly varied in the recap, where the ascending semitonal motion continues upward to an A♭^{7} which is then reinterpreted as the German sixth of C major; as a result, the entire passage modulates down by minor third rather than down by semitone.[29]) Once again, the majority of the modulations use efficient chromatic voice leading among triads and seventh chords. To the extent that we can familiarize ourselves with the major- and minor-third systems, we can begin to see that Schubert's kaleidoscopic key changes reuse a small number of familiar contrapuntal moves.

Let me clarify that I am not claiming that Schubert and Chopin explicitly conceptualized these different chromatic systems; it is entirely possible that they simply sat at the piano and exploited the most efficient voice leadings that came to hand. My point

Figure 6.6.3 An outline of the modulations in the scherzo to Schubert's C major String Quintet. Local tonics are shown with open noteheads. Of the eleven modulations, nine involve the major- and minor-third systems; only two employ traditional pivot chords.

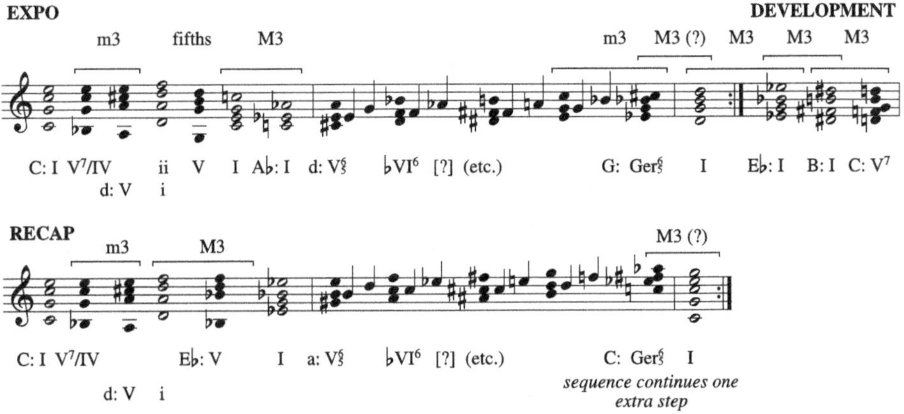

28 Thanks to Andrew Jones, who made a number of the observations in this paragraph.

29 This compensates for the fact that the recap's D minor moves up to E♭ major rather than back to C major, leaving Schubert in an inconvenient key.

is that the geometry of chord space ensures that this sort of intuitive exploration will necessarily result in music that can be described using the major- and minor-third systems. It is useful here to revisit the analogy of the mountain climber, though now representing an individual composer rather the development of Western music as a whole. Chromatic composers, like mountaineers, will be constrained by the environment in which they operate, and the geometrical spaces of Part I are literally the terrain through which chromatic music moves. Insofar as we understand this geometry, we will also understand why intuitive musical exploration produces the results it does—in this case a plethora of major-third-related triads and minor-third- or tritone-related seventh chords.

It seems to me that a deep appreciation of nineteenth-century music requires a systematic grasp of *all* the voice-leading possibilities between familiar sonorities. This, of course, was a central theme of Part I. The notion of "near symmetry" (§2.9) allows us to understand how a chord's internal structure determines its contrapuntal capabilities: thus, given a particular sonority such as the C dominant seventh, we can identify other structurally similar chords that are nearby. This, in turn, leads us to notice that triads can typically be connected smoothly to their major third transpositions while seventh chords can be efficiently linked to their minor-third and tritone transpositions. The geometrical spaces of Chapter 3 offer a convenient way to visualize these facts, allowing us to draw "maps" in which the major-third and minor-third systems are clearly represented. Furthermore, by focusing on crossing-free voice leadings—treating voice crossings as embellishments of these more basic templates—we saw that we can reduce the vast number of voice-leading possibilities to a much more manageable set of categories (§4.9–10). Taken together, these tools allow us to evaluate composers' choices in light of a robust understanding of the options available to them. Or, to revert to the metaphor, they allow us to understand the mountaineer's decisions in light of a systematic knowledge of the rock face. If we can internalize these principles, understanding the logic of chromatic voice leading, then chromatic music will start to seem much more coherent: instead of describing Chopin or Schubert's music as resulting from capricious acts of musical fancy, Romantic lawbreaking that obeys no fixed principles, we will instead see a small collection of familiar paths through chromatic space.

6.7 TWENTIETH-CENTURY SCALAR MUSIC

The first half of the nineteenth century witnessed a tremendous expansion of harmonic options; new chords were permitted and new chromatic voice leadings were used to connect formerly distant chords. But it saw relatively few extensions to music's scalar or modal vocabulary. This imbalance eventually led to a palpable compositional dilemma: what *melodic notes* should be used to accompany the chords of the chromatic tradition?

This problem became particularly acute when composers required a large number of melodic notes to accompany a single chromatic sonority. To see why, consider Figure 6.7.1. Suppose you would like to associate each chord with a complete scale—

say, a run that spans at least an octave. One option is simply to use the C major scale, creating a clash with the chromatic notes of the altered harmonies. Another is to incorporate the chordal alterations by inserting additional chromatic notes into the passage. A third is to replace diatonic notes with their "altered" forms, fusing the basic scale of the key (here, C diatonic) with alterations belonging to the chords themselves. These three alternatives represent the main nineteenth-century solutions to the problem of associating chord and scale, as illustrated by Figure 6.7.2.

Twentieth-century tonality instead exploits the fact that the sonorities of chromatic harmony can all be embedded in a small number of familiar scales. (Recall from §4.4 that just seven kinds of scale contain every "cluster-free" chord.) Twentieth-century composers treat these scales as ready-to-hand accompaniments for particular chromatic chords. Thus, for example, a composer might use the D and B♭ acoustic scales to harmonize the augmented and minor triads in Figure 6.7.3. This solution is noteworthy for several reasons. First, the acoustic scales would traditionally be associated with the keys of A minor and F minor, keys that are quite distant from one another. Second, though the acoustic scale is familiar from the classical tradition, it is used here in unfamiliar modes (treating C as the tonic). And third, since the acoustic scale has just seven notes, it creates a smallish macroharmony that is not overwhelmingly chromatic. As a result, the passage has a kind of rigorous logic, even while departing from the procedures of traditional tonality.

Figure 6.7.4 illustrates this technique in the context of Ravel's String Quartet, where a G^9–$C^{\flat 9}$–F^{add6} progression gives rise to three separate scales: the G^9 chord has a pronounced whole-tone flavor; the $C^{\flat 9}$ is accompanied by the octatonic scale,

Figure 6.7.1 Accompanying chromatic chords with scales. In (*a*), the scale does not contain the chromatic chords; in (*b–c*) it does. The music in (*b*) augments the diatonic scale with the altered notes, while the music in (*c*) replaces diatonic with altered notes.

Figure 6.7.2 (*a*) In Strauss' *Till Eulenspiegel* (R7), the harmony B♭-D♭-E-G♯ serves as an altered dominant chord resolving semitonally to the tonic F. The scale in the bass, however, is a simple A♭ major that does not contain the E♮ of the harmony, resulting in a fleeting dissonance. (*b*) In Wagner's *Parsifal* (mm. 668–9, Schirmer vocal score p. 40), a diminished seventh chord is harmonized with a melody touching on all the chromatic notes except F♯ and G. The effect is of a wash that creates a sense of motion, but does not clearly suggest any familiar scale. (*c*) In m. 86 of the first movement of Mozart's Piano Sonata K. 533, a familiar augmented sixth chord gives rise to an unusual ("gypsy") scale. This scale is derived by combining the notes of C diatonic with the alterations belonging to the German augmented sixth.

Figure 6.7.3 Twentieth-century scalar composers might use acoustic scales to harmonize altered chords. The result is a melodic texture without augmented seconds or consecutive semitones.

and the F major chord is accompanied by F diatonic. The bottom staves of Figure 6.7.4 interpret the harmonies. Level (*c*) is purely diatonic, and depicts a relatively standard ii^9–V^9–I^6 progression. Level (*b*) includes chromatic embellishments of this pattern: in the first two chords, diatonic B♭ becomes the applied leading tone B♮ and diatonic D becomes C♯, producing a $G^{\sharp 11}$ chord and a $C^{\flat 9}$.[30] Finally, level (*a*) embellishes this progression with whole-tone and octatonic scales. What is remarkable is that each level suggests a different stage in our overarching historical narrative. Level (*c*) is purely diatonic, and uses a functional chord progression inherited from classical tonality. Level (*b*) uses chromatic embellishments that evoke nineteenth-century chromatic practice. Level (*a*) adds a distinctively twentieth-century contribution, as

30 Note that the C♯ resolves upward by semitone to the D, so that the $C^{\flat 9}$–F^{add6} progression combines elements of a V–I progression in F major with a vii^{o7}–i progression in D minor.

Figure 6.7.4 (*a*) Whole-tone and octatonic scales in Ravel's String Quartet. (*b*) The underlying progression, and its diatonic logic (*c*).

Figure 6.7.5 Bill Evans using the octatonic scale in his Town Hall recording of "Turn Out the Stars."

the altered chords give rise to additional scales that are neither diatonic nor chromatic. Chapters 9 and 10 will show that jazz musicians inherit and systematize these techniques. Thus in Figure 6.7.5, Bill Evans uses the octatonic scale to accompany the V chord, very much in the manner of Ravel's String Quartet. Jazz theorists are both systematic and explicit when describing these relations between chord and scale, providing recipes that show students which scales to play over the altered chords of jazz harmony. In this sense, jazz manages to standardize the intuitive scalar exploration of earlier decades.

The two examples we have considered represent a relatively traditional strain of twentieth-century scalar thinking, in which nondiatonic scales are used to accompany functionally harmonic progressions. Chapter 9 will also present examples that reject the ii–V–I paradigm, drawn from impressionist pieces by Debussy, Ravel, and Janáček; minimalist and postminimalist works by Reich, Adams, and Nyman; and nonfunctional jazz by the Miles Davis quintet. These examples, though stylistically quite diverse, reuse the same basic scales and the same basic compositional techniques. To my mind, this package of scalar procedures represents one of the most interesting recent developments in the thousand-year tradition that is Western tonality—a thread of common practice linking a wide variety of recent tonal styles, equal in its significance to the other developments surveyed in this chapter.

6.8 THE EXTENDED COMMON PRACTICE

The eighteenth and nineteenth centuries are often called the "common practice period" in Western music.[31] The term suggests a compositional consensus transcending national and temporal boundaries: Italian music of 1720, it is claimed, is quite similar to the German music of the 1880s, and both styles are quite different from any of the music composed prior to 1700 and subsequent to 1900. Other Western styles, such as Renaissance polyphony or contemporary jazz, may involve shared musical practices that are distantly related to those of the eighteenth and nineteenth centuries. But any similarities are overwhelmed by the differences. Consequently, there is no substantive sense in which Palestrina or Duke Ellington can be said to participate in the same musical tradition as the musicians of the eighteenth and nineteenth centuries.

The view sketched here is a different one. I have claimed that when we step back far enough, we can see a much broader common practice that includes not just classical composers, but also jazz musicians like Ellington and Renaissance musicians like Palestrina. Central to this extended common practice is the technique of connecting harmonically significant chords by efficient voice leading. We have seen this in each of our musical excerpts. In our simple medieval style, efficient voice leading connects consonant intervals; in later music, it connects structurally similar triads and seventh chords. Classical music introduces modulation, applying efficient voice leading to scales as well as chords. Chromaticism shifts freely between the diatonic and chromatic realms. Finally, twentieth-century tonality develops a consistent technique of associating chromatically altered chords with a small number of familiar scales. At this level of abstraction, it looks like the tonal composers of the Western tradition are all playing fundamentally the same game, creating music that is both melodically and vertically coherent, and incorporating the various innovations of their predecessors.

I think there is something sublime about this. It is amazing that contemporary rock guitar fingerings are directly related to voice-leading practices more than half a millennium old (Figures 6.3.9 and 6.3.10), or that Bill Evans' improvisations develop ideas found in Ravel's carefully notated String Quartet (Figures 6.7.4 and 6.7.5). And though I am mindful of the need to remain ever vigilant against the temptations of Hegelian or Whiggish history, I am fascinated by the way certain stylistic developments in Western music seem to respond to, or arise out of, technical problems faced by earlier composers—for example, the way nondiatonic scales provide a solution to melodic challenges inherent in chromatic harmony (§6.7), or the way triads provide a solution to the problem of writing consonant three-voice counterpoint (§6.3). By focusing on the very general mechanisms of tonal coherence, by developing a bird's-eye view of Western tonal practice, we can start to see these connections more clearly.

Geometry has helped us here, providing a different space for each of our five styles. We used the two-dimensional Möbius strip to represent early medieval

31 The term seems to have originated with Walter Piston, who used it in his 1941 harmony textbook. See Harrison (forthcoming) for perceptive comments on the notion of a "common practice period."

two-note counterpoint. Later, the circle of diatonic thirds proved helpful in modeling Renaissance triadic voice leading. The turn to baroque music required us to introduce the scale lattice, a three-dimensional region in seven-dimensional scale space. The chromaticism of Schumann, Schubert, and Chopin led us to supplement our earlier diatonic models with more complex chromatic spaces, in which we find a wealth of "shortcuts" between once-distant chords. Finally, Chapter 9 will show that twentieth-century scalar music involves a much more complex sort of scalar voice leading, involving a correspondingly sophisticated use of the scale lattice. Thus the development of musical style can be represented, at least in part, as a process of exploring an increasingly sophisticated array of musical spaces. Our earlier theoretical work allows us literally to visualize this process, giving us a unified set of geometrical models that help us comprehend the development of Western music.

Pedagogically, I find this perspective to be extremely fruitful. My own musical education was a traditional one, centered almost exclusively on a bifurcated diet of musty Germanic classics and bracing twentieth-century atonality. The introductory music-theory class at my undergraduate institution devoted an entire year to Bach chorales. Second-year theory was devoted exclusively to classical and very early Romantic music, while subsequent classes discussed twelve-tone music, Schenkerian analysis, and baroque counterpoint. Not once in my entire four years of undergraduate education did I hear a pedagogical word about jazz, rock, or minimalism—except in an unguarded moment, when one of my professors, an atonal composer and theorist, let slip that he preferred *Sgt. Pepper's* to any piece of atonality.

I believe we can do better. Part of what interests me about the narrative in this chapter is the way it suggests a more inclusive pedagogy, more suited to the pluralism of contemporary culture. I teach a year-long, introductory music-theory class based on the five musical styles we have just considered. Students begin by writing faux-medieval two-voice counterpoint in which parallel fifths are permitted. After a brief detour into contemporary rock harmony, they progress to simplified four-voice Renaissance music along the lines of Josquin's "Tu pauperum refugium." By the time the common practice is introduced, they are already somewhat adept at the business of connecting triads by efficient voice leading while also avoiding forbidden parallels. This makes the introduction of classical harmonic norms (including modulation) considerably less painful than it usually is. The final sections of the course provide a systematic introduction to chromatic voice leading and twentieth-century scalar techniques. At the end of the year, students have learned that musical styles change, that tonality is a living tradition, and that when you dig deep enough, you can find nonobvious connections between very different musical styles. My hope is that these lessons prepare them to confront today's wide open, polystylistic, multicultural, syncretistic, and postmodern musical culture.

CHAPTER 7

Functional Harmony

This chapter reconsiders four basic topics in tonal theory: chord progressions, sequences, key distances, and the Schenkerian critique of Roman numeral analysis. My aim here is not to provide a detailed restatement of tonal theory, a project that would require a book in itself, but rather to indicate some points of intersection with our theoretical work. In particular, I'll show how we can use the ideas of Part I to model the elementary harmonic and modulatory procedures of classical music.

7.1 THE THIRDS-BASED GRAMMAR OF ELEMENTARY TONAL HARMONY

In many broadly tonal styles, chord progressions are relatively unconstrained: in Renaissance music, contemporary popular music, and many folk styles, virtually any diatonic triad can progress to any other. From this point of view, Western classical music is exceptional—here, a root position V chord is overwhelmingly likely to progress to a root position I chord, whereas it moves to root position IV only rarely. Chords thus seem to obey specifically *harmonic* laws, with some progressions being common while others are rare. This is one of the features of Western music that is most suggestively language-like. For just as in English, the subject normally precedes the verb, which in turn precedes the object, so too does Western music seem to have a harmonic "grammar" according to which subdominant chords precede dominants that in turn precede tonics.[1]

Figure 7.1.1 models the major-mode version of this harmonic grammar.[2] Here, the diatonic chords other than iii are arranged as a chain of descending thirds, with the mediant being omitted because it is rare. Chords can move rightward by any number of steps along this chain from tonic to dominant; however, they can move leftward only along one of the labeled arrows. (I will say that a sequence of rightward

1 Note that I am not claiming that music *is* a language, only that it involves recurring patterns somewhat analogous to linguistic syntax. See Patel 2008 for more discussion. Gjerdingen 2007 offers a nice counterweight to the syntactical point of view, emphasizing idioms and schemas rather than abstract rules.

2 Here I am ignoring inversion; in actual music, vii° is almost always in first inversion, and vi is almost always in root position. The resulting model resembles that in Kostka and Payne 2003. The thirds-based arrangement of diatonic triads also plays a role in Agmon 1995, Meeus 2000, Tymoczko 2003b, and Quinn 2005.

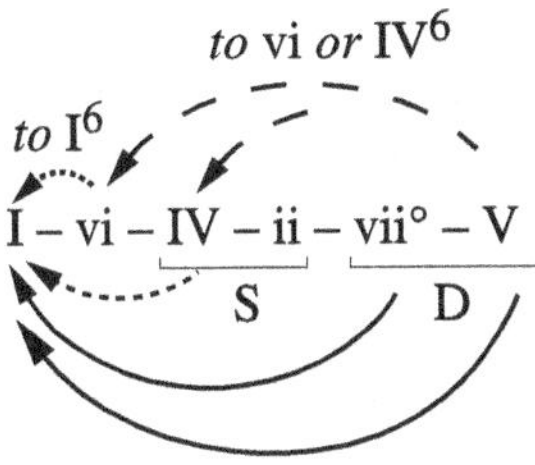

Figure 7.1.1 A simple model of the allowable chord progressions in major-mode functional harmony. Chords can move rightward by any amount, but can move left only along the arrows. "S" and "D" stand for "subdominant" and "dominant," respectively.

- *Any major or minor triad can be preceded by an applied dominant.*
- *Root-position* V *can be preceded by* I^6_4

motions from the tonic, followed by a leftward return, constitutes a *harmonic cycle.*) Each Roman numeral can represent either a pure triad or a seventh chord, with the sevenths on ii and V being particularly common. The V chord can be preceded by I^6_4, and any chord other than vii° can be preceded by its own "applied dominant."[3]

This model privileges certain chords by assigning them distinctive roles, with tonics typically beginning harmonic cycles, dominants (vii° and V) ending them by progressing back to I, and subdominants (ii and IV) preceding dominants.[4] In addition, the model privileges certain kinds of *motion:* descending thirds and fifths are more often permissible than ascending thirds and fifths, while ascending steps are more often permissible than descending steps. This asymmetry arises as a consequence of the graph's spatial layout. Since rightward motion is always permitted, every chord except V can progress by descending third, every chord except vii° can progress by descending fifth, and every chord except ii can progress by ascending step. By contrast, only two chords (I and IV) can progress by ascending fifth, only two (I and vi) can progress by descending step, and only one can progress by ascending third. Descending thirds, descending fifths, and ascending steps are often called "strong" progressions, with the remaining progressions said to be "weak."[5] Our model predicts that chords closer to the dominant side of the spectrum should be more likely to move "strongly"—a claim that is borne out by actual music (Figure 7.1.2).

For the most part, functionally tonal music cycles through the graph in a few stereotypical ways: classical pieces consist largely of progressions such as I–V–I, I–ii–V–I, I–vii°–I, and I–IV–I. Occasionally, however, composers will employ more extended

3 Some theorists consider vii° to be a V^7 with a missing root. However, this view cannot account for the regular root motions in sequences such as C–G–a–e°–F-. . ., where diminished triads are on par with major and minor triads (cf. Haydn's Piano Sonata No. 49 in E♭ major, I, 50, and Beethoven Piano Sonata in D major, Op. 28, IV, 130ff). Other pedagogues disallow the progression vii°–V. However, in Mozart's piano sonatas, vii° is about nine times more likely to move to V than V is to move to vii°. Readers who would prefer to disallow vii°–V can imagine placing the two chords on top of each other, so that neither can progress rightward to the other.

4 Note that these functional labels ("subdominant," "dominant") provide only an approximate description of harmonic behavior, and do not explain why the progressions IV–ii and IV–I are more common than ii–IV and ii–I. For more, see Tymoczko 2003b.

5 See Rameau 1722/1971, Schoenberg 1969, Sadai 1980, and Meeus 2000.

Figure 7.1.2 The relative tendency of major-mode triads to progress "strongly" (by descending third or fifth, or ascending step) in a sample of 70 Bach chorales (top line) and in Mozart's piano sonatas (bottom line). The asymmetry increases as one moves from tonic to dominant by descending third.

I (53%) → vi (53%) → IV (76%) → ii (100%) → vii° (96%) → V (95%) (Bach)
I (32%) → vi (67%) → IV (66%) → ii (97%) → vii° (99%) → V (97%) (Mozart)

segments of the descending thirds cycle, as in Figure 7.1.3. The idea behind our model is to portray these falling thirds progressions as the fundamental path from tonic to dominant. Falling fifths are "composite" progressions insofar as they can typically be "factored" into a pair of falling thirds: I–IV can become I–vi–IV, vi–ii can become vi–IV–ii, and so on. By contrast, thirds cannot generally be factored into fifths. We can conclude that falling thirds are more *fundamental* than falling fifths, even though falling fifths may be more *common*.[6] It is interesting here that tonal composers sometimes utilize the full circle of diatonic thirds, interposing a mediant triad between dominant and tonic (Figure 7.1.4). In these passages, the engine of falling thirds harmony temporarily overcomes the V–I paradigm, blurring the expected resolution of the dominant chord.

Minor-mode harmony is slightly more complicated, as it involves frequent digressions to the relative major. However, if we treat these as brief changes of key, we can use virtually the same graph for minor (Figure 7.1.5). This symmetry between

Figure 7.1.3 The chorale "Bach's chorale "Auf, auf, mein Herz, und du mein ganzer Sinn" (Riemenschneider No. 124).

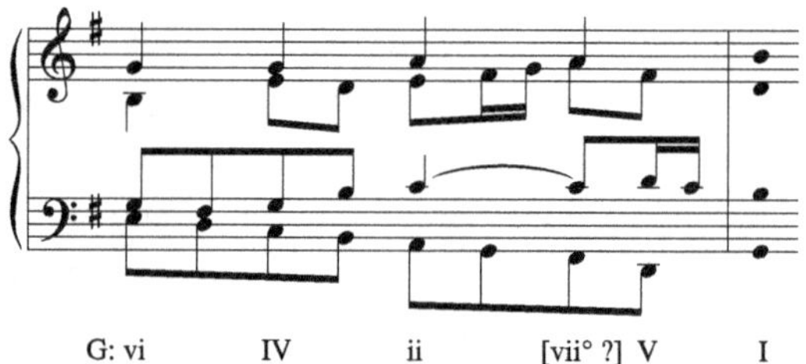

Figure 7.1.4 Bach's duet (BWV 803, mm. 22–26) interposes iii between V and I.

6 It is important here to distinguish the *permissible* from the *probable*. Root progressions by descending fifth are more common than root progressions by third; however, when describing the *permissible* progressions, it is useful to treat falling-thirds progressions as basic.

Figure 7.1.5 The allowable progressions in minor are largely the same as the allowable progressions in major. Again, chords can move rightward by any amount, but can move left only along the arrows.

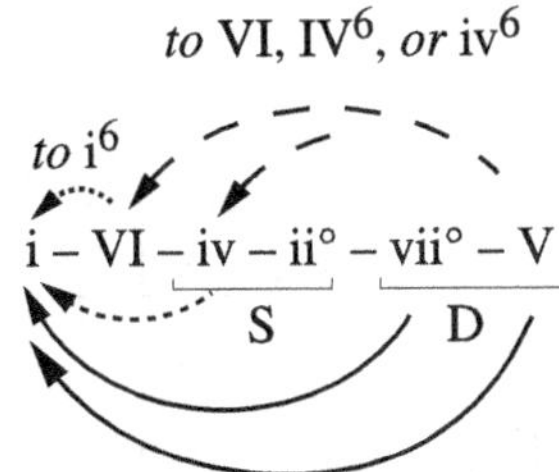

- *Any major or minor triad can be preceded by an applied dominant.*
- *Root-position* V *can be preceded by* i^6_4

major and minor is quite remarkable, particularly when one reflects that in other tonal styles modes often have their own distinctive harmonic repertoires. (For instance, the natural minor progression i–VII–VI–VII–i is quite common in contemporary popular music, while its major-mode analogue, I–vii°–vi–vii°–I, is virtually unknown.[7]) This sort of modal asymmetry would seem to be the default situation: after all, there is no reason to expect that progressions as dissimilar as VII–VI and vii°–vi should function in the same way. Classical harmony is from this point of view atypical, imposing a rigorous consistency on all its modes and keys. The payoff, of course, is that composers can present "the same" musical material in two dramatically different emotional contexts.

To evaluate the thirds-based model, we need a substantial collection of harmonic analyses of traditional tonal works. There are, to my knowledge, only two: a collection of 70 Bach chorales, and a much larger collection of the complete Mozart piano sonatas, both produced in conjunction with the writing of this book.[8] Figure 7.1.6 identifies the probability of each two-chord diatonic progression in the two repertoires, while Figure 7.1.7 identifies the most common harmonic cycles. The results are quite consistent with the descending thirds model: in Bach, 95% of roughly 3000 two-chord diatonic progressions conform to our predictions, as do 97–99% of all Mozart's roughly 10,000 diatonic progressions; furthermore, every one of our allowable progressions appears reasonably frequently.[9] Almost all the exceptions belong to familiar categories: sequences (discussed shortly), chromatic chords, and other common tonal devices. Given the simplicity of the model, the accuracy of fit is quite remarkable. One geometrical picture, which can be explained to students in a single hour, accounts for the vast majority of the chord progressions they will ordinarily encounter.[10]

---

7 See also van der Merwe (1989, ch. 11).

8 Earlier databases, such as those of Craig Sapp and Philip Norman, do not attempt to indicate key changes, and hence are of limited utility: a G major ii–V–I is labeled vi–V/V–V if the overall key of the piece is C major. My analyses, which were produced with the help of more than thirty theorists, do show modulations, and will hopefully be published soon.

9 The slightly lower number (95% in Bach, rather than 97–99% in Mozart) reflects Bach's somewhat broader diatonic vocabulary.

10 To be sure, the model is just a first approximation to actual tonal procedures: it does not incorporate chromatic chords like augmented sixths; it makes no attempt to model variation across musical styles; and it ignores a number of important tonal "idioms," including sequences, motion by parallel stepwise first-inversion triads, and three-chord idioms such as the progression vi–I^6–(IV/ii^6).

Figure 7.1.6 Two-chord progressions in Mozart's major-key passages (*a*), Mozart's minor-key passages (*b*), Bach's major-key passages (*c*), and Bach's minor-key passages (*d*). Values represent the probability that, given the row-label chord, it will move to the column-label chord (expressed as a percentage). Sequences, passages in parallel triads, and I^6_4 chords have been omitted. Of the vi–I progressions, the large majority terminate in I^6; of the V–IV progressions, the large majority terminate in IV^6.

(*a*)

	I	vi	IV	ii	vii°	V	iii
I	*	5	15	13	5	62	0
vi	9	*	14	52	4	21	0
IV	50	0	*	19	10	21	0
ii	1	1	1	*	18	77	0
vii°	82	0	1	0	*	16	1
V	94	4	1	0	1	*	0
iii	67	33	0	0	0	0	*

(*b*)

	i	VI	iv	ii°	vii°	V	III
i	*	5	8	9	11	67	0
VI	3	*	19	58	13	6	0
iv	43	0	*	10	9	39	0
ii°	2	0	0	*	27	71	0
vii°	74	0	1	1	*	25	0
V	81	8	5	0	5	*	0
III	0	0	100	0	0	0	*

(*c*)

	I	vi	IV	ii	vii°	V	iii
I	*	9	28	15	6	41	1
vi	12	*	11	30	9	33	5
IV	22	2	*	13	23	39	0
ii	1	1	0	*	25	71	0
vii°	91	3	2	0	*	4	1
V	82	9	7	1	0	*	0
iii	3	32	52	3	3	6	*

(*d*)

	i	VI	iv	ii°	vii°	V	III
i	*	9	20	18	12	41	1
VI	3	*	14	54	8	19	3
iv	22	0	*	14	15	48	0
ii°	1	0	0	*	7	89	3
vii°	81	0	3	0	*	15	1
V	80	10	6	0	2	*	2
III	6	31	25	6	13	19	*

Figure 7.1.7 (*a*) The most popular major-mode harmonic cycles in a selection of 70 Bach chorales. All of them conform to the thirds-based model. (*b*) The most popular major-mode harmonic cycles in the Mozart piano sonatas. Once again, all conform to the thirds-based model.

(*a*)

I–V–I	90
I–ii–V–I	30
I–IV–V–I	26
I–IV–I	22
I–vii°–I	21
I–ii–vii°–I	13
I–IV–ii–V–I	9
I–IV–vii°–I	7
I–vi–ii–V–I	5
I–V–IV^6–V–I	4

(*b*)

I–V–I	1026
I–ii–I^6_4–V–I	204
I–vii°–I	127
I–IV–I	122
I–ii–V–I	82
I–IV–I^6_4–V–I	68
I–vi–ii–V–I	61
I–I^6_4–V–I	60
I–ii–vii°–I	27
I–V/IV–IV–I	23
I–IV–V–I	20
I–V/IV–IV–vii°–I	19
I–IV^6–I^6_4–V–I	18
I–vi–IV–ii–V–I	17
I–V/ii–ii–V–I	15
I–V–vi–V–I	15

7.2 VOICE LEADING IN FUNCTIONAL TONALITY

In Part I, we saw that triads and seventh chords divide the octave nearly evenly, and hence can be linked to all their transpositions by reasonably efficient voice leading. It follows that virtually any collection of purely harmonic rules (such as "IV can go to ii but not iii") can be realized by progressions exhibiting efficient voice leading. By contrast, "clustered" chords such as {B, C, D♭} are not so close to all of their transpositions, and would require harmonic laws specifically tailored to their voice-leading capabilities. In this sense, the internal structure of the triad underwrites the independence of traditional harmonic laws.

However, attentive readers will have noticed that there is an interesting connection between the two domains. In §6.3 we saw that the circle of thirds can be used to represent single-step voice leadings among diatonic triads. Here the circle is purely *contrapuntal*, describing minimal voice-leading relationships among chords. But we have just seen that the chain of third-related chords can also be used to model *harmonic* successions in functionally tonal music. Thus the passage shown in Figure 7.2.1 has a double significance: its upper voices are at once a sequence of triads linked by maximally efficient voice leading, as well as a complete statement of all the potential intermediaries between tonic and dominant. Harmony and counterpoint here work hand in hand, creating a unified structure in which horizontal and vertical forces are in delicate balance.

One reason for this is that common tones and efficient voice leading together produce a kind of harmonic *similarity*.[11] As shown in Figure 7.2.2, a root position F major triad is very similar to a first-inversion D minor triad, since the chords can be linked by single-step voice leading.[12] It follows that a first-inversion D minor triad can replace a root position F major triad without much disrupting the music's harmonic or contrapuntal fabric: the "substitute" chord will share the bass note and upper third (F and A), substituting a consonant sixth for a perfect fifth (D for C; Figure 7.2.2b). This may help explain how the circle of thirds comes to play its two different roles: by linking chords according to efficient voice leading, the circle defines a psychologically

Figure 7.2.1 Here, the upper voices are connected by single-step voice leading, while the harmonies move along the descending circle of thirds from tonic to dominant.

11 This notion of similarity is explored in Callender, Quinn, and Tymoczko 2008.

12 The F major triad is also very similar to a second-inversion A minor triad, but second-inversion triads play only a very small role in functional tonality.

Figure 7.2.2 (*a*) Third-related triads sound similar, since they share two of their three notes and can be connected by single-step voice leading. (*b*) One can often replace a diatonic chord with a third-related chord, without much disrupting the harmonic or contrapuntal fabric of a passage.

robust notion of similarity, one that in turn influenced the developing conventions of functional harmony.

We can therefore say that functional tonality permits two different kinds of substitution. In *bass-line substitution,* the same chord progression appears over different bass notes, as in Figure 7.2.3a. (Traditional Roman numeral analysis was in fact developed to capture the similarity between such progressions.) In *third substitution,* a root position chord is replaced with a first-inversion chord on the same bass, or vice versa (Figure 7.2.3b). Here the bass stays the same while the content of the harmony is subtly altered. (The potential for this sort of substitution might be thought to be implicit in figured-bass notation, in which the bass is fundamental to a chord's identity.) Third substitution explains why there are so many third-related chords that can play similar musical roles: I/vi^6, vi/IV^6, IV/ii^6, vii°/V^6, and even V/III+^{6}.[13] The challenge in describing functional harmony is to make room for both perspectives, combining the advantages of the root-functional and figured-bass approaches. Our model does so by way of geometry: by placing third-related triads adjacent to one another, it asserts that these chords can typically substitute for one another in the rightward progression from tonic to dominant.

13 Riemannian "function theory" (Riemann 1893) allows all third-related triads other than ii and vii° to represent the same "harmonic function." Contemporary anglophone pedagogues do not typically endorse full-blown function theory, though many incorporate some of its features. Aldwell and Schachter (2002, ch. 11), for example, emphasize the similarity of vi and IV^6.

Figure 7.2.3 Bass-line and third substitution. In (*a*) a same I–IV–V–I chord progression appears over two different bass lines. In (*b*), root position and first-inversion chords (over the same bass note) play similar harmonic roles.

Figure 7.2.4 rewrites the circle of thirds so as to identify the pitch classes in each chord. It is clear that short rightward motions (i.e. "strong" progressions) will produce pitch classes that descend by third. For example, the triadic progression I–ii–V–I can be articulated by the pitch-class sequence (G, E, C)-(A, F, D)-(D, B, G)-(G, E, C), in which each new note is a third below its predecessor; other familiar progressions, such as I–IV–V–I, can be analyzed similarly. Tonal composers often exploit this fact by writing descending melodic thirds over familiar progressions—a device that was a particular favorite of Bach's (Figure 7.2.5). Sometimes, as in Figure 7.2.6, we even find bare sequences of falling thirds that do not articulate individual chords. Such passages present the raw material of functional harmony in an unusually pure manner, revealing a falling thirds essence that is typically encountered in only a refined or processed form.

Note that strong *triadic* progressions are most efficiently realized by ascending voice leading: in voice leadings like (C, E, G)→(C, E, A) or (C, E, G)→(C, F, A) notes move up by step. Since descending melodic steps are somewhat more common than ascending steps, harmonic cycles will often contain at least one voice leading in which efficiency is sacrificed for the sake of descending motion. This is illustrated by Figure 7.2.7.

Figure 7.2.4 Short motions along the descending-thirds sequence of triads can produce descending-thirds sequences of pitch classes.

GEC	ECA	CAF	AFD	FDB	DBG
I –	vi –	IV –	ii –	vii^{o6} –	V

Figure 7.2.5 Bach's music often features descending-thirds sequences of pitch classes. (*a*) The third movement of the third Brandenburg Concerto, mm. 11–12. (*b*) The F major two-part invention, mm. 21–23.

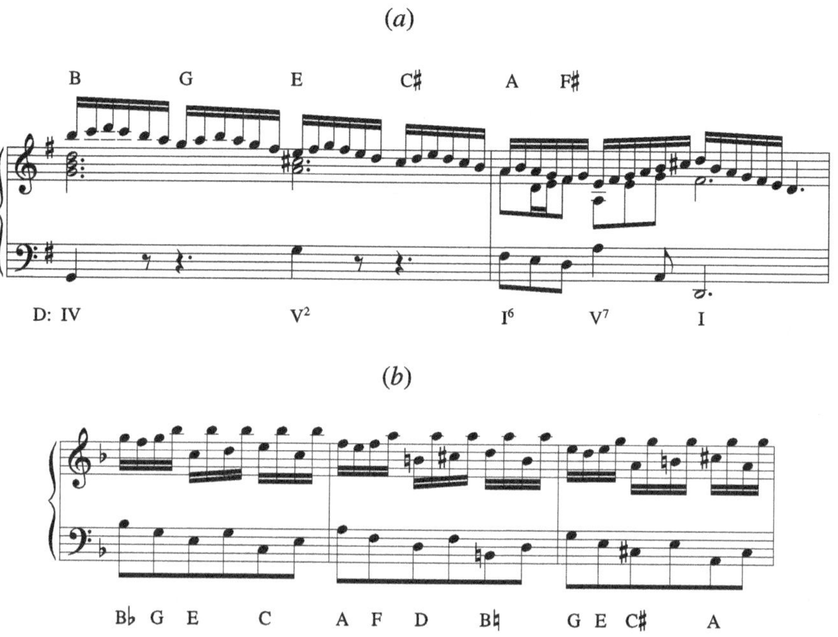

Figure 7.2.6 Two passages in which melodic descending thirds do not clearly determine harmonies. (*a*) Bach's fourteenth Goldberg Variation, mm. 9–10. (*b*) The opening of Brahms' Op. 119 No. 1.

Seventh chords are very different in this regard. Figure 7.2.8 shows that diatonic sevenths can be arranged in a circle of thirds very similar to the triadic circle, but with descending-thirds progressions producing descending voice leading: to move the seventh chord C^{maj7} down by third to A^{min7} we lower the note B to A; by contrast, to move the C major triad down by third to A minor, we need to *raise* G to A. It follows that any "strong" seventh-chord progression can be realized by stepwise descending voice leading (Figure 7.2.9). (In this sense, seventh-chord harmony is somewhat more straightforward than the triadic version taught in harmony textbooks.[14]) The association between seventh chords, strong progressions, and descending stepwise voice leading plays an increasingly important role in late nineteenth-century harmony, and is fundamental to pieces like Chopin's E minor prelude and Wagner's *Tristan*. As we will see, it also provides the nucleus of jazz voice leading.

Figure 7.2.7 Ascending motion provides the most efficient voice leading between strongly related triads (top three voices of *a*). Since tonal phrases often feature descending melodic lines, composers typically have to use at least one non-minimal voice leading per harmonic cycle (*b*–*c*).

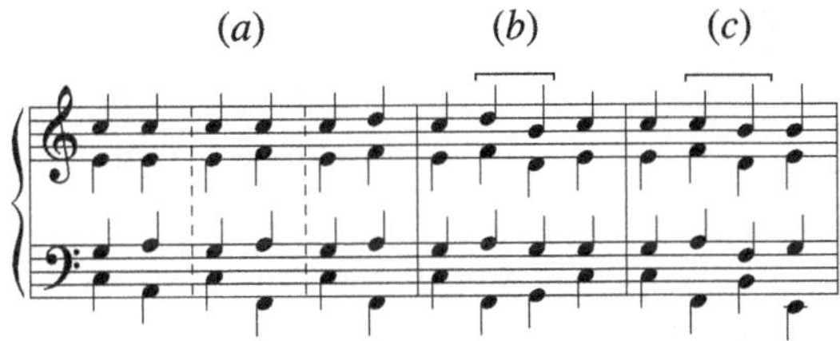

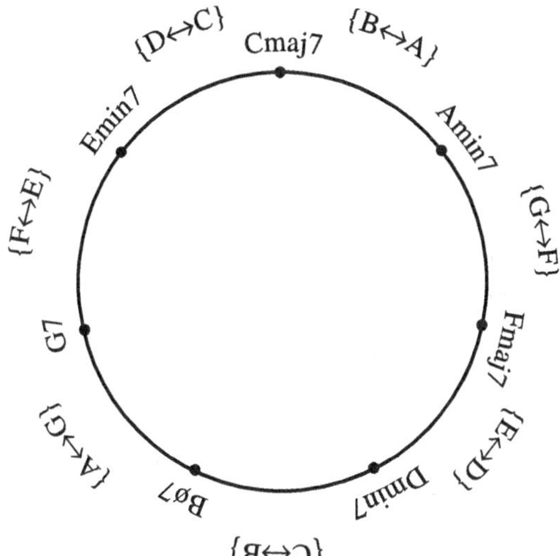

Figure 7.2.8 Voice-leading relations among diatonic seventh chords can be modeled with a circle of thirds. Here descending-third progressions are articulated by descending stepwise voice leading.

14 Mathieu 1997 (cited in Ricci 2004) makes similar points.

Figure 7.2.9 Efficient voice leading between strongly related seventh chords descends (top four voices of *a*). Harmonic cycles and descending-fifths sequences can therefore be realized with maximally efficient, descending voice leading (*b–c*).

Finally, a word about four-voice voice leading among triads. In Chapter 6, we encountered the 3 + 1 schema, in which three voices move between complete triads in a strongly crossing-free way. But Figure 7.2.10 shows that we can also connect triads by *nonfactorizable* voice leadings, in which no voice can be eliminated without creating an incomplete chord. Clearly, a four-voice triadic voice leading will be nonfactorizable only when it has the general form of Figure 7.2.11: a note in the first chord "splits" into two adjacent notes in the second, while two notes in the first "merge" onto the remaining note in the second.[15] There are 3 × 3 = 9 basic possibilities, depending on whether the splitting and merged-upon notes are the root, third, or fifth of their respective triads. For example, the first voice leading in Figure 7.2.10 maps a chord with doubled root to a chord with doubled root, while the second maps a chord with doubled root to a chord with doubled third. Remarkably, the various forms of the nonfactorizable schema exploit a variety of triadic near symmetries, including the triad's proximity to the tritone and diminished seventh chord; readers who are interested in exploring this issue should attempt the exercises in Appendix F.[16]

Figure 7.2.10 These voice leadings are nonfactorizable, because eliminating any voice creates an incomplete triad.

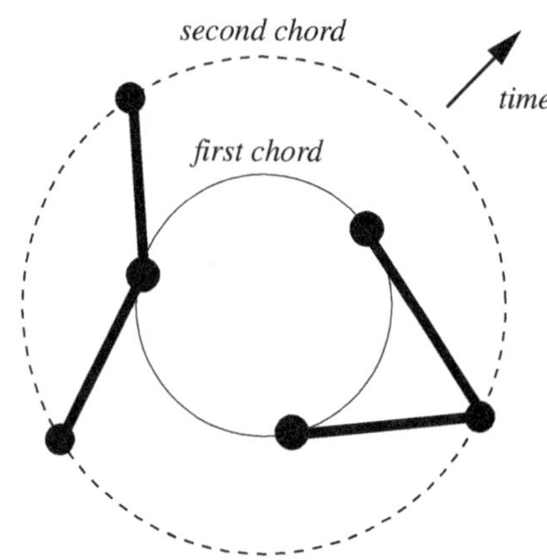

Figure 7.2.11 A nonfactorizable, strongly crossing-free, four-voice triadic voice leading embodies this basic schema: two notes in the first chord "merge" onto a note in the second, while the third note of the first chord "splits" into the remaining two notes of the second chord. Here, time progresses radially from the inner circle toward the outer.

15 Proof: if the merged-onto note were a destination of the splitting note, the voice leading would be factorizable.

16 In particular, nonfactorizable voice leadings of the form (r, r, t, f)→(t, f, r, r), which map a chord with doubled root to a chord with doubled root, exploit the chord's closeness to the tritone; voice leadings of the form (r, r, t, f)→(r, t, f, f) exploit its closeness to the quadruple unison; while voice leadings of the form

Figure 7.2.12 shows that these nonfactorizable voice leadings, combined with the 3 + 1 schema discussed earlier, account for a substantial proportion of the four-voice triadic voice leadings in the music of composers from Dufay to Bach.[17] At first blush, this might seem shocking, as if all the glories of the Renaissance could be reduced to just two basic contrapuntal tricks. But on reflection it is not terribly surprising: after all, there are only so many ways to connect triads, and our two schemas together produce *all* the strongly crossing-free four-voice triadic voice leadings—including all of those in which each note in the first chord moves to its nearest (upper or lower) neighbor in the second. Insofar as composers are interested in efficient voice leading, then we should expect them to make heavy use of these two basic techniques. This reinforces the claim that there are important continuities between contrapuntal practices in Renaissance modality and functional tonality: on the basic chord-to-chord level, we find virtually the same voice-leading schemas dominating the two repertoires. Rather than a broad difference between styles, we instead see an interesting sort of composer-by-composer variation: for example, nonfactorizable voice leadings account for more than 20% of the voice leadings in Palestrina, but only about 5% of those in Lassus. This seems less like a matter of large-scale historical change than of individual composerly preference.

Figure 7.2.13 shows how the nonfactorizable pattern might appear in keyboard-style passages: in each case, a close position triad in the right hand moves to an

Figure 7.2.12 The 3 + 1 and nonfactorizable schemas together account for a very large proportion of the four-voice triadic voice leadings in a wide range of music. There are, however, some individual differences between composers.

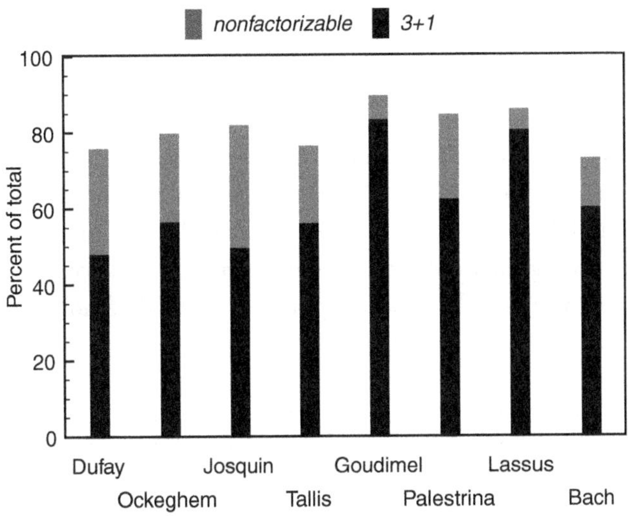

(r, r, t, f)→(f, r, t, t) exploit its closeness to the diminished seventh. These three categories exhaust all the possibilities up to permutation of the labels "r," "t," and "f."

17 The Goudimel pieces, from 1564, are four-voice harmonizations of the complete Geneva Psalter. These chorales are highly stereotypical and very homophonic.

incomplete chord—either an octave enclosing another note or an interval with one doubling—while the bass voice completes the second triad.[18] This means that our voice-leading formulas are associated with simple physical gestures that can easily be taught to young musicians: when using the 3 + 1 schema, a keyboardist moves the right hand between complete triads, while allowing the bass to move independently; to use the nonfactorizable schema, the keyboardist switches from complete to incomplete triads with the right hand, while completing the second chord with the left. In fact, these two gestures are embedded, with varying degrees of explicitness, in traditional figured-bass pedagogy: early theorists such as Heinichen discuss the 3 + 1 schema, while later writers (including C. P. E. Bach) provide numerous examples of the nonfactorizable alternative.[19] (Two centuries later, the techniques are still taught in universities, and I learned both as a college freshman.) This, I think, is a wonderful example of the practical pedagogical tradition solving a relatively complex mathematical problem. More than three centuries ago, figured-bass theorists had devised a simple set of physical gestures that produce all the strongly crossing-free voice leadings between triads—gestures that are straightforward enough to use improvisationally, yet powerful enough to generate an extraordinary degree of contrapuntal variety.

Figure 7.2.13 Nonfactorizable voice leadings in keyboard style. In each case, a complete triad in the right hand moves to an incomplete chord.

7.3 SEQUENCES

So far we have no reason to believe that functional tonality involves *short* motions along the descending circle of thirds: our thirds-based model permits arbitrary rightward motions on Figure 7.1.1 and does not privilege short steps over longer leaps.[20] However, tonal music also involves *sequences,* in which the same musical material is repeated at multiple pitch levels.[21] Here there is a notable bias toward small motions along the descending circle of thirds. The most compact sequence, when represented on the circle of thirds, is (of course) a repeating series of descending thirds itself—a

---

18 This simple physical schema (along with its retrograde) can be used to produce any nonfactorizable voice leading that exemplifies the basic pattern in Figure 7.2.11. However, not every voice leading that moves from a close triad to an incomplete triad in the right hand will be nonfactorizable: for example, (C3, E4, G4, C5)→(F3, C4, A4, C5) is factorizable.

19 Heinichen's 1728 figured-bass treatise always recommends a complete triad in the right hand (see Buelow 1992, p. 28). C. P. E. Bach's *Essay on the True Art of Playing Keyboard Instruments* (Bach 1949, pp. 202ff, originally published in 1753 and 1762) discusses a wider range of right-hand possibilities, including the nonfactorizable schema.

20 For example, the progression vi–V involves a four-step rightward motion, with the triads vi and V being maximally distant from the standpoint of voice leading.

21 See Caplin 1998, ch. 2, Harrison 2003, and Ricci 2004.

progression that appears periodically in the literature, though it is not extremely common (Figure 7.3.1a). (Note that sequences frequently use the iii chord, which is rare in nonsequential harmony.) The second-most compact sequence alternates descending thirds with ascending fourths, and is widespread (Figure 7.3.1b). The ubiquitous descending fifth sequence is the third-most compact sequence (Figure 7.3.1c), consisting of a series of two-step motions along the circle. The pattern in Figure 7.3.1d is a close variant, in which a single descending third alternates with an ascending second, moving successively by one and three steps along the circle of thirds. (We will discuss this sequence in a moment.) Another variant is shown in Figure 7.3.1e, consisting of two descending thirds followed by a descending fifth. The resemblances between Figures 7.3.1c–e are particularly striking: in each case, a series of short motions along the circle of thirds produces a sequential pattern that repeats at the interval of a descending second, yielding slight variations on the same fundamental paradigm. Figure 7.3.2 provides some examples of these sequences in actual music.

Figure 7.3.3 lists all 18 diatonic sequences whose repeating unit contains at most two chords; the list is ordered by compactness on the descending circle of thirds, with inversionally related sequences sharing the same line. (Thus if a sequence on the left features short descending motions along the circle of thirds, its partner on the right features short *ascending* motions along the circle.) In each of the first five rows, the sequence on the left is considerably more common than that on the right, suggesting that descending thirds are indeed preferred.[22] The sixth and seventh rows feature

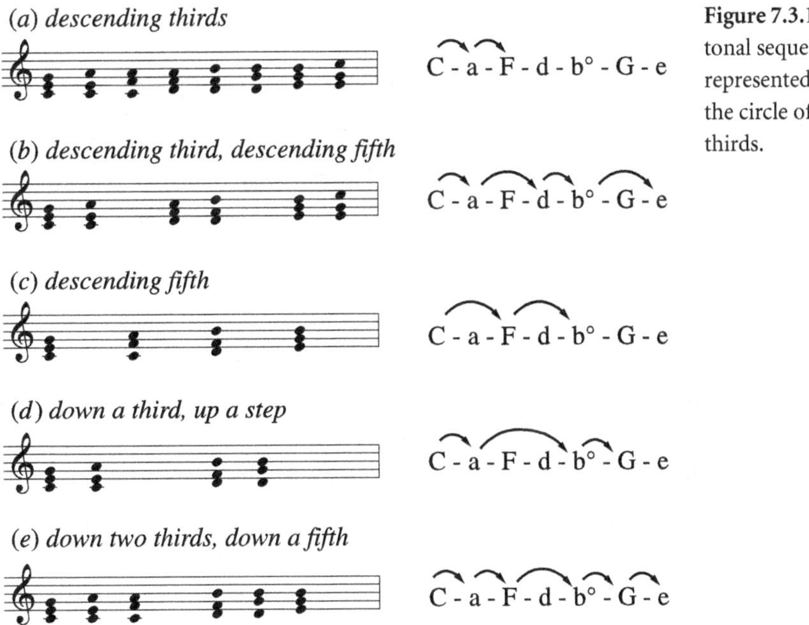

Figure 7.3.1 Five tonal sequences represented on the circle of thirds.

22 One possible explanation for this is that tonal harmony involves a fundamental preference for descending fifths progressions; third substitution could then transform descending fifths into either descending thirds or ascending steps.

Figure 7.3.2 (*a*) Haydn's E minor Piano Sonata, Hob. XVI/34, mm. 72–75. (*b–c*) The "down a third, up a step" sequence in Fauré's *Pavane*, mm. 2–5 and Bach's B♭ two-part invention, mm. 15–16 (bottom). (*d*) The "down a third, down a third, down a fifth" sequence in the D major fugue from Book I of Bach's *Well-Tempered Clavier,* mm. 9–10.

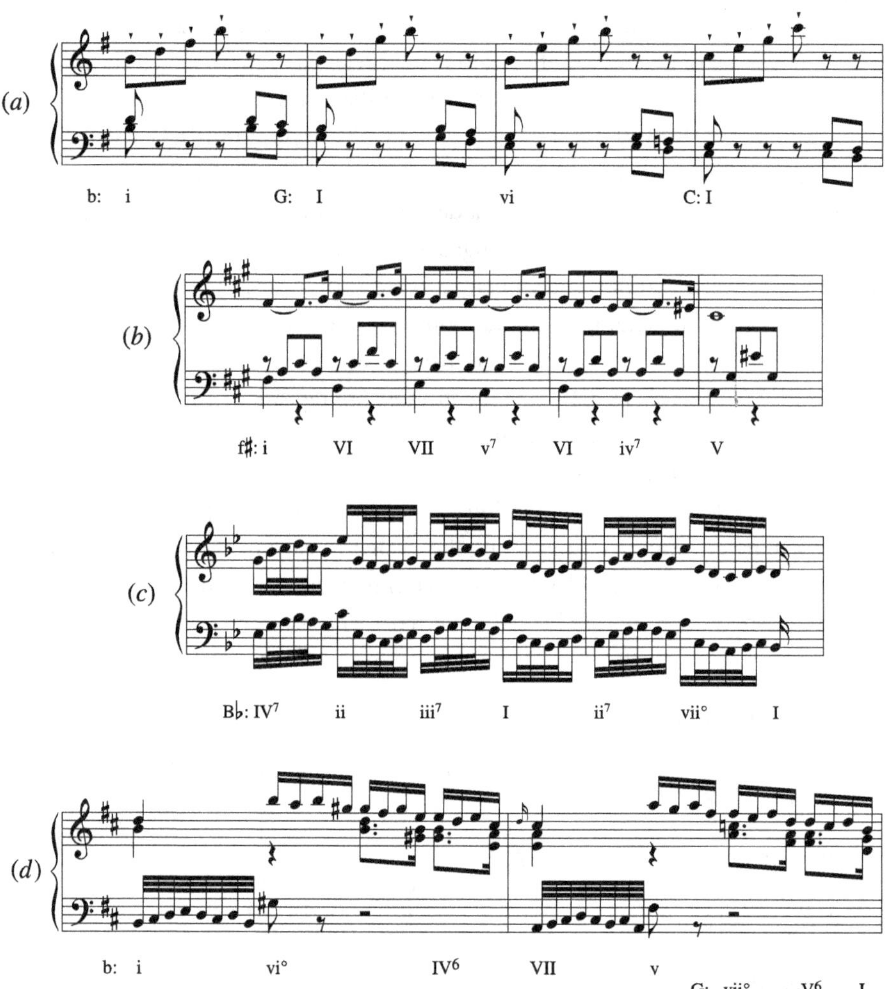

sequences that combine ascending and descending motion: though all four of these appear, there is a notable preference for those on the left, which repeat at the interval of a descending third. (Here the descending thirds motion appears between successive units of the sequence, rather than between adjacent chords.) The sequences in the eighth row are virtually unknown. (The stepwise progressions in the last row are common, but play a unique rhetorical role in tonal harmony; they typically appear in the context of brief "fauxbourdon"-style gestures, rather than sequences proper.) Figure 7.3.4 shows the distribution of sequences in the Mozart piano sonatas; the asymmetry between columns is quite striking.

Thus there is a subtle connection between what François-Joseph Fétis identified as the two basic components of tonal practice: in "harmonic tonality" the music moves

Figure 7.3.3 The eighteen diatonic sequences whose unit of repetition contains at most two chords. The (*a*) columns describe the sequence, the (*b*) columns estimate its frequency in the baroque and classical literature. Sequences featuring only "strong" progressions are considerably more common than their counterparts. Among those that mix strong and weak motions, sequences that repeat at the interval of a descending third are more common than those that repeat at the interval of the ascending third. The starred sequences in the last row, moving by parallel step, are common in both ascending and descending forms; however, they tend to play a slightly different role in the literature.

Sequence		**Inverted Form**	
a	*b*	*a*	*b*
↓third ↓third	*exists* (C-a-F-d-)	↑third ↑third	*very rare* (C-e-G-b°-)
↓third ↓fifth	*very common* (C-a-d-b°-)	↑third ↑fifth	*very rare* (C-e-b°-d-)
↓fifth ↓fifth	*very common* (C-F-b°-e-)	↑fifth ↑fifth	*exists* (C-G-d-a-)
↓third ↑step	*exists* (C-a-b°-G-)	↑third ↓step	*very rare* (C-e-d-F-)
↑step ↓fifth	*common* (C-D^7-G-A^7-)	↓step ↑fifth	*very rare* (C-b°-F-e-)
↑third, ↓fifth	*common* (C-E^7-a-C^7-)	↓third, ↑fifth	*exists* (C-G-e-b°-)
↑fifth, ↑step	*common* (C-G-a-e-)	↓step, ↓fifth	*exists* (a-G^7-C-B^7-e-)
↑step, ↑third	*very rare* (C-d-F-G-)	↓step, ↓third	*very rare* (C-b°-G-F-)
↑step ↑step	*exists** (C-d-e-F-)	↓step ↓step	*exists** (C-b°-a-G-)

from tonic to dominant along the circle of descending thirds, often forming "strong" progressions along the way. However, the gravitational attraction of tonic, subdominant, and dominant is strong enough to obscure this descending thirds structure: progressions such as I–V–I and I–IV–I move symmetrically along the circle and betray no preference for strong progressions. In "sequential tonality" the tonic and dominant lose their attractive power as a single musical pattern is whirled through diatonic space. Here the preference for strong progressions shines forth more clearly. What is interesting is that the descending circle of thirds plays a distinctive role in each of these two kinds of tonality: harmonic tonality uses the circle to organize motion from tonic to dominant, while sequential tonality emphasizes short steps along it.

To see how we might use these ideas in analysis, consider the fetching sequence from the last movement of Mozart's first piano sonata (Figure 7.3.5). I interpret this passage as a version of the "down a third, up a step" sequence in Figure 7.3.1; however, since the melodic pattern repeats after four chords, the sequence sounds to the

Figure 7.3.4 Two-unit sequences, of at least six chords in length, in the Mozart piano sonatas.

Sequence		Inverted Form	
↓third ↓third	2	↑third ↑third	0
↓third ↓fifth	6	↑third ↑fifth	0
↓fifth ↓fifth	33	↑fifth ↑fifth	0
↓third ↑step	8	↑third ↓step	0
↑step ↓fifth	22	↓step ↑fifth	0
↑third, ↓fifth	1	↓third, ↑fifth	0
↑fifth, ↑step	9	↓step, ↓fifth	0
↑step, ↑third	0	↓step, ↓third	0

casual listener like it descends by third. When the sequence returns to start the development section, Mozart makes an intriguing substitution: the music now begins D–G–c♯ø7 rather D–e–c♯°, moving down by fifths rather than down by third and up by step. (This alteration is retained throughout the sequence.) Figure 7.3.5c represents Mozart's variation on the descending circle of thirds, showing that he has simply moved the second chord leftward by one unit. The two versions, in other words, are related by *third substitution,* represented geometrically by replacing a diatonic triad with its nearest neighbor.

Something rather similar occurs in the A♭ major fugue from the second book of Bach's *Well-Tempered Clavier*. The fugue theme, an embellished sequence of fifths, is typically

Figure 7.3.5 (*a*) The "down a third, up a step" sequence in the third movement of Mozart's first Piano Sonata, K. 279. (*b*) When the sequence returns at the start of the development, Mozart alters it so that it begins with a pair of descending fifths. (*c*) This change is a minimal perturbation when represented along the circle of thirds.

accompanied by a chromatically descending countersubject. The first two harmonizations feature the "down a third, up a step" sequence and are illustrated in Figure 7.3.6a; the remaining harmonizations use descending fifths, as in Figure 7.3.6b. The figure shows that the two versions are related by third substitution: the countersubject's initial A♭ is simply repeated, transforming all the first-inversion triads into seventh chords. However, this transformation is rather cleverly disguised by the sixteenth-note figuration (not shown in the example), which moves from the middle voice to the soprano. As a result, the middle voice takes over the role of chromatically descending countersubject, appearing an octave rather than an eleventh above the subject's initial note. (This is double counterpoint on the cheap: since the upper voices both feature descending stepwise voice leading, the difference between the two countersubjects is largely a matter of figuration.) The interesting point, from our perspective, is the fluidity with which Bach moves between the "descending fifths" and "down a third, up a step" sequences. Like Mozart, he seems to view them as fundamentally similar.

For a final example, consider the "sequence" in mm. 16–18 of the F minor fugue in the first book of the *Well-Tempered Clavier* (Figure 7.3.7). The scare quotes acknowledge that the passage is not truly sequential: although the stuttering, descending melodic lines are always related by transposition, the interval is not uniform. (The descending passage begins first on, then a third above, then a third below the root of the preceding harmony; as a result, the chords within each measure are related by descending fifth, descending third, and ascending step.) Across bar lines the passage always articulates a V^7–I progression, so that the resulting harmonic sequence is entirely composed of strong progressions: descending twice by fifth (f–B♭^{7}–E♭), by third (E♭–C^7), by fifth (C^7–f), ascending by step (f–G^7), and descending once again

Figure 7.3.6 An interpretation of two passages from Bach's A♭ major fugue from WTC II. (*a*) Measures 6–7 involve the "down a third, up a step" sequence, while mm. 13–15 involve the descending fifths sequence (*b*). In the original music, the middle voice of (*a*) and the top voice of (*b*) involve sixteenth-note figuration; thus the chromatic descent moves from soprano (*a*) to middle voice (*b*).

Figure 7.3.7 A sequence-like passage from the F minor fugue in book I of Bach's *Well-Tempered Clavier*, mm. 16–18. Harmonically, the passage involves an unsystematic collection of "strong" progressions.

by fifth (G^7–C). This succession of strong progressions, articulated by descending-thirds melodies, creates a strong sense that the passage is both functionally tonal and sequence-like. (Indeed, I played it for years before noticing that it was not an exact sequence.) One hears the omnipresent engine of descending thirds—typical of tonal sequences in general and of Bach's sequences in particular—and fails to notice the subtle deviations from exact transposition.

Figure 7.3.8 (*a*) The "down a third, up a step" sequence can be derived from more familiar sequences by exchanging root position and first-inversion chords. Here, the four forms on the bottom staff are derived from the descending-fifth and descending-step sequences in the upper staff. (*b*) Measures 62–66 from Contrapunctus X in Bach's *Art of the Fugue*. Here, root substitution over a sequential bass line changes the "down a third, up a step" progression into the descending fifths progression.

These examples suggest that it might be worth reconsidering the role of the "down a third, up a step" sequence in functional tonality. Although rare, the sequence does appear sporadically throughout the literature. Yet in my experience, theorists are reluctant to acknowledge its existence—as if it were an anomaly so inexplicable that its very presence threatened to undermine the solid foundations of classical theory. From my point of view the sequence is anything but inexplicable: it results from a simple thirds substitution for the more common descending-fifths sequence (Figure 7.3.8). Figure 7.3.9 shows that it can appear in four basic forms, depending on which of its chords are in inversion. Our theoretical approach, by providing a home for this sequence, may help us learn to hear it, and thus to resist the almost overwhelming temptation to deny its existence.

Figure 7.3.9 (*a–d*) There are four basic forms of the "down a third, up a step" sequence, depending on which inversions are used. An example of each is provided. (*e*) Haydn's D major Piano Sonata Hob. XVI/42, II, mm. 11–12. (*f*) The opening of the "Crucifixus," from Bach's B minor Mass (BWV 232). (*g*) Brahms' F minor Piano Quintet, Op. 34, I, mm. 8–9. (Note that the dynamics and musical context all suggest that the sevenths should not be understood as suspensions.) (*h*) Bach's G major fugue, Book II of the *Well-Tempered Clavier*, mm. 66–69.

7.4 MODULATION AND KEY DISTANCE

Functional tonality employs conventionalized motions on both the level of the chord and the key: just as a V chord is overwhelmingly likely to progress to I, so too is a classical-style major-key piece overwhelmingly likely to modulate to its dominant. However, it is much harder to describe the syntax of key changes than of chord-to-chord progressions. The first problem is cross-stylistic variability: where harmonic grammar remains relatively constant over time, there is considerably more variation in modulations.[23] For example, much jazz obeys classical ii–V–I harmonic norms, though its key changes are anything but classical. (To take an extreme case, John Coltrane's "Giant Steps" involves a series of ii–V–I progressions that modulate by major third.) The second problem is that we continue to find significant variation even if we narrow our focus to the tonality of the eighteenth and early nineteenth centuries. Indeed, sonatas, fugues, and rondos all involve slightly different modulatory norms.

That said, it is still possible to identify some basic modulatory principles that are common to multiple genres: most obviously, pieces typically start and end in the same key; the first modulatory destination in major is the dominant key, while in minor it is either the dominant or relative major; and the subdominant key area often appears toward the end of the piece (Figure 7.4.1). Furthermore, theorists generally agree that tonal pieces often modulate between "closely related" keys. The most widely accepted model of key distance is the "chart of the regions" usually attributed to Gottfried Weber, though actually originating with F. G. Vial.[24] Figure 7.4.2 shows an equal-tempered version of the chart: motion along the SW/NE diagonal links modally matched fifth-related keys; motion along the SE/NW diagonal changes mode, alternating between the "parallel" (or tonic-preserving) and "relative" (or diatonic-scale-preserving) relationships. Though more than 200 years old, the Vial/Weber model continues to play a role in contemporary theory, particularly in the work of Carol Krumhansl and Fred Lerdahl. In fact, both of these theorists have attempted to *derive* the model from more basic principles: Krumhansl from the results of psychological experiments, and Lerdahl from the deeper postulates of his theoretical system.[25]

Figure 7.4.1 Common sequences of keys in functionally tonal music.

	First Key	Second Key	Third Key	Other Keys	Often Found Near the End	Last Key
Major	I	V	often ii, v, or vi	various	IV	I
Minor	i	III or v	often VII, iv, VI	various	iv	i

23 Stein 2002 argues that the chordal syntax of classical harmony antedates the modulatory syntax.

24 See Lester 1992, p. 230.

25 See Krumhansl 1990, ch. 7 and Lerdahl 2001, ch. 2. Both theorists derive the Weber model from a combination of experimental data and theoretical assumptions. In this sense, the model is (partially) a theoretical construct, rather than the simple output of psychological experiments. As far as I know, there are no experiments that directly test key distances, or even establish their perceptual reality.

Figure 7.4.2 The "chart of the regions" in its equal-tempered form. Major keys are capitalized, minor keys are shown in small letters. Fifth-related keys are on the SW/NE diagonal lines, while "parallel" and "relative" keys are on the SE/NW diagonals. The figure is a torus whose top edge should be glued to the bottom, and whose left edge should be glued to the right.

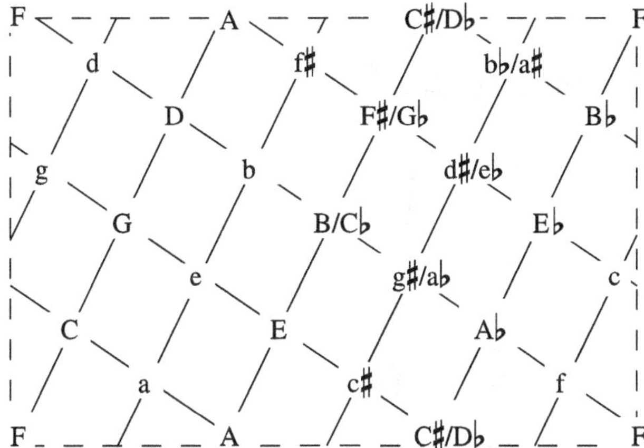

Weber's chart suggests that fifth-related major keys are particularly close, but it does not explain *why* this is so. One possibility is that fifth-related *tonic notes* or *tonic chords* are themselves close—in other words, C major pieces modulate to G major because the G major chord (or the note G) has a particular affinity for the C major chord (or note C). (This in turn may be due to the acoustic relationship between perfect fifths.) Another possibility, however, is that fifth-related major keys are close because their associated *scales* are close. From this point of view, what links the keys of C and G major is the fact that the single-semitone shift F→F♯ transforms the C diatonic scale into G diatonic. Similarly, C major and A minor are close because the C major scale shares the same notes as A natural minor, and because a single-semitone shift (G→G♯) transforms C major into A harmonic minor. Thus we have two plausible but distinct theories of key distance, one based on chords (or notes), the other on scales.

Let's see if we can use our geometrical models to investigate this issue. Recall from §4.6 that the familiar seven-note scales of the Western tradition are contained on a three-dimensional cubic lattice, reproduced here as Figure 7.4.3. According to the scalar model of key distance, keys are close if their associated scales are near each other on this lattice. If we limit our attention to major keys, then the lattice simply reduces to the familiar circle of fifths. Minor tonalities present a challenge, however, as they can use any of three distinct scale forms. How should we measure the distance from C major to E minor? Should we, for example, choose the E minor scale that is closest to C major? Or should we choose the farthest scale instead? One sensible solution is to take the *average* of the distances between the scales belonging to each key. This means that the distance from C major to E minor would be $(1 + 2 + 3)/3 = 2$

Figure 7.4.3 The three-dimensional lattice showing voice-leading relations between familiar scales. The three A minor scales lie along the solid dark line, while the three E minor scales lie along the dotted dark line.

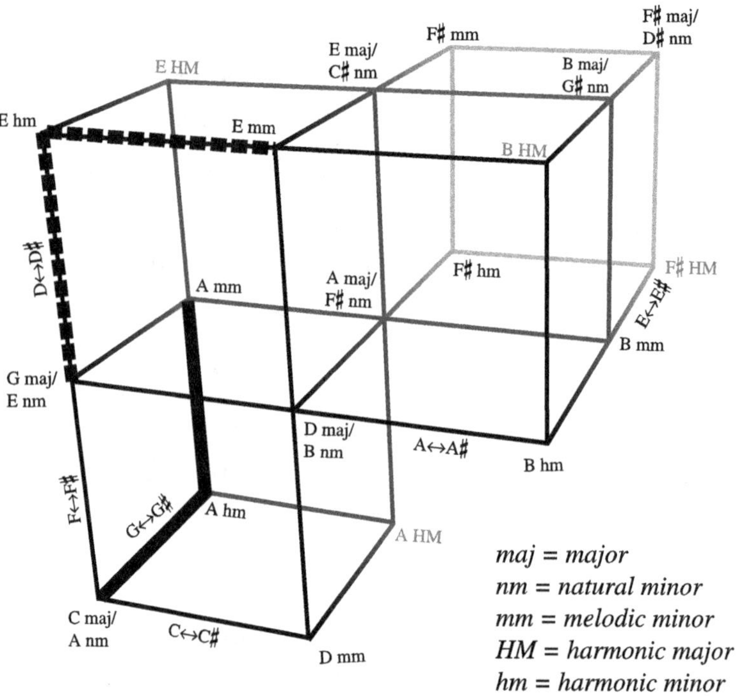

(Figure 7.4.4).[26] When measuring the distance between minor keys, we can average the distances in the most efficient *pairing* between their scales, as illustrated by the figure.[27]

Figure 7.4.5 lists the resulting distances. According to this model, major keys are particularly close to their dominant major (V), subdominant major (IV), and relative minor keys (vi), with the supertonic minor (ii) being just a little farther away. A minor key is maximally close to its relative major. In second place is the subtonic major (VII), with the subdominant minor (iv), dominant minor (v), submediant major (VI), and parallel major (I) being slightly farther. While these key distances are broadly similar to Weber's, there are some intriguing differences: notably, the scalar model helps explain why minor keys would be more likely to modulate to the relative major than to the dominant. Note also that from the scalar perspective, the keys of C major and D minor are particularly close, since two of the D minor scales can be linked to C major by single-semitone voice leading (Figure 7.4.6). Compared to the Weberian model, then, the scalar perspective would lead us to expect more

26 For simplicity, I am adopting the "smoothness" metric, which counts the total number of semitones moved by all voices (Appendix A).

27 Alternatives tend to produce counterintuitive results. For instance, one might try to measure key distances using the smallest distance between two sets of minor scales, but this means that C minor and E♭ minor are maximally close, since C natural minor is one semitone away from E♭ melodic minor ascending. Similarly, one might try to take the average of all nine distances between two sets of minor scales, but this means that a minor key is not distance zero from itself.

Figure 7.4.4 Using voice leading to calculate distances between keys. (*a*) For major keys, the distances are simply the voice-leading distances between the relevant diatonic collections. (*b*) For distances between major and minor, we calculate the size of the voice leadings from the major scale to each minor scale, and take the average. Here, the average distance between C major and the three A minor scales is 1. (*c*) For minor scales, we take the average of the three voice leadings in the most efficient pairing of the scales in one key with those in the other. Here, the average distance for the best pairing between A minor and E minor scales is 2.3.3.

modulations between a major key and its supertonic minor (or conversely, a minor key and its subtonic major), and less fifth motion among minor keys.

To evaluate these competing models of key distances, we can compare them to actual modulation frequencies in baroque and classical music. (The assumption here is that composers modulate more frequently to nearby keys.) To this end, Figure 7.4.7 shows the results of a crude statistical survey of a large number of pieces by Bach, Haydn, Mozart, and Beethoven.[28] The results are quite interesting. First, there

28 The analysis was simplistic but hopefully unbiased: I simply programmed a computer to look through MIDI files to find moderately long sections (15 notes or more) belonging to a single diatonic, harmonic minor, or melodic minor ascending scale. (I assumed that minor keys do not normally reside in the diatonic collection.) Each successive modulation was then categorized according to root relationship and mode: thus a modulation from G major to A minor was treated as "root moves up by two semitones, mode changes from major to minor," regardless of the global tonic of the piece. To test the data, I correlated the resulting modulation frequencies with those in human analyses of Mozart's piano sonatas. The correlation was very high (.96) for modulations beginning in major keys, and somewhat lower (.86) for those beginning with minor keys, in part because the computer stayed in minor keys longer than the humans did.

Figure 7.4.5 Key distances, calculated using voice-leading distance between scales. The smallest distances are shown in boldface.

	C major	C minor
C major	0	**2**
C♯ major	5	3
D major	2	4
E♭ major	3	**1**
E major	4	5.33
F major	**1**	2.33
F♯ major	6	4
G major	**1**	3
A♭ major	4	**2**
A major	3	5
B♭ major	2	**1.33**
B major	5	5
C minor	2	0
C♯ minor	5	4.33
D minor	**1.33**	2.67
E♭ minor	5	3
E minor	2	4
F minor	3	**2.33**
F♯ minor	4	4.67
G minor	2.33	**2.33**
G♯ minor	5.33	4
A minor	**1**	3
B♭ minor	4	2.67
B minor	3	4.33

Figure 7.4.6 A major key is particularly close to its supertonic minor, just as a minor key is very close to its subtonic major.

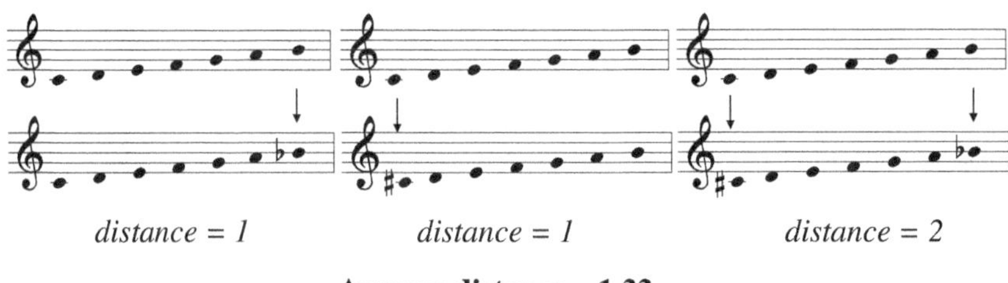

is a marked asymmetry between major and minor: for all four composers, the four most common major-key destinations are V, IV, vi, and ii. (Note that these numbers are calculated relative to the immediately preceding key: a modulation from C major to G major is treated as I→V, no matter what the global key of the piece.) For minor keys, however, the two most common modulatory destinations are III and VII, often by a wide margin. This represents a striking deviation from the Weber model, which

Figure 7.4.7 Estimated modulation frequencies in Bach's *Well-Tempered Clavier* and the piano sonatas of Haydn, Mozart, and Beethoven. The left column indicates the directed chromatic interval of root motion from source key to target key. (For example, a modulation from F major to G major or B minor to C♯ major is represented by the number 2.) Under each composer's name, the "min" and "maj" columns refer to the modality of the target key. The two or three largest values in each column are in boldface.

(*a*) from major keys

Root	**Bach**		**Haydn**		**Mozart**		**Beethoven**	
Motion	maj.	min.	maj.	min.	maj.	min.	maj.	min.
0	-	2.3	-	4.5	-	4.7	-	4.1
1	0	0	0.2	0.1	0.3	0	0.3	0.1
2	3.3	**8.8**	1.8	**7**	5.3	**7.1**	1.9	**12.7**
3	0.8	0	1.3	0	1.8	0.3	1.7	0.2
4	0	4.9	0.5	3.2	1.2	2.1	0.6	6.7
5	**26**	0.1	**29.8**	1.4	**24.6**	1.5	**23.3**	1.8
6	0	0.1	0	0	0	0	0.2	0.2
7	**26.8**	2.9	**28.4**	2.1	**28.2**	2.1	**20.8**	2.5
8	0.5	0	0.6	0	0.9	0	1.1	0.5
9	0.4	**20.2**	0.8	**15.7**	2.1	**13.1**	1.2	**14.6**
10	2	0	1.9	0.1	3.6	0.3	2.8	0.3
11	0.3	0.4	0	0.5	0	0.9	0.5	1.7

(*b*) from minor keys

Root	**Bach**		**Haydn**		**Mozart**		**Beethoven**	
Motion	min.	maj.	min.	maj.	min.	maj.	min.	maj.
0	-	1.9	-	**11.2**	-	6.9	-	**9.2**
1	0	1.4	0	1	0	2.8	0.6	2
2	0.8	0	2.4	1.2	0.7	0	2.2	1
3	0.8	**31.1**	2.1	**28.3**	0.7	**21.5**	1.3	**20.3**
4	0.3	0	0.3	0	1.4	0	0.7	0.3
5	**12.3**	3.8	**8.6**	4	**7.6**	4.9	**9**	2.2
6	0	0	0	0.2	0	0.7	0.2	0.6
7	**9.8**	1.9	**6.6**	2.9	**9.7**	4.2	**10.1**	2.5
8	0.3	**10.7**	0	6.4	2.1	**8.3**	0.9	**10**
9	0	0	1.2	0	2.1	0	0.6	0.3
10	1.9	**23**	1.8	**21.4**	2.1	**24.3**	3.8	**21.5**
11	0	0	0.3	0.2	0	0	0.6	0.2

predicts that the two modes should modulate in essentially similar ways. Furthermore, our data confirm that there is a particularly close relation between a major key and the minor key two semitones above it: major keys modulate to their supertonic minor more often than to the parallel minor, with minor keys modulating to their subtonic major more frequently than to any key except the relative major. All of these results are more consistent with the scalar model than the Weberian chart of the regions.[29]

Let me be clear that I do not take this to show that the scalar approach explains everything about tonal modulation. First, the statistical tests I have conducted are relatively simplistic and need to be confirmed by more careful investigation. Second, other musical factors no doubt play a role: the close relation between parallel keys, such as C major and C minor, surely has *something* to do with the fact that they share the same tonic note. And third, we need to recognize the role of individual preferences, since distance alone will not explain the fact that Mozart modulates to the parallel minor more frequently than Bach. That said, however, I think it is interesting that simple scale-based voice-leading models work as well as they do. Their success does seem to show that eighteenth- and nineteenth-century composers were sensitive to the twisted three-dimensional geometry shown in Figure 7.4.3.

It's worth saying a word or two about why this is important. We have seen that there are two fundamentally different ways to understand the "closeness" of fifth-related keys: one based on the acoustic relation between their tonic notes, the other based on the voice-leading relationships between their associated scales. These theories suggest very different generalizations to unfamiliar musical contexts. For example, in Chapter 9, we will find composers such as Debussy, Ravel, Shostakovich, and Reich exploiting efficient voice leading between a wide range of scales and modes. If we neglect the role of scale-to-scale voice leadings in classical music, then we will miss the way in which these twentieth-century composers are generalizing traditional modulatory practices. And this in turn could lead us to think that they had somehow gone wrong, for instance, by abandoning the use of fifth-related keys. This shows that both historians and composers have an interest in understanding the mechanisms underlying traditional modulation: the former, because they need to understand the connections between twentieth-century tonality and earlier styles; the latter, because they may want to develop analogues to modulation in as-yet-unexplored musical situations.

7.5 THE TWO LATTICES

We've now used two different circles to model functional tonality: the circle of thirds, which identifies single-step voice leading among triads, and the circle of fifths, which represents single-semitone voice leading among diatonic scales. There is of course a very close structural analogy between them, arising from the fact that both depict

29 More sophisticated quantitative tests confirm the intuition that modulation frequencies are closely related to voice-leading distance between scales. For example, I constructed quantitative models based on the assumption that keys are most likely to modulate to their n nearest neighbors on either the Weber model or the scale lattice. Scalar models consistently outperformed the Weberian models, achieving correlations in the range of .91–.96, for the repertoire in Figure 7.4.7, compared to .77–.84 for the best Weberian models.

Figure 7.5.1 The diatonic triad and the major scale both divide the octave nearly (but not precisely) evenly. The circle of thirds arises from changing the position of the three-step interval; the circle of fifths arises from shifting the position of the six-semitone interval.

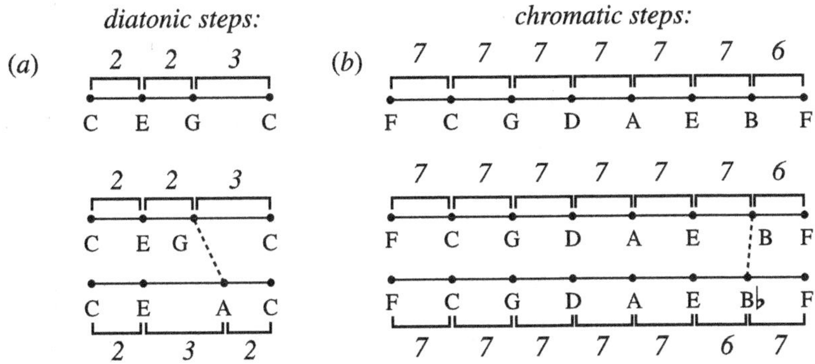

voice leading among "near interval cycles": the triad trisects the diatonic octave into two, two, and three scale steps, while the major scale divides four chromatic octaves into six perfect fifths and one "near fifth" (Figure 7.5.1). As explained in §3.11, the circle of thirds and the circle of fifths are formed by shifting the position of the unusual interval—a process that links transpositionally related collections by single-step voice leading. Geometrically, the resulting circles lie near the center of their respective chord spaces, as described back in Figure 3.11.6.

From this, there follows a remarkable consequence: voice-leading relations among nearly even three-note diatonic chords are fundamentally analogous to those among nearly even seven-note scales. Recall from §3.11 that we can scramble the voice leadings on a generalized circle of fifths to produce higher dimensional voice-leading lattices. If we scramble adjacent voice leadings on the circle of thirds, we obtain the two-dimensional structure shown in Figure 7.5.2—a lattice of squares each sharing an edge with its neighbors. This two-dimensional lattice contains triads and fourth chords, and is analogous to the "scale lattice" containing diatonic and acoustic scales (Figure 3.11.8b). Here the fourth chord plays the role of the acoustic scale, since it is generated by reversing a pair of adjacent voice leadings on the triadic circle. This means that the progression from C to G by way of the suspension {C, D, G} is structurally similar to the shift from D major to C major by way of the D melodic minor scale (Figure 7.5.3).

Pressing on, we note that it takes three single-step motions to move from C major to D minor on the circle of thirds. By scrambling these we obtain "incomplete seventh chords" such as {D, F, G} and {D, E, G}—the structural analogues of the harmonic major and minor collections (Figure 7.5.4).[30] Proceeding in this way, we arrive at the three-dimensional structure in Figure 7.5.5, which has the

30 Observe that the incomplete seventh chords are related by diatonic inversion, just as the harmonic major and minor scales are related by chromatic inversion; the diatonic triad and diatonic fourth chord are symmetrical under diatonic inversion, just as the diatonic and acoustic scales are symmetrical under chromatic inversion.

Figure 7.5.2 (*a*) On the circle of thirds, we move from C to G by way of E minor. (*b*) If we reverse the order of the voice leadings C→B and E→D, we can move from C to G by way of the "suspension chord" C-D-G. By scrambling every adjacent pair of voice leadings on the circle of thirds, we produce a lattice of squares each sharing an edge with their neighbors.

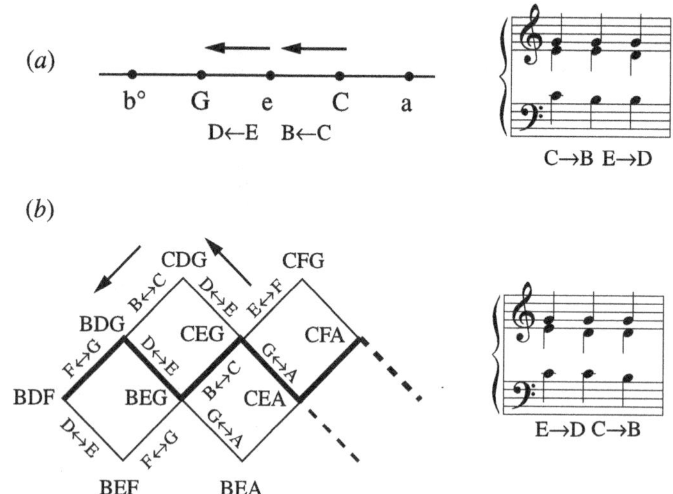

Figure 7.5.3 The move from C major to G major by way of the suspension chord C-D-G is precisely analogous to the shift from D major to C major by way of D melodic minor.

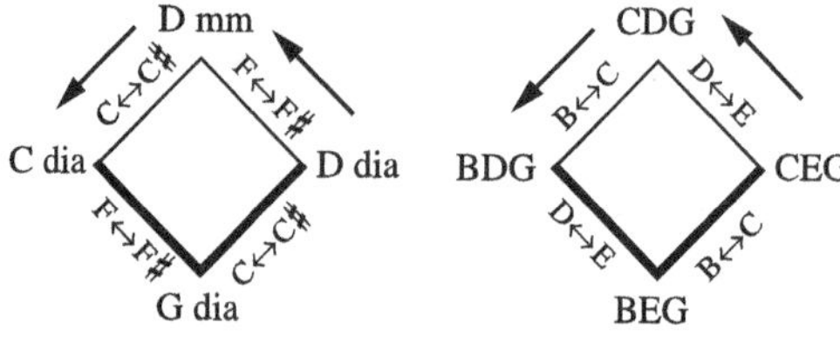

same basic form as our scale lattice: the circle of diatonic thirds is analogous to the diatonic circle of fifths and runs through the center of the figure in a zigzag fashion; nontriadic chords form a second circle, which winds its way around the triads as described in Figure 4.6.1. This lattice contains all the three-note diatonic sonorities that can resolve to a triad by one or two descending steps—in other words, the chords that can be formed by either a single or double suspension (Figure 7.5.6).[31] Figure 7.5.7 shows how these chords can act as waystations between the genuinely harmonic triads on the lattice's central spine, allowing composers to break large melodic motions into smaller steps. By enabling us to visualize these possibilities, the chord lattice can help us conceptualize them. For example, Figure 7.5.8 identifies four ways in which suspensions can be used to embellish a sequence of descending first-inversion triads: in each case, a single voice alternates with a pair of simultaneous descents. Figure 7.5.9 shows two passages in which composers exploit these pathways: in the first, the eighteenth-century composer (and chess master) François-André Danican Philidor alternates standard 7–6 suspensions with more

31 The chord lattice does not include diatonic clusters (such as {C, D, E}) or multisets (such as {C, C, D}). It is of course possible to create a larger three-dimensional lattice that contains these chords.

Figure 7.5.4 (*a*) On the circle of thirds, we move from C major to D minor by way of A minor and F major. (*b*) If we scramble the order of the voice leadings G→A, E→F, and C→D, we obtain a cube containing four triads (on C, A, F, and D), two fourth chords (CFG and DEA) and two incomplete seventh chords (DFG and DEG).

(*a*)

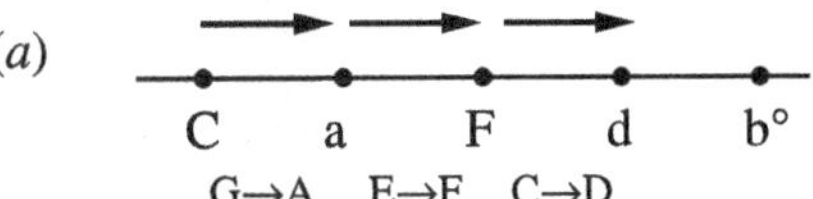

(*b*)

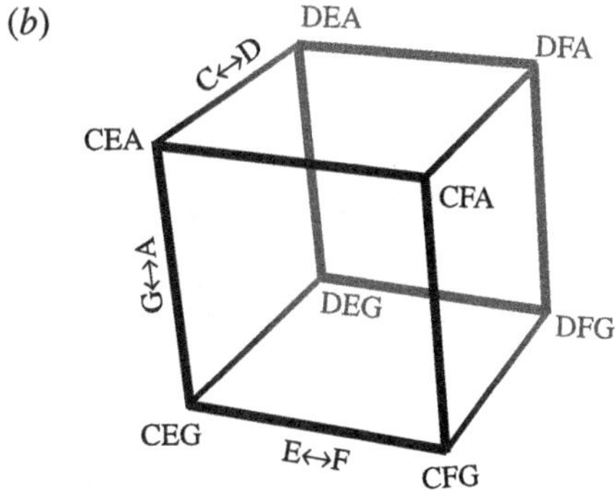

Figure 7.5.5 We can stack the cubes in Figure 7.5.4 to create a diatonic "chord lattice" precisely analogous to the scale lattice we investigated earlier (e.g. Figure 7.4.3). The triadic circle of thirds runs through the center of the space, taking a right-angled turn at each step. (From the lower left, we have CEG→CEA→CFA→etc.) The nontriadic chords are contained on a second circle, which winds around the first: from the lower right front we have CFG→DFG→DEG→DEA→. . ., a sequence that repeats every three chords at the interval of a descending third.

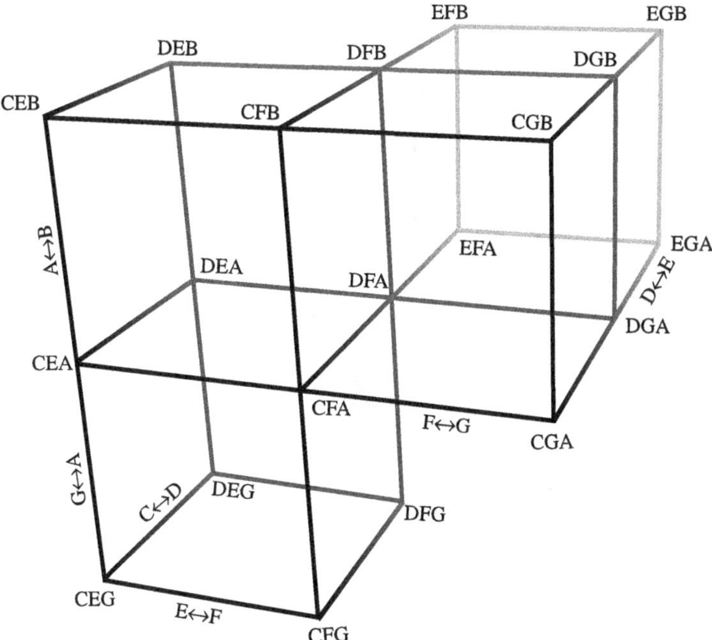

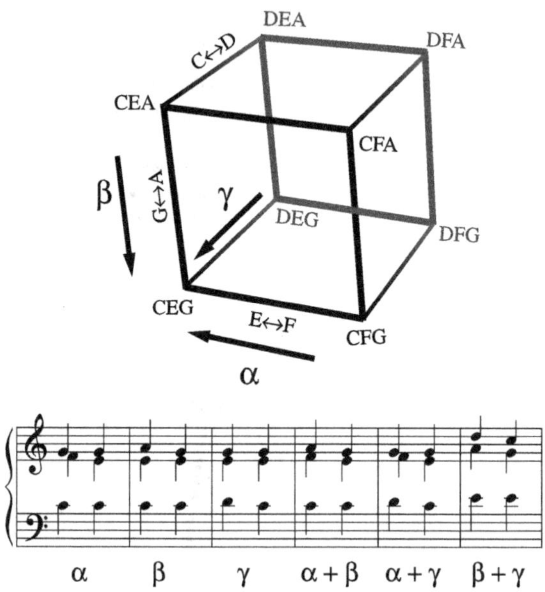

Figure 7.5.6 The diatonic chord cube contains all the sonorities that can resolve to CEG by either a single or double suspension.

Figure 7.5.7 The sonorities on the chord lattice provide waystations allowing composers to break large movements into smaller steps. Instead of moving directly from DGB to CEG, as in (*b*), a composer can use nonharmonic tones to smooth out the journey (*c*). The path in (*a*) depicts the music in (*c*). Historically, the F in the bass voice of (*c*) originated as a nonharmonic passing tone, but was eventually granted harmonic status as part of the seventh chord on G.

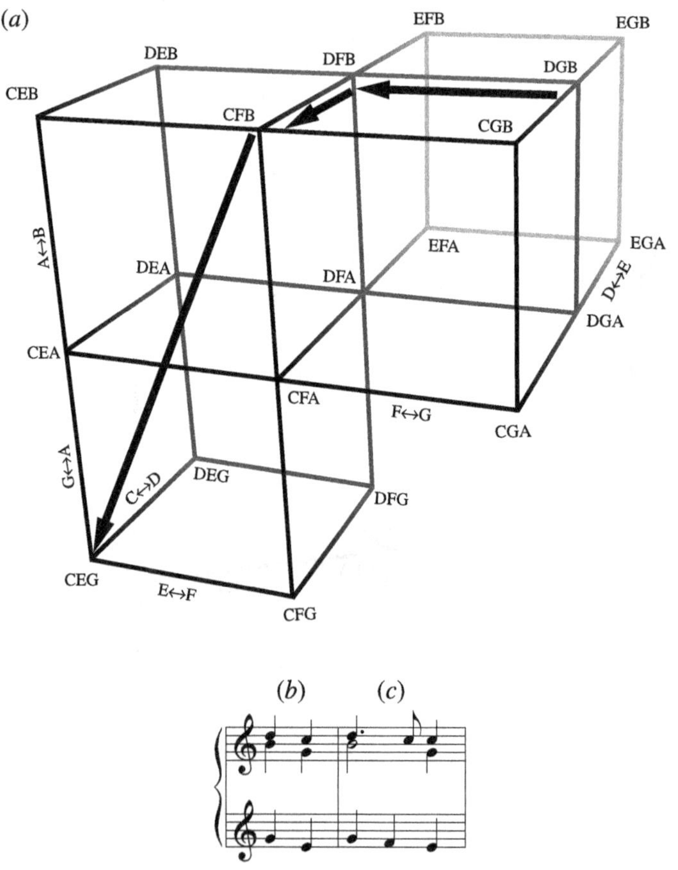

Figure 7.5.8 Four ways to use suspensions to decorate a series of descending first-inversion triads, represented on the chord cube. The first produces the ubiquitous 7–6 suspension, while those in (*b*) and (*c*) interpose an additional (root position or second-inversion) triad between consecutive first-inversion triads; the path in (*d*) creates a double suspension that sounds like an incomplete seventh chord.

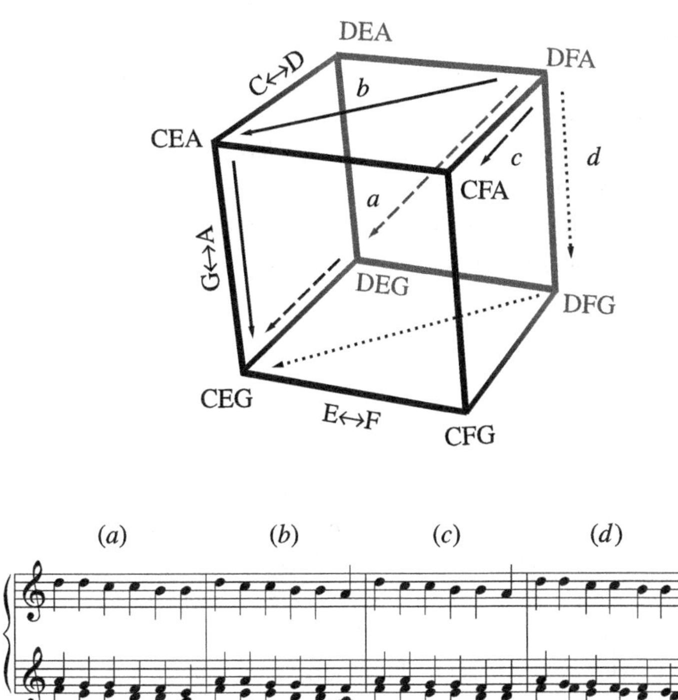

Figure 7.5.9 (*a*) Philidor's "Art of Modulation" (Sinfonia V, Fuga, mm. 36–38) alternates between 7–6 and 4–3 suspensions, utilizing paths *a* and *b* in Figure 7.5.8. (*b*) The Prelude to Grieg's suite "From Holberg's Time" uses the unusual double suspension represented by path (*d*).

unusual $^{6}_{4-3}$ suspensions, exploiting paths (*a*) and (*b*) on the cube in Figure 7.5.8; in the second, Grieg uses the path in (*d*).[32]

Earlier, I observed that tonal music is hierarchically self-similar, combining harmonic consistency and efficient voice leading at both the level of the chord and the level of the scale. We can now sharpen this observation considerably. Not only is there a loose analogy between the techniques composers use to relate chords and scales, but there is in fact a very precise structural similarity between the underlying voice-leading graphs. Indeed, chords and scales can be represented by *essentially the same geometry*. This extraordinary degree of self-similarity evokes fractals, mathematical shapes that exhibit the same structure no matter how they are magnified.[33] In much the same way, functional harmony exemplifies the same contrapuntal relationships whether we zoom out to the level of key relations, or zoom in to the level of chords.

7.6 A CHALLENGE FROM SCHENKER

The ideas in this chapter have been inspired by traditional tonal theorists such as Rameau, Weber, and Riemann. On my view, tonal music obeys purely harmonic principles that specify how chords can move, while modulations involve voice leadings between scales. Insofar as we can specify something like a "grammar" or "syntax" of functional tonality, it is largely concerned with local rules that tell us how to connect adjacent scales and chords. There are, however, a number of contemporary theorists who would object to these ideas: many followers of Heinrich Schenker seem to deny that functional tonality involves harmonic rules, asserting instead that its putative "harmonic grammar" can be explained contrapuntally.[34] (As Schenker wrote, the horizontal domain takes "precedence" over the vertical, and is the "only generator of musical content."[35]) Since Schenker's theories are highly influential, it will be worth considering them more closely, with the goal of understanding whether they do indeed conflict with the ideas we have been investigating.

Schenker is a highly complex figure who by every account made enormous contributions to music theory: in particular, he made a compelling case that there is more to musical coherence than the simple chord-to-chord constraints discussed in §7.1. Much of his work was devoted to elucidating these additional mechanisms of tonal

32 Thanks to Hank Knox and David Feurzeig for these examples.

33 True fractals are *infinitely* self-similar, no matter how far we zoom in or out, whereas tonal music is self-similar only on two levels. Nevertheless, there is something compelling, and even beautiful, about the symmetry between scale and chord.

34 The *locus classicus* of Schenker's antagonism to traditional harmonic theory is his essay "Rameau oder Beethoven?" (Schenker 1930 and 1997). More moderate critiques of traditional harmonic theory can be found throughout the Schenkerian literature, including Salzer 1982 and Schenker 2001. See also Rothstein 1992: "[early] Schenker conceived of tonal music as a kind of battleground on which the forces of harmony, voice leading, rhythm, and motivic repetition contest with each other.... The notion of semi-independent musical forces, in perpetual conflict with each other, seems to have been largely abandoned by Schenker as he developed his theory. I believe this was a serious mistake."

35 Schenker 1930, p. 20 ("Vorrecht") and p. 12 ("allein den musicalischen Inhalt hervorbringt"). For an English translation, see Schenker 1997, p. 7 ("prerogative") and p. 2.

organization, ranging from simple idioms (including progressions such as I–vii$^{\circ 6}$–I^{6}), to recurring melodic patterns (such as voice exchanges and linear progressions), to larger phenomena (such as the centrality of the return to V in the development section of a classical sonata). All of this is important and welcome. But in the course of making these arguments, he ended up advocating a radical model of musical organization according to which entire pieces were massively recursive structures, analogous to unimaginably complex sentences. The complexity of these hierarchical structures far outstrips those found in natural language, and seems incompatible with what we know about human cognitive limitations.[36] Further, and more directly relevant to our present concerns, the recursive model has an uncertain relationship to the chord-to-chord constraints that play an indisputable role in classical harmony.

Let's consider this point in the context of an elementary example of Schenkerian practice. Figure 7.6.1 analyzes the opening phrase of Mozart's variations on "Ah, vous dirai-je, Maman" better known in English as "Twinkle, Twinkle Little Star." The analysis is taken from Cadwallader and Gagné's undergraduate textbook *Analysis of Tonal Music: A Schenkerian Approach.* Beneath their example, I have provided a standard Roman numeral description. My chord-by-chord analysis includes two chords that Cadwallader and Gagné omit: where I interpret the opening measures as

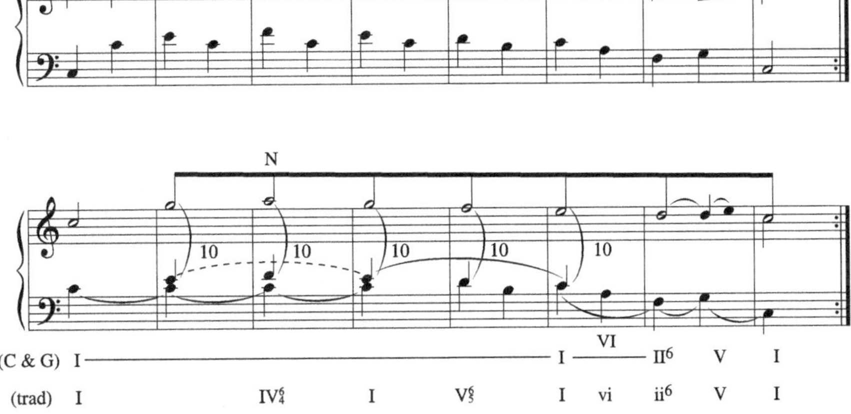

Figure 7.6.1 Mozart's variations on "Ah, vous dirai-je, Maman," (K. 265), along with Cadwallader and Gagné's Schenkerian analysis.

36 By drawing an analogy to sentences, I mean to be registering the fact that Schenker conceives of musical passages as being *nested* within one another, much like linguistic clauses (§7.6.3). Picking up on this analogy, Lerdahl (2001) uses linguistic tree structures to express essentially Schenkerian ideas. Schenker himself periodically made comparisons to language, as at the opening of "Further Considerations of the Urlinie: II," where he decries the simplification of German syntax, associating it with a degradation of musical comprehension (Schenker 1996, p. 1). (See also Schenker's analogy to linguistic grammar, quoted below.) Ultimately, however, the analogy is a suspicious one: spoken English contains sentential units that are about 13 words long, as compared to written English, in which the units are 22 words long (O'donnell 1974). (Cf. Miller 1956, which emphasizes the "7 ± 2" limits on human short-term memory.) This contrasts dramatically with the length of classical pieces, which can be 20 minutes long, and can contain hundreds of measures and tens of thousands of notes. Given the centrality of language to human survival, it is evolutionarily reasonable to take the limits on hierarchical linguistic cognition as a rough guide to the limits on hierarchical musical cognition.

a I–IV$^6_4$–I–V$^6_5$–I progression, Cadwallader and Gagné label the first five measures "I." Thus, they describe my "IV$^6_4$ chord" as a "neighboring chord" (indicated by the label "N") and my "V$^6_5$ chord" as "passing." The implication seems to be that these chords are produced by contrapuntal rather than harmonic forces. In Schenkerian analysis, this process of identifying (and removing) "merely contrapuntal" harmonies produces ever-more abstract summaries of a piece, until entire movements, no matter how large, resemble simple I–V–I progressions.

There is room to debate whether traditional harmonic theorists need to recognize the notion of a "passing chord," as opposed to simply acknowledging the existence of a few harmonic idioms. But insofar as they do, the term "passing chord" will presumably describe those rare sonorities that violate the harmonic syntax of §7.1. (Figure 7.6.2 provides a potential example.) By contrast, Cadwallader and Gagné's "neighboring" and "passing" chords participate in *perfectly well-formed harmonic cycles*. That is, if we simply place Roman numerals under each and every chord, as shown at the bottom of Figure 7.6.1, we find a series of harmonies conforming to conventions described in §7.1. We therefore need to understand what it means to assert that some of these apparently syntactical harmonies are the "byproducts" of contrapuntal motion. In particular, we need to understand how this description relates to that provided by traditional harmonic theory.

Figure 7.6.2 The first movement of Mozart's Piano Sonata K. 279, mm. 25–30. A traditional theorist might consider the I$^6_4$ to be a "passing chord," since it violates the expectation that I$^6_4$ goes to V. By treating it as the product of linear motion (as shown in *b*), we obtain a syntactical progression from an apparently nonsyntactical surface.

It seems to me that there are essentially four options here:

1. *Nihilism.* Harmonic nihilists simply deny that harmonies in functionally tonal music exhibit regularities of the sort described in §7.1.
2. *Monism.* Monists acknowledge that tonal harmonies appear to obey harmonic rules, but assert that these regularities can be explained contrapuntally. The traditional theorist is therefore *wrong* to find a harmonic grammar in Mozart's music; the deeper and more correct explanation invokes the melodic processes described by Schenker.
3. *Holism.* The holist asserts that it is impossible to separate harmony and counterpoint, because the very distinction is ill-defined. Traditional harmonic theory, by postulating purely harmonic principles, illicitly tries to treat the harmonic realm on its own, without adequately considering counterpoint.
4. *Pluralism.* The pluralist believes that independent harmonic laws govern functionally tonal music. On this view, Schenkerian theory adds additional information to, but does not replace, traditional harmonic analysis. The traditional harmonic theorist correctly observes that Mozart's music obeys independent harmonic laws; the Schenkerian *augments* this observation by pointing out that the notes also have additional contrapuntal functions.

We can discount the first of these, as it is inconsistent with the evidence presented in §7.1. Each of the remaining views is worth considering in more detail.

7.6.1 Monism

According to the monist, the first five measures of Mozart's "Twinkle, Twinkle" should be explained contrapuntally rather than harmonically. Figure 7.6.3 attempts to test this theory by replacing Mozart's initial I–IV–I progression with a I–vi–I, and by eliminating the leading tone from the fifth measure. The resulting chord progressions are very rarely found in tonal music, even though they are perfectly legitimate contrapuntally: the I–vi^6–I progression is produced by neighboring motion in the upper voice, while the I–ii–I^6 motion can be understood as a passing chord. The awkwardness of the resulting progressions strongly suggests that Mozart's compositional choices are indeed motivated by harmonic considerations. Absent harmonic laws, we simply have no way of explaining why I–vi–I and I–ii–I^6 should be so much less common than I–IV–I and I–V–I.[37]

Figure 7.6.4 presents a number of contrapuntally unobjectionable progressions that are quite rare in functionally tonal music. All feature efficient melodic motion, avoid forbidden parallel fifths and octaves, and resolve the leading tone upward by step; all would be perfectly acceptable in sixteenth- or twentieth-century music. Yet Figure 7.6.5 shows that they are virtually absent in Mozart's piano sonatas. The challenge for the monist is to explain this using recognizably contrapuntal principles.

37 This point has been made by numerous commentators, including Smith (1986), Rothstein (1992), and Agmon (1996).

Figure 7.6.3 These "neighboring" and "passing" chords are contrapuntally unobjectionable, though the resulting chord progressions are harmonically unusual.

Figure 7.6.4 Three progressions that are contrapuntally unobjectionable, but which rarely appear in baroque or classical music: a root position V–IV (*a*), a major-key I–iii–V–I (*b*), and the analogous progression in minor (*c*).

Figure 7.6.5 Chord progressions in Mozart's sonatas. Starred progressions occur across phrase boundaries (e.g. K. 311, third movement, mm. 71–72). Schenkerians have asserted that the last two progressions are basic to tonal music, whereas traditional tonal theory claims that they are rare.

V-vi	103
I-I^6-V	56
V-IV^6	48
i-i^6-V	10
V-IV-I	2*
I-iii-V	0
i-III-V	0

To my knowledge, no theorist has ever even attempted to do so—at least not in clear, principled language that would be comprehensible to students or scientists. It seems reasonable to conclude that we cannot replace harmonic principles with purely contrapuntal laws. In the words of the noted Schenkerian (and pluralist) William Rothstein,

> [H]ow is it that all those passing and neighboring tones time and again just happen to dispose themselves in ways that produce what appear to be tonics, dominants, and other familiar chords, often moving in exactly the ways predicted by the harmony books?... It takes a very large leap of faith to believe that so many chordal structures and successions, exhibiting so many regular patterns are to be ascribed to contrapuntal happenstance.[38]

---

38 Rothstein (1992) is paraphrasing Smith (1986).

7.6.2 Holism

Let's now turn to the claim that traditional harmonic theory imposes an illegitimate separation between harmony and counterpoint. The idea is that, in actual music, harmony and counterpoint are so intimately intertwined that we must always consider both together. One obvious response is that *there currently exists an accurate theory of functional harmony,* one that is largely independent of contrapuntal considerations. Taken literally, holism would seem to imply that we cannot produce a purely harmonic theory such as that in §7.1. The holist therefore needs some explanation of how traditional theory manages to achieve the impossible. Furthermore, this explanation will need to explain how it is that very similar harmonic laws govern tonal styles with very different contrapuntal norms, including baroque music, classical music, and many varieties of jazz, rock, and pop. (This fact alone would seem to imply that harmonic principles can indeed be separated from counterpoint.) To my knowledge, no such explanation has ever been offered.

More generally, it seems likely that the holist fails to distinguish three separate questions:

1. Is it the case that composers' choices are guided at every point both by harmonic and contrapuntal considerations?
2. When analyzing a piece of music, does the dutiful analyst typically consider both harmony and counterpoint?
3. Can we provide an informative *theory* of the harmonic progressions found in tonal music that is largely independent of counterpoint?

The key point is that a traditional harmonic theorist is perfectly free to answer "yes" to all three. *Yes,* actual composers, in the heat of the creative process, invariably think about both harmony and counterpoint; and *yes,* a responsible analyst typically considers both factors together. But despite this in-practice entanglement of harmony and counterpoint, we can still provide an enlightening and largely harmonic *theory* of tonal chord progressions. This is because the theoretical project of characterizing the grammar of elementary tonal harmony is completely distinct from the analytical project of *saying interesting things about particular pieces.* Just as the grammarian of the English language can remain resolutely neutral on the proper method of interpreting Romantic poetry, so too can the supporter of traditional harmonic theory remain completely agnostic about how to analyze specific works. In particular, harmonic theorists need *not* assert that composers think first about harmony before thinking about counterpoint, nor that one has said all there is to say about a piece simply by placing Roman numerals under its chords. (Indeed, Schenkerian theory has provided an important corrective to these very tendencies.) To my mind, the point cannot be emphasized strongly enough: the project of constructing a harmonic grammar is totally independent of the enterprise of musical analysis—as independent as linguistics is from literary criticism.[39]

7.6.3 Pluralism

Pluralist Schenkerians believe that traditional harmonic theory is correct as far as it goes. Thus when the pluralist declares that the IV^6_4 and V^6_5 chords in Figure 7.6.1 are "passing" or "neighboring," she does not thereby deny that these chords are *also* genuinely harmonic objects that participate in syntactic harmonic cycles; instead, she means to assert that there is another level of description in which these chords can be discounted. It follows that, for pluralists, harmony and counterpoint will often suggest very different ways of organizing a single passage of music. Harmonically, music is organized into a series of concatenated cycles like beads on a string. Contrapuntally, however, it is organized hierarchically, nested like a series of Russian "matryoshka" dolls (Figure 7.6.6).[40] The result is a fundamentally *disunified* conception of musical structure, in which harmony and counterpoint work against each other, providing very different ways of organizing one and the same piece.[41]

I will not consider this view in much detail, as it is largely irrelevant to our present concerns. The important point is that traditional theorists and pluralist Schenkerians can agree about many things: that functionally tonal music involves distinctively harmonic laws; that the local voice-leading moves in Renaissance and classical music are quite similar; that modulations involve, among other things, voice leadings between scales; that nineteenth-century harmony often exploits efficient voice leading in chromatic space; that harmonic consistency, efficient voice leading, acoustic consonance, macroharmony, and centricity all contribute to our sense of tonality; and so on. Ultimately, the question is whether a theory emphasizing these facts will be embedded into a larger theory incorporating insights from Schenker. For the purposes of this book I am happy to remain agnostic about this larger issue. There is plenty of work to do, even if we restrict ourselves to matters about which traditional theorists and (pluralist) Schenkerians agree.

However, I would like to close with two general observations. First, it is unclear whether pluralist Schenkerianism is supposed to provide a grammar-like theory describing music's objective structure or a psychological theory about listeners' sub-

---

39 Imagine someone who objected to linguistics as follows: "your claim that English has a normal subject–verb–object ordering suggests that we have said everything there is to say about a sentence by labeling its constituents, but this leaves us unable to distinguish beautiful sentences from horrific ones." As far as I can see, this obviously silly argument is exactly analogous to the suggestion that traditional harmonic theory implies an impoverished analytical method.

40 The analysis in Figure 7.6.6 is taken from an article by David Beach (1983). In traditional Schenkerian theory, it is linear patterns—rather than chords—that are the focus of attention, and are understood to be recursively nested. Nevertheless, this has the effect of creating nested patterns of Roman numerals.

41 One important task for the pluralist is to re-examine Schenker's emphasis on musical unity in light of this manifest disunity. Is it the case that different musical parameters—not just harmony and counterpoint, but also form, theme, and motive—might in general suggest different ways of parsing a piece? And if so, does this reduce the importance of the "unity" that Schenker identified? See Cohn 1992a for related discussion.

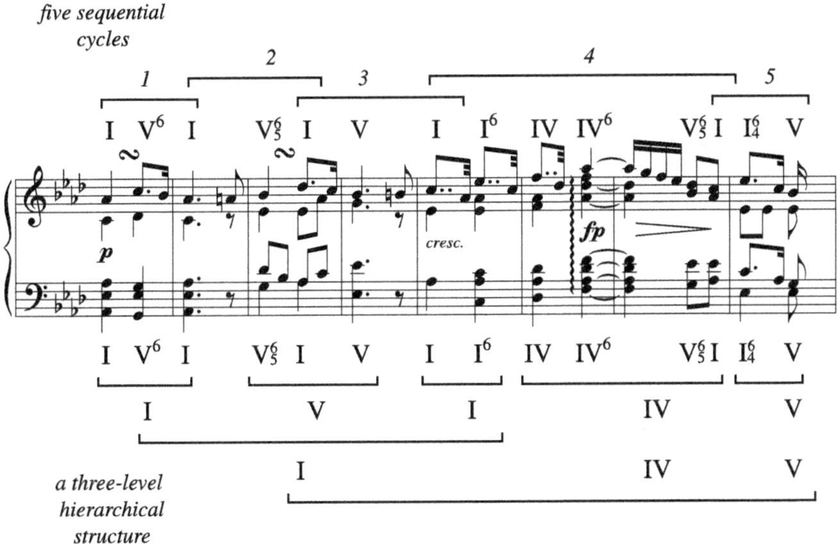

Figure 7.6.6 The opening of the slow movement of Beethoven's Sonata in C minor, Op. 10 No. 1, along with two ways of parsing its structure. In the traditional tonal analysis (*top*) five harmonic cycles are concatenated like beads on a string. In the Schenkerian reading (*bottom*) harmonies are nested recursively. (For example, the progression IV–IV^6–V$^6_5$–I, which belongs to the fourth harmonic cycle, is taken to represent a single IV chord on level 2.) Schenkerians believe that these sorts of recursive structures, which cut across the articulation into harmonic cycles, can be reliably inferred from a piece's contrapuntal structure. Ultimately, the recursive embedding proceeds until entire pieces are reduced to one of just a few basic templates, each resembling a I–V–I progression.

jective (and possibly variable) responses.[42] I have stressed that traditional harmonic theory is more like a grammar than a theory of phenomenological introspection. In analyzing Figure 7.6.7, for example, you do not need to ask yourself whether the D5 in the second beat *sounds like* a passing tone: if you know that tonal harmony is fundamentally triadic then you know enough to say that the D5 is indeed passing; and if experience tells you otherwise, then so much the worse for experience.[43] (In much the same way, a traditional theorist can describe the I$^6_4$ chord in Figure 7.6.2 as a "passing chord" without implying anything about how it sounds.) If Schenkerians mean to be making similarly objective claims about musical organization, then they need to spell out explicit procedures for making their recursive analyses—procedures that will allow us to test the theory in something like the way we tested the simple

42 Among contemporary theorists inspired by Schenker, Lerdahl (2001) models listeners' subjective responses, while Brown (2005) models objective musical organization. Schenker himself wrote "my teaching describes for the first time a genuine grammar of tones, similar to the linguistic grammar that is presented in schools" (Schenker 1956, p. 37; the sentence is translated only very loosely in Oster's English edition).

43 This is not to say that we never need to appeal to our psychology in resolving very difficult, ambiguous passages. In general, however, I think the goal of constructing Roman numeral analyses is to show how a particular passage relates to existing harmonic conventions; if so, then statements about *how we hear it* may be beside the point. This is one reason why it is possible to train a deaf person, or a computer, to become reasonably proficient at traditional harmonic analysis (Taube 1999 and Raphael and Stoddard 2004).

Figure 7.6.7 If we were to consider every note to be harmonic, we would confront an array of unusual sonorities, such as the A-D-E on beat 2. By eliminating nonharmonic tones, we reveal a "deeper level" of musical structure, in which triadic harmonies progress in familiar ways. The violation of our expectations (e.g. that harmonies should be triadic) is what motivates our reductive analysis.

harmonic grammar of §7.1.[44] If, on the other hand, pluralist Schenkerians mean to be making purely phenomenological claims, then their appropriation of the traditional terms like "passing" and "neighboring" is misleading at best. For the (psychological, subjective) Schenkerian "passing chord" is a different animal from the (grammatical, and more objective) passing tones of traditional theory. Furthermore, there are some delicate and as-yet-unexplored questions about the reliability and normative status of this sort of phenomenological introspection.[45]

Second, I want to remind you that there is an alternative way to formulate broadly Schenkerian claims about tonal unity. One of the primary attractions of Schenkerian theory, at least to my mind, is that it promises to show that classical music has a kind of hierarchical self-similarity, with its large-scale procedures mirroring the local details of chord-to-chord voice leading. This chapter has identified another route to a rather similar conclusion: for as we have seen, modulation involves scale-to-scale voice leadings that do indeed echo the contrapuntal techniques on the chordal level. To establish this analogy, we do not need to resort to musical reduction, nor to the analogy between musical pieces and enormous sentences, nor again to the claim that composers have cognitive capacities far exceeding those of ordinary listeners. Scale-to-scale voice leadings are right there in the score, transparent even

44 Temperley (2007, p. 172) makes a similar point.

45 It is quite possible to be deceived about what one hears. In part, this is because it can be difficult, introspectively, to distinguish *hearing as* from *hearing plus thinking*. It is one thing to have certain thoughts while listening to music (such as "aha, we're returning to the tonic key!"), but it is quite another for those thoughts to be embodied within the perceptual experience itself. See Wittgenstein 1953 (IIxi) for discussion of the analogous distinction between "looking plus thinking" and "seeing as."

to casual observation. Furthermore, it is not at all implausible to suggest that tonal composers might have sensed that F *moves to* F♯, when modulating from C major to G major, or that this is somewhat analogous to the way C moves to B as the C major triad changes to E minor. Our inquiry into voice leading thus provides a minimalist alternative to the more robust hierarchies of Schenkerianism proper. No doubt true Schenkerians will feel that this approach pales in comparison to the richly imbricated structure of an authentic Schenker graph. But there may be some readers who prefer the more modest—and perhaps empirically grounded—approach that I have outlined here.

CHAPTER 8

Chromaticism

We'll now consider some of the ways in which nineteenth-century composers exploited efficient voice leading, both as a tool for embellishing traditional progressions and as an alternative to these same routines. We'll begin with chromatic progressions that decorate a functionally tonal substrate: augmented sixths, Neapolitans, and examples of "modal mixture." We then turn to more exotic instances of chromaticism, comparing short pieces by Brahms and Schoenberg, and examining a few passages from Schubert. This sets the stage for a more in-depth discussion of two nineteenth-century warhorses: Chopin's E minor Prelude, Op. 28 No. 4, and Wagner's *Tristan* prelude.

My goal here is to present chromaticism as an orderly phenomenon rather than an unsystematic exercise in compositional rule breaking. Lacking a comprehensive understanding of voice leading, it is easy to become overwhelmed by the variety of nineteenth-century chromatic practices—a bewildering collection of techniques that do not display any obvious organization. From here it is just a small step to deciding that chromaticism is a matter of the Romantic Composer's Unexplainable Whim. If, on the other hand, we have absorbed the theoretical lessons of Part I, then we can adopt a more systematic attitude: once we can determine for ourselves the various contrapuntal paths from chord to chord, once we feel at home with the geometrical perspective of Chapter 3, we can begin to see that chromatic music reuses, over and over again, a relatively small number of musical tricks. This allows us to recognize the complex voice-leading relationships that bind together individual pieces while connecting them to one another.

8.1 DECORATIVE CHROMATICISM

Figure 8.1.1a contains a trio of dominant–tonic progressions in the key of C major. To a composer with a diatonic frame of reference, the voice leading is as small as it can be: each voice is either held constant or moves to its destination by a single step. But to composers who think chromatically, the counterpoint is not maximally efficient since notes sometimes move by two semitones. It is therefore tempting to use chromatic alterations to "fill in the gaps," perhaps in the hope that this will create an increased yearning for the tonic chord. Figure 8.1.1 shows that chromatic alterations produce a variety of familiar tonal chords, including the diminished

Figure 8.1.1 Intensifying diatonic dominant-tonic chord progressions with chromatic notes.

seventh, the dominant seventh with an augmented fifth, and the dominant seventh "flat five" chord.[1]

The chords (*d*)–(*f*) require special comment. Here, the chromatically altered note creates an augmented sixth that resolves outward to an octave. Each of these chords has a flattened second scale degree, and can be labeled only awkwardly with traditional Roman numerals.[2] But as *secondary* dominants they are very familiar, having long ago acquired picturesque names: the Italian, French, and German augmented sixth chords. One curious feature of Western music history is that these altered sonorities first appear as applied dominant (V-of-V) chords. It was only during the first few decades of the nineteenth century that they begin to appear as dominant sonorities in their own right. (Figure 8.1.2 provides a pair of representative examples.) This tendency reaches its apogee in twentieth-century jazz, where these altered dominants—conceived as "tritone substitutions" for the V^7—become virtually mandatory.[3]

1 This table is similar to Table 2 in Smith 1986. Smith's approach to chromaticism is in general very congenial to my own.

2 The chord {D♭4, F4, G4, B4} is often labeled "G$^{4\flat 5}_{3}$," with the numbers "$^{4}_{3}$" referring to intervals above the bass D♭4 and the symbol "♭5" referring to the interval above the root G.

3 Biamonte (2008) contrasts the voice-leading behavior of classical augmented sixths and jazz tritone substitutes. To my mind, however, these differences arise from the fact that classical music is largely triadic, whereas jazz makes heavier use of seventh chords. Modulo these differences, there is a clear connection between the two kinds of chords.

Figure 8.1.2 Chromatically altered dominants at the final cadence of Schubert's C major String Quintet (*a*) and at the opening of Chopin's C♯ minor Nocturne, Op. 27 No. 1 (*b*).

This historical contingency creates something of a pedagogical conundrum: most harmony textbooks, mirroring the historical development of Western music, introduce these sonorities first as secondary dominant chords, alterations of iv or V-of-V, rather than as dominants in their own right. (In fact, theorists sometimes debate whether augmented sixth chords have "secondary dominant" or "predominant" function.[4]) As a result, many textbooks pay relatively short shrift to the underlying similarity between the chords in Figure 8.1.1. This is symptomatic of a more general tendency to depict chromatic harmony as a series of disconnected idioms, often presented in a "one chord per chapter" format. This "object-based" (or harmonic) approach to chromaticism is diametrically opposed to the "process-based" (or contrapuntal) approach I am advocating. From my point of view, what is important is that the progressions in Figure 8.1.1 can all be obtained by a fundamentally similar process of chromatic embellishment.

One advantage of my approach can be seen by considering the chords in Figure 8.1.1g–h. These altered dominant sonorities do not have standard theoretical names, and appear only rarely in nineteenth century music. Figure 8.1.1g is the central progression of Strauss' *Till Eulenspiegel*, and is sometimes called the "Till Sixth." Figure 8.1.1h appears in the upper voices of the final progression of Scriabin's *Poem of Ecstasy*,

4 I think of augmented sixths as being secondary dominants for two reasons: first, in sequences they often alternate with ordinary dominants (see Mozart's C minor fantasy, K. 475, mm. 1–3, as well as Figure 8.3.4); second, in recapitulations they often replace the exposition's secondary dominants (cf. Beethoven's F minor piano sonata, Op. 2 No. 1, I, mm. 41 and 140; Mozart's D major sonata, K. 311, II, mm. 14 and 50). They only rarely substitute for genuine predominants in these contexts.

and has probably been given a silly name at some point (the "Ecstatic Sixth?"). Students who have learned chromatic harmony as a series of idioms tend to panic when they first confront such chords. ("What is *that* and why wasn't it in my textbook?") What they need, I think, is not an extensive list of chords to memorize, but rather a sense of how to *think for themselves* chromatically—a sense, in other words, for the cognitive processes that might lead composers to invent sonorities of this kind. Students who realize that there are countless chromatic alterations in nineteenth-century music, only some of which have standard names, are more capable of confronting the harmonic unknown, both analytically and in their own music.

Of course, chromatic techniques can be applied to other progressions as well. Figure 8.1.3 presents a few standard embellishments of ii and IV. As discussed in Chapter 6, the I–IV–I progression is often decorated by interposing an augmented triad between I and IV and a minor triad between IV and I. (A very similar alteration, when applied to a V–I$^6_4$–V progression, intensifies the dominant by way of the minor tonic triad.) Other changes transform ii$^6_5$ into a half-diminished chord and ii^{o6} into the Neapolitan sixth. As a teacher, I try to emphasize the general structural principle that links all these progressions: in nearly every case, diatonic tones are modified to create efficient chromatic voice leading, smoothing the transition from chord to chord. Although students must still be introduced to these chords individually, and coached in their various voice-leading particularities, I find that it is much easier to teach this material when the deeper musical principles are explained.

In fact, it can even be interesting to ask whether there are chromatic alterations that do *not* commonly appear in nineteenth-century music. For example, the standard V$^4_3$–i progression can be embellished by lowering the second and fourth scale degrees as shown in Figure 8.1.4. This chord is extremely rare, perhaps because Romantic composers regarded the minor mode as the dual or shadow of the major. (That is: since the lowered fourth scale degree is not available in major, composers may have shied away from it in minor.) However, it does occasionally appear in later music—

Figure 8.1.3 Other chromatic embellishments.

Figure 8.1.4 In the nineteenth century, the lowered fourth scale degree is extremely rare. However, it does appear in later music.

for instance, at the end of the slow movement of Shostakovich's G minor Piano Quintet.[5] This, then, is an example of the continued development of chromatic tonality in twentieth-century music: just as the dominant seventh "flat-five" chord was rare in the eighteenth century, becoming common only later, so too is lowered scale-degree four uncommon in Romantic music—coming into its own only in the extended tonality of the more recent past.

8.2 GENERALIZED AUGMENTED SIXTHS

So far, we have examined chromaticism that decorates or embellishes traditional tonally functional progressions. Let's now turn to music in which chromaticism provides an alternative language, a kind of "second practice," distinct from the routines of ordinary functional tonality. Figure 8.2.1 shows five passages in which a seventh chord moves by stepwise motion to a triad. The first, from the opening of Schubert's "Am Meer" uses what theory books would call a "German augmented sixth," here acting as an incomplete neighbor to a root position tonic. Next is the opening of Schoenberg's song "Erwartung," Op. 2 No. 1 (not to be confused with the atonal monodrama of the same name), which presents a less familiar progression: a sounding B minor seventh acting as a neighbor to the tonic E♭ major, all over a pedal E♭.[6] The third is derived from the penultimate progression of Wagner's *Tristan,* with a (sounding) F half-diminished seventh moving semitonally to E minor.[7] The fourth, from Act III, Scene 4 of Debussy's *Pelléas et Mélisande,* presents a very similar progression, in which $G^{2[\sharp5]}$ again resolves to E minor. The final passage, from the opening of the last movement of Brahms' Second Piano Concerto, has D^7 resolving to E♭, the subdominant of the underlying key; it can be understood tonally as a deceptive resolution of an applied dominant. From a traditional point of view, some of these are "normal" progressions with familiar names ("German sixth," "deceptive resolution"), while others are nameless and unusual. However, from our perspective they are all quite closely related: in each case, the seventh chord is dissonant, unstable, and neighboring, resolving efficiently to a more stable triad. Our goal is to think systematically about how these progressions relate.

---

5 The lowered fourth scale degree sometimes appears in heavy metal, as in the second part of the Black Sabbath song "Sabbath, Bloody Sabbath." This alteration is probably derived from the blues, though here it takes on a more sinister character.

6 The adjective "sounding" indicates that I am ignoring spelling.

7 Here I remove *Tristan's* characteristic voice crossing, as discussed in §8.6.

Figure 8.2.1 Chromatic voice leading in Schubert's "Am Meer" (*a*), Schoenberg's "Erwartung," Op. 2 No. 1 (*b*), Wagner's *Tristan* (*c*), Debussy's *Pélleas et Mélisande* (*d*), and the last movement of Brahms' Second Piano Concerto, Op. 83 (*e*).

To this end, it helps to begin with a more general theoretical problem. Suppose we would like to find an efficient (four-voice) voice leading from a seventh chord to a triad. The principle of avoiding crossings tells us that we should map ascending steps in the seventh chord to either unisons or ascending steps in the triad. This means that the voice leading can be represented schematically as shown in Figure 8.2.2: two adjacent notes in the seventh chord converge on a single note in the triad, while the other two voices connect the remaining notes. It is therefore possible to categorize such voice leadings based on two pieces of information: the converging notes in the seventh chord and the converged-upon note in the triad. This is illustrated by Figure 8.2.3, which shows that there are twelve abstract possibilities to consider—four pairs of converging notes times three possible targets. Figure 8.2.4 provides concrete examples of these voice-leading schemas, in the particular case where the first chord is a dominant seventh and the second is a triad. (Of course, not all of these voice leadings are equally useful; they are shown merely to illustrate the possibilities.) Voice leadings in the same square of the table are individually T-related (§2.6).

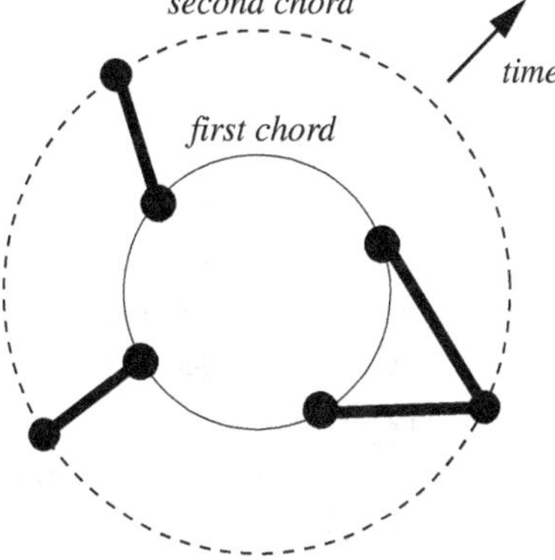

Figure 8.2.2 A four-voice crossing-free voice leading from a four-note chord to a three-note chord. Two notes in the four-note chord converge on a single note in the three-note chord.

Figure 8.2.3 In a crossing-free voice leading from a four-note to a three-note chord, there are twelve abstract possibilities to consider. The converging pair of voices is listed at the top of each column, while the note converged upon is listed to the left of each row.

	Root, Third	**Third, Fifth**	**Fifth, Seventh**	**Seventh, Root**
	r→r	t→r	f→r	s→r
Root	s→f	r→f	t→f	f→f
	f→t	s→t	r→t	t→t
	t→r	f→r	s→r	r→r
	r→t	t→t	f→t	s→t
Third	s→r	r→r	t→r	f→r
	f→f	s→f	r→f	t→f
	t→t	f→t	s→t	r→t
	r→f	t→f	f→f	s→f
Fifth	s→t	r→t	t→t	f→t
	f→r	s→r	r→r	t→r
	t→f	f→f	s→f	r→f

Figure 8.2.4 Instances of the twelve schemas in Figure 8.2.3. In each case, a dominant seventh chord moves to a major triad. Voice leadings separated by a dotted line are individually T-related.

	Root, Third		**Third, Fifth**		**Fifth, Seventh**		**Seventh, Root**	
	F→G	F→F♯	A→B♭	A→B	C→D♭	C→D	E♭→E	E♭→E♭
Root	E♭→D	E♭→C♯	F→F	F→F♯	A→A♭	A→A	C→B	C→B♭
	C→B	C→A♯	E♭→D	E♭→D♯	F→F	F→F♯	A→G♯	A→G
	A→G	A→F♯	C→B♭	C→B	E♭→D♭	E♭→D	F→E	F→E♭
	IV^7→V		V→I		V→♭III		Ger. 6	
	F→G	F→F♯	A→B♭	A→B	C→D	C→C♯	E♭→E	E♭→F
Third	E♭→E♭	E♭→D	F→G♭	F→G	A→B♭	A→A	C→C	C→D♭
	C→B♭	C→A	E♭→D♭	E♭→D	F→F	F→E	A→G	A→A♭
	A→G	A→F♯	C→B♭	C→B	E♭→D	E♭→C♯	F→E	F→F
	V^6→IV^6		V→♭VI		V→I		"blues"	
	F→G	F→F♯	A→B♭	A→A	C→D♭	C→D	E♭→E	E♭→F
Fifth	E♭→E	E♭→D♯	F→G	F→F♯	A→B♭	A→B	C→C♯	C→D
	C→C	C→B	E♭→E♭	E♭→D	F→G♭	F→G	A→A	A→B♭
	A→G	A→F♯	C→B♭	C→A	E♭→D♭	E♭→D	F→E	F→F
			V/V→I^6_4		V→♭VI	IV→V	Ger. 6	

Augmented sixth chords are a special subset of these voice leadings—those in which the converging notes are separated by two semitones, and they converge on the note that lies between them.[8] These voice leadings are important because they permit all four voices to move *semitonally* to the subsequent triad, as in the first four progressions of Figure 8.2.1. Augmented sixths, understood in this general sense, need not have dominant function: where the chords in Figure 8.2.5a–c contain a leading tone that resolves upward, and clearly sound "dominant-like," those in (*f*–*g*) do not. From this point of view, the familiar augmented sixths are simply a noteworthy species within the genus of efficient voice leadings from four-note to three-note chords. Such chords can be expected to occur frequently in chromatic music, and need not be conceptualized as modifications of the Italian, French, and German sixths of introductory tonal theory.

Now back to our musical examples (Figure 8.2.1). The first four are all augmented sixths in which the voices move semitonally to their destinations. Figure 8.2.6 shows that Schubert and Schoenberg's progressions exemplify the abstract schema (r, t, f, s)→(f, r, t, f)—that is, the seventh chord's (sounding) root moves to the triad's fifth, its third moves to the triad's root, the fifth moves to the third, and the seventh moves to the fifth. (Schoenberg simply lowers the third of the German sixth, lending the chord a dominant quality.) Wagner's progression exhibits the schema (r, t, f, s)→(r, t, f, r), resolving the root and seventh to the root of the following triad. The very similar passage from *Pélleas,* meanwhile, reimagines this augmented sixth as the raised fifth and seventh of a G^7 chord; this is a rare example in which a generalized augmented sixth occurs between notes other than the sounding root and seventh. (Note that Wagner and Debussy's progressions are quite closely related, just as Schubert and Schoenberg's are.) Finally, the opening of Brahms' movement does *not* feature augmented-sixth voice leading; here the

Figure 8.2.5 In an "augmented sixth" resolution, two voices are separated by ten semitones, and converge semitonally to an octave, doubling one of the notes in a major or minor triad; typically, the augmented sixth lies between what sound like the first chord's root and seventh, though in (*c*) this is not the case. If the resolution contains a leading tone resolving upward to the tonic, then the chord can typically function as an altered dominant.

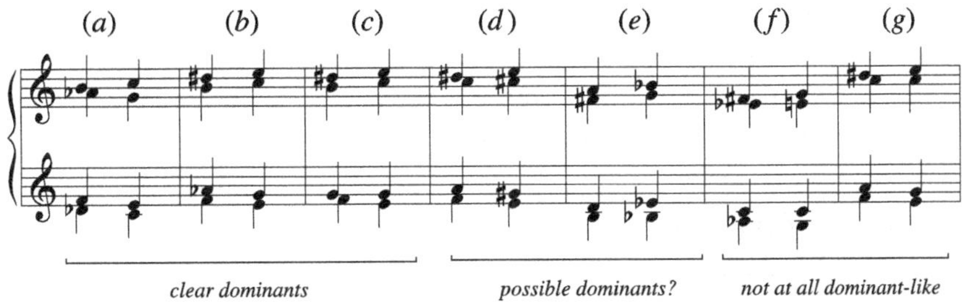

8 See Harrison 1995 for an alternative perspective that emphasizes tonal function.

Figure 8.2.6 The voice leadings at the start of Schubert's "Am Meer" (*a*) and Schoenberg's "Erwartung" (*b*) both exemplify the abstract schema (r, t, f, s)→(f, r, t, f). The voice leading in *Tristan* is (r, t, f, s)→(r, t, f, r) (*c*), while in *Pélleas* it is (s, r, t, f)→(r, t, f, r) (*d*). All four of these voice leadings are generalized "augmented sixth" resolutions. The voice leading in the last movement of Brahms' Second Piano Concerto (*e*) employs the schema (f, s, r, t)→(t, f, r, t), in which the converging voices are separated by nine semitones. This is not a generalized augmented sixth.

seventh chord's third and fifth are separated by nine semitones, and converge on the triad's third. Our theoretical ideas thus provide a precise vocabulary for specifying how the first four progressions relate, while differing from the last.

As I said earlier, to be initiated into the mysteries of chromatic tonality one needs to develop an understanding of *all* the voice-leading possibilities between familiar chords. This requires sorting through the analogues to the voice leadings in Figure 8.2.3 for any pair of chords we might encounter—identifying in the process the most useful possibilities. Furthermore, we need to be able to deploy this knowledge relatively quickly, so that we immediately recognize the relationships between various voice leadings. Nineteenth-century composers no doubt developed this sort of knowledge intuitively, through hours and hours of hands-on experimentation at the piano keyboard. Twenty-first-century musicians need to experiment as well, but we have the advantage of theoretical tools that allow us to conceptualize more abstract voice-leading relationships—grouping musical possibilities into more manageable categories and revealing structural principles linking superficially different progressions.

8.3 BRAHMS AND SCHOENBERG

For a more complex artifact of the nineteenth-century "second practice," we turn to Brahms' Intermezzo, Op. 76 No. 4, a teasing piece that begins on a dominant seventh chord that resolves only at the end. My reduction, shown in Figure 8.3.1, tries to separate the two "systems" of nineteenth-century tonality, using open noteheads for chords that behave in functionally harmonic ways, and closed noteheads for instances of chromatic voice leading. The piece opens by oscillating between F^7 and what I will call the "Tristan chord" {F, G♯, B, E♭}.[9] The two chords are con-

9 Some of you may prefer to think of the E♭ as a pedal tone, in which case the relevant sonority is {F, G♯, B, D}. Others may prefer to postulate a five-note sonority containing both D and E♭. Brahms' piece proceeds by exploiting alternate resolutions of this chord, however it may be understood.

Figure 8.3.1 A reduction of Brahms' Intermezzo, Op. 76 No. 4. Resolutions of the Tristan chord {F, A♭, C♭, E♭} and E♭ minor triad are identified with the letters "α" and "β" respectively.

nected by the voice leading (F, G♯, B, E♭)→(F, A, C, E♭), which moves two notes by semitone. At α_2, Brahms resolves the same Tristan chord in a different way: here, F and E♭ collapse onto E♭, and B♮ rises to C, producing an A♭ major triad.[10] Immediately thereafter, the V^7 of A♭ major gets reinterpreted as an augmented sixth of G minor, resolving directly to a first-inversion tonic. (Note that the "augmented-sixth resolution," though it has a familiar name, can be interpreted as just another

10 Abstractly, this involves the schema (r, t, f, s)→(f, r, t, f).

chromatic voice leading.) Brahms thus modulates from B♭ major to G minor by way of the more distant key of A♭ major, deliberately taking a scenic detour in tonal space.

The opening of the middle section, shown in Figure 8.3.2, provides a nice illustration of individually T-related voice leadings: here, Brahms takes a voice leading from the first ending and transposes the second chord up by semitone, leading to a contrasting passage in C♭ major.[11] (Of course, the root position tonic triad never appears: the middle section is "in the dominant of C♭," just as the opening is "in the dominant of B♭.") The section starts with a long dominant pedal, discharged (in my reading) by the "down by third, up by step" sequence of §7.3. The third section begins much as the first did, alternating between the Tristan chord and the F^7. Once again, the piece moves away from the tonic by resolving the Tristan chord to A♭ major; however, Brahms immediately follows this resolution with yet another resolution of the Tristan chord, this time to E♭ major. (The voice leading here has the root and seventh converging on E♭, reinterpreting the Tristan chord as $ii^{ø7}$ of E♭.) This E♭ major triad initiates a descending sequence of chromatically embellished harmonies, culminating in a $ii^{ø7}$–♭II^7–I progression. (Jazz musicians would call the ♭II^7 a "tritone substitution" for the dominant, while classical theorists would say it is an augmented sixth resolving directly to I.) Given Brahms' prominent use of the Tristan chord, it is amusing to note that the $ii^{ø7}$–♭II^7 voice leading evokes the very opening of Wagner's opera.

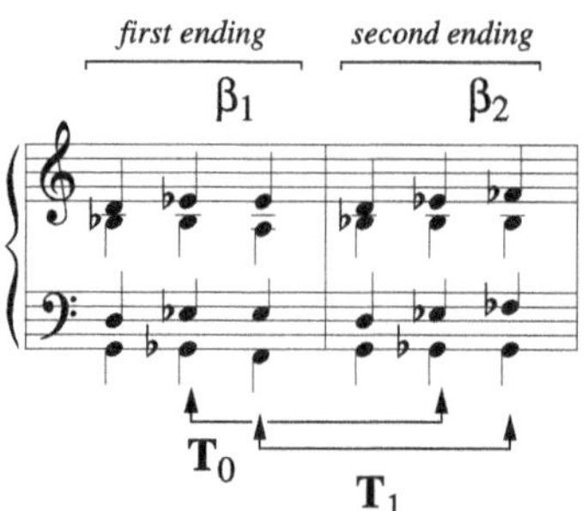

Figure 8.3.2 Individual T relatedness in Op. 76 No. 4.

Brahms' piece thus progresses by exploiting multiple resolutions of a few basic sonorities, including the Tristan chord and the E♭ minor triad (marked on the reduction as "α" and "β"). The multivalence of these chords propels the music while also endowing it with a kind of harmonic unity, allowing the composer to return again and again to the same basic chords. A very similar technique appears in Schoenberg's "Erwartung," whose opening progression was discussed in the previous section. In Figure 8.3.3, I have provided a reduction, once again using black stemless noteheads for nonfunctional chromatic chords. A glance at the reduction shows that Schoenberg's song, like Brahms' piece, is delicately balanced between two musical worlds. Once again, it explores a variety of ways to resolve a few chromatic sonorities—in particular, the "augmented sixth" at the opening (enharmonically, {B, D, F♯, A} over an E♭ pedal), which resolves semitonally as a neighboring chord to E♭ major while also acting as a passing chord to IV^7. And once again, we find a mix of familiar and unfamiliar progressions: A♭^{7}, the third chord of the piece, resolves as a German sixth to {E♭, G, C}, while {C♭, E♭,

11 As in Mozart's C minor fantasy, K. 475, the individual transposition changes iv^6–V^7 into iii^6–V^7 (§2.6).

G♭, A} in third system—a standard German sixth in E♭—"normalizes" the song's unusual second sonority. (Both of these German sixths are denoted by asterisks on the example.) Curiously, the end of the piece once again contains a progression that evokes the opening measures of Wagner's *Tristan* ($C\sharp^{ø7}$–$B\flat^{7}$, bracketed on the reduction).

The middle section of Schoenberg's song, shown on the second line of Figure 8.3.3, is an embellished ascending-fifths sequence of dominant seventh chords. Each sequential unit hints at a I^6_4–$V^{\flat 9}$ progression, with the $V^{\flat 9}$ chord becoming the subsequent I^6_4. (For instance, $G^{\flat 9}$ leads to G^6_4, which is then reinterpreted as I^6_4 of the subsequent dominant.) This sequence exploits a technique first discussed in §3.8, whereby stepwise descending voice leading produces ascending-fifths root progressions. Figure 8.3.4 identifies the basic voice-leading pattern, and compares Schoenberg's sequence to a rather similar sequence in one of Haydn's late piano sonatas. Although the two passages are separated by almost a century, they arguably make use of the same basic underlying relationships—testifying to the way music theory can help us understand hidden roads connecting superficially different styles.

Figure 8.3.3 A reduction of Schoenberg's song "Erwartung," Op. 2 No. 1.

Figure 8.3.4 (*a*) An ascending fifths sequence that uses descending stepwise voice leading. (*b*) A sequence from the development of the first movement of Haydn's Piano Sonata Hob. XVI/49 in E♭ major, mm. 117–122, which decorates this basic voice-leading pattern. (c) Schoenberg's sequence, transposed up by semitone for ease of comparison with the earlier examples. In Haydn's sequence, explicit i$^6_4$–v resolutions ascend by fifth, linked by secondary dominants; Schoenberg's progression only hints at the i$^6_4$ harmonies, subsuming them within extended dominants. Here the dotted line signifies that the G5 in the first measure can be considered "the same" as the G4 in the second measure—or in Schenkerian terms, a "voice transfer."

8.4 SCHUBERT AND THE MAJOR-THIRD SYSTEM

In a moment, we'll examine two pieces that make sophisticated use of seventh chords' four-dimensional geometry, exploiting what I have called the "minor-third system." Before doing so, however, it will be useful to warm up with some triadic music, where the relevant geometry is three-dimensional and hence easier to grasp. Having honed our skills on the simpler "major-third system," we can then turn to the more complex relationships among seventh chords.

Figure 8.4.1 outlines the opening of Schubert's D major Piano Sonata, D. 850, Op. 53. The first phrase is intense but traditional, touching briefly on the subdominant before cadencing in the tonic D major. The second phrase switches abruptly to the parallel minor, but otherwise begins as the first. Having reached F major (the relative major of the parallel minor of the tonic key), Schubert then leaves traditional tonality in favor of the major-third system: a pair of efficient chromatic voice

Figure 8.4.1 A reduction of the opening of Schubert's D major Piano Sonata, D. 850, Op. 53.

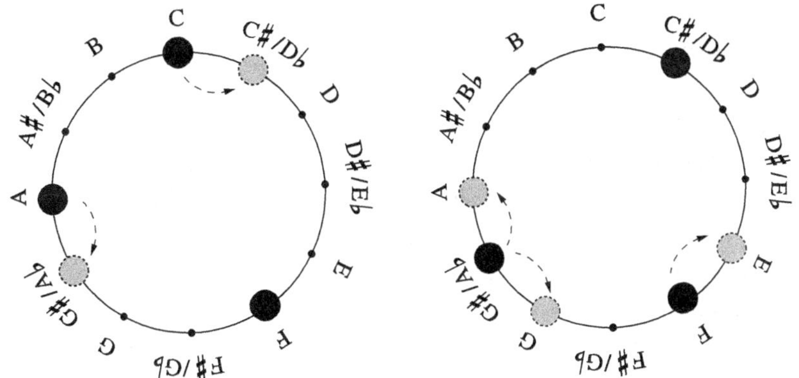

Figure 8.4.2 A geometrical representation of the voice leadings (F, A, C)→(E♯, G♯, C♯) and (E♯, G♯, G♯, C♯)→(E, G, A, C♯), which exploit the near major-third symmetry of the triad.

leadings connecting F major to C♯ major to A^7, which in turn leads back to the tonic. We can think of this passage as exploiting the fundamental geometry of three-note chord space, in which the major triads F, C♯, and A are all adjacent (Figure 3.10.2b). From this point of view the seventh is inessential—an embellishment that merely decorates the more basic triadic relationship. (An alternative interpretation, shown in Figure 8.4.2, uses the pitch-class circle and retains the seventh.[12]) No matter how we conceptualize it, the progression represents a dazzling, gratuitous, and over-the-top transition from F major to A^7—"gratuitous" since F major and A^7 are harmonically quite close, and do not require the intermediation of a C♯ chord.[13]

There is, in fact, an interesting precedent for these sorts of major-third juxtapositions: in both baroque and classical music, one occasionally finds major-third-related triads across phrase boundaries (Figure 8.4.3). Typically, the earlier phrase ends with a half cadence on the dominant of the relative minor, while the next phrase begins

12 Note that the progression from C♯ to A^7 uses the standard German-sixth resolution in retrograde.

13 A classical composer would have no problem moving directly from F major to A^7, the dominant of the relative minor.

Figure 8.4.3 Cross-phrase mediant progressions in Bach (Riemenschneider chorale 163) (*a*) and Mozart (K280, III, 104) (*b*).

directly with a tonic.[14] We can understand these progressions as exhibiting an attenuated dominant-tonic functionality: the fifth of the dominant is the leading tone of the relative major, rising by semitone to the root of the subsequent tonic triad, while the third of the dominant acts enharmonically as $\flat\hat{6}$, falling semitonally to the fifth of the subsequent tonic. Schubert in effect liberates these major-third juxtapositions from their traditional role, allowing them to occur within phrases rather than across phrase boundaries, and weakening their status as pseudo-dominants. (In particular, the speed of the sonata's juxtapositions make it hard to hear the chords as tonally functional.) Here, as elsewhere, the boundaries between musical styles are somewhat porous: it is not so much that Schubert uses absolutely new progressions, never used by his predecessors, but rather that he uses familiar progressions in unfamiliar ways.

Figure 8.4.4 contains two sequences from Schubert's *Quartett-Satz* in C minor, D. 703, which make a more subtle use of the major-third system. In both cases, descending stepwise voice leading articulates unusual triadic progressions: the first is a sequence of I–V progressions that descend by major second, while the second moves upward by fifths from G major to G minor to D major to D minor, and so on.[15] (This latter sequence is somewhat reminiscent of the central section of Schoenberg's "Erwartung" in Figure 8.3.3.) Geometrically, the two sequences present different ways of moving downward, level by level, along the cubic lattice in three-note chord space (Figure 8.4.5). Using only major chords, there are six possible sequences that can be formed in this way, each of which can be derived by applying major-third

14 This gesture is particularly common at the beginning of sonata-form recapitulations, though it can be found elsewhere as well. See, among many examples, the end of the development of Clementi's G major sonata, Op. 25 No. 2, I, and the opening of Beethoven's F major sonata, Op. 10 No. 2, I, mm. 17–18. The Decemberists' song "The Legionnaire's Lament" includes two cross-phrase mediants: the verse, d–F–g^7–A, ends on a V that progresses directly to the relative major, while the chorus, F–C–g–B♭–b♭, ends on a iv that progresses back to the relative minor.

15 A number of other passages in the piece involve stepwise descending voice leading, including the opening measures, the accompaniment to the second theme, and the ascending step sequence at m. 70ff.

Figure 8.4.4 Descending triadic sequences in Schubert's *Quartett-Satz*, D. 703, m. 173ff (*a*) and m. 105ff (*b*). (The second has been transposed up by minor third to facilitate comparison.) The sequences can be derived by applying "major-third substitution" to a chromatic descending sequence.

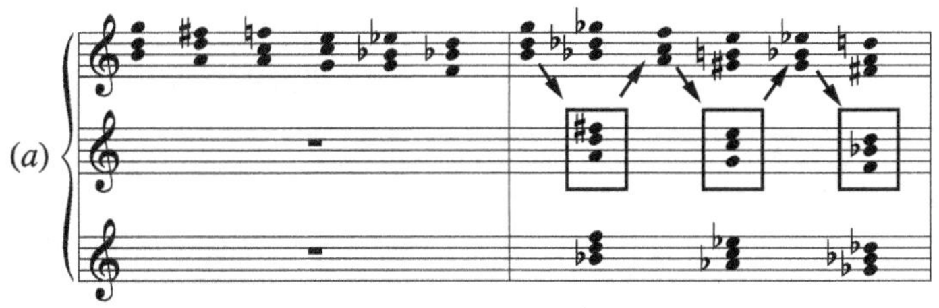

substitution to a sequence of semitonally descending triads.[16] (Cf. the right side of Figure 8.4.4, where the semitonal sequences are in the top row, and the various third substitutes are contained on the lower lines.) If we allow minor chords, there are nine possible two-chord sequences, which can again be derived by applying major-third substitution to a more straightforward chromatic sequence.

The underlying principle here is related to an idea that we encountered in §7.2: since major-third-related triads can be connected by efficient voice leading, they can substitute for one another without much disrupting the music's contrapuntal or harmonic fabric.[17] In other words, we are concerned here with the *chromatic* analogue to the diatonic third substitutions found in functional harmony. When compared to the diatonic version, chromatic third substitution is of course significantly more disruptive: C major and E major are nowhere near as similar as IV^6 and vi, and the resulting sequences are harmonically quite distinct. Nevertheless, the descending voice leading does create a clear sense of family resemblance—a palpable sinking feeling that contrasts with the buoyant harmony. This quality can be used to great effect, particularly in passages that try to convey a melancholic or gloomy mood. For example, in Goffin and King's "Natural Woman" (made famous by Aretha Franklin) the "up a fifth, up a minor third" sequence represents the narrator's psychic anomie, while in "Hey Joe" (asso-

16 Here I am considering only sequences whose repeating unit is one or two chords long.

17 Diatonic third substitution has a less dramatic effect on harmony than chromatic major-third substitution. In replacing F♯ major with D♯ minor (or replacing IV with ii^6), we preserve two of the original chord's notes; in replacing F♯ major with D major (as in the sequence we are considering), we preserve fewer notes, creating a much more dramatic harmonic change.

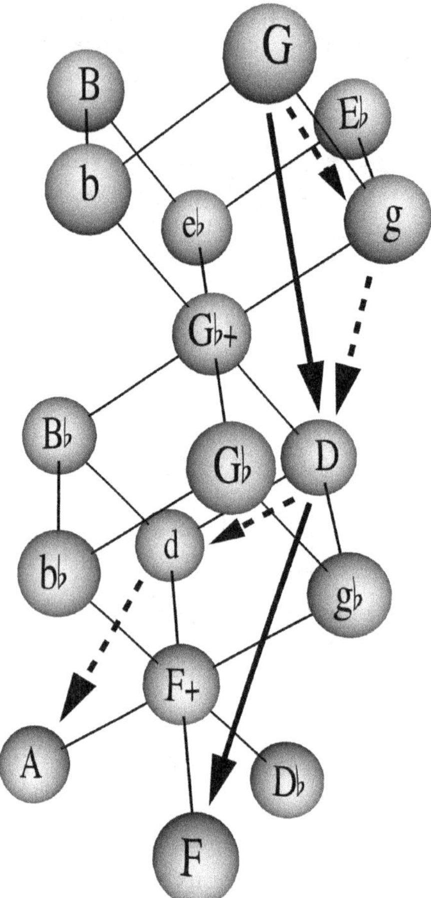

Figure 8.4.5 Schubert's sequences as they move along the lattice at the center of three-note chord space. The solid line is the sequence in Figure 8.4.4a, the dashed line is the sequence in Figure 8.4.4b.

ciated with Jimi Hendrix, and possibly written by Billy Roberts) the progression C maj–G maj–D maj–A maj–E maj implies descending voice leading that elegantly mirrors the narrator's descent into murderous depravity.

8.5 CHOPIN'S TESSERACT

Figure 8.5.1 shows the opening of Chopin's F minor Mazurka, Op. 68 No. 4 (1849?), perhaps the last piece he ever composed.[18] The music is blurred and chromatic, moving through a series of dominant seventh chords without articulating a clear tonal center. Beneath the music, I have provided a reduction of its basic harmonies. In constructing this analysis, I considered the left-hand notes on the third beat of each measure to sound through the following first-beat rest—thus, for example, I imagine that {G, D♭, F} still sounds at the downbeat of measure 3.

My analysis portrays the piece as moving through a series of numbered "cycles" that transpose a dominant seventh chord by a staggered series of single-semitone descents. For example, the third cycle, shown on the third staff, moves F^7 to E^7 by lowering the fifth (C→C♭), third (A→A♭), seventh (E♭→D), and root (F→E) in turn. The music thus exhibits an interesting combination of freedom and constraint. If we look only at the first chord in each cycle, we see a straightforward sequence of semitonally descending chords: G^7, $G♭^7$, F^7, and E^7. However, if we look at the voice-leading motions within each cycle, we do not recognize a regular pattern: sometimes the third moves first (as in Cycles 1 and 3), and sometimes the fifth moves first (Cycle 4). In other cases, Chopin moves two voices at the same time—as in Cycle 2, where the fifth and seventh descend simultaneously.

Furthermore, in the second phrase of the piece, shown on the bottom staff of the example, Chopin repeats the basic sequence of dominant sevenths, but embellishes

18 Kallberg (1985) presents some interesting but circumstantial evidence that the piece was composed earlier.

Figure 8.5.1 An analysis of Chopin's Mazurka, Op. 68 No. 4. The harmonies form a series of cycles which are labeled numerically: chords 1a, 1b, and 1c belong to the first cycle, chords 2a, 2c, and 2d belong to the second, and so on.

them slightly differently. The music thus seems to embody what twentieth-century composers would call an "open form"—a set of rules that only partially determine the musical result, of the sort that might be used as the basis for improvisation. This combination of freedom and constraint challenges the formal categories that we typically use to describe nineteenth-century music: the harmonic progression here is neither an exact sequence, in which the same music is repeated verbatim, nor free composition. Instead, it resembles the kind of open-ended musical game more commonly associated with recent music.

To describe the game's rules, we need to recognize that the piece exhibits a rather subtle kind of harmonic consistency: throughout, we hear only dominant sevenths, diminished sevenths, minor sevenths, half-diminished sevenths, and French sixth chords. In particular, there are no nontertian sonorities such as {G♭, A, C, F} and no chords with major sevenths. This harmonic consistency results in turn from a subtle contrapuntal regularity: within each cycle, the root is always the last note to descend. (Were Chopin to violate this rule he would generate strange harmonies, such as those in Figure 8.5.2.) We can thus imagine Chopin creating the piece by following the instructions in Figure 8.5.3. What is fixed is the descending chromatic sequence of dominant sevenths, along with the injunction that the bass voice descends last; what is free is the precise order of the semitonal motions in the other voices. Since Chopin was in fact an improvising composer, it is quite possible that these rules capture something about how he was thinking: indeed, it is easy to imagine him sitting at the piano, exploring the various ways of sliding between semitonally related dominant seventh chords.[19]

Figure 8.5.4 uses a cube to represent Chopin's "open form." The G dominant seventh appears at the apex, while the next level contains minor sevenths on G and E

19 A daring performer might choose to reflect this by departing from the written notes in favor of an improvisatory tour through Chopin's musical space—a performance that would be unfaithful to the written notation while also capturing something about his musical concerns.

Figure 8.5.2 In Chopin's piece, the root of the chord always descends after the other voices. If this rule were violated, unusual harmonies would result. These chords cannot be conceived as stacks of thirds, and are very rare in nineteenth-century music.

Figure 8.5.3 The "directions for improvisation" that might produce Chopin's F minor Mazurka.

F Minor Mazurka
1. Begin with a dominant seventh chord.
2. Successively lower the third, fifth, and seventh of the chord by semitone, in any order, eventually producing a diminished seventh chord.
3. Lower the note of diminished seventh chord that was the root of the initial dominant seventh, producing a new dominant seventh chord a semitone lower than the original.
4. Repeat.
Bonus rule: it is possible to eliminate one or more chords in the resulting sequence, lowering multiple notes by semitone at the same time.

and a French sixth on G/C♯ (labeled "gFr" on the figure). Each of these chords can be reached by semitonally lowering a note of the initial G⁷. Level 1c contains half-diminished seventh chords on C♯, E, and G. (Again, these chords can be reached by lowering a note in a chord on level 1b.) The G diminished seventh appears at the bottom of the cube and is the only chord on level 1d. Finally, there is a line leading from the base of the cube to G♭⁷, signifying that the process begins again, a semitone below the original G⁷ chord. (Hence the label "2a.") A musician improvising according to Chopin's directions must follow the edges of the cube in a descending manner, from level 1a to 1b to 1c and 1d: at the apex of the cube there are three choices, since one can lower the third, fifth, or seventh. Having made that choice, there are two remaining options, corresponding to the two voices that have yet to descend. Finally, there is just a single possibility, which takes us to the diminished seventh chord at the bottom of the cube. Here

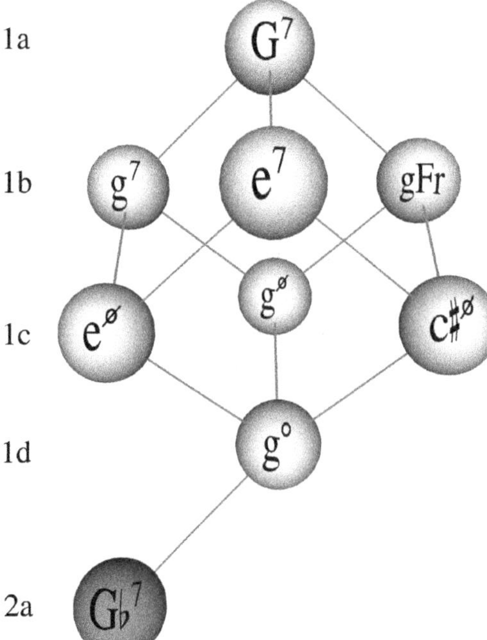

Figure 8.5.4 A geometrical representation of Chopin's "directions for improvisation."

again, the improviser's hand is forced, since there is only one semitonal descent that transforms the G diminished seventh into the G♭ dominant seventh. This cubic geometry thus encapsulates in a single image rules that would otherwise require careful verbal specification—presenting a kind of musical "game board" whose internal structure mirrors Chopin's presumed compositional process.

So far, we have been treating the F minor Mazurka as an object in itself, unconnected to the rest of Chopin's *oeuvre.* Things get more interesting when we observe that the mazurka is a virtual rewriting of one of Chopin's most famous pieces—the E minor Prelude, Op. 28 No. 4. Remarkably, the two pieces use virtually the same voice-leading procedures to embellish very different harmonic sequences. To see how this works, consider Figure 8.5.5, which presents the chords in the prelude's opening phrase. Here again, the music is organized in a sequence of cycles, each transforming one dominant seventh into another by way of a diminished seventh.[20] Chopin again lowers third, fifth, and seventh of the initial dominant seventh until he has created a diminished seventh on the same root; this time, however, he joins the successive cycles by lowering the voice that contained the *fifth* of the original dominant seventh chord, so that the resulting dominant sevenths descend by fifth rather than by semitone. As in the F minor Mazurka, we find a recognizable progression when we consider only the first chord in each cycle. But between these harmonic pillars the piece freely interpolates descending semitones, resulting in a liquid, Romantic texture that utterly disguises its sequential skeleton.[21]

Figure 8.5.5 The opening of Chopin's E minor Prelude, Op. 28 No. 4.

20 In making this reduction, I have eliminated the upper neighbor tones in the right hand on the fourth beat of each measure, as well as the E♮ suspension in the alto voice of measure 2; otherwise, I have simply transcribed every vertical sonority that appears in the passage.

21 The interpretation I present here is similar to that in Marciej Golab's *Chopins Harmonik: Chromatik in ihrer Beziehung zur Tonalität* (Golab 1995). (See also Callender 2007 for some brief but suggestive remarks and Russ 2007 for an extensive discussion of semitonal voice leading between half-diminished and dominant sevenths, including references to several of the pieces discussed here.) Many published analyses interpret the E minor Prelude as a chain of parallel, first-inversion triads in the left hand, decorated with suspensions (Parks 1976, Schachter 1994). Sometimes it is implied that the harmonic content of the opening phrase is insignificant—a long chromatic series of passing tones from the "structural" opening tonic chord to the "structural" dominant that closes the phrase. By contrast I interpret the piece as a four-voice texture exemplifying one of the most basic progressions in all of tonal music—the descending-fifths sequence, albeit freely embellished by chromatic passing tones.

Figure 8.5.6 A comparison between the two "directions for improvisation."

F Minor Mazurka	E Minor Prelude
1. Begin with a dominant seventh chord.	1. Begin with a dominant seventh chord.
2. Successively lower the third, fifth, and seventh of the chord by semitone, in any order, eventually producing a diminished seventh chord.	2. Successively lower the third, fifth, and seventh of the chord by semitone, in any order, eventually producing a diminished seventh chord.
3. Lower the note of the diminished seventh chord that was the **root** of the initial dominant seventh, producing a new dominant seventh chord a **semitone** lower than the original.	3. Lower the note of the diminished seventh chord a semitone below the **fifth** of the initial dominant seventh, producing a new dominant seventh chord a **perfect fifth** lower than the original.
4. Repeat.	4. Repeat.
Bonus rule: it is possible to eliminate one or more chords in the resulting sequence, lowering multiple notes by semitone at the same time.	Bonus rule: it is possible to eliminate one or more chords in the resulting sequence, lowering multiple notes by semitone at the same time.

Figure 8.5.6 contrasts the directions for improvisation that might produce the prelude and the mazurka. The similarities are striking: in both cases, the third, fifth, and seventh of the dominant seventh chord move down by semitone until they produce a diminished seventh chord. At this point, one of the notes of the diminished seventh moves down to produce another dominant seventh. The chief difference lies here: in the F minor Mazurka, Chopin always lowers the note in the voice that contained the *root* of the original dominant seventh chord, producing a semitonally descending sequence; in the E minor Prelude, Chopin lowers the note that is in the voice that contained the *fifth* of the dominant seventh chord. This small change is enough to make the difference between descending semitones and descending fifths.

Of course, the diminished seventh chord is completely symmetrical, so we can lower any of its four notes to produce a dominant seventh. Thus, there are two other possibilities beyond those we have already considered: we could lower the voice that contained the third of the original dominant seventh, producing a sequence that ascends by major second; or we could lower the voice that contained the seventh of the dominant seventh chord, producing a sequence that descends by major third. The four possibilities are illustrated musically and geometrically in Figures 8.5.7 and 8.5.8. Once we have sensitized ourselves these possibilities, we start to find them again and again throughout Chopin's music; indeed, they are a familiar "lick" to which he repeatedly returned. Figure 8.5.9 shows a few of the many passages in which the lick appears: the first, from the A minor Mazurka, Op. 7 No. 2, combines the ascending second and descending semitone versions of the sequence; the second, from the F♯ minor Mazurka, Op. 6 No. 1, largely descends by fifths but ends with a descending semitone; the third, from the D♭ major nocturne, Op. 27 No. 2, again mixes descending fifths and descending semitones.

Although it is not completely obvious, the graph in Figure 8.5.8 is contained within a structure that we encountered in §3.11: the *tesseract*, or four-dimensional cube, lying at the center of four-note chromatic chord space (Figure 8.5.10). This hypercube has four horizontal layers, as indicated by the labels "1a," "1b," "1c," and "1d," and shares a vertex with the hypercube immediately below it, whose layers are

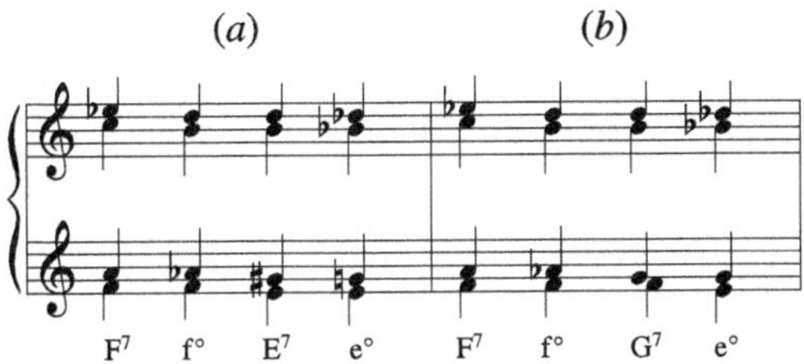

Figure 8.5.7 There are four fundamentally similar sequences that can be formed using these "directions for improvisation," depending on which of the diminished seventh chord's notes is lowered.

labeled "2a," "2b," "2c," and "2d." Essentially, Chopin's two pieces move down this hypercubic lattice by taking one or two steps at a time. The resulting progressions are constrained by the basic geometry of the space, and in particular by the fact that minor-third- and tritone-related sevenths are near each other. Thus Chopin's descending semitonal motion will produce harmonic progressions that can be obtained by applying *minor-third substitution* to a descending semitonal sequence: this gives root motions by descending semitone, descending major third, descending fifth, and ascending major second. (By contrast, stepwise descending motion between triads produces root progressions by descending semitone, ascending fifth, or ascending minor third, as we saw in the previous section.[22]) The similarities between the Prelude and the Mazurka therefore testify to a more fundamental similarity between descending-semitone and descending-fifth progressions—a relationship that lies at the root of the jazz "tritone substitution," illustrated here by Figure 8.5.11 and discussed further in Chapter 10.

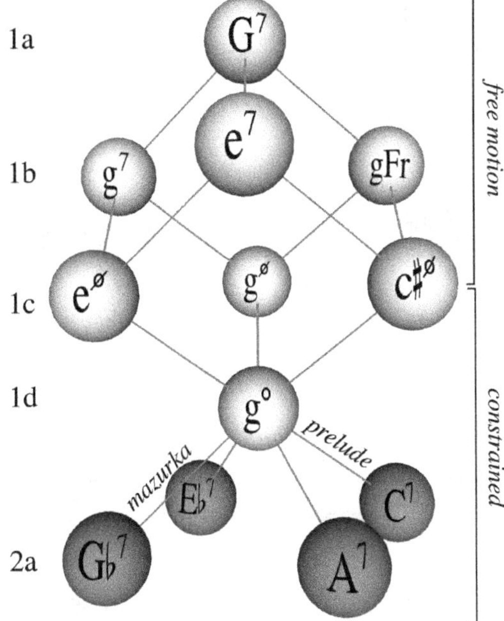

Figure 8.5.8 A geometrical representation of the four possibilities in Figure 8.5.7.

22 The root progressions (−1, −5, and −9 semitones for triads; −1, −4, −7, and −10 semitones for seventh chords) are determined by the formula −1 (mod 12/n), where n is the size of the chord.

Figure 8.5.9 The sequence as it appears in Chopin's A minor Mazurka (*a*), F♯ minor Mazurka (*b*), and D♭ major Nocturne. In each analysis, the letters "a," "b," "c," refer to levels on the cubic structure shown in Figure 8.5.8; the numbers refer to adjacent cubes in the lattice.

Since there is nothing particularly radical about the idea of using descending voice leading to connect familiar seventh chords, we should not be too surprised to find similar passages in other composers' music as well. Figure 8.5.12a shows a sequence from the development of the first movement of Mozart's Symphony No. 40, in which seventh chords descend by fifths. The harmonies, though more conventional than Chopin's, can be generated by a series of one- and two-step motions

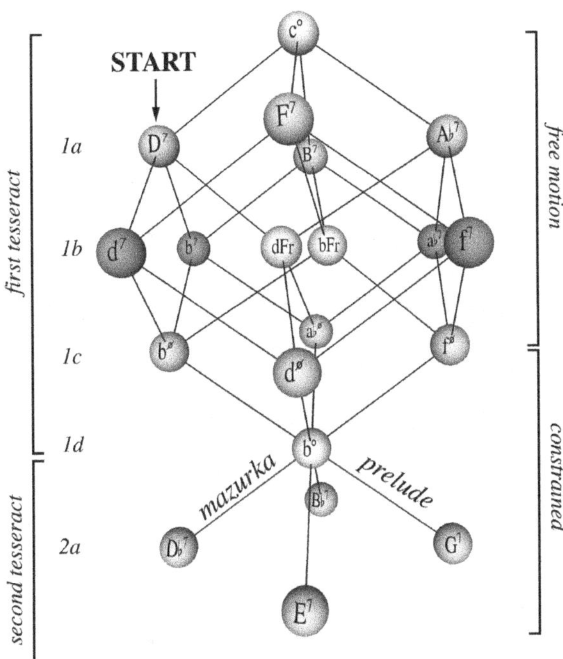

Figure 8.5.10 The musical possibilities we have been exploring can be represented using the four-dimensional cubic lattice at the center of four-note chord space. This lattice is another (and more complete) way of looking at the possibilities in Figure 8.5.8.

Figure 8.5.11 Chopin's F minor Mazurka and E minor Prelude are related by way of a tritone substitution. The mazurka is based on a semitonally descending sequence of seventh chords (top line), while the prelude uses a descending-fifths sequence. One can transform each sequence into the other by replacing every other chord with its tritone transposition.

along the same tesseract.[23] The passage in Figure 8.5.12b, from the second movement of Beethoven's Piano Sonata in F major, Op. 54, is nicely intermediate between Mozart and Chopin: here the dominant seventh chords descend once by semitone and five times by perfect fifth, returning to the initial A♭^{7} after six complete cycles. (Note the alternation between mazurka-like semitones and prelude-like fifths, characteristic of jazz harmonic practice and tritone substitution more generally.) And while Beethoven typically precedes each dominant seventh with a ii^{ø7} chord, he also interposes some additional chords, including a fully diminished seventh and a French augmented sixth. Figure 8.5.13 collects a few related passages from early twentieth-century American music, hinting at some of the connections between nineteenth-century chromaticism and twentieth-century jazz.[24]

---

23 The pianist Al Tinney, one of the pioneers of bebop, suggested that dominant seventh chords resolving to predominant sevenths was a hallmark of the bebop harmonic style (Patrick 1983). It is interesting to find this bebop hallmark in Mozart!

24 For some other related passages, consider the "Crucifixus" from Bach's B minor Mass; Mozart's Piano Sonata K. 576, I, mm. 84ff and 137ff, which use the descending-fifth and ascending-major-second versions of the pattern; the opening of the second movement of Schubert's "Rosamunde" Quartet (D. 804, Op. 29 No. 1, mm. 13–14); Schubert's *Quartett-Satz* (D. 703, mm. 72–75), which uses a slightly disguised version of the ascending-major-second pattern; and Wagner's *Tristan* prelude, to be discussed below.

Figure 8.5.12 Precursors to Chopin's procedures in (*a*) Mozart's Symphony No. 40, movement 1, start of the development section; and (*b*) Beethoven's Piano Sonata Op. 54, movement 2, mm. 64ff.

Figure 8.5.13 (*a–c*) In his 1898 operetta "The Serenade," Victor Herbert uses chromatic voice leading to connect dominant sevenths by way of various intermediaries. The examples are from nos. 3a (Schuberth vocal score, p. 35), 4 (p. 46), and 5b (p. 59). (*d*) In "Shreveport Stomp," Jelly Roll Morton uses descending stepwise voice leading to connect dominant sevenths.

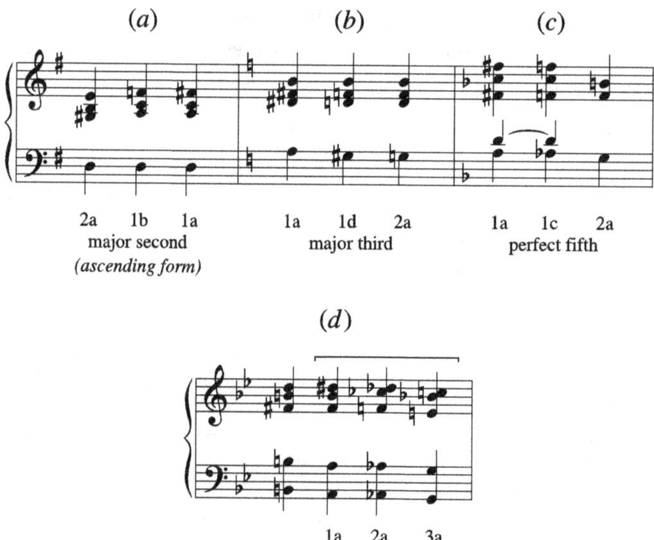

So did Chopin understand four-dimensional geometry? In one sense, the answer is clearly "no": certainly, he lacked the mathematical concepts we have used to dissect his pieces, and he might have struggled to describe what he was doing in precise music-theoretical language. (Something similar could be said of Chopin's mathematical contemporaries, as the study of higher dimensional geometry was in its infancy in the 1830s.) But at the same time, he clearly had a sophisticated intuitive understanding of the musical possibilities in Figure 8.5.10, and hence had knowledge that *can be usefully described* geometrically. (He may not have *conceived* of these possibilities as constituting a geometry, but they in fact do so, and his knowledge of the possibilities is in some sense a geometrical knowledge.) I find it marvelous to reflect that there was a period in human history in which *music* provided the most powerful language for expressing this kind of higher dimensional understanding: though nobody in 1840 could have written a treatise on four-dimensional quotient spaces, Chopin could express his understanding of one particular quotient space by writing beautiful Romantic piano music. Here there is something particularly compelling about the fact that Chopin recomposed the E minor Prelude at the very end of his life, as if the earlier piece did not say everything he had wanted to say. And in a sense, it could not, for the E minor Prelude displays just one of many routes through the hypercubic lattice: ultimately, the F minor Mazurka and E minor Prelude together demonstrate a much more profound understanding of musical space than does either piece on its own.

8.6 THE *TRISTAN* PRELUDE

Suppose you would like to find efficient (four-voice) voice leadings between half-diminished and dominant seventh chords. The principle of avoiding voice crossings says that you can organize the relevant possibilities according to whether they move the root of the half-diminished chord to the root, third, fifth, or seventh of the dominant seventh (§4.10). Figure 8.6.1 identifies the most efficient (four-voice) voice leading from $F^{ø7}$ to each of the twelve dominant sevenths: seven of the voice leadings involve just two semitones of total motion, one involves four single-semitone motions, and the rest involve six total semitones. Putting these last voice leadings aside, we see that the remaining eight can be grouped into pairs: two move root to root, two move root to third, two move root to fifth, and two move root to seventh. In each case, one voice leading in the pair involves predominantly descending motion, while the other involves predominantly ascending motion.

Figure 8.6.2 shows how these eight voice leadings are located in four-dimensional chord space. Chords on the same vertical line participate in similar voice leadings: for example, E^7 and F^7 lie directly above each other, and the minimal voice leading from $F^{ø7}$ to both chords moves root to root. Similarly, $D♭^7$ and D^7 lie directly above each other and in both cases the minimal voice leading from $F^{ø7}$ maps root to third.[25] Note

25 Or to put the point the other way around: the four chords E^7, G^7, $B♭^7$, and $D♭^7$, all of which lie on the same horizontal plane on Figure 8.6.2, are most directly reached by different kinds of voice leadings: to transform $F^{ø7}$ into E^7, one moves root to root; to transform $F^{ø7}$ into $D♭^7$, one moves root to third; and so on.

Figure 8.6.1 (*a*) Suppose you want to move from a Tristan chord to a dominant seventh by efficient voice leading. Which voice leading would you choose? (*b*) The most efficient (four-voice) voice leadings from the F^{ø7} chord to each of the twelve dominant sevenths.

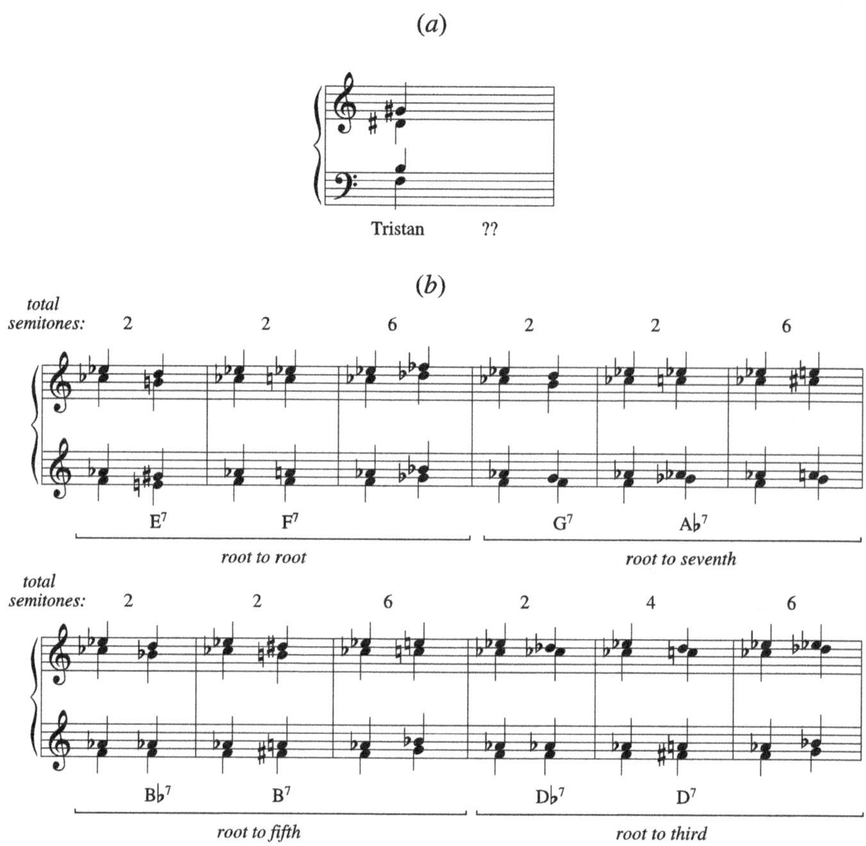

that when moving from F^{ø7} to any of the lower four dominant seventh chords (E^7, G^7, B♭^{7}, and D♭^{7}) we can pass through F diminished along the way, but when moving to the upper four dominant seventh chords (F^7, A♭^{7}, B^7, and D^7) it is instead possible to pass through minor sevenths and French sixths. Figure 8.6.3 presents two excerpts from Wagner's *Tristan* where these intervening sonorities appear.

Turning now to the opera's prelude, we are dismayed to find that its voice leadings are *not* maximally efficient. For example in Figure 8.6.4, the melody climbs yearningly from G♯ to B, while the tenor voice swoons from B down to G♯. Were each voice to remain stationary, as in Figure 8.6.4b, we would have a two-semitone voice leading between F^{ø7} and E^7, one that is nicely modeled by our hypercube. But Wagner deliberately rejects this option in favor of an alternative in which the voices take the long way to their destinations—suggesting that all our work on efficient voice leadings has been wasted!

Well, when confronting lemons, one should study the feasibility of lemonade. Suppose we hypothesize that Wagner's voice crossings decorate a deeper structure in which efficient voice leading is important. (This may seem like a stubborn refusal to face facts, but let's see where it takes us.) As we look through the *Tristan* prelude, and indeed through the rest of the opera, we see that this perspective sheds light on a number of passages: for example, each of the progressions in Figure 8.6.5 can be represented as an extremely efficient voice leading that has been embellished with a voice crossing. (Note that the crossing always involves three- or four-semitone motion in two separate voices.[26]) In other words, these examples suggest that Wagner's *harmonic* choices are influenced by voice-leading relationships not directly manifested by the surface of his music. In particular, he seems to avoid the four most distant dominant sevenths, which require six-semitone voice leadings, in favor of those that are closer to the initial half-diminished seventh.

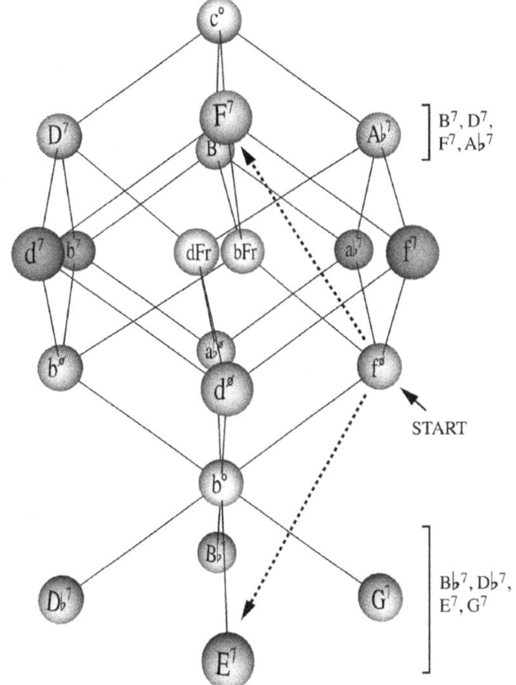

Figure 8.6.2 The eight most efficient voice leadings in Figure 8.6.1 connect $F^{ø7}$ to the eight nearest dominant sevenths in four-note chord space. The two voice leadings represented by the dotted lines both map root to root.

(*a*)

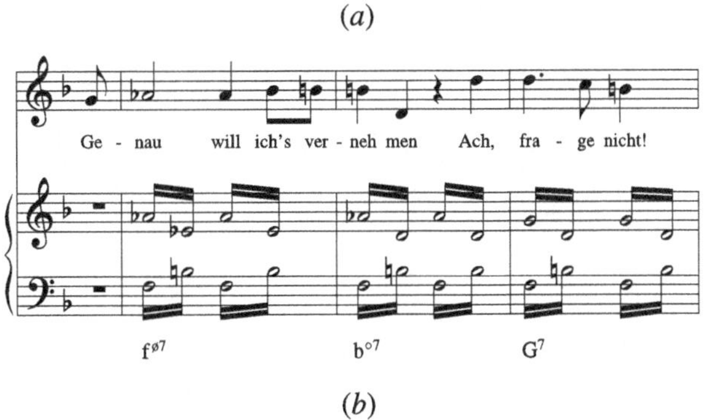

(*b*)

Figure 8.6.3 In moving from a Tristan to half-diminished seventh, Wagner often passes through one of the intervening chords in four-note chord space.

Thinking a little more about this, we realize that the opera's omnipresent ascending third motive is most effectively realized as an embellishment of an efficient "background" voice leading. For suppose we would like to find a voice leading from $F^{ø7}$ to E^7 in which at least one voice ascends chromatically by minor third. One possibility is to

26 The idea that these voice crossings are surface events is a relatively old one. For example, both William Mitchell (1973) and Robert Gauldin (1997) analyze the prelude's opening voice leading by removing crossings. See also Boretz 1972.

Figure 8.6.4 Unfortunately, the actual voice leadings in *Tristan* often have crossings.

use an interscalar transposition by ascending step, in which case *each* of the voices ascends (Figure 8.6.6). But this is somewhat unsatisfactory, both because it is inefficient and because the pervasive melodic motion distracts from the ascending melody we would like to highlight. It is more sensible to begin with a voice leading in which all the voices remain roughly fixed in register, embellishing it with a crossing that yields the desired ascending third motion. (Since we are using tertian sonorities it will typically be possible to find such a crossing.) Thus we arrive at the original "Tristan" voice leading, in which two voices

Figure 8.6.5 Other passages in Tristan that seem to embellish a crossing-free substrate: mm. 10–11 (*a*), mm. 22–23 (*b*), and m. 81 (*c*).

Figure 8.6.6 Suppose we would like to combine an F^{ø7}–E^{7} progression with melody that ascends chromatically by minor third. One possibility is to use an interscalar transposition by ascending step (*a*), producing ascending motion in all four voices. Another possibility is to begin with an efficient voice leading (*b*), which is then embellished by a voice crossing (*c*).

move efficiently, one falls discretely by third, and the final voice presents the ascending chromatic leitmotif. In this sense, Wagner's voice leadings, though not themselves maximally efficient, can be derived from more basic voice leadings that are crossing free.

Figure 8.6.7 presents five voice leadings from the opening 20 measures of the prelude, omitting the voice crossings as just discussed. The first two are related by (uniform) transposition at the minor third, and map the root of the Tristan chord to the root of the succeeding dominant seventh. The third and fourth map the root of the half-diminished to the *third* of the dominant seventh: the third sends D^{ø7} to B^{7}, moving each of the four voices by semitone; the fourth sends F♯^{ø7} to D^{7}, holding three common tones fixed.[27] (We can also perhaps hear a fifth voice leading from F♯^{ø7} directly to G^{7}, treating the D in the melody as an anticipation.) These examples suggest that *Tristan* begins with a relatively systematic exploration of the voice leadings between half-diminished and dominant sevenths. In the opening measures of the prelude, Wagner systematically shows us what his chord can do—rather like a traveling salesman eagerly demonstrating the capabilities of his new vacuum cleaner.

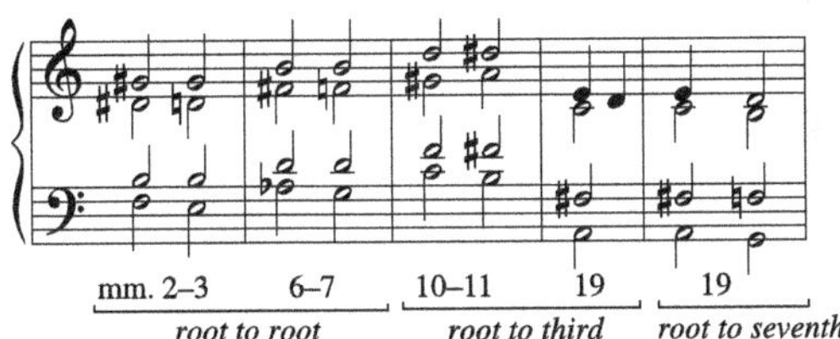

Figure 8.6.7 When we remove Wagner's voice crossings, we typically end up with a highly efficient voice leading.

These opening voice leadings reappear throughout the opera, often without their voice crossings. In Figure 8.6.8a, the root and seventh of the B half-diminished chord move down by semitone, forming a B♭ dominant seventh; this is the opening voice leading, reregistered, shorn of its crossings, and transposed by tritone. In (*b*), which occurs just prior to the preceding example, we find the root, third, and fifth of a D^{ø7} chord moving up by semitone, while the seventh moves down by way of a descending scalar run; this is the third voice leading in the prelude, using the very same pitch classes. Finally, in (*c*), which occurs between the two previous examples, we see the prelude's fourth voice leading, where the seventh of the half-diminished chord moves down by two semitones. (Note that the pitches here are those of the opera's opening chord.) If we have sensitized ourselves to these voice-leading schemas, then the resemblance to the start of the prelude will be quite striking, particularly since all these later examples occur in short succession.

27 Some of you may consider the E to be a nonharmonic tone, but I would caution against an uncritical use of the term. Throughout the prelude, nonharmonic tones conspire to produce a sounding half-diminished seventh chord; this conspiracy is what needs to be explained. Furthermore, later passages—such as the beginning of Act I, Scene IV—emphasize this particular voice leading to the point where the half-diminished seventh seems more clearly "harmonic."

Figure 8.6.8 The voice-leading schemas in the Prelude return many times throughout the opera. These three passages are taken from Act I, scene iii: (*a*) p. 51/98, (*b*) p. 49/96, (c) p. 49/95. (Page numbers refer to the Schirmer vocal score and Dover full score, respectively.)

Note that in the beginning of the prelude it is the half-diminished chords, rather than the dominant sevenths, that are harmonically anomalous: we expect E^7, G^7, and B^7 in an A minor context, but not $F^{\varnothing 7}$, $G\sharp^{\varnothing 7}$, or $D^{\varnothing 7}$. This might lead us to wonder whether these chords result from a process of "substitution," whereby one half-diminished seventh replaces another (cf. the major-third substitutions of §8.4). For example, we might propose that Wagner applies a tritone substitution to the standard $B^{\varnothing 7}$–E^7 progression, giving us the more remarkable $F^{\varnothing 7}$–E^7.[28] The effect is to replace an efficient but traditional voice leading with an unfamiliar but equally efficient alternative. In much the same way, the progression $D^{\varnothing 7}$–B^7 perhaps results from a major-third substitution whereby a $D^{\varnothing 7}$ appears in place of $F\sharp^{\varnothing 7}$. (Note that the geometry of four-note space allows for both major-third and minor-third substitutions in this context: given $F\sharp^{\varnothing 7}$–B^7, one can obtain an efficient voice leading by replacing $F\sharp^{\varnothing 7}$ with either $D\sharp^{\varnothing 7}$ or $D^{\varnothing 7}$.[29]) In fact, there are places in the opera where Wagner explicitly engages in this sort of substitution: for example, Figure 8.6.9 shows a pair of passages

28 Hansen 1996 makes this observation.

29 This is because the dominant seventh chords in Figure 8.6.2 lie between two different "layers" of half-diminished sevenths. The voice leading (D♯, F♯, A, C♯)→(D♯, F♯, A, B) involves more common tones while (D, F, A♭, C)→(D♯, F♯, A, B) involves smaller motions in the voices. Cook (2005) calls this latter voice leading "extravagant," since it moves every voice by semitone.

Figure 8.6.9 "Tritone substitution" applied to Tristan chords in Wagner's opera.

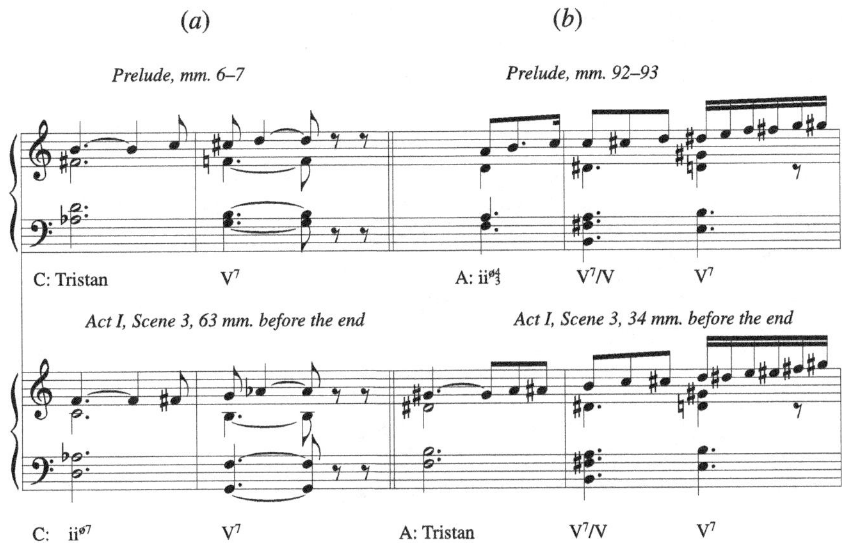

from the prelude, along with variants from the end of Act I, Scene III; in the variants, the half-diminished seventh chords have been replaced by their tritone transpositions, exchanging a "Tristan progression" for a more prototypical ii^{ø7}–V^7.

Formally, the prelude's opening uses an AAB schema ("bar form"), with the A and B sections featuring different resolutions of the Tristan chord: the progression F^{ø7}→E^7 (A) is transposed up by minor third to produce A♭^{ø7}→G^7 (A), which is then followed by the contrasting D^{ø7}→B^7 (B). Figure 8.6.10 shows that the same formal schema returns midway through the prelude, where a trio of French sixths resolve to dominant sevenths: the initial French sixth on D♭ resolves conventionally to C^7; this passage is then transposed exactly by major second; but in the third iteration, the French sixth resolves to B^7, a perfect fifth away from the expected E^7. (Although it is not obvious, this alternate resolution is individually T-related to the preceding two, with one voice moving upward by semitone, rather than the other three moving down.) Here again we have the AAB schema, with the two A sections related by exact transposition and the B section featuring an alternate resolution of the initial sonority. It is also relevant that the French sixths are minimal perturbations of the half-diminished sevenths—a point that Wagner makes explicit at the end of the prelude, when he repeats the music with the half-diminished {F, A, B, D} substituting for the French sixth {F, A, B, D♯}.

The climax of the prelude, shown in Figure 8.6.11, articulates a series of predominant-dominant progressions, decorated with a variety of passing chords. The liquid, semitonal voice leading here is strongly reminiscent of Chopin's E minor Prelude, and can in fact be modeled using the very same geometry. (Figure 8.6.12 shows a passage from Act III, in which the relation to Chopin is even more clear.) The music reaches a peak in mm. 81–83 (Figure 8.6.11a, last two measures), where two different resolutions of the "Tristan" chord compete: a standard ii^{ø7}–V^7 resolution suggesting E♭

Figure 8.6.10 Measures 36ff of the prelude mirror the form of the opening: an initial voice leading is transposed exactly, whereupon the opening chord type is resolved in a new way. Here the initial chord is a French augmented sixth and the third voice leading is individually T-related to the first (*b*). Note that when this music repeats at the end of the prelude, Wagner uses D♮ instead of D♯ in the second-to-last measure of (*a*).

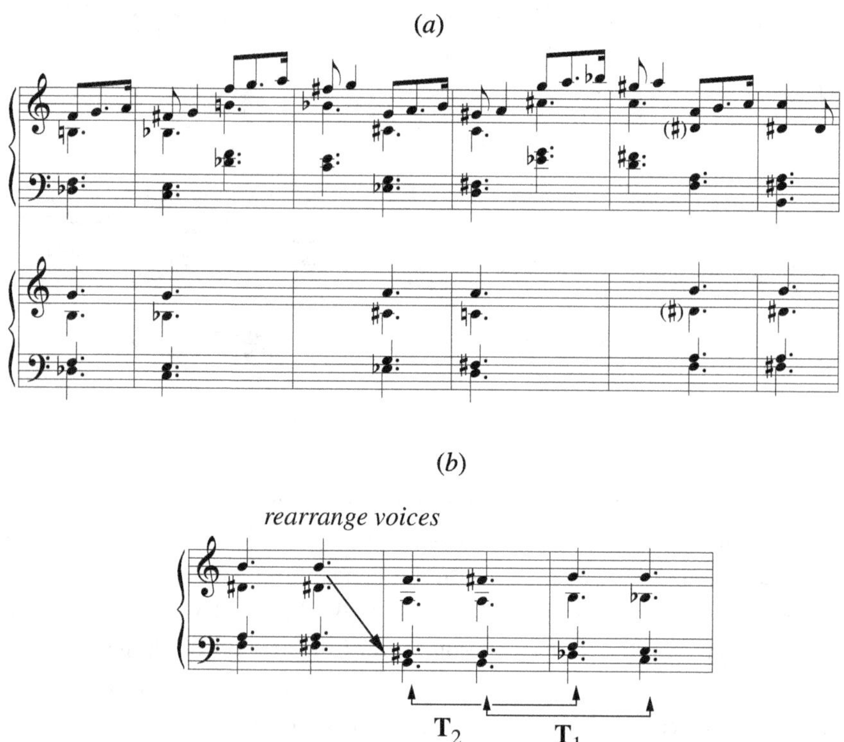

minor, and the alternative resolution from the opera's opening.[30] This explicit statement of the Tristan chord's multivalence, at the emotional highpoint of the prelude, is a not-so-subtle clue that the music is in some sense "about" the various ways of resolving the chord. It is difficult to avoid investing this moment with symbolic significance: the competition between resolutions is a competition between functional orthodoxy and chromatic perversity, with the victorious Wagnerian resolution subverting musical propriety—much as Tristan and Isolde reject their social obligations in favor of a doomed passion.

Figure 8.6.13 collects prominent Tristan-chord resolutions from the opera, removing voice crossings and transposing so that they begin on the F half-diminished chord. (All but two of these have appeared in previous examples; the sources for the newcomers are given in Figure 8.6.14.) Comparing these to Figures 8.6.1b and 8.6.2, we see that Wagner indeed makes use of the eight most efficient Tristan resolutions—exploiting *all* of the shortest pathways between half-diminished and dominant sev-

30 This procedure is reminiscent of traditional "pivot chord" modulations, in which a single chord (here, the "Tristan chord") is given two different harmonic interpretations.

Figure 8.6.11 A reduction of two passages from the Tristan prelude, both of which move along the lattice at the center of four-note chord space. Labels below each chord again show how the music moves through the connected hypercubes. Where Chopin moves steadily forward, Wagner moves backward and forward in a stuttering manner.

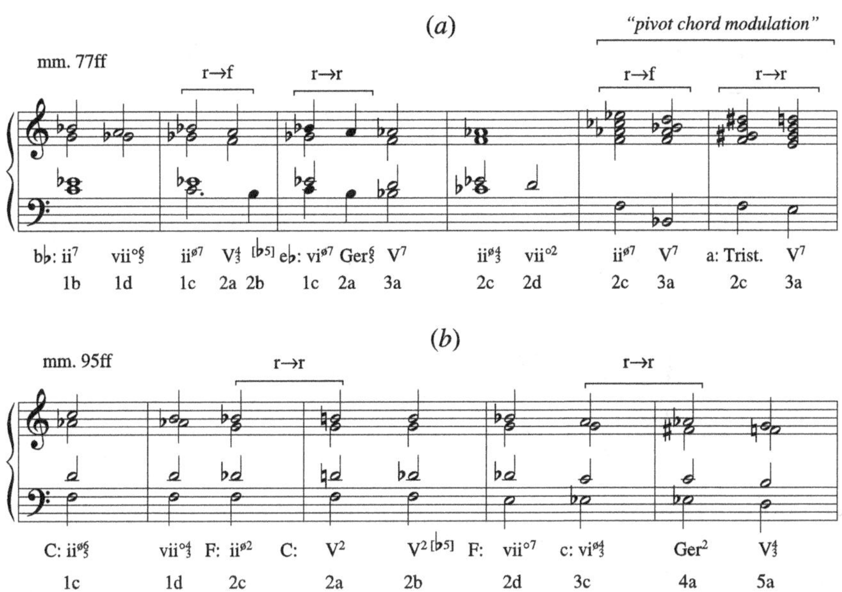

Figure 8.6.12 A passage from Act III, Scene I, p. 233/494 that can also be described using Chopin's techniques.

enth chords. To my mind, this suggests that the fundamental logic of the opera is a *contrapuntal* logic, and that Figure 8.6.2 is indeed the space through which Wagner's music moves. And though time does not permit us to delve deeply into the prelude, even this cursory sketch shows Wagner demonstrating a sophisticated understanding of four-dimensional chord space: utilizing all of the most efficient voice-leading possibilities from half-diminished to dominant seventh (Figure 8.6.13), substituting one half-diminished chord for another (Figure 8.6.9), moving between chords by way of their chromatic intermediaries (Figure 8.6.3), reusing the same basic contrapuntal schema with different sonorities (Figure 8.6.10), and even reproducing the open-ended quasi-sequences of Chopin's E minor prelude. Chromaticism here starts to achieve an impressive degree of autonomy; loosening itself from tonal functionality, it becomes an independent force with its own distinctive logic.

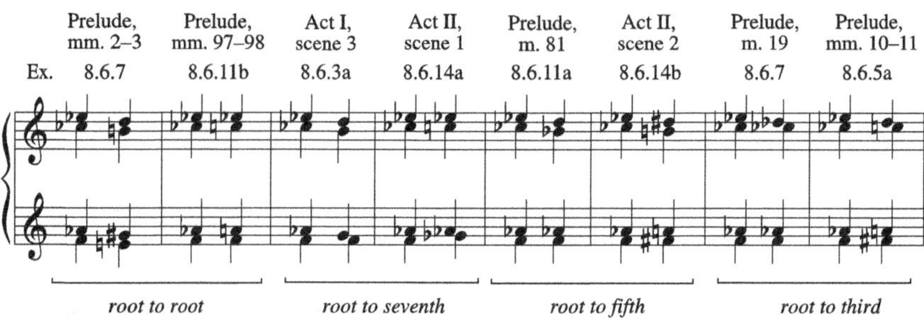

Figure 8.6.13 Resolutions of the Tristan chord from throughout the opera. Compare Figure 8.6.1b.

Figure 8.6.14 Two additional resolutions of the Tristan chord from later in the opera: Act II, Scene 1, p. 121/239 (root to seventh) (*a*), and Act II, Scene 2, p. 141/287 (root to fifth) (*b*).

8.7 ALTERNATIVE APPROACHES

I have argued that nineteenth-century composers exploit chromatic voice leading as an alternative to traditional tonal syntax, citing a variety of musical passages as evidence. But readers may legitimately wonder whether my examples establish the broader point. After all, couldn't it be that composers chose these chord progressions for other reasons, applying the efficient voice leading only as an afterthought? Why, in other words, should we believe that voice leading helps *explain* or *motivate* the examples I have chosen?

For specificity, let's consider the F–C♯–A^7 progression in Schubert's D major sonata (Figure 8.4.1). Over the years, theorists have advanced a variety of purely harmonic explanations for progressions of this sort: Gregory Proctor, for example, has argued that Romantic composers often exploited "equal divisions of the octave," such as F-C♯-A; David Kopp has singled out "chromatic mediant relations," in which chord roots move by major or minor thirds; and Richard Cohn and Fred Lerdahl have argued for the importance of hexatonic scales such as E-F-G♯-A-C-C♯.[31] (Still others, such as Suzannah Clark, emphasize *common-tone retention* rather than voice leading proper: from this point of view, it is the shared F that motivates Schubert's move from F major to C♯ major, and the shared C♯ that links C♯ major and A^7.[32]) These accounts suggest that the *harmonic* relations among Schubert's chords may be as important as their contrapuntal relations. To be sure, the passage *does* exhibit efficient voice leading—but then again, so does most other tonal music. Perhaps voice leading is a secondary matter, subservient to deeper harmonic forces.

I can offer three responses. First, nineteenth-century music uses an enormous variety of voice leadings between familiar tonal sonorities. Consider just the examples in this chapter: the decorated functional progressions of §8.1, Schubert and Schoenberg's nonstandard augmented sixths, Brahms' and Wagner's explorations of the various resolutions of the Tristan chord, Chopin's exquisite use of the hypercube at the center of four-note chord space, and so on. As far as I know, nobody has ever attempted to provide a purely harmonic explanation for these different chromatic techniques. (Certainly, not all of them exhibit equal division of the octave, mediant relationships, or the hexatonic scale.) Yet they seem to be importantly similar. Insofar as we want to acknowledge this similarity, we need to accept that voice leading is a motivating force in nineteenth-century music.

Second, as I have stressed, there are asymmetries between chromatic routines involving triads and those involving seventh chords: in particular, triads very frequently move by major third, while seventh chords often move by minor third or tritone. Where I explain this asymmetry using the intrinsic geometry of chord space, the harmonic approach does not explain it at all: the assumption that composers were concerned with equal divisions of the octave, mediant relations, or hexatonic scales gives us no reason to think that triads should be any different from seventh chords. From the harmonic perspective, the difference remains an unexplained mystery.

Third, voice leading can potentially *explain* the sorts of harmonic relationships identified by theorists such as Proctor, Kopp, and Cohn. Suppose, for example, we postulate that composers were interested in particularly efficient voice leadings between major triads or dominant seventh chords. A concern with voice-leading efficiency would therefore be expected to give rise to mediant relations of the sort Kopp discusses: after all, geometry shows that triads are particularly close to their major-third transpositions, while seventh chords are close to their minor-third and tritone transpositions. Furthermore, by repeatedly exploiting these relationships, composers will generate passages exhibiting Proctor's "equal divisions." (This is because major and minor thirds evenly divide the twelve-semitone octave.) Finally, as we saw in Chapter 4, the resulting progressions will necessarily produce subsets of hexatonic

31 Proctor 1978, Kopp 2002, Cohn 1996 and Lerdahl 2001. Cohn's views are subtle, and also emphasize voice leading

32 Clark 2002.

and octatonic scales.[33] Thus, voice leading can potentially *subsume* the harmonic explanations proposed by other theorists. From the standpoint of explanatory parsimony, then, it makes sense to focus on chromatic voice leading rather than these derivative phenomena.

In saying this, I do not mean to suggest that a progression like Schubert's F–C♯–A^7 is entirely contrapuntal, or that Schubert was 100% unconcerned with harmonic relationships. As I stressed in Chapter 7, composers almost always think simultaneously about harmony and counterpoint, and it is quite likely that Schubert attached some genuinely harmonic significance to major-third relations. (Indeed for a composer who thinks seriously about voice leading, the C and A♭ major triads will come to have an affinity, even when they are juxtaposed in a way that hides their contrapuntal connections.[34]) No doubt there are some chromatic passages in nineteenth-century music that can be attributed to harmonic factors such as common-tone retention or mediant relations. Nevertheless, I think we have good general reasons to prioritize voice leading over harmony: absent indications to the contrary, it is reasonable to assume that a particular instance of efficient voice leading is just that—an example of a near-ubiquitous procedure that provided the principal nineteenth-century alternative to conventional functional syntax. Voice leading may not be the last word in the analysis of nineteenth-century music, but it certainly is a very reasonable starting point.

8.8 CONCLUSION

The preceding pages should make it clear that I am not proposing a simple method or rule for doing musical analysis: there is no royal road to musical understanding, geometrical or otherwise. Instead, my claim is that appreciating the grammar of nineteenth-century music requires a flexible grasp of the various voice-leading possibilities among familiar triads and seventh chords. Chromatic composers were for the most part extraordinarily intelligent people who spent their lives exploring the resources of the piano keyboard. As a result, they developed a deep understanding of the various contrapuntal routes from chord to chord.

Generally speaking, early nineteenth-century chromaticism tends to embellish traditional tonal progressions. Over the following decades, chromatic procedures gain autonomy, to the point where they eventually compete with or even supersede traditional principles: although Chopin's E minor Prelude may be based on a descending fifths background, the descending semitonal chromaticism is much more salient. By

33 Recall in this connection that each cube in the center of three-note chromatic space contains chords belonging to a single hexatonic scale, while each hypercube in the center of four-note chord space contains chords belonging to a single octatonic scale (§3.11). Thus we can expect these scales to arise as the mere byproduct of chromatic voice leading. Indeed I would suggest that in the nineteenth century this is often the case: deliberate compositional exploration of these scales is largely a twentieth-century phenomenon.

34 In twentieth-century music one often finds direct juxtapositions of major-third-related triads in which there is no efficient voice leading; this is particularly common in Prokofiev, for example.

the time of Wagner's *Tristan*, the chromatic and the diatonic are in extremely delicate balance, with chromaticism at times threatening to eradicate tonal functionality altogether. This is precisely what leads theorists to talk of late-nineteenth century music as having a Janus-faced quality, combining a functional "first practice" with a chromatic "second practice." (Cohn aptly draws an analogy to bilingual communities in which speakers switch rapidly between languages, sometimes within the span of a single sentence.[35]) Figure 8.8.1, from Strauss' *Salome*, provides a sense of where this development would eventually lead: here, familiar tonal concepts lose their purchase,

Figure 8.8.1 In Strauss' *Salome*, extensive chromatic voice leading is accompanied by equally chromatic melodic motion, leading to a saturated pitch-class space in which all twelve notes are constantly in play.

35 See Cohn 2007.

as incessant chromatic voice leading produces a highly chromatic macroharmony without any strong sense of tonal center.

In older histories of twentieth-century music, this trend toward increasing chromaticism is sometimes presented as inevitable, a simple matter of musicians following the signpost of Historical Progress. And in truth, the claim of inevitability is not obviously wrong: for insofar as chromatic techniques are used incessantly, as in *Salome,* the result will be textures whose tonality can be quite difficult to discern. From here it is a relatively small step to the more robustly atonal works of the second Viennese school. (Indeed, Chapter 5 already broached this thought, pointing out that chromatic tonality and free atonality often share similar statistical profiles, including similar rates of pitch-class circulation and a similar absence of centricity.) Musicians who recoiled from these post-Wagnerian extremes, but who did not want to write traditional music, would therefore need to go back to the drawing board, devising new approaches that could coexist more peacefully with our five basic components of tonality.

CHAPTER 9

Scales in Twentieth-Century Music

While nineteenth-century chordal procedures can be stunningly sophisticated, the exploration of modality and nondiatonic scales tends to be relatively cautious by comparison. As a result, the music often has an asymmetrical quality, combining intensive investigation in one domain with a seeming indifference toward another. Indeed, this asymmetry between chord and scale may help to explain why late-nineteenth-century composers start to flirt with atonality: for as we have just seen, omnipresent chromatic voice leading can start to weaken the sense of centricity and macroharmony, dissolving tonality in the universal solvent of semitonal motion. Insofar as one's musical world is circumscribed by the opposition between chromatic counterpoint and functional harmony, and insofar as one resolves to avoid functional harmony altogether, then one will inevitably be driven out onto the seas of relentless chromaticism.

In this chapter I consider three techniques that twentieth-century composers used to counteract chromaticism's pull. The first, *chord-first* composition, exploits efficient chordal voice leading to generate a sequence of otherwise unrelated scales; it thus augments nineteenth-century chordal procedures with additional scales that piggyback on the chordal level. The second technique, *scale-first* composition, uses efficient voice leading to connect *scales* rather than chords; the technique thus generalizes traditional modulation by extending nineteenth-century chordal practices to a new scalar domain. Finally, there is the *subset technique*, which links scales by way of common chords or common chord types. As we will see, this last technique is intermediate between the first two: when the shared subsets are small and chordlike, it can be understood as a species of chord-first composition; when they are large, it is closer to scale-first composition.

My ultimate goal here is to propose an alternative to historical narratives that center on atonality and the avant garde. Reading these accounts, one sometimes gets the sense that twentieth-century tonality is fundamentally static and backward-looking, as if the language had remained unchanged since the time of Brahms and Wagner. My own view, by contrast, is that the nineteenth century bequeathed a genuine and pressing problem to subsequent composers, namely synthesizing its contrapuntal innovations with the five components discussed in Chapter 1. As we will see, a large number of twentieth-century musicians solved this problem in an essentially similar way, using scales to ameliorate the destabilizing effects of chromatic motion. To my ear, the result is a tonality that is renewed, refreshed, and clearly distinct from that of earlier centuries: listening to Debussy or Miles Davis or Steve Reich, one recognizes a genuinely novel approach in which scales play a new and fundamental role.

9.1 THREE SCALAR TECHNIQUES

Central to all three techniques is what jazz theorists call the *principle of chord-scale compatibility,* illustrated in Figure 9.1.1. Here, chords are understood as subsets of familiar five-to-eight-note scales. (Jazz theorists would say that the chord and scale are "compatible.") Given this two-tiered structure, it is possible for one element to take the lead, determining the changes that occur on the other level. This relationship might be compared to that between harmony and counterpoint: although both elements are important, passages can be more harmonic or more contrapuntal, depending on which property seems to be controlling the music at a particular time. In much the same way, chord and scale can at different points seize control over the music's fundamental logic.

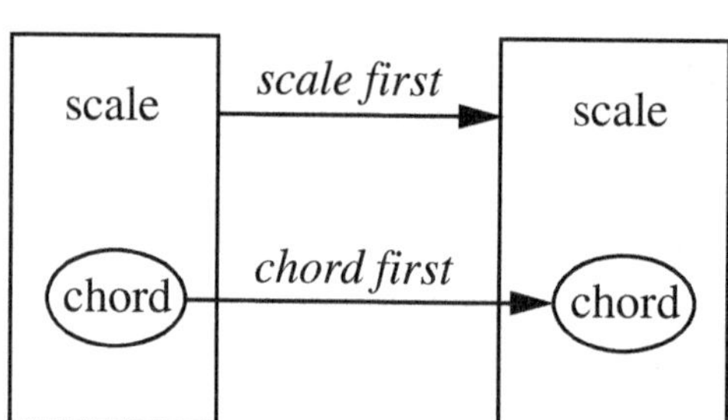

Figure 9.1.1 Scale-first and chord-first composition.

A key component of this approach is that scales are understood to be more than mere byproducts—that is, they are recognizable objects in themselves, with their own syntactical role to play. The top staff of Figure 9.1.2 provides an example in which scales might be described as derivative: the second chord, with A♭ and F♯, is accompanied by the unusual scale C-D-E-F♯-G-A♭-B; the third chord, with D♯, is accompanied by the equally unusual C-D♯-E-F-G-A-B. In this passage, the scales are parasitic on the chords, being determined by the chordal accidentals; no attempt is made to produce a scale that divides the octave evenly, or contains a large number of consonances, or possesses any of the other virtues discussed in Chapters 4 and 5. By contrast, the second staff accompanies the same chords with collections that possess desirable scalar qualities. The presence of these "virtuous" scales suggests a compositional mind that is attuned to *both* the chordal and scalar levels—a musical "twofoldness" that is our current concern.

Turning now to the techniques themselves, in *chord-first* composition, the chordal level predominates: thus, an efficient voice leading like (E, G♯, B, D)→(F, A♭, B♭, D) might give rise to an E acoustic scale (containing E^7) followed by a B♭ mixolydian scale (containing $B♭^7$). The second of Scriabin's Op. 48 Preludes, composed in 1905, provides a particularly clear example (Figure 9.1.3). The three upper voices contain a standard nineteenth-century progression in which semitonal voice leading connects D minor, B♭ minor, and an incomplete C major seventh, C-E-B; however, Scriabin departs from post-Wagnerian practice by assigning a different scale to each chord. Chords seem to be leading the scales in the following sense: we can easily imagine

Figure 9.1.2 The unfamiliar scales in the top staff simply apply the chords' accidentals to the underlying C diatonic collection, and do not suggest particular attentiveness toward scales as such; by contrast, those on the second staff are quite familiar, and exhibit many of the virtues discussed in Chapter 4.

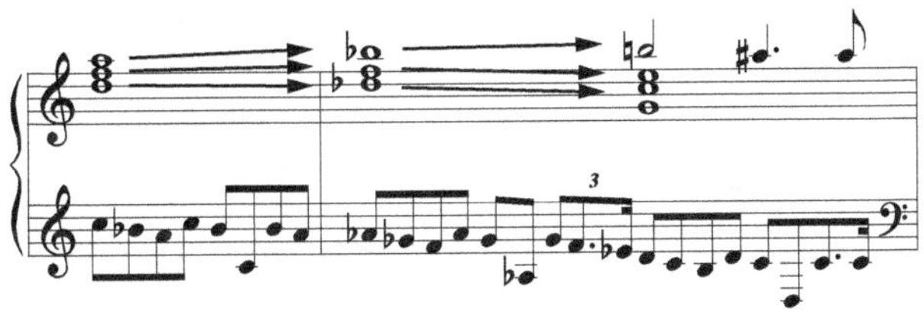

Figure 9.1.3 Scriabin's prelude, Op. 48 No. 2, in which efficient voice leading in the upper staff gives rise to a series of scales.

composing the efficient chordal voice leadings prior to the scales, but it is much more difficult to imagine starting with the F, D♭, and G diatonic scales, composing the chords only later.[1]

By contrast, in *scale-first* composition, music progresses by way of efficient voice leading between scales themselves. The opening of Ravel's *Ondine,* shown in Figure 9.1.4, begins with a shimmering wash featuring the C♯ mode of B acoustic, C♯-D♯-E♯-F♯-G♯-A-B ("C♯ mixolydian ♭6").[2] A series of single-semitone changes creates, successively, C♯ harmonic major, C♯ diatonic, and G♯ acoustic. (Note that many of these collections are incomplete.) Unlike Scriabin's piece, one gets the sense of a distinctively *scalar* logic, as if Ravel deliberately moved between closely related scales by changing one or two notes at a time. Figure 9.1.5 uses our familiar scale lattice to

1 Note that I am considering the notes A♯, C♯, and E♭ to be nonharmonic.

2 See also Tymoczko 1997.

Figure 9.1.4 The opening of Ravel's "Ondine," from *Gaspard de la nuit*, suggests a series of single-semitone voice leadings among familiar scales.

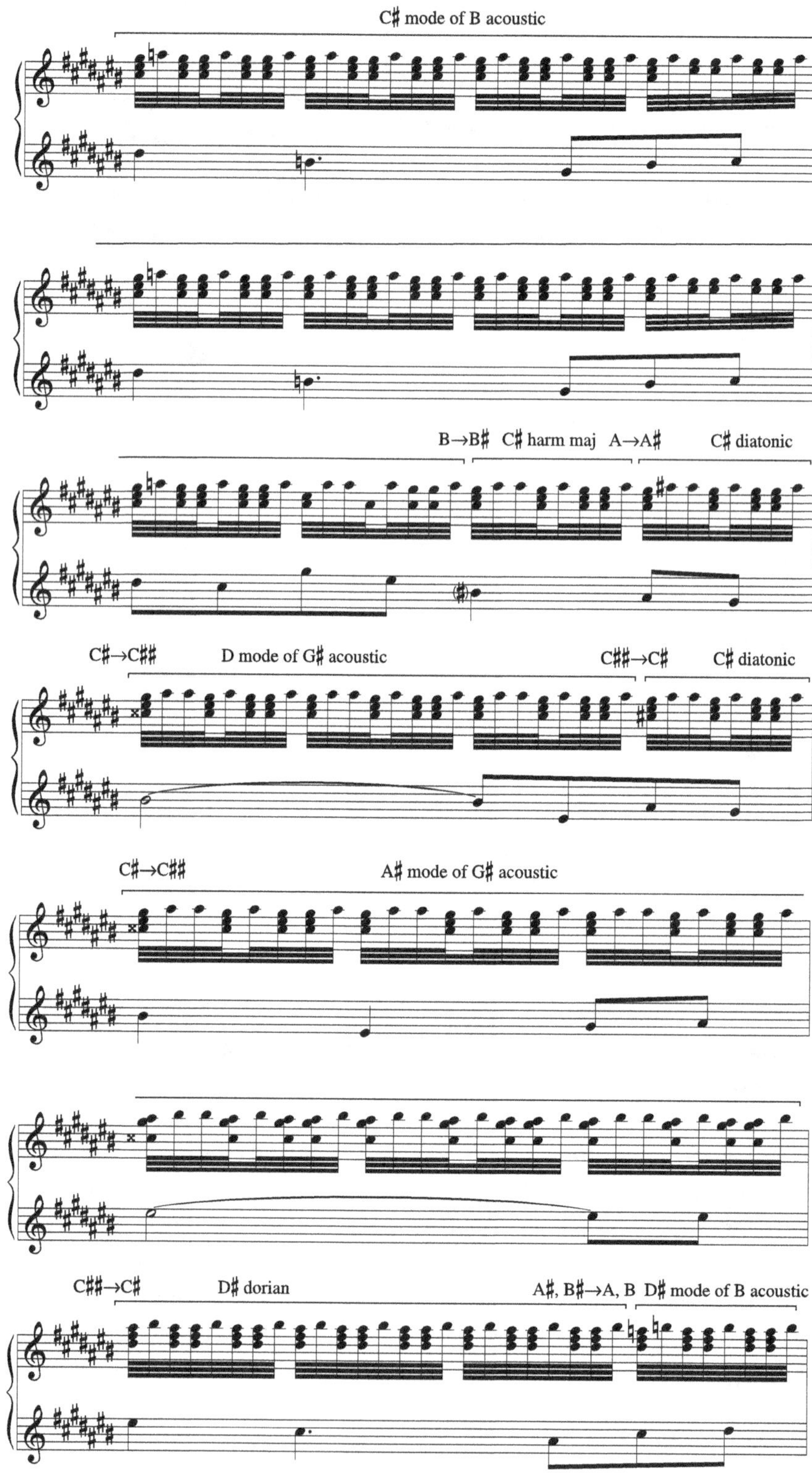

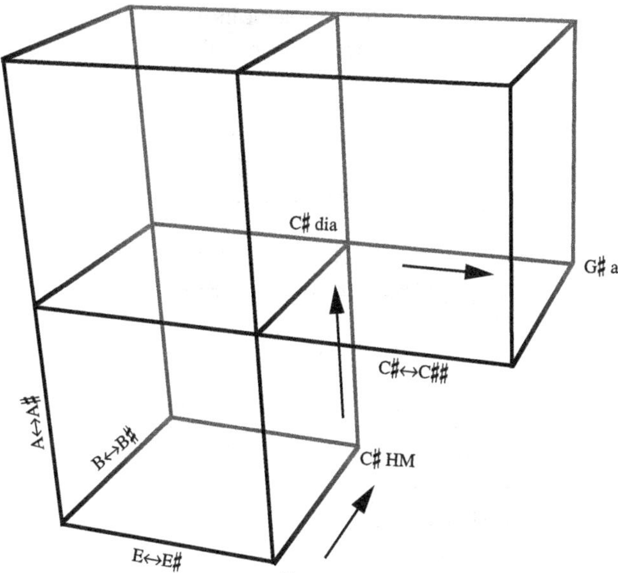

Figure 9.1.5 Ravel's scales plotted on the scale lattice.

show that Ravel systematically explores a small region of the space, moving between nearby collections. This is just the efficient chromatic voice leading of Chapter 8, applied now to *scales* rather than *chords.*

Finally, the *subset technique* juxtaposes scales sharing some contextually salient set of notes. For example, Debussy's "Collines d'Anacapri" presents the opening pentatonic theme B-F♯-C♯-E-G♯-B in three distinct scalar contexts: B diatonic, E diatonic, and E acoustic (Figure 9.1.6).[3] One could say that the music has five "fixed" scale degrees (B, C♯, E, F♯, G♯) and two "mobile" degrees (D/D♯ and A/A♯). This technique can sometimes be hard to distinguish from the scale-first technique: for example, since all three scales in Figure 9.1.6 can be linked by efficient voice leading, one could in principle say that the music exemplifies scale-first composition. But it is important here that the "fixed" collection comprises the main theme of the piece. In describing this music as an example of the subset technique, I am therefore making the claim that the subset relationship is *more important* than voice leading: common tones, more than counterpoint, determine the modulations in the prelude.

Clearly, the subset technique is intermediate between the other two approaches. When the subsets are small, we can think of the technique as a special case of chord-first composition: where chord-first composition features *efficient* voice leading, such as (C, E, G)→(B, E, G♯), the subset technique uses "trivial" voice leadings, such as (C, E, G)→(C, E, G), in which all the voices are left unchanged. However, when the subsets in question are large (as in "Collines d'Anacapri") the subset technique more closely resembles scale-first composition. (This is simply because two scales that share a large number of notes can typically be linked by efficient voice leading.) Musical context is important here: when composers emphasize the fixed subset—for

3 See Tymoczko 2004 and Kopp 1997 for more thorough analyses.

Figure 9.1.6 In Debussy's "Les collines d'Anacapri," the pentatonic theme B-F♯-C♯-E-G♯-B acts as a fixed subset, and appears in the context of several different scales: B diatonic (*a*), E diatonic (*b*), and E acoustic (*c*).

instance by using it in important themes or melodies—then we may want to highlight shared subsets rather than voice leading; in other situations, however, it may be that the voice-leading relationships are paramount. Thus the distinction between the subset technique and the others is one of emphasis rather than fundamental technique.

Of course, the three techniques all have their antecedents in earlier music. In the nineteenth century, the chord-first technique sometimes occurs across modulations: for example, Figure 9.1.7 presents the modulation from exposition to development in the first movement of Schubert's B♭-major sonata, D. 960; the semitonal voice leading between F major and C♯ minor chords drags the rest of the music along for the ride, leading to a dramatic shift in scale and key. Chapter 7 argued that the scale-first technique is used in ordinary modulations between closely related keys. (That is, the distance between keys is largely a function of the size of the voice leadings between the relevant scales.) Figure 9.1.8 provides a rare nineteenth-century example that employs nonstandard modes: here, the C♯ phrygian theme of Chopin's Mazurka, Op. 41 No. 1, returns as the fifth mode of F♯ harmonic minor. Finally, Figure 9.1.9 presents an example of the subset technique, from Chopin's G♭ major Etude, Op. 10 No. 5. In this piece, the right hand plays only black keys, which act as a fixed subset contained in both the tonic dominant scales. (Again, the two scales are also related by efficient voice leading; the point is that Chopin emphasizes the fixed subset compositionally.) These examples suggest that what is new in twentieth-century music is

Figure 9.1.7 Chord-first modulation in the transition from exposition to development of Schubert's B♭ major Sonata, D. 960, movement I.

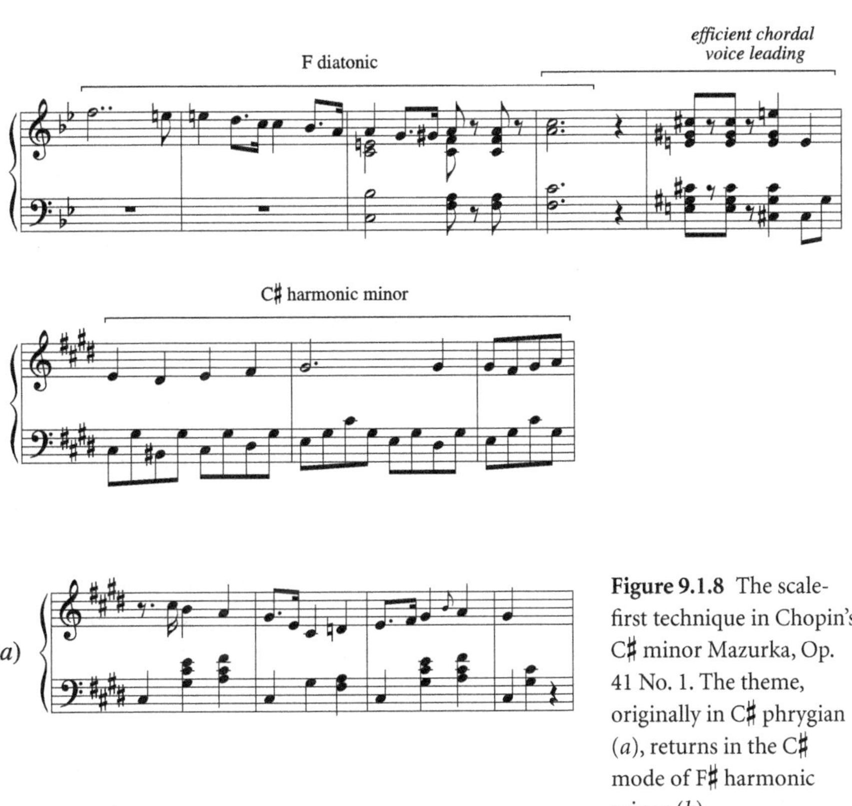

Figure 9.1.8 The scale-first technique in Chopin's C♯ minor Mazurka, Op. 41 No. 1. The theme, originally in C♯ phrygian (*a*), returns in the C♯ mode of F♯ harmonic minor (*b*).

Figure 9.1.9 The subset technique in Chopin's G♭ major ("black key") Etude, Op. 10 No. 5. Throughout the piece, the right hand plays only black keys, which serve as a fixed subset common to the two primary scales in the piece.

not the techniques themselves, but rather the willingness to apply them more consistently, more frequently, and to a much wider range of scales and modes.

9.2 CHORD-FIRST COMPOSITION

We'll begin with examples in which the musical logic resides in chords rather than scales: on their own, the scales need not have any particular significance; instead, they are related by virtue of the chords they contain.

9.2.1 Grieg's "Drömmesyn" ("Vision"), Op. 62 No. 5 (1895)

The opening of Grieg's short piece, shown in Figure 9.2.1, is based on a progression that uses descending semitonal voice leading to connect familiar seventh chords, one that might easily appear in Chopin's music. (In fact, it can be modeled on the four-dimensional lattice used in the previous chapter.) Unlike nineteenth-century composers, however, Grieg treats the chords as a skeleton to be fleshed out by diatonic scales. On their own, these scales would seem arbitrary, without discernable logic or pattern. But when we consider the chords, their significance is clear: the chords are connected by semitonal voice leading, while the scales just happen to contain them.

A traditionalist might hear Grieg's piece as moving successively through the keys of A, D♭, G♭, and C major. But to my ear, the seventh chords are stable objects in themselves rather than unstable objects that need to resolve. This is, in part, because of the piece's static harmony and avoidance of V^7–I resolutions. But it is also a function of the subtle and shifting relationship between melody, chord, and scale: in the first and third phrases, the melody starts on the added sixth of the underlying harmony, while in the second and fourth phrases, the melody starts on the chordal *seventh*. Furthermore, the chords themselves move relative to the purported tonic: the bass of the first chord is the first scale degree of A major, the bass of the second chord is the fifth degree of D♭ major, and the bass of the third chord is the second degree of G♭ major. What results is an extremely subtle counterpoint between the scale, tonic, and melody, in which the three elements never once move in parallel (Figure 9.2.2). Given this complexity, my ear tends to gravitate toward the bass as the most stable

Figure 9.2.1 Grieg's Lyric Piece "Drömmesyn" (Vision), Op. 62 No. 5. The piece is built around a series of efficient voice leadings between four-note chords (*a*), which give rise to diatonic scales (*b*).

Figure 9.2.1 (Continued)

Figure 9.2.2 Grieg's piece articulates an abstract counterpoint between the melody's starting note, the diatonic collection, and the root or bass.

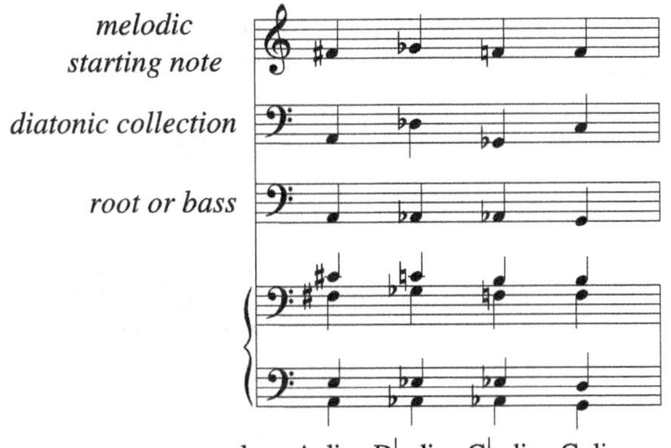

note—which means that I conceive the melody as successively beginning on the sixth degree of A major, the seventh degree of A♭ mixolydian, the sixth degree of A♭ dorian, and the seventh degree of G mixolydian.

9.2.2 Debussy's "Fêtes" (1899)

Figure 9.2.3 outlines the basic voice leading in the central section of "Fêtes," the second of Debussy's orchestral *Nocturnes*. The music is largely sequential, with its 16-bar model divided into two eight-bar halves. The harmonies in the first half of the second 16-bar unit (chords 9–12 on the example) are transposed up by minor third, while the rest of the phrase is transposed by tritone: instead of B^{ø7}–G^{7}–B^{ø7}–G♯^{o7}, we hear D^{ø7}–B♭^{7}–D^{ø7}–B^{o7}. The last 16 bars of the section repeat the harmonies of the first 16 bars, but now accompanied by the movement's opening theme—a running scalar passage featuring G♭, E♭, and A diatonic (Figure 9.2.4). As in Grieg's piece, the theme remains fixed in register, beginning twice on B♭ despite the change from D♭^{7} to B♭^{7}.

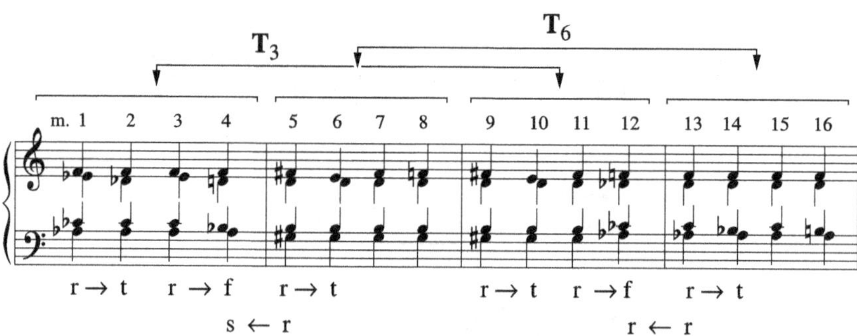

Figure 9.2.3 Voice leadings in the middle section of "Fêtes." Each measure represents four bars of music.

Figure 9.2.4 In the third phrase of the middle section of "Fêtes," the opening chords return, though now accompanied by scales articulating the movement's main theme.

Thus it begins successively on the third degree of G♭ diatonic, the fifth degree of E♭ diatonic, and the third and seventh degrees of A diatonic.

Figure 9.2.3 indicates the relevant interscalar transposition under each voice leading from half-diminished to dominant seventh. (Voice leadings from dominant seventh to half-diminished use a backwards arrow, labeling relative to the root of the half-diminished chord.) We see that the music exploits *all* of the different types of (crossing-free) voice leadings between the two types of chord, mapping the root of the half-diminished to the third, fifth, seventh, and root of the dominant seventh.[4] The technique here is essentially that of Wagner's *Tristan,* albeit now accompanied by a variety of diatonic modes. It follows that we can use our four-dimensional geometrical models to describe the passage: Figure 9.2.5 shows that Debussy's chords lie on the adjacent vertices of two hypercubes, with the half-diminished sevenths appearing just above the b^{o7} chord, and the dominant sevenths just below.[5] The voice leading connecting F^{ø7} to D♭^{7} (as well as G♯^{ø7} to E^{7}, and D^{ø7} to B♭^{7}) moves one note by two semitones, and passes directly through the diminished seventh chord to the chord on the other side.[6] The remaining voice leadings, such as F^{ø7}→B♭^{7} and D♭^{7}→D^{ø7}, move two notes by semitone, and do not pass through the diminished seventh chord.

The procedures in "Fêtes" can be found throughout Debussy's compositions, and are particularly salient in the *Prelude to "The Afternoon of a Faun"* (Figure 9.2.6). This testifies to a significant degree of continuity between Wagnerian Romanticism and Debussian impressionism: we find the same fascination with half-diminished and dominant seventh chords, and the same systematic use of the various voice leadings connecting them.[7] The big difference, to my mind, lies in the two composers' attitude toward scales. For Wagner, chromatic voice leading is just that—a *chromatic* technique that invariably brings the chromatic scale into play at the melodic level. For Debussy, these chromatic voice leadings occur at a much slower rate, and give rise to

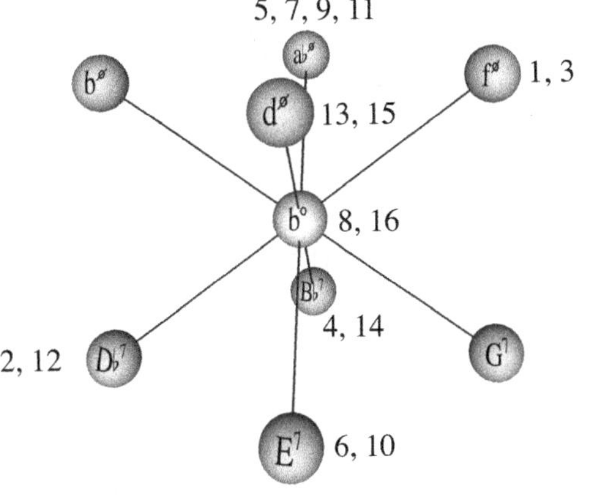

Figure 9.2.5 A geometrical depiction of Debussy's chords.

4 In the actual music, some of these voice leadings are slightly disguised.

5 Compare with Figure 8.5.10 to see how this figure is contained in the more familiar structure.

6 The fact that Debussy restricts himself to these chords strongly suggests that his harmonic choices were motivated by voice-leading facts, even though the relevant voice leadings are sometimes disguised.

7 Cf. Holloway 1982 and Pople 2001.

Figure 9.2.6 Efficient voice leadings between half-diminished and dominant seventh chords in Debussy's *Prelude to "The Afternoon of a Faun"*: mm. 6–9 (*a*), 17–19 (*b*), and 44–46 (*c*).

additional scales at the musical surface. By remaining in a single scale for a significant length of time, Debussy endows his music with a simple, classicist quality that is in marked contrast to the relentless churning of Wagnerian chromaticism.

9.2.3 Michael Nyman's "The Mood That Passes Through You" (1993)

For a more contemporary example, we turn to one of Michael Nyman's cues for the movie *The Piano*. Nyman's music is not so much a traditional "piece" as it is a vignette or musical moment, meant to fulfill a specific dramatic need. (Part of its interest, in fact, lies in its vernacular quality, demonstrating that chord-first composition has become part of a broader common practice.) Figure 9.2.7 shows that the music has two basic sections, each based on a repeating chord progression. In the first, we hear

B♭ minor, D major, and E major triads, each in root position, and each lasting for two measures. (Note that the right hand contains a concealed ostinato figure, indicated by the beamed noteheads.) In the second, we hear a sequence of four descending triads, first g♯^{6}–e^6–B$^6_4$–A$^6_4$, and then B–e^6–B$^6_4$–A$^6_4$, with a root position B major triad substituting for the first-inversion G♯ minor. (This is of course the "third substitution" of §7.2.) The voice leading is mostly parallel and owes more to popular music than to classical. Nevertheless, it is easy to hear echoes of the nineteenth-century concern for efficient voice leading, particularly in the repeated juxtapositions of major-third-related triads. Figure 9.2.8 shows that the ostensibly parallel voice leading articulates semitonal connections in pitch space.

As in the previous example, chords give rise to scales at the musical surface. In the first part of the cue, the B♭ minor triad is accompanied by B♭ natural minor, while

Figure 9.2.7 Michael Nyman's "The Mood that Passes Through You," from the soundtrack to the movie *The Piano*. The brackets indicate two instances of major-third juxtapositions: B♭ minor–D major, and G♯ minor–E minor.

Figure 9.2.8 Nyman's left-hand arpeggios articulate a semitonal voice leading between major-third-related triads.

the D and E major triads are accompanied by A diatonic. In the second part, the G♯ minor and B major triads are accompanied by B diatonic, E minor is accompanied by G acoustic, and A major is accompanied by D diatonic.[8] (Of particular interest here is the appearance of G acoustic, one of the most important nondiatonic collections in twentieth-century tonal music and a favorite of Debussy's.) Once again, the scalar logic seems secondary: it is chords rather than scales that are determining the music's progress.[9] Comparable passages can be found throughout postminimalist music, in the works of composers such as Glass, Reich, Adams, Torke, and Lansky (Figure 9.2.9).

Note that the major-third system appears in twentieth-century styles as diverse as Russian modernism, American minimalism, and film music. (In particular, it plays a role in both Figures 9.2.7 and 9.2.9.) The progressions in our examples—and in recent music more generally—are distinctive insofar as they replace the *major triads* typical of Schubert's music with *minor* triads that produce a more ominous and brooding sound, an effect that is often highlighted by driving or asymmetrical rhythms. Figure 9.2.10, from Prokofiev's *Overture on Hebrew Themes,* exemplifies these qualities, juxtaposing A♭ minor, E major and C minor triads over pulsating eighth notes.[10] Figure 9.2.11 shows some related

Figure 9.2.9 Chord-first voice leading in Adams' *Nixon in China,* Act I, Scene I, mm. 141–148.

8 Most of the scales are incomplete—unsurprisingly, given the length of the excerpt.

9 However, it is true that G acoustic shares six notes with D diatonic, which in turn shares six notes with A diatonic.

10 Thanks to Daniel Zimmerman for pointing me to this piece.

Figure 9.2.10 Major-third-related triads in Prokofiev's *Overture on Hebrew Themes*, R42.

Figure 9.2.11 The major-third system in (*a*) the G minor prelude from Shostakovich's Twenty-four Preludes and Fugues, (*b*) Philip Glass' *Einstein on the Beach*, and (*c*) the opening credits of the 2004 television series *Battlestar Galactica*.

passages from Shostakovich, Philip Glass, and television music, which combine a Schubertian (or Wagnerian) harmonic sense with a rhythmic impulse whose roots lie in Stravinsky and popular music.[11] Taken together, they suggest a genealogy by which the major-third system passes from Schubert's Vienna to contemporary America by way of Russian modernist composers like Prokofiev and Shostakovich, acquiring in the process a darker, more ominous quality.

9.3 SCALE-FIRST COMPOSITION

Next, we'll consider passages that extend nineteenth-century *chordal* techniques to scales themselves, generalizing traditional modulation to a broader range of scales and modes.

9.3.1 Debussy's "Des Pas Sur La Neige" (1910)

Figure 9.3.1 contains the score to Debussy's "Des pas sur la neige" ("Footprints in the Snow"). As shown in Figure 9.3.2, Debussy's piece explores a collection of five closely related scales, all containing the ostinato D-E-F.[12] These can be considered a kind of "tonic region," since each provides a different coloring of a basically D minor tonality. In addition, the piece also contains three other scales forming a contrasting harmonic region—A♭ mixolydian, A♭ dorian, and C whole tone. The first two are again related by single-semitone voice leading, and emphasize A♭, the note a tritone away from the tonic D. None of these is particularly close to the first network, and the two regions are audibly quite distinct.

The first transition between these regions is worth examining more closely. In mm. 8–9, C^7 alternates with $C\sharp^7$, while in m. 11, G^7 alternates with $G\flat^{maj7}$ (Figure 9.3.3). This semitonal shifting leads us into the foreign scale area: the C^7 of mm. 8–9 belongs to the F diatonic of mm. 1–3, while the $C\sharp^7$ and $G\flat^{maj7}$ belong to the G♭ diatonic of mm. 29–31. The next harmonic move, from D♭ diatonic to C whole tone, occurs by way of the shared subset G♭-A♭-B♭-C, emphasized by the left hand in mm. 13–14. The subsequent whole-tone passage represents the piece's greatest point of distance from the opening diatonicism. The transition back to D natural minor illustrates one of Debussy's characteristic modulatory devices, the use of an acoustic scale as an intermediary between whole-tone and diatonic collections. As shown in Figure 9.3.3b, B♭ acoustic shares five of the whole-tone scale's six notes, while also

11 The overtly Romantic harmony in Figure 9.2.11c is unusual in Stravinsky's own music.

12 For this reason, one could also consider Debussy's piece as an example of the subset technique described in §9.4. (This is essentially the approach taken in Tymoczko 1997.) However, successive scales are typically linked by small voice leadings, suggesting that both techniques are in play.

Figure 9.3.1 (1 of 2) Debussy's "Des pas sur la neige."

sharing six of the diatonic scale's seven notes—a hybrid of whole tone and diatonic that smoothes the transition between them.[13]

Figure 9.3.4 summarizes the relations among the prelude's scales. On the left is the tonic region, containing C and F diatonic, A and D harmonic minor, and B♭ acoustic. On the right we have the contrasting key area of D♭ and G♭ diatonic, with C whole

13 See Whitall 1975.

Figure 9.3.1 (2 of 2) Debussy's "Des pas sur la neige."

tone connected to both regions. The music initially moves to the secondary region by way of upward semitonal transposition, returning to the tonic area via the C whole-tone scale. A substantial number of Debussy pieces are constructed around similar networks of scales, including "Le vent dans la plaine," "Les collines d'Anacapri," "La fille aux cheveaux de lin," *L'isle joyeuse,* "Les sons et les parfums tournent dans l'air du soir," and "Voiles." Indeed, Debussy's use of these techniques is so pervasive and systematic that one could easily write an entire book about the subject.[14]

14 For more, see Tymoczko 2004.

Figure 9.3.2 The tonic region in "Des pas sur la neige" contains five scales that are near each other on the scale lattice.

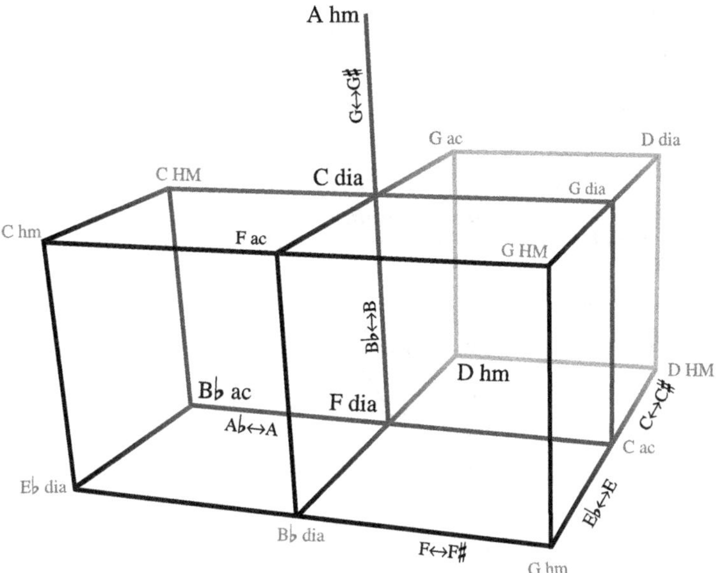

Figure 9.3.3 (*a*) The transition between the tonic (D-centered) scalar region and the secondary (black-note) scalar region occurs by way of semitonal shift upward. (*b*) The transition back occurs by way of the C whole-tone and B♭ acoustic scales.

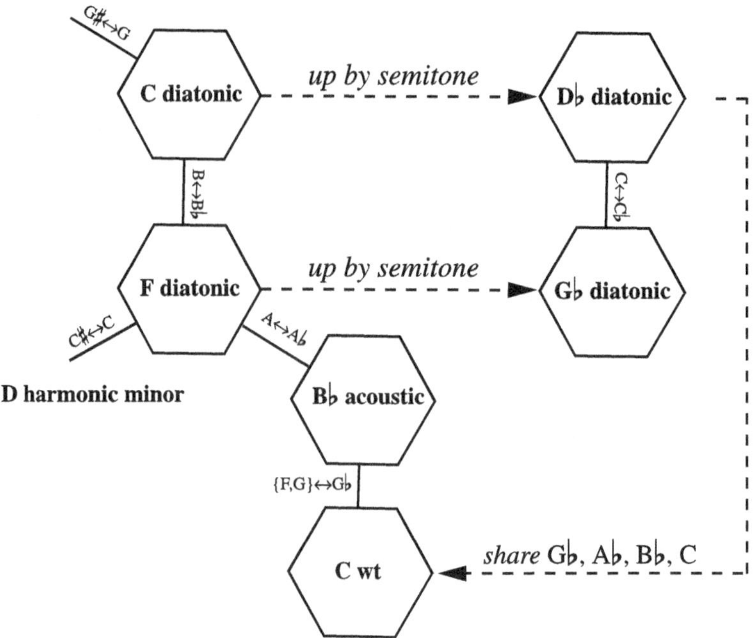

Figure 9.3.4 The scales in "Des pas sur la neige."

9.3.2 Janáček's "On an Overgrown Path," Series II, No. 1 (1908)

Janáček's piece is similar in spirit to Debussy's, though with a distinctive Eastern European flavor. Figure 9.3.5 provides the score for the opening, while Figure 9.3.6 summarizes its scalar content. The first section uses a different scale for each phrase: beginning with E♭ harmonic major, we hear E♭ harmonic minor, the A♭ "Gypsy" scale (equivalent to A♭ harmonic minor with raised fourth scale degree), E♭ major, and what is either a whole-tone scale on E♭ or the "Gypsy major" scale E♭-F-G-A-B♭-C♭-D. The next section changes the texture somewhat, introducing a pedal note marked by triplet octaves. We hear a pair of diatonic collections (C♯ dorian and C♯ natural minor) that are somewhat distant from the opening scales. Phrase 8 uses interscalar transposition to shift phrase 7 into E♭ harmonic major, creating a harmonic but not thematic recapitulation. Phrase 9 deepens the sense of recapitulation by repeating the melodic and harmonic content of phrase 2, though with the initial notes slightly altered (E♭-G♭-E♭ rather than E♭-A♭-F, reiterating the pattern established by phrase 1). Phrase 10 oscillates between E♯ and E♮, as if undecided between B Gypsy and B harmonic minor.

Figure 9.3.6 arranges the piece's eight scales into two networks, each connected by single-semitone displacements. The tonic network contains scales that are a semitone away from the initial E♭ harmonic major, arranged in a hub-and-spoke design.[15] The

15 If we were to examine seven-dimensional chord space, we would see that these "spokes" were all at right angles to one another; since we cannot visualize seven dimensions, however, we need to flatten the space so that it lies in two dimensions.

Figure 9.3.5 The opening of Janáček's "On an Overgrown Path," Series II, No. 1.

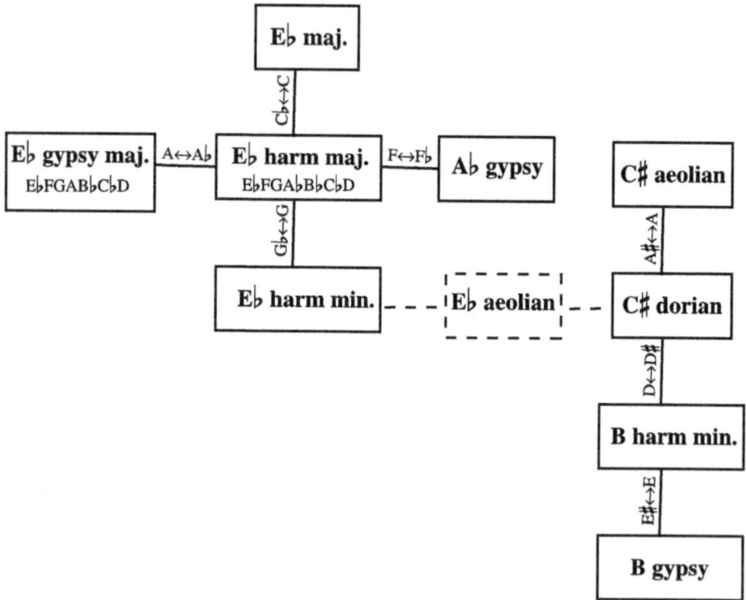

Figure 9.3.6 The scales in Janáček's piece.

nontonic network contains C♯ dorian, C♯ natural minor, B harmonic minor, and B Gypsy, arranged like railroad cars rather than the spokes of a wheel. The two networks are closer together than those in Debussy's prelude, since C♯ dorian could be connected to E♭ harmonic minor by way of an E♭ natural minor that does not appear in the piece. Janáček's scales are also somewhat more exotic, largely because he begins with a harmonic major rather than diatonic collection; semitonal alteration thus generates a series of colorful scales that include Gypsy and Gypsy major.

Although somewhat tangential to our current concerns, it is worth noting that the B section of Janáček's piece recalls Chopin's F minor Mazurka (Figure 9.3.7). Here we have a 10-measure phrase in which a series of first-inversion triads descend in a "staggered" fashion. (Note also the clever use of double counterpoint: the first half of the melody begins on the fifth of the underlying B minor triad, but the second half starts on the *root* of the G♯ minor triad.) Figure 9.3.8 represents its chords using the cubic lat-

Figure 9.3.7 The middle section of Janáček's "On an Overgrown Path," Series II, No. 1.

Figure 9.3.8 The middle section of Janáček's piece, plotted on the portion of the cubic lattice that is near (but not at) the center of three-note chord space. Here, capital and small letters refer to major and minor triads, "b°" and "B♭+" are diminished and augmented triads, "D♭4" refers to the fourth chord D♭-G♭-B, and "D♭7" refers to the incomplete seventh chord D♭-F-C♭.

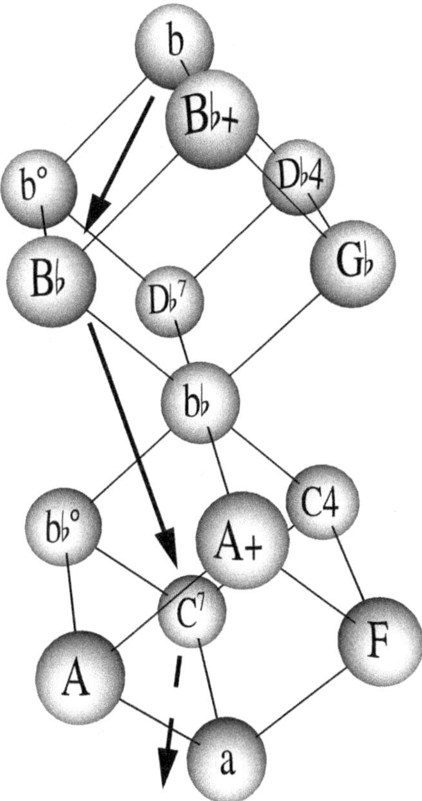

tice that is *near* (but not exactly at) the center of three-note chord space.[16] Like Chopin, Janáček traverses the lattice downward, by moving one, two, or three voices by step at each turn, producing a "liquefied" version of a familiar descending step sequence.

9.3.3 Shostakovich's F♯ Minor Prelude and Fugue, Op. 87 (1950)

Traditional composers raised the notes of the natural minor to bring it closer to major. Shostakovich, however, was more likely to *lower* its notes, creating unfamiliar "hyperminor" tonalities with a distinctive sinister character.[17] Figure 9.3.9

16 The cubic lattice at the center of the space, shown in Figure 3.11.2a, contains augmented triads at the shared vertex and major and minor triads elsewhere; the lattices adjacent to the center have major or minor triads at the shared vertices, and contain a greater variety of chord types.

17 For more on Shostakovich's scales, see Carpenter 1995.

Figure 9.3.9 F♯ natural minor has four degrees that can be lowered by semitone, represented here by the closed noteheads.

shows that F♯ natural minor offers four opportunities for semitonal lowering: the second scale degree can be lowered to produce the phrygian mode; the fourth can be lowered to produce a chromatic mode I will call "natural minor ♭4"; the fifth can be lowered to produce the F♯ mode of D acoustic; and the seventh can be lowered to produce another chromatic mode with half-steps C♯-D-E♭ ("natural minor ♭7"). The remaining notes are not good candidates for alteration, since lowering A or D would produce note duplications, while lowering F♯ would change the tonic.

The four lowerings can be combined to produce 16 different seven-note scales, including F♯ locrian (which lowers both G♯ and C♯) and the F♯ mode of G harmonic minor (which lowers all four notes). We can represent these 16 possible combinations with a familiar geometrical structure, the four-dimensional cube in Figure 9.3.10.

Figure 9.3.10 The four lowerings can be combined to produce sixteen scales, eight of which appear in Shostakovich's F♯ minor Prelude and Fugue. I have labeled only the scales relevant to Shostakovich's piece.

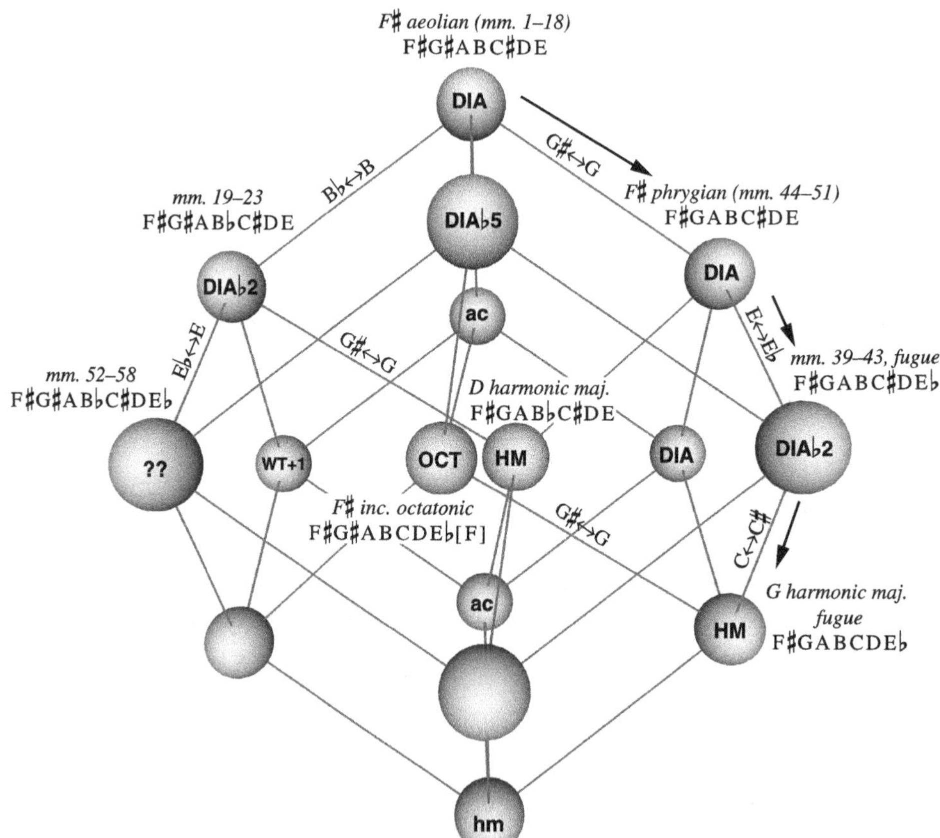

(This graph depicts a portion of seven-dimensional chord space, near but not at its center.) Eight of its sixteen scales appear either in the prelude or in the opening of the subsequent fugue, and Shostakovich does not employ any scales not found on the figure.[18] In this sense, the "scale tesseract" represents the modulatory space through which Shostakovich moves.

Figure 9.3.11 shows the tonic-key passages from the prelude and the opening of the fugue. The prelude begins with 18 measures of F♯ aeolian, disrupted by brief

Figure 9.3.11 Tonic-key passages in Shostakovich's F♯ minor Prelude and Fugue. These involve a progressive sequence of lowerings, leading ultimately to the harmonized fugue theme.

18 One possible exception is the B major chord on the second page of the prelude, which might be thought to imply F♯ dorian. However, the complete scale is not stated explicitly, and in any case it could easily be added to the graph as a point above F♯ natural minor.

moments of chromaticism; the recapitulation lowers G♯ to G♮, transforming F♯ natural minor into F♯ phrygian. The fugue subject suggests a "phrygian ♭7" scale F♯-G-A-B-C♯-D-E♭, which lowers the E of the preceding phrygian. (Note that while the subject itself does not contain a second scale degree, the note appears in both the countersubject and the subject's continuation.) The harmonization of the fugue subject, meanwhile, moves from the F♯ mode of G harmonic major to F♯ phrygian. If we look only at these tonic-key passages, we see a sequence of semitonal descents, beginning at natural minor and concluding with a "hyperminor" that has lowered second, fifth, and seventh degrees. We can represent this journey as a descending motion along the right edge of Figure 9.3.10, much as we represented Chopin's E minor Prelude as a systematic series of descents along the four-dimensional chord lattice.[19] (Needless to say, it is amazing that such similar geometries can represent both chords in Chopin and scales in Shostakovich!) Musically, this sequence of lowerings serves to prepare us for the unfamiliar tonality of the fugue: by moving gradually from a standard F♯ natural minor to the hyperminor of the harmonized fugue subject, Shostakovich slowly acclimates us to his unusual scalar vocabulary, fulfilling the traditional function of a prelude in an unfamiliar manner.

9.3.4 Reich's *New York Counterpoint* (1985)

Figure 9.3.12 lists the scales in Steve Reich's *New York Counterpoint* for eleven clarinets, one live and ten prerecorded.[20] The first movement opens with pulsating chords implying A♭ and E♭ diatonic. These eventually give way to rhythmic canons in A♭ diatonic, with the six voices divided into three pairs playing mostly parallel tenths. As shown in Figure 9.3.13, the top voice in each pair plays the notes (G, C, F), with the pitches A♭, B♭, and E♭ being ordered differently in each line; the result of this permutation is that the dotted quarter note occurs on a different pitch in each part. The movement then combines these canons with the original pulsating chords, leading to modulations that produce subtle alterations in the canonic pitches.[21]

The second movement is exclusively in B diatonic and again combines canons with repeated chords (Figure 9.3.14). Two of the pairs now play exactly the same music, with the third presenting a very slight variant. The canonic structure is consequently much clearer, sounding almost as if it had been produced by a digital delay. The third movement begins with a D♭ acoustic scale that is related by single-semitone

19 Shostakovich's prelude suggests a variety of other scales as well: mm. 17–23 vacillate between B♮ and B♭, suggesting F♯-G♯-A-B♭-C♯-D-E♭; mm. 29–30 suggest an explicit but fleeting octatonic scale, which can be associated with the collection F♯-G♯-A-B-C-D-E♭ on Figure 9.3.10; and the end of the prelude suggests the doubly lowered F♯-G-A-B♭-C♯-D-E♭. These scales, however, are often incomplete or accompanied by extraneous notes—a mild sort of polytonality typical of Shostakovich's music.

20 For simplicity, the following discussion will use the notated pitches, rather than the sounding pitches a major second below.

21 The live clarinet also plays noncanonic "resultant melodies" that draw their pitches from the canonic parts; for simplicity, my discussion omits these.

voice leading to the opening A♭ diatonic.[22] The six canonic voices are now divided into two groups, each playing mostly triads. At rehearsal 67, shown in Figure 9.3.15, the bass clarinets enter in canon with the notes E♭-A-E♭, producing the seven-note "whole tone plus one" scale E♭-F-G-A♭-A-B-D♭. (The rhythm of each bass clarinet part is the four-against-three cross-rhythm, for which the phrase "pass the goddamn butter" is a useful mnemonic.) The piece ends by oscillating between the "whole-tone plus one" and diatonic collections, closing with the pitches G♯, B, C♯, and D♯—the four notes common to the D♭ acoustic, E diatonic, and B diatonic scales.

Figure 9.3.16 graphs the scales using a two-dimensional scale lattice: the opening A♭ diatonic is connected by single-semitone voice leading to both E♭ diatonic and to D♭ acoustic, and D♭ acoustic is in turn connected by single-semitone voice leading to the "whole-tone plus one" scale. Similarly, the B diatonic of movement 2—three steps flatward from A♭ diatonic—is connected by single-semitone voice leading to the E diatonic of movement 3. Note that the "whole-tone plus one" collection appears naturally on the graph, as a third layer of scales surrounding the central zigzag of fifths: in particular, the "D♭ whole-tone + A♭" scale is connected by single-semitone voice leading to both B acoustic and D♭ acoustic.[23] Such graphs are characteristic of Reich's later pieces: like many of his works, *New York Counterpoint* makes very heavy use of the diatonic collection, occasional use of the acoustic scale (as well as other familiar scales such as the harmonic minor), and more sporadic use of exotic scales such as the "whole-tone plus one." Scales are often linked by efficient voice leading and frequently demarcate compact regions in scale space. However, Reich's modulations themselves give the sense of a relatively free journey through the space, rather than a systematic oscillation around a single tonic region.

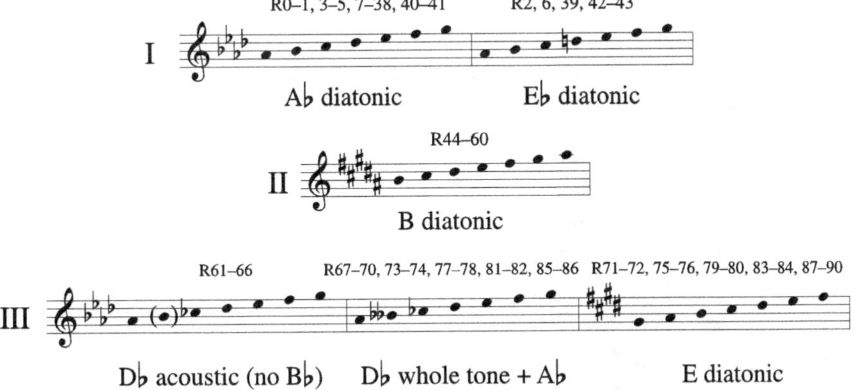

Figure 9.3.12 Scales in Steve Reich's *New York Counterpoint.*

22 The acoustic scale's B♭ is never stated. My analysis is influenced by the fact that Reich frequently uses the scale in other pieces.

23 This graph of diatonic, acoustic, and "whole-tone plus one" scales has analogues in some (but not all) of the situations in which there is a generalized circle of fifths: for instance, it exists in the case of diatonic seventh chords, but not diatonic triads. Interested readers are invited to explore this.

Figure 9.3.13 Canons in the first movement of *New York Counterpoint* (*a*). The canonic upper voices reorder the last three pitches, so that a different note is held in each part (*b*).

Figure 9.3.14 Canons in the second movement of *New York Counterpoint*. The paired voices play almost exactly the same music, the one exception being starred at the end of the second measure of the second staff.

Figure 9.3.15 Canons in the third movement of *New York Counterpoint*.

Before moving on, I should mention the fascinating relationship between the harmonic and rhythmic structures in Reich's music. Since *New York Counterpoint* is written in twelve-beat measures, its various rhythmic patterns are structurally analogous to familiar equal-tempered chords. For example, the opening measure of the third movement contains attacks on beats 0 (the downbeat), 2, 4, 5, 7, 9, and 11 (Figure 9.3.15). As pitch classes, these are the C diatonic scale.[24] Figure 9.3.15 shows that the first canon enters at a delay of two eighth notes, which means that there are five common attack points between the original rhythm and its canonic statement; this is the rhythmic analogue to the five common tones between C and D major. Thus, just as Reich frequently juxtaposes scales that share nearly all of their notes, so too do his rhythmic canons often maximize (or nearly maximize) their common attack points. It would be an interesting project to trace this parallelism more carefully, with an

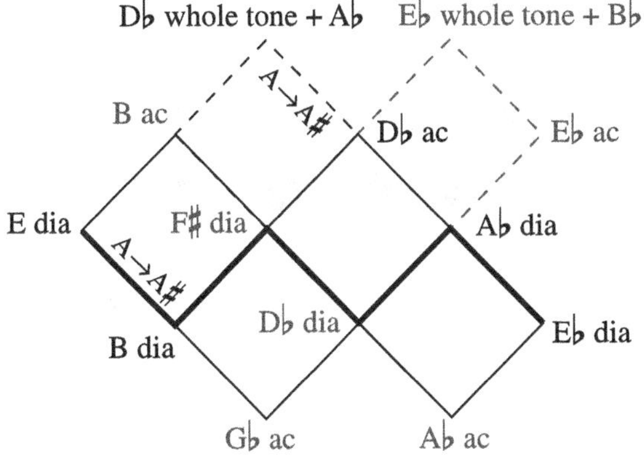

Figure 9.3.16 The scales in the third movement of *New York Counterpoint*, graphed on an extended version of the two-dimensional scale lattice.

24 For more on the pitch-class/rhythm isomorphism see Babbitt 1962, Pressing 1983, and Cohn 1992b. Note that, for simplicity, I am just talking about the rhythm in the first measure of the two-measure pattern.

eye toward understanding the relationship between these two musical domains. For instance, it is suggestive that the first explicit appearance of the "diatonic rhythm" in *New York Counterpoint* occurs precisely at the introduction of the first nondiatonic pitch collection.

9.3.5 Reich's *The Desert Music,* Movement 1 (1984)

The Desert Music, for orchestra and chorus, explores the ideas in *New York Counterpoint* on a much grander scale.[25] As in *New York Counterpoint,* the first movement opens with pulsating eighth-note chords, moves eventually to rhythmic canons, and concludes by synthesizing the two textures.[26] The music begins with four repetitions of a five-chord sequence, stated in pulsating eighth notes, with the chorus singing the syllable "de." Figure 9.3.17 shows that the vocalists' chords contain five or six pitch classes and suggest a number of familiar scales: the first belongs to E♭ acoustic and F harmonic major; the second to E♭ acoustic and A♭ diatonic; the third to E♭ acoustic and B♭ whole tone; the fourth to C♯ harmonic major and B acoustic; and the fifth to C and F diatonic. The instrumental parts add extra notes, creating a series of six- and seven-note sonorities (Figure 9.3.18). The first, third, and fourth sound like altered dominants, by virtue of combining a major third and minor seventh; the second and final chords sound like extended minor chords.

The logic of this opening progression can be clarified by imagining that it begins "in medias res," with the true (and hidden) starting point being the final D dorian. We then have a sequence of five scales that move efficiently and in a flatward direction: D dorian, F harmonic major, A♭ diatonic, E♭ acoustic, and a "strange" scale

Figure 9.3.17 Reich's *The Desert Music* opens with a sequence of five chords in the chorus, each suggesting a variety of scales.

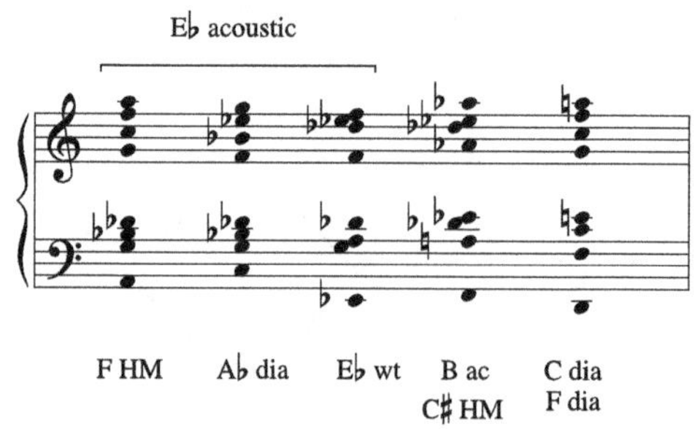

25 I am indebted here to Quinn (2002), who discusses scale-to-scale voice leadings in Reich's music. Callender 1998 and Morris 1987 are also relevant.

26 Interestingly, the middle movement of *The Desert Music* contains the same rhythmic pattern as the middle movement of *New York Counterpoint,* suggesting that the later piece consciously reuses ideas from *The Desert Music.*

F-G-A♭-B♭♭-C-D♭-E♭.[27] (Note the resemblance to Shostakovich's prelude and fugue, which also moves flatward through closely related scales.) Both the efficient voice leading and the flatward tendency are clear on Figure 9.3.19a, which represents the modulations on our three-dimensional scale lattice. (Since the strange scale does not appear on the lattice proper, I have added it to the bottom of the graph using dotted lines.) It is also clear why Reich begins with F harmonic major rather than D dorian: by reserving the most dramatic harmonic shift for the end of the phrase, he creates a striking

Figure 9.3.18 (1 of 2) A reduction of Reich's *The Desert Music,* movement 1.

27 This strange scale can be understood as an A♭ diatonic collection with lowered second scale degree; it is somewhat reminiscent of the jazz "altered scale," the fourth mode of the acoustic collection.

Figure 9.3.18 (2 of 2) A reduction of Reich's *The Desert Music*, movement 1.

cadential "brightening"—as if the clouds had suddenly parted to reveal a glittering blue sky, illuminated by a ray of D-dorian sunshine.[28]

The second half of the movement cycles through similar scales while introducing both freely composed choral parts and Reich's trademark rhythmic canons. The canons start in F mixolydian, a scale not previously heard in the piece. The music then articulates a series of single-semitone voice leadings, from F mixolydian to E♭ acoustic to A♭ diatonic and back to E♭ acoustic. From there the modulations become more dramatic as we move to a mode of B acoustic by a four-semitone shift. (This mode, called "F altered" by jazz musicians, is connected to the "strange" scale by two-semitone voice leading; it can be understood as a "normalization" of this earlier scale, since both harmonize the five-note choral chord F-A♭-A-D♭-E♭.) In Figure 9.3.19b, I map this second part on the scale lattice. Once again it is clear that the music moves in a generally descending (flatward) direction, frequently exploiting efficient voice leading between nearby scales. Figure 9.3.19 clarifies at a glance the similarity between the modulations in the two parts of the piece—a relationship that would be rather tedious to describe verbally.

28 It is interesting that for both Reich and Shostakovich, the dorian mode represents a comparatively bright tonality—as if their scalar palette had been shifted toward the darker end of the harmonic spectrum.

Figure 9.3.19 Scales in *The Desert Music*, movement 1. (*a*) The progression of scales from R5–R9, and (*b*) the progression from R20–R44. The progression from R45–54 is the same as that in (*b*), but without B♭ diatonic (F mixolydian).

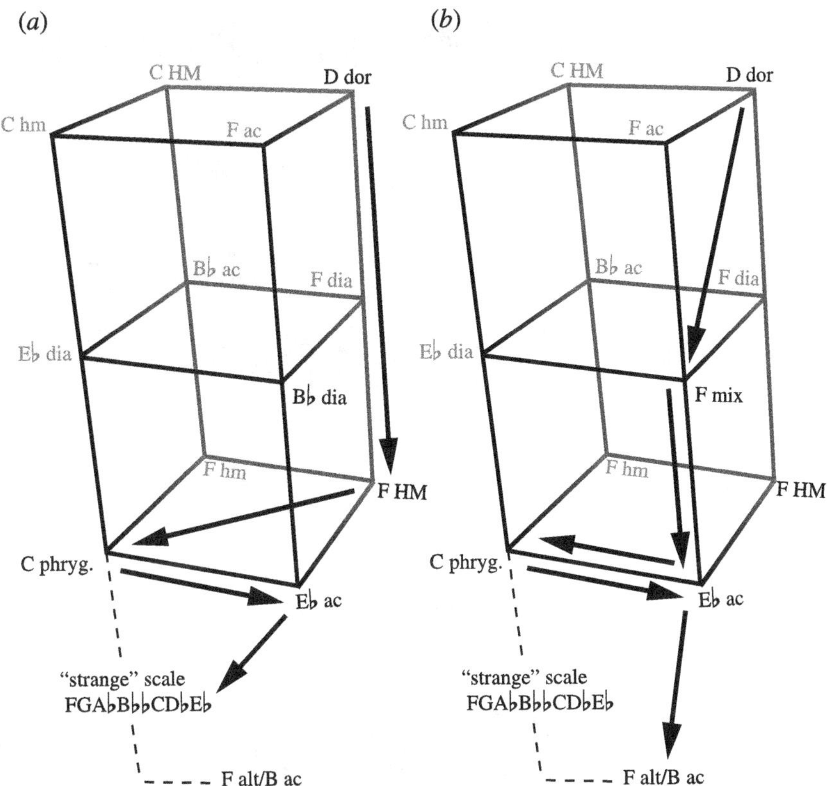

The fifth and final movement of *The Desert Music* returns to these ideas, cycling through the same basic scalar progression eight more times, and ending with the pulsing chords of the opening. The beginning of the movement is particularly interesting: in Figure 9.3.20, I show that it moves between four different modes, each suggesting an E♭ dominant sonority—E♭ acoustic, E♭ mixolydian, E♭ mixolydian ♭6, and E♭ whole tone plus A♭. It is significant that the "whole-tone plus one" scale appears almost exactly as it did in *New York Counterpoint:* tritone motion in the bass transforms a mixolydian ♭6 mode (missing its fourth scale degree) into a "whole-tone plus one" scale sharing six of its seven notes. In fact, Figure 9.3.21 traces the passage on the same graph we used to represent *New York Counterpoint,* showing that it explores very similar harmonic territory. Here we see clear evidence of a common practice linking one Reich piece to another, and more generally to a broader tradition of twentieth-century scalar thinking.

9.3.6 The Who's "I Can't Explain" (1965) and Bob Seger's "Turn the Page" (1973)

Figure 9.3.22a shows the chords in the Who's "I Can't Explain." The verse is constructed around a I–VII–IV progression in E mixolydian, while the chorus is a standard I–vi–IV–V progression in E major. The two parts of the song therefore involve

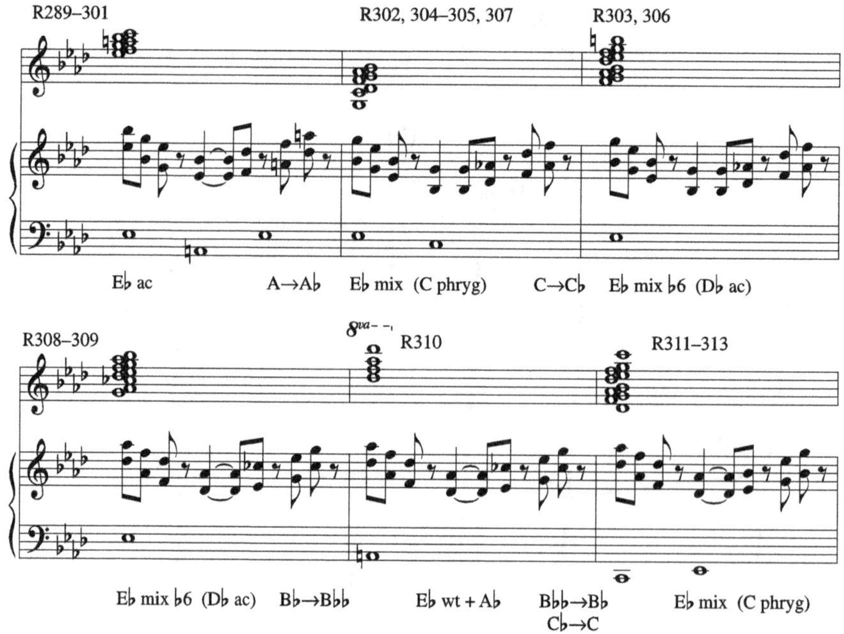

Figure 9.3.20 A summary of the opening *The Desert Music,* movement 5.

Figure 9.3.21 Scales in the opening *The Desert Music,* movement 5.

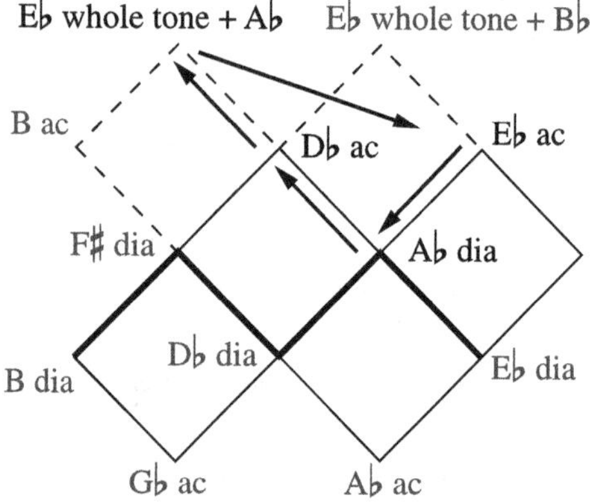

a single-semitone change over a fixed tonic, exactly analogous to the opening of Debussy's "Des pas sur la neige."[29] Bob Seger's "Turn the Page," shown in Figure 9.3.22b, is a kind of dorian-mode dual to The Who's song. The verse contains virtually the same chord progression, i–VII–IV–i, though with a minor tonic rather than major. (Note that The Who's mixolydian and Seger's dorian modes are related by the single-semitone shift G♯→G.) At the end of the chorus, Seger switches briefly to natural minor, employing a standard rock VI–VII–i progression.

29 In Debussy's prelude, the semitonal voice leading B♭→B connects D natural minor to D dorian; here the voice leading D→D♯ connects E mixolydian to E major.

Figure 9.3.22 Scales in The Who's "I Can't Explain" (*a*) and Bob Seger's "Turn the Page" (*b*).

Of course, these two songs have been arbitrarily selected from among thousands that use closely related modes. I cite them chiefly to make the point that the procedures we have been discussing have entered the musical vernacular: not only can they be found in works of self-conscious "art music," but also in film music, jazz, rock, and no doubt in other styles as well. At this point in musical history, it is totally unremarkable to find musicians of virtually any stripe exploiting efficient voice leadings between the full range of diatonic modes. Scale-first composition, in other words, is simply an accepted part of our contemporary tonal language.

9.4 THE SUBSET TECHNIQUE

We now turn to the subset technique, whereby a composer uses scales that all contain some prominent collection of notes. These notes are held fixed and remain stable across scale changes, while the remaining notes are "mobile" and are altered to form a variety of different collections.[30]

9.4.1 Grieg's "Klokkeklang" ("Bell Ringing"), Op. 54 No. 6 (1891)

Figure 9.4.1 presents the opening of the "Klokkeklang," one of Grieg's most unusual and inventive works.[31] Discarding functional harmony in favor of open fifths, the piece creates an austere soundworld that perfectly captures the effect of distant tintinnabulation. The first phrase is in C diatonic, featuring a C-G/F-C drone in the left hand and a series of (mostly) descending parallel fifths in the right. The phrase is comprised of four two-measure groups, each immediately echoed. The first two "echoes" fill in the bare fifths of the right hand with an additional note, forming diatonic triads; in the third "echo" the right hand is transposed down by step, while the ostinato shifts downward by minor third, leading to a cadence on G.

30 Clark (2002) discusses the subset technique in Schubert's music, but applied to chords rather than scales.

31 For another perspective, see Sutcliffe 1996.

Figure 9.4.1 The opening of Grieg's Lyric Piece "Klokkeklang" (Bell Ringing), Op. 54 No. 6.

In the second phrase, outlined by Figure 9.4.2, the ostinato shifts to G-D-A, and the fifths ascend by diatonic third.[32] The echoing process is now extended, with each two-measure idea appearing four times: as in the first phrase, the first echo fills in the bare fifth with an additional note, but the second and third echoes repeat the preceding four measures with added sharps. (This sort of systematicity evokes the algorithmic practice of "change ringing," which in turn anticipates the music of later composers such as Nancarrow, Reich, and Ligeti.) As shown in Figure 9.4.2, the right hand combines with the ostinato bass to form two different diatonic collections: the white-note C diatonic and the two-sharp D diatonic. We can think of the music as containing five "fixed" pitches D-E-G-A-B and two "mobile" pitches F/F♯ and C/C♯.

The end of the phrase brings a surprise: when the white-note collection ascends by thirds to B5, completing the diatonic circle of thirds, its echo adds a G♯ that creates an A diatonic collection. This G♯ clashes with the G♮ and A in the ostinato, creating a mild polytonal dissonance.[33] (It is possible that Grieg meant this G/G♯ clash to evoke the bells' inharmonicity.) The climactic gesture concludes with a long passage in which the fifths descend by diatonic thirds, from E5-B5 to G3–D4. Once again, there is a clash between different forms of a note in different registers: the top note of the gesture (B♮) suggests C diatonic, while the bottom note (B♭) suggests F diatonic. The next two measures present a pair of mysterious sonorities, G minor and F augmented. As shown in Figure 9.4.2, these combine with the ostinato to imply D harmonic minor, here missing only its E♮. The final chord "normalizes" C♯ to C♮, preparing for the recapitulation.

Surveying the whole of Grieg's piece, then, we can say that there are three "fixed" notes (D, A, E) and four "mobile" notes that can appear either inflected or unin-

32 Note that the tonal center shifts to D before the scale itself changes, a possibility discussed in §4.5.

33 As in much polytonal music, the different scales are clearly distinguished by register: all the notes below E5 belong to D diatonic, while those above A2 belong to A diatonic. Furthermore, the wide registral separation between the G♯5 in the right hand and the clashing G3 in the left ameliorates the sense of dissonance, creating a sense of independent auditory streams, each with its own macroharmony.

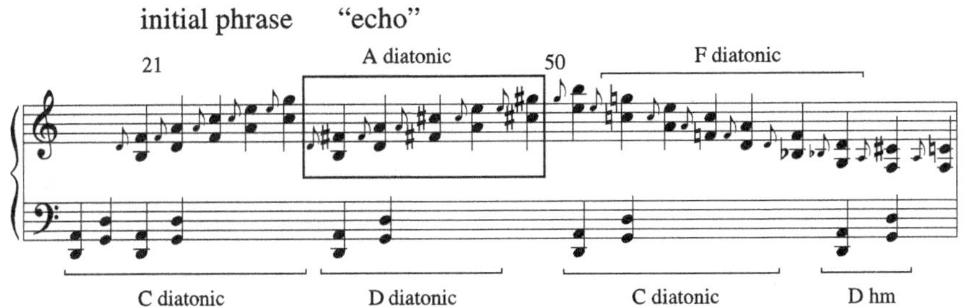

Figure 9.4.2 A reduction of the central section of "Klokkeklang."

flected (B♭/B, F/F♯, C/C♯, and G/G♯). The play of inflections suggests a variety of different scalar collections, each stated fairly explicitly: C diatonic, D diatonic, A diatonic, F diatonic, and D melodic minor. (Figure 9.4.3 shows that these five collections are all contained within two adjacent cubes of the scale lattice.) The piece progresses from a neutral "white-note" state in which all notes appear uninflected, to a climactic section in which all four inflections are presented within the span of eleven measures (mm. 43–53). Interestingly, the B section begins by contrasting two scales that are close but not adjacent on the lattice (C and D diatonic), with the separation increasing as the music progresses: D diatonic moves sharpward to A diatonic, while C diatonic moves flatward to F diatonic, and thence to the nondiatonic D harmonic minor (see the arrows in Figure 9.4.3). This progression brings to mind a pistol duel, in which the participants begin back to back and walk several paces away from each other.

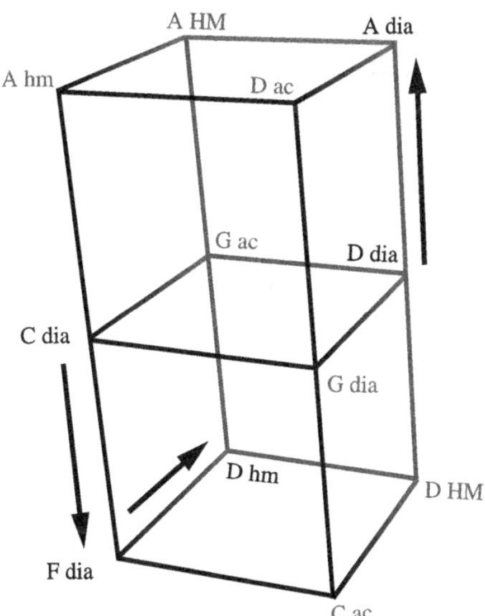

Figure 9.4.3 Scales in "Klokkeklang."

9.4.2 "Petit Airs," from Stravinsky's *Histoire du Soldat* (1918)

Stravinsky's "Petit airs au bord du ruisseau" exhibits an easygoing folksiness, depicting a wandering soldier relaxing by a brook, enjoying his newfound (and hard-to-tune) fiddle. On the surface, the music would seem to have nothing to do with Grieg's austere tone painting. But when we dig deeper, we find that there are interesting resemblances between the pieces, beginning with their ostinati: the double bass in "Petit airs" plays a "walking" motif G-D-A-G that outlines the same three pitch classes as those in the B section of Grieg's "Klokkeklang" (Figure 9.4.4). As in Grieg's piece, Stravinsky seems to divide his pitch material into "fixed" notes that always appear in the same form (G-D-A-E-B) and "mobile" notes that can either be inflected or uninflected (F/F♯, C/C♯). Not surprisingly, Stravinsky juxtaposes these "mobile" notes

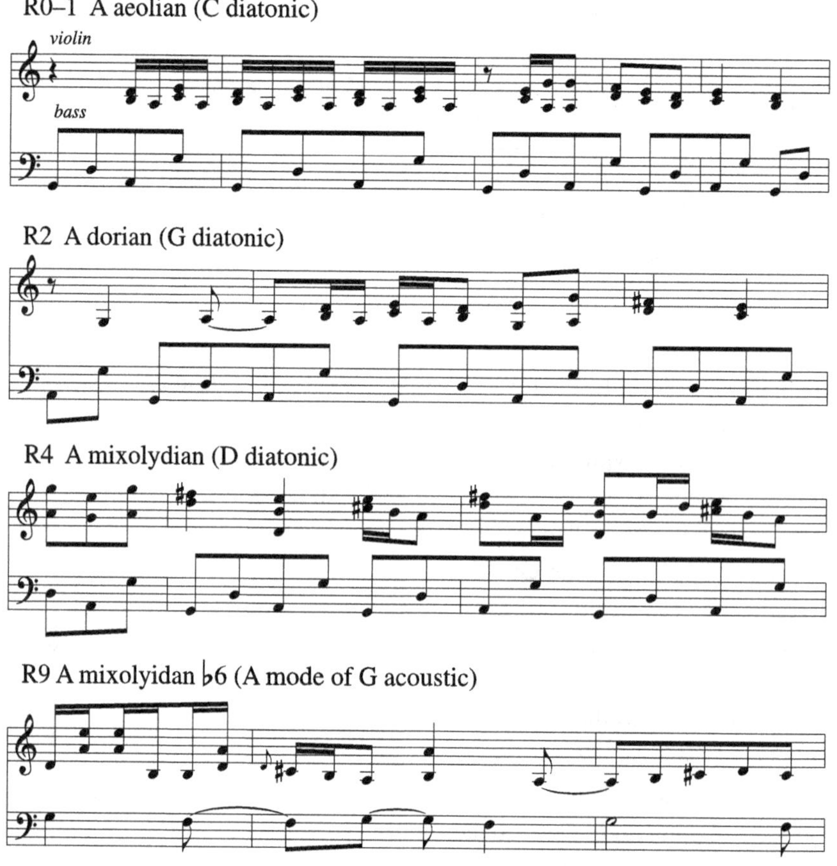

Figure 9.4.4 Scales in Stravinsky's "Petit airs," from *Histoire du soldat.*

more freely than Grieg, often assigning different accidentals to different instruments: for instance, in mm. 29–37, shown in Figure 5.6.9, the clarinet and bassoon play in D diatonic while the violin adds F♮ and C♮, creating two tonally distinct "strata." Polytonality, which occurs only fleetingly in "Klokkeklang," is much more pervasive in Stravinsky.

There are four familiar scales that contain the five "fixed" notes, and they can all be represented by a square face of our scale lattice (Figure 9.4.5). Like Grieg, Stravinsky systematically explores the scales that can be constructed in this way. Figure 9.4.4 shows that each of the collections appears prominently in "Petit airs." Particularly noteworthy are mm. 53–60, which present an explicit statement of the G acoustic collection. (See the bottom system of Figure 9.4.4.) This nondiatonic scale acts somewhat like Grieg's D harmonic minor, providing a striking point of contrast with the surrounding diatonic and polytonal music.

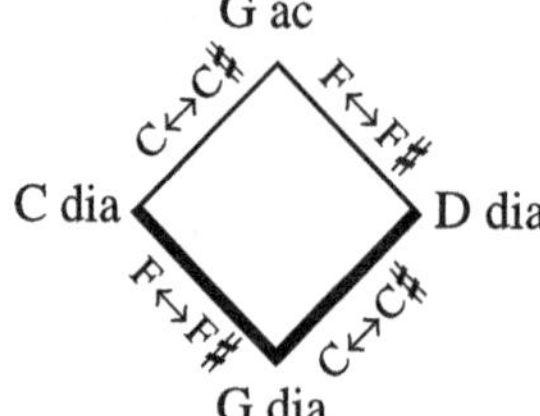

Figure 9.4.5 "Petit Airs" uses the diatonic and acoustic scales combining F/F♯ and C/C♯.

9.4.3 Reich's *City Life* (1995)

The third movement of Steve Reich's *City Life* features a repeating ostinato built upon the fifth D-A. The movement is divided into three sections, each beginning with the sampled words "It's been a honeymoon." (The unhappy tone of the sampled voice creates a striking contrast with the text's meaning.) After about 20 seconds, the remaining instruments enter, filling out the D-A fifth with scale fragments. Figure 9.4.6 shows that these fragments suggest D lydian, the fourth mode of A harmonic minor, and D mixolydian. Reich's music therefore exemplifies, in a particularly obvious and systematic fashion, the same procedures at work in both Grieg and Stravinsky. Once again, we have a set of "fixed" scale degrees stacked in fifths, filled out by additional "mobile" degrees that appear in a variety of forms.[34]

The resemblances among Grieg's "Klokkeklang," Stravinsky's "Petit airs," and Reich's *City Life* might initially seem to be completely fortuitous, purely superficial similarities with no deeper significance. But in fact, there are important historical and musical connections among the three composers. At a purely musical level, all three were interested in exploring alternatives to functional harmony, while stopping short of complete atonality. In particular, all three embraced a wide variety of scales and modes, and devised creative ways to generalize traditional modulatory procedures.[35] And then there are specific historical connections as well: Grieg was an important influence on Ravel, whose music in turn was important to Stravinsky; and both Stravinsky and impressionism influenced the language of jazz, which was in turn important to Reich.[36] So it should perhaps not be terribly surprising to find these three composers mining similar musical territory.

Indeed, it would not be too surprising even if there were no historical connections among them. For as we have seen in Part I, the familiar scales of the Western tradition—such as the diatonic, acoustic, and harmonic scales—are in many ways natural objects of musical exploration. Furthermore, the idea of writing music that exploits scales containing a particular fixed subset is reasonably intuitive, and we can well imagine each composer happening upon it independently. Thus, rather than considering the resemblances among our three pieces to be insignificant coin-

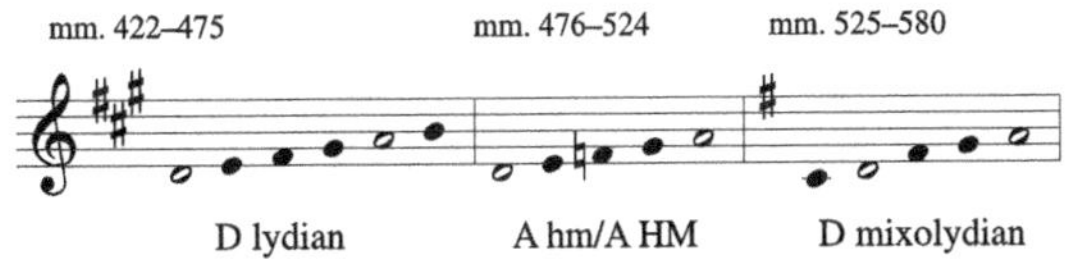

Figure 9.4.6 A summary of Steve Reich's *City Life*, movement 3.

34 Reich's movement again uses the "diatonic rhythm" {0, 2, 4, 5, 7, 9, 11}. The music opens by setting this rhythm in canon with itself at a distance of an eighth note. This is analogous to combining the C and D major scales, and leads to five shared attacks. Later in the piece, the canonic distance increases to a quarter note, analogous to combining C and E diatonic collections, which decreases the number of shared attacks to three. The music thus exhibits a common Reichian technique of moving from relative rhythmic alignment toward increased disalignment. See Cohn 1992.

35 See Tymoczko 1997, 2002, 2003a, 2006.

36 See, among many other sources, Herresthal 2005 and Strickland 2000.

cidences, I prefer to think of them as symptomatic of shared musical concerns crossing stylistic boundaries.

9.4.4 The Beatles' "Help" (1965) and Stravinsky's "Dance of the Adolescents" (1913)

In "Help!," John Lennon's lead vocal largely confines itself to the first five pitches of the A major scale, with a sixth note (F♯) appearing only in the song's introduction (Figure 9.4.7). This simple melody, almost obsessive in its repetitiveness, becomes a fixed set of pitches that are contextualized within two different scales, A major and A mixolydian. Here timbre reinforces the distinction between the fixed subset and the mobile pitches: the lead vocal confines itself to the fixed notes, while both the guitar and backup vocals articulate the mobile pair G/G♯. (Note that the resulting scales, A major and A mixolydian are the only two diatonic collections containing the fixed pitches.) Particularly interesting is the mixolydian cadence that accompanies the lead vocal D→C♯: in the key of A major, melodic D→C♯ would likely be harmonized with V^7–I; in "Help!," however, this archetypal schema is replaced by a striking modal progression in pure major triads, D–G–A. (This technique, whereby common melodic schemas are modally reharmonized in pure triads, seems characteristic of the Beatles in particular and rock music more generally.) Note also that the opening progression b–G–E^7, familiar from §3.10, links three chords that share the notes B and D; it again introduces the seventh chord precisely when the root motion changes from major third to minor third.

Stravinsky's "Dance of the Adolescents" uses a somewhat more abstract version of the same technique, in which it is not particular notes that are held fixed, but rather more abstract intervallic patterns. The scales in Figure 9.4.8a share the major pentachord {G, A, B, C, D}, and hence are related by the subset technique. Those in Figure 9.4.8b do *not* share any five-note subset; nevertheless, they are audibly similar by virtue of the fact that they all contain *some* major pentachord—that is, they contain a five-note segment that is transpositionally equivalent to {G, A, B, C, D}. Just as two major scales sound very similar, by virtue of being transpositionally related, so too do these scales sound *somewhat* similar by virtue of the fact that they contain large, transpositionally related subsets. (Or to put it another way, the scales all contain the

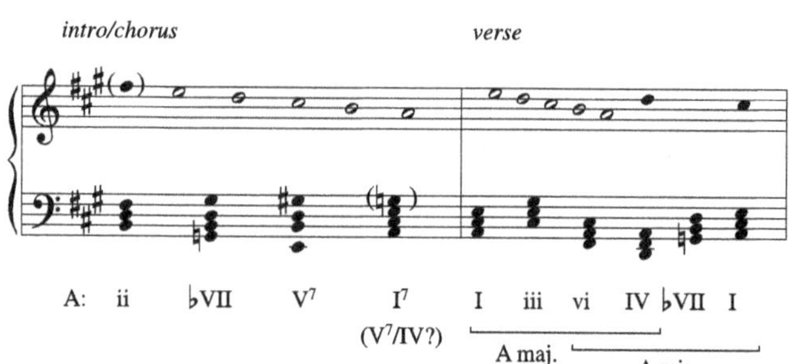

Figure 9.4.7 A sketch of the Beatles song "Help!" The upper staff contains the notes in the lead vocal line, while the lower staff outlines the harmonies.

Figure 9.4.8 The subset technique in its concrete (*a*) and abstract (*b*) forms.

interval pattern 2-2-1-2.) This is particularly true when the composer chooses to emphasize these subsets in some salient way.

In the "Dance of the Adolescents," the major pentachord forms the basis of the folksy theme shown in Figure 9.4.9. (Here A is the tonic, suggesting natural minor or dorian.[37]) The theme can be embedded within familiar scales in three ways: we can add E and F, producing A aeolian; we can add E and F♯, producing A dorian; or we can add E♭ and F, producing the "locrian ♯2" mode of F acoustic.[38] These scales can then be transposed to produce three general modal categories, aeolian, dorian, and locrian ♯2. Figure 9.4.10 shows that the folksy theme appears in each of these modal contexts in the second half of the "Dance of the Adolescents."[39] Since each of our three mode types appears at least once, we can say that Stravinsky exhaustively exploits the various ways of embedding his theme in familiar modal contexts.

Though it might again seem fanciful to compare Stravinsky to the Beatles, the resemblance is upon reflection relatively clear. Both "Help!" and "The Dance of the Adolescents" exploit melodic material that is deliberately simple or even primitive. Indeed, in both pieces the fixed material is remarkably similar, with the fixed pitches being A-B-C♯-D-E-(F♯) in "Help!" and the fixed intervallic pattern being 2-2-1-2

Figure 9.4.9 The folk-like melody used in the "Dance of the Adolescents."

37 This folksy melody seems to be original to Stravinsky. For an extended discussion of Stravinsky's borrowings, see Chapter 12 of Taruskin 1996.

38 A fourth possibility combines E♭ and F♯, producing a mode of G harmonic major; here, however, the augmented second is melodically awkward. The three possibilities in the main text represent the only way to embed the theme in a scale whose steps are at most two semitones large, and whose thirds are at least three semitones large (§4.4).

39 In each case, the music also adds some characteristically Stravinskian polytonal elements, such as bassoon trills foreign to the underlying scale; nevertheless, the underlying scales are fairly clear. Note also that consecutive scales, such as G locrian ♯2, B♭ dorian, and B♭ natural minor, are often linked by minimal voice-leading. Interestingly, Stravinsky uses both of the single-semitonal voice leadings connecting acoustic and diatonic scales, one of which preserves the fixed subset (R31–32) and one of which does not (R25–27).

Figure 9.4.10 Stravinsky presents his folk-like melody in five scalar contexts.

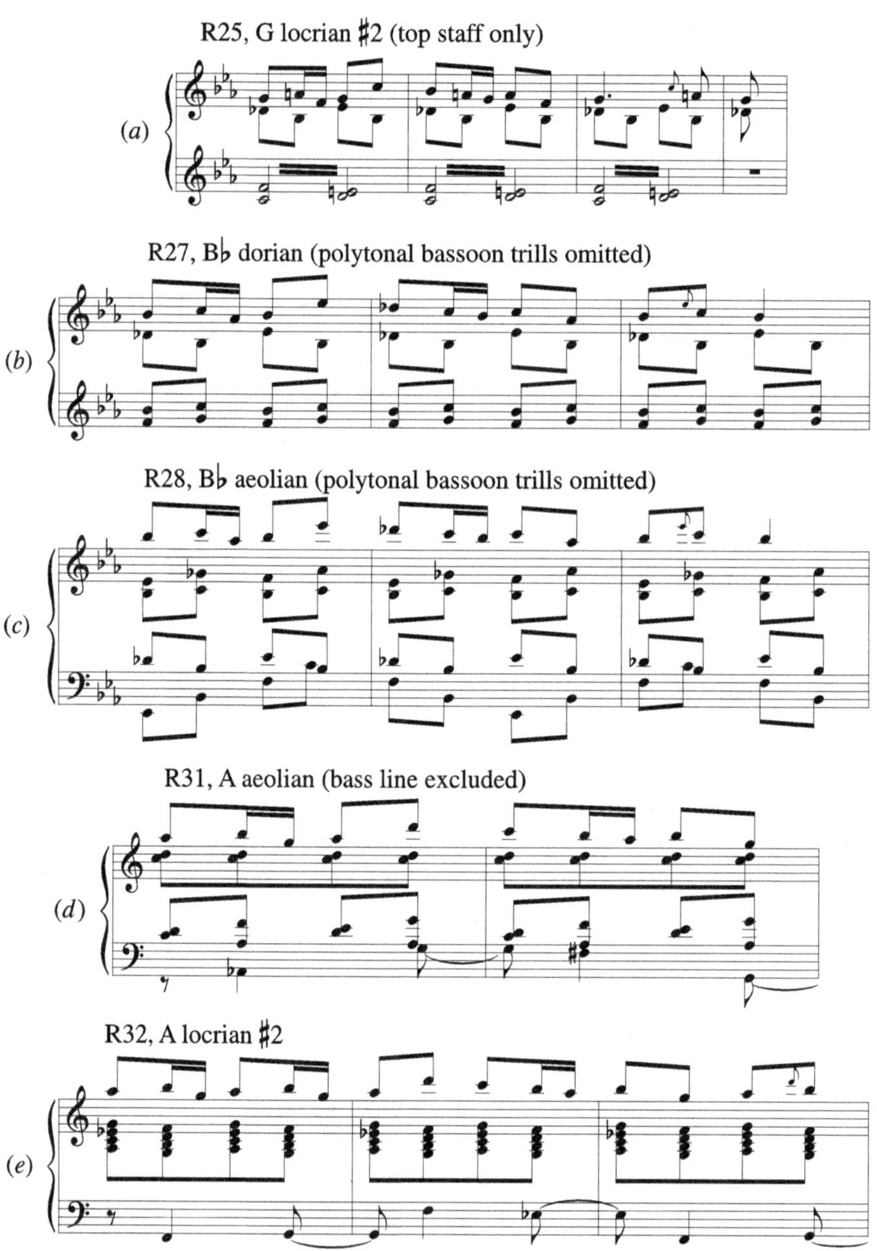

in "Dance of the Adolescents." Both pieces contextualize this simple melodic material within musical textures that are anything but primitive, adding sophisticated harmonies, countermelodies, and orchestrational embellishments. (In fact, both pieces use Debussyian parallel triads, the first in the chorus's vocal harmonies, the second in the orchestral wash.) And both pieces use an expanded scalar vocabulary in which scalar and chromatic transposition are available, and in which ionian and mixolydian are more or less on equal footing. (Note that by ignoring transposition and centricity, we can see that both pieces augment their "fixed" pitches in essentially similar ways, extending A-B-C♯-D-E with either G or G♯ to form two different diatonic collections.) All of which is just to say that both pieces make relatively straightforward use of the possibilities afforded by an expanded scalar vocabulary.

9.4.5 The Miles Davis Group's "Freedom Jazz Dance" (1966)

We'll close with what might seem like a trivial example of the subset technique, one in which the shared collection is a perfect fifth—or maybe just a single note. The Miles Davis Group's "Freedom Jazz Dance," from the album *Miles Smiles*, consists in a series of improvisations over a static B♭ harmony. Although one might casually say that the piece is "in B♭," this description masks an important subtlety: it is actually in a *variety* of B♭s, since the soloists interpret the tonic drone differently. The piece thus provides an interesting improvisational counterpart to the precomposed music we have been considering.

Since it would take us too far afield to discuss the entire piece, a few brief remarks must suffice. The bass line, played by Ron Carter, is based on B♭ and often features fourths-based riffs such as F-E♭-B♭. The harmonic accompaniment, played by Herbie Hancock, often uses chords such as E-B♭-E♭, drawn from the blues scale on B♭ (B♭-D♭-E♭-E♮-F-A♭). Hancock's relatively sparse accompaniment leaves the soloists plenty of freedom, and they respond by "coloring" the B♭ drone in a variety of ways. Figure 9.4.11 provides a series of excerpts from the solos, showing that the improvisers play a number of familiar scales—B♭ natural minor, B♭ melodic minor ascending, B♭ mixolydian, B♭ acoustic, A♭ harmonic minor, and the B♭-C♭ octatonic scale. (Of course, there is also a lot of nonscalar playing in the piece as well.) From the standpoint of the current chapter, the interesting point is that the Miles Davis Group's notion of "being in B♭," like Debussy's notion of being "in D," is general enough to encompass natural minor, dorian, the acoustic scale, and even the octatonic. In other words, the relevant conception of tonality is not the major-minor system of the eighteenth and nineteenth centuries, but rather the extended scalar system of the twentieth.

9.5 CONCLUSION: COMMON SCALES, COMMON TECHNIQUES

In this chapter, we have seen numerous appearances of scales such as the acoustic and octatonic. When I first started thinking seriously about twentieth-century tonality, I was amazed to find so many different composers using such similar scales. Why do these collections reappear in so many different styles? Was there a kind of underground commerce in scales, with composers cluing each other in to their most important discoveries? Did Debussy and Stravinsky talk scales and modes during their conversations in Paris? Did George Gershwin teach impressionist techniques to the early beboppers? Did Steve Reich learn the "altered scale" from some jazz harmony book? The alternative, that so many different composers had *independently*

Figure 9.4.11 Excerpts from the solos in the Miles Davis Group's version of "Freedom Jazz Dance." Miles Davis favors traditional B♭ minor scales, Wayne Shorter makes heavy use of B♭ acoustic, and Herbie Hancock uses even more exotic octatonic and harmonic minor scales. (Asterisks indicate notes outside the scale.)

found their way to the same basic collections, seemed even more improbable: for how could so much haphazard investigation converge on such similar outcomes?

Now, of course, this strikes me as considerably less surprising. Although there may have been some composer-to-composer commerce in scales, we can explain the convergence without it. After all, one of the main claims of Chapter 4 is that traditional scales are overdetermined, with a variety of different considerations pointing toward the same basic scalar collections—*viz.* familiar scales divide the octave relatively evenly, contain large numbers of consonant intervals, avoid consecutive semitones while having relatively small gaps between their successive notes, and are generally optimal from a variety of independent perspectives. Thus we should not be astonished to find composers of different stylistic proclivities using octatonic or acoustic scales. *Of course* composers would independently find their way to these collections—much in the way that different mountain climbers tend to follow the most obvious routes up a particular cliff.

This is not to say that these scales are the only important ones, or that all twentieth-century tonal music makes use of them. Some tonal composers, including Messiaen and Shostakovich, constructed idiosyncratic scales that do not possess the virtues I have highlighted. (Messiaen used seven symmetrical "modes of limited transposition" whereas Shostakovich sometimes constructed ad hoc modes out of octatonic and other scale fragments.) Others—particularly "neoclassical" composers—eschewed nondiatonic scales in favor of a pervasive (and occasionally somewhat brittle) diatonicism. Still others created polytonal effects by superimposing multiple scales at the same time, leading to musical textures poised delicately between tonality and atonality. There is plenty of variety in twentieth-century tonal music, with scalar procedures playing only one part in an ensemble cast.

Nevertheless, it is striking that at least three major twentieth-century tonal styles—impressionism, jazz, and postminimalism—make use of the same basic collection of nondiatonic scales and modes. These scales, along with the three techniques in this chapter, constitute a twentieth-century "common practice" that is larger than any particular tonal composer, and indeed than any particular tonal style. Although the outlines of this common practice may be less clear than the outlines of earlier common practices, its very existence indicates that the difference between the nineteenth and twentieth centuries is more a matter of degree than of kind. The naive contrast between nineteenth-century homogeneity and twentieth-century individualism is misleading: if there is an enormous harmonic gulf between Mussorgsky and Johann Strauss, then there are also interesting threads of continuity between Debussy, jazz, and Reich. Indeed, I would go so far as to say that the scales and techniques described in this chapter represent the single most interesting example of a twentieth-century tonal common practice—one that results not just from conscious imitation, but also from a simultaneous convergence on an intrinsically fertile territory.

CHAPTER 10

Jazz

This last chapter reviews some central features of jazz harmony, emphasizing connections with earlier styles. For reasons of space, I focus on a collection of ideas that evolved in the late 1950s and early 1960s, and that now form a kind of *lingua franca* for contemporary improvisers. My goal is to show that jazz synthesizes the contrapuntal preoccupations of late nineteenth-century chromaticism with the scale-based procedures of early twentieth-century modernism, creating a contemporary "common practice." This common practice has influenced composers such as Steve Reich and John Adams, resulting in a network of relationships that cross the boundaries between notated and non-notated music (sometimes called "serious" and "popular"). Given these pervasive influences, it is reasonable to wonder whether we make too much of the boundaries between styles: if jazz is both inheritor of early modernism and progenitor of late twentieth-century postminimalism, then at what cost do we segregate it from "legitimate" concert music? My answer is that the cost is large indeed. We can obtain a full picture of twentieth-century tonality only by considering notated and non-notated music as part of an integral tradition.[1]

In saying this, I do not mean to efface the obvious differences between improvised and notated music, but rather to suggest that we sometimes take these differences too seriously. Ask yourself whether a highly avant-garde composer like Xenakis is more or less like Debussy than is an improvising musician like Bill Evans. True, both Xenakis and Debussy use notation, but once we move past this fact there are few similarities in their specific approaches to melody, harmony, and rhythm. Meanwhile, Bill Evans is an improviser who self-consciously borrowed ideas from impressionism, whose chords and scales relate to Debussy's in very clear ways, and who helped transmit certain musical techniques from Debussy to late-twentieth-century tonal composers. From this point of view, it seems short-sighted to say that Schoenberg, Xenakis, and Lachenmann "belong with" Grieg and Debussy, simply because they all happen to use musical notation. To say so is to fetishize superficial resemblances at the expense of more profound and purely musical connections.

1 For an alternative approach, see Taruskin 2005, which attempts to treat the notated tradition in isolation from other styles.

10.1 BASIC JAZZ VOICINGS

Basic jazz harmony derives from an elementary voice-leading schema first described in Chapter 7, in which fifth-related diatonic seventh chords are connected by descending stepwise voice leading. Figure 10.1.1 moves the schema up by diatonic third, so that it connects the four *upper voices* of a series of ninth chords. Here we have a five-voice passage in which the bass leaps while the upper voices move by step. Figure 10.1.1c embellishes this pattern once more, suspending the ninth of the ii^9 chord into the dominant and replacing the seventh of the tonic sonority with a sixth.[2] The resulting chords are fundamental to modern jazz, and are sometimes called the A and B "left hand" voicings, as they leave the pianist's right hand free to improvise (Figure 10.1.2).

Figure 10.1.1 (*a*) A basic nineteenth-century voice-leading schema, linking fifth-related diatonic triads by stepwise voice leading. (*b*) The same schema, now interpreted as the upper four voices of a sequence of ninth chords. (*c*) A variant that suspends the ninth of the ii chord into V, forming a thirteenth; the note B in the C^{maj9} chord is also replaced with A, so that all four upper voices move down by step from V to I.

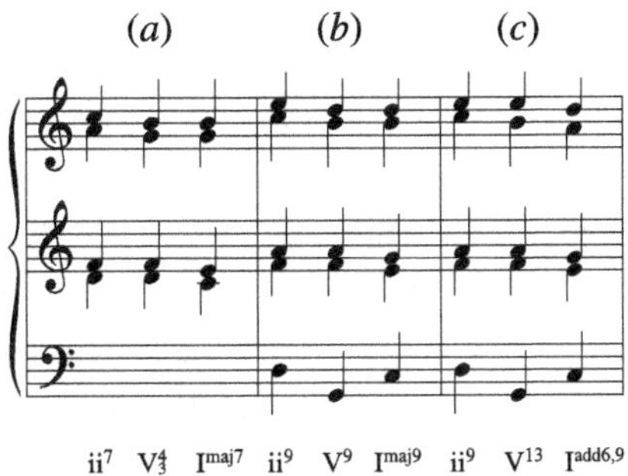

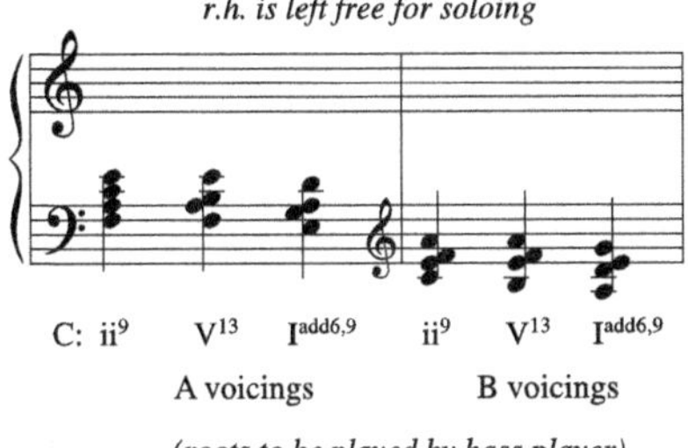

Figure 10.1.2 The "left hand voicings" in their A and B forms.

2 The form E-G-B-D does appear, though E-G-A-D seems to be preferred. (See McGowan 2005 on "dialects of consonance" in jazz.) This preference is sometimes attributed to the desire to avoid the minor ninth that can result when a melodic C is played above the chordal B. However, the change may also reflect the fact that the voicing E-G-A-D is a diatonic "fourth chord"(§10.2). Relevant here is the fact that a diatonic seventh chord like E-G-B-D is already somewhat "fourthy," as it contains two component fourths (B-E and D-G) and can be written as a stack of fourths with one missing note (that is, as B-E-[A]-D-G). When substituting E-G-A-D for E-G-B-D, a jazz musician can use efficient voice leading to change E-B into E-A, heightening the fourthiness without drastically changing the sound of the chord.

Since each of these chords contains all but two of the notes in the diatonic scale, jazz pedagogues sometimes describe chord voicings negatively, by identifying the diatonic notes that a particular chord should *not* contain: for example, they say that a ii voicing can contain any diatonic note except the leading tone; that a V voicing can contain any diatonic note except the tonic; and that the I voicing can contain any diatonic note except the fourth scale degree. These forbidden tones are sometimes called "avoid" notes, indicating that they should be avoided if a chord is to have a particular harmonic function.[3] The underlying idea is that there are certain basic voice-leading motions that are essential to defining harmonic function: the introduction of scale degree 4 as one moves from tonic to predominant, the resolution $\hat{1}\rightarrow\hat{7}$ as one moves from predominant to dominant, and the resolution $\hat{4}\rightarrow\hat{3}$ coupled with the return of scale degree 1, as one progresses from dominant to tonic (Figure 10.1.3). "Avoid notes" obscure this skeleton by introducing certain notes prematurely. (For instance, including the leading tone in the ii chord tends to blur the difference between predominant and dominant, just as including the tonic note in V tends to blur the difference between dominant and tonic.) The advantage is that this approach conveys the freedom inherent in jazz: as long as the fundamental voice-leading skeleton is reasonably clear, notes can be freely added without disturbing the effect of functional harmony.[4] Indeed, even the basic voice-leading skeleton can sometimes be slightly obscured, as in Figure 10.1.4.

Figure 10.1.3 The basic voice-leading structure of the ii–V–I. As long as these contrapuntal motions are clear, the schema can be embellished with a large variety of additional notes.

This sort of harmonic flexibility would lead to incoherence, were it not for several important facts. First, jazz makes extremely heavy use of root position chords, providing unambiguous clues as to a chord's identity.[5]

Figure 10.1.4 The schema in Figure 10.1.3 need not always be presented in its entirety. In (*a*) the root of the V chord is transposed by tritone; while in (*b*) the leading tone is absent from the V chord. In both examples, the open noteheads show tones involved in the basic schema of Figure 10.1.3.

3 The term "avoid note" is often associated with Mark Levine (1989), though he says he heard it at Berklee in the 1950s.

4 It is interesting that the ascending semitonal resolution of the leading tone, so central to classical harmonic practice, is *not* among the basic voice-leading motions in jazz.

5 Temperley (2007) makes the same point.

Second, where classical composers use many highly similar chord progressions (such as I–IV–vii°–I and I–ii–V–I), jazz musicians tend to use the ii–V–I schema almost to the exclusion of the others. This prevents confusion between chords with closely related pitch content. Third, jazz tunes typically repeat the same chord progressions over and over, giving listeners many opportunities to identify a tune's harmonic structure. Furthermore, many jazz compositions reuse the same progressions: ostensibly distinct tunes like "Oleo," "Anthropology," and "Rhythm-a-ning," all use the chord progression from George Gershwin's "I Got Rhythm"; while others, including "Au Privave," "Blue Monk," and "Collard Greens and Black-Eyed Peas," use variants on the standard blues progression. (In fact, the blues and "rhythm changes" together account for a substantial fraction of the jazz repertoire.) Taken together, these simplifications make it much easier to identify jazz harmonies. And because listeners have a pretty good idea what chord is coming, improvisers can be correspondingly free in their harmonic embellishments.

Not surprisingly, the preceding ideas can sometimes be useful for analyzing twentieth-century notated music.[6] Figure 10.1.5 shows several classical anticipations of the jazz A and B voicings, while Figure 10.1.6 shows a series of six- and seven-note chord voicings, all avoiding precisely the notes that jazz pedagogy recommends. Furthermore, twentieth-century composers have a noticeable tendency to place the root in the bass of "extended" chords: pieces like Debussy's "Sirènes" and Reich's *The Desert Music,* for

Figure 10.1.5 A and B voicings in classical music. (*a*) Ravel, "Forlane" from *Le tombeau de Couperin*, m. 130, presenting the A voicings on V and IV (upper staff). (*b*) Grieg's Lyric Piece "Salon," Op. 65 No. 4, m. 1 outlines the dominant B voicing with its ascending sixteenth notes. (*c*) The same piece has a variant of the A dominant voicing, in which the root of the chord replaces the ninth. (*d*) Scriabin's Etude, Op. 65 No. 3. The four highest notes of the G^7 chord outline an A voicing.

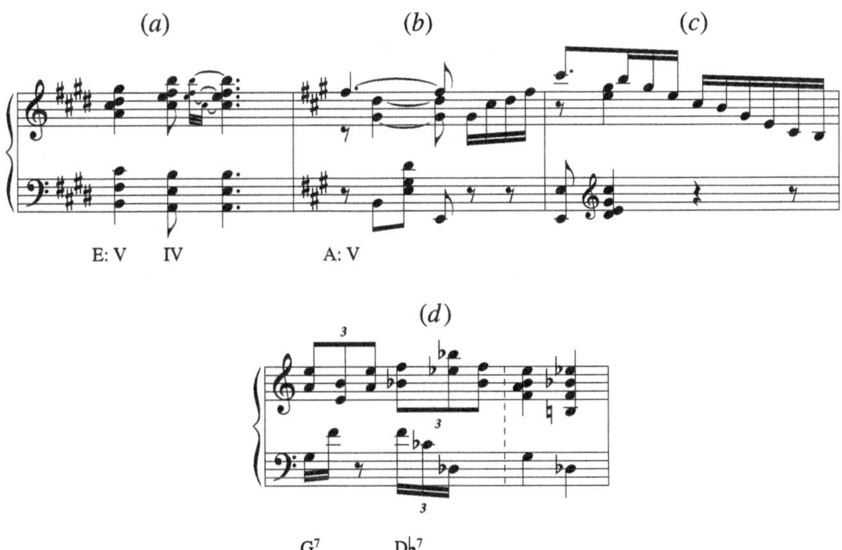

6 See Tymoczko 1997, 2002, and 2003.

Figure 10.1.6 Concert-music chords that omit the jazz "avoid notes." The first three examples present tonic voicings that omit the fourth above the root. (*a*) Debussy's "Sirènes," m. 8. (*b*) Ravel *Jeux d'eau*, m.1 (*c*) Reich, *Different Trains*, movement 1. (*d*) A ii^{11}–$\mathrm{V}^{\mathrm{sus}}$–I in Ravel's "Rigaudon," from *Le tombeau de Couperin*, mm. 1–2. The dominant voicing is a suspended chord, analogous to Figure 10.1.4b; as in jazz practice, the leading tone becomes the "avoid note" in the suspended chord. (*e*) An extended predominant in Ravel's *Pavane pour une infante défunte*, mm. 67–68. (*f*) Altered dominant chords in the opening of Reich's *The Desert Music*, movement 1, all conspicuously omitting the fourth above the root. (*g*) Debussy, *Prelude to "The Afternoon of a Faun,"* R10, is similar.

example, consist largely of extended root position dominant chords, embellished with sevenths, ninths, and other tones.[7] We should not, of course, be too surprised by such correspondences, both because of the historical connections between notated music and jazz, and because many of these principles are tantamount to common sense: it is only natural, when using extended sonorities, to want to avoid harmonic confusion by placing the root in the bass; just as it is only natural to want to clarify harmonic function by avoiding the tonic note in dominant voicings.

---

7 Some of the ideas in this section have been explored by Dan Harrison (1994) in the context of late nineteenth-century music. Like jazz pedagogues, Harrison argues that a chord with a prominent leading tone and fifth scale degree can often be interpreted as a dominant chord, no matter what other notes it contains. However, he diverges from jazz pedagogy by interpreting tonal harmony as fundamentally triadic, and by taking IV to be the characteristic predominant. McGowan 2005 adapts Harrison's ideas to a jazz context.

10.2 FROM THIRDS TO FOURTHS

Traditional tonal theory teaches that harmonies are generated by extending thirds upward from the root. But as chords grow larger, their identity as stacks of thirds becomes less and less determinate. Postwar jazz musicians exploit this fact to reconceive traditional chords as quartal rather than tertian in origin: for example, Figure 10.2.1 rearranges the dominant and tonic A voicings as stacks of diatonic fourths, producing a distinctively modern feel. (A pianist might play these voicings when accompanying a soloist; guitarists—whose instruments are tuned in fourths—play them as a matter of course.) As shown in the figure, each voicing can be extended upward by one or two fourths before encountering an avoid note.

These quartal voicings suggest that we might want to look for a fourth-based predominant voicing as well. The most common option here, shown in Figure 10.2.2, is called the "'So What' chord," since it appears prominently in Bill Evans' playing on the Miles Davis tune of the same name. The "'So What' chord" consists of three perfect fourths and one major third, and is often encountered in the form shown in Figure 10.2.2b, with the lowest note doubled in the soprano. (Guitar players will recognize this as the open strings of the guitar, tuned down a major second.) We, of course, recognize the chord as a stack of two-step intervals in the pentatonic scale. If we begin on a different pentatonic note—as in Figure 10.2.2c—we obtain all the various chords that insert a major third into a sequence of five perfect fourths. (In each case, the chord exhausts the notes of a pentatonic scale.) Figure 10.2.3 combines a "'So What' chord" with quartal V–I voicings to produce a fourth-based version of the ii–V–I schema. Such quartal voicings have been important to jazz since the 1950s, and many pianists play three-note quartal voicings as a matter of course. Often associated with McCoy Tyner, they create an "open" feel that evokes the sound world of Stravinsky, Bartók, and Hindemith.[8]

Not surprisingly, the trend toward quartal voicings goes hand in hand with an increasing use of melodic fourths in solos. Passages in melodic fourths can occasionally be found in the recordings of the 1940s, particularly by musicians associated with Lennie Tristano, but they become much more common in the early 1960s, largely

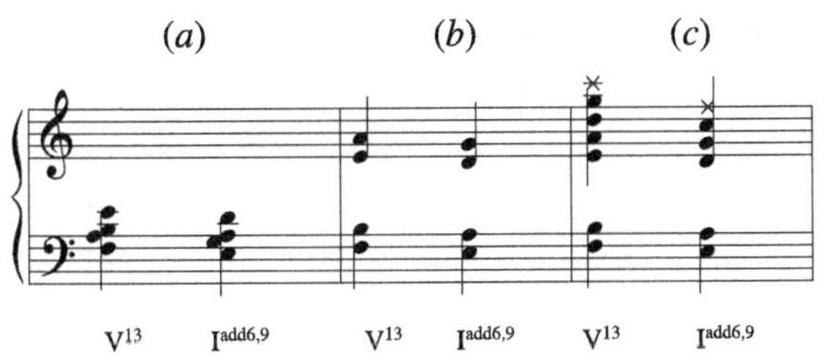

Figure 10.2.1 The dominant and tonic A voicings reinterpreted as stacks of fourths. In (*c*) the stacks are extended until they reach an "avoid note."

8 Scriabin's "mystic chord" is often voiced as a stack of acoustic scale fourths: C-F♯-B♭-E-A-D. Fourths appear prominently in Stravinsky (*Firebird Suite* [1919], "Infernal Dance," R26), Bartók (*Out of Doors*, movement 2), and Hindemith (*Ludus Tonalis*).

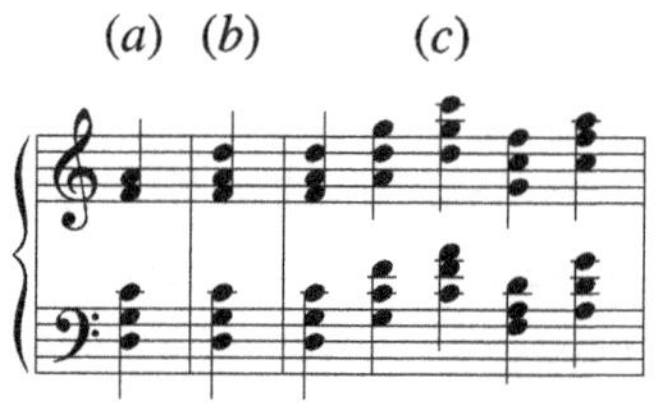

Figure 10.2.2 Quartal predominant voicings. (*a*) The "So What" voicing. (*b*) The same voicing with the bass note doubled in the soprano. This is a complete stack of pentatonic thirds: **D**-F-**G**-A-**C**-D-**F**-G-**A**-C-**D**. (*c*) Other inversions of the "'So What' chord" begin the stack of thirds on a different note of the F pentatonic scale. Each voicing has four perfect fifths and one four-semitone "near fifth."

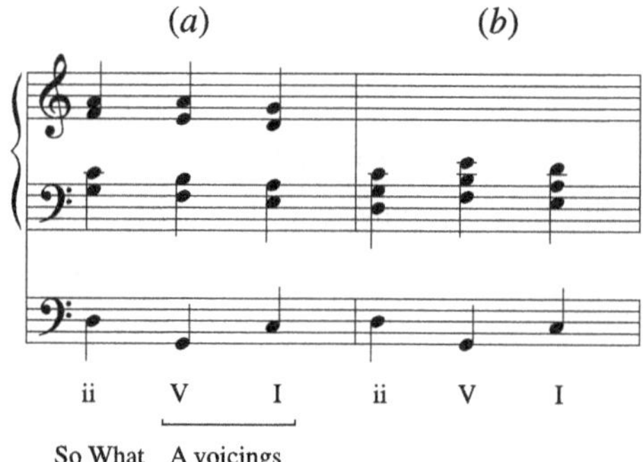

Figure 10.2.3 Quartal ii–V–I voicings played with both hands (*a*) and with the left hand alone (*b*).

through the influence of the John Coltrane Quartet. One way to create quartal melodies is to use small collections of notes that are themselves stacks of fourths: by randomly selecting notes from among a small stack-of-fourths collection, one will obtain a high proportion of fourths, allowing the improviser a degree of melodic freedom while still ensuring that the resulting music will sound reasonably "fourthy."[9] Figure 10.2.4a presents a passage from the fifth chorus of Keith Jarrett's solo on "You and the Night and the Music" (from *At the Deer Head Inn*) in which the four-note stack of fourths {F, G, B♭, C} expands to a five-note pentatonic scale in the last measure of the example. Figure 10.2.5, the opening of the tune "Freedom Jazz Dance," is quite similar: here, a pentatonic arpeggio (F, B♭, E♭, G, C, F) is augmented by the note D to form a six-note stack of fifths.[10]

In Chapter 4, we noted that the pentatonic scale is a minimal perturbation of a pure stack of fourths, returning to its starting point without passing through all twelve pitch classes (§4.4). It is interesting to think that similar considerations might play a role in explaining the more spontaneous improvisational choices made in 1960s jazz. For suppose you are an improviser who would like to play melodic fourths

9 Two thirds of the intervals randomly selected from the notes F-G-C will be perfect fourths or fifths, 50% of the intervals in F-G-B♭-C are perfect fourths or fifths, and 40% of the intervals in E♭-F-G-B♭-C are perfect fourths or fifths.

10 Pentatonic scales also appear in early jazz, though their effect is more folksy than quartal. My sense is that the pentatonic playing in the 1960s is only loosely connected to these earlier procedures.

Figure 10.2.4 Two passages from Keith Jarrett's solo on "You and The Night and The Music," which exploits stacks of fourths.

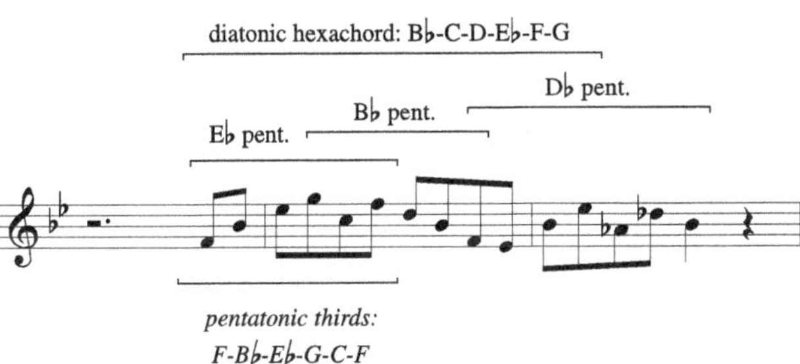

Figure 10.2.5 The opening of "Freedom Jazz Dance" begins by arpeggiating the E♭ pentatonic scale, adds a D to create a diatonic hexachord, and concludes with the D♭ pentatonic scale.

in a largely diatonic environment: like the designer of scales, you have an interest in ensuring that your melodic fourths do not lead you too far away from the underlying harmony (Figure 10.2.6). One natural solution is to incorporate a four-semitone "near fourth," so that the sequence of intervals returns to its starting point after just five notes. Virtually the same considerations apply to the abstract problem of designing five-note scales, and indeed to the problem of tuning an instrument in fourths: thus guitars, lutes, and viols often include an anomalous major third to ensure that the top string sounds the same note as the lowest, although the precise location of the third varies from instrument to instrument. It is somewhat remarkable that the same fundamental facts can help such disparate musical phenomena.

Fourth chords and pentatonic scales are now so central to jazz as to be virtually identified with the style. In fact, the enormous popularity of 1960s jazz means that composers who build quartal harmonies are more likely to be heard as referencing jazz than (say) the earlier works of Stravinsky, Hindemith, or Bartók. Of course, jazz musicians were in turn influenced by these same composers, deliberately borrowing quartal harmonies from the notated tradition in order to evoke a more modern sound.[11] To my mind, this is a remarkable instance of the oft-neglected interaction between jazz and concert music: quartal harmony, originally the province of the

11 James Moody, in a personal conversation, recalled that a number of musicians in the 1940s and 1950s were interested in Hindemith's fourth chords.

Figure 10.2.6 (*a*) An extended sequence of melodic fourths will generate notes that clash with the underlying harmony or scale. (*b–c*) To correct this problem one can add a "near fourth," producing a pentatonic or diatonic collection.

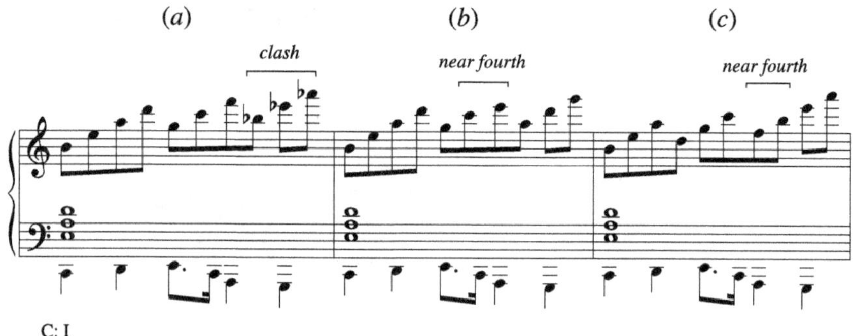

notated avant-garde, moved eventually into jazz, where it became incorporated into the canons of functional harmony; from there, it moves back into notated music as various contemporary composers borrowed jazz sounds in their own compositions. It would hardly be possible to write a coherent history of quartal harmony, itself a crucial component of twentieth-century tonality, without considering jazz and concert music together.

10.3 TRITONE SUBSTITUTION

Perhaps the most mysterious feature of jazz harmony, from a classical standpoint, is the practice of replacing a dominant seventh chord with its tritone transposition. For a musician with a classical education, these "tritone substitutions" can seem like harmonic sorcery—chaotic acts of rule breaking that defy all musical logic, yet nevertheless produce compelling musical effects. But as we will see, the tritone substitution is anything but mysterious: indeed, it is a straightforward generalization of traditional chromatic procedures, one that can easily be explained using our familiar geometrical models.

Figure 10.3.1 applies a tritone substitution to the second chord in the $\text{ii}^7\text{–V}^4_3\text{–I}^{\text{maj7}}$ progression discussed at the start of the chapter. The tritone in the upper staff is unaffected by the change, while the notes in the lower staff move semitonally in contrary motion. The substitution's effectiveness can thus be attributed to two factors: it preserves the leading tone and seventh of the V^7 chord, the "tendency tones" most directly responsible for pushing it forward toward the tonic; and it does not radically disrupt the contrapuntal flow in the remaining voices, transforming descending *diatonic* steps into descending *chromatic* steps. Figure 10.3.2 provides an example that uses quartal voicings. (Here an additional voice plays the root of the chords; for the time being, we can imagine that the bass player has miraculously intuited that the pianist intended to make the substitution.) Once again, tritone substitution preserves the tendency tones B-F and moves the remaining voices by semitone: A and E, the ninth and thirteenth of a G^7 chord, become B♭ and E♭, the thirteenth and ninth of D♭^{7}. Again, the substituted notes fit naturally within the contrapuntal framework of the original progression, leading to familiar voice-leading motions in each of the individual lines: in fact, the A-B♭-G motion in the soprano of Figure 10.3.3 recalls a gesture common in classical minor-key harmony.

Figure 10.3.1 (*a*) A familiar seventh-chord ii–V–I voice-leading schema. (*b*) The dominant chord can be replaced with its tritone transposition so as to preserve the notes in the upper staff, moving those in the lower staff by semitone.

If we think about this a bit more, we will eventually notice that both of these examples exploit the fact that tritones are unchanged by tritone transposition, while perfect fourths can be connected to their tritone transpositions by semitonal voice leading. It follows that as long as a chord can be *decomposed* into perfect fourths and tritones, it can be replaced by its tritone transposition without much disrupting the music's harmonic or contrapuntal fabric. In effect, the substitution takes advantage of the symmetry, or near symmetry, of the chord's two-note constituents. Figure 10.3.4 reminds us that tritone transposition corresponds to reflection around the central horizontal line of the two-note Möbius strip: every chord gets sent to the point where its image would appear, if the "line of tritones" were in fact a mirror. Since tritones are at the mirror's location, they are identical to their tritone transpositions, and since perfect fourths (or fifths) are very close to the mirror, tritone transposition does not move them very far. Musically, this means that tritone substitution preserves tritones while minimally perturbing fourths and fifths.

Three points are important here. First, tritone substitution relies crucially on the fact that jazz harmony uses seventh chords rather than triads. A four-voice dominant seventh chord can be decomposed into a perfect fifth and tritone, whereas a plain triad cannot. (Similarly, the *upper voices* of a five-note ninth chord can be

Figure 10.3.2 Tritone substitution as applied to the quartal version of the A voicing. The notes in the middle staff are preserved, while those in the upper staff move by semitone.

Figure 10.3.3 Tritone substitution produces a $\flat\hat{7}\rightarrow\hat{5}$ leap reminiscent of the $\flat\hat{7}\rightarrow\flat\hat{6}\rightarrow\hat{5}$ motion in classical minor-key harmony.

Figure 10.3.4 (*a*) Tritones can be linked to their tritone transpositions by zero-semitone voice leading, while perfect fourths can be linked to their tritone transpositions by semitonal voice leading. (*b*) These facts reflect the geometry of two-note chord space.

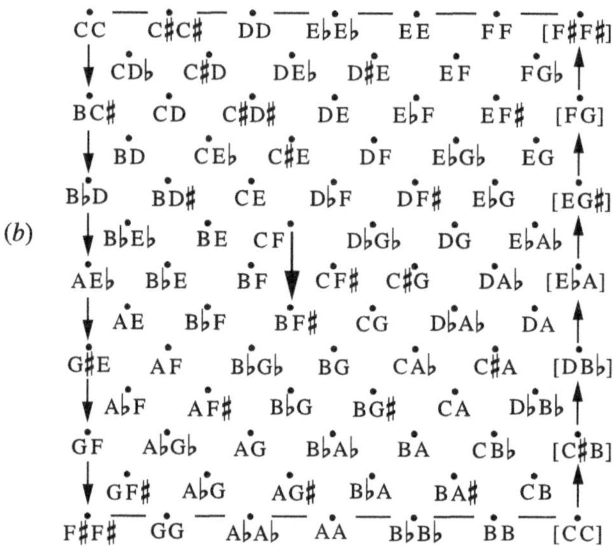

decomposed into tritones and fifths.[12]) Second, tritone substitution is most naturally applied to the dominant chord, since it preserves the all-important tritone between leading tone and fourth scale degree. *Contrapuntally*, it may be possible to apply tritone substitutions very broadly, but many of these substitutions disrupt the basic musical skeleton described in §10.1 (Figure 10.3.5). Not surprisingly, jazz musicians most often apply tritone substitution to dominant chords, less frequently apply it to predominant chords, and almost never apply it to the tonic. Finally, tritone substitution and quartal chord voicings go hand in hand. Originally, jazz harmonies were much more clearly tertian, and tritone substitution was most often found in the basic form shown in Figure 10.3.1. The increased use of added notes eventually allowed jazz musicians to reinterpret traditional harmony quartally while also making manifest the underlying logic of tritone substitution. (When a chord is arranged in fourths, it is clear that tritone substitution preserves its quartal

12 In fact, efficient voice leading between seventh chords (or the upper voices of ninth chords) preserves this partitioning when chord-roots relate by fourth, fifth, or tritone: the voice-leading schema in Figure 10.1.1a sends the third and seventh of D minor into the seventh and third of G^7, while sending the root and fifth of D minor into the fifth and root of G^7. This is also apparent in the upper voices of Figure 10.1.3. With other root progressions, the third/seventh pair exchanges places with the root/fifth pair, as in (C, G, E, B)→(C, G, E, A).

organization.) The happy convergence between quartal voicings and tritone substitution may therefore have contributed to the increased systematization of what was originally a more ad hoc collection of musical practices.

Readers will no doubt notice that this discussion echoes ideas in earlier chapters. In §7.2, we discussed diatonic "third substitution" in classical music—the process of replacing a diatonic triad, such as IV, with a third-related diatonic triad, such as ii^{6}. Our explanation was that the substitution kept two notes fixed while moving the remaining note by diatonic step (Figure 10.3.6). The preceding explanation of tritone substitution has the same essential structure: here, *tritone*-related dominants share two common tones (the crucial third and seventh) while the remaining notes move by chromatic step. Tritone substitution, like diatonic third substitution, therefore preserves something of the harmonic and contrapuntal character of the original chord, with the difference between the cases lying in the intrinsic geometry of the relevant chord spaces: since three-note diatonic triads divide the octave into three nearly even parts, they can be linked to their third transpositions by very efficient voice leading; since fourths and fifths divide the octave into two nearly even parts, they can be linked efficiently to their tritone transpositions. This example nicely illustrates the power of the geometrical approach: were it not for our intensive exploration of the geometry of chord space, we might never think to associate the third substitutions of the eighteenth century with the tritone substitutions of the twentieth. And thus we would miss an important connection between these two very different periods.

Since the tritone substitution has its roots in basic musical facts, we should expect it to appear in earlier styles as well. Figure 10.3.7a reminds us that the standard German sixth chord can be understood as a tritone substitution for the applied dominant chord V^{7}/V. (Indeed, tritone substitution presumably originates with augmented sixth chords, as discussed in Chapter 8.) Figure 10.3.7b applies the tritone substitution to the standard vii$^{ø4}_{3}$–I^{6} progression. The result is a striking progression from iv^{ø7} to I^{6}, commonly associated with Strauss' *Till Eulenspiegel*. The progression demonstrates a principle close to any jazz musician's heart: if a particular half-diminished chord works

Figure 10.3.5 Tritone substitution applied to tonic (*b*) and predominant (*c*) chords. The tonic substitution is not very effective, while the predominant substitution is somewhat more so.

Figure 10.3.6 Diatonic third-substitution (*a*) and chromatic tritone-substitution (*b*). Both substitutions preserve important notes in the first chord while moving the remaining notes by short distances.

Figure 10.3.7 Classical chord progressions that can be understood as tritone substitutions. (*a*) The augmented sixth chord can be seen as a tritone substitution for V^7/V. (*b*) The central chord progression in *Till Eulenspiegel* can be seen as a tritone substitution for a common $\text{vii}^{\circ 4}_{3}$–I progression. (*c*) The initial progression of *Tristan* can be seen as a tritone substitution for $\text{ii}^{ø 4}_{3}$–V. (*d*) In the "Forlane" from *Le tombeau de Couperin,* Ravel embellishes a descending-fifth sequence with tritone transpositions.

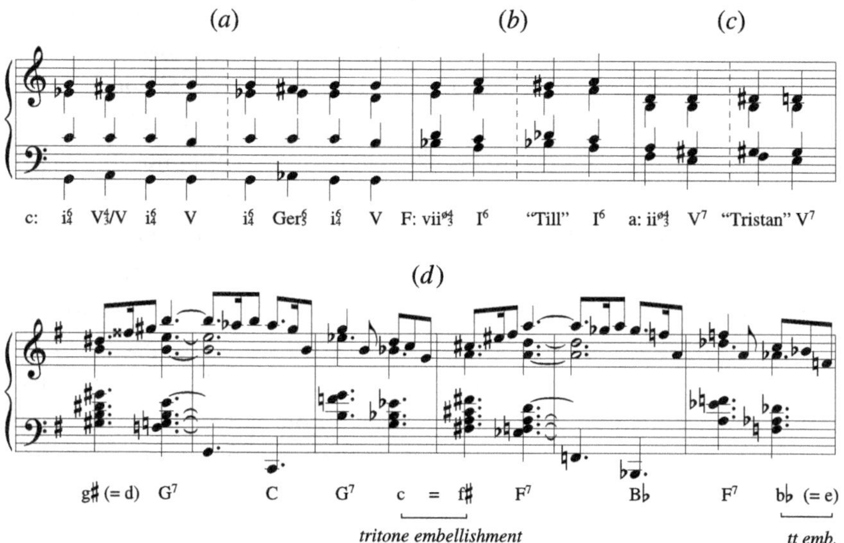

as a dominant sonority, then its tritone transposition will probably work as well. Figure 10.3.7c shows that the Tristan chord can be derived by applying the tritone substitution to the first chord in a standard $\text{ii}^{ø 4}_{3}$–V^7 progression. (Recall from Chapter 8 that Wagner explicitly uses these substitutions in *Tristan.*) Finally, Figure 10.3.7d presents one of many passages from Ravel that can be analyzed in terms of tritone substitution—a beautiful g♯–G^7–c–f♯–F^7–B♭ progression that embellishes descending fifths with tritone-related chords. (Since the music presents both chords in the tritone-related pair, the term "tritone embellishment" might be more appropriate here.) These are just some of the countless passages from nineteenth- and early twentieth-century music that involve something like tritone substitution. From this perspective, jazz simply codifies procedures that are already present, at least in embryo, in notated music.

Figure 10.3.8 Voice leading between fifth-related (*a*) and tritone-related (*b*) dominant seventh chords. The two voice leadings are individually T-related, and are nearly the same size.

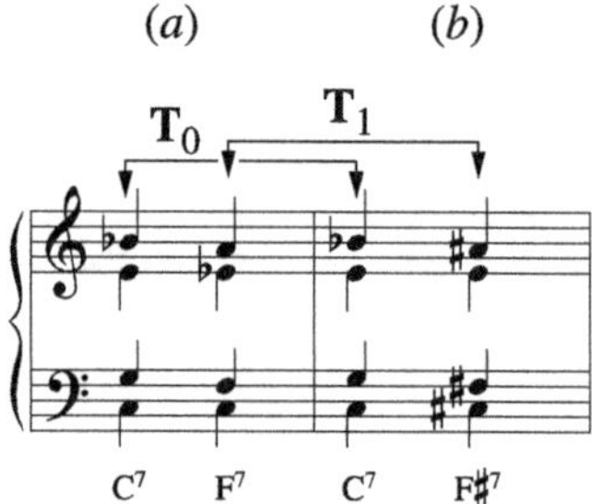

Finally, it is worth noting that the tritone substitution depends on the very same features of chord structure at play in descending-fifths progressions. The two voice leadings in Figure 10.3.8 are roughly the same size, since their second chords differ only by semitone. Traditional tonal syntax exploits the first voice leading to *connect* fifth-related dominant seventh chords in sequence. Tritone substitution exploits the second to *replace* one dominant seventh chord with its tritone transposition. In this sense, the possibility of tritone substitution is latent in the basic routines of traditional tonality. Over the course of its history, tonal harmony exploits this possibility with increasing frequency—beginning with augmented sixths in the eighteenth century, progressing through the occasional use of tritone substitutions in the early nineteenth century, leading to more daring impressionist uses of the technique, and culminating in its universal acceptance in modern jazz.

10.4 ALTERED CHORDS AND SCALES

In composed music, it is possible for chords to change as rapidly as the melody. In improvisation, however, very high rates of harmonic change have the effect of constraining a player's freedom; he or she expends so much mental energy thinking about chords that little is left for melodic invention. As a result, jazz typically features at most one or two chords per measure, with improvisers playing four, eight, or more notes per chord. For exactly this reason, *scales* provide invaluable guidance about which melodic notes will sound good, particularly when improvisers need to negotiate the altered and extended chords central to jazz harmony.

The lower staves in Figure 10.4.1 show the basic voice-leading skeleton from the beginning of the chapter. Since the harmonies all belong to C diatonic, it would be possible to play that scale for the entire passage. But doing so requires the player to handle the avoid notes with some care: for instance, the tonic scale degree, when played over the dominant chord, will typically need to be treated as a passing or neighboring tone. Figure 10.4.1 identifies an alternative approach, where the avoid

Figure 10.4.1 An improviser who plays diatonically will need to handle the "avoid notes" with care, for instance by making them into passing or neighboring notes. Another alternative is to raise the avoid notes by semitone, in which case they can be used more freely. The resulting ii–V–I progression uses three different scales.

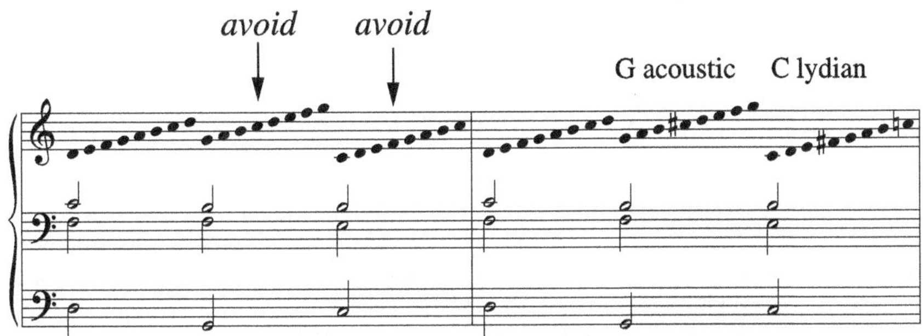

notes are raised by semitone to create altered chords.[13] Since there are no avoid notes, the improviser is now free to treat all seven scale tones as if they were harmonic: for instance it becomes possible to leap in and out of the altered notes, sustain them for long durations, and so on. But notice that the passage now involves a series of three different scales: ii^{7} is accompanied by C diatonic, V^{7} by G acoustic, and I^{maj7} by G diatonic. The simple ii–V–I progression, the archetype of functional harmony, has become a fundamentally polyscalar construction.

Figure 10.4.2 shows that the G acoustic scale combines a lower whole-tone fragment G-A-B-C♯ with an upper octatonic fragment C♯-D-E-F-G, each spanning a tritone. (Jazz musicians sometimes call this the "lydian dominant scale."[14]) Now it can happen that one musician will spontaneously use a tritone substitution while others do not, as in Figure 10.4.2b: here, the pianist plays ♭II^{7} while the bass player plays the fifth scale degree. Given the bass, listeners are likely to hear G as being the most important note in the chord, understanding the scale to be the fourth mode of D♭ acoustic. Notice

Figure 10.4.2 (*a*) The lydian dominant mode of the acoustic scale combines a whole-tone lower tritone with an octatonic upper tritone. (*b*) Here, the pianist makes a tritone substitution, playing the D♭ lydian dominant mode, while the bass player does not. (*c*) The result is a G altered scale, which combines an octatonic lower tritone with a whole-tone upper tritone.

13 George Russell's *Lydian Chromatic Concept* (1953, but reprinted in 2001) explicitly discusses this practice. However, the technique itself was used by Debussy and other early twentieth-century composers.

14 The term is symptomatic of a widespread tendency to elide the difference between scale and mode.

that here the whole-tone and octatonic fragments have switched positions: it is the lower tritone G-A♭-B♭-B-C♯ that is octatonic, and the upper tritone C♯-D♯-F-G that is whole tone. Jazz musicians call this new scale the G "altered scale," since it contains many more nondiatonic "alterations" than G lydian dominant: rather than the solitary ♯$\hat{4}$, the altered scale has ♭9, ♯9, ♯11/♭5, and ♯5/♭13.[15] Perhaps its clearest precedent in classical music occurs in the minor mode, where the lowered and raised forms of the leading tone sometimes collide (Figure 10.4.3).[16]

We have now considered two ways to fill the tritones G-C♯ and C♯-G with whole-tone or octatonic scale fragments. Since each tritone can contain either fragment, it is reasonable to wonder what happens when we combine them freely. It turns out that we can form three different scales in this way—whole tone, acoustic, and octatonic, with the acoustic appearing in both lydian dominant and altered modes (Figure 10.4.4). Each contains the notes {G, B, C♯, F} and hence can appear over either V⁷ or its tritone substitute. These scales, together with the diatonic, are in many ways the central scales of jazz harmony: they are played by countless improvisers and are highlighted in virtually every jazz textbook I have encountered.[17] They have also reappeared at various points throughout this book. Chapter 4 argued that these scales are theoretically interesting, since they are the only scales with one-or-two semitone steps and three-or-four semitone thirds. Chapter 9 showed that the same scales play an important role in a wide variety of twentieth-century notated music.[18] Here we see that they are essential to jazz as well.

Figure 10.4.3 (*a*) A harmonic minor scale with an additional (neighboring) ♭$\hat{7}$. (*b*) The resulting notes are very similar to the altered scale.

Figure 10.4.4 There are four ways to combine octatonic and whole-tone upper and lower tritones, producing one whole tone scale, one octatonic scale, and two modes of the acoustic scale.

Figure 10.4.5 reproduces a number of extended and altered dominant sonorities

15 The altered scale is often spelled with two thirds and no fourths, as in G-A♭-B♭-B♮-D♭-E♭-F-G (Figure 9.3.18, R43).

16 It would be interesting, in fact, to investigate whether early jazz players played this quasi-harmonic minor scale in contexts where later musicians use the altered scale.

17 See Tymoczko 1997 for a survey of various textbooks' treatments of scales.

18 Interestingly, it was jazz theorists—in their role as practical-minded pedagogues—who first isolated this collection of scales and asserted their importance. And though more academic theorists were aware of the individual scales, they did not begin to emphasize the group until well after they had been discussed in jazz. Indeed, the first published theoretical discussion of the four scales seems to be Tymoczko 1997, which was preceded—and directly inspired—by Levine 1989.

from the beginning of Chapter 8, showing that each belongs to one of our four scales. One might wonder whether one of these scales will inevitably contain any given altered dominant chord. The answer is "almost." Recall from §4.4 (and Figure 10.4.6) that seven types of scale contain *every* "nonchromatic chord"—that is, every chord that does not include a chromatic cluster such as {C, C♯, D}. To incorporate *all* of these chords we would need to expand our four-scale vocabulary to include the hexatonic and harmonic collections. (Jazz musicians typically use chromatic clusters only as a special effect, so we do not need to worry about chords with clusters.) Interestingly, however, it turns out that the hexatonic and harmonic scales are in practice rarely needed. Figure 10.4.7 shows that there are only four nonchromatic set classes with five or fewer notes not contained within some diatonic, acoustic, whole-tone, or octatonic scale. Consequently, the four basic scales are sufficient for most musical circumstances.

Of course, jazz musicians use other scales as well (Figure 10.4.8). Pentatonic scales can impart a "fourthy" flavor to predominant, dominant, and tonic chords. The

Figure 10.4.5 Scales that are compatible with common altered-dominant chords.

Figure 10.4.6 The transpositions of these seven scales contain all the sets that do not themselves contain a chromatic subset such as {C, C♯, D}, and hence all of the common extended or altered tonal harmonies.

Figure 10.4.7 The first column lists the number of set classes containing a chromatic cluster such as {C, C♯, D}. The second lists the number of set classes contained in the diatonic, acoustic, whole tone, and octatonic scales. The third lists the number of set classes that do not contain a chromatic cluster, but are not contained in one of these four scales. All set classes belong to one of these three categories.

	Chromatic	Dia, Aco, Wt, Oct	Other
Three Notes	1	11	0
Four Notes	5	23	1
Five Notes	16	19	3
Six Notes	32	13	5

Figure 10.4.8 Other scales commonly played in jazz. Pentatonic scales are often used over ii, V, and I. The hexatonic scale can be played against a tonic major seventh. The acoustic scale often appears over ii^{ø7} in the "locrian ♯2" mode; the same scale sometimes appears against a bare tonic triad (without the seventh). Harmonic minor is sometimes used for minor-key dominant chords, as in classical music, and harmonic major can be used over a major-seventh tonic.

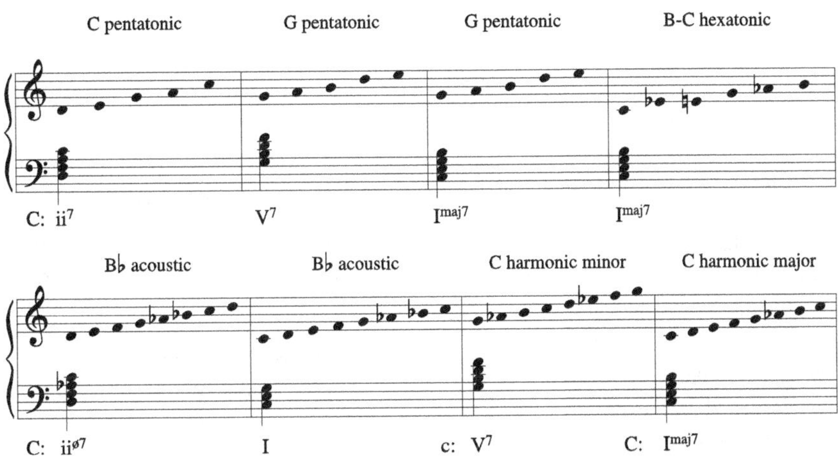

acoustic scale can be played over a ii^{ø7} or I chord, lending a minor coloring to the major mode ii–V–I. Acoustic and harmonic minor scales often appear in minor-mode contexts, while the hexatonic can be played over a major or minor tonic chord. More unusual scales, such as the gypsy scale, are sometimes used to evoke an exotic or non-Western ambience. Taken together, these conventions provide a fairly robust set of rules for associating chords and scales, thus synthesizing functional harmony, nineteenth-century chordal techniques, and impressionist scale use.[19] And

19 Jazz pedagogues, as noted in Chapter 9, describe these conventions as "the principles of chord-scale compatibility."

though these fundamental principles are familiar from the twentieth-century notated tradition, they are applied in jazz with a systematic rigor that far exceeds anything found earlier.

10.5 BASS AND UPPER VOICE TRITONE SUBSTITUTIONS

I have already mentioned that a bass player or pianist will sometimes make a tritone substitution without alerting the other musicians. In *bass-only* tritone substitutions, the same upper voices are reinterpreted as belonging to a new root a tritone away. This is illustrated in Figure 10.5.1a, where the seventh, ninth, third, and thirteenth of a G^7 voicing become the third, flat thirteenth, seventh, and sharp ninth of a $D\flat^7$ altered chord. (This could occur if the bass player, but not the pianist, decided to apply a tritone substitution.) In the upper voice version of the substitution, the bass stays fixed, while the upper voices move by tritone. For instance, in Figure 10.5.1b, the seventh, ninth, third, and thirteenth of the G^7 voicing become the third, flat thirteenth, seventh, and sharp ninth of a G^7 altered chord.[20] (This could happen if the pianist applied the tritone substitution independent of the bass player.) Note that this substitution changes the macroharmony more dramatically than the bass-only version, since many more notes are affected: both voicings in Figure 10.5.1a belong to the same G acoustic collection, while in (*b*) the second belongs to D♭ acoustic.

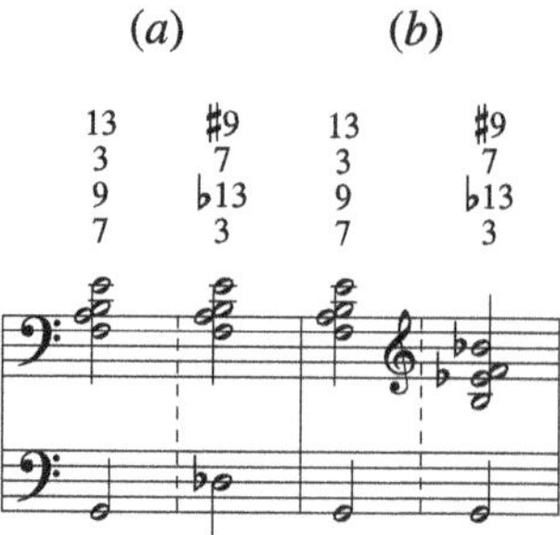

Figure 10.5.1 Bass substitution and upper-voice substitution. Here either the bass player or pianist makes the substitution, but not both. In each case, the effect is to transform a diatonic voicing containing the seventh, ninth, third, and thirteenth above the root into an altered voicing containing third, flat thirteenth, seventh, and sharp nine.

Scales provide a useful way to conceptualize these transformations. The whole-tone, octatonic, lydian dominant, and acoustic scales all contain both the dominant note ($\hat{5}$) and its tritone substitute ($\flat\hat{2}$); thus as long as a chord's notes are chosen from one of these scales, they will be consistent with either of the chord roots a bass player might play (Figure 10.5.2). Furthermore, since both whole tone and octatonic are tritone symmetrical, upper voice substitution will send a whole-tone voicing to another whole-tone voicing, and an octatonic voicing to another octatonic voicing. (Since any of the notes in these scales can reasonably be played over a V^7 chord, these new chords will be guaranteed to work reasonably well.) Meanwhile, upper-voice substitution exchanges the G lydian dominant mode for G altered: hence any collection of upper voices drawn from one of these scales can

20 This is just the A voicing of $D\flat^7$ over a G bass.

Figure 10.5.2 Upper-voice substitution leaves the whole-tone and octatonic scales unchanged (top two lines), exchanges the lydian dominant and altered modes of the acoustic scale (line three), and sends the diatonic scale to its tritone transposition (bottom line).

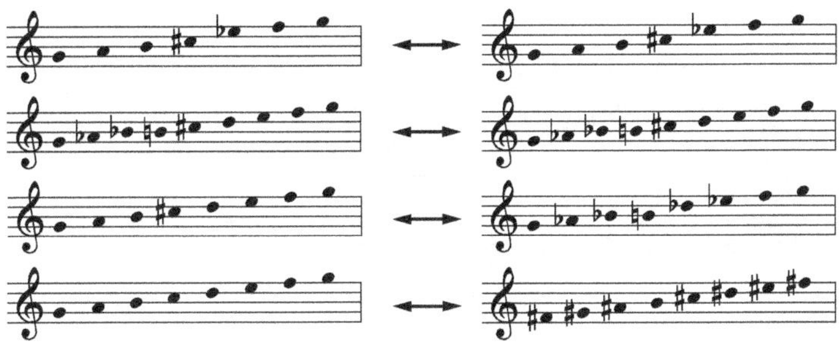

Figure 10.5.3 Independent applications of the tritone transposition can clash with purely diatonic voicings. Here, the diatonic notes C and D clash with the bass player's (tritone substitute) D♭; similarly, the unsubstituted G in the bass clashes with the pianist's G♭ diatonic.

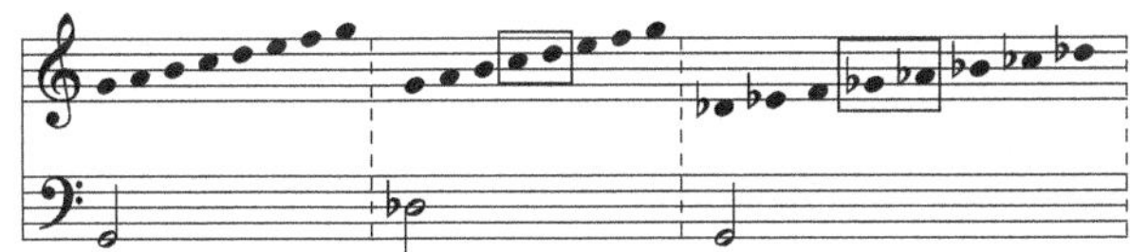

be transposed by tritone to produce a voicing drawn from the other. By contrast, this same procedure can lead to problems in diatonic contexts: since upper-voice substitution sends the C diatonic scale to F♯ diatonic, it can create clashes with the bass line, as in Figure 10.5.3.

One important musical consequence is that a soloist can always play a descending-by-semitone melodic sequence over a sequence of dominant harmonies that descend by fifths. In effect, the soloist applies the upper-voice tritone substitution to every other chord, as shown in Figure 10.5.4. The harmonic meaning of the notes thus alternates between chords: for example, in Figure 10.5.4a, the augmented triad represents the seventh, sharp eleventh, and ninth in the first and third chords, and the third, root, and sharp fifth of the second and fourth chords (Figure 10.5.5). Similarly, the melodic fourths in 10.5.4b alternate between lydian dominant and altered voicings. This idiom, by which dominant voicings move chromatically over a descending fifth bass line, is ubiquitous in jazz, providing an easy way to cope with fast descending fifth sequences.

Readers will not be shocked to learn that these ideas are again anticipated, often very explicitly, in the music of Debussy, Ravel, and other early twentieth-century composers. Debussy in particular was extremely fond of the lydian dominant mode, and often constructed textures in which a dominant seventh chord is accompanied

Figure 10.5.4 Chromatically descending voicings can always accompany descending-fifths patterns in the bass. In effect, tritone transposition is applied to every other chord in the sequence.

by a sharp eleventh. (See Figure 10.5.6a.) Both Debussy and Ravel also apply tritone substitution independently to either the bass or upper voices: for instance, in Figure 10.5.6b, Ravel begins by alternating between C^{7} (expressed by the "mixolydian ♭6 mode") and G♭^{7} (expressed by a voicing that belongs both to G♭ diatonic and lydian dominant); when the music returns, however, the bass stays fixed, producing an "altered" voicing of the C^{7}. In (*c*), from Debussy's "La danse de Puck," a C♯ altered scale alternates with standard V^{7} voicing, suggesting an upper-voice substitution. Finally, Figure 10.5.6d presents a much-discussed passage from Debussy, in which semitonally descending A voicings in the right hand appear over descending fifths in the bass, exactly as in Figure 10.5.4. (This passage includes an upper voice A♭ pedal.[21]) In light of the preceding examples, it does not seem entirely anachronistic to describe this as a series of Debussian dominants, in which diatonic voicings alternate with their tritone substitutes.

Figure 10.5.5 This table shows how tritone substitution affects the notes in a dominant voicing. The root of the dominant chord becomes the ♯4 (or ♯11) and vice versa. (Notes here are labeled according to their intervals above the bass.) The ♭9 and fifth are exchanged, and so on.

Interval ↔TT sub	
root	♯4
♭9	5
9	♯5
♯9	6
3	7

21 This progression echoes a similar passage in Berg, as discussed in Stuckenschmidt 1965.

Figure 10.5.6 Impressionist composers prefigured many central ideas of jazz harmony. In (*a*), from *Prelude to "The Afternoon of a Faun,"* mm. 61–62, Debussy uses an acoustic scale over V^7, as in Figure 10.4.1. In (*b*), from Ravel's "Ondine," bass substitution is applied to the dominant chord at the end of m. 46 and m. 51. In (*c*), from the Prelude "La danse de Puck," Debussy applies something like upper-voice substitution, moving between altered and diatonic dominant voicings. In (*d*), from *Six épigraphes antiques,* No. 4, Debussy uses descending-semitone voicings over a descending-fifths bass line, applying the upper-voice substitution to every other chord in the sequence.

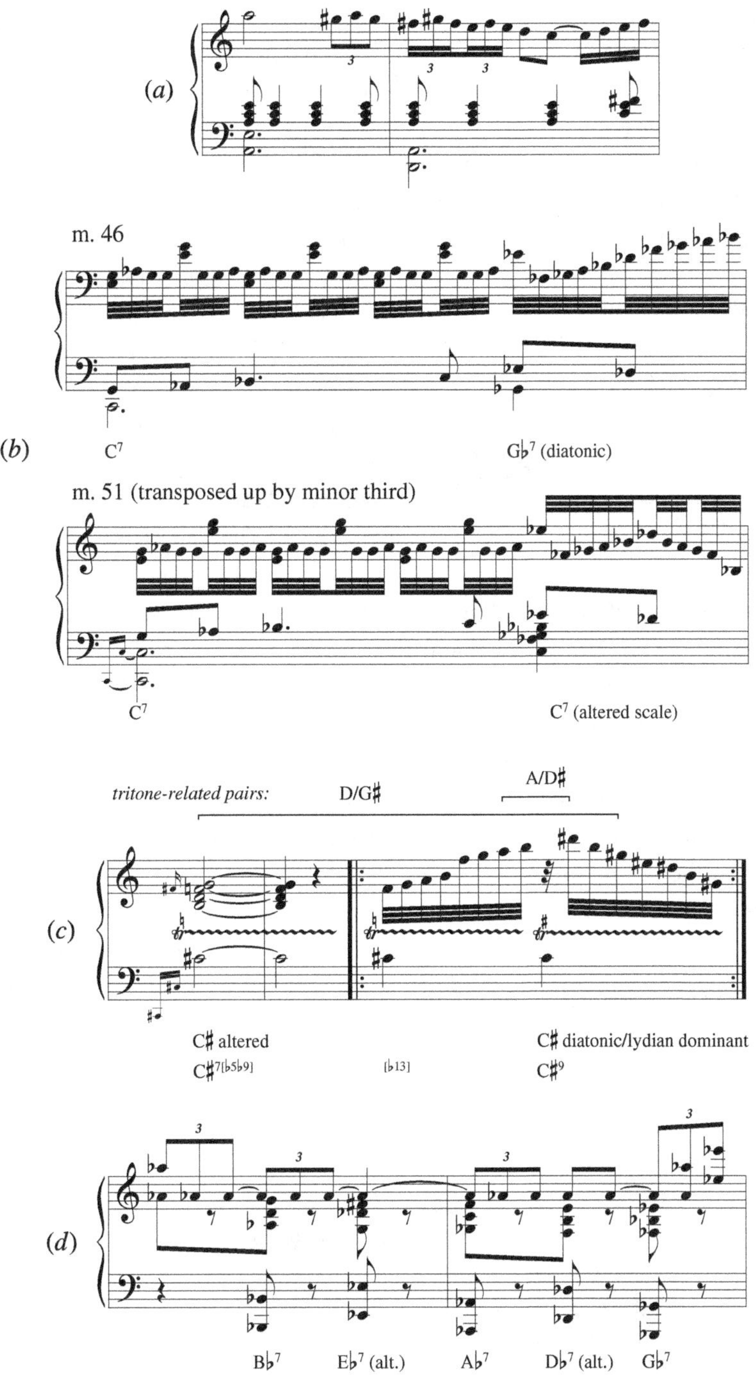

10.6 POLYTONALITY, SIDESTEPPING, AND "PLAYING OUT"

So far we have been imagining an idealized performance situation in which players are always perfectly in synch, and their notes systematically related. But of course this is unrealistic: in the blur of the improvisatory moment, there is room for a good deal of asynchrony, as players go their own way by stepping outside of the underlying harmony. One of the most interesting features of contemporary jazz is the way players negotiate and exploit this possibility—deliberately moving between states of being together and being apart.

The origins of this technique can perhaps be traced to the blues, which is characterized by "blue notes" that create a delicious dissonance with the underlying harmony. In Figure 10.6.1, scale degrees ♭3 and ♭5 are superimposed above a dominant seventh. The music thus suggests a kind of polytonality, or clash between independent harmonic streams, in which an upper-register (African American) "blues scale" contrasts with a lower-register European harmony. Figure 10.6.2 presents a more audacious example, drawn from Warne Marsh's solo on the tune "Smog Eyes." The underlying harmony here is a tonic E♭ major, but Marsh begins his solo with a wonderfully brash E major chord a half step too high. What is more, he embellishes the top note of the line with an upper neighbor. As ♯$\hat{4}$ in E♭ major, A♮ would typically resolve upward to the B♭; but as the fourth scale degree in E major, it is an upper neighbor to the G♯. The authority of Marsh's phrasing is such that the downward resolution feels utterly compelling, suggesting that we hear E major as being both locally stable (relative to the A♮, which wants to resolve downward to it) and globally unstable (relative to the key of the rest of the ensemble). Marsh intensifies the feeling of resolution by lowering G♯ to G♮, initiating a descending arpeggio that resolves *the entire E major triad* down by semitone to the tonic E♭. (Note how register and tonality interact: the line ascends to the doubly dissonant A♮, the upper neighbor to the third of a chord that is itself an upper neighbor; then

Figure 10.6.1 The blues often features polytonal clashes between melody and harmony.

Figure 10.6.2 Out-of-key playing in Warne Marsh's solo on "Smog Eyes." Marsh plays an E major figure over an E♭ harmony; the A is an upper neighbor to the G♯, and the entire E major triad resolves downward to E♭.

the descent brings the music back into the key.) All of this, of course, occurs over a supposedly stable tonic triad. Marsh thus exploits two fundamentally different mechanisms of tension and release: there is the standard tonal oscillation between dominant and tonic, but also the oscillation between states of being in the same key and states of being apart.

These concepts can again be applied, *mutatis mutandis,* to music in the classical tradition. Chopin, for example, was an improvising musician who also liked to exploit sudden shifts between semitonally related keys. For example, the B section of his first Nocturne, shown in Figure 10.6.3a, contains a four-measure phrase that shifts from D♭ major to D major and back. This semitonal shift—which a jazz musician might call "sidestepping"—is perhaps comparable to Marsh's temporary shift from E♭ to E major. Figure 10.6.3b shows an example from Chopin's second Nocturne, where a cadence on B♭ major immediately leads to a dazzling digression to E major. The underlying musical impulse here is again not so foreign to jazz: the music briefly and dramatically shifts to a distant and colorful key, before settling back to its proper home. Of course, an improviser like Marsh typically shifts key *independently* of the rest of the ensemble, creating a polytonal clash. Chopin, who

Figure 10.6.3 Sidestepping in Chopin. (*a*) In the first Nocturne (Op. 9 No. 1), Chopin shifts suddenly from D♭ major to D major, in the middle of the phrase. (*b*) In the second Nocturne (Op. 9 No. 2), he returns from B♭ to E♭ by way of E major.

as a solo player was in complete control of the music, and who was in any case uninterested in polytonality, shifts the entire texture at the same time.[22]

There are some jazz pieces in which the ii–V–I architecture of functional harmony disappears almost entirely, being replaced by this process of moving in and out of synchrony. (The ambiguous term "modal jazz" is sometimes used in this context, though it can also refer to other musical phenomena.[23]) McCoy Tyner's "Passion Dance" is a good example: although the tune itself contains a few chord changes, the solo section is entirely based on a tonic F^7 chord, implying a drone-like mixolydian. In his solo, Tyner reinforces this drone-like feeling by continually reverting to a low F-C fifth in the bass. Above this, the right hand plays melodic stacks of fourths, with the fourths F-B♭-E♭ and G-C-F representing the tonic voicings, and formations like F♯-B-E representing the nontonic (out-of-key) states.

Figure 10.6.4 shows two phrases that occur near the beginning of Tyner's solo, each exhibiting the same basic oscillation between in-key and out-of-key playing. In the first, Tyner repeats the descending stepwise pattern G-F-E♭ in an unsystematic

Figure 10.6.4 Harmonic motion in "Passion Dance" largely consists in oscillations between in-key and out-of-key playing.

22 The semitonal shifts in Prokofiev and Shostakovich sometimes *do* create polytonal effects, and are perhaps even closer to those in jazz. See Frankenhauser 2008.

23 "Modal jazz" can be used to describe either highly diatonic pieces with very few chord changes, or relatively chromatic music in which harmonic tension is generated by out-of-key playing.

chromatic sequence, presenting it on E♭ (in a variant form), F♯, F, D, D♯, C♯, C and B♭, before returning to F mixolydian. (Note that the out-of-key section begins with the hands moving in contrary motion, with the right-hand scale fragment descending while the left-hand fourths ascend.) The second phrase departs from F mixolydian only in its fourth measure, moving to the black-note pentatonic collection while the quartal voicing shifts up to F♯-B-E. One can hear this music as suggesting a dominant seventh sonority on F♯, a semitone away from the tonic. However, the musical impression is not so much of motion between well-defined chords as of oscillation between two basic harmonic states—"home" and "away," with the "away" state potentially manifesting itself in a variety of different harmonic colors.

While the solos on "Passion Dance" are almost entirely devoid of traditional chord progressions, many jazz pieces combine this sort of "playing outside" with traditional tonal functionality. Harmonic tension in this music thus arises from motion within a key (from stable I to unstable V and back), from motion between keys (from the global tonic to various subsidiary regions), from neighboring and passing tones (creating fleeting dissonances with the underlying harmony), and from more radical motion between states of being together and being apart. The interaction between these four kinds of tension can produce music of extraordinary subtlety, in which the choice between functional tonality and other modes of pitch organization can be made anew every few seconds.

I should also mention one more way in which jazz musicians evoke a sense of polytonality or "being apart": the use of dominant voicings that contain a triad foreign to the tonic key. (Pedagogues sometimes call these "upper structure" voicings.) Figure 10.6.5 shows how to combine the essential notes of the dominant harmony (root, third, and seventh) with a triad foreign to the underlying key. (The figure eliminates those voicings that contain an F♯, which would create a chromatic cluster with F-G in the dominant voicing, or a C, which would prematurely anticipate the resolution

Figure 10.6.5 "Upper structure" dominant voicings combine root, third, and seventh in the bass with a foreign triad in the upper voices. Upper-voice tritone substitution leaves the lowest three notes unchanged, transposing the triad by tritone. This provides a convenient way to remember and categorize these voicings.

of the leading tone.) Jazz soloists can create polychordal effects by emphasizing the "upper structure" triads, for instance by playing prominent E-major or E♭-major arpeggios over an accompanimental G^7 chord. Although these upper structure arpeggios could in principle be described as altered dominant chords, they evoke a sensation of polytonality not too dissimilar from the cases we have been considering.

10.7 BILL EVANS' "OLEO"

We'll now use these ideas to analyze Bill Evans' version of Sonny Rollins' "Oleo," from the 1958 trio album *Everybody Digs Bill Evans*. It's an unusual and austere piece, like Bach in its stripped-down rigor: for much of the recording, Evans plays only with his right hand, while the drummer Philly Joe Jones lays out, leaving the bass player (Sam Jones) to improvise two-part counterpoint with the solo line. By omitting left-hand chords, Evans creates space to depart from the tune's underlying framework—playing outside the key for a significant portion of the solo. (Because of the wide registral and timbral separation between the instruments, clashes between melody and bass are not at all jarring.) The coordination in the ensemble is itself virtuosic—the tempo is fast (approximately 240 beats per minute) and the music replete with destabilizing syncopations and polyrhythms. Yet the players manage not only to make musical sense, but also to swing.

The piece is a repeating 32-bar AABA form, based on the chord changes to Gershwin's "I Got Rhythm" (Figure 10.7.1). (Each AABA unit is called a "chorus.") Traditionally, the B section of "Oleo" is improvised, with only the chords being fixed. In the first three choruses, Philly Joe Jones drums normally only in the B section; in the A sections he either remains silent or plays a dotted half-note polyrhythm on the hi-hat. (At the start of the fourth chorus, he explodes into activity in what is, to my mind, one of the most dramatic entrances in all of jazz.) Two features of the tune are noteworthy. First, the B section (mm. 17–24) features a series of whole-tone voicings that descend semitonally over descending fifth chords, discussed earlier in §10.5. Second, Evans begins the dotted-quarter figure on the second eighth note of measure 17, creating a continuous dotted-quarter pulse that lasts until the second half of measure 20. This is a common technique, whereby soloists start a polyrhythm so that it will synchronize with the main pulse at a structurally important moment—here the downbeat of m. 19.

10.7.1 Chorus 1

The solo opens with a blues gesture emphasizing ♭5 and ♭3, shown in Figure 10.7.2. The phrase is delayed so as to start on beat three of the first measure, although the casual listener might easily miss this. The sixth measure of the solo features an octatonic scale over $E\flat^7$ and is followed by a pair of two-measure phrases that recall the blues-inflected opening. (These phrases develop the B♭-F-E♭-D motive bracketed on the example.) Evans then plays two repetitions of a two-and-a-half-measure phrase,

Figure 10.7.1 Sonny Rollins' tune "Oleo," as played by Bill Evans.

each divided into six-beat units. These phrases sidestep between a B major triad, whose third is embellished with an upper neighbor, and a B♭ major triad embellished in the same way. The B major chord can be understood either as an out-of-key element or as a (triadic!) tritone substitution for a dominant F major triad.

The B section begins with a development of this six-beat idea: what was once a second-inversion B major triad becomes a root position G major triad, representing the seventh, ninth, and eleventh of an A^{ø7} chord. Figure 10.7.3 interprets this as an efficient voice leading between B♭ and G major triads—reminiscent of the chromatic progressions we find in nineteenth-century music, although here the G major triad is an upper structure of A^{ø7}. (The B♮ suggests the A mode of the F acoustic scale, also known as "locrian ♯2.") The next phrase spins out this idea into a longer melodic line. The final A section begins with another example of sidestepping, as second-inversion major triads slide chromatically back and forth between B♭ and C, leading

Figure 10.7.2 The first chorus of Evans' solo.

to an embellished scalar descent from F5 to A3. It is interesting that the final sixteen bars of the chorus feature four appearances of the same basic musical shape, marked on the score with the Greek letter β. Having somewhat less individuality than a classical motive, this "shape" is more like a turn or melodic curlicue, a stylized way to get from one place to another.[24] This particular pattern is characteristic of Evans' playing, and appears repeatedly in many of his solos; almost every jazz improviser has a similar collection of favorite melodic devices, small "signatures" that help define the player's style or sound.

24 In this respect it is perhaps analogous to the small cells that contribute to the identity of an Indian Rag.

Figure 10.7.3 Measures 47–49 articulate an efficient voice leading between B♭ and G major triads. However, the G triad represents the upper notes of an extended A^ø7 chord.

10.7.2 Chorus 2

The second chorus, shown in Figure 10.7.4, begins by linearizing a set of four-note voicings. Figure 10.7.5 shows that the C♯ minor seventh can be understood as a tritone substitution for, or upper structure of, G⁷, though it is also possible to understand it as a chromatic passing chord.[25] The next phrase features rhythmic displacement of a sort that is quite common to jazz: the rhythmic and registral accents are on beats 2 and 4, as if the entire phrase had been shifted forward by one beat (Figure 10.7.6).

Figure 10.7.4 The second chorus of Evans' solo.

25 One implication of Figure 10.5.4 is that "tritone substitute" and "chromatic passing chord" are intimately connected.

Figure 10.7.5 The first phrase of the chorus linearizes a collection of four-note voicings, similar to those discussed earlier in the chapter.

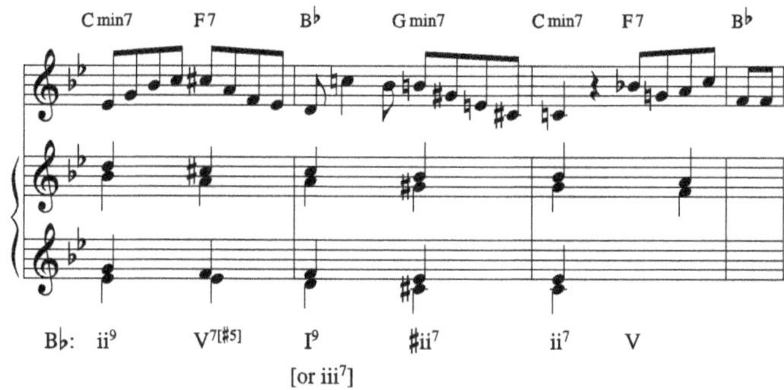

Figure 10.7.6 The second phrase of the chorus displaces the accent: on its own, the melody would be heard with the registrally accented notes on strong beats (lower line); as played, however, the notes are rhythmically weak, creating a kind of polyrhythm.

The B section begins with a trick that appears in the statement of the tune: the augmented triad D-B♭-F♯, originally the root, flat thirteenth, and third of the chord, is shifted down by semitone as the chord roots fall by fifth, producing C♯-A-F, the sharp eleventh, ninth, and seventh of the chord. The pitches of the sixth phrase recall the very opening of the solo (Figure 10.7.2, mm. 33–35), except here the E♮ is treated as a lower neighbor to the F; meanwhile, the dotted-quarter rhythm sets up the virtuosic polyrhythms of the next chorus. The end of the phrase returns to eighth notes, delaying the resolution of the B♭^{7} chord until the third beat of m. 94. Philly Joe Jones enters precisely when Evans ends his phrase, one bar before the end of the chorus—an incredibly brash entrance that sets the stage for the dazzling music that is to follow.

10.7.3 Chorus 3

The climactic chorus, shown in Figure 10.7.7, reaches a peak of rhythmic density, chromaticism, and polyrhythmic complexity. It is built on a common rhythmic device, an extended series of dotted sixteenth notes grouped in fours. On the page, the rhythm looks almost unplayable, particularly at this tempo, but it is not actually that difficult. (To practice it, begin by playing a series of dotted quarters against a quarter-note pulse; then, while holding the dotted-quarter pulse firmly in mind, let your fingers play four notes in the span of each dotted quarter.) Although conceptually straightforward, the device produces a spectacular impression and has been adopted by a number of musicians.

Evans' playing here is largely chromatic and outside the tonal system: he moves the motive F-G♭-F-D up and down by semitone, with no regard for the underlying chord changes—an apotheosis of the more cautious sidestepping earlier in the solo. (Note, by the way, that both the rhythm and the contour of this motive are anticipated by the seemingly throwaway turn in mm. 5 and 13 of the tune.) Since the dotted-sixteenth groups fall on the downbeat of every third measure, the rhythm

Figure 10.7.7 The third chorus of Evans' solo.

articulates three-measure units. However, the pitches articulate a phrase of nine dotted-quarters that is repeated a half step lower (Figure 10.7.8).[26] Evans breaks off his polyrhythm on the fourth beat of the seventh measure of the chorus, taking a one-bar rest that allows him to resynchronize with the tune's eight-bar units. After this brief pause, the second phrase begins a five-group unit that descends chromatically (mm. 105–106), repeated at the interval of an ascending major third (mm. 107–108). (Note that here Evans observes the two-measure phrasing of the tune, reigning in the dotted quarters' tendency to group the measures into threes.) The next phrase (mm. 109–112) begins with another chromatically descending five-group unit, but continues diatonically, creating a subtle feeling of resolution as the chromatic macroharmony clarifies. Note that the sequence picks up right on schedule on the second eighth note of m. 109, suggesting that there is a missing dotted-quarter unit across the barline of mm. 108–109.

Figure 10.7.8 The rhythm of the dotted sixteenth-note figure articulates three-measure groups. However, the pitches articulate a nine dotted-quarter sequence.

The B section opens with the last appearance of the dotted-sixteenth-note idea, this time using a G harmonic minor scale over a D^7 chord. The next phrase returns to the shapely melodic playing of the earlier sections of the solo: we hear a G altered scale over G^7; a G♭^{7} arpeggio that suggests an upper structure of (or tritone substitution for) the C^7; and a slightly chromaticized C^{-7} arpeggio. The phrase ends with a little octatonic fillip over F^7. Evans marks the return of the A section by introducing a new harmonic idea, a quartal passage articulating the notes F-G-B♭-C.

10.7.4 Chorus 4

Like the last act of a Shakespeare play, Chorus 4 lowers the energy level of the climactic Chorus 3, bringing the solo to a satisfying close (Figure 10.7.9). The music opens by developing the quartal idea introduced in the last eight bars of Chorus 3. (Jazz players pride themselves on this sort of flexible phrasing, in which the improvised motives blur the tune's section boundaries.) The subtle process of variation in these measures is illustrated in Figure 10.7.10: we begin by moving straight up and down the inverted stack of fourths F-B♭-C-F. Evans then varies the gesture's contour and rhythm, playing a series of "down by step, up by third" motions along the "scale" F♯-B-C♯-[F♯]. He repeats this varied form a semitone lower in the "tonic" stack of fourths. The fourth statement moves the pattern backward in time by one

26 I have my doubts about whether Evans meant to do this, though I feel uncomfortable betting against his ingenuity.

eighth note. Finally, the fifth iteration recalls the beginning of the first, though with the triplet now displaced forward in time. The impression is of a kaleidoscopic series of ever-changing variations, as the same basic elements are recombined in new ways.

A relatively simple descending line in mm. 134–136 leads to an idea whose overt bluesiness recalls the very beginning of the solo. Figure 10.7.11 shows how Evans plays with this musical idea in these next few measures: the second statement shifts the pattern upward so that it starts on F♮ rather than D♮—transposing the motive up by step along the non-octave repeating scale (D4, F4, B♭4, D♭5, E♭5, E5). He also compresses the third note so the repetitions occur on weak eighth notes. The third statement uses the same pitches and rhythms as the second, but begins an eighth note later, so that the repeated notes are now on the beat again. (Note that these two phrases also vary the number of repeated notes.) Once more, the impression is

Figure 10.7.9 The fourth chorus of Evans' solo.

Figure 10.7.10 Motivic development at the opening of the fourth chorus.

Figure 10.7.11 Development of the bluesy motif.

of a dazzling process of continuous musical variation, wherein the same basic elements are constantly reconfigured—as if you could never step twice into the same musical river.

The B section begins with a series of chromatically filled-in major thirds; these ascend by minor third while the harmonies descend by fifth ($A^{ø7}$, D^7, G^7). Figure 10.7.12 interprets the underlying musical logic: in the lower staves, we find augmented triads descending semitonally over descending fifths harmonies as in mm. 17–24 and 82–83. Evans, not content to use this stock pattern for a third time, hits upon a clever variation: instead of moving down by semitone from one augmented triad to the next, he moves *up by minor third*—producing the same series of augmented triads, but now in an ascending fashion. This spontaneous stroke of music-theoretical inspiration exploits two different kinds of substitution: tritone substitution, which allows semitonally descending augmented triads to accompany dominant seventh chords descending by fifth, and what might be called "major-third substitution" (deriving from the augmented triad's threefold symmetry), which allows Evans to replace aug-

Figure 10.7.12 With augmented triads, ascending minor thirds and descending semitones produce the same sequence of chords.

mented triads that *descend by semitone* with augmented triads that *ascend by minor third*.[27]

The rest of the phrase is more typical, using scales and arpeggios to outline the underlying harmonies. The solo ends by returning to the bluesy idea of m. 137, doubling its repeated notes at the major third, evoking Stravinsky as much as the blues proper. Evans ends his solo by developing the last two notes of this gesture, falling chromatically to A-C♯. Noticing the waning intensity, Philly Joe Jones stops drumming in preparation for the bass solo.

These sorts of relationships would be interesting if they were found in a piece of composed music, carefully constructed over weeks or months. But their appearance in such a rhythmically complex improvisation is truly remarkable. Many classical musicians, I suspect, would be hard pressed simply to keep time with Evans' rhythm section—indeed, it can be hard enough to follow the form while listening to the record. (Philly Joe Jones, with his dotted half-note polyrhythms, certainly doesn't help!) That Evans is able to do so, while spontaneously developing a coherent musical statement, must be counted an act of genuine virtuosity. Whether we look at the large-scale form of the piece, with its recurrent motives and organic formal development, or at small-scale processes of variation, the improvisation seems logical, clear, and carefully constructed. This is not simply a virtuosity of the body but of the mind as well—the spontaneous expression of a deep understanding of the fundamental principles of twentieth-century tonal composition.

10.8 JAZZ AS MODERNIST SYNTHESIS

Arnold Schoenberg and Walter Piston both observed that theirs was an age marked by the proliferation of styles.[28] Like many of their contemporaries, they despaired of trying to synthesize these diverse trends into a coherent body of knowledge,

27 It is interesting to compare this passage to the opening of Radiohead's "Just," where the triads C–E♭–D–F support a melodic octatonic scale. Radiohead's progression can be understood as an ascending minor-third pattern (C–E♭–F♯–A) that has been transformed by a major-third substitution (F♯→D) which changes an ascending minor third into a descending semitone. (After this substitution the ascending minor thirds continue apace.) The F♯→D substitution preserves the chord tone F♯, so that the octatonic scale sounds the root of the first two chords and the third of the second two. In Evans' solo, descending augmented triads become ascending minor-third augmented triads; in Radiohead's song, ascending minor-third *major triads* instead descend by semitone. Underlying both procedures is the same fundamental geometry.

28 See Piston 1941 and Schoenberg 1975.

explaining that they were too close to the developments they surveyed. (Indeed, it was precisely Piston's despair that gave rise to modern American pedagogy, centering on the "common practice period" of the eighteenth and nineteenth centuries.) Instead, both prophesied that there would come a time in which the various developments of the early twentieth century would be clarified, coalescing into a coherent musical language. I find it marvelous to reflect that these prognostications were essentially correct. For there *is* a late twentieth-century musical language that synthesizes many of the developments of nineteenth and early twentieth-century music, including chromatic voice leading, quartal harmony, polychords, impressionist scales, and polytonality. This musical language has been codified in textbooks, is taught at (some) conservatories, and can be heard on any given night in New York, Riga, Dubrovnik, Tokyo, and throughout much of the rest of the world.

Of course, Schoenberg and Piston would have been shocked to see the form in which their prophecies were realized. First, the synthesis was not achieved by the inheritors of the European notated tradition—composers of string quartets and symphonies, trained in the best conservatories and having access to the finest orchestras and concert halls. Instead the language was forged by improvising musicians, many poor and African American, who carved an alternative musical tradition out of the materials afforded by popular culture. Second, the modernist synthesis did not take the form of a robust *alternative* to tonality: instead, it created a hybrid style that incorporates modernist devices while continuing to exploit functionally tonal ideas. For the contemporary jazz musician, chromatic voice leading, octatonic scales, quartal harmonies, and polychords are just more grist for the tonal mill. Figure 10.8.1 shows that a simple jazz ii–V–I is an accretion of musical techniques formed over the ages: at its core, we have a ii–V–I schema dating from the time of Monteverdi; in the upper voices of the piano's right hand, we find an efficient chromatic voice leading between

Figure 10.8.1 A simple jazz progression incorporates techniques from the entire history of tonality.

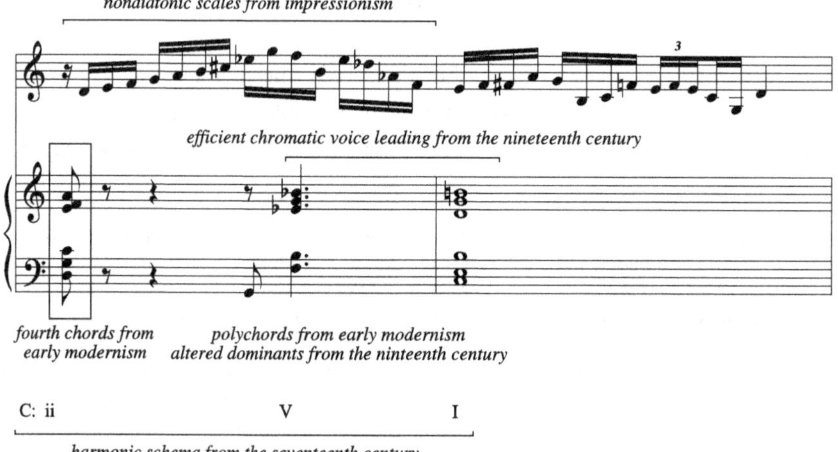

third-related major triads (E♭, G, B♭)→(D, G, B), reminiscent of the progressions that fascinated Schubert, Brahms, and Wagner. On top of this we find scales characteristic of early twentieth-century modernism: an acoustic scale over the V chord, and the lydian mode over the tonic chord. This routine passage, in other words, is a musical synthesis literally centuries in the making, incorporating and domesticating the ideas of previous revolutionary eras.

From an economic point of view, there are clear reasons why jazz musicians would emphasize synthesis and shared musical practices. Notated music is a highly individualized business, created by composers who largely work alone. Jazz, as an inherently social form of music making, is more fertile ground for constructing a genuinely shared musical language: the constant formation and reformation of musical ensembles facilitates an exchange of musical ideas, and the necessity of playing together forces musicians to agree on a set of common principles. As a result, innovations in jazz tended to accumulate, forming an ever-growing common practice. Notated composers, on the other hand, are free to rethink musical syntax from the ground up. Not surprisingly, then, twentieth-century concert music contains a multitude of highly individual musical languages, stunning in their diversity, but sometimes completely disconnected from one another.

Ultimately, this economic difference allowed jazz musicians to act as custodians of a tradition of advanced tonal thinking, bridging the gap between the tonality of Debussy and Ravel, and that of Louis Andreissen, Steve Reich, and John Adams. To composers who grew up during the modernist ascendancy—a time when atonality was in fashion and tonality was occasionally dismissed as a remnant of the past—jazz must have provided a beacon of hope, an example of a sophisticated tonal language that drew on the past, yet went beyond it in significant ways. For these composers, jazz would have provided a major source, if not *the* major source, for ideas about how to compose in a distinctively modern and tonal style. Certainly this was true in my own case: it was pieces like Bill Evans' "Oleo" (as well as the music of Art Tatum, John Coltrane, and Miles Davis) that convinced me that tonality had continued to develop and grow throughout the twentieth century, unnoticed by official academic culture. And I learned as much about the mechanics of tonal harmony from jazz theorists like Mehegan and Levine, as I did from the atonal composers who taught me about Bach and Schubert.

Today, of course, both tonality and jazz have made some inroads into elite musical culture. Nevertheless, it remains true that jazz continues to occupy a subordinate position in American music theory and music education (Figure 10.8.2). Students continue to receive music degrees from major American universities without ever engaging seriously with jazz. It is possible that this represents only the intrinsic difficulties of teaching non-notated music, exacerbated by a serious case of institutional inertia: for a long time, jazz education was an oral tradition, and there were few good written resources to be found. (Furthermore, even under the best of circumstances, academic institutions are like ocean liners, requiring a long time to turn around.) But it is also possible that the current status of jazz reflects, at least in some ways, the legacy of decades of systematic bias. It is sobering to think that many of the most

Figure 10.8.2 According to online databases of academic journals, jazz plays a relatively minor role in contemporary music scholarship. For example, just a handful of articles mention tritone substitution, whereas thousands mention serial music.

	Hits	
Search Subject	**JSTOR**	**RILM**
Arnold Schoenberg	2421	2545
John Cage	2368	1448
"serial music" or serialism	2688	2433
Duke Ellington	1227	354
John Coltrane	453	210
tritone substitution	15	3

important jazz innovations occurred during a time when it was still illegal, in some parts of this country, for people of different races to marry. Given this, it is perhaps not surprising that a musical style that married African and European approaches might have had difficulty making inroads into university curricula. One can only hope that the recent election of the first African-American president of the United States foreshadows a future, however distant, in which irrational barriers may mean less than they once did, and in which we can start to appreciate the profound connections between jazz and other musical styles.

Conclusion

Imagine yourself as a European composer at the beginning of the twentieth century, when the world was changing at an unimaginable pace. The decreasing cost of travel had made it possible to bring, say, a gamelan to Paris, or to mount strangely terrifying exhibitions of "primitive" art. Unprecedented scientific and technological discoveries were expanding your sense of what was possible: suddenly, images and sounds could be preserved for posterity, information could be transmitted instantaneously across vast distances, and the very distinction between space and time was in question. Under the circumstances, it would be perverse not to wonder whether there could be musical analogues to this revolutionary ferment. Surely, there were some features of Western music that were just conventions—parochial habits that went unchallenged simply because no one had ever thought to challenge them. Perhaps the V–I cadence was one of these, or the use of familiar meters, or even the notion of consonance itself....

Composers, in other words, faced the broadly scientific problem of determining which features of musical language were arbitrary and which were rooted more firmly in our biology or unchangeable cultural habits. Different musicians responded in different ways, arraying themselves along the spectrum from extreme conservatives (almost in denial about the changes sweeping the world) to utopian radicals (who in retrospect seem somewhat naive about humanity's appetite for musical revolution).[1] For a time, music really was "experimental," as composers drew and redrew the line between what would be different and what would remain the same. The problem is that in music, unlike science, "experiments" rarely produce unequivocal answers: it is entirely likely that a particular compositional style—be it impressionism, atonality, or bebop—will attract some adherents while repulsing others. And so, a century later, we are still struggling with the aftershocks of the modernist explosion. Rather than reaching consensus on the fundamental mechanisms of musical coherence, the musical world has split into distinct and sometimes hostile camps. For every musician who thinks that tonality is a thing of the past, there is another who thinks that atonality was a vast and horrible mistake—the musical analogue, as Milan Kundera once wrote, of the Dictatorship of the Proletariat.

1 Interestingly, music theorists like Riemann and Schenker tended toward the conservative end of the spectrum, insisting on the naturalness of traditional Western music well into the twentieth century.

This situation is exacerbated by the fact that music occupies an intermediate position in our psychic economy. It is possible to splash paint relatively haphazardly on canvas without creating something that is truly noxious—at worst, the result will be bland but inoffensive, a kind of apocalyptic wallpaper. By contrast, imagine the situation of the avant-garde cook who simply combines *all possible tastes* in the way Jackson Pollock splashed paint. (Please note that I am not limiting myself to *food* tastes!) It's safe to say that the culinary avant-gardist would have to close up shop relatively quickly, and that even the most diehard aesthetes would give Aleatoric Eatery a pass. Somewhere between these two extremes lies the situation of the avant-garde composer, who faces an audience less tolerant than the audience for paintings, but more tolerant than the audience for food. It is quite possible to develop a taste for atonal music, and as a result there are more fans of atonal music than there will ever be for Atonal Food. But at the same time, developing a taste for atonality often involves a significant investment of time, and it is not for everybody—meaning that avant-garde music will never be as popular as avant-garde painting. Atonality is neither so abrasive as to die out completely, nor so attractive as to achieve widespread acceptance.[2]

My initial motivation in writing this book was to try to imagine a time in which the aftershocks of modernism were no longer so keenly felt, and in which we could begin to glimpse rudimentary answers to the old modernist questions. To my mind, the five properties of Chapter 1 are fairly basic to the Western conception of musical coherence and not likely to be supplanted soon: for the foreseeable future, the majority of successful Western music will continue to exploit acoustic consonance, small melodic motions, consistent harmonies, clear tonal centers, and identifiable macroharmonies. (Whether this is a matter of biology, deep cultural inertia, or some combination of the two is practically speaking not that important.) And this in turn means that familiar chords and scales—overdetermined and multiply optimized as they are—will continue to play a central role in our musical life. Thus the goal of Part I, to provide a conceptual framework for composers who are less interested in *replacing* tonality than in devising new tonal styles. I like to think of the five features as basic flavors that can be combined and recombined endlessly—as if the composer were a chef attempting to create new musical dishes with the same basic set of ingredients.

From a purely theoretical perspective, the important point is that it is extremely difficult to satisfy all five features simultaneously. This can be seen by considering the continuous geometrical spaces in Chapter 3. To combine harmonic consistency and conjunct melodic motion is to utilize short-distance line segments between structurally similar chords, and this is possible only if we exploit some unusual feature of the geometry: either the global "twist" by which opposite faces are identified, or

2 There is also the fact that painters sell one-of-a-kind commodities which often appreciate in value, whereas composers (like cooks) sell repeatable experiences and depend for their profits on a high volume of sales. This results in a tragicomic disparity between avant-garde painters and composers: while it is almost *de rigueur* for successful visual artists to buy their own palaces and islands, even the most successful atonal composers typically need to augment their modest compositional income by teaching.

the boundaries that act like mirrors. (These two possibilities can be associated with traditional tonality and 1960s "micropolyphony," respectively.) But there are other, more subtle forms of constraint as well, leading us to expect that composers would naturally gravitate toward scales that (for example) contain many consonances while also dividing the octave nearly evenly. In this sense, tonality is not one among an infinitude of habitable planets, all easily accessible by short rocket flight; instead, it is much closer to being the *only* habitable planet that we have discovered so far. And just as we have an interest in conserving the ecology of this, our only habitable planet, so too might we have an interest in protecting the sophisticated tonal languages that manage to survive in today's unfriendly economic climate.

This is not to say that there is nothing new under the sun, or that the music of the future is doomed to repeat the procedures of the past. Over the course of the book, I have described a number of new ideas—including individual T-relatedness, near symmetry, pitch-class circulation, global macroharmonic profiles, chord lattices, interscalar transposition, and so on—that naturally suggest directions for further musical exploration. Previous composers have explored these ideas in a fairly intuitive and unsystematic manner. My hope is that a deeper theoretical understanding will open new compositional doors, suggesting new ways in which we might transmute the basic materials of tonality into something rich and strange. (Even the simple harmonic "grammar" of §7.1 is potential grist for the twenty-first-century compositional mill, providing a way to tweak or automate or parody the ancient procedures of functional tonality.) And while I had initially envisioned an entire chapter describing the potential compositional applications of these ideas, I eventually decided against this. For it seemed to me that readers might prefer to discover *for themselves* how to use these new concepts to create new music. And I thought that I myself might prefer to be surprised by what readers come up with, rather than pushing them to walk along the paths that I had already made.

As I said, my initial goal in writing this book was to explore basic theoretical and compositional issues. But during the course of my thinking, I gradually began to realize that my five features could also provide a helpful framework for understanding the development of Western music. The narrative sketched in Chapter 6—and fleshed out by the rest of Part II—suggests a reasonably systematic progression wherein composers repeatedly grappled with the problems and opportunities bequeathed to them by their predecessors. Increasing interest in three- and four-voice composition led to triadic harmony, which eventually paved the way for the functional conventions of the classical era. The gradual standardization of major and minor modes led to an increased emphasis on chromatic transposition, which eventually underwrote the expanded modal vocabulary of twentieth-century tonality. Nineteenth-century chromatic voice leading led to more chromatic macroharmonies, resulting in a split between atonal composers who followed the vector of increasing chromaticism to its logical conclusion, and scalar composers who ameliorated chromaticism with the three scalar techniques of Chapter 9.

My hope is that these sorts of ideas might inspire theorists and historians to do more careful and detailed work. My chief goal has been to introduce (or reframe) basic theoretical concepts such as voice leading, pitch-class intervals, chord similarity, key distance, scale, mode, centricity, and so on. I have provided some hints about how we might use these concepts, both in traditional analysis and in statistical investigations of larger trends. But in a book such as this, it is impossible to consider these issues in anything like the detail that they deserve. Forced to play the dual role of tool salesman and carpenter, I have left you with a frame rather than a completed house. Consequently, there is more to be said about the varieties of nineteenth-century chromaticism, or the various statistical approaches to musical analysis, or really any of the historical topics broached in this book. Hopefully, readers will see this as an invitation to future work, rather than a defect of the book as it stands.

To my mind, the most novel feature of my historical narrative concerns the transition from the nineteenth to the twentieth century. I am fascinated by the thought that, amid the fog and confusion of recent history, it is just possible to discern the outlines of a genuine common practice, stretching from impressionism through jazz to contemporary postminimalism. This common practice fuses nineteenth-century voice leading with a distinctively twentieth-century interest in scales, combining a flexible attitude toward centricity with a serious concern for macroharmony. I do not want to suggest that this is the only twentieth-century music worth paying attention to, but for me it forms a kind of central core, the twentieth century's most obvious contribution to elementary mechanisms of tonality. Particularly interesting here is the thought that jazz, rather than being some marginal offshoot of classical music, is actually more continuous with early twentieth-century tonality than many forms of more avant-garde music. Thus my claim that the history of twentieth-century tonality runs straight through jazz: we cannot possibly hope to understand the development of notated tonal music without understanding its relation to non-notated styles.

This brings me to my final point. I began by suggesting that early twentieth-century composers faced the difficult problem of determining which aspects of musical practice might be changed and which were more deeply ingrained. Twenty-first-century composers confront a very different challenge. In the past, notated composers had a monopoly on high-culture respectability, since notation was virtually the only way to preserve and transmit one's music. Over the last hundred years, however, the primary means of musical dissemination has shifted from scores to recordings. And while the notated tradition was conducting its experiments in musical coherence, alienating audience members in the process, jazz and rock were becoming increasingly sophisticated, to the point where they now challenge the status of notated music. New instruments—the electric guitar, the synthesizer, the drum set—changed our sonic frame of reference, so that there is now something archaic about the very sound of string quartet or orchestra. The upshot is that young composers not only have to answer the metaphysical questions of their modernist ancestors, but also have to figure out how notated music fits into this new cultural context. They need to think about what it means to write string quartets in the world of Metallica—or, failing that, to establish how best to marry the strengths of notation to the raw power of the electric guitar.

This, then, is contemporary composers' biggest challenge: to rebuild interest on the part of audiences who are largely indifferent to avant gardism, who think that notated music begins and ends with the classics, and who in any case care more about jazz, rock, rap, and electronica. The task is to show that notation—and more generally, a certain kind of sophisticated musical *thinking*—has something to contribute to contemporary culture. I myself believe that this is possible, and that there is music waiting to be written that combines the intellectuality of Bach (or Debussy) with the raw energy of Coltrane (or The Pixies or Einstürzende Neubauten). I would love to think that something in this book had inspired some young musician to grapple with this challenge, perhaps by exploring some of the ideas I have described. But failing that, it would be enough to say something useful about the deep questions of tonality and atonality, still with us a century after the advent of modern music.

APPENDIX A

Measuring Voice-Leading Size

My view is that measures of voice leading should depend only on the distance moved by each voice. Mathematically, we take the absolute value of the difference between the initial and final pitches: thus the distance from C4 to D4 is $|60 - 62|$ or 2, while the distance from C♯4 to C5 is $|60.5 - 72|$ or 11.5. (In some cases, we might want to measure relative to a scale, but we will ignore that complication as it does not change the underlying mathematics.) When several voices move simultaneously, then a measure of voice-leading distance should depend only on the *collection* of distances moved by each voice. For instance, the first voice leading in Figure A1 moves its three voices by two, zero, and zero semitones, while the second moves its voices by one, one, and one semitones.[1] A measure of voice-leading size therefore needs to tell us whether the collection {2, 0, 0} is larger or smaller than {1, 1, 1}. We can assume that larger motions in any individual voice do not result in smaller overall voice leadings; thus the collection {6, 3, 1} should be at least as large as {4, 3, 1}, since six is greater than four.

Unfortunately, as mentioned in Chapter 2, it is not obvious how to compare collections. One possibility is to compare their *largest* element, in which case {2, 0, 0} is larger than {1, 1, 1} (since 2 > 1). (I call this the "largest-distance metric.") Another possibility is to *add* the distances in the two collections, in which case the first (total distance = 2) is smaller than the second (total distance = 3). (This is sometimes called the "taxicab metric.") Yet a third possibility is to treat the set of distances as determining the coordinates of a line segment in Euclidean space, with the length of the line segment representing the size of the collection. Here again, the first collection is larger than the second, since the line segment (2, 0, 0) is 2 units long, whereas (1, 1, 1) is only $\sqrt{3}$ units long. (This is called the "Euclidean metric."[2])

Figure A1 The first voice leading moves one note by two semitones, while the second moves three notes by one semitone each.

Since each of our methods is in itself perfectly reasonable, we have no reason to choose one rather than another. Faced with this embarrassment of riches, we could

1 Note that the distance is always a positive number and does not depend on whether the voice moves up or down.

2 The formula for computing distance in n-dimensional Euclidean space is $\sqrt{x_1^2 + x_2^2 + ... + x_n^2}$.

arbitrarily choose one and hope for the best. (This is what music theorists have traditionally done.[3]) Alternatively, we might note that there are some facts about which "reasonable" metrics should agree: surely, for example, no reasonable metric can treat the voice leading (C, G)→(F♯, C♯), in which both voices move by tritone, as being smaller than (C, G)→(C♯, F♯), in which the voices move by semitone![4] This suggests the strategy of trying to demarcate the "zone of agreement" among reasonable metrics. In the best-case scenario, we might find that all of the claims we would like to make are valid for all reasonable metrics—and thus there is no need to choose one rather than another. Less optimistically, we might find that we occasionally need to select a method of measuring voice leading; but by charting the "zone of agreement," we will at least be able to see where particular choices lie in the space of reasonable alternatives.

This is the strategy I follow here. I propose that *any method of measuring voice leading is acceptable, as long as it does not have the counterintuitive consequence that "voice crossings" make a voice leading smaller* (Figure 2.7.2).[5] It is actually quite easy to formulate this principle mathematically: if a metric is not to favor voice crossings, then it must treat the collection of distances $\{x_1 + c, x_2, \ldots, x_n\}$ as being at least as large as $\{x_1, x_2 + c, \ldots, x_n\}$, whenever $x_1 > x_2$ and $c \geq 0$. Furthermore, $\{x_1, x_2 + c, \ldots, x_n\}$ should be at least as large as $\{x_1, x_2, \ldots, x_n\}$. Intuitively, this means that the metric should not prefer an uneven distribution of distances, such as {4, 0, 0} over a more even distribution, such as {1, 1, 2}. This well-known mathematical principle can be stated in a number of equivalent ways.[6] Originating in early twentieth-century economics, it is called the *submajorization partial order,* and it appears in an extraordinarily wide range of applications.[7] The principle determines a "partial order" because it provides a way to compare some but not all collections of numbers. For instance, it tells us that {1, 1} can be no larger than {2, 0}, but it does not tell us anything about the relative sizes of {3, 3} and {4, 1}.

Figure A2 uses the Möbius strip to illustrate the geometry underlying this approach. The arrows in the upper left show that the musical "no-crossings principle" is equivalent to the geometrical principle that voice leadings bouncing off the mirror (which contain crossings) should never be shorter than those that directly

3 See, for example, Straus (2003), who chooses the taxicab metric, and Callender (2004), who chooses Euclidean distance. For early (and somewhat vague) discussions of voice leading size, see Masson 1697/1969, Hostinský 1879, and Schoenberg 1975.

4 To be clear, there may be some notions of distance according to which, say, G is closer to C than C♯ is, but I claim that these alternatives measure something other than *voice-leading distance.*

5 Composers regularly employ voice crossings, but there is no reason to think that in doing so they are reducing voice-leading size.

6 For instance, here is a not obviously equivalent formulation: given two voice leadings *A* and *B*, *A* is no larger than *B* if the largest distance moved by any single voice in *A* is less than or equal to the largest distance moved by any voice in *B*, and if the sum of the largest *two* distances in *A* is less than or equal to the sum of the largest two distances in *B*, and if the sum of the largest *three* distances in *A* is less than or equal to the sum of the largest three distances in *B*, and so on.

7 See Marshall and Olkin 1979, and Hall and Tymoczko 2007.

Figure A2 Two connections between geometry and voice-leading distance. (*Möbius strip, upper left*) To say that voice crossings never make a voice leading smaller is to say that the two edges of this triangle are not shorter than the third. Since the voice leading β contains a crossing, it bounces off the mirror boundary. The "uncrossed" alternative (α) forms the triangle's third edge. According to all reasonable measures of voice-leading size, the uncrossed voice leading in α is no larger than the crossed voice leading in β. (*Möbius strip, lower right*) The figure provides a geometrical illustration of the submajorization partial order. All voice leadings in the inner diamond are smaller than (C, G)→(D, F). All voice leadings outside the shaded area are larger. The shaded area represents the zone of acceptable disagreement among reasonable metrics.

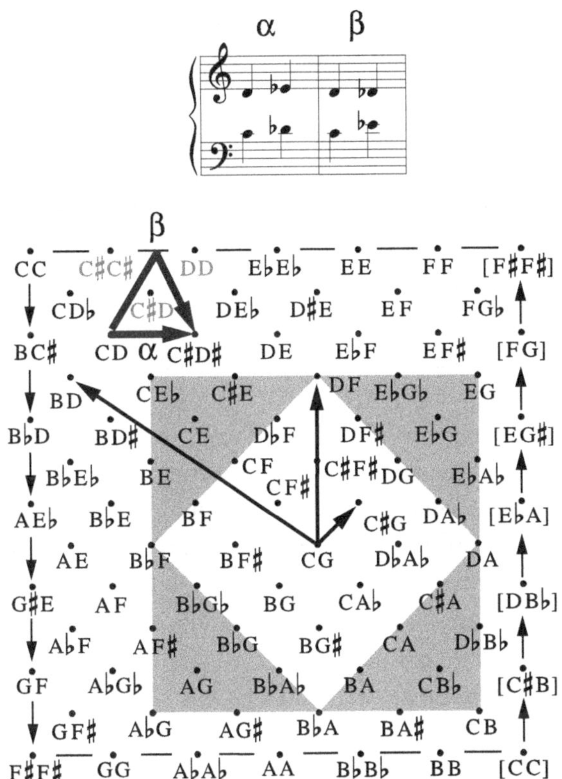

connect their endpoints.[8] (This, in turn, is related to what mathematicians call "the triangle inequality.") In the lower right, I show how the no-crossings principle gives us a method of comparing some, but not all, voice leadings. The vertical arrow corresponds to the voice leading (C, G)→(D, F). The inner diamond determines the voice leadings that, according to any reasonable metric, must be at least as small as this one. The outer white space contains voice leadings that must be at least as large as the vertical arrow. The shaded area, meanwhile, represents the zone of acceptable disagreement; arrows that terminate in this area may reasonably be considered to be either

8 Any voice leading with a crossing in pitch space is represented by a line segment that bounces off the mirror boundary at the point where two voices cross.

smaller or larger than (C, G)→(D, F).[9] If we are interested in making comparisons between similar-sized voice leadings we therefore need to choose a specific metric, but when comparing very different voice leadings we often do not: for instance, we can say that the arrow (C, G)→(B, D) on Figure A2 is at least as large as the two other arrows originating at the same point *for any reasonable metric whatsoever*.

It turns out that reasonable metrics agree about a surprisingly large number of musically interesting facts. For instance, they agree that more-even chords in general have smaller voice leadings to their various transpositions.[10] They also agree that "inversionally symmetrical" voice leadings are particularly small: suppose $A \rightarrow B$ is a voice leading such as (C, E, G)→(B, E, G♯), in which, for every voice that moves up by x semitones, there is also a voice that moves down by x semitones; reasonable metrics will all agree that $A \rightarrow B$ is at least as small as any other individually T-related voice leading $A \rightarrow \mathbf{T}_x(B)$. From this it follows that, for any reasonable metric, major triads can be connected by minimal voice leading when they are related by major third, and dominant seventh chords can be connected by minimal voice leading when they are related by minor third or tritone. (In other words, reasonable metrics agree about the importance of the major-third and minor-third systems.) Thus we need not always select one voice-leading metric from among the many equally plausible alternatives: in many cases, we can assume only that our voice-leading metric is a "reasonable" one obeying the submajorization partial order.[11]

It bears repeating that my distinction between "reasonable" and "unreasonable" metrics applies only when we are interested in measuring voice-leading size. In other contexts, there are other conceptions of musical distance that we might want to consider. For example, we might sometimes want to consider G4 to be particularly close to C3, since the upper note is the lower note's third harmonic.[12] Although this is a legitimate measure of musical distance, it cannot be considered a measure of voice-leading size, as I use the term: voice-leading size has to do with *how far the hands move on the piano keyboard from one chord to another*. It is, in other words, a measure of the aggregate effort needed to move along a specific path between two musical "places." This quantity is known to be relevant to listeners' psychology, determining our ability to separate notes into individual melodic streams.[13] And it is this quantity, rather than the other distances considered above, that composers seem to try to minimize as they move from one chord to another.

---

9 Strictly speaking, this is true only of voice leadings that do not touch the edges; once a voice leading passes into the exterior white region it is necessarily larger than the vertical arrow.

10 See Tymoczko 2006. Here I am considering only bijective voice leadings.

11 This principle is general enough that it can plausibly be attributed to composers' individual psychology: it is certainly hard to imagine that a composer would think that the voice leading (C, G)→(B, D) on Figure A2 is smaller than (C, G)→(D, F). By contrast, it is much harder to imagine that, say, Mozart used the largest-distance metric rather than the taxicab metric.

12 Or we might consider the chord {C, C♯, E, F♯} to be close to {C, D♭, E♭, G}, since they contain the same collection of intervals (Tymoczko 2008c); in still other cases, we might measure distance by counting how many voices are moving.

13 See Huron 2001. Wessel 1979 contains an important caveat.

APPENDIX B

Chord Geometry: A More Technical Look

This appendix offers a more technical description of the higher dimensional chord spaces. My goal is to provide enough information to allow you to work with the spaces directly, either by hand or using a computer. My treatment will presuppose only elementary mathematics, explaining technical terms (such as "fundamental domain" and "quotient space") along the way. However, I will not shy away from messy details omitted from the main text.

Musically, a pitch can be represented by a number, as discussed in §2.1. An ordered sequence of n pitches is therefore represented by an ordered sequence of n numbers, or in mathematical parlance an "n-tuple." (Chapter 2 refers to these n-tuples as "basic musical objects.") Geometrically, an n-tuple determines a point in infinite n-dimensional Cartesian space, or "ordered pitch space." To generate the space of *un*ordered sequences of *pitch classes,* we need to "fold" this space to eliminate octave and order information. (Mathematicians would say that this folding produces a *quotient* of the original space.) In other words, we move from an infinite, periodic "wallpaper space" to the finite space representing one of its individual tiles (§3.2). In three dimensions we obtain the tile by gluing together all points such as (x_1, x_2, x_3), (x_2, x_3, x_1), and (x_2, x_1, x_3), which represent different ways of ordering the same pitches, as well as all points such as (x_1, x_2, x_3) and $(x_1 + 12, x_2, x_3)$, in which the same pitch classes appear in different octaves.

The easiest way to approach this process is to find a region of the original space that contains exactly one point for each unordered set of n pitch classes. This region, by itself, will not have any interesting mathematical or topological qualities: as a portion of plain-vanilla Euclidean space, it will be completely unremarkable, just like the space from which it is drawn. (Mathematicians would say that this region is a *fundamental domain,* which is not yet a quotient space.) Our region becomes mathematically interesting only when we ascribe unusual properties to its boundaries: for instance, when we assert that some points act like mirrors, or are glued together in various ways. We make these assertions because we would like to use the region to model distances or trajectories in the original, infinite space—much as we used the single tile of wallpaper to record the ant's progress in §3.2.

This distinction between a fundamental domain (a region of ordinary Euclidean space) and a quotient space (a more topologically exotic space) is worth illustrating. Figure B1a depicts the infinite, one-dimensional line containing single pitches. To convert this into a space of pitch classes, we need to glue together all octave-related pitches x and $x + 12$. We begin by constructing a *region* of the original space containing one point for every pitch class. This is an ordinary line segment such as that in Figure B1b, consisting of all points greater than or equal to zero, and less than 12. (Note that our figure does not include the point 12, since it represents the same pitch class as zero; however, it contains every point less than 12, including points infinitesimally close to 12.) Because this is just a line segment, there is no reason (yet!) to say that the points at different ends are close together. It is only when we start to use the space to represent distances or trajectories in our original pitch space that we notice that it its endpoints are related: for instance, the motion shown in Figure B1c disappears off the right edge of our line segment to reappear on the left. This tells us that the two edges of the line segment should be glued together, and that two points near

Figure B1 (*a*) Pitch space is a line. (*b*) The region $0 \leq x < 12$ contains one point for every pitch class. (*c*) The line segment 59→64 disappears off the right edge of our region, reappearing on the left. (*d*) This tells us that we should attach the right edge to the left, forming a *quotient space*. We can represent this quotient space as a circle in two dimensions. Alternatively, we could simply add a new point, 12, to the right edge of our space and declare it to be the same as the point at the left edge.

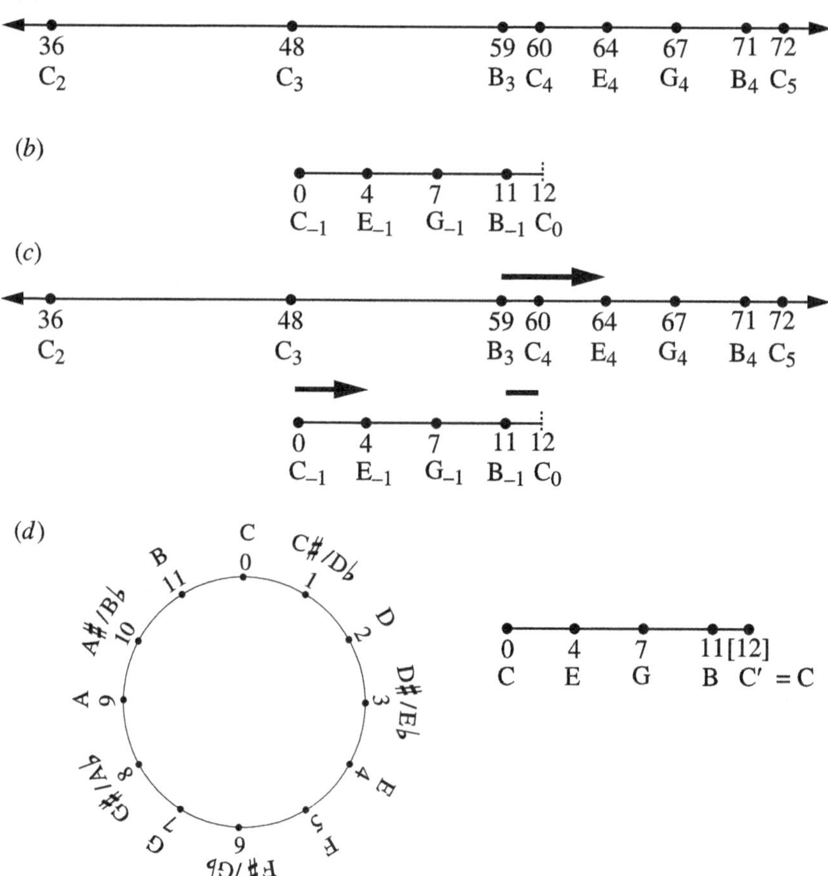

opposite ends are actually close together. We can express this visually by bending the line segment, producing the familiar pitch-class circle shown in Figure B1d. Alternatively, we could simply add the point 12 to the right edge, declaring it to be the same as the point 0 on the left.[1]

Our goal, then, is to determine how to identify a region of n-dimensional Euclidean space containing one point for every unordered set of n pitch classes.[2] To do this, we can choose the region containing all and only those chords whose pitches (1) are in nondescending order, (2) span no more than an octave, and (3) together sum to a number less than 12 and greater than or equal to zero.[3] Clearly, by reordering and octave transposing, we can transform any sequence into one that meets the first two criteria: for instance, we can turn (G4, C3, E5) into (C4, E4, G4), which is in nondescending order and spans no more than an octave. However, the pitches (C4, E4, G4) do not meet the third criterion, since the numbers (60, 64, 67) sum to 191. Observe, though, that we can reduce their sum by 12 by transposing the last note down by octave and moving it to the front of the list. (In Chapter 4 we describe this process as transposition by one descending step along the "scale" C-E-G.) The resulting sequence, (G3, C4, E4), sums to 179 (or 191 − 12), while still meeting the other criteria. By repeating this process, therefore, we can eventually bring the sum into the range $0 \le x < 12$.[4]

Our region is therefore bounded by the following mathematical inequalities:

$$x_1 \le x_2 \le \ldots \le x_n \le x_1 + 12 \tag{B.1}$$

$$0 \le x_1 + x_2 + x_3 + \ldots + x_n < 12 \tag{B.2}$$

Equation B.1 says that the pitches are in nondescending order, spanning no more than an octave. Equation B.2 says that the sum of the pitches is greater than or equal to zero, and less than 12. Together, these inequalities determine a region of infinite n-dimensional Cartesian space, in which there is exactly one point for every collection of n unordered pitch classes. Of course, points in this region still represent *ordered pitch sequences,* and not chords proper; in this sense the region, like a single tile of wallpaper, is a kind of steppingstone between our original "ordered pitch space" and the topologically complex "unordered chord space" we are trying to construct.

Before I try to explain what this region looks like, I should note that in some sense, complicated mathematics is unnecessary. For if we wanted to, we could simply program a computer to display the lower dimensional chord spaces directly. There are numerous computer graphics packages that allow users to draw in two- or

---

1 In fact, this might be preferable since it shows that our quotient space is intrinsically one-dimensional; the circular representation may falsely suggest that the space has two dimensions.

2 There will actually be many different regions satisfying this criterion, of varying shapes; in what follows, I will describe a region that is particularly useful.

3 I use "nondescending" rather than "ascending" because I want to include chords that have pitch duplications, such as (C4, C4, C4, E4).

4 This process will never run afoul of the other two constraints, since the original ordering spans no more than an octave.

three-dimensional space; using the algorithm in Figure B2, we can transform any arbitrary ordered pitch sequence into a point lying in our region, and can thus graph arbitrary chords in the space. Furthermore, as explained in Chapters 2 and 3, we can graph voice leadings simply by imagining that each voice glides smoothly from its origin to the destination. (A computer can be programmed to provide the illusion of a smooth glide by taking discrete steps that are too small for the eye to follow.) At each stage along the glide, we project the current point into our fundamental region. Were we to do this, we would immediately see the shapes in Figures 3.3.1 and 3.8.2. Furthermore, as we plotted various voice leadings on the figure, we would find that our algorithm automatically accounts for the space's "exotic" boundary points: some boundaries would act like mirrors, while others would seem to be glued together. (That is, we would sometimes see a trajectories disappear off one part of the figure to reappear on another.) For someone who is not comfortable with geometry or abstract mathematics, or for someone who does not recognize what shapes Eqs. B.1 and B.2 correspond to, this sort of direct, intuitive hands-on exploration may perhaps be the easiest way to proceed.

However, my job here is to try to explain—in a principled way—how to understand the two sets of inequalities. In preparation for this task, I will review several elementary musico-geometrical facts.

Fact 1. Transposition is represented by adding a constant to every note in a chord: $(x_1 + t, x_2 + t, \dots, x_n + t)$ is the transposition of $(x_1, x_2, \dots, x_n)$ by t semitones (§2.1).

Fact 2. Geometrically, adding t to every note in a chord corresponds to moving in parallel to the "unit diagonal" that connects $(0, 0, \dots, 0)$ to $(1, 1, \dots, 1)$ (Figure B3).

Figure B2 An algorithm for moving any ordered pitch set into the fundamental region defined by equations (1) and (2).

Algorithm	Example
1. Convert pitches into pitch-class numbers lying in the range $0 \le x < 12$.	1. We begin with {E4, B2, G♯3} or {64, 47, 56}. Converting to pitch-class notation gives {4, 11, 8}.
2. Order these numbers from low to high.	2. Ordering gives us (4, 8, 11).
3. If the sum of the pitch classes in the chord is 12 or larger, subtract 12 from the last note and move it to the front of the list. This new number will be less than 0.	3. Since $4 + 8 + 11 \ge 12$, we subtract 12 from the last number and move it to the front, producing (–1, 4, 8).
4. Repeat step 3 until the sum of the pitch classes is less than 12.	4. Since $-1 + 4 + 8 < 12$, we are done.

Fact 3. The equation $x_1 + x_2 \dots x_n = c$ determines a higher dimensional analogue to the plane—a "hyperplane"—perpendicular to the unit diagonal described in Fact 2 (Figure B3).[5]

Fact 4. There is exactly one transposition of any ordered pitch sequence with elements that sum to any particular value. The number $t = (c - x_1 - x_2 - \dots - x_n)/n$ is the unique transposition such that $(x_1 + t, x_2 + t, \dots, x_n + t)$ sums to c. Geometrically, this means that there is a unique way to move any point p parallel to the unit diagonal until it reaches an arbitrary plane perpendicular to that diagonal (Figure B3).

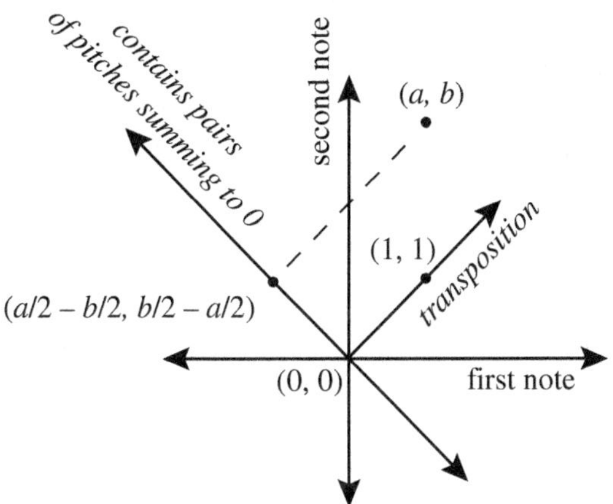

Figure B3 Transposition is represented by motion parallel to the line stretching from (0, 0) to (1, 1). The planes perpendicular to this line contain chords summing to a constant value.

Armed with these facts, let us return to our two equations:

$$x_1 \le x_2 \le \dots \le x_n \le x_1 + 12 \tag{B.1}$$

$$0 \le x_1 + x_2 + x_3 + \dots + x_n < 12 \tag{B.2}$$

Fact 3 tells us that Eq. B.2 determines a collection of hyperplanes perpendicular to the line connecting (0, 0, 0,…, 0) to (1, 1, 1…, 1), with sums in the range $0 \le c < 12$. By Fact 2, these hyperplanes are related by transposition.[6] Next, we observe that if any

5 The term "hyperplane" refers to a flat Euclidean space with one fewer dimension than the n-dimensional space in which it resides. To see that the equation $x_1 + x_2 + \dots + x_n = c$ determines a hyperplane, it helps to know that any *linear* equation $a_1x_1 + a_2x_2 + \dots + a_nx_n = c$, with the a_i all real numbers, determines a hyperplane. (Intuitively, we can freely choose $n - 1$ of the n coordinates, with the final coordinate being determined by our earlier choices.) To see that the plane is perpendicular to the line connecting (0, 0,…, 0) to (1, 1,…, 1) recall that two vectors are perpendicular when $x \cdot y = 0$. (Here "•" is the dot product of linear algebra: $x_1y_1 + x_2y_2 + \dots + x_ny_n$.) That is, $(x_1, x_2, \dots, x_n) \cdot (1, 1, \dots, 1) = 0$, or $x_1 + x_2 + \dots x_n = 0$. Thus the $(n - 1)$-dimensional plane $x_1 + x_2 + \dots x_n = 0$ contains vectors perpendicular to the vector (1, 1,…, 1). The expression $(x_1, x_2, \dots, x_n) \cdot (1, 1, \dots, 1) = c$, or $x_1 + x_2 + \dots x_n = c$, identifies the hyperplane that is c units away along the line connecting (0, 0,…, 0) to (1, 1,…, 1).

6 If two of our hyperplanes sum to c_1 and c_2, then they are related by $(c_2 - c_1)/n$ semitone transposition, with n being the size of the chord.

ordered pitch sequence satisfies the first set of inequalities (Eq. B.1), then so do all its transpositions. (This is just to say that if an ordered pitch sequence is in nondescending order spanning less than an octave, then its transpositions are, too.) It follows that Eq. B.1 determines the same shape in each of the cross sections $x_1 + x_2 \ldots + x_n = c$. The space of musical chords is therefore some sort of *prism:* the inequalities $x_1 \leq x_2 \leq \ldots \leq x_n \leq x_1 + 12$ determine the shape of the cross section, while the equation $x_1 + x_2 + x_3 + \ldots + x_n = c$ identifies the particular cross section containing pitch sequences summing to c.

The next problem is to determine the shape of the cross section. We begin by reviewing the definition of a "simplex"—an n-dimensional figure bounded by the lines interconnecting $n + 1$ vertices.[7] (A simplex is so-called because it is, in some sense, the "simplest" n-dimensional figure, with the minimal number of vertices.) In two dimensions, the simplex's three vertices determine a triangle. In three dimensions, the four vertices determine a tetrahedron. Mathematicians sometimes use the term "the standard simplex" to refer to the simplex bounded by the endpoints of the basis vectors in n-dimensional Cartesian space. Figure B4 shows that the basis vectors in two-dimensional space define a one-dimensional simplex stretching from (0, 1) to (1, 0); the three basis vectors in three-dimensional space determine a simplex stretching from (1, 0, 0) to (0, 1, 0) to (0, 0, 1). (The higher dimensional figures, although harder to visualize, are analogous.) Every point in these two simplexes is represented by coordinates that are all nonnegative and sum to one. For this reason, these simplexes are important in applications in which a total quantity of "stuff" is divided up into a fixed number of parts: for example, the one-dimensional simplex in Figure B4 might be used to represent the result of an election featuring two candidates, while the two-dimensional simplex might be used for a three-party election.

Figure B4 The "standard simplex" in two-dimensional space is a one-dimensional line segment (i.e. a one-dimensional simplex) stretching from (1, 0) to (0, 1); in three dimensional space, it is a two-dimensional triangle (two-dimensional simplex) bounded by (1, 0, 0), (0, 1, 0), and (0, 0, 1). The standard simplex contains all points with nonnegative coordinates summing to 1.

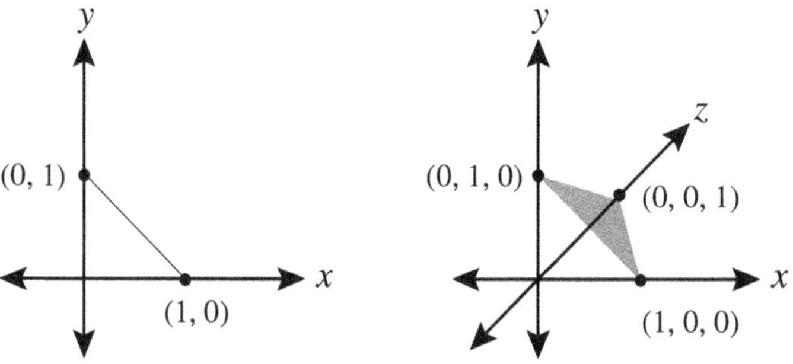

7 Strictly speaking, the vertices must be "affinely independent"—that is, that there should be no c-dimensional plane containing more than $c + 1$ of the points.

Now a mathematician would immediately recognize that the equation $x_1 \leq x_2 \leq \ldots \leq x_n \leq x_1 + 12$ determines a simplex in the hyperplane $x_1 + x_2 + x_3 + \ldots + x_n = c$. There are a number of ways to see why this is so.[8] Perhaps the most instructive is to note that there is a close relation between our equations and the standard simplex described in the previous paragraph. To see why, note that we can rewrite the inequalities $x_1 \leq x_2 \leq \ldots \leq x_n \leq x_1 + 12$ as

$$x_i - x_{i-1} \geq 0 \text{ for } 1 < i \leq n$$
$$x_1 + 12 - x_n \geq 0$$

Since $x_i - x_{i-1}$ is the interval from note x_{i-1} to x_i, our new inequalities simply say that the intervals between adjacent notes in the sequence are all nondescending, including the "wraparound" interval from the last note, x_n, to the note an octave above the first, $x_1 + 12$. Furthermore, these n positive numbers must sum to 12, since they begin with x_1 and end with $x_1 + 12$. Dividing by 12 therefore gives us the coordinates of a point in the standard simplex.[9] Conversely, for any point in the standard simplex, we can multiply its coordinates by 12 and construct a pitch sequence with those numbers as its consecutive intervals. According to Fact 4, there will be one and only one transposition of this sequence lying in the hyperplane $x_1 + x_2 + x_3 + \ldots + x_n = c$.[10] We conclude that there is a "coordinate transformation" sending our original simplex, in which numbers represent *pitches*, into the standard simplex, in which the numbers represent *intervals*, as measured in fractions of an octave (Figure B5). Mathematicians will recognize that this coordinate change is an "affine transformation," which means that it transforms one simplex into another. It follows that our original inequalities determine a simplex as well.[11]

Figure B5 The coordinate transformation from pitch-class space, in which coordinates represent numbers, to interval space, in which they represent intervals.

Original Coordinate	New Coordinate
x_1	$(x_2 - x_1)/12$
x_2	$(x_3 - x_2)/12$
...	...
x_n	$(x_1 + 12 - x_n)/12$

8 The simplest is to note that each of the inequalities $x_i \leq x_j$ carves the space into two halves, bounded by the hyperplane $x_i = x_j$. If n such half-spaces determine a finite region in $(n - 1)$-dimensional space, then that region is bounded by n hyperplanes, which is just to say that it is a simplex.

9 For example, beginning with the pitch sequence (60, 64, 67) we can construct the interval sequence (4, 3, 5) representing the interval from 60 to 64, from 64 to 67, and from 67 to the note an octave above 60. Dividing by 12 gives us (4/12, 3/12, 5/12) which is a point on the standard simplex.

10 For instance, we multiply (½, ½, 0) by 12 to obtain the sequence of intervals (6, 6, 0). We then construct a sequence of pitches whose successive notes are separated by these intervals, for instance (F♯2, C3, F♯3) or (42, 48, 54). These values sum to 144; transposing down by four octaves gives (−6, 0, 6), which sums to zero.

11 Suppose x and y are two points that the coordinate transformation sends to x' and y'. An affine transformation sends the point $x + b(y - x)$ to the point $x' + b(y' - x')$, thus transforming a line in the original space into a line in the second. (It is easily checked that the coordinate transformation in Figure B5 is affine.) Algebraically, affine transformations represent the new coordinates as linear functions of the old coordinates—e.g. functions like $x_1' = ax_1 + bx_2 + c$, which do not involve higher powers of the original variables x_1 and x_2.

We conclude, therefore, that our fundamental region is a prism whose face is a simplex. The lower face is determined by the equations

$$x_1 + x_2 + x_3 + \ldots + x_n = 0 \text{ and } x_1 \le x_2 \le \ldots \le x_n \le x_1 + 12$$

This simplex is "extruded" along the line connecting $(0, 0, \ldots, 0)$ to $(1, 1, \ldots, 1)$, a process that corresponds musically to transposing upward, and algebraically to increasing the sum of the chords in the cross section

$$x_1 + x_2 + x_3 + \ldots + x_n = c \text{ and } x_1 \le x_2 \le \ldots \le x_n \le x_1 + 12,$$

with the parameter c varying from 0 to 12. Each layer of the prism contains pitch sequences with a different sum; we can transpose until the sum is equal to 12, at which point we return to the chords that appear on the sum-zero face.

Fact 4 tells us that any ordered pitch sequence satisfying Eq. B.1 has exactly one transposition in each cross section of the space. This means that no two ordered pitch sequences in the same cross section are transpositionally related. However, the cross sections will contain sequences that are transpositionally related *when we ignore octave and order*. For suppose $(x_1, x_2, \ldots, x_n)$ satisfies Eqs. B.1 and B.2. Then,

$$(x_2 - 12/n, x_3 - 12/n, \ldots, x_n - 12/n, x_1 + 12 - 12/n)$$

will as well. (Those of you who have read Chapter 4 will note that this operation combines a chromatic transposition by $-12/n$ semitones with a scalar transposition by one ascending step.[12]) As ordered pitch sequences, these are *not* transpositionally related, but if we disregard octave and order, they are.[13] Thus, given an n-note sequence meeting our criteria, we can easily construct another by moving the first note of the sequence to the end, adding 12 to it, and subtracting $12/n$ from every note in the resulting sequence. For example, starting with (0, 4, 7), we generate (4 – 12/3, 7 – 12/3, 12 – 12/3) or (0, 3, 8). Repeating this procedure gives (3 – 4, 8 – 4, 12 – 4) or (−1, 4, 8). A final repetition returns us to (0, 4, 7), where we began. Musically, the sequences (0, 4, 7), (0, 3, 8), and (−1, 4, 8) represent C major, A♭ major, and E major triads, each in a different mode or registral inversion: (0, 4, 7) is a C major chord whose first note is its root, (0, 3, 8) is an A♭ major chord starting on its third, and (−1, 4, 8) is an E major chord starting with its fifth.[14] In general, every n-note chord type will appear in each cross section n times, in each of its modes.

To determine the vertices of our cross section, we can exploit the relation with the standard simplex. In three dimensions, the standard simplex is bounded by the points (1, 0, 0), (0, 1, 0), and (0, 0, 1), which will correspond to the vertices of our cross section. Multiplying by 12 transforms these numbers into the interval sequences (12, 0, 0),

12 That is, it sends $(x_1, x_2, \ldots, x_n)$ to $(x_2, \ldots, x_n, x_1 + 12)$, transposing up by one scale step, and then subtracts $12/n$ from these coordinates, transposing chromatically downward by $12/n$.

13 If we ignore octave and order $(x_1, x_2, \ldots, x_n)$ is the same as $(x_2, \ldots, x_n, x_1 + 12)$. Subtracting $12/n$ from each number transposes the chord downward.

14 Remember that to find the pitch class to which a number belongs, add or subtract 12 until it lies in the range $0 \le x < 12$. Thus the number −1 refers to the pitch class B.

(0, 12, 0), and (0, 0, 12). Each determines a unique sequence of pitches on the face that sums to 0: (−8, 4, 4), (−4, −4, 8), and (0, 0, 0), or in scientific pitch notation (E–2, E–1, E–1), (G♯–2, G♯–2, G♯–1), and (C–1, C–1, C–1). In other words, they represent the three "modes" of the "scale" containing just one pitch class (Figure B6). The same procedure of course works in other dimensions: the boundaries of the cross section can always be determined by finding the pitch sequences summing to zero, and whose one-step scalar intervals are (12, 0,…, 0), (0, 12, 0,…, 0), (0, 0, 12,…, 0),…, and (0, 0,…, 0, 12).

Two Notes	Three Notes	Four Notes	Five Notes
(0, 0)	(0, 0, 0)	(0, 0, 0, 0)	(0, 0, 0, 0, 0)
(–6, 6)	(–4, –4, 8)	(–3, –3, –3, 9)	(–2.4, –2.4, –2.4, –2.4, 9.6)
	(–8, 4, 4)	(–6, –6, 6, 6)	(–4.8, –4.8, –4.8, 7.2, 7.2)
		(–9, 3, 3, 3)	(–7.2, –7.2, 4.8, 4.8, 4.8)
			(–9.6, 2.4, 2.4, 2.4, 2.4)

Figure B6 The vertices of the zero-sum cross section in various dimensions.

The final step is to understand the "strange" points on the boundary of our region. We begin by considering how to attach the sum-zero face at one edge of the prism to the opposite, sum-12 face.[15] Suppose that $(x_1, x_2, \ldots, x_n)$ lies on the face of the prism summing to zero. Recall that the following chords all lie on the same face.

$$A_1 = (x_1, x_2, \ldots, x_n)$$
$$A_2 = (x_2 - 12/n, x_3 - 12/n, \ldots, x_n - 12/n, x_1 + 12 - 12/n)$$
$$A_3 = (x_3 - 24/n, x_4 - 24/n, \ldots, x_n - 24/n, x_1 + 12 - 24/n, x_2 + 12 - 24/n)$$
$$\vdots$$
$$A_n = (x_n - 12 + 12/n, x_1 + 12/n, \ldots, x_{n-1} + 12/n)$$

If we transpose these chords up by $12/n$ semitones, we obtain a series of chords that sum to 12:

$$A_1' = (x_1 + 12/n, x_2 + 12/n, \ldots, x_n + 12/n)$$
$$A_2' = (x_2, x_3, \ldots, x_n, x_1 + 12)$$
$$A_3' = (x_3 - 12/n, x_4 - 12/n, \ldots, x_n - 12/n, x_1 + 12 - 12/n, x_2 + 12 - 12/n)$$
$$\vdots$$
$$A_n' = (x_n - 12 + 24/n, x_1 + 24/n, \ldots, x_{n-1} + 24/n)$$

15 Note that we have excluded this sum-12 face from our fundamental domain, since it contains the same chords as the sum-0 face. However, when we are constructing the quotient space, we need to think about how to attach various points on the boundaries. As in Figure B1d, we therefore add extra points, declaring them to be "the same" as some that we have already included.

As ordered pitch sequences, A'_1 is the transposition of A_1, A'_2 is the transposition of A_2, and so on. But when we disregard octave and order, then A_1 and A'_2 are *the same chord*, as are A_2 and A'_3, A_3 and A'_4, etc. Therefore we need to imagine that the sum-zero face of the prism should be attached to the opposite (sum-12) face with a "twist." This twist acts as a *cyclic permutation* of the simplex's vertices, connecting A_i to A'_{i+1}.

Finally, we consider the boundary points such as (x, y, y), which contain pitch duplications. Consider a point in the interior of our simplex, such as $(x_1, x_2 - c, x_2 + c)$, with c some small positive number. As c goes to zero, the point $(x_1, x_2 - c, x_2 + c)$ approaches (x_1, x_2, x_2), moving in a line toward the boundary of the cross section. When c becomes negative, the ordered pitch sequence $(x_1, x_2 - c, x_2 + c)$ lies outside of our fundamental region, since the second number is now greater than the third. According to the algorithm in Figure B2, then, we need to reorder the sequence so that it returns to our region. This reordering returns us to a point on the line segment along which we have just been traveling, since $(x_1, x_2 - (-c), x_2 + (-c))$ is a reordering of $(x_1, x_2 - c, x_2 + c)$. It follows that the boundaries containing pitch duplications act like mirrors: a point moving directly toward the boundary is "reflected" backward along its approaching trajectory.[16]

Putting it all together then, the space of n-note chords is an n-dimensional prism whose simplicial ("simplex-shaped") faces are glued together with a twist, and whose remaining boundaries act like mirrors. By attributing this behavior to our boundary points, we have finally managed to convert our fundamental region—an unremarkable portion of ordinary Cartesian space—into a *quotient space* (or *orbifold*), an exotic mathematical space with a nontrivial topology. Mathematicians would describe our quotient space as "the n-torus modulo the symmetric group that acts on n elements"—symbolically, $\mathbb{T}^n/S_n$. Here, $\mathbb{T}^n$ is the mathematical symbol for the n-torus, the space of ordered pitch-class sequences; S_n refers to the collection of operations that reorder n elements; and the division symbol instructs us to glue together points related by the operations that follow. Thus the mathematical symbol "$\mathbb{T}^n/S_n$" means "the space that results when you start with ordered pitch-class sequences and disregard order." As discussed in Chapter 3, this is something very much like the space of *chords* as musicians ordinarily conceive of them.[17]

Readers are now prepared to plot voice leadings in the space. To do this, we must augment the algorithm in Figure B2 with two additional rules. First, when transposing or reordering the notes in a voice leading, we must always do so uniformly, applying the same operations to both chords: if we transpose the first note in the first chord up by octave, then we must transpose the first note in the second chord up by octave as well; similarly, if we exchange the first and second notes in the first chord,

16 This argument considers trajectories moving perpendicular toward the boundary. More general trajectories can be decomposed into a perpendicular and parallel components; the argument can then be applied to the perpendicular component.

17 Of course, musicians typically consider (C, C, E, G) to be the same as (C, E, G). When modeling voice leading, however, we often do not want to do this, as it can disrupt the relationship between distance and voice-leading size. See Callender, Quinn, and Tymoczko 2008.

then we must do the same in the second. Second, we may sometimes find that we can move a line segment into our fundamental domain only by breaking it into pieces. For example, suppose we would like to plot the voice leading (C4, E♭4, G♭4)→(E♭4, G♭4, C5), or (60, 63, 66)→(63, 66, 72), which shifts the C diminished chord up by one scale step. To get the sum of the first chord's notes to lie between 0 and 12, we must transpose down by five octaves; this means we need to transpose the second chord down by five octaves as well, producing (0, 3, 6)→(3, 6, 12). Here we encounter a problem. The first part of this line segment—from (0, 3, 6) to just before (1, 4, 7)—lies within our region, since its chords sum to less than 12. However, the rest of the line segment—(1, 4, 7)→(3, 6, 12)—sums to 12 or more. We therefore split the voice leading into two parts: (0, 3, 6)→(1, 4, 7) and (1, 4, 7)→(3, 6, 12). To move the second part of the voice leading into our fundamental region, we lower the final note in each chord by 12 and move it to the front of the list. (Once again, we do this uniformly, applying the same transposition and reordering to both chords.) This gives us (−5, 1, 4)→(0, 3, 6), which is a line segment that begins on the lowest (sum-zero) face of the prism and moves to (0, 3, 6). Our voice leading (C4, E♭4, G♭4)→(E♭4, G♭4, C5) therefore disappears off the top face of the fundamental region, reappearing on the bottom. A little experimentation will show that *any* one-step ascending scalar transposition, in any chord space of any dimension, moves off the top face to reappear on the bottom in a very similar way.

The fundamental idea here—and it is both simple and profound—is that ordinary numbers provide a natural and musically meaningful set of geometrical coordinates, with points representing chords and line segments representing voice leadings. Any sequence of numbers can be understood as an ordered list of pitches, while any pair of (equal-length) sequences can be understood as a voice leading in pitch space. When we disregard octave and order information, we are restricting our attention to a region of Cartesian space defined by Eqs. B.1 and B.2 above. This involves moving arbitrary points and line segments into our region. If we do this carefully and thoughtfully, we realize that the boundaries of this region have special properties. In other words, we make the transition from regions of ordinary Euclidean space to quotient spaces proper.[18]

---

18 Note that it is often possible to work with the original Cartesian coordinates: it is obvious that the voice leading (60, 64, 67)→(64, 60, 67) exchanges two notes, and hence bounces off a mirror boundary, and that (60, 64, 67, 70)→(64, 67, 70, 72) is an ascending one-step scalar transposition, and hence is represented by a path that disappears off the sum-12 face to reappear on the sum-zero face, returning to its starting point. After a little practice, you will start to feel comfortable with statements such as "there is a tritone halfway between (C4, G4) and (C♯4, F♯4)"—and even with more difficult tasks, such as imagining the cross section of an arbitrary voice leading in three-note chord space.

APPENDIX C

Discrete Voice-Leading Lattices

In recent decades, music theorists have produced a number of graphs representing voice-leading relationships. Often, these graphs seem to imply something like the following methodology. First, one selects some interesting domain of chords and some interesting set of voice-leading relationships among them. (For example, semitonal voice leading among major, minor, and augmented triads.) Second, one constructs a graph representing all of the voice-leading relationships among all of the objects in question. Third, one interprets the resulting graph as providing a measure of distance between the objects it contains. Thus, for example, one might use the graph to analyze music that moves between nonadjacent chords, or claim that larger leaps on the graph are musically disfavored in some way.

However, this third step involves a subtle logical leap. For while the method generates graphs whose *local* structure is perfectly clear, it does not follow that the graphs' *global* structure is equally meaningful. Consider, for example, the familiar *Tonnetz*—invented by Leonhard Euler, made famous by Hugo Riemann, and resurrected by contemporary theorists such as Lewin, Hyer, and Cohn (Figure C1).[1] Two triads are adjacent on the *Tonnetz* if they can be linked by what Cohn calls "parsimonious" voice leading, voice leading in which a single voice moves, and it moves by just one or two semitones. However, there is no similarly intuitive way to characterize larger distances in the space. On the *Tonnetz,* C major is two units away from F major but *three* units from F minor—even though it takes just two semitones to move from C major to F minor, and three to move from C major to F major (Figure C2). (This is precisely why F minor so often appears as a passing chord between F major and C major.) It follows that we cannot use the *Tonnetz* to model the ubiquitous IV–iv–I progression, in which the two-semitone motion $\hat{6}\rightarrow\hat{5}$ is broken into the semitonal steps $\hat{6}\rightarrow\flat\hat{6}\rightarrow\hat{5}$. More generally, it shows that *Tonnetz* distances do not correspond to voice-leading distances. (Nor do they correspond to common tone distances: both F minor and E♭ minor are three *Tonnetz* steps away from C major, even though C major and F minor have one common tone, while C major and E♭ minor have none.) Indeed, it is an open question whether there is any intuitive notion of musical distance that is being modeled here.[2]

---

1 For a history of the *Tonnetz,* see Mooney 1996. For a general discussion of recent work featuring various analogous discrete lattices, see Cohn 1998a.

2 Tymoczko 2009a notes that the *Tonnetz* may capture an *acoustic* conception of distance, according to which C3 is particularly close to its second overtone G4; the point here is that this is very different from voice-leading or common-tone distance.

Figure C1 Two versions of the *Tonnetz*. In (*a*) points represent notes, and chords are represented by triangles. In (*b*), points represent chords, and hexagons represent single notes. (For example, the hexagon containing C and f can be associated with the note C, common to all six of its triads.)

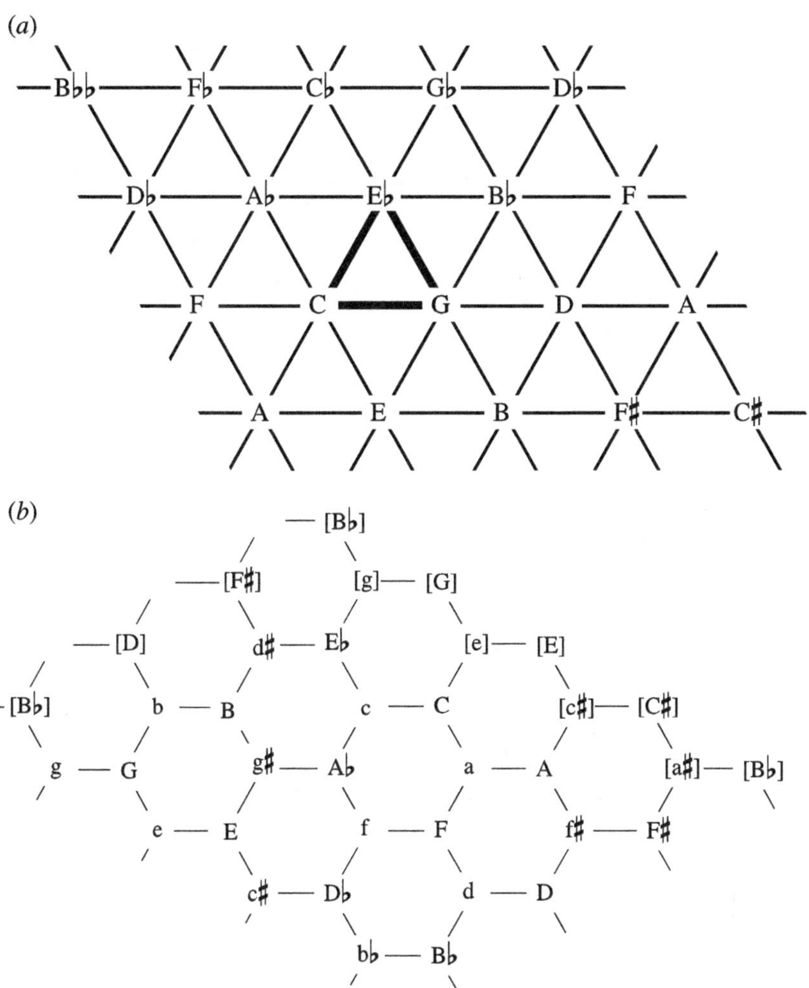

A surprising number of discrete music-theoretical graphs suffer from similar problems. For example, the graph in Figure C3 shows single-semitone voice leadings among diminished, dominant, French sixth, and half-diminished seventh chords.[3] While it would be entirely appropriate to use it to analyze a passage that moves by single-semitone voice leading between these chords, it is problematic to use it to model voice-leading distance between nonadjacent chords: the graph contains no two-step path between C^7 and $A^{ø7}$, even though the chords can be connected by two-semitone voice leading. For another example, consider Figure C4a, which represents single semitone voice-leading among major thirds and perfect fourths. On this graph, {C, F}

3 This graph is quite similar to Douthett and Steinbach's "Power Towers" (1998).

Figure C2 (*a*) On the *Tonnetz,* F major (triangle 3) is closer to C major (triangle 1) than F minor (triangle 4) is. Consequently, the voice leading (C, E, G)→(C, F, A) is represented as a two-step motion, while it takes at least *three* steps to represent (C, E, G)→(C, F, A♭). (*b*) In actual music, however, F minor frequently appears as a passing chord between F major and C major.

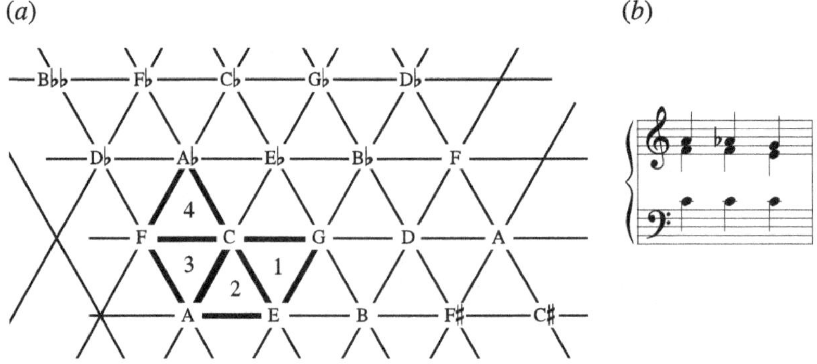

Figure C3 A graph of single-semitone voice-leading relations among diminished, dominant, half-diminished and French sixth chords. On the graph it takes four steps to get from C7 to $A^{ø7}$, even though the chords can be connected by two single-semitone shifts.

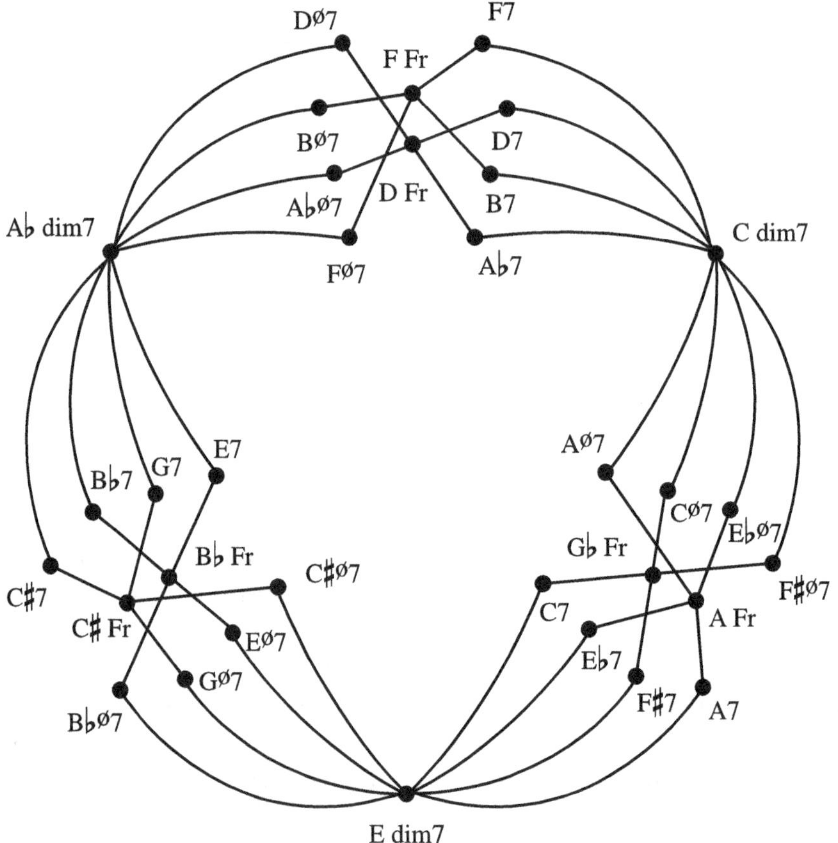

Figure C4 (*a*) A graph of single-semitone voice-leading relations between major thirds and perfect fourths. (*b*) Since it does not contain tritones, it cannot represent voice leadings such as (C, F)→(B, F♯), which move vertically across the center of the space.

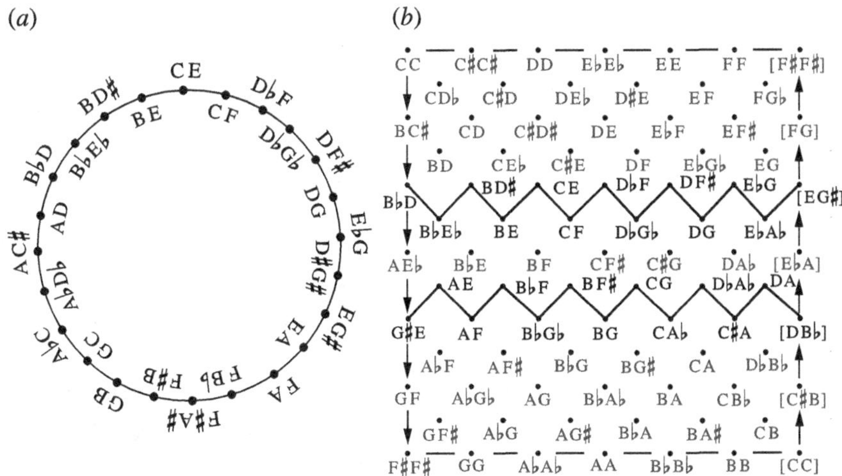

and {F♯, B} are twelve steps apart, even though the minimal voice leading between them moves each voice by just a semitone. Once again, local voice-leading concerns give rise to a graph whose global distances are difficult to interpret.

This last example provides a key to understanding what is going on. Figure C4b embeds the circular graph within the Möbius strip representing two-note chords, showing that one can move from {C, F} to {B, F♯} across the center of the larger space. We cannot take advantage of this shortcut if we stay on the discrete lattice, because the lattice forces us to go "the long way around"—off one side of the strip and onto the other. A little thought will show that these sorts of voice-leading "shortcuts" always pass through chords dividing the octave *at least as evenly* as those we happen to be interested in. (This is obvious in two-note chord space and less than obvious in higher dimensions; but the general principle holds there as well.) This leads to a very useful rule of thumb: in general, we should expect that a faithful representation of voice-leading possibilities will contain whatever chords we are interested in, *as well as all the chords that divide the octave at least as evenly as those chords.* Thus if we are interested in voice leading among major thirds and perfect fourths, we should also include tritones. This is precisely why the lattices in §3.11 are all reliable: they include the most even chords in any given scale, and hence faithfully represent voice-leading distances.

More generally, we can specify criteria ensuring that a graph's global structure faithfully represents voice-leading distances:

1. Every edge on the graph should represent voice leading in which a single voice moves by a single scale step or chromatic semitone (a condition violated by the *Tonnetz*).

2. For any two of its chords, the graph should contain all the interscalar transpositions between them (§4.9). This implies that the graph should not present the appearance of multiple disjoint segments in a cross section of the space of all chords, a condition violated by Figure C4b.
3. The chords on the graph should all have the same size.[4]
4. The paths representing these interscalar transpositions should not involve ascending and descending motion in the same voice (a condition violated by the *Tonnetz* and Figure C3 above).
5. The graph should not contain any multisets.

It is relatively easy to see that any graph satisfying these three requirements will faithfully reflect voice-leading distances, even between nonadjacent chords: condition 2 implies that the graph contains the shortest voice leading between any of its chords (§4.9); condition 1 implies that edges have unit voice-leading length; and condition 3 implies that the edges representing an interscalar transposition do not cancel each other out.[5] The five requirements are satisfied by all of the lattices in §3.11.

Of course, geometry can also provide a deeper perspective on these "faithful" voice-leading graphs. For instance, Douthett and Steinbach's "Cube Dance" (Figure C5a).

Figure C5 Douthett and Steinbach's "Cube Dance" (*a*) and the lattice at the center of three-note chord space (*b*).

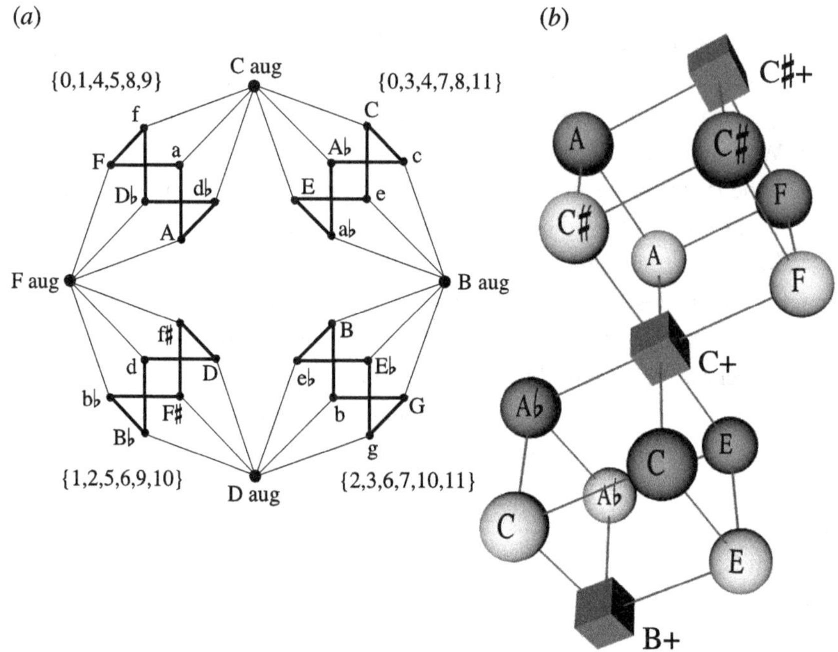

4 For discussion of the problems arising when graphs combine chords of different sizes, see Callender, Quinn, and Tymoczko 2008 and Tymoczko 2010.

5 Note that if we are measuring paths by counting the number of edges they contain, then we are using the "taxicab" metric of voice-leading size.

is virtually identical to the lattice at the center of three-note chord space, and was discovered almost a decade before the continuous spaces of Chapter 3. However, it turns out that we can extract much more information from the graph when we understand how it is embedded within the continuous space. For example, geometry tells us that the graph represents all and only the *strongly crossing-free voice leadings* between its chords; that the three spatial axes correspond to motion in the three musical voices; that these spatial axes can only be defined locally, since the figure has a global topological twist; and that two paths on the figure represent the same voice leading if they have the same "winding number" (that is, if they take the same number of clockwise or counterclockwise steps). All of which shows that the geometrical perspective can do more than just reveal *that* some graphs faithfully represent voice leading; it can also help us use these graphs in a more sophisticated and musical fashion.

APPENDIX D

The Interscalar Interval Matrix

Chapter 4 noted that strongly crossing-free voice leadings can be decomposed into chromatic and interscalar transpositions. As it happens, there is a useful mathematical way to represent this idea. Figure D1 depicts what I call an *interscalar interval matrix,* representing the four interscalar transpositions that take a half-diminished seventh chord to a dominant seventh chord with the same root. The numbers in the matrix are paths in pitch-class space, showing how far and in what direction each note moves. To combine these scalar transpositions with chromatic transpositions, we simply add a constant value to the relevant matrix row. For instance, the first row represents the voice leading (C,E♭, G♭,B♭)$\xrightarrow{0,\ 1,\ 1,\ 0}$(C, E,G,B♭), which sends the root of the C half-diminished chord to the root of the C dominant seventh chord; by subtracting one from the values (0, 1, 1, 0), we get (−1, 0, 0, −1), representing the voice leading (C, E♭, G♭, B♭)$\xrightarrow{-1,\ 0,\ 0,\ -1}$(B, D♯, F♯, A). In effect, we have transposed the second chord down by chromatic semitone, from C^7 to B^7. (The two voice leadings are individually T-related since they differ only by the transposition of their second chord.) Every strongly crossing-free (four-voice) voice leading from half-diminished to dominant seventh can be obtained by adding some constant to some row of the interscalar interval matrix: for example, to obtain (C, E♭, G♭, B♭)$\xrightarrow{0,0,-1,-1}$(C, E♭, F, A), subtract seven from the values in the third row. This is equivalent to combining interscalar transposition upward by two steps with chromatic transposition downward by seven semitones.

With a little practice, we can learn to "read" these matrices, seeing at a glance the voice-leading possibilities between all the transpositions of any two chord types. For example, suppose we want to find the most efficient voice leading between C half-diminished and A dominant seventh. Our matrix contains voice leadings that send a half-diminished chord to the dominant seventh with the same root. Since we want a voice leading that moves the root down by third, we will be subtracting three from the numbers in some row of the matrix.[1] To find the ascending scalar transposition that most nearly offsets descending chromatic transposition by three semitones, we

1 Note that the matrix contains ascending scalar transpositions, which we will be attempting to neutralize with descending chromatic transpositions; hence we transpose by subtracting three rather than by adding nine.

Figure D1 (*a*) The rows of this matrix correspond to the voice leadings in (*b*). All of the strongly crossing-free (four-voice) voice leadings from half-diminished to dominant seventh can be derived by adding a constant number to some row of this matrix. For example, to combine interscalar transposition up by two steps with chromatic transposition downward by seven semitones, subtract 7 from the values in the third row of the matrix, as illustrated by (*c*).

(*a*)

	C	E♭	G♭	B♭
zero steps	0	1	1	0
up one step	4	4	4	2
up two steps	7	7	6	6
up three steps	10	9	10	9

(*b*)

$$(\text{C, E}\flat\text{, G}\flat\text{, B}\flat) \xrightarrow{0,1,1,0} (\text{C, E, G, B}\flat)$$
$$(\text{C, E}\flat\text{, G}\flat\text{, B}\flat) \xrightarrow{4,4,4,2} (\text{E, G, B}\flat\text{, C})$$
$$(\text{C, E}\flat\text{, G}\flat\text{, B}\flat) \xrightarrow{7,7,6,6} (\text{G, B}\flat\text{, C, E})$$
$$(\text{C, E}\flat\text{, G}\flat\text{, B}\flat) \xrightarrow{10,9,10,9} (\text{B}\flat\text{, C, E, G})$$

(*c*)

$$(\text{C, E}\flat\text{, G}\flat\text{, B}\flat) \xrightarrow{7,7,6,6} (\text{G, B}\flat\text{, C, E})$$
$$+\quad (\text{G, B}\flat\text{, C, E}) \xrightarrow{-7,-7,-7,-7} (\text{C, E}\flat\text{, F, A})$$

$$(\text{C, E}\flat\text{, G}\flat\text{, B}\flat) \xrightarrow{0,0,-1,-1} (\text{C, E}\flat\text{, F, A})$$

simply look for the row of the matrix whose values come closest to three. This is clearly the second row: subtracting three from these values gives (1, 1, 1, −1), representing $(\text{C, E}\flat\text{, G}\flat\text{, B}\flat) \xrightarrow{1,\,1,\,1,\,-1} (\text{C}\sharp\text{, E, G, A})$.[2]

After a bit of time, this sort of computation becomes automatic; one virtually starts to see the voice leading $(\text{C, E}\flat\text{, G}\flat\text{, B}\flat) \xrightarrow{1,\,1,\,1,\,-1} (\text{C}\sharp\text{, E, G, A})$ directly in the matrix in Figure D1. To test yourself, try to use the matrix to identify the most efficient voice leading from a C half-diminished chord to an E♭ dominant seventh chord.[3] Then use

2 Interscalar interval matrices provide another way to understand the relationship between near evenness and efficient voice leading: for two nearly even chords, the rows of the interscalar interval matrix will all be very close to a constant value, which means that the interscalar transpositions and chromatic transpositions will nearly cancel each other out. Hence we can find reasonably efficient voice leadings between that chord and all of its various transpositions.

3 To do this, simply subtract nine from the row of the matrix whose values are closest to nine. (Again, we want to combine a descending chromatic transposition with an ascending scalar transpositions in the matrix, and hence will be subtracting nine rather than adding three to some row.) In this case, the relevant row is the last one: subtracting nine from the values in the fourth row gives us (1, 0, 1, 0), representing $(\text{C, E}\flat\text{, G}\flat\text{, B}\flat) \xrightarrow{1,0,1,0} (\text{D}\flat\text{, E}\flat\text{, G, B}\flat)$.

it to find the minimal voice leading that maps the root of the half-diminished chord onto the fifth of some dominant seventh.[4]

Analogous matrices can be constructed for any pair of chords, using the following algorithm[5]:

1. Assign scale degree numbers to the two scales *A* and *B*.
2. Arrange chord *A* in pitch space in ascending scale degree order (i.e. with the first scale degree at the bottom and the last scale degree at the top) such that the top and bottom notes are no more than an octave apart. Arrange chord *B* similarly.
3. Write down the voice leading that maps the lowest note of *A* to the lowest note of *B*, the second-lowest note of *A* to the second-lowest note of *B*, and so on. Write this voice leading as a pitch-class voice leading of the form $(a_1, a_2, \ldots, a_n) \xrightarrow{x_1, x_2, \ldots, x_n} (b_1, b_2, \ldots, b_n)$ (§2.5). The numbers above the arrow are the first row of the interscalar interval matrix.[6]

Figure D2 Constructing the interscalar interval matrix from (C, D, E, F, G, A, B) to (C, D, E, F♯, G, A, B♭). The resulting matrix is shown in Figure D3.

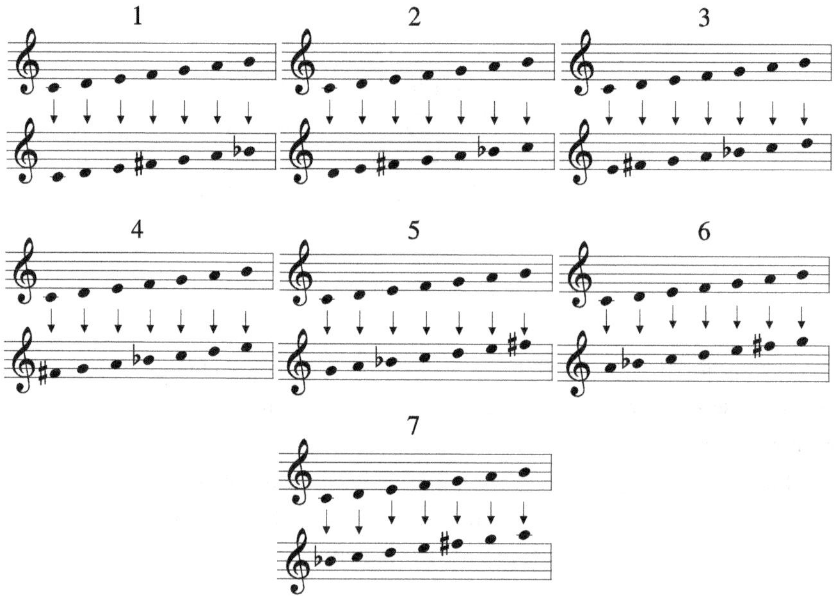

4 Here, we begin with the third row of the matrix (which maps root to fifth) and ask what chromatic transposition comes closest to neutralizing these values. There are two equally good possibilities: subtracting six gives us a two-semitone voice leading from C^{ø7} to F♯^{7}, while subtracting seven gives us a two-semitone voice leading from C^{ø7} to F^7.

5 It is assumed that *A* and *B* have the same number of notes. One can always add "doublings" to the smaller chord so that it has the same number of notes as the larger chord. However, there are multiple ways to do this.

6 Or more mathematically: the numbers are obtained by subtracting the pitches of *B* componentwise from those of *A*.

4. Transpose the lowest note of *B* up by octave and move it to the end of the sequence, replacing $(b_1, b_2, \ldots, b_n)$ with $(b_2, b_3, \ldots, b_n, b_1 + 12)$.
5. Repeat steps 3–4 to obtain the second row of the interscalar interval matrix. Continue repeating until the chord *B* has been transposed upward by octave.

Figure D2 generates the interscalar interval matrix that takes the C diatonic scale to the C acoustic scale. Note that the result is affected both by how we assign scale degrees to the two chords, and by how we arranged them register. For example, suppose we had numbered the C acoustic scale so that D was its first scale degree, and arranged it in register so that it began 10 semitones below middle C: (D3, E3, F♯3, G3, A3, B♭3, C4). This would yield an interscalar interval matrix whose first row is (−10, −10, −10, −10, −10, −11, −11) rather than (0, 0, 0, 1, 0, 0, −1). Figure D3 compares the matrix that results with the matrix we originally generated: each row of Figure D3b is either identical to a row in Figure D3a, or can be obtained from one by subtracting 12. In principle, the difference between these two matrices is immaterial; they contain the same information and can be used in more or less the same way. However, it is in practice easier to work with the matrix in Figure D3a.

In the special case where the second chord is the same as the first, then we have a *scalar* (rather than an interscalar) interval matrix. One can construct these matrices in exactly the same way, though we should always label the scale degrees so that the first row of the matrix contains only zeros. Figure D4 generates the scalar interval matrix that takes the dominant seventh chord to itself. Its four rows correspond to the voice leadings at the bottom of the figure.

Again, the matrix can be used to represent every combination of scalar and chromatic transpositions. For example, to combine scalar transposition by ascending step with chromatic transposition downward by three semitones, subtract three from the second row of the matrix, giving (C, E, G, B♭)$\xrightarrow{1,0,0,-1}$(C♯, E, G, A).

Figure D3 Two equivalent interscalar interval matrices. Each of the first six rows in the right matrix can be obtained by subtracting twelve from the next row down in the left matrix. The last row of the right matrix is identical to the first row of the left.

(*a*)

	C	D	E	F	G	A	B
0 steps	0	0	0	1	0	0	–1
1 step	2	2	2	2	2	1	1
2 steps	4	4	3	4	3	3	3
3 steps	6	5	5	5	5	5	5
4 steps	7	7	6	7	7	7	7
5 steps	9	8	8	9	9	9	8
6 steps	10	10	10	11	11	10	10

(*b*)

	C	D	E	F	G	A	B
0 steps	–10	–10	–10	–10	–10	–11	–11
1 step	–8	–8	–9	–8	–9	–9	–9
2 steps	–6	–7	–7	–7	–7	–7	–7
3 steps	–5	–5	–6	–5	–5	–5	–5
4 steps	–3	–4	–4	–3	–3	–3	–3
5 steps	–2	–2	–2	–1	–1	–2	–2
6 steps	0	0	0	1	0	0	–1

Figure D4 The four voice leadings corresponding to the four rows of the scalar interval matrix that takes (C, E, G, B♭) to itself.

	C	E	G	B♭
0 steps	0	0	0	0
1 step	4	3	3	2
2 steps	7	6	5	6
3 steps	10	8	9	9

$$(\text{C, E, G, B}\flat) \xrightarrow{0,0,0,0} (\text{C, E, G, B}\flat)$$

$$(\text{C, E, G, B}\flat) \xrightarrow{4,3,3,2} (\text{E, G, B}\flat\text{, C})$$

$$(\text{C, E, G, B}\flat) \xrightarrow{7,6,5,6} (\text{G, B}\flat\text{, C, E})$$

$$(\text{C, E, G, B}\flat) \xrightarrow{10,8,9,9} (\text{B}\flat\text{, C, E, G})$$

The key point is that these scale-theoretic ideas provide another way to think about the geometrical spaces described in Chapter 3. Consider Figure D5, which reproduces the cross section of three-note chord space (§3.8). The line segments on the figure represent the three paths connecting 047 to a minor triad without touching the boundary: (0, 4, 7)→(0, 3, 7), (0, 4, 7)→(0, 5, 8), and (0, 4, 7)→(0, 4, 9). Each line segment corresponds to a different category of interscalar transposition between major and minor triads. The first, (0, 4, 7)→(0, 3, 7), links root to root; the second, (0, 4, 7)→(0, 5, 8), links root to fifth; and the third, (0, 4, 7)→(0, 4, 9), links root to third. In fact, there is a very close connection between the idea of isolating the purely contrary component of a voice leading and the techniques we are discussing here: roughly speaking, the interscalar transposition corresponds to the pure contrary component of a crossing-free voice leading, while the chromatic transposition corresponds to the pure parallel component.[7] What is particularly useful about the scalar approach is that it can be applied to large chords, without requiring that we try to visualize higher dimensional geometry. The interscalar

7 More precisely: each of the strongly crossing-free, purely contrary voice leadings between chord *A* and a chord transpositionally related to *B* involves a distinct interscalar transposition. By focusing on pure contrary voice leadings or interscalar transpositions, we select one voice leading from among a class of individually T-related voice leadings, using it as the representative of that larger class.

Figure D5 The cross section of three-note chord space contains three line segments that connect 047 to a minor triad without touching the boundary (*a*). Each corresponds to a different interscalar transposition between major and minor triads (*b*).

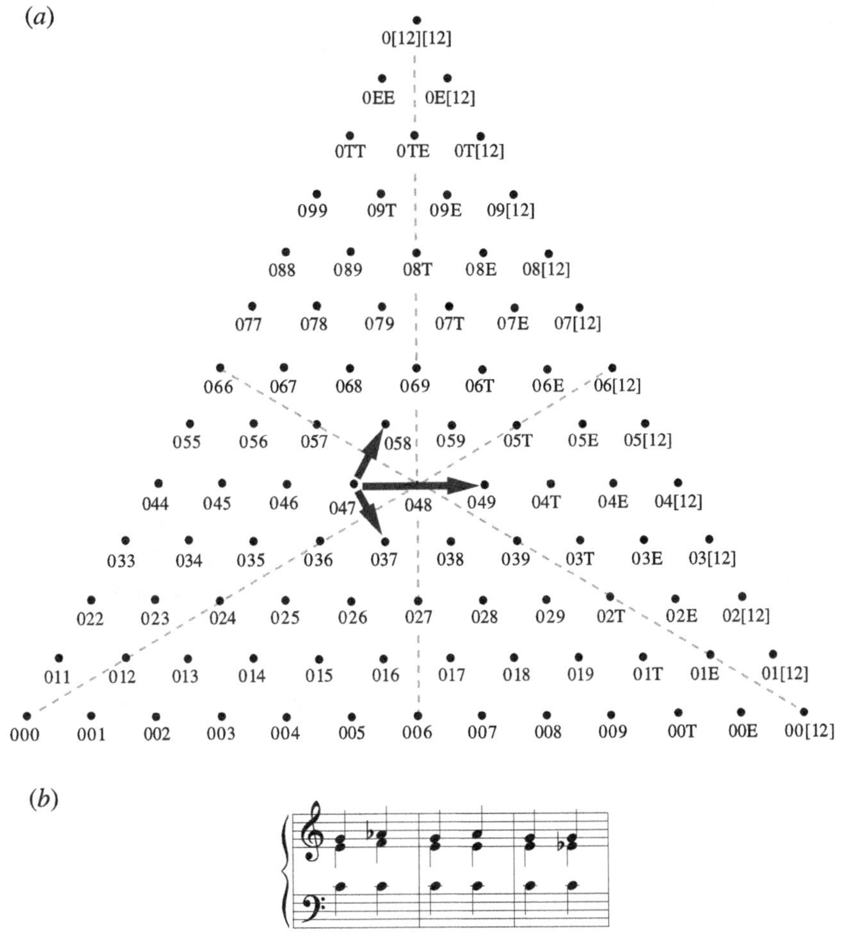

interval matrix thus provides a kind of "road map" of chord space, displaying the most commonly traveled routes between any two points. In many cases, the language of interscalar transpositions is considerably more intuitive than its higher dimensional, geometrical equivalent. I find it wonderful that these two languages—one heavily geometrical, the other more recognizably musical—are essentially saying the same thing.

APPENDIX E

Scale, Macroharmony, and Lerdahl's "Basic Space"

In some ways, Fred Lerdahl and I have very different approaches to music theory. Lerdahl postulates a kind of lossless listening in which ordinary people typically recover *all* of the details in a musical score; I emphasize the importance of information loss in music perception. Lerdahl is strongly influenced by Schenker, believing that entire tonal pieces can be described by giant, recursive "tree structures" analogous to those found in linguistics; I am skeptical of these approaches, preferring to emphasize local harmonic norms such as "IV goes to ii but not vice versa." (Lerdahl does not discuss harmonic norms in *Tonal Pitch Space,* leading me to suspect that he does not consider them to be particularly important.[1]) Finally, Lerdahl is primarily concerned with modeling cognitive structures in the *listener's* mind, whereas I am interested in how contemporary musicians might think about composing music.

Nevertheless, there are some ways in which our views are rather similar. On a very general level, Lerdahl and I both present theoretical models that seek to integrate the local ("chordal") and larger ("scalar") levels. Furthermore, we use very similar graphs to represent "centricity" or pitch prominence. Figure E1 presents a five-tiered pitch-class profile that is very similar to what Lerdahl calls the "basic space" for the key of C major; indeed, to the casual observer they are virtually indistinguishable. There are, however, two subtle but important differences between our figures. First, Lerdahl uses his graphs to represent not just macroharmony and centricity, but also music's *scalar structure.* And second, Lerdahl's basic space does double duty, representing both global harmonic stability and the local harmonic expectations associated with being on the tonic chord in a particular key.

Let's consider these points in more detail. Lerdahl's basic space encodes the claim that listeners hear tonal melodies relative to five melodic "alphabets": the chromatic scale (level *e*), diatonic scale (level *d*), the triad (level *c*), the perfect fifth (level *b*), and the unison (level *a*). By contrast, the pitch-class profiles in Chapter 5 represent only

1 He also suggests (2001, p. 215) that terms like "tonic" and "dominant" can be translated into statements about "prolongational position," a position that seems to court monism (§7.6).

Figure E1 A five-tiered pitch-class profile for the key of C major (*a*) and Fred Lerdahl's "basic space" (*b*).

(*a*)

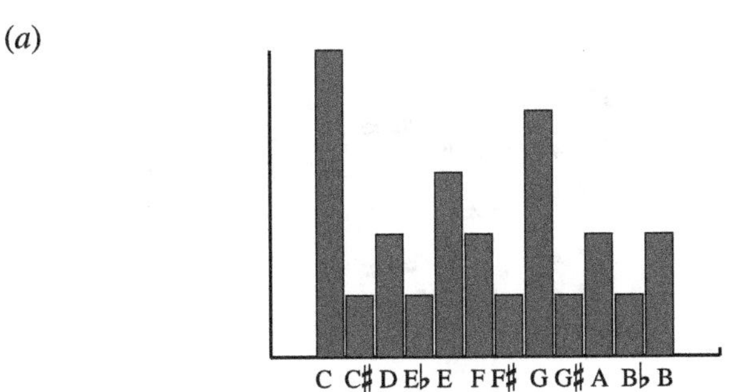

(*b*)

level *a*	C												(C)
level *b*	C							G					(C)
level *c*	C				E			G					(C)
level *d*	C		D		E	F		G		A		B	(C)
level *e*	C	D♭	D	E♭	E	F	F♯	G	A♭	A	B♭	B	(C)

the stability of individual notes, and do not reflect anything about music's melodic or scalar structure. I think this is an advantage of my approach. Lerdahl is surely correct to assert that traditionally tonal melodies are *often* interpreted relative to his five melodic alphabets, but I am not sure that they always or necessarily are. Figure E2a presents the end of the Chopin "black-key" etude. Intuitively, I would imagine that listeners interpret this passage relative to the pentatonic scale, which does not constitute a distinct layer of Lerdahl's space. The same is true of Figures E2b–c, which also feature melodic pentatonic scales. To me, these examples strongly suggest that tonal music sometimes uses a pentatonic "melodic alphabet"—one that is not included in Lerdahl's basic space.

The deep issue here, it seems to me, is that scale, macroharmony, and centricity are in principle independent, even though they are often linked in practice. This is precisely what allows a musician like Chopin to use pentatonic melodies to articulate pitch-class profiles like the one in Figure E1a. From the contemporary composer's perspective, or from the standpoint of the theorist interested in charting the full space of tonal possibilities, Lerdahl's basic space is therefore too confining, precisely because it forces us into a relatively traditional understanding of the relation between scale, macroharmony, centricity. By separating scale from macroharmony, we sever the link between pitch-class profiles and melodic alphabets, thereby allowing ourselves to consider more ambiguous profiles such as that in Figure 5.6.12.

Lerdahl also means for his basic space to play two similar but related roles: it represents both the *global* stability of notes within a key and also the *local* stability of notes relative to a sounding tonic chord. In its first role, the basic space expresses

Figure E2 Pentatonic scales playing a prominent melodic role at the conclusion of Chopin's Op. 10 No. 5 (*a*), in Dvorák's Op. 96 "American" Quartet (*b*), and at the opening of McCoy Tyner's solo on "Pursuance" (*c*).

thoughts like "in the key of C major, C is the most important pitch, then G, then E, then the remaining white notes, then the black notes—no matter what chord is actually sounding." In its second role, the basic space expresses sentiments like "when I am hearing a C major chord in the key of C major, the C is the most stable note *because it is the root of the chord I am hearing,* then G, because it is the fifth of the chord that I am hearing, then E, then the white notes, *because they belong to the main scale of the key I am in.*" Lerdahl not unreasonably assumes that these two kinds of stability should correspond: the global importance of notes relative to a key should reflect the local stability of notes *when the tonic chord is sounding.*

But in many modern tonal styles, this requirement is inappropriate. For example, a contemporary jazz pianist might regularly play the tonic chord of an F blues as a stack of fourths F-B♭-E♭ (Figure E3). Relative to this particular voicing of the tonic

F[7] chord, the B♭ might be conceived as more stable than the A—in fact, a melodic A played over this voicing will produce a distinctive "bite" since it forms a semitone with the B♭ in the harmony. However, it would be odd to interpret this *local* chord voicing as upsetting the *global* stability of notes in the key: jazz musicians conceive of voicings as flexible things that can be altered and changed spontaneously, without restructuring the key itself. (The chord voicing does not, for example, destroy the sense that B♭ is attracted melodically to A.) Here, then, the stability of notes within the key diverges from the local stability of notes when the tonic chord is sounding.[2]

Figure E3 The opening of Chick Corea's solo on "Matrix," from *Now he sings, now he sobs* (transcribed by Bill Dobbins in Corea 1988). In jazz, the global harmonic stability of notes need not correspond to their local stability over tonic chords: Corea often plays F-B♭-E♭ for the F[7] chord, but this does not mean that B♭ is globally more stable than A.

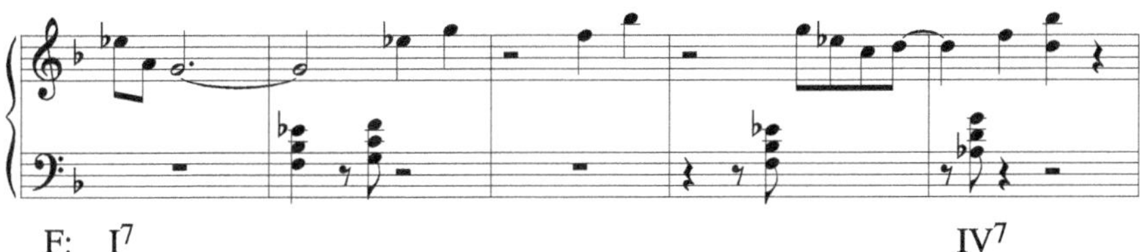

Of course, Lerdahl's theory is optimized for the purpose of modeling listeners' responses to classical music, in which these complications typically do not arise. My points should therefore be taken as obstacles to extending Lerdahl's methods to other styles, rather than intrinsic problems within its own domain. It is also important to reiterate that Lerdahl and I are pursuing fundamentally different aims: unlike Lerdahl, I am not trying to develop an accurate quantitative model of listeners' responses to the classical style in particular; instead, my goal is to develop more general representations that can help musicians think about a much wider range of tonal styles, including those of the past hundred years. To this end, I want more flexible tools that are sensitive to the ways in which macroharmony, scale, and centricity can sometimes diverge.

2 Jazz is filled with examples of this phenomenon—as when improvisers play the lydian mode over the tonic triad (Chapter 10).

APPENDIX F

Some Study Questions, Problems, and Activities

CHAPTER 1

1. Compose a short etude, about a minute long, exploring one or more combinations of the five features.
2. Write a simple melody exploiting a small voice leading between two closely related scales.

CHAPTER 2

1. Using the formulas in §2.3, show that transposition and inversion are distance-preserving functions (requires basic algebra).
2. Using the formulas in §2.3, show that every inversion leaves some pitch unchanged and moves every other point by twice the distance to this "fixed point" (requires basic algebra).
3. Determine which (if any) combination of O, P, T, I, and C is required to transform

    a. (C4, E4, G4) into (A3, C♯5, E3)
    b. (C4, E4, G4) into (E♭3, G4, C3, E♭2)
    c. (C4, E♭4, G4, B♭4) into (B♭4, G4, G4, E♭4, C4)
    d. (C4, D4, E♭4) into (A3, F♯2, G5)
    e. (C4, D4, F4) into (B5, A5, F♯5)
    f. (C4, E4, F4) into (G4, F♯4, D4, C4)

4. Choose a Bach chorale and write the voice leadings in the first measure as shown in Figure 2.7.1. Ignore nonharmonic tones.
5. How (if at all) are the following pitch-class space voice leadings related?

    a. (C, E, G)→(B♭, E♭, G) and (C, E♭, G)→(C, E, A)
    b. (C, E, G, B♭)→(B, E, G♯, B) and (C, E♭, G♭, A)→(C, E, G, G)
    c. (C, E, G)→(C, E, A) and (E, G, C)→(E, A, C)
    d. (F♯, A, C, E)→(F♯, A, C, D) and (D, F, A♭, C)→(D♯, F♯, A, B)
    e. (C, E, G, B♭)→(C, E♭, F, A) and (F♯, A, C, D)→(F♯, A♭, C, E♭)

f. (C, D, E, F, G, A, B)→(D, E, F, G, A, B, C) and (C, D, E, F, G, A, B)→(C, D, E♭, F, G, A, B♭)
g. (C, E, G)→(C, E, G♯) and (C, E♭, G)→(C, E♭, G♭)

6. Find a symmetrical chord that is very close to the following chords and describe its symmetries. Construct a voice leading that exploits the near symmetries of the chords below.

   a. {E, G, B, D♯}
   b. {C, E, G, B♭}
   c. {C, F, F♯}
   d. {C, C♯, D, F♯}
   e. {C, D, E♭, F, G, A♭, B}

7. Nearly even chords are also nearly inversionally symmetrical. Why? What about chords whose notes are clustered very close together?
8. Compose a small musical etude that exploits the near symmetries of some chord.

CHAPTER 3

1. Make several copies of the two-note Möbius strip (Figure 3.3.1), and draw the following voice leadings:

   a. (E♭4, A♭4)→(E♭4, B♭4)
   b. (E♭4, A♭4)→(B♭3, E♭4)
   c. (E♭4, A♭4)→(E♭4, B♭3)
   d. (E♭4, A♭4)→(E♭3, B♭4)
   e. (C4, E4)→(A3, F4)
   f. (A♭3, B♭3)→(A3, G3)

2. On the two-note Möbius strip, choose two major thirds and draw two different generalized line segments between them, neither of which touches the mirror boundary. In ordinary musical notation, write voice leadings corresponding to these two paths.
3. On the two-note Möbius strip, choose two major thirds and draw two generalized line segments between them: one bouncing off the lower mirror boundary and one bouncing off the upper mirror boundary. Write voice leadings in pitch space corresponding to these two paths.
4. On the triangular cross section of three-note chord space (Figure 3.8.6), represent the pure contrary component of the following voice leadings:

   a. (C, E, G)→(B, E, G)
   b. (C, G, E)→(C, A♭, F)
   c. (C, F, A♭)→(C, E♭, A)

d. (C, D♭, G)→(D♭, C, G)
e. (G, B, D)$\xrightarrow{-7,1,-2}$(C, C, C)
f. (A, C, E)→(A♭, C, F)→(G, B, F)

5. On the triangular cross section of three-note chord space, choose a point representing a minor triad. Draw the three line segments that connect this point to major triads without touching the mirror boundary. Then come up with *diatonic* voice leadings (i.e. voice leadings between chords belonging to the same diatonic scale) whose "purely contrary" component is represented by these line segments.
6. The chord {A, C♯, F, F♯} has two notes clustered together, and there is one efficient voice leading that permutes the clustered notes; the chord {A, D, D♯, E} has three notes clustered close together, and there are five efficient voice leadings that permute the clustered notes. Explain this geometrically, in terms of the chords' positions in the cross section of four-dimensional chord space. What about a chord like {A, B♭, B, C}?
7. Locate the inversionally symmetrical set classes in the cross section of three-dimensional space.
8. Write out a new Möbius strip, labeling only the points contained in seven-note equal temperament. (You can identify scale degrees using the letters A through G, but note that this scale is not the familiar major scale—it divides the octave into seven completely equal parts, rather than having steps of two different sizes.) Compare the cross sections of this space to those of the chromatic Möbius strip. Are there any interesting differences?
9. (*Advanced*) Chapter 2 showed that the chord (B, C, E, F♯) is near its tritone transposition. Explain this fact using the geometry of four-note chord space. *Hint:* consider the two-dimensional "slice" of the space containing all chords with both C and F♯. What does this slice look like? How is the voice leading (C, E, F♯, B)→(C, F, G♭, B♭) represented in it?
10. (*Advanced*) Consider the slice of four-note chord space containing chords that can be decomposed into two perfect fourths. What does it look like? What voice leadings does it depict? How does this slice differ from the slice containing chords that can be decomposed into a perfect fourth and a major third? *Optional:* use this space to analyze a passage from Bartók's "Fourths," no. 131 in the *Mikrokosmos*.

CHAPTER 4

1. What is the smallest (three-voice) voice leading between the D minor and E major triads if you measure distance according to the A harmonic minor scale? What if you measure distance according to the chromatic scale?
2. Compose a brief etude using one of the scales described in §4.4.

3. Figure F1, at the end of this appendix, contains several unlabeled graphs. Select the appropriate graph and label the chords described in the following list. In each case, measure distances using scale steps. Consult §3.11 for help.

   a. The most even two-note chords in the acoustic scale
   b. The most even two-note chords in the octatonic scale
   c. The most even three-note chords in the hexatonic scale
   d. The most even four-note chords in the octatonic scale (Note: you may need to use multiple copies of the graph to do this completely.)
   e. The "generalized circle of fifths" at the center of four-note diatonic space. (That is, the one-dimensional space representing voice-leading relations among the most even type of four-note diatonic chord.)
   f. The two-dimensional graph representing the two most even types of four-note diatonic chords.
   g. The three-dimensional analogue of the graph in the previous problem, containing four types of nearly even diatonic chords.
   h. The most even four-note chords in the chromatic scale (don't look back at Chapter 3).

4. Using Appendix D, construct the scalar interval matrix for

   a. the major triad considered as an object in chromatic space
   b. the triad considered as an object in diatonic space
   c. the acoustic scale

5. Use the scalar interval matrices from the previous problem to find the most efficient voice leading between

   a. two major triads in chromatic space
   b. two triads in diatonic space
   c. two acoustic scales

6. Write the most efficient (three-voice) voice leadings from a C major triad to each of the twelve minor triads and catalogue them according to which interscalar transposition is used.
7. Choose a sequence of five diatonic, acoustic, and harmonic scales that are related by efficient voice leading. Now chart this sequence on both the scale lattice (Figure 4.6.1) and the alchemistical diagram (Figure 4.6.5). Use this opportunity to familiarize yourself with the alchemistical diagram.
8. (*Very advanced*) Consider any single-step voice leading between two chords belonging to the same scale. This voice leading defines a unique single-step voice leading between the *complements* of those chords. (The complement of a chord relative to a scale contains all the notes of the scale not in the chord.) For instance, the diatonic voice leading (C, E, G)→(C, E, A) defines a complementary voice leading among seventh chords (B, D, F, A)→(B, D, F, G).

This seems to show that the lattices representing complementary chords are structurally similar, even though they have different dimension. (For instance, the space representing diatonic triads has three dimensions, whereas that representing diatonic seventh chords has four dimensions.) Explain.

9. Explain why the scales discussed in §4.4 have a compact appearance on the *Tonnetz* (Figure C1a).

CHAPTER 5

1. Use pitch-class profiles to imagine one or more "generalized keys" and write a short etude in this "key."

CHAPTER 7

1. Identify the appearances of the 3 + 1 and "nonfactorizable" schemas in some phrase of a Bach chorale.
2. (*Advanced*) Consider the nonfactorizable voice leading (C, C, E, G) →(A, C, F, F). Show that this voice leading exploits the fact that the major triad is near the tritone. (*Hint:* show that the size of the voice leading can be continuously shrunk to zero by moving E and G closer to F♯ (in the first chord) and A and C closer to B (in the second), while also changing the transpositional relationship between the triads from five semitones to six.) Can you find analogues to this voice leading that use other three-note chords?
3. (*Advanced*) Now consider the voice leading (C, C, E, G)→(B, D, F, F). What near symmetries of the triad does this voice leading exploit? How can it be shrunk to zero? Can you find analogues to this voice leading that use other three-note chords? (*Hint:* consider the triad as an object in diatonic space.)
4. (*More advanced*) Provide a similar analysis of the voice leading (C, C, E, G)→(B, D, D, G).
5. Show that every instance of the "nonfactorizable" schema falls into one of the cases considered in the previous three questions.

CHAPTER 8

1. Analyze the development section of the first movement of Dvorak's *New World Symphony,* paying attention to the role of the major-third and minor-third systems.

CHAPTER 9

1. Analyze Debussy's prelude "Les tierces alternées" (Book II, no. 11), paying particular attention to scales.

CHAPTER 10

1. Transcribe and analyze a jazz solo.

Figure F1 Unlabeled graphs that can be used to represent voice leading relations among various sorts of chords.

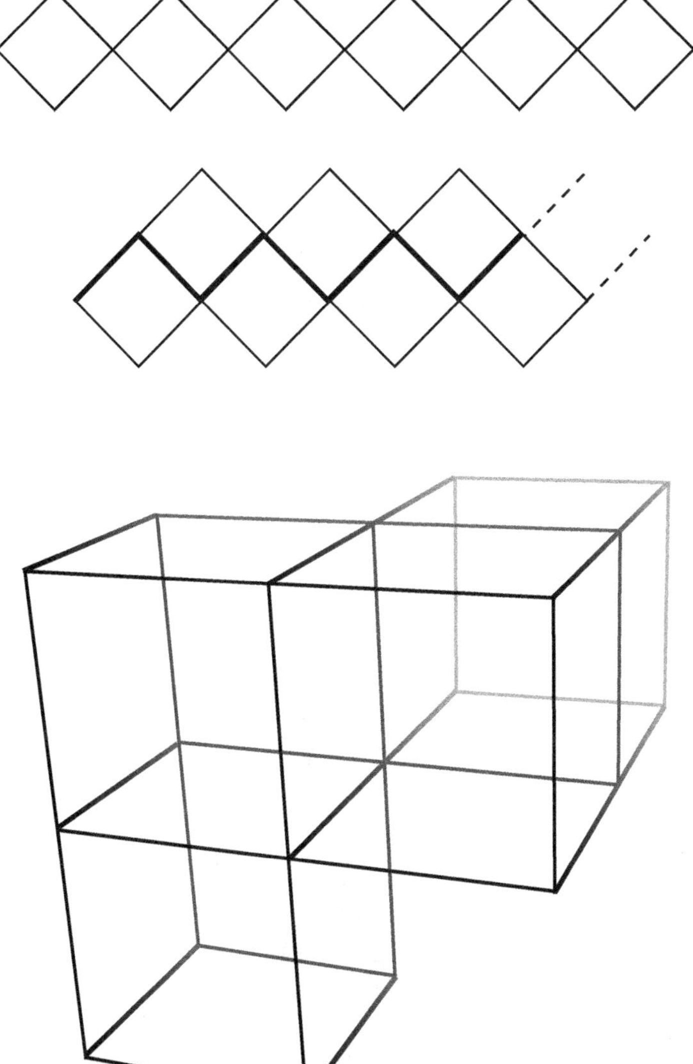

Figure F1 (Continued)

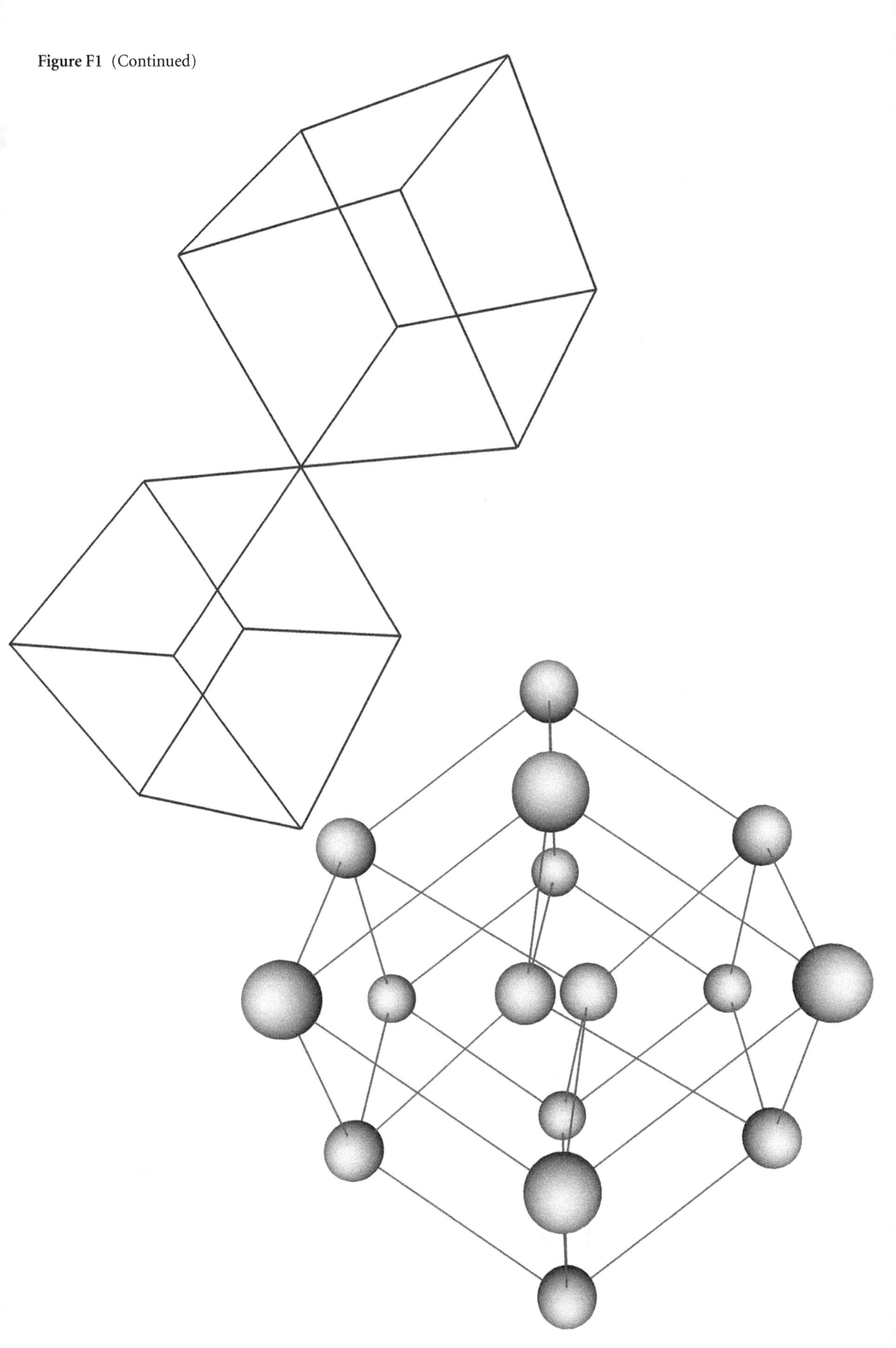

REFERENCES

Agmon, Eytan. 1989. "A Mathematical Model of the Diatonic System." *Journal of Music Theory* 33(1): 1–25.

Agmon, Eytan. 1991. "Linear Transformations Between Cyclically Generated Chords." *Musikometrika* 46(3): 15–40.

Agmon, Eytan. 1995. "Functional Harmony Revisited: A Prototype-Theoretic Approach." *Music Theory Spectrum* 17(2): 196–214.

Agmon, Eytan. 1996. "Conventional Harmonic Wisdom and the Scope of Schenkerian Theory: A Reply to John Rothgeb." *Music Theory Online* 2(3).

Aldwell, Edward and Carl Schachter. [1969] 2002. *Harmony and Voice Leading*, 3rd ed. Belmont: Wadsworth.

Antokoletz, Elliott. 1984. *The Music of Béla Bartók*. Berkeley: University of California Press.

Antokoletz, Elliott. 1993. "Transformations of a Special Non-Diatonic Mode in Twentieth-Century Music: Bartók, Stravinsky, Scriabin, and Albrecht." *Music Analysis* 12(1): 25–45.

Babbitt, Milton. 1958. "Who Cares if You Listen?" *High Fidelity* 8(2): 38–40.

Babbitt, Milton. 1962. "Twelve-Tone Rhythmic Structure and the Electronic Medium." *Perspectives of New Music* 1(1): 49–79.

Bach, Carl Philipp Emanuel. [1753/1762] 1949. *Essay on the True Art of Playing Keyboard Instruments*. Ed. and trans. William J. Mitchell. New York: Norton.

Barnett, Gregory. 1998. "Modal Theory, Church Keys, and the Sonata at the End of the Seventeenth Century." *Journal of the American Musicological Society* 51(2): 245–281.

Bartók, Béla. 1976. *Essays*. Ed. Benjamin Suchoff. Lincoln: University of Nebraska Press.

Beach, David. 1974. "The Origins of Harmonic Analysis." *Journal of Music Theory* 18(2): 274–230.

Beach, David. 1983. "Schenker's Theories: A Pedagogical View." In *Aspects of Schenkerian Theory*, ed. David Beach, 1–38. New Haven: Yale University Press.

Berger, Arthur. 1963. "Problems of Pitch Organization in Stravinsky." *Perspectives of New Music* 2(1): 11–42.

Berry, Wallace. 1976. *Structural Functions in Music*. New York: Dover.

Biamonte, Nicole. 2008. "Augmented-Sixth Chords vs. Tritone Substitutes." *Music Theory Online* 14(2).

Blum, Fred. 1959. "Another Look at the Montpellier Organum Treatise." *Musica Disciplina* 13: 15–24.

Boretz, Benjamin. 1972. "Meta-Variations, Part IV: Analytic Fallout (1)." *Perspectives of New Music* 11(1): 146–223.

Bregman, Albert. 1990. *Auditory Scene Analysis: The Perceptual Organization of Sound*. Cambridge: MIT Press.

Brown, Matthew. 2005. *Explaining Tonality*. Rochester: University of Rochester Press.

Buelow, George. 1992. *Thorough-Bass Accompaniment According to Johann David Heinichen*. Lincoln: University of Nebraska Press.

Burns, Edward M. 1999. "Intervals, Scales and Tuning." In *Psychology of Music,* 2nd ed., ed. Diana Deutsch, 215–264. San Diego: Academic Press.

Caballero, Carlo. 2004. "Multimodality in Fauré." Paper presented to the joint meeting of the Society for Music Theory and American Musicological Society, Seattle, Washington.

Cadwallader, Allen and David Gagne. 1998. *Analysis of Tonal Music: A Schenkerian Approach.* New York: Oxford University Press.

Callender, Clifton. 1998. "Voice-Leading Parsimony in the Music of Alexander Scriabin." *Journal of Music Theory* 42(2): 219–233.

Callender, Clifton. 2004. "Continuous Transformations." *Music Theory Online* 10(3).

Callender, Clifton. 2007. "Interactions of the Lamento Motif and Jazz Harmonies in György Ligeti's *Arc-en-ciel.*" *Intégral* 21: 41–77.

Callender, Clifton, Ian Quinn, and Dmitri Tymoczko. 2008. "Generalized Voice Leading Spaces." *Science* 320: 346–348.

Callender, Clifton, and Nancy Rogers. 2006. "Judgments of Distance between Trichords." In *Proceedings of the Ninth International Conference on Music Perception and Cognition,* eds. Mario Baroni, Anna Rita Addessi, Roberto Caterina, and Marco Costa, 1686–1691. Bologna: The Society for Music Perception and Cognition.

Caplin, William. 1998. *Classical Form: A Theory of Formal Functions for the Instrumental Music of Haydn, Mozart, and Beethoven.* New York: Oxford University Press.

Cariani, Peter. 2001. "Temporal Codes, Timing Nets, and Music Perception." *Journal of New Music Research* 30(2): 107–135.

Carey, Norman and David Clampitt. 1989. "Aspects of Well-Formed Scales." *Music Theory Spectrum* 11(2): 187–206.

Carpenter, Ellon. 1995. "Russian Theorists on Modality in Shostakovich's Music." In *Shostakovich Studies,* ed. David Fanning, 76–112. New York: Cambridge University Press.

Clark, Suzannah. 2002. "Schubert, Theory and Analysis." *Music Analysis* 21(2): 209–243.

Clough, John and Jack Douthett. 1991. "Maximally Even Sets." *Journal of Music Theory* 35: 93–173.

Clough, John, Nora Engebretsen, and Jonathan Kochavi. 1999. "Scales, Sets, and Interval Cycles: A Taxonomy." *Music Theory Spectrum* 21(1): 74–104.

Clough, John and Gerald Myerson. 1985. "Variety and Multiplicity in Diatonic Systems." *Journal of Music Theory* 29(2): 249–270.

Cohn, Richard. 1991. "Bartók's Octatonic Strategies: A Motivic Approach." *Journal of the American Musicological Society* 44: 262–300.

Cohn, Richard. 1992a. "The Autonomy of Motives in Schenkerian Accounts of Tonal Music." *Music Theory Spectrum* 14(2): 150–170.

Cohn, Richard. 1992b. "Transpositional Combination of Beat-Class Sets in Steve Reich's Phase-Shifting Music." *Perspectives of New Music* 30(2): 146–177.

Cohn, Richard. 1996. "Maximally Smooth Cycles, Hexatonic Systems, and the Analysis of Late-Romantic Triadic Progressions." *Music Analysis* 15(1): 9–40.

Cohn, Richard. 1997. "Neo-Riemannian Operations, Parsimonious Trichords, and their 'Tonnetz' Representations." *Journal of Music Theory* 41(1): 1–66.

Cohn, Richard. 1998a. "Introduction to Neo-Riemannian Theory: A Survey and a Historical Perspective." *Journal of Music Theory* 42(2): 167–180.

Cohn, Richard. 1998b. "Square Dances with Cubes." *Journal of Music Theory* 42(2): 283–296.

Cohn, Richard. 1999. "As Wonderful as Star Clusters: Instruments for Gazing at Tonality in Schubert." *Nineteenth-Century Music* 22(3): 213–232.

Cohn, Richard. 2000. "Weitzmann's Regions, My Cycles, and Douthett's Dancing Cubes." *Music Theory Spectrum* 22(1): 89–103.

Cohn, Richard. 2003. A Tetrahedral Model of Tetrachordal Voice-Leading Space. *Music Theory Online* 9(4).

Cohn, Richard. 2007. "Review of Fred Lerdahl's *Tonal Pitch Space*." *Music Theory Spectrum* 29(1): 101–114.

Corea, Chick. 1988. *Now He Sings, Now He Sobs*. Transcr. Bill Dobbins. Rottenberg: Advance Music.

Cook, Nicholas. 1987. "The Perception of Large-Scale Tonal Closure." *Music Perception* 5(2): 197–205.

Cook, Nicholas. 1994. "Music and Psychology: A Mutual Regard?" In *Musical Perceptions*, ed. Rita Aiello and John Sloboda, 64–95. Oxford: Oxford University Press.

Cook, Robert. 2005. "Parsimony and Extravagance." *Journal of Music Theory* 49(1): 109–140.

Crocker, Richard. 1962. "Discant, Counterpoint, and Harmony." *Journal of the American Musicological Society* 15(1): 1–21.

Crowder, Robert, J. Steven Reznick, and Stacey L. Rosenkrantz. 1991. "Perception of the Major/Minor Distinction: V. Preferences among Infants." *Bulletin of the Psychonomic Society* 29: 187–188.

Dahlhaus, Carl. 1990. *Studies in the Origins of Harmonic Tonality*. Trans. Robert Gjerdingen. Princeton: Princeton University Press.

De La Grange, Henry-Louis. 1973. *Mahler*. New York: Doubleday.

Deutsch, Diana and John Feroe. 1981. "The Internal Representation of Pitch Sequences in Tonal Music." *Psychological Review* 88: 503–522.

Diamond, Jared. 1997. *Guns, Germs, and Steel*. New York: Norton.

Douthett, Jack and Peter Steinbach. 1998. "Parsimonious Graphs: A Study in Parsimony, Contextual Transformations, and Modes of Limited Transposition." *Journal of Music Theory* 42(2): 241–263.

Dowling, W. Jay and Dane L. Harwood. 1986. *Music Cognition*. San Diego: Academic Press.

Dubiel, Joseph. 1997. "What's the Use of the Twelve-Tone System?" *Perspectives of New Music* 35(2): 33–51.

Duffin, Ross. 2006. *How Equal Temperament Ruined Harmony (and Why You Should Care)*. New York: Norton.

Fétis, François-Joseph. [1840] 1994. *Esquisse de l'Histoire de l'Harmony*. Trans. Mary Arlin. Stuyvesant: Pendragon.

Feynman, Richard. 1994. *The Character of Physical Law*. New York: Modern Library.

Forte, Allen. 1955. *Contemporary Tone Structures*. New York: Columbia University Press.

Forte, Allen. 1973. *The Structure of Atonal Music*. New Haven: Yale University Press.

Forte, Allen. 1987. "Liszt's Experimental Music and the Music of the Early Twentieth Century." *Nineteenth-Century Music* 10: 209–228.

Forte, Allen. 1990. "Musorgsky as Modernist: The Phantasmic Episode in *Boris Godunov*." *Music Analysis* 9: 3–45.

Forte, Allen. 1991. "Debussy and the Octatonic." *Music Analysis* 10: 125–169.

Frankenhauser, Gabe. 2008. "Flat Primary Triads, Harmonic Refraction, and the Harmonic Idiom of Shostakovich and Prokofiev." In *Musical Currents from the Left Coast*, eds. Jack Boss and Bruce Quaglia. Newcastle upon Tyne: Cambridge Scholars Publishing.

Fuller, Ramon. 1975. "A Structuralist Approach to the Diatonic Scale." *Journal of Music Theory* 19(2): 182–210.

Gann, Kyle. 2006. *Music Downtown: Writings from the Village Voice*. Berkeley: University of California Press.

Gauldin, Robert. 1997. *Harmonic Practice in Tonal Music.* New York: Norton.

Gervais, Françoise. 1971. "Etude Comparée des Langues Harmoniques de Fauré et de Debussy." *La Revue Musicale* 272–273: 3–152, 7–131.

Gjerdingen, Robert. 2007. *Music in the Galant Style.* New York: Oxford University Press.

Golab, Marceij. 1995. *Chopins harmonik: Chromatik in ihrer Beziehung zur Tonalität.* Köln: Bela Verlag.

Gut, Serge. 1976. "La Notion de Consonance Chez les Théoriciens du Moyen Age." *Acta Musicologica* 48(1): 20–44.

Hall, Rachel. 2009. "Geometrical models for modulation in Arab music." Paper presented to the national meeting of the Society for Music Theory, Montreal.

Hall, Rachel, and Dmitri Tymoczko. 2007. "Poverty and polyphony: a connection between music and economics." Paper presented to the 2007 Bridges Conference on Mathematical Connections in Art, Music, and Science, Donostia, Spain.

Hansen, Finn. 1996. "The Tristan Chord Is Nothing but a Tritone Substitution of the Characteristic Subdominant." In *Jan Maegaard Festschrift,* ed. Mogens Andersen, Niels Bo Foltmann, and Claus Røllum-Larsen, 165–183. Copenhagen: Engstrom and Sodring.

Harrison, Daniel. 1994. *Harmonic Function in Tonal Music: A Renewed Dualist Theory and an Account of Its Precedents.* Chicago: University of Chicago Press.

Harrison, Daniel. 1995. "Supplement to the Theory of Augmented-Sixth Chords." *Music Theory Spectrum* 17(2): 170–195.

Harrison, Daniel. 2003. "Rosalia, Aloysius, and Arcangelo: A Genealogy of the Sequence." *Journal of Music Theory* 47: 225–272.

Helmholtz, Hermann von. [1863] 1954. *On the Sensation of Tone.* New York: Dover.

Herresthal, Harald. 2005. "Edvard Grieg und Frankreich: Zur Grieg-Rezeption." *Musik-Konzepte* 127: 23–44.

Hindemith, Paul. [1937] 1984. *The Craft of Musical Composition,* vol. 1. Trans. Arthur Mendel. London: Schott.

Holloway, Robin. 1982. *Debussy and Wagner.* New York: Da Capo.

Hook, Julian. 2007a. "Cross-Type Transformations and the Path Consistency Condition." *Music Theory Spectrum* 29(1): 1–39.

Hook, Julian. 2007b. "Enharmonic Systems: A Theory of Key Signatures, Enharmonic Equivalence, and Diatonicism." *Journal of Mathematics and Music* 1: 99–120.

Hook, Julian. 2008. "Signature Transformations." In *Music Theory and Mathematics: Chords, Collections, and Transformations,* eds. Jack Douthett, Martha M. Hyde, and Charles J. Smith, 137–160. Rochester: University of Rochester Press.

Hostinský, Ottokar. 1879. *Die Lehre von den musikalischen Klangen.* Prague: H. Dominicus.

Howat, Roy. 1983. *Debussy in Proportion.* New York: Cambridge University Press.

Hulse, Stewart H., Daniel J. Bernard, and Richard F. Braaten. 1995. "Auditory Discrimination of Chord-Based Spectral Structures by European Starlings (*Sturnus vulgaris*)." *Journal of Experimental Psychology: General* 124: 409–423.

Huovinen, Erkki. 2002. *Pitch-Class Constellations: Studies in the Perception of Tonal Centricity.* Turku: Acta Musicologica Fennica.

Huron, David. 1994. "Interval-Class Content in Equally-Tempered Pitch-Class Sets: Common Scales Exhibit Optimum Tonal Consonance." *Music Perception* 11(3): 289–305.

Huron, David. 2001. "Tone and Voice: A Derivation of the Rules of Voice-Leading from Perceptual Principles." *Music Perception* 19(1): 1–64.

Huron, David. 2007. *Sweet Expectation: Music and the Psychology of Expectation.* Cambridge: MIT Press.

Hyer, Brian. 2002. "Tonality." In *The Cambridge History of Western Music Theory*, ed. Thomas Christensen, 726–752. New York: Cambridge University Press.

Isacoff, Stuart. 2001. *Temperament: The Idea That Solved Music's Greatest Riddle*. New York: Knopf.

Izumi, A. 2000. "Japanese Monkeys Perceive Sensory Consonance of Chords." *Journal of the Acoustical Society of America* 108: 3073–3078.

Joseph, Charles. 1978. "Architectural Control in Josquin's *Tu pauperum refugium*." *College Music Symposium* 18: 189–195.

Judd, Cristle Collins. 2006. *Reading Renaissance Music Theory*. Cambridge: Cambridge University Press.

Kallberg, Jeffrey. 1985. "Chopin's Last Style." *Journal of the American Musicological Society* 38(2): 264–315.

Kaye, Philip. 1989. *The "Contenance Angloise" in Perspective: A Study of Consonance and Dissonance in Continental Music, c. 1380–1440*. New York: Garland.

Kindermann, William and Harold Krebs, eds. 1996. *The Second Practice of Nineteenth Century Tonality*. Lincoln: University of Nebraska Press.

Kopp, David. 1997. "Pentatonic Organization in Two Piano Pieces of Debussy." *Journal of Music Theory* 41(2): 261–287.

Kopp, David. 2002. *Chromatic Transformations in Nineteenth-Century Music*. New York: Cambridge University Press.

Kostka, Stefan and Dorothy Payne. 2003. *Tonal Harmony*, 4th ed. New York: Alfred A. Knopf.

Krumhansl, Carol. 1990. *Cognitive Foundations of Musical Pitch*. New York: Oxford University Press.

Krumhansl, Carol. 2004. "The Cognition of Tonality: As We Know it Today." *Journal of New Music Research* 33(3): 253–268.

Krumhansl, Carol L. and Mark A. Schmuckler. 1986. "Key-Finding in Music: An Algorithm Based on Pattern Matching to Tonal Hierarchies." Paper presented to the 19th annual Mathematical Psychology Meeting, Cambridge, Massachusetts.

Krumhansl, Carol L. and Roger Shepard. 1979. "Quantification of the Hierarchy of Tonal Functions within a Diatonic Context." *Journal of Experimental Psychology: Human Perception and Performance* 5: 579–594.

Kurth, Ernst. 1920. *Romantische Harmonik und ihre Krise in Wagners 'Tristan.'* Berlin: Max Hesses Verlag.

Larson, Steve. 1992. "Scale-Degree Function: Cognition Research and Its Application to Aural-Skills Pedagogy." CRCC technical report no. 67. Bloomington: Indiana University, Center for Research on Concepts and Cognition.

Lendvai, Erno. 1971. *Béla Bartók: An Analysis of His Music*. London: Kahn & Averill.

Lerdahl, Fred. 1988. "Cognitive Constraints on Compositional Systems." In *Generative Processes in Music*, ed. John Sloboda, 231–259. New York: Oxford University Press.

Lerdahl, Fred. 2001. *Tonal Pitch Space*. New York: Oxford University Press.

Lester, Joel. 1974. "Root-Position and Inverted Triads in Theory around 1600." *Journal of the American Musicological Society* 27(1): 110–119.

Lester, Joel. 1992. *Compositional Theory in the Eighteenth Century*. Cambridge: Harvard University Press.

Levine, Mark. 1989. *The Jazz Piano Book*. Petaluma: Sher Music.

Lewin, David. 1987. *Generalized Musical Intervals and Transformations*. New Haven: Yale University Press.

Lewin, David. 1998. "Some Ideas about Voice-Leading between PCSets." *Journal of Music Theory* 42(1): 15–72.

Lowinsky, Edward. 1961. *Tonality and Atonality in Sixteenth-Century Music*. Berkeley: University of California Press.

Marshall, Albert and Ingram Olkin. 1979. *Inequalities: Theory of Majorization and Its Applications*. New York: Academic Press.

Marvin, Elizabeth West and Alexander Brinkman. 1999. "The Effect of Modulation and Formal Manipulation on Perception of Tonic Closure by Expert Listeners." *Music Perception* 16(4): 389–408.

Masson, Charles. [1697] 1969. *Nouveau Traité des Regles pour la Composition de la Musique*. New York: Da Capo.

Mathieu, William. 1997. *The Harmonic Experience: Tonal Harmony from its Natural Origins to Its Modern Expression*. Rochester, Vt.: Inner Traditions.

Mazzola, Guerino, et al. 2002. *The Topos of Music*. Basel: Birkhauser.

McDermott, Josh, and Marc Hauser. 2005. "The Origins of Music: Innateness, Uniqueness, and Evolution." *Music Perception* 23(1): 29–59.

McGowan, James. 2005. "Dynamic Consonance in Selected Piano Performances of Tonal Jazz." PhD diss., Eastman School of Music.

Meeus, Nicolas. 2000. "Toward a Post-Schoenbergian Grammar of Tonal and Pre-tonal Harmonic Progressions." *Music Theory Online* 6(1).

Miller, George. 1956. "The Magical Number, Seven Plus or Minus Two." *The Psychological Review* 63(2): 81–97.

Mitchell, William. 1962. "The Study of Chromaticism." *Journal of Music Theory* 5: 2–31.

Mitchell, William. 1973. "The *Tristan* Prelude: Techniques and Structure." *Music Forum* 1: 162–203.

Mooney, Kevin. 1996. "The 'Table of Relations' and Music Psychology in Hugo Riemann's Harmonic Theory." PhD diss., Columbia University.

Morris, Patrick. 1987. "Steve Reich and Debussy: Some Connexions." *Tempo* 160: 8–14.

Morris, Robert. 1998. "Voice-Leading Spaces." *Music Theory Spectrum* 20(2): 175–208.

Morton, David. 1976. *The Traditional Music of Thailand*. Berkeley: University of California Press.

Narmour, Eugene. 1990. *The Analysis and Cognition of Basic Melodic Structures: The Implication-Realization Model*. Chicago: University of Chicago Press.

Norman, Philip. 1945. *A Quantitative Study of Harmonic Similarities in Certain Specified Works of Bach, Beethoven, and Wagner*. Boston: Carl Fischer.

Norton, Richard. 1984. *Tonality in Western Culture*. University Park: Pennsylvania State University Press.

O'donnell, Roy. 1974. "Syntactic Differences between Speech and Writing." *American Speech* 49(1–2): 102–110.

Parks, Richard. 1976. "Voice Leading and Chromatic Harmony in the Music of Chopin." *Journal of Music Theory* 20(2): 189–214.

Parks, Richard. 1989. *The Music of Claude Debussy*. New Haven: Yale University Press.

Patel, Aniruddh. 2008. *Music, Language, and the Brain*. New York: Oxford University Press.

Patrick, James. 1983. "Al Tinney, Monroe's Uptown House, and the Emergence of Modern Jazz in Harlem." *Annual Review of Jazz Studies* 2: 150–179.

Perle, George. 1984. "Scriabin's Self-Analyses." *Music Analysis* 3: 101–122.

Perle, George. 1996. *The Listening Composer*. Berkeley: University of California Press.

Piston, Walter. 1941. *Harmony*. New York: Norton.

Pople, Anthony. 2001. "Styles and Languages at the Turn of the Century." In *The Cambridge History of Nineteenth-Century Music,* ed. Jim Samson, 601–620. Cambridge: Cambridge University Press.

Powers, Harold. 1958. "Mode and Raga." *The Musical Quarterly* 44(4): 448–460.

Powers, Harold. 1981. "Tonal Types and Modal Categories in Renaissance Polyphony." *Journal of the American Musicological Society* 34(3): 428–470.

Powers, Harold. 1992. "Is Mode Real? Pietro Aron, the Octenary System, and Polyphony." *Basler Jahrbuch für Historische Musikpraxis* 16: 9–52.

Pressing, Jeff. 1978. "Towards an Understanding of Scales in Jazz." *Jazz Research* 9: 25–35.

Pressing, Jeff. 1982. "Pitch Class Set Structures in Contemporary Jazz." *Jazz Research* 14: 133–72.

Pressing, Jeff. 1983. "Cognitive Isomorphisms Between Pitch and Rhythm in World Musics: West Africa, the Balkans and Western Tonality." *Studies in Music* 17: 38–61.

Proctor, Gregory. 1978. "Technical Bases of Nineteenth-Century Chromaticism." PhD diss., Princeton University.

Quinn, Ian. 1996. "Fuzzy Transposition of Pitch Sets." Paper presented to the national meeting of the Society for Music Theory, Baton Rouge, Louisiana.

Quinn, Ian. 2001. "Listening to Similarity Relations." *Perspectives of New Music* 39(2): 108–158.

Quinn, Ian. 2002. "Foundations of Steve Reich's Later Harmonic Practice: The *Variations* and *Tehilim*." Paper presented to the national meeting of the Society for Music Theory, Columbus, Ohio.

Quinn, Ian. 2005. "Harmonic Function without Primary Triads." Paper presented to the national meeting of the Society for Music Theory, Boston, Massachusetts.

Quinn, Ian. 2006. "General Equal-Tempered Harmony." *Perspectives of New Music* 44(2): 5–60.

Quinn, Ian. 2007. "General Equal-Tempered Harmony: Part II." *Perspectives of New Music* 45(1): 6–65.

Raffman, Diana. 2003. "Is Twelve-Tone Music Artistically Defective?" *Midwest Studies in Philosophy* 27: 69–87.

Rahn, Jay. 1991. "Coordination of Interval Sizes in Seven-Tone Collections." *Journal of Music Theory* 35(1–2): 33–60.

Rameau, Jean Paul. [1722] 1971. *Treatise on Harmony*. Trans. Philip Gossett. New York: Dover.

Randel, Don. 1971. "Emerging Triadic Tonality in the Fifteenth Century." *The Musical Quarterly* 57(1): 73–86.

Raphael, Christopher and Joshua Stoddard. 2004. "Functional Harmonic Analysis Using Probabilistic Models." *Computer Music Journal* 28(3): 45–52.

Rappaport, David. 2006. "Musical Scales, Integer Partitions, Necklaces, and Polygons." *Proceedings of the 2006 Bridges Conference on Mathematical Connections in Art, Music, and Science,* ed. Reza Sarhangi and John Sharp, 595–598. St. Albans: Tarquin.

Reti, Rudolf. 1958. *Tonality Atonality Pantonality*. London: Rockliff.

Ricci, Adam. 2004. "A Theory of the Harmonic Sequence." PhD diss., Eastman School of Music.

Riemann, Hugo. 1893. *Vereinfachte Harmonielehre*. London: Augener.

Riley, Matthew. 2004. "The 'Harmonic Major' Mode in Nineteenth-Century Theory and Practice." *Music Analysis* 23(1): 1–26.

Rivera, Benito. 1979. "Harmonic Theory in Musical Treatises of the Late Fifteenth and Early Sixteenth Centuries." *Music Theory Spectrum* 1: 80–95.

Roeder, John. 1984. "A Theory of Voice Leading for Atonal Music." PhD diss., Yale University.

Roeder, John. 1987. "A Geometric Representation of Pitch-Class Series." *Perspectives of New Music* 25(1–2): 362–409.

Roeder, John. 1994. "Voice-leading as Transformation." In *Musical Transformation and Musical Intuition: Eleven Essays in Honor of David Lewin,* ed. Raphael Atlas and Michael Cherlin, 41-58. Roxbury: Ovenbird.

Rothstein, William. 1992. "The True Principles of Harmony: Or, Schulz, Schenker, and the *Stufe*." Paper presented to the Second International Schenker Symposium, New York, New York.

Russ, Michael. 2007. "Some Observations on $P_{M,N}$ Relations Between Set Classes." *Music Analysis* 26(1–2): 111–158.

Russell, George. 1959. *The Lydian Chromatic Concept of Tonal Organization for Improvisation.* Brookline: Concept.

Russom, Philip Wade. 1985. "A Theory of Pitch of Pitch Organization for the Early Music of Maurice Ravel." PhD diss., Yale University.

Sadai, Yizhak. 1980. *Harmony in Its Systemic and Phenomenological Aspects.* Jerusalem: Yanetz.

Salzer, Felix. [1952] 1982. *Structural Hearing.* New York: Dover.

Salzer, Felix and Carl Schachter. [1969] 1989. *Counterpoint in Composition.* New York: Dover.

Samson, Jim. 1977. *Music in Transition: A Study of Tonal Expansion and Atonality, 1900–1920.* New York: Norton.

Santa, Matthew. 1999. "Defining Modular Transformations." *Music Theory Spectrum* 21(2): 200–229.

Schachter, Carl. 1994. "The Prelude in E Minor Op. 28 No. 4: Autograph Sources and Interpretation." *Chopin Studies* 2: 161–182.

Schenker, Heinrich. 1930. *Das Meisterwerk in der Musik,* vol. 3. Munich: Drei Masken Verlag.

Schenker, Heinrich. [1935] 1956. *Der freie Satz.* Ed. Oswald Jonas. Vienna: Universal.

Schenker, Heinrich. 1996. *The Masterwork in Music: Volume 2, 1926: A Yearbook.* Ed. William Drabkin. New York: Cambridge University Press.

Schenker, Heinrich. 1997. *The Masterwork in Music: Volume 3, 1930: A Yearbook.* New York: Cambridge University Press.

Schenker, Heinrich. 2001. *Free Composition.* Hillsdale: Pendragon.

Schoenberg, Arnold. [1954] 1969. *Structural Functions of Harmony.* Ed. Leonard Stein. New York: Norton.

Schoenberg, Arnold. [1950] 1975. *Style and Idea: Selected Writings of Arnold Schoenberg.* Ed. Leonard Stein, trans. Leo Black. New York: St. Martins Press.

Schoenberg, Arnold. [1911] 1983. *Theory of Harmony.* Berkeley: University of California Press.

Sethares, William. 1999. *Tuning, Timbre, Spectrum, Scale.* New York: Springer.

Simms, Bryan. 1975. "Choron, Fétis, and the Theory of Tonality." *Journal of Music Theory* 19(1): 112–138.

Slonimsky, Nicolas. [1937] 1994. *Music Since 1900.* New York: Schirmer.

Smith, Charles. 1986. "The Functional Extravagance of Chromatic Chords." *Music Theory Spectrum* 8: 94–139.

Starr, Daniel and Robert Morris. 1977. "A General Theory of Combinatoriality and the Aggregate (Part I)." *Perspectives of New Music* 16(1): 3–35.

Stein, Beverly. 2002. "Carissimi's Tonal System and the Function of Transposition in the Expansion of Tonality." *The Journal of Musicology* 19(2): 264–305.

Strickland, Edward. 2000. *Minimalism: Origins.* Bloomington: Indiana University Press.

Straus, Joseph. 2003. "Uniformity, Balance, and Smoothness in Atonal Voice Leading." *Music Theory Spectrum* 25(2): 305–352.

Straus, Joseph. 2005. *Introduction to Post-Tonal Theory*. Upper Saddle River: Pearson Prentice Hall.

Stuckenschmidt, Hans Heinz. 1965. "Debussy or Berg? The Mystery of a Chord Progression." *The Musical Quarterly* 51(3): 453–459.

Sutcliffe, W. Dean. 1996. "Grieg's Fifth: The Linguistic Battleground of 'Klokkeklang.'" *The Musical Quarterly* 80(1): 161–181.

Taruskin, Richard. 1985. "Chernomor to Kashchei: Harmonic Sorcery; or, Stravinsky's 'Angle.'" *Journal of the American Musicological Society* 38: 262–300.

Taruskin, Richard. 1987. "*Chez Petrouchka:* Harmony and Tonality *Chez* Stravinsky." *Nineteenth Century Music* 10: 265–286.

Taruskin, Richard. 1996. *Stravinsky and the Russian Traditions*. Berkeley: University of California Press.

Taruskin, Richard. 2005. *The Oxford History of Western Music*. New York: Oxford University Press.

Taube, Heinrich. 1999. "Automatic Tonal Analysis: Toward the Implementation of a Music Theory Workbench." *Computer Music Journal* 23(4): 18–32.

Temperley, David. 2007. *Music and Probability*. Cambridge: MIT Press.

Terhardt, Ernst. 1974. "Pitch, Consonance, and Harmony." *Journal of the Acoustical Society of America* 55: 1061–1069.

Thomson, William. 1991. *Schoenberg's Error*. Philadelphia: University of Pennsylvania Press.

Thomson, William. 1999. *Tonality in Music: A General Theory*. San Marino: Everett Books.

Trainor, Laurel J. and Becky M. Heinmiller. 1998. "The Development of Evaluative Responses to Music: Infants Prefer to Listen to Consonance over Dissonance." *Infant Behavior and Development* 21: 77–88.

Trainor, Laurel J., Christine D. Tsang, and Vivian H. W. Cheung. 2002. "Preference for Sensory Consonance in 2- and 4-Month-Old Infants." *Music Perception* 20: 187–194.

Tramo, Mark Jude, Peter Cariani, Cris Koh, Nikos Makris, and Louis Braida. 2005. "Neurophysiology and Neuroanatomy of Pitch Perception: Auditory Cortex." *Annals of the New York Academy of Sciences* 1060: 148–174.

Tymoczko, Dmitri. 1997. "The Consecutive-Semitone Constraint on Scalar Structure: A Link Between Impressionism and Jazz." *Integral* 11: 135–179.

Tymoczko, Dmitri. 2002. "Stravinsky and the Octatonic: A Reconsideration." *Music Theory Spectrum* 24(1): 68–102.

Tymoczko, Dmitri. 2003a. "Octatonicism Reconsidered Again." *Music Theory Spectrum* 25(1): 185–202.

Tymoczko, Dmitri. 2003b. "Progressions Fondamentales, Functions, Degrés: une Grammaire de l'Harmonie Tonale Élémentaire." *Musurgia* 10(3–4): 35–64.

Tymoczko, Dmitri. [2007] 2004. "Scale Networks in Debussy." *Journal of Music Theory* 48(2): 215–292.

Tymoczko, Dmitri. 2005. "Voice Leadings as Generalized Key Signatures." *Music Theory Online* 11(4).

Tymoczko, Dmitri. 2006. "The Geometry of Musical Chords." *Science* 313: 72–74.

Tymoczko, Dmitri. 2007. "Recasting K-nets." *Music Theory Online* 13(3).

Tymoczko, Dmitri. 2008a. "Lewin, Intervals, and Transformations: A Response to Hook." *Music Theory Spectrum* 30(1): 164–168.

Tymoczko, Dmitri. 2008b. "Scale Theory, Serial Theory, and Voice Leading." *Music Analysis* 27(1): 1–49.

Tymoczko, Dmitri. [2010] 2008c. "Set-Class Similarity, Voice Leading, and the Fourier Transform." *Journal of Music Theory* 52(2): 251–272.

Tymoczko, Dmitri. 2009a. "Three Conceptions of Musical Distance." In *Mathematics and Computation in Music*, eds. Elaine Chew, Adrian Childs, and Ching-Hua Chuan, 258–273. Heidelberg: Springer.

Tymoczko, Dmitri. [2010] 2009b. "Generalizing Musical Intervals." *Journal of Music Theory* 53(2): 227–254.

Tymoczko, Dmitri. 2010. "Geometrical Methods in Recent Music Theory." *Music Theory Online* 16(1).

Tymoczko, Dmitri. Forthcoming. "Dualism and the Beholder's Eye." In *Riemann Perspectives*, ed. Alex Rehding and Ed Gollin. New York: Oxford.

van der Merwe, Peter. 1989. *Origins of the Popular Style*. New York: Oxford.

van den Toorn, Pieter. 1983. *The Music of Igor Stravinsky*. New Haven: Yale University Press.

Vos, Piet and Jim Troost. 1989. "Ascending and Descending Melodic Intervals: Statistical Findings and Their Perceptual Relevance." *Music Perception* 6: 383–396.

Weeks, Jeffrey. 2002. *The Shape of Space*. New York: Marcel Dekker.

Weitzmann, Carl Friedrich. 1853. *Der übermässige Dreiklang*. Berlin: T. Trautweinschen.

Weitzmann, Carl Friedrich. 1860. "Erklärende Erläuterung und musikalisch-theoretische Begründung der durch die neuesten Kunstschöpfungen bewirkten Umgestaltung und Weiterbildung der Harmonik," *Neue Zeitschrift für Musik* 52: 1–3, 9–12, 17–20, 29–31, 37–39, 45–46, 53–54, 65–66, 73–75.

Wessel, David. 1979. "Timbre Space as a Musical Control Structure." *Computer Music Journal* 3(2): 45–52.

Whittall, Arnold. 1975. "Tonality and the Whole-Tone Scale in the Music of Debussy." *The Music Review* 36: 261–271.

Wittgenstein, Ludwig. 1953. *Philosophical Investigations*. Trans. G. E. M. Anscombe. Oxford: Basil Blackwell.

Wright, Anthony A., Jacquelyne J. Rivera, Stewart H. Hulse, Melissa Shyan, and Julie Neiworth. 2000. "Music Perception and Octave Generalization in Rhesus Monkeys." *Journal of Experimental Psychology: General* 129: 291–307.

Yasser, Joseph. 1975. *Theory of Evolving Tonality*. New York: Da Capo.

Zentner, Marcel R. and Jerome Kagan. 1996. "Perception of Music by Infants." *Nature* 383: 29.

Zentner, Marcel R. and Jerome Kagan. 1998. "Infants' Perception of Consonance and Dissonance in Music." *Infant Behavior and Development* 21: 483–492.

Zimmerman, Daniel. 2002. *Families Without Clusters in the Early Works of Sergei Prokofiev*. PhD diss., University of Chicago.

INDEX